PHILIP'S

STREET ATLAS
Norfolk

www.philips-maps.co.uk

First published in 2003 by
Philip's, a division of
Octopus Publishing Group Ltd
www.octopusbooks.co.uk
Endeavour House, 189 Shaftesbury Avenue
London WC2H 8JY
An Hachette UK Company
www.hachette.co.uk

Third edition with interim revision 2012
First impression 2012
NORCA

ISBN 978-1-84907-206-9 (pocket)

© Philip's 2012

Ordnance Survey®

This product includes mapping data licensed from
Ordnance Survey® with the permission of the
Controller of Her Majesty's Stationery Office. ©
Crown copyright 2012. All rights reserved. Licence
number 100011710.

No part of this publication may be reproduced,
stored in a retrieval system or transmitted in any
form or by any means, electronic, mechanical,
photocopying, recording or otherwise, without the
permission of the Publishers and the copyright
owner.

While every reasonable effort has been made to
ensure that the information compiled in this atlas
is accurate, complete and up-to-date at the time
of publication, some of this information is subject
to change and the Publisher cannot guarantee its
correctness or completeness.

The information in this atlas is provided without
any representation or warranty, express or
implied and the Publisher cannot be held liable
for any loss or damage due to any use or reliance
on the information in this atlas, nor for any
errors, omissions or subsequent changes in such
information.

The representation in this atlas of a road, track
or path is no evidence of the existence of a right
of way.

Ordnance Survey and the OS Symbol are registered
trademarks of Ordnance Survey,
the national mapping agency of Great Britain.

Speed camera data provided by
PocketGPSWorld.com Ltd

Post Office is a trade mark of Post Office Ltd in the
UK and other countries.

Printed in China

Contents

II Mobile safety cameras

III **Key to map symbols**

IV **Key to map pages**

VI **Route planning**

X Major administrative and Postcode boundaries

1 **Street maps** at 1⅓ inches to 1 mile

132 **Street maps** at 2⅔ inches to 1 mile

178 **Street map of Norwich city centre**
at 5⅓ inches to 1 mile

179 **Index** of towns and villages, streets, hospitals,
industrial estates, railway stations, schools, shopping
centres, universities and places of interest

Digital Data

The exceptionally high-quality mapping found in this atlas is available as digital data in TIFF format,
which is easily convertible to other bitmapped (raster) image formats.

The index is also available in digital form as a standard database table. It contains all the details
found in the printed index together with the National Grid reference for the map square in which each
entry is named.

For further information and to discuss your requirements, please contact
philips@mapsinternational.co.uk

Mobile safety cameras

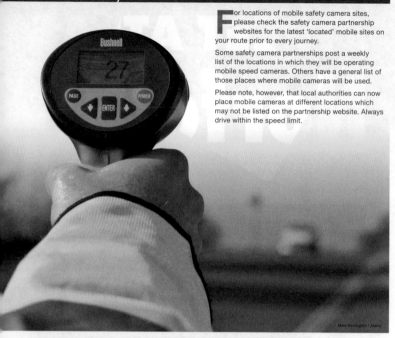

Bushnell

27

PAGE   ENTER   POWER

For locations of mobile safety camera sites, please check the safety camera partnership websites for the latest 'located' mobile sites on your route prior to every journey.

Some safety camera partnerships post a weekly list of the locations in which they will be operating mobile speed cameras. Others have a general list of those places where mobile cameras will be used.

Please note, however, that local authorities can now place mobile cameras at different locations which may not be listed on the partnership website. Always drive within the speed limit.

Mike Harrington / Alamy

Useful websites

Norfolk Safety Camera Partnership
http://norfolk-safety-camera.org.uk/

Cambridgeshire and Peterborough Road Safety Partnership
http://www.cprsp.gov.uk/

Lincolnshire Road SafetyPartnership
http://microsites.lincolnshire.gov.uk/LRSP

Suffolk Safecam
http://www.suffolk.police.uk/safetyadvice/roadsafety/safecam.aspx

Further information
www.dvla.gov.uk

www.thinkroadsafety.gov.uk

www.dft.gov.uk

www.road-safe.org

Key to map symbols

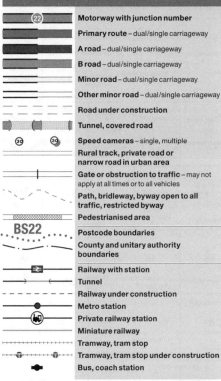
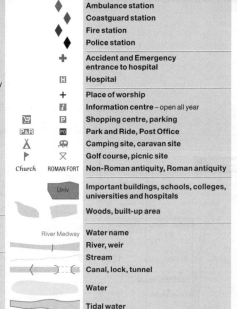

Motorway with junction number	Ambulance station
Primary route – dual/single carriageway	Coastguard station
A road – dual/single carriageway	Fire station
B road – dual/single carriageway	Police station
Minor road – dual/single carriageway	Accident and Emergency entrance to hospital
Other minor road – dual/single carriageway	Hospital
Road under construction	Place of worship
Tunnel, covered road	Information centre – open all year
Speed cameras – single, multiple	Shopping centre, parking
Rural track, private road or narrow road in urban area	Park and Ride, Post Office
Gate or obstruction to traffic – may not apply at all times or to all vehicles	Camping site, caravan site
Path, bridleway, byway open to all traffic, restricted byway	Golf course, picnic site
Pedestrianised area	Non-Roman antiquity, Roman antiquity
Postcode boundaries	Important buildings, schools, colleges, universities and hospitals
County and unitary authority boundaries	Woods, built-up area
Railway with station	Water name
Tunnel	River, weir
Railway under construction	Stream
Metro station	Canal, lock, tunnel
Private railway station	Water
Miniature railway	Tidal water
Tramway, tram stop	Adjoining page indicators and overlap bands – the colour of the arrow and band indicates the scale of the adjoining or overlapping page (see scales below)
Tramway, tram stop under construction	The dark grey border on the inside edge of some pages indicates that the mapping does not continue onto the adjacent page
Bus, coach station	The small numbers around the edges of the maps identify the 1-kilometre National Grid lines

Abbreviations

Acad	Academy	Meml	Memorial
Allot Gdns	Allotments	Mon	Monument
Cemy	Cemetery	Mus	Museum
C Ctr	Civic centre	Obsy	Observatory
CH	Club house	Pal	Royal palace
Coll	College	PH	Public house
Crem	Crematorium	Recn Gd	Recreation ground
Ent	Enterprise	Resr	Reservoir
Ex H	Exhibition hall	Ret Pk	Retail park
Ind Est	Industrial Estate	Sch	School
IRB Sta	Inshore rescue boat station	Sh Ctr	Shopping centre
Inst	Institute	TH	Town hall / house
Ct	Law court	Trad Est	Trading estate
L Ctr	Leisure centre	Univ	University
LC	Level crossing	W Twr	Water tower
Liby	Library	Wks	Works
Mkt	Market	YH	Youth hostel

Enlarged maps only

	Railway or bus station building
	Place of interest
	Parkland

The map scale on the pages numbered in green is 1⅓ inches to 1 mile
2.1 cm to 1 km • 1:47620

0	½ mile	1 mile	1½ miles	2 miles
0	500m	1km	1½km	2km

The map scale on the pages numbered in blue is 2⅔ inches to 1 mile
4.2 cm to 1 km • 1:23810

0	¼ mile	½ mile	¾ mile	1 mile
0	250m	500m	750m	1km

The map scale on the pages numbered in red is 5⅓ inches to 1 mile
8.4 cm to 1 km • 1:11900

0	220yds	440yds	660yds	½ mile
0	125m	250m	375m	500m

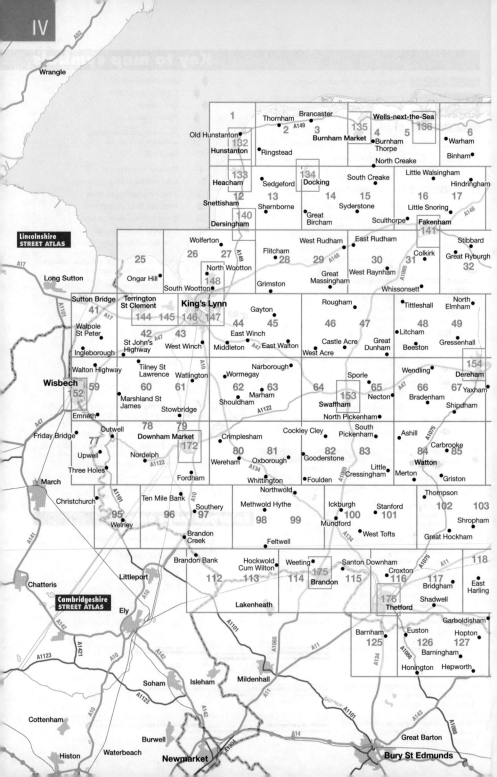

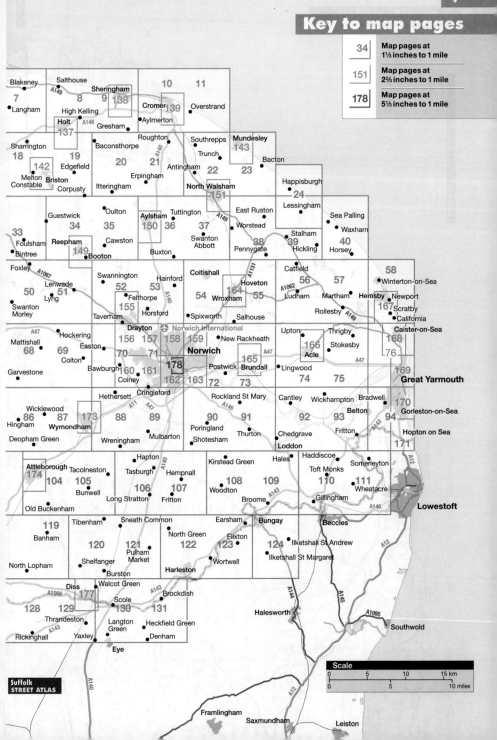

V

Key to map pages

34	Map pages at 1⅓ inches to 1 mile
151	Map pages at 2⅔ inches to 1 mile
178	Map pages at 5⅓ inches to 1 mile

Blakeney
Langham
7
A149
Salthouse
8
Sheringham
9
138
10
11
Cromer
139
Overstrand
High Kelling
Holt
137
A148
Gresham
Aylmerton
Roughton
Southrepps
Trunch
Mundesley
143
Sharrington
18
Edgefield
19
Baconsthorpe
20
Erpingham
21
Antingham
22
Bacton
23
Happisburgh
24
Melton Constable
142
Briston
Corpusty
Itteringham
North Walsham
151
Lessingham
Guestwick
Oulton
Tuttington
East Ruston
Sea Palling
58
33
34
35
Aylsham
150
36
37
Worstead
Waxham
Foulsham
Reepham
149
Cawston
Swanton Abbott
Stalham
39
40
Bintree
Booton
Buxton
Pennygate
Hickling
Horsey
Foxley
A1067
Swannington
Hainford
Coltishall
Catfield
56
57
Winterton-on-Sea
Lenwade
52
53
164
Hoveton
A1062
Martham
Hemsby
Newport
50
51
Lyng
Felthorpe
155
54
Wroxham
55
Ludham
167
Scratby
Swanton Morley
Horsford
Taverham
Spixworth
Salhouse
Rollesby
A149
California
Caister-on-Sea
168
A47
Hockering
Drayton
Norwich International
Upton
Thrigby
166
76
Mattishall
68
Easton
69
156
157
158
159
New Rackheath
Acle
Stokesby
A47
169
Colton
70
71
Norwich
165
Garvestone
Bawburgh
160
161
178
Postwick
Brundall
Lingwood
74
75
Great Yarmouth
Colney
162
163
72
73
Cringleford
Rockland St Mary
Cantley
Wickhampton
Bradwell
170
Wicklewood
Hethersett
A11
A47
A146
Belton
Gorleston-on-Sea
86
87
173
88
89
90
91
92
93
94
Hingham
Wymondham
Poringland
Thurton
Chedgrave
Fritton
Hopton on Sea
171
Deopham Green
Wreningham
Mulbarton
Shotesham
Loddon
Attleborough
174
Tacolneston
Hapton
Kirstead Green
Hales
Haddiscoe
Somerleyton
104
105
Tasburgh
Hempnall
108
109
Toft Monks
110
111
Bunwell
106
107
Woodton
Broome
A143
Gillingham
Wheatacre
Old Buckenham
Long Stratton
Fritton
A146
Lowestoft
119
Tibenham
Sneath Common
Earsham
Bungay
Beccles
Banham
North Green
Flixton
120
121
122
123
124
Ilketshall St Andrew
A12
North Lopham
Shelfanger
Pulham Market
Wortwell
Ilketshall St Margaret
A145
Burston
Harleston
A1095
Diss
Walcot Green
177
Brockdish
128
129
Scole
130
131
Halesworth
Southwold
Thrandeston
A1066
Langton Green
Heckfield Green
A143
Rickinghall
Yaxley
Denham
A143
Eye

Scale
0 ----- 5 ----- 10 ----- 15 km
0 ----- 5 ----- 10 miles

Suffolk STREET ATLAS

Framlingham
Saxmundham
Leiston

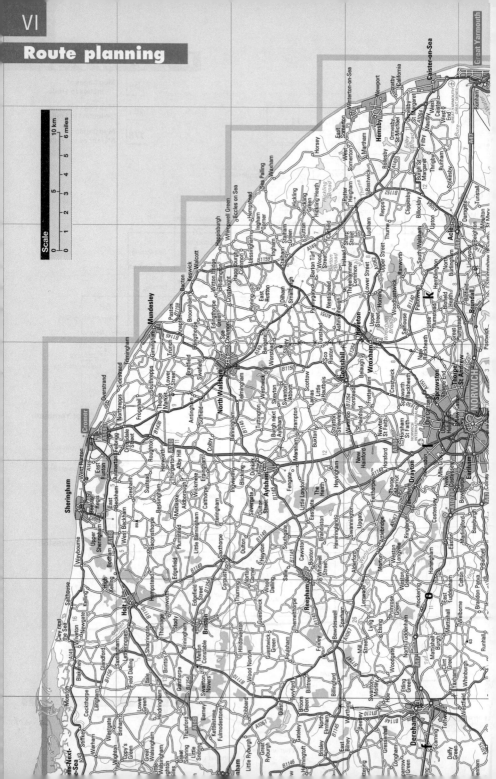

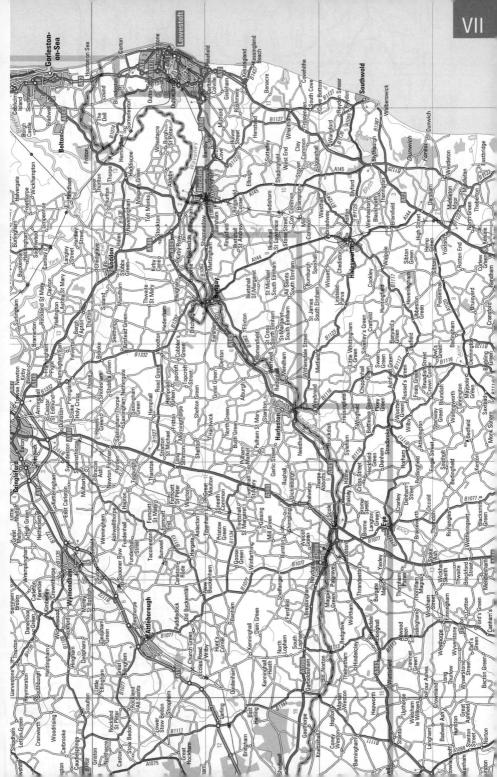

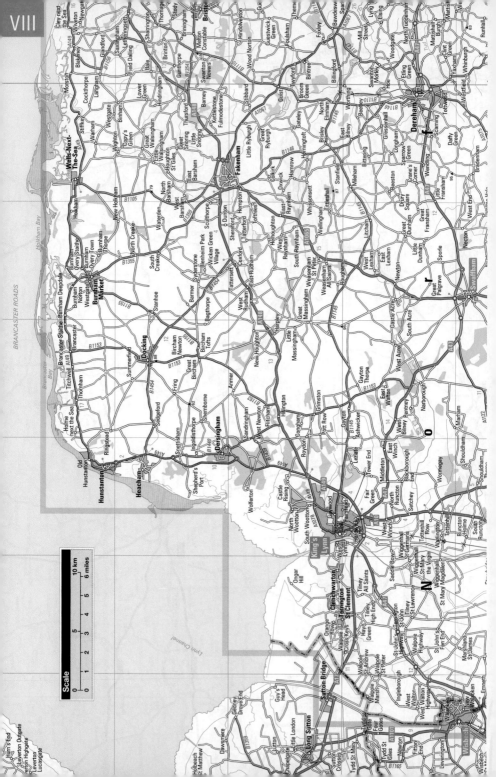

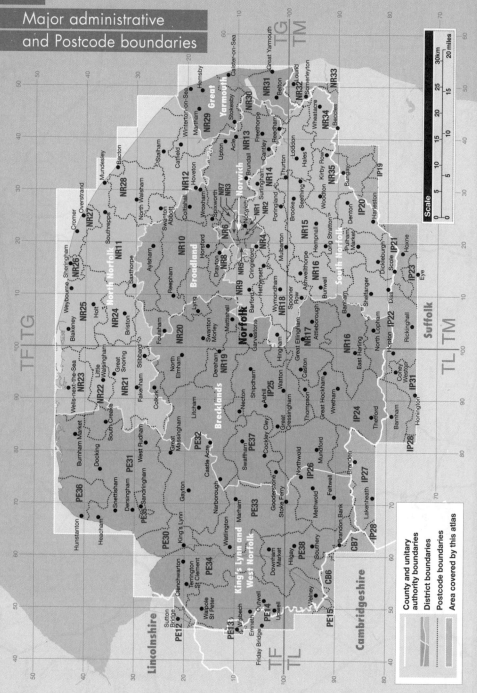

A   B   C   D   E   F

8

45

7

44

BROADWATER RD

6

Peddars Way & Norfolk Coast Path   WESTGATE RD

43

132

CH Hotel

Old Hunstanton

WODEHOUSE RD
HAMILTON RD
Motel
St Edmund's Point
GOLF COURSE ROAD
OLD HUNSTANTON RD

A149

5

LIGHTHOUSE CL.
St Edmund's Chapel   B1161

Chalkpit Wood
Birthday Wood
Hunstanton Hall
Deodara Wood
Ilex Wood

42

CLIFF PARADE
BERNARD CRESCENT
PEDDARS DR.
CLARENCE RD
VICTORIA AVE
CROMER ROAD
CHAPEL BANK

Kimberley Plantation
Ada Grove
Heart Plantation

132

PE36

4

Glebe House Sch

Sensory Park

HUNSTANTON

Hunstanton Park Earthwork

Cross
PO
HARTLEY CL.
DOWNS RD

132

Oak Grove
Half Moon Plantation

41

3

Hunstanton Sea Life Sanctuary

Liby
CRESCENT LA.
MELTON
SOUTHEND ROAD
KING'S LYNN RD

Smithdon High Sch
Lodge Farm

Old Bank Wood

Cemy
OASIS WAY
Sch
B1161
WINDSOR RISE

South Hill Wood
Larch Plantation

40

MANOR
SOUTH BEACH ROAD
WINDSOR DR.
REDGATE HILL

St Andrew's Chapel (remains of)
Downs Farm
Hill Wood
Ringstead Downs Nature Reserve

133

2

The Firs
Redgate Hill
Ringstead Downs

CH

RINGSTEAD ROAD

39

Searles Golf Course

Pit

PE31

Manor Farm
MANOR RD.
Long Wood

Little Wood

133

Whin Covert

1

HUNSTANTON RD
A149
CHURCH FARM RD
Church Farm

Heacham Park

38

64   A   65   B   66   C   67   D   68   E   69   F

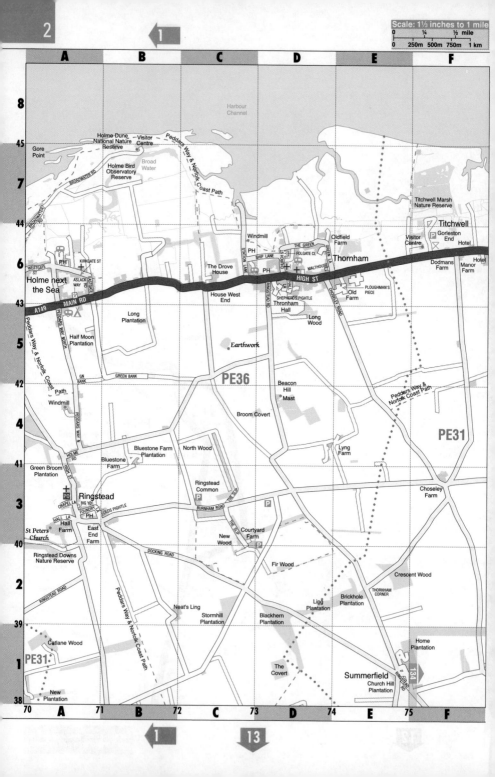

Scale: 1½ inches to 1 mile

0   ¼   ½ mile
0   250m 500m 750m 1 km

8

Harbour
Channel

45

Holme Dune
National Nature
Reserve

Visitor
Centre

Gore
Point

Peddars Way & Norfolk Coast Path

Broad
Water

Holme Bird
Observatory
Reserve

BROADWATER RD

7

Titchwell Marsh
Nature Reserve

44

BROOMFIELD

Windmill

Oldfield
Farm

Titchwell

Gorleston
End

Visitor
Centre

Hotel

P/H

KIRKGATE ST

WESTGATE

6

THE GREEN

FOLGATE CL

STATION LANE

SHIP LANE

PH

CHURCH ST

MALTHOUSE

Thornham

Dodmans
Farm

Hotel

Manor
Farm

ASLACK
WAY

KIRKGATE RD

Holme next
the Sea

The Drove
House

HIGH ST

43

MAIN RD

A149

Peddars Way & Norfolk Coast

House West
End

SHEPHERD'S PIGHTLE

Thornham
Hall

Old
Farm

PLOUGHMAN'S
PIGHTLE

CHOSELEY ROAD

Long Plantation

Long
Wood

5

Half Moon
Plantation

Earthwork

Path

GN
BANK

GREEN BANK

42

PE36

Beacon
Hill

Mast

Peddars Way & Norfolk Coast Path

Windmill

4

Broom Covert

Lyng
Farm

PE31

PEDDARS WAY

HOLME
RD

Bluestone Farm
Plantation

North Wood

41

Green Broom
Plantation

HIGH LA

Bluestone
Farm

Ringstead
Common

P

THE SLIP

Choseley
Farm

CHAPEL LA

BIG YD

Ringstead

BURNHAM ROAD

P

3

FOUNDRY

GOLDS PIGHTLE

PH

St Peters
Church

HALL LA

Hall
Farm

East
End
Farm

New
Wood

Courtyard
Farm

P

40

Ringstead Downs
Nature Reserve

RINGSTEAD ROAD

DOCKING ROAD

Fir Wood

Crescent Wood

THORNHAM
CORNER

2

Neat's Ling

Stormhill
Plantation

Blackhern
Plantation

Ling
Plantation

Brickhole
Plantation

Peddars Way & Norfolk Coast Path

39

Catlane Wood

The Covert

Summerfield

Home
Plantation

PE31

A14

1

New
Plantation

Church Hill
Plantation

38

70   **A**   71   **B**   72   **C**   73   **D**   74   **E**   75   **F**

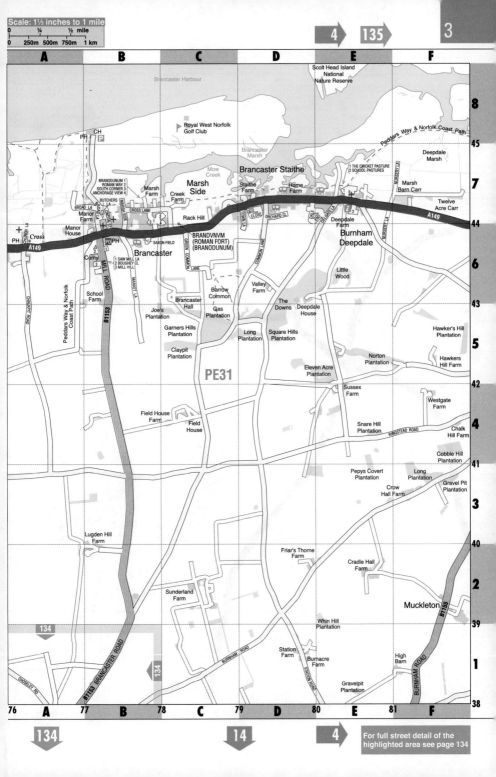

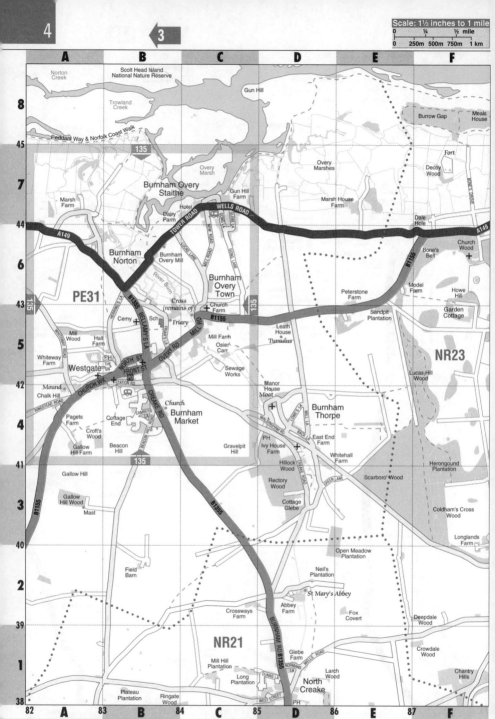

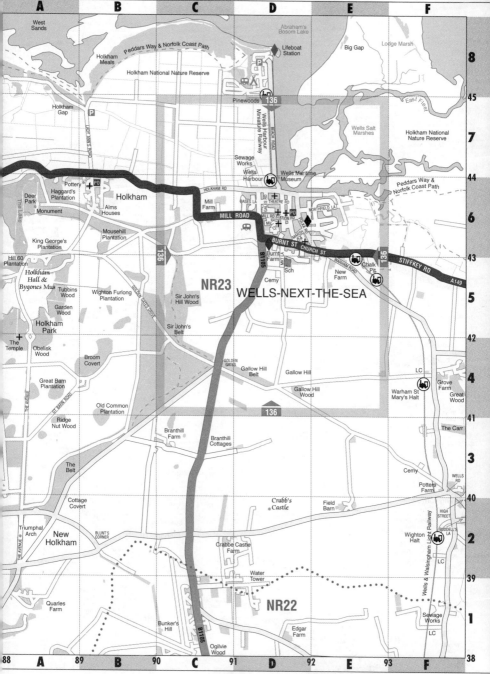

A   B   C   D   E   F

West Sands

Abraham's Bosom Lake

Lifeboat Station

Big Gap

Lodge Marsh

8

Holkham Meals

Peddars Way & Norfolk Coast Path

Holkham National Nature Reserve

Pinewoods

136

East Fleet

45

Holkham Gap

P

Wells Harbour Miniature Railway

BEACH ROAD

Wells Salt Marshes

Holkham National Nature Reserve

7

LADY ANNS ROAD

Sewage Works

Wells Harbour

Wells Maritime Museum

Peddars Way & Norfolk Coast Path

44

Deer Park

Pottery

Haggard's Plantation

PO

Holkham

HOLKHAM RD

Mill Farm

BASES LA

ST THEATRE RD

MILL RD STATION RD

NORTHFIELD LA

6

THE LAKE

Monument

Alms Houses

MILL ROAD

PO

Mousehill Plantation

BURNT ST

CHURCH ST

STIFFKEY RD

A149

43

Hill 60 Plantation

King George's Plantation

136

B1105

Burnt Farm

Sch

WARHAM ROAD

136

Holkham Hall & Bygones Mus

Tubbins Wood

Wighton Furlong Plantation

NR23

Sir John's Hill Wood

Cemy

New Farm

Chalk Pit

5

Garden Wood

HOLKHAM ESTATE DRIVE

WELLS-NEXT-THE-SEA

Holkham Park

Sir John's Belt

42

The Temple

Obelisk Wood

Broom Covert

GOLDEN GATES

Gallow Hill Belt

Gallow Hill

LC

Grove Farm

4

Great Barn Plantation

THE AVENUE

ST MARY RD

Gallow Hill Wood

Warham St Mary's Halt

Great Wood

41

Ridge Nut Wood

Old Common Plantation

136

The Carr

3

The Belt

Branthill Farm

Branthill Cottages

Cemy

Wells & Walsingham Light Railway

WELLS RD

Potters Farm

Cottage Covert

40

Triumphal Arch

New Holkham

BLUNT'S CORNER

Crabb's Castle

Field Barn

HIGH STREET

Wighton Halt

BIDDELL'S LA

2

Quarles Farm

Crabbe Castle Farm

Water Tower

NR22

LC

39

Bunker's Hill

B1105

Edgar Farm

Sewage Works

1

Ogilvie Wood

LC

88   A   89   B   90   C   91   D   92   E   93   F   38

16

6

For full street detail of the highlighted area see page 136

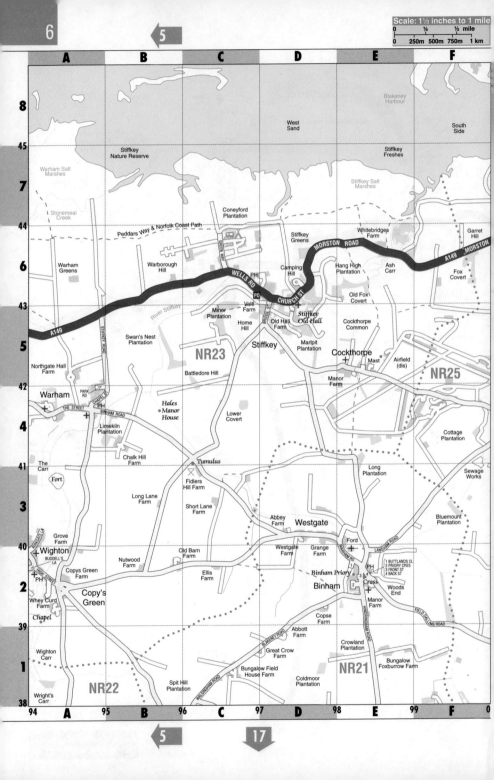

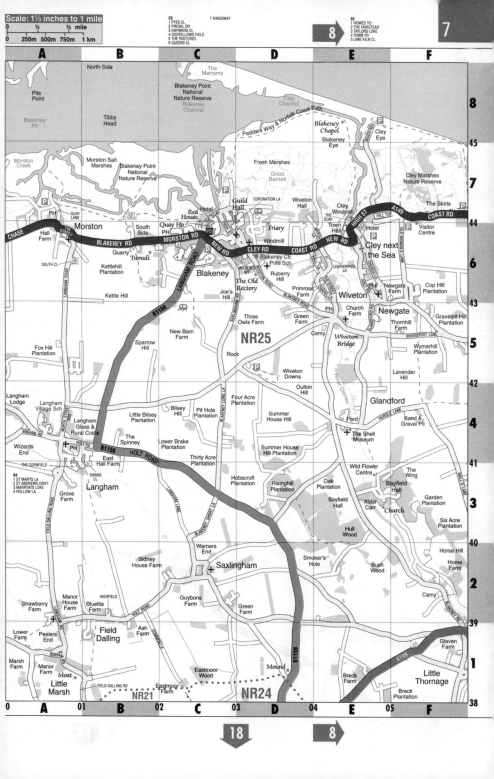

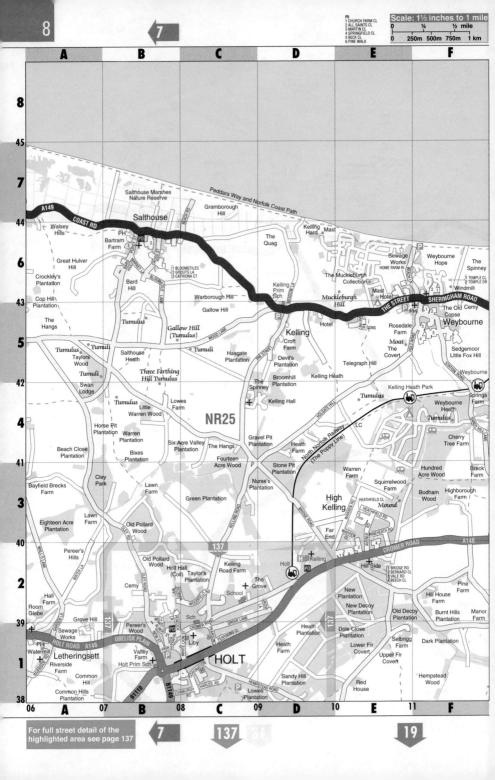

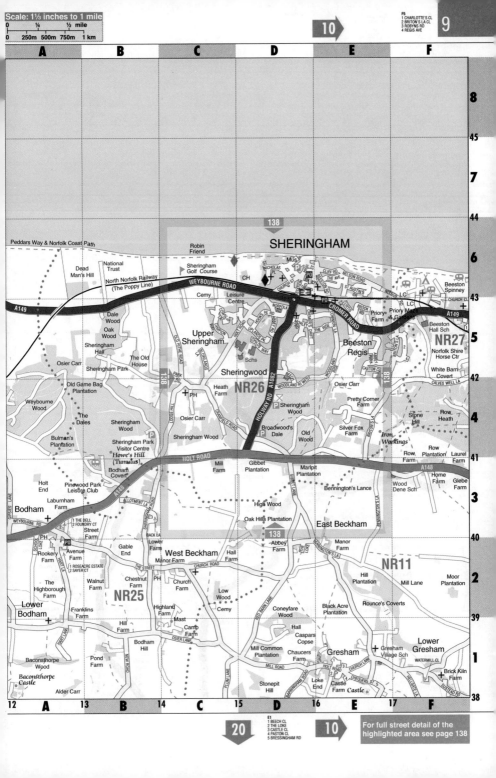

Scale: 1⅓ inches to 1 mile

| 0 | ¼ | ½ mile |
| 0 | 250m 500m 750m | 1 km |

10

9

F5
1 CHARLOTTE'S CL
2 BRITON'S LA CL
3 ROBYNS RD
4 REGIS AVE

| | A | | B | | C | | D | | E | | F | |

8

45

7

44

138

SHERINGHAM

6

Peddars Way & Norfolk Coast Path

Dead Man's Hill

National Trust

Robin Friend

Sheringham Golf Course

ST NICHOLAS

MUS

CLIFF RD

NELSON ROAD

Beeston Spinney

43

A149

North Norfolk Railway (The Poppy Line)

WEYBOURNE ROAD

CH

Cemy

Leisure Centre

ST AUSTIN'S

NETN

LC

Beeston Hall Sch

LC

CHURCH CL

A149

5

Dale Wood

Oak Wood

Sheringham Hall

The Old House

Upper Sheringham

UPLANDS RD

CROMER ROAD

Priory Farm

Priory Maze & Gardens

Beeston Regis

Norfolk Shire Horse Ctr

NR27

1

Osier Carr

Sheringham Park

HOLWAY RD

A1002

Sheringwood

Schs

CHUR WAY

Sheringwood

NR26

Heath Farm

WOODLAND RD WEST

White Barn Covert

CALVES WELL LA

42

Old Game Bag Plantation

PH

Osier Carr

Osier Carr

Pretty Corner Farm

Stone Hill

Row Heath

4

Weybourne Wood

The Dales

Sheringham Wood

Sheringham Wood

Broadwood's Dale

Old Wood

Silver Fox Farm

Iron Workings

Row Farm

Row Plantation

Laurel Carr

Bulman's Plantation

Howe's Hill (Tumulus)

Sheringham Park Visitor Centre

Bodham Covert

A148

Mill Farm

Gibbet Plantation

Marlpit Plantation

Wood Dene Sch

Home Farm

Glebe Farm

41

Holt End

HOLT ROAD

A148

Pinewood Park Leisure Club

A148

High Wood

Bennington's Lance

3

Bodham

Laburnham Farm

Street Farm

BACK LA

Oak Hills Plantation

East Beckham

40

PH

PO

1 THE DELL
2 FOUNDRY CT

Gable End

Lower Farm

138

Abbey Farm

Manor Farm

Rookery Farm

Avenue Farm

1 ROSEACRE ESTATE
2 SAYER CT

THE STREET

West Beckham

Manor Farm

Hall Farm

NR11

2

The Highborough Farm

Walnut Farm

Chestnut Farm

PH

Church Road

Church Farm

Low Wood

Hill Plantation

Mill Lane

Moor Plantation

Lower Bodham

Franklins Farm

Highland Farm

Mast

Cemy

Coneyfare Wood

Black Acre Plantation

Rounce's Coverts

Gresham Village Sch

Lower Gresham

39

Hill Farm

Camp Farm

OSIER LANE

Hall Farm

Caspars Copse

WATERMILL CL

1

Baconsthorpe Wood

Pond Farm

Bodham Hill

Mill Common Plantation

Chaucers Farm

Gresham

Gresham

Brick Kiln Farm

Baconsthorpe Castle

Alder Carr

Stonepit Hill

Loke End

Castle Farm Castle

38

| 12 | A | 13 | B | 14 | C | 15 | D | 16 | E | 17 | F | |

20

E1
1 BEECH CL
2 THE LOKE
3 CASTLE CL
4 PASTON CL
5 BRESSINGHAM RD

10

For full street detail of the highlighted area see page 138

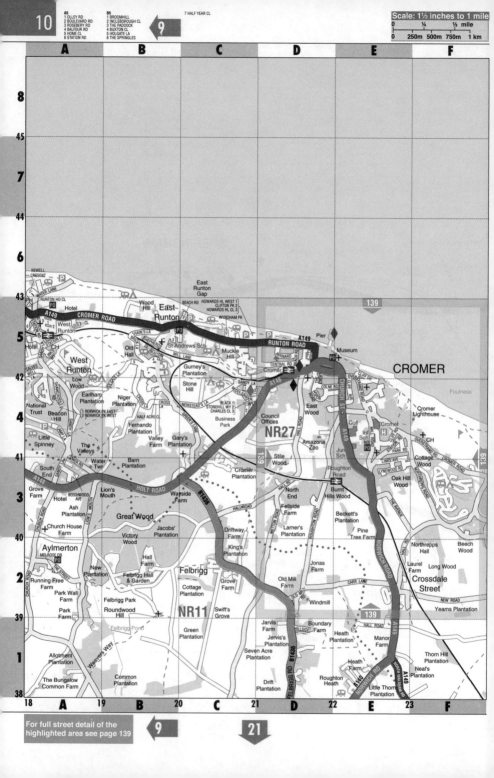

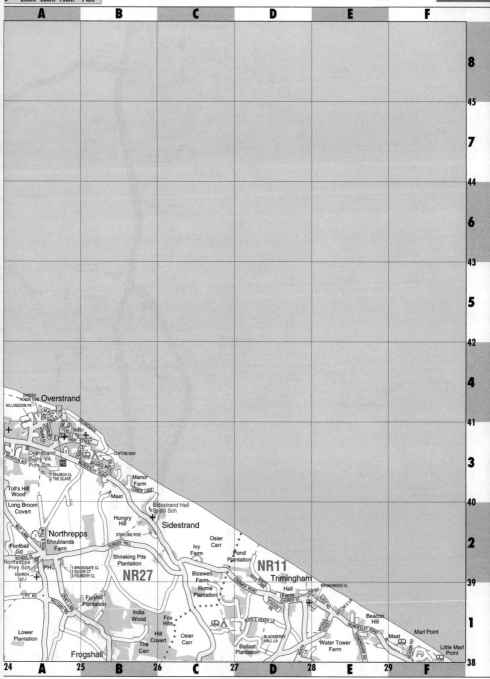

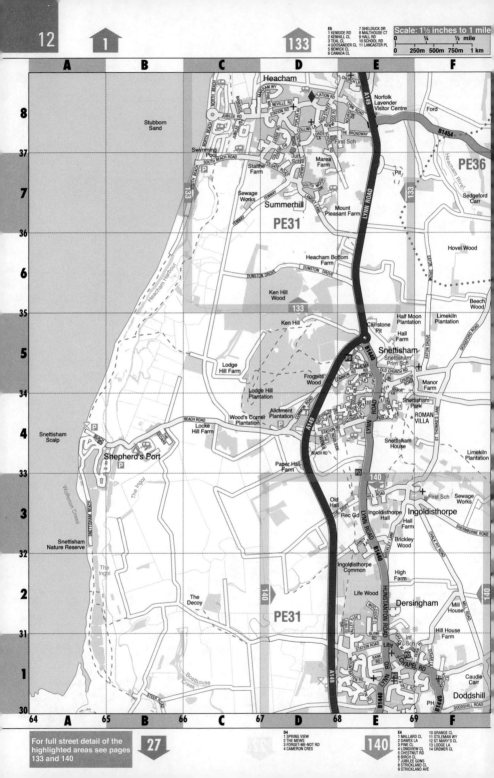

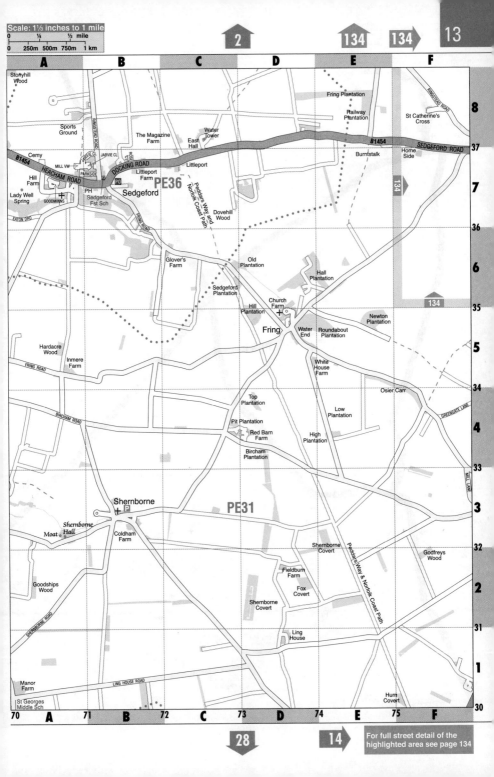

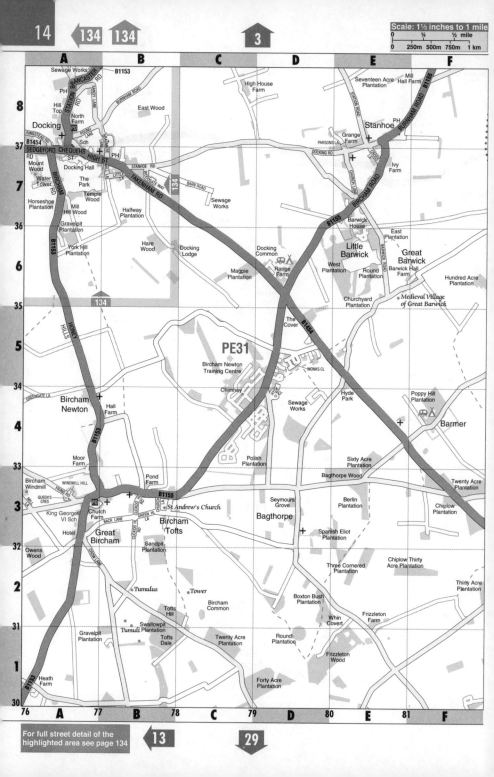

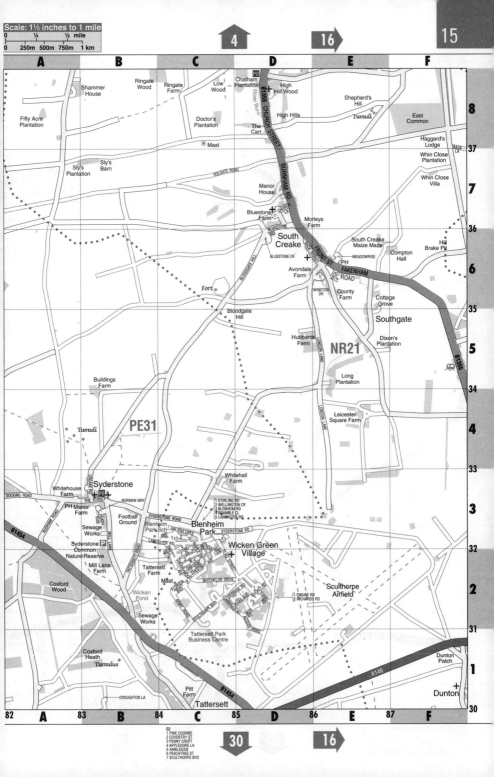

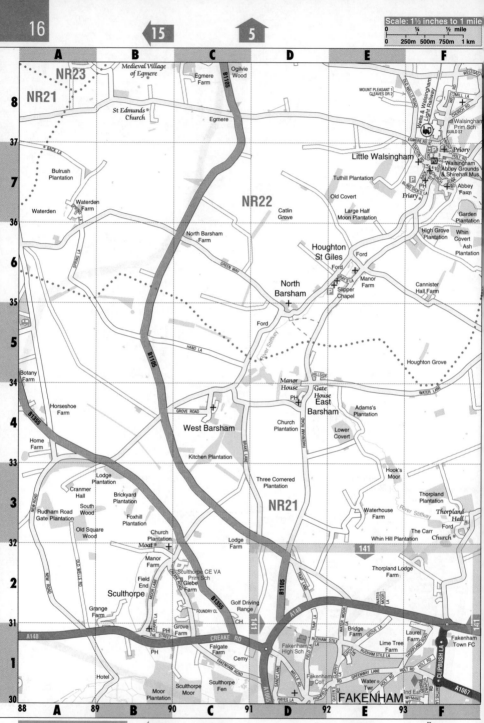

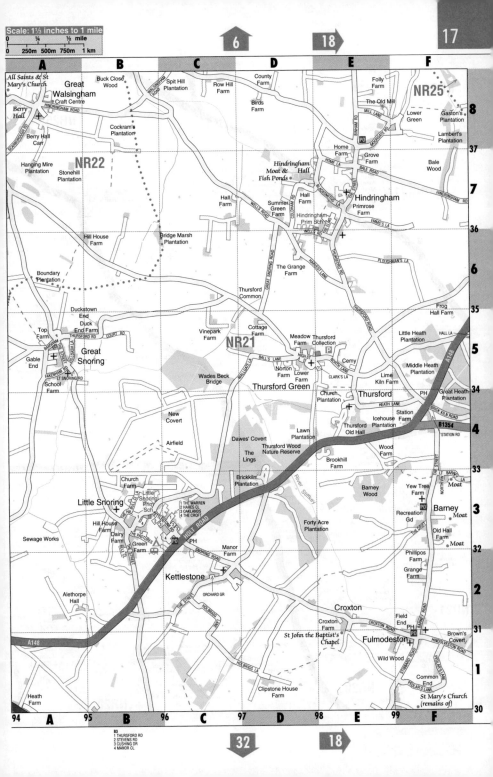

A   B   C   D   E   F

NR25

Patch Plantation
Clipstreet Farm
Bale Hall
Henry's Wood
Wells Glebe Farm
Bale Wood
The Covert
Church Farm
CLIPSTREET LA
Manor Farm
Cemy
NR21
Bale
Oak Moat
The Carr
Hurrel's Grove
SLADE RD
SHARRINGTON ROAD
HINDRINGHAM ROAD
FIELD DALE RD
Rectory Farm
Bulfer Grove

8

37

7

36

Daubney Hall Farm
Stowe Ollands
Sharrington Hall
Sharrington Cross
Valley Farm
Church Farm
BALE RD
THE STREET
UPR VILLA
UPR HALL RD
A148
B1155

Osier Carr Farm
Sharrington

Breck Plantation
NR25
Thornage New Plantation
Hill House
LETHERINGSETT RD
Ash End
Thornage Hall
Town Farm
HOLT RD
THE STREET
B1110
Thornage
Beck Farm

Stew Pond Plantation
Turf Common Plantation
Old Hall Farm
Brinton
The Coppice
STODY RD
Church Farm
Lady Astley's Grove
THE STREET
Grange Farm
White House Farm
North Meadow Covert
Stody
Coronation Covert
Kendles Farm
BRINTON RD
142

6

35

Woodhouse Farm
Rookery Farm
White Horse Farm
Roydon Green Plantation
Hall Farm
A148
HALL LANE
HEATH LANE
NEAPS LANE
SHARRINGTON ROAD
SWANTON ROAD
Gunthorpe Hall
Gunthorpe Park
Pond Plantation
Gunthorpe
Gravelpit Plantation
Townland Plantation
Briningham Plantation
Great Heath Plantation
Boundary Farm
BRICK KILN ROAD

NR24

BAYSE'S LANE
Orchard Plantation
Field End
Lobb's Valley
Hall Farm
Bayse's Wood
Home Farm
Sharpens Farm
Home Woods
DEREHAM RD
HOLY RD
GUNTHORPE LA
Laburnham Farm
Holmlea Farm
Burgh Stubbs
Foxburrow Plantation
Wormwood Plantation

5

34

Sou' Meadow Plantation
Tower
Celia's Wood
Briningham
B1110
Bellevue Plantation
Oakhills Plantation
St Mary's Church
Burgh Hall
Burghbeck Plantation
Manor Farm

4

B1354

33

Guybon's Wood
New Plantation
Osier Carr
LT BARNEY LANE
GALLOWHILL LANE
Pigg's Grave
Hempit Plantation
Old Limekiln Plantation
Park Farm
Sinks' Plantation
Industrial Estate
BRISTON RD
WELLINGTON RD
GARDEN CL
Melton Constable
FAKENHAM ROAD
B1354
Astley Prim Schl
THE LANE
PH
142

3

Church Farm
Rudds Farm
Old Hall Farm
Dogkennel Wood
THE STREET
ST GILES RD
Swanton Novers
THE CROFT
Stud Farm
Icehouse Plantation
Rondlane Plantation
Melton Park
Church Plantation
Jewel's Grove
Moat

32

Neat's Close
Barney Hills Covert
Little Wood
Brick Kiln Farm
Alder Carr
Swanton Great Wood
Woodlane Plantation
Melton Constable Hall
Deer Park
Dairy Farm
Foxburrow Plantation
Three Acre Plantation
Six Acre Plantation
Ridlands Wood
Hatchet Plantation
RIDLANDS ROAD
Markshall Game Farm

NR21

2

31

Brown's Covert
Round Plantation
Menagerie Belt
Bunker's Hill
The Lake
Workhouse Plantation
Culpits Farm
Dark Covert
Queen's Wood
Culpits Plantation
Holmes's Wood
142
RIDLANDS RD
Craymere Beck

Fulmodeston Common
HINCOLVESTON ROAD
Gill's Covert
NR20
B1110
Tipples' Farm
Gardiner's Meadow Plantation
Wood Severals
Old Rough Plantation
MELTON ROAD
NR20
THE DYES
Craymere Farm
CRAYMERE BECK RD
THE DRIFT

1

30

Raw Hall Farm
MOUSTON RD

00   A   01   B   02   C   03   D   04   E   05   F

River Glaven

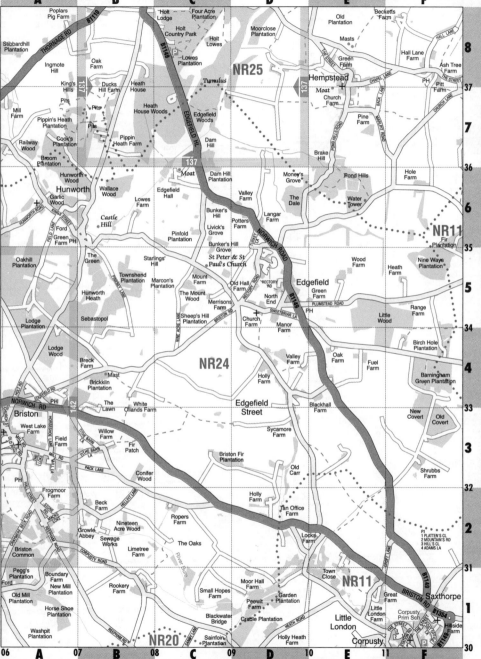

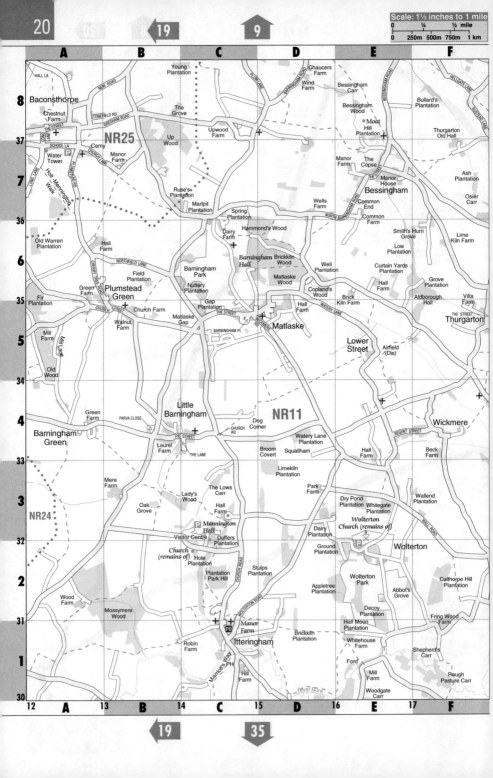

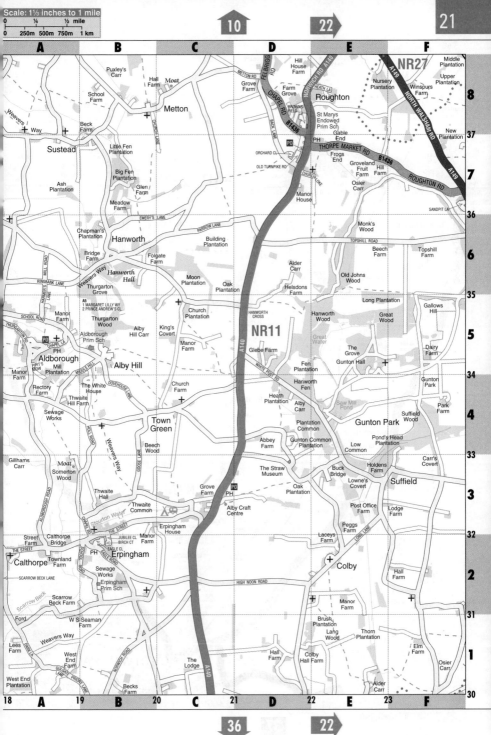

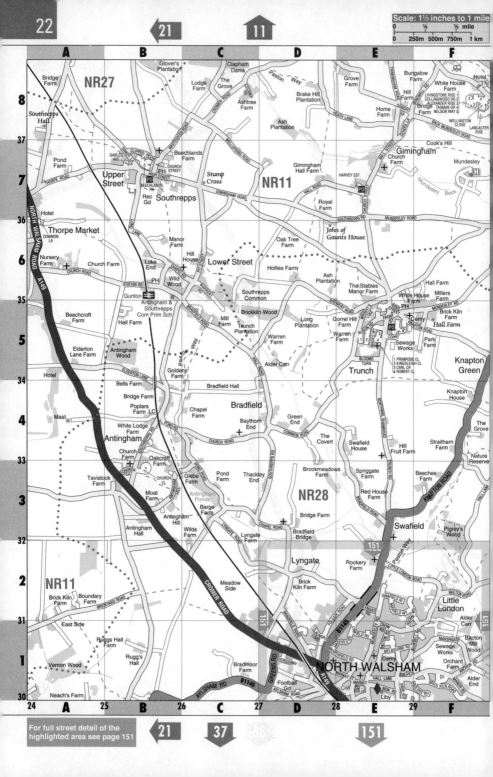

A   B   C   D   E   F

143

Cliftonville

Liby

Mundesley Maritime Museum

Mundesley

SEA VIEW RD   CROMER ROAD

P

LINKS ROAD

Water Tower

HIGH ST

Hotel

PASTON LANE

Sch

BECKMEAD

WATER LANE

TRUNCH ROAD

Stow Mill

Stow Hill Farm

Holiday Centre

143

Stow Hill

Paston Way

NR11

B1145 KNAPTON RD

MUNDESLEY ROAD

The Spinney

PERO LANE

Paston

VICARAGE RD

BEANS CHAPEL RD

Great Barn

Hall Farm

Gas Distribution Station

Knapton

Church Farm

BACTON RD

CHURCH RD

Rookery Plantation

Mast

Mast

B1159 BACTON ROAD

COAST ROAD

BEACH RD

Bacton Green

Bacton

Watch House Gap

Water Tower Sewage Works

143

Paston Green

Lowlands Farm

WODEHOUSE RD

Church Farm

CHURCH ROAD

PH

PO

BEACH RD

PH

THE PADDOCKS

Bromholm Field End

Keswick

ANNE STANNARD WAY

KESWICK RD

Old Hall Street

Paston Way

P

Parrs Farm

Croft Farm

SCHOOL LANE

Church Farm

RECTORY ROAD

NR12

Hall Farm

Bacton-on-Sea First Sch

BLUEHOUSE LANE

SANDY LANE

Broomholm

Abbey Farm

ABBEY STREET

PRIORY RD

WALCOTT RD (COAST RD)

B1159

PH

Gap End

ST HELENS RD

HELENA RD

THE CEDARS

PO

Rudram's Gap

Dead Man's Grave

Hill Farm

The Grove

Church Farm

Edingthorpe

CHURCH LANE

Stories Farm

The Grange

Grange Farm

Pollard Street

POPLAR DR

Barchams Farm

Honeytop Farm

Clay Lane Farm

THE STREET

CLAY LANE

NORTH WALSHAM ROAD

NR28

Park Farm

WEST STREET

Ash Tree Farm

Odessa Farm

Mill Common

Rookery Farm

COAST RD

Heath Farm

HENNESSEY'S LOKE

Cooper's Covert

North Plantation

Witton Hall

Common Farm

Stonebridge Cottage Selfs Carr

Batrington Farm

PH

Edingthorpe Green

Green Farm

P

Church Plantation

STONEBRIDGE ROAD

MILL COMMON ROAD

MCHROFTS LANE

BACK LANE

NORTH WALSHAM RD

Edingthorpe Heath

MILL ROAD

Road Plantation

BACTON ROAD

Manor Farm

MARSH LOKE

Witton Bridge

Church Farm

HAPPISBURGH ROAD

Ridlington

NASHS LANE

NR12

Spa Common

Muckle Hill Farm

Bacton Wood

Philip's Grove

Verona Plantation

TMH RD

HALL ROAD

Old Hall

Ivy Farm

NORTH WALSHAM ROAD

Hoole House

Primrose Farm

THE STREET

South Side

Ridlington Street

Bransmeadow Carr

Heath Farm

Nashs Farm

Ridlington Plantation

OLD LANE

Witton Heath

Tumulus

A   B   C   D   E   F

8

29

7

28

The Wash

6

Breast
Sand

27

5

Peter Scott Walk

26

4

Boat Creek

Peter Scott Walk

Admiralty
Point

25

New Inclosed
Marsh

Admiral's
Farm

PE34

BILT ROAD

Ongar
Hill

3

Admiral's
Marsh

Wingland Marsh

Walkers
Marsh

Horseshoe
Hole Farm

New
Marsh

Pierrepont
Farm

24

Terrington
Marsh

Bankside
Farm

Balaclava
Farm

Governor's
Marsh

The Laurels
Farm

2

Sharpes
Bank Farm

Burman
Farm

Grove
Farm

Fern House
Farm

Old New
Marsh

23

New Common
Marsh Farm

Myrabella
Farm

Weatherall
Farm

Creek
Farm

LONG ROAD

Green
Marsh

Marshland
Farm

Bentinck
Farm

1

Sycamore
Farm

Bungalow
Farm

RHON RD

Bentinck
Marsh

Welbeck
Marsh

Tommyshop
Farm

GREEN MARSH RD

22

52   A   53   B   54   C   55   D   56   E   57   F

Lincolnshire Street Atlas

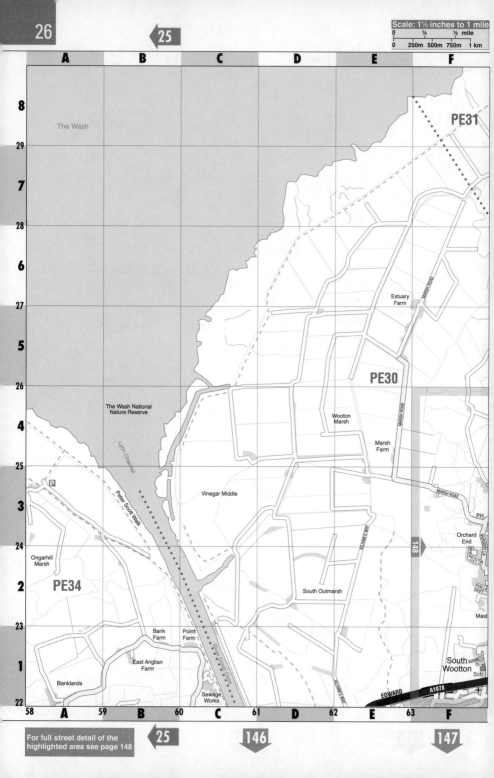

Scale: 1½ inches to 1 mile

0   ¼   ½ mile

0   250m   500m   750m   1 km

The Wash

PE31

PE30

The Wash National
Nature Reserve

Lynn Channel

Peter Scott Walk

Vinegar Middle

Wooton
Marsh

Estuary
Farm

Marsh
Road

Marsh
Farm

Marsh Road

PH

Orchard
End

148

Ongarhill
Marsh

PE34

South Outmarsh

KILDRUM'S WAY

KINGSLEY RD

WHEATLEY DR

RYALLA
DRIVE

Mast

Bank
Farm

Point
Farm

East Anglian
Farm

Banklands

Sewage
Works

Peter Scott Walk

South
Wootton

Sch

BIRKBECK

EDWARD
BENEFER WAY

A1078

For full street detail of the
highlighted area see page 148

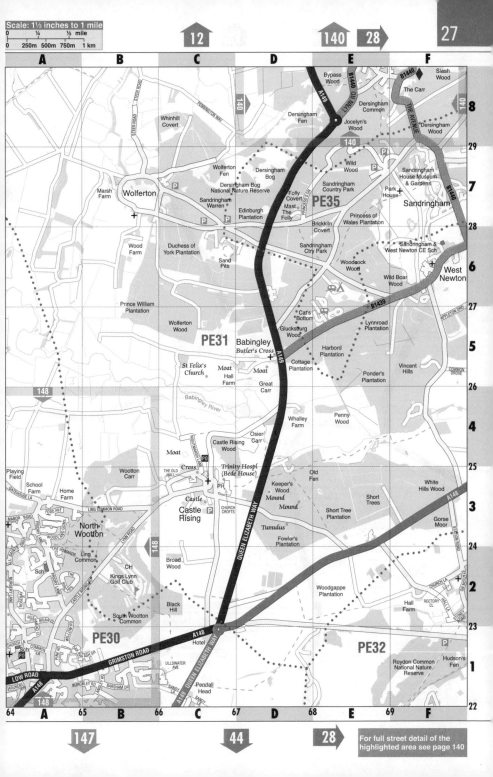

Scale: 1⅓ inches to 1 mile

0   ¼   ½ mile
0   250m 500m 750m 1 km

12   140   28

A   B   C   D   E   F

Bypass Wood
B1440
Slash Wood
The Carr
B1440
Dersingham Common
Dersingham Wood
Dersingham Fen
Jocelyn's Wood
THE AVENUE
8
140
Whinhill Covert
PENNINGTON WAY
A149
LYNN RD

140

29
Wild Wood
P
Wolferton Fen
Dersingham Bog
Sandringham Country Park
P
Sandringham House Museum & Gardens
Marsh Farm
Wolferton
P
Dersingham Bog National Nature Reserve
Sandringham Warren
Edinburgh Plantation
Folly Covert
Mast The Folly
PE35
Brickkiln Covert
Park House
+
Sandringham
B1440
7

Wood Farm
Duchess of York Plantation
Sand Pits
Sandringham Ctry Park
Princess of Wales Plantation
Sandringham & West Newton CE Sch
28

Prince William Plantation
Woodcock Wood
Wild Boar Wood
+
West Newton
6

Wolferton Wood
PE31
B1439
Lynnroad Plantation
APPLETON DRO
27

Babingley
Butler's Cross
A149
Cat's Bottom
Glucksburg Wood
Harbord Plantation
Ponder's Plantation
Vincent Hills
COMMON DROVE
5

St Felix's Church
Moat Hall Farm
Moat
Great Carr
Cottage Plantation
26

Babingley River
Whalley Farm
Penny Wood
4

Moat
Castle Rising Wood
Osier Carr
NORTHGATE LANE
P
Keeper's Wood Mound
Old Fen
White Hills Wood
A148
25

Playing Field
School Farm
Home Farm
GATEHOUSE LA
Wootton Carr
THE OLD HALL
Cross
PH
Trinity Hospl (Bede House)
Mound
Short Tree Plantation
Short Trees
Gorse Moor
STATION ROAD
3

MANOR ROAD
FORD AVE
Ling Common Road
North Wootton
148
Castle
Castle Rising
P
CHURCH CROFTS
QUEEN ELIZABETH WAY
Tumulus
Fowler's Plantation
24

Sch
Ling Common
Kings Lynn Golf Club
Broad Wood
Black Hill
Woodgappe Plantation
Hall Farm
RECTORY CL
CHURCH LA
+
2

PE30
South Wootton Common
A148
Hotel
QUEEN ELIZABETH WAY
PE32
P
23

CHURCH LA
PO
+
LOW ROAD
A148
GRIMSTON ROAD
ULLSWATER AVE
A149
Pendall Head
SANDY
Royalton Common National Nature Reserve
Hudson's Fen
1

64   65   66   67   68   69

148   44   28

For full street detail of the highlighted area see page 140

147

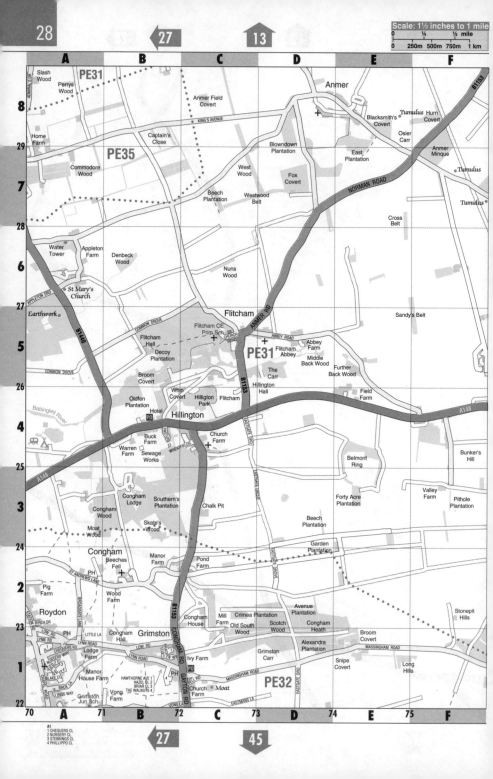

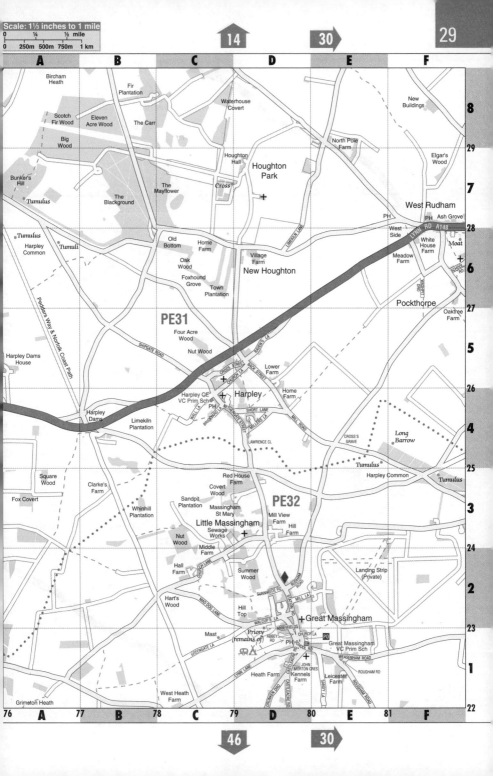

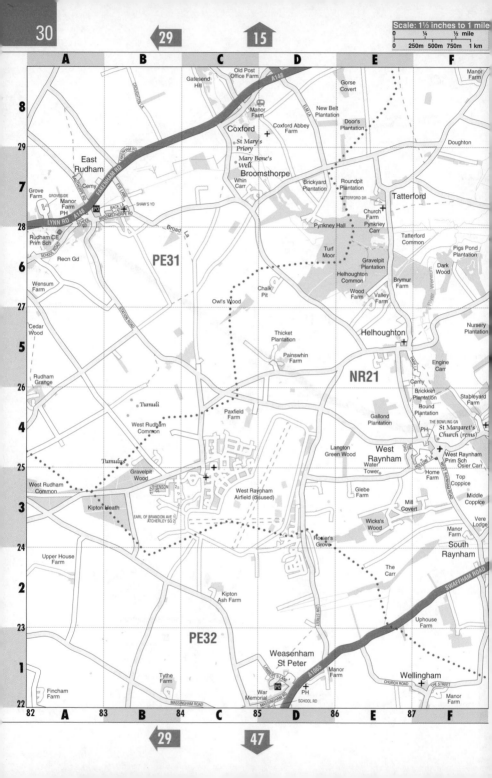

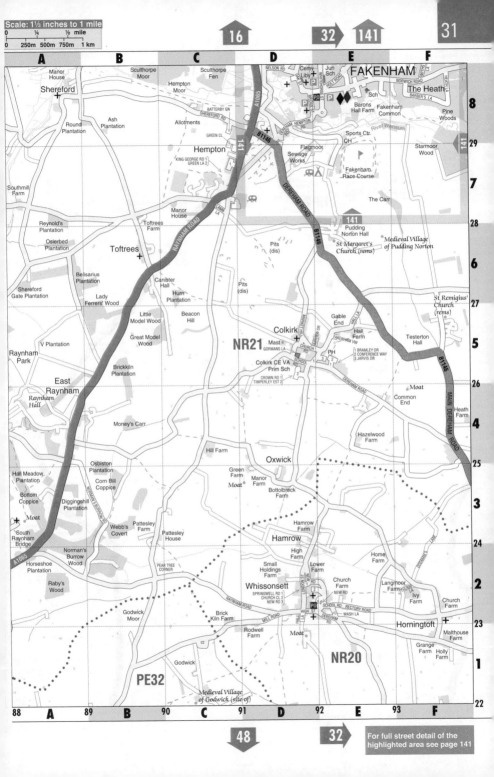

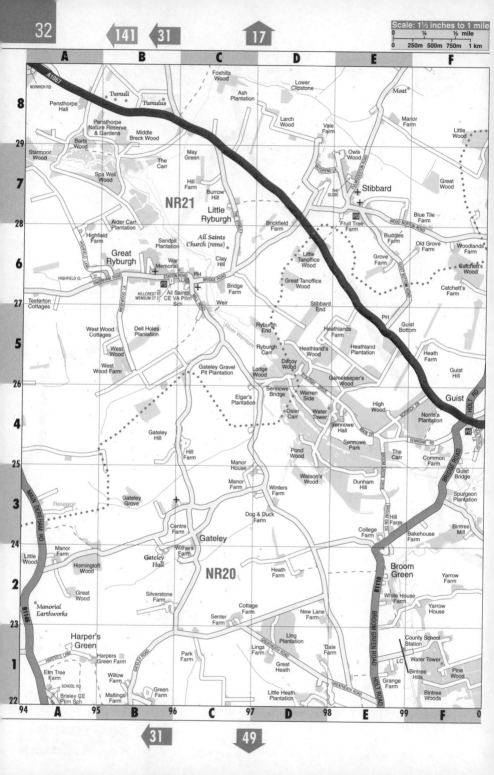

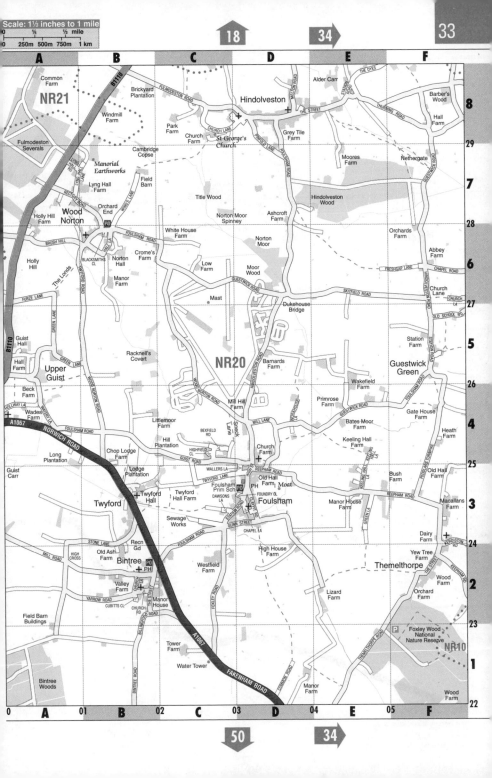

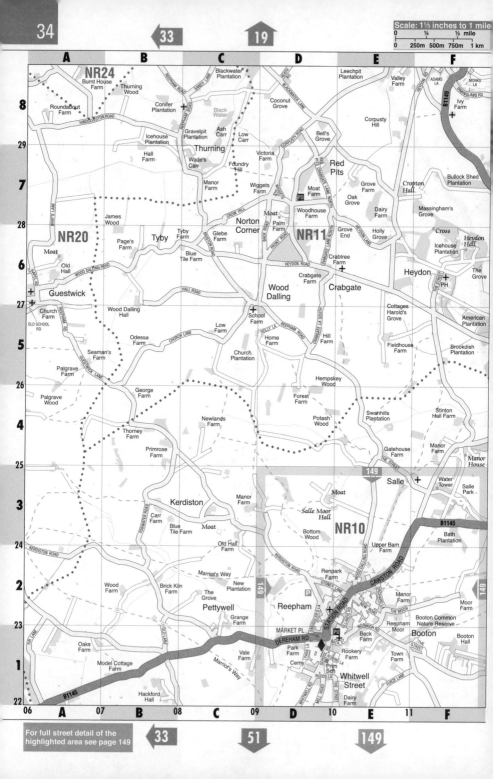

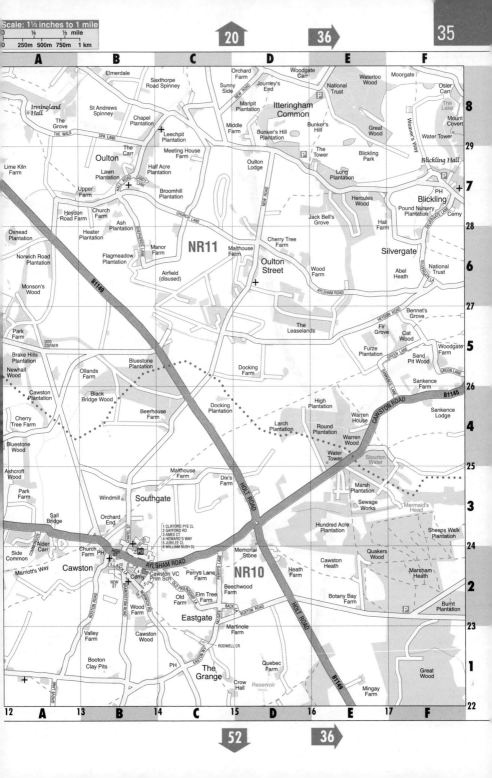

Scale: 1⅓ inches to 1 mile

| 0 | ¼ | ½ mile |
| 0 | 250m | 500m 750m | 1 km |

Park Farm
Mount Covert
Ingworth
Manor Farm
Cemy
Church Farm
Ingworth Bridge
Aylsham Wood
Banningham
Holly Farm
Sunnyside Farm
Chapel Farm
Mill Farm
Home Farm
PH
Colby Prim Sch
Laurel Farm
Cedar Wood
Hyltons Crossways
Cubitt's Carr
Little Cubitt's Carr
Poplar Farm
Manor Farm
NORTH WALSHAM ROAD
Osier Carr
Beck Farm
Squirrel's Carr
Toll Bar Wood
Hill Top Plantation
Abbotts Hall Farm
Abbot's Hall Pond Plantation
Church Farm
B1145
Brick Kiln Farm
Pinetree Farm
Rose Farm
Old Mill Farm
NR28
Brick Kiln Plantation
Holly's Grove
Lodge Farm
Ashtree Farm
Common Farm
Meadows Farm
The Meadows
Meadow Way
Holly Side
Drabblegate
Dunkirk
Weavers' Way
Coldham Hall
HEATH FARM LA 1
THIEVES LA 2
TUTTINGTON ROAD
Heath Farm
Common Farm
Oakfield Farm
Weavers' Way
Oak Plantation
The Carr
The Plantation
Tumulus
Chapel Farm
Lower Farm
Tuttington
BLACKWATER CORNER
Millgate
Aylsham High Sch
Sch
P
Hall Farm
NR11
Carrot Plantation
NR10
Chy
Sewage Works
Ashlands Farm
King's Covert
Aylsham Schs
Cemy
Hall Farm
Round Hill Moat
Kings Bridge
Hill Plantation
AYLSHAM
Kettle Brigg Farm
Stonegate Farm
Abbey Farm
Spa Farm
Motel
Bure Valley Farm
Stapletons Farm
Spratts Green Farm
FAIRFIELDS WY
Burgh next Aylsham
WHITE CROSS
North Farm
PH
Nut Plantation
Burgh Bridge
Church Farm
THE STREET
Brampton
Lime Kiln Farm
Broomhill Plantation
The Mermaid
Cherry Tree Farm
Fengate Farm
Bolwick Hall Farm
ROMAN BUILDINGS
Bolwick Hall
The Mermaid
Low Farm
Church Plantation
Hall
Oxnead
Alder Carr
Long Plantation
Top Farm
Fengate
Cambridge Farm
PH
Rodgate Farm
Marsham
1 CHURCH LA
2 LE NEVE RD
3 OLD NORWICH RD
Brampton
Belt Wood
Bure Valley Railway and Walk
Buxton Lodge
Little London
White House Farm
ALLISON STREET
NR10
Buxton
Buxton Prim Sch
Burnt Plantation
Rounce Farm
Home Farm
MILL ROAD
Vickers Lane
Mill Farm
Red House
Dudwick Farm
BULWER RD 1
MANOR CL 2
ST ANDREWS CL 3
Buxton
Lion Plantation
PH
Wood Farm
Mast
Kempton Park Farm
Holly Farm
Manor Farm
Rippon Hall
Ash Plantation
Hill Farm
Lodge Farm
Kempton Park Farm
Allotments
Glebe Farm
CHURCH LA
CHURCH LANE
Dudwick House

For full street detail of the highlighted area see page 150

F1
1 STRACEY RD
2 SEWELL RD
3 DRAKES LOKE
4 CHURCH CL
5 MILL REACH

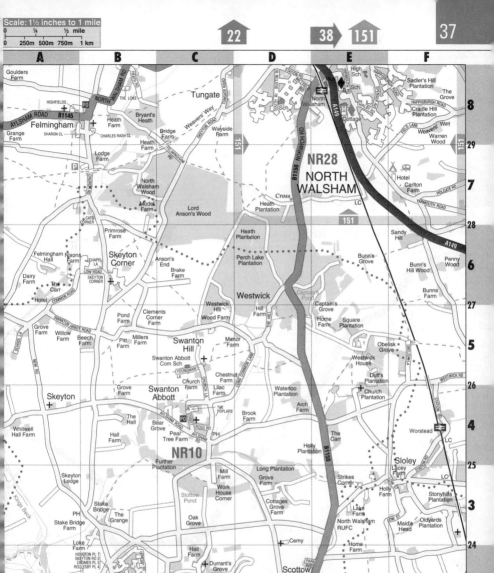

A   B   C   D   E   F

Goulders Farm
HIGHFIELDS
B1145
PO
NORTH
THE LOKE
HEATH RD
NORTH WALSHAM RD

Felmingham
AYLSHAM ROAD
B1145
Heath Farm
CHARLES RASH CL
SHARON CL
Bryant's Heath
Tungate
TUNGATE ROAD
STATION RD
BUXTON RD
SOUTH RD
STATION RD

High Sch
Sadler's Hill Plantation
The Grove
HAPPISBURGH RD

8

Grange Farm
Lodge Farm
P
Heath Farm
Heath Farm
Bridge Farm
WEAVERS WAY
SKEYTON ROAD
Wayside Farm
Weavers Way
North Walsham
Sch
North Walsham
NORWICH RD
A149
Cottage
Cradle Hill Plantation
FIELD LANE
Weavers Way
Warren Wood

29

CHURCH RD
North Walsham Wood
Model Farm
B1150
NR28
NORTH WALSHAM
Hotel
Carlton Farm
HOLGATE RD
YARMOUTH ROAD

7

CATS CORNER
Primrose Farm
Lord Anson's Wood
Cross
Heath Plantation
LC
151

28

Felmingham Hall
Nixons Farm
CHAPEL LA
LOW ROAD
SKEYTON CORNER
Skeyton Corner
Anson's End
Brake Farm
Heath Plantation
Perch Lake Plantation
Bunn's Grove
Sandy Hill
Bunn's Hill Wood
Penny Wood

6

Dairy Farm
The Carr
Hotel
COMMON ROAD
SWANTON ABBOTT ROAD
Westwick
Captain's Pond
Captain's Grove
Bunns Farm

27

Grove Farm
Willow Farm
Beech Farm
Pond Farm
Clements Corner Farm
Pitt Farm
Millers Farm
Westwick Hill
Wood Farm
Hill Farm
Home Farm
Square Plantation

NEW RD
SCHOOL LA
Swanton Hill
Swanton Abbott Com Sch
Manor Farm
Obelisk Grove
Westwick House
Duff's Plantation

5

YOUNGMANS LA
Church Farm
Chestnut Farm
Waterloo Plantation
Church Plantation

26

Skeyton
Grove Farm
Swanton Abbott
Lilac Farm
THE POPLARS
CHURCH LA
Brook Farm
Arch Farm

Whitwell Hall Farm
The Hall
Briar Grove
Pear Tree Farm
CROSS RD
AYLSHAM RD
PH
Holly Plantation
B1150
The Carr
Worstead
LC

4

Hall Farm
NR10
Further Plantation
Mill Farm
Long Plantation
Grove Farm
Strikes Corner
Sloley
Lacey Farm

25

Skeyton Lodge
Stake Bridge
The Grange
Work House Corner
Stottow Pond
Cottages Grove Farm
Lake Farm
North Walsham RUFC
Holly Farm
Stonyhills Plantation

Kings Beck
PH
Stake Bridge Farm
Loke Farm
Oak Grove
Home Farm
Maid's Head
Oldyards Plantation

3

HOVETON PL 1
SKEYTON RD 2
CROMES PL 3
ROLLESBY PL 4
Hall Farm
Durrant's Grove
Cemy
Scottow
PH
POUND LANE

24

Hall Farm
OLD HALL GDNS
THE STREET
Sports Gd
BARTON RD
The Douglas Bader School
Steward's Plantation
THE FAIRSTEAD
Home Farm
Sloley Hall
NR12

2

Lamas
SCOTTOW RD
HMP Bure
Chimney
Malthouse Farm
NORTH WALSHAM RD

23

Fendyke Farm
Sewage Works
Mast
Coltishall Airfield (Disused)
FROGGE LA
B1150
Long Plantation
Manor Farm
Tunstead
CHURCH LA
TUNSTEAD ROAD
LC
Tunstead Prim Sch

1

LC

22

24   25   26   27   28   29

A   B   C   D   E   F

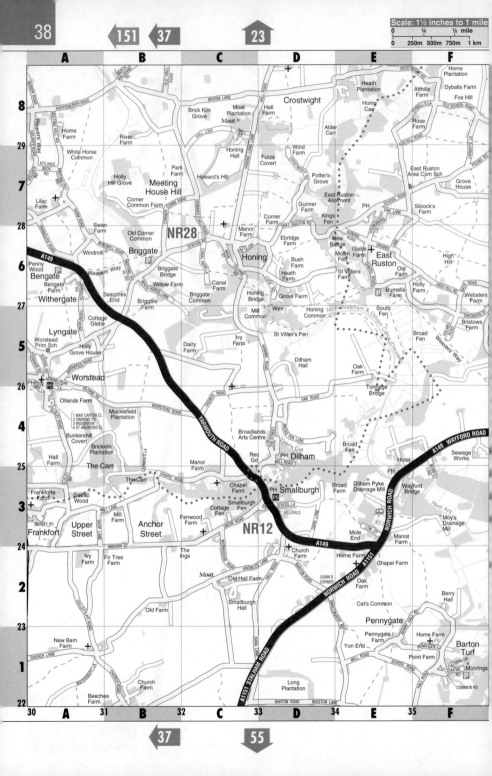

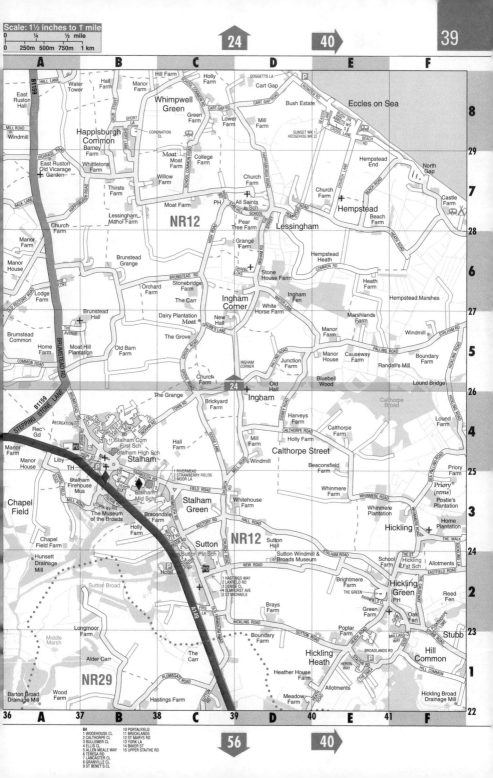

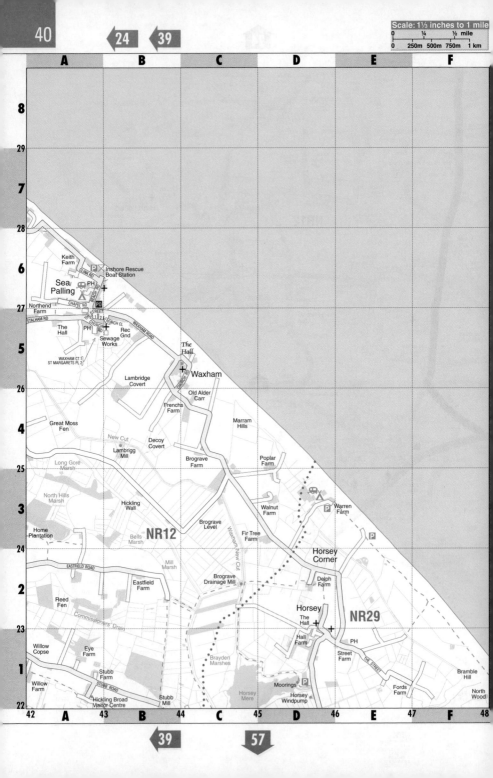

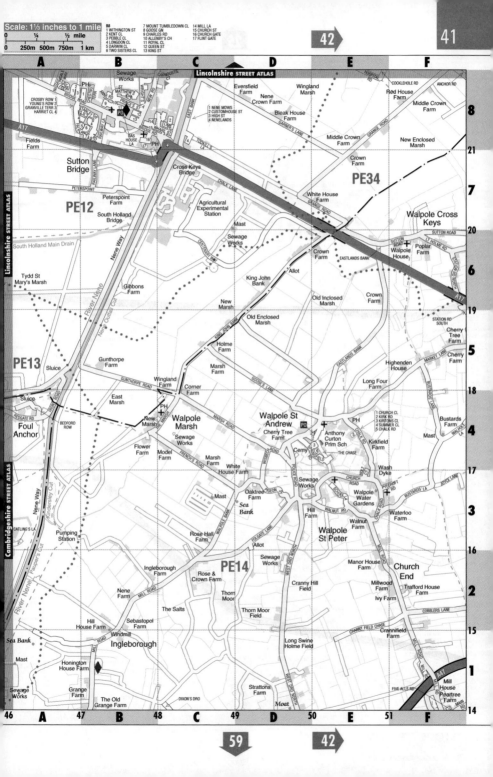

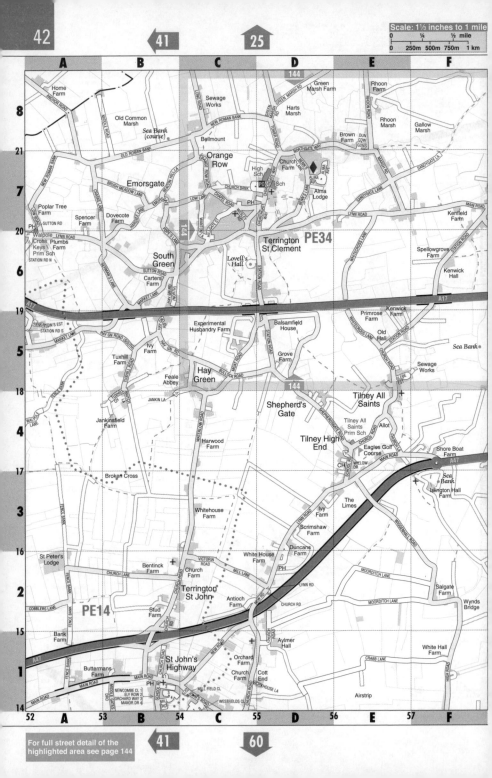

Scale: 1½ inches to 1 mile
0   ¼   ½   mile
0   250m 500m 750m 1 km

A   B   C   D   E   F

144

Home Farm

8

Old Common Marsh

Sea Bank (course)

Green Marsh Farm

Harts Marsh

Rhoon Farm

Rhoon Marsh

Gallow Marsh

Sewage Works

Bellmount

New Roman Bank

21

Orange Row

Emorsgate

High Sch

Church Sch

Brown Farm

DUN COW GDNS

NORTHGATE WAY

ALMA AV

RHOON ROAD

MASSIT RD

SANDYGATE LA

7

Poplar Tree Farm

Spencer Farm

Dovecote Farm

Church Bank

PO

Sch

PH

Almia Lodge

Lynn Road

Sandygate Lane

Kenfield Farm

MAIN ROAD

20

Walpole Cross Keys

Plumbs Farm

Prim Sch

STATION RD N

LYNN ROAD

SUTTON RD

PH

Low Lane

CHAPEL ROAD

PH

Terrington St Clement

PE34

Spellowgrove Farm

WHITECROSS LANE

Kenwick Hall

STATION ROAD

6

South Green

Carters Farm

SUTTON ROAD

MARKET LANE

Lovell's Hall

SPICER ROAD

Kenwick Farm

Primrose Farm

Old Hall

Sewage Works

A17

19

STATION RD S

MARKET LANE

HAY GN ROAD (SOUTH)

Experimental Husbandry Farm

Balsamsfield House

STATION ROAD

WHITECROSS LANE

Sea Bank

5

Ivy Farm

Tuxhill Farm

HAY GN RD

Grove Farm

GLEBE LEST

Feale Abbey

Hay Green

BULLOCK ROAD

144

Tilney All Saints

JANKIN LA

18

Jankinsfield Farm

WATERLOO ROAD

Shepherd's Gate

SHEPHERDSGATE RD

Tilney All Saints Prim Sch

Allot

4

Harwood Farm

Tilney High End

CHURCH RD

Eagles Golf Course

MAIN ROAD

Shore Boat Farm

A47

17

Broken Cross

Whitehouse Farm

CH

WILLOW DR

Sea Bank

Islington Hall Farm

3

The Limes

Ivy Farm

LYNN ROAD

Scrimshaw Farm

WISBECH ROAD

16

St Peter's Lodge

FENCE BANK

Bentinck Farm

VICTORIA ROAD

White House Farm

Duncans Farm

PH

CHURCH ROAD

MILL LANE

LYNN RD

MOORDITCH LANE

Salgate Farm

2

COBBLERS LANE

PE14

Church Farm

Terrington St John

Antioch Farm

NEW ROAD

CHURCH RD

MOORDITCH LANE

Wynds Bridge

15

Bank Farm

Stud Farm

Aylmer Hall

CRABB LANE

White Hall Farm

A47

1

Buttermans Farm

MAIN ROAD

NEWCOMBE CL 1
ELY ROW 2
ORCHARD WAY 3
MANOR DR 4

PH

St John's Highway

SCHOOL RD

ST SWAIN'S ROAD

MILL FIELD CL

Orchard Farm

Church Farm

Cott End

WOODHOUSE LA

Airstrip

HIGH ROAD

14

MAIN ROAD

WESTFIELDS CL

52   A   53   B   54   C   55   D   56   E   57   F

For full street detail of the highlighted area see page 144

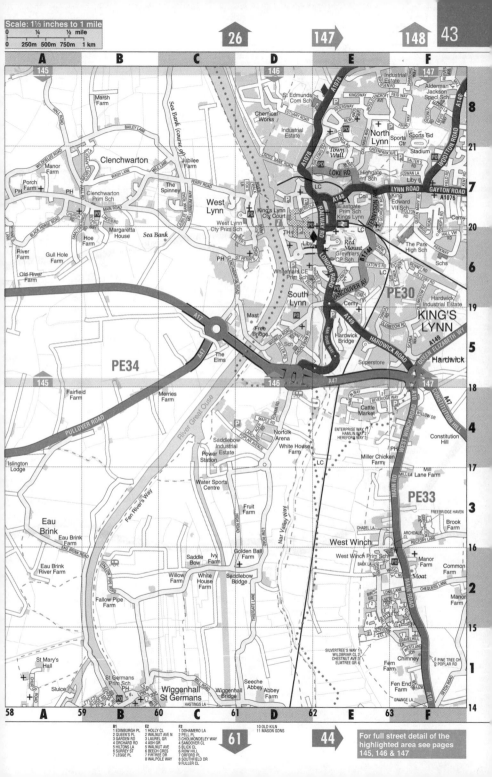

A   B   C   D   E   F

145   146   147

8
21
7
20
6
19
5
18
4
17
3
16
2
15
1

Marsh Farm

Manor Farm

Porch Farm PH
PH

Clenchwarton Prim Sch

Hoe Farm

River Farm

Gull Hole Farm

Old River Farm

Sea Bank (course of)

Jubilee Farm

Clenchwarton

The Spinney

Margaretta House

Sea Bank

West Lynn

Ferry Road

West Lynn Cty Prim Sch

King's Lynn Cty Court

PH

St Peter's

St Edmunds Com Sch

Chemical Works

Industrial Estate

Cross Bank Road

Town Wall

North Lynn

Sports Ctr

Sports Gd Stadium

Highgate Inf Sch

Loke Rd

King's Lynn

Eastgate Prim Sch

King Edward VII Sch

Cemy

The Park High Sch

Schs

Red Mount

Greyfriars CP Sch

Whitefriars CE Prim Sch

South Lynn

Mast

Free Bridge

PE30

King's Lynn

Hardwick Industrial Estate

Vancouver Av

Cemy

Hardwick Bridge

Hardwick Road

Superstore

Hardwick

Queen Elizabeth Wy

PE34

The Elms

Fairfield Farm

Merries Farm

River Great Ouse

Pullover Road

Islington Lodge

Saddlebow Industrial Estate

Power Station

Norfolk Arena

White House Farm

Cattle Market

Beveridge Way

Enterprise Way 1
Hamlin Way 2
Hereford Way 3

Miller Chicken Farm

Constitution Hill

Mill Lane Farm

Water Sports Centre

Fruit Farm

Fen River's Way

Eau Brink

Eau Brink Farm

Eau Brink River Farm

Fallow Pipe Farm

Saddle Bow

Willow Farm

Ivy Farm

White House Farm

Golden Ball Farm

Saddlebow Bridge

Nar Valley Way

West Winch

West Winch Prim Sch

PE33

Freebridge Haven

Brook Farm

Manor Farm

Moat

Common Farm

Manor Farm

Chapel La

Rectory Lane

Chequers Lane

St Mary's Hall

Sluice

St Germans Prim Sch
PH

Wiggenhall St Germans

Wiggenhall Bridge

Hastings La

Seeche Abbey Farm

Silvertree's Way 1
Wildbriar Cl 2
Chestnut Ave 3
Elmtree Gr 4

Chimney

Fen Farm

Fen End Farm

Pine Tree Cl 1
Poplar Rd 2

Grange La

58   A   59   B   60   C   61   D   62   E   63   F   14

B1
1 EDINBURGH PL
2 QUEEN'S PL
3 GARDEN RD
4 ORCHARD RD
5 HILTONS LA
6 SURREY ST
7 LEGGE PL

E2
1 HOLLY CL
2 WALNUT AVE N
3 LAUREL GR
4 ASH GR
5 WALNUT AVE
6 BEECH CRES
7 FIRTREE DR
8 WALPOLE WAY

F2
1 DOHAMERO LA
2 PELL PL
3 CHOLMONDELEY WAY
4 SANDOVER CL
5 BLICK CL
6 ROW HILL
7 ORFORD PL
8 SOUTHFIELD DR
9 FULLER CL

10 OLD KILN
11 MASON GDNS

For full street detail of the highlighted area see pages 145, 146 & 147

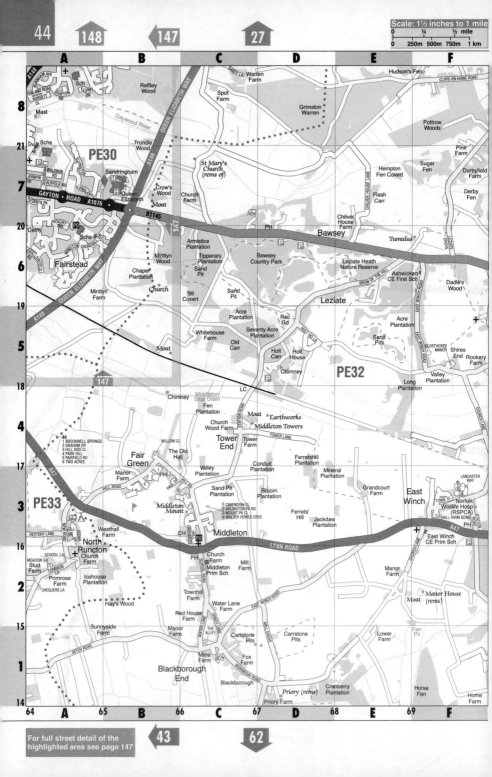

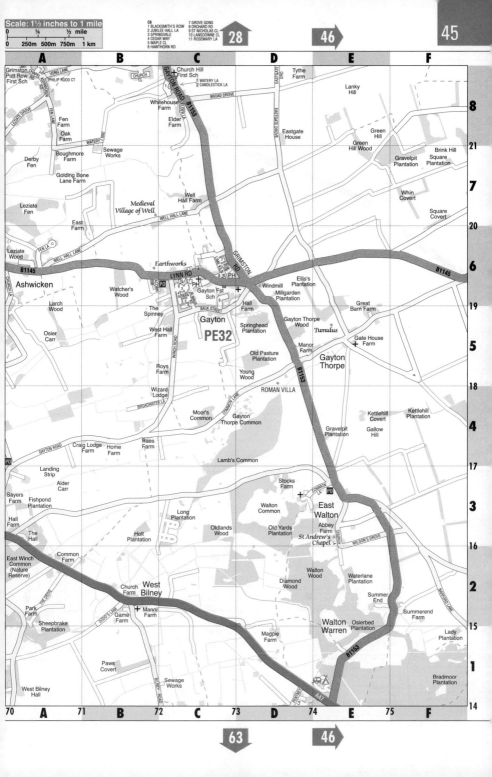

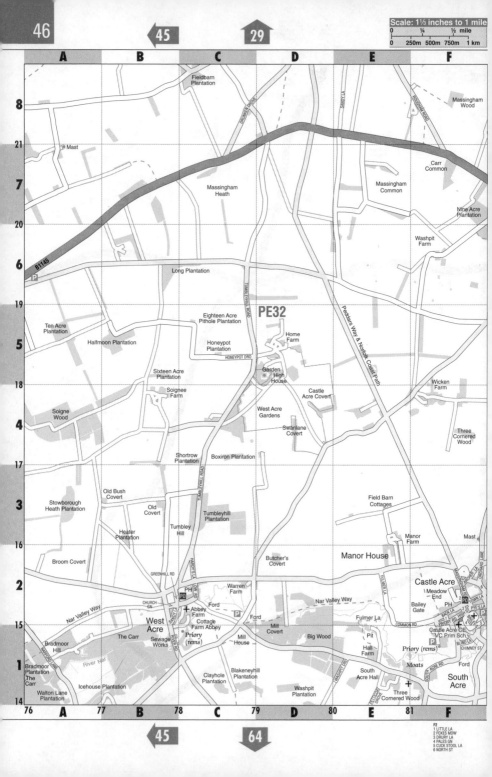

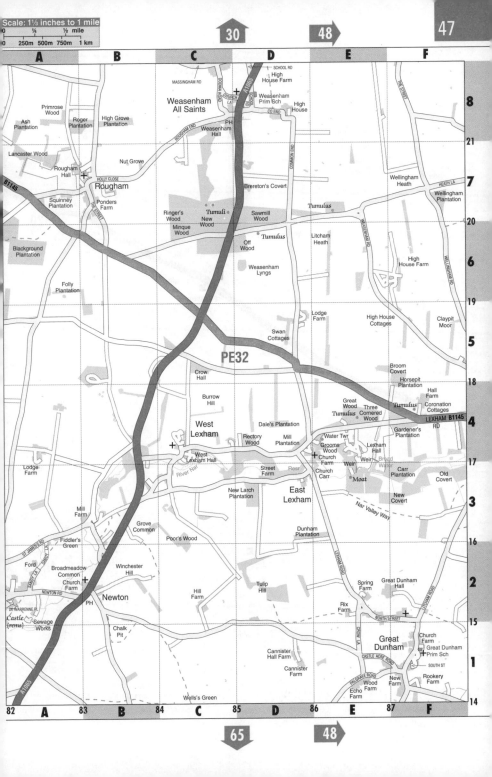

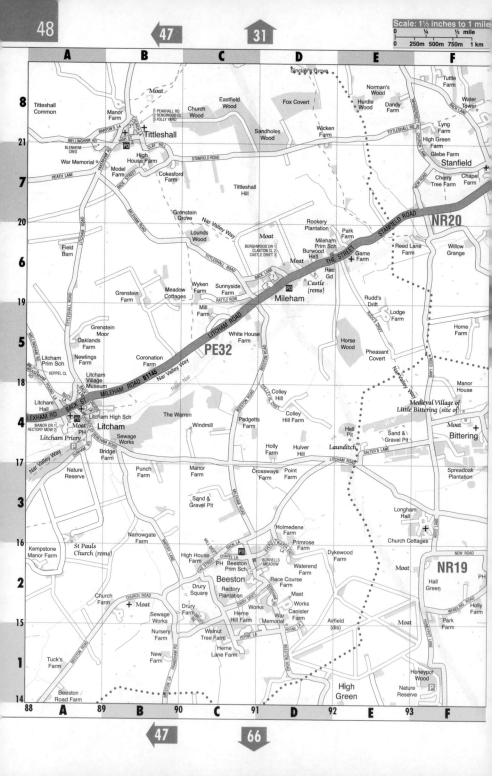

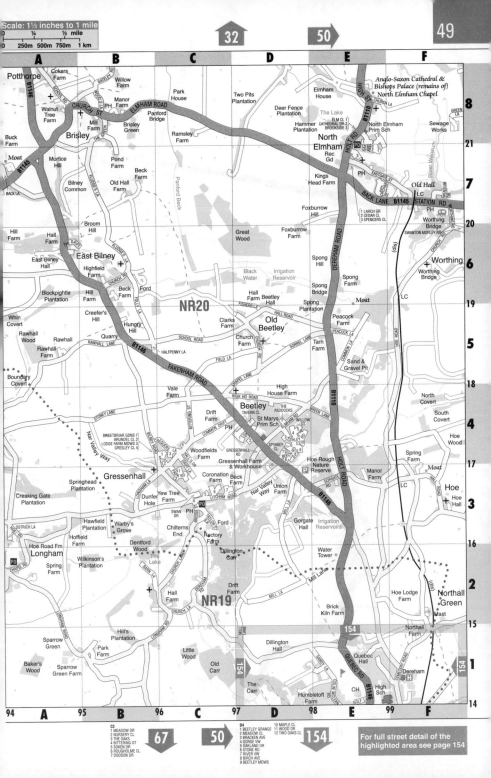

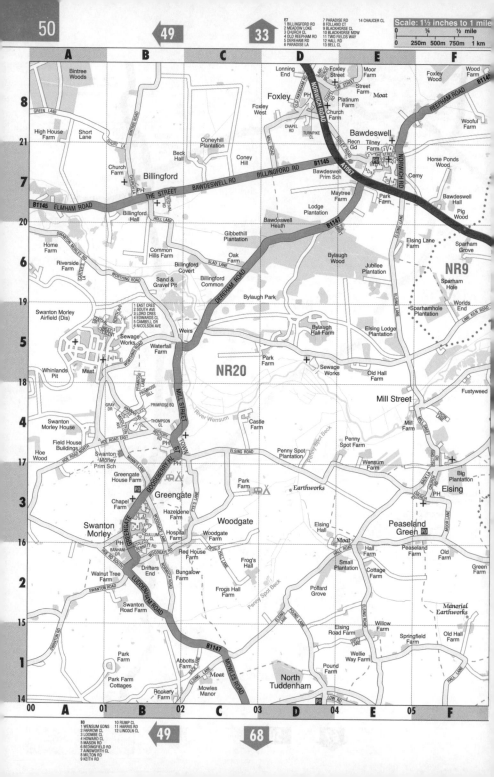

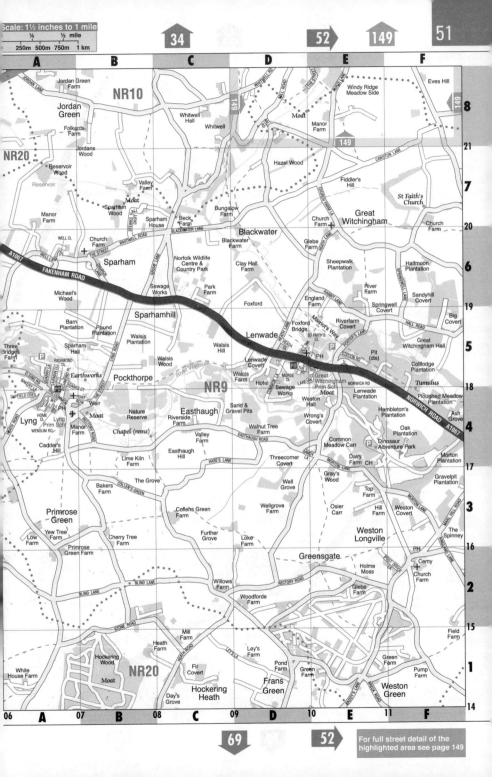

A   B   C   D   E   F

NR10

Jordan Green Farm
Jordan Green
Folkards Farm
Jordans Wood

NR20

Reservoir Wood
Reservoir

Manor Farm
Michael's Wood

Whitwell Hall
Whitwell

Windy Ridge Meadow Side
Moat
Manor Farm

Eves Hill

8

149

21

Hazel Wood

Cawston Lane

Fiddler's Hill

St Faith's Church

7

Valley Farm
Moat
Sparham Wood
Sparham House
Beck Farm
Blackwater Lane

Bungalow Farm

Blackwater

Great Witchingham

Church Farm

Church Farm

20

A1067
FAKENHAM ROAD

WELL CL
Church Farm
THE STREET
Sparham

Blackwater Farm
Norfolk Wildlife Centre & Country Park
Park Farm

Foxford

Clay Hall Farm

Glebe Farm

Sheepwalk Plantation

River Farm

Springwell Covert

Halfmoon Plantation

Sandyhill Covert

6

19

Barn Plantation
Pound Plantation
Sparhamhill
Sparham Hall

Walsis Plantation

Walsis Wood

River Wensum

Walsis Hill

Lenwade

Foxford Bridge
St Faith's CL

Marriot's Way
Riverfarm Covert

Big Covert

Great Witchingham Hall

Colllodge Plantation

Springwell Covert

5

18

Three Bridges Farm
Earthworks
RICHMOND

Pockthorpe

NR9

Walsis Farm

Hotel

Lenwade Covert

Sewage Works

PH

Weston Hall

Pit (dis)

Great Witchingham Prim Schl
Moat
Lenwade Plantation

Tumulus

NORWICH ROAD
A1067

Ploughed Meadow Plantation

Ash Grove

4

17

Lyng
Lyng Prim Sch
WENSUM RD
Manor Farm
Moat
Cadder's Hill

Chapel (rems)

Nature Reserve

Easthaugh
Riverside Farm
Valley Farm
Easthaugh Hill

Sand & Gravel Pits
Walnut Tree Farm
EASTHAUGH ROAD
HASE'S LANE

Wrong's Covert

Threecorner Covert

Common Meadow Carr

Hambleton's Plantation
Oak Plantation

Dairy Farm

Dinosaur Adventure Park

CH

Morton Plantation

Gravelpit Plantation

3

16

Bakers Farm
COLLEN'S GREEN
The Grove

Primrose Green
Yew Tree Farm
Low Farm
Primrose Green Farm

Cherry Tree Farm

Coffehs Green Farm

Further Grove

Well Grove

Wellgrove Farm

Loke Farm

Gray's Wood

Osier Carr

Top Farm

Hill Farm

Weston Covert

Weston Longville

The Spinney

PH
Cemy
Church Farm

2

15

BLIND LANE
STONE ROAD

Willows Farm

Woodforde Farm

Greensgate

RECTORY ROAD

Holme Moss

Glebe Farm

Green Farm

Field Farm

1

14

White House Farm
NR20
Moat
Hockering Wood
Heath Farm
Mill Farm
HEATH ROAD
Fir Covert
Day's Grove
Hockering Heath

LEY'S LA
Ley's Farm

Pond Farm
Frans Green

Green Farm

Weston Green

Green Farm
Pump Farm

06   A   07   B   08   C   09   D   10   E   11   F

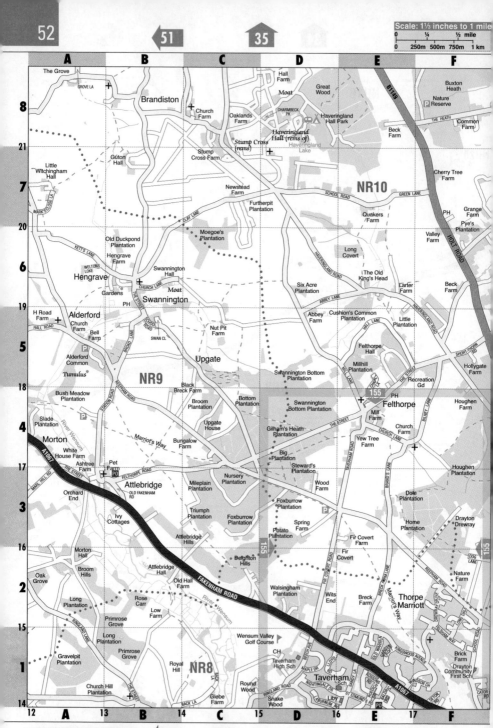

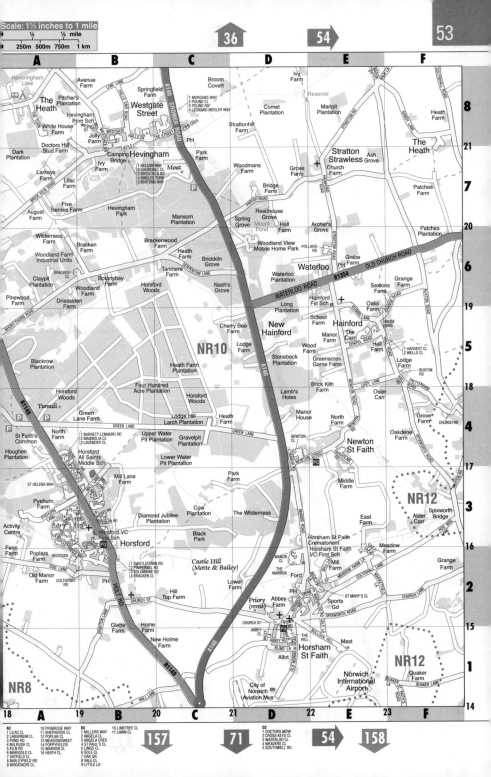

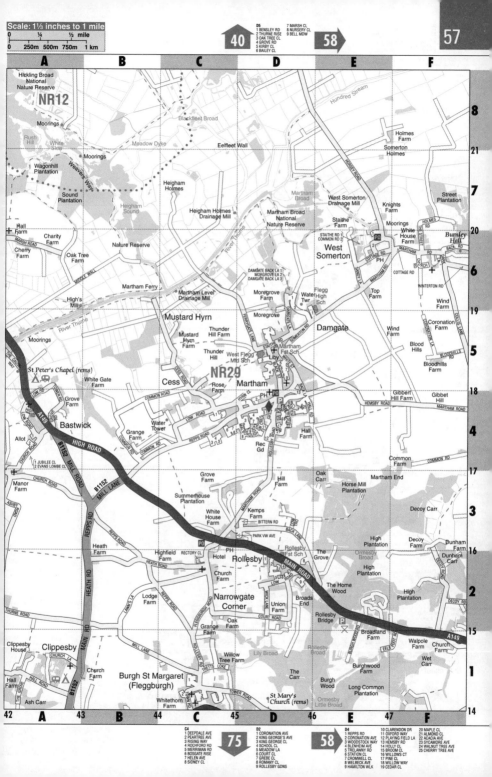

B6
1 BACK PATH
2 OLD CHAPEL RD
3 BACK RD
4 THE LOKE
5 MARINE CRES
6 WINNER AVE
7 ACKLAND CL
8 GEORGE BECK RD
9 THE COBBLEWAYS
10 GREENCOURTS
11 SPINDRIFT CL
12 LAVENDER CT
13 SANDPIPER CT
14 MARKET PL

57

Scale: 1⅓ inches to 1 mile

North Wood
Winterton Ness
South Wood

Decoy Wood

Winterton Dunes National Nature Reserve

Home Covert

Manor Farm
East Somerton
St Mary's Church (rems)
The Spinney
Winterton First Sch
Church Farm
WINTERTON RD
BACK RD
SOMERTON RD
LOW RD
BLACK ST
BEACH RD
KING ST
Winterton-on-Sea
PO
Hermanus Leisure Centre
PH
THE LANE
BURNELL LA
HORSEY ROAD
HILLVIEW DR
THE HOLWAY

High Barn Farm
Rainbows End
Mill Farm
EDWARD RD

NR29

Hemsby
MARTHAM ROAD
NORTH ROAD
Fengate Farm
COMMON RD
COMMON
Sch
FINE STREET
KINGS LOKE
THE CLOSE
THE AVENUE
Sch
PH
THE LURES
BEACH ROAD
IRB Station
THOMAS'S
PH
KINGS WAY
BACK MKT LA
PO
FAIRLEIGH WAY
HALL ROAD
BRIDGECOURT 1
BRIDGE MDW 2
SUMMERFIELD RD 3
SPRINGFIELD RD 4
SPRINGFIELD RD 5
SPRINGFIELD N 6
The Spinney
NEWPORT ROAD
YARMOUTH ROAD
ORMESBY ROAD
FAKES RD
FAKES RD
Newport
Cross (rems)
Swimming Pool
SEAGULL RD

167

167

Dowe Hill Farm
Dowe Hill
Scratby Hall
Mill Farm
THOROUGHFARE LANE
BECK AVE
DECOY
Pettingills Farm
Home Farm
Barn Farm
Manships Farm
Manor Farm
Ormesby St Margaret
Gables Farm
HEATHER AVE
BEACH ROAD
PO
LADY HAMILTON CL
FRITTON CL
YAXHAM DR
Sch
Sch
PO
PH
PRIVATE RD
THE PROMENADE
EDWARDS RD
Scratby
California
PH
California Farm
California Rd
CALIFORNIA CR
OLD COAST ROAD
STATION ROAD
MAIN RD
A149
CROMER RD
Ormesby St Michael
Manship's Plantation
MILL LANE
Filby Lane Farm
FILBY LA
NOVA
Ormesby Hall
BRIDECAMP CL
Willow Farm
YARMOUTH ROAD
PH Hotel
NR30

For full street detail of the highlighted area see page 167

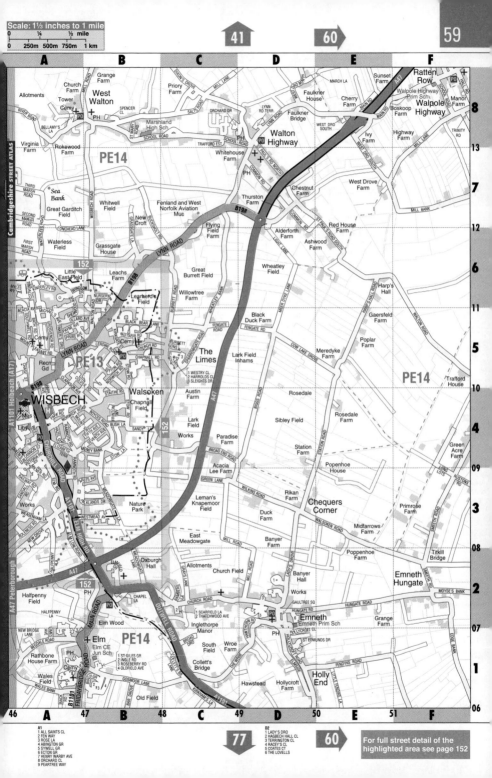

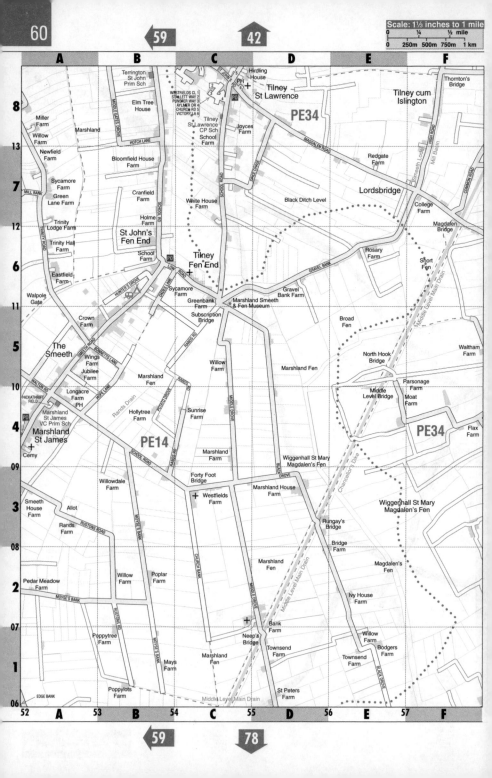

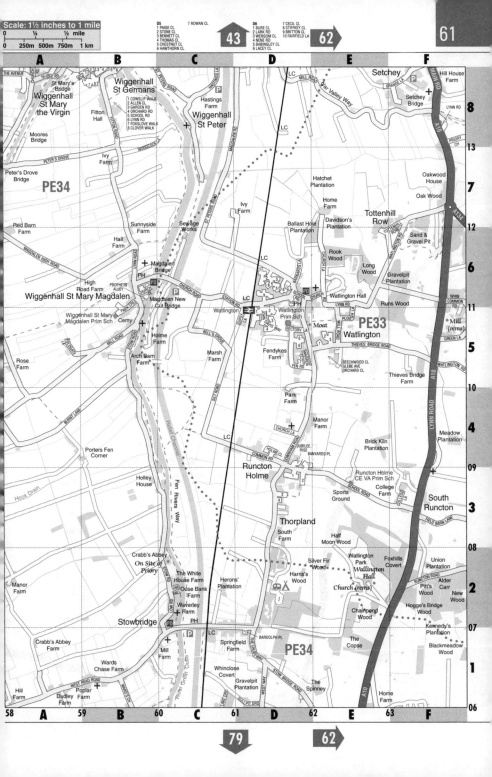

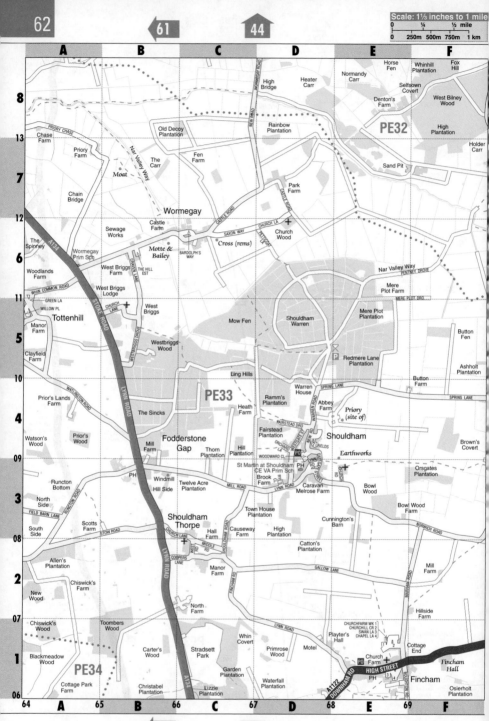

A B C D E F

8

13

7

12

6

11

5

10

4

09

3

08

2

07

1

06

PE32

Horse Fen
Whinhill Plantation
Fox Hill

Normandy Carr
Selfsown Covert
West Bilney Wood

Denton's Farm
High Plantation
Holder Carr

Sand Pit

PRIORY CHASE
Chase Farm

Old Decoy Plantation
Rainbow Plantation

Heater Carr

High Bridge

WORMEGAY ROAD
NEW ROAD

Priory Farm
The Carr
Fen Farm

Nar Valley Way

Moat

Park Farm

CASTLE ROAD

Chain Bridge

Wormegay

Castle Farm

SAXON WAY
CHURCH LA
Church Wood
Cross (rems)

The Spinney
A134
Sewage Works
Motte & Bailey
BARDOLPH'S WAY

Nar Valley Way
PENTLEY DROVE

Woodlands Farm
Wormegay Prim Sch
West Briggs Farm
THE HILL EST
CHURCH LANE

Mere Plot Farm
MERE PLOT DRO

WHIN COMMON ROAD
West Briggs Lodge

STOKE ROAD

GREEN LA
WILLOW PL
Tottenhill
CHURCH LANE
West Briggs
LYNN BRANCH RD

Mow Fen

Shouldham Warren
Mere Plot Plantation

Button Fen

Manor Farm
Westbriggs Wood

Redmere Lane Plantation

Button Farm
Ashholt Plantation

Clayfield Farm

Ling Hills

PE33

Prior's Lands Farm
WATLINGTON ROAD

The Sincks
Heath Farm

Ramm's Plantation
Warren House

SPRING LANE

SPRING LANE

Watson's Wood
Prior's Wood

Abbey Farm

Priory (site of)
Brown's Covert

LYNN ROAD

Fodderstone Gap
Thorn Plantation
Hill Plantation
FAIRSTEAD DRO
Fairstead Plantation
ORCHARD LA
WOODWARD CL

Shouldham
Earthworks

Orsgates Plantation

Mill Farm
PH
Windmill Hill Side
Twelve Acre Plantation

St Martin at Shouldham CE VA Prim Sch
Brook Farm
PH
PYE RD

Bowl Wood

Runcton Bottom

MILL ROAD

Caravan
Melrose Farm

Bowl Wood Farm

North Side
FIELD BARN LANE
Scotts Farm
STOW ROAD
Shouldham Thorpe
CHURCH LANE
Town House Plantation
Causeway Farm
High Plantation

Cunnington's Barn

NORWICH ROAD

South Side

Hall Farm
WEST RD
MIDDLE RD
SHOULDHAM RD

Catton's Plantation

GALLOW LANE

Mill Farm

Allen's Plantation
COOPERS LANE

Manor Farm
FINCHAM RD

MARHAM ROAD

Chiswick's Farm
New Wood

North Farm

Hillside Farm

Chiswick's Wood
Toombers Wood

LYNN ROAD

CHURCHFARM WK 1
CHURCHILL CR 2
SWAN LA 3
CHAPEL LA 4
Player's Hall

Cottage End

Blackmeadow Wood

PE34

Carter's Wood
Stradsett Park

A134

Whin Covert

Primrose Wood

Motel

A1122
HIGH STREET
Church Farm
PH
DOWNHAM RD
Fincham

Fincham Hall

Cottage Park Farm

Christabel Plantation
Lizzie Plantation

Garden Plantation
Waterfall Plantation

Osierholt Plantation

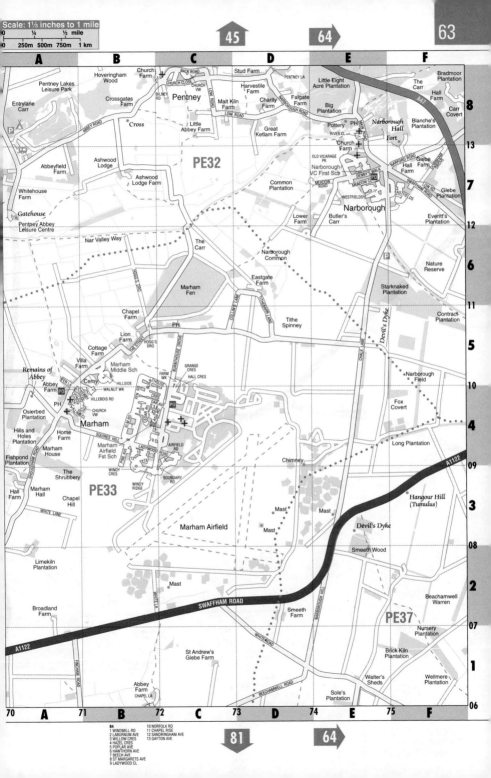

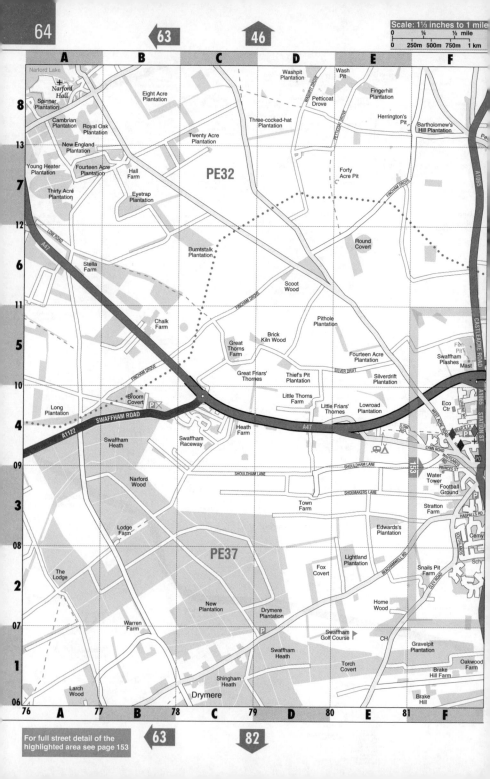

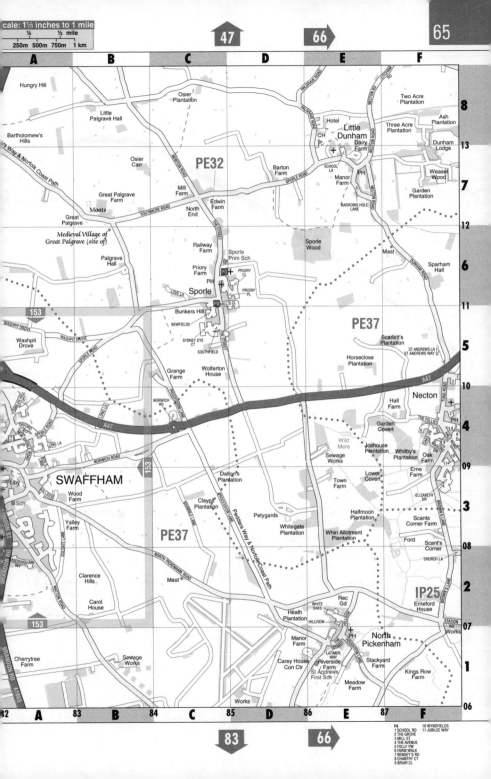

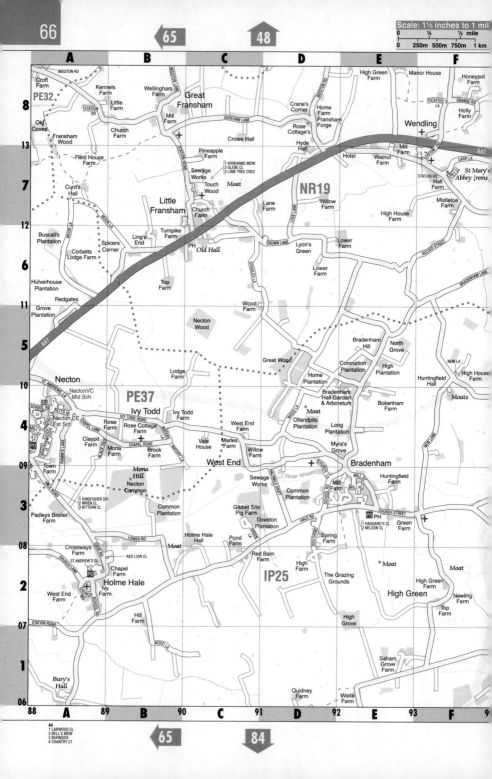

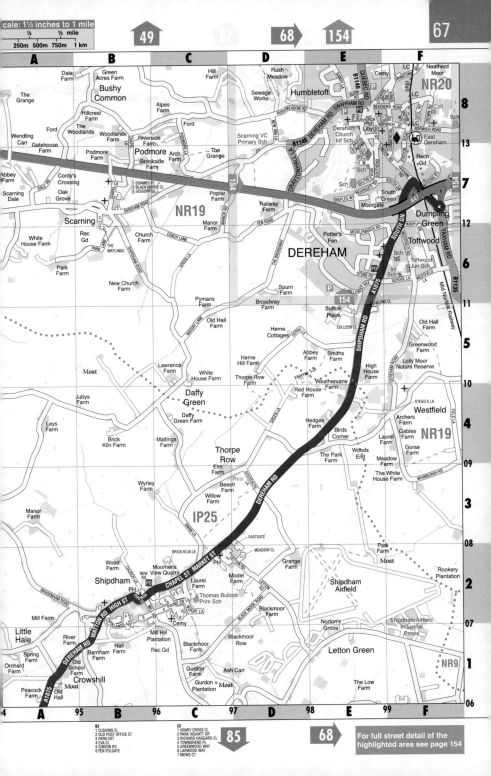

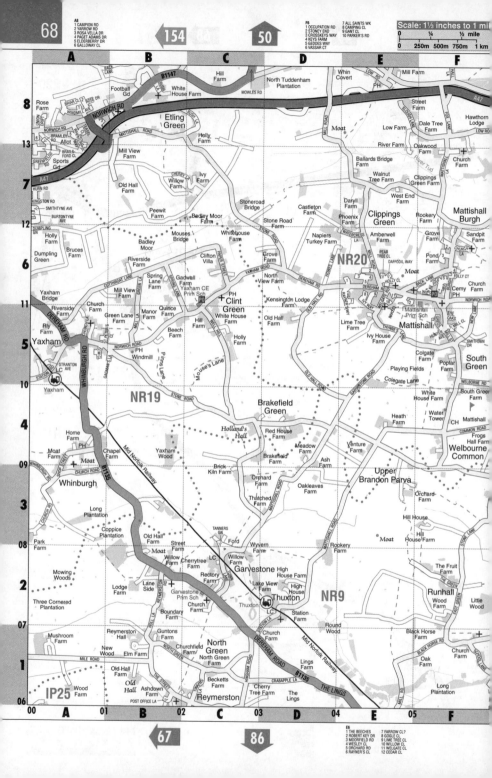

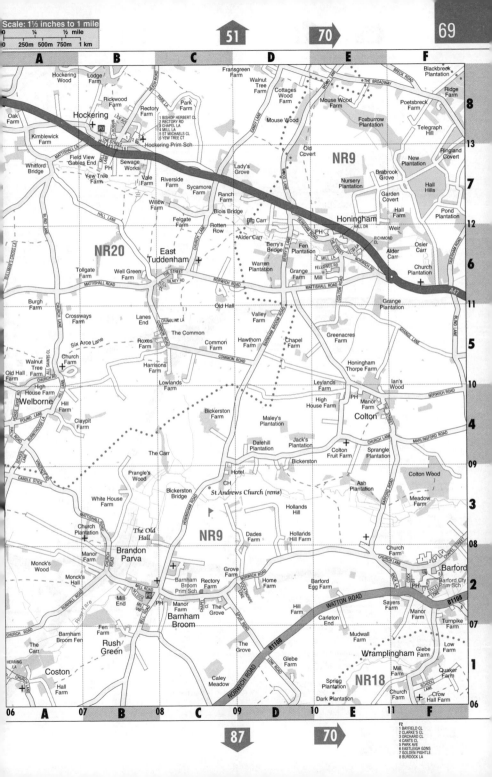

Scale: 1½ inches to 1 mile

0   ¼   ½ mile
0   250m   500m   750m   1 km

A   B   C   D   E   F

8

13

7

12

6

11

5

10

4

09

3

08

2

07

1

06

Blackbreck Plantation
Poets Breck Farm
Poetbreck Plantation
Barn Plantation
Harman's Grove
Hill Farm
Riverside Farm

Manor Farm
Ringland
Jennis' Wood
Dryhill Plantation
Slade Hills
Ave's Gap
Stonyhole Plantation
Spruce Plantation
Snake's Hills
Paddock Plantation
Hill Grove Plantation

PH
THE STREET
Low Common
Ringland Wood
NR8
Blyth's Wood
Three Corner Plantation
Ringland Hills
Ringland Plantation
Old Wood
Holly Wood
Weir
Westlodge Hills
Longdell Hills

Snake Wood
Taverham Hall Sch
Church Farm
Blackhill Wood
Sch
Lord's Hills
Queen's Hills
Snake's Hills
Bog Wood
Reservoir Hill
Sand & Gravel Pit

Taverham Mid Sch
Ghost Hill Fst Sch
Taverham
Place Farm
Church Farm
Transport Plantation
Brickfield Farm
Tower Hill
CH
Costessey Park

A1067 FAKENHAM RD
Costessey
Green Hills
Cemy
Costessey High Sch
Bunkers Hill
Cleves Way
River Tud

A47
A47
Water Tower
Easton
Four Acre Plantation
St Peters CE VC Prim Sch
Fit Covert
Model Farm
Broom Farm
BUXTON CL 1
EDDINGTON WAY 2
PARKER'S CL 3
RINGLAND LA 4
ST PETERS DR 5
KENNEDY CL 6
PEGG CL 7
PEACOCK CL 8
CARDINAL CL 9
Mast
NR9
Marlingford Sports Club
Cobb's Grove Plantation

Dereham Road
Royal Norfolk Showground
Stafford's Plantation
Sand Pit
Dunham's Plantation
Playing Fields
Easton Coll
Three Cornered Plantation
The Harrings
Valley Farm
Glen Lodge Farm

A1074 DEREHAM ROAD
Hotel
P&R
Lodge Farm
Round Well
Beech Plantation
NR5
Sand & Gravel Pits

Water Tower
Hotel
Costessey Jun Sch
PO
Sch   Sch
Bowthorpe
PO

Marlingford
Blue Cedar Farm
PH
Morris' Grove
Home Farm
The Common
Chapel Farm
The Old Hall

Bawburgh Road
River Yare
Beech Grove
Algarsthorpe Farm
St Walston's Well
Bridge
CHURCH ST

Woods End
Bawburgh
Bawburgh Prim Sch
Lodge Farm
Clinkhill Plantation

St Michael's Church (rems)
Sand & Gravel Pits
Summer House Plantation

Moat
Bungalow Farm
Marlingford Hall
Earthworks
Common Farm
Four Oak Plantation
River Plantation
Bow Hill
Swan's Harbour
Ryehill Plantation

Admiral's Wood
High House Farm
Port Arthur Wood

WATTON ROAD
Thorn Pit Plantation
Gravel Pit Plantation
Sewage Works
Bawburgh Hill
Villa Farm
Mast
Colney Wood
NR4
Rybeck Plantation
Limekiln Wood
Milestone Plantation
WATTON ROAD   B1108

B1108
NR18
Oak Pollard
Coleseed Plantation
Hall Farm
Pockthorpe
Great Melton
School Plantation
Melton Hall (rems)
Furze Ground
Lodge Plantation
Church Plantation
Church (rems)
Market Lane
Coronation Wood
Church Farm
Walnut Tree Farm
Beckhithe
Little Melton
PH
Sch
Manor Farm
Hospital Farm
Elm Farm
Braymeadow Bottom
Braymeadow Farm
Norfolk & Norwich
Great Melton Road

A   B   C   D   E   F

12   13   14   15   16   17

For full street detail of the highlighted area see pages 156 and 160

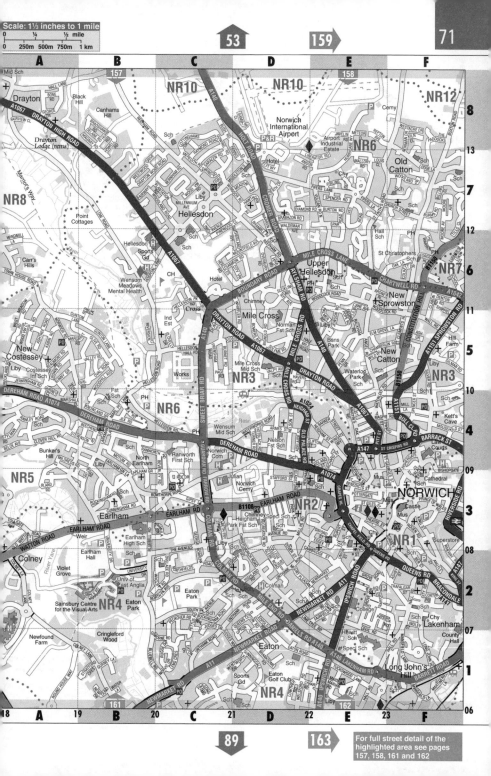

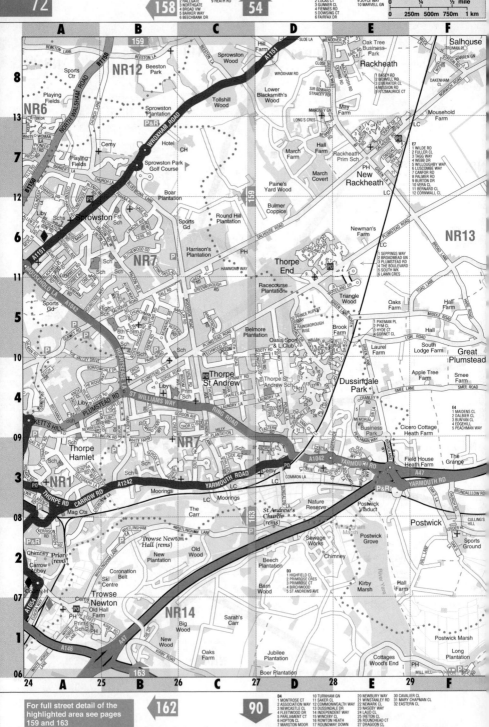

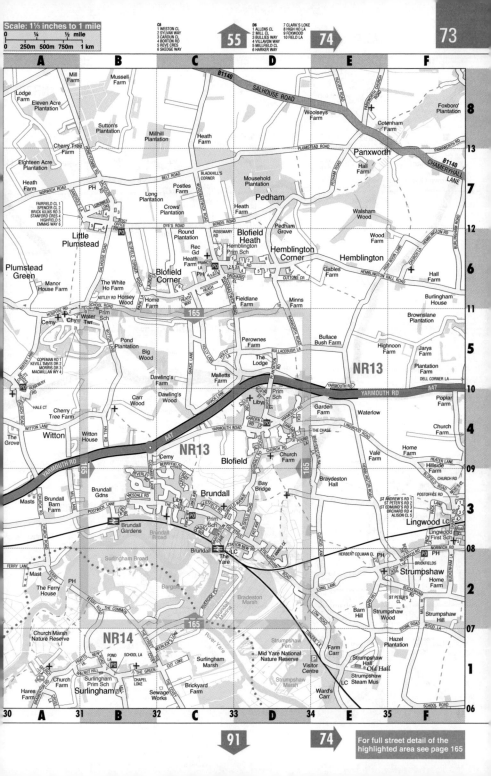

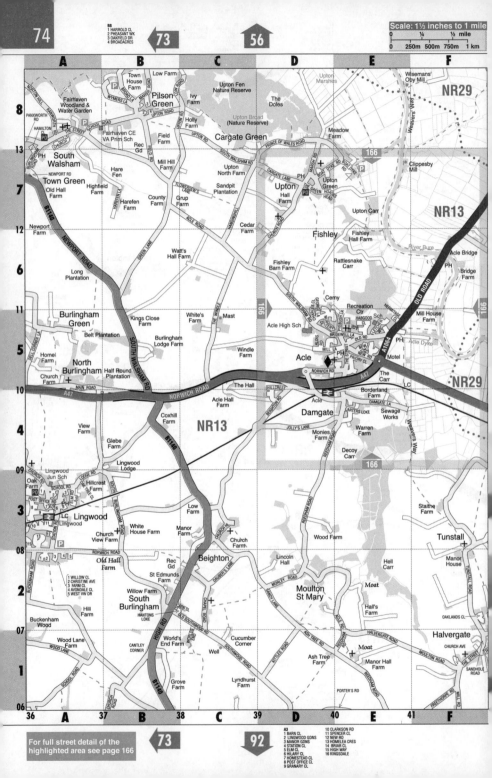

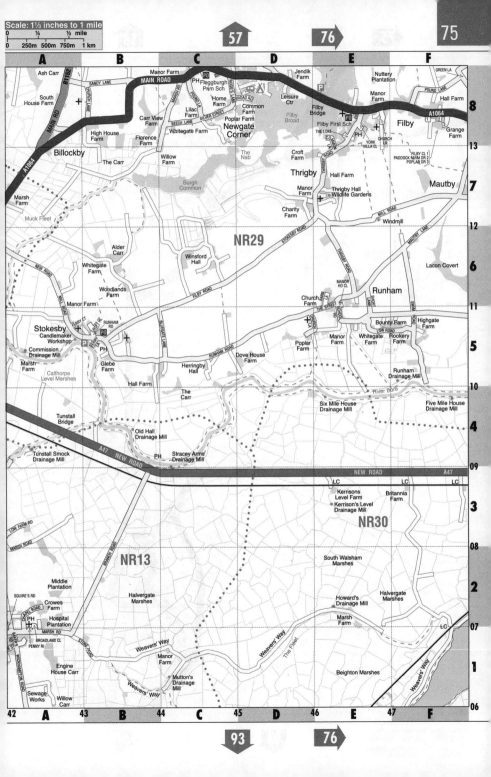

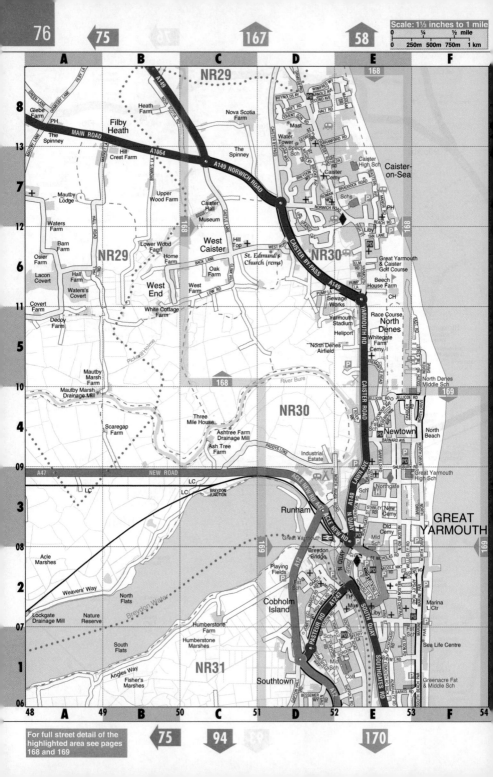

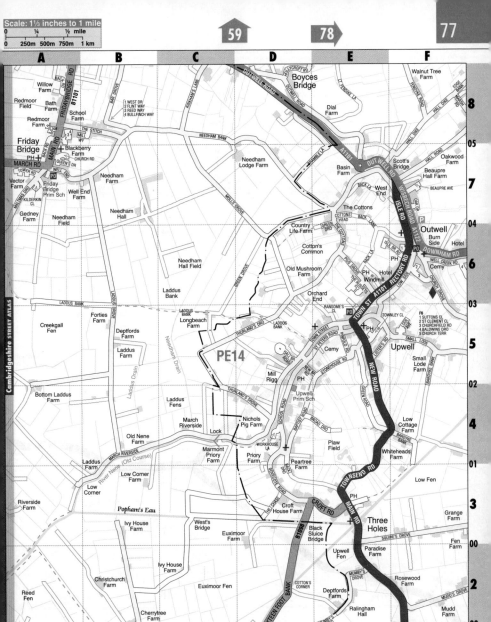

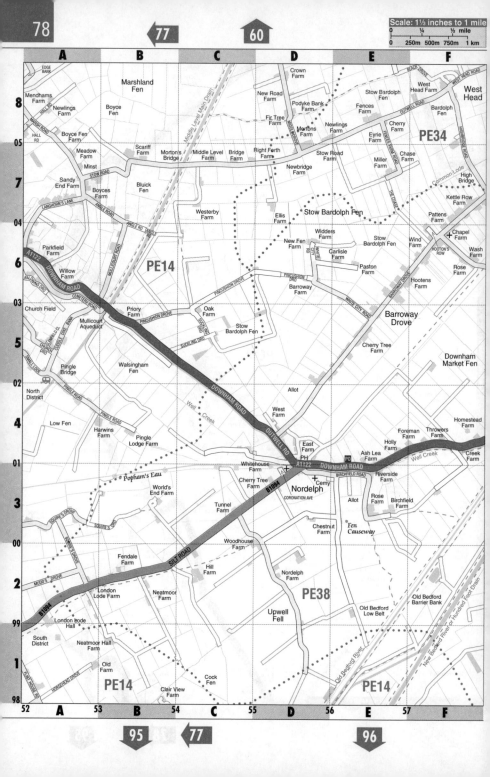

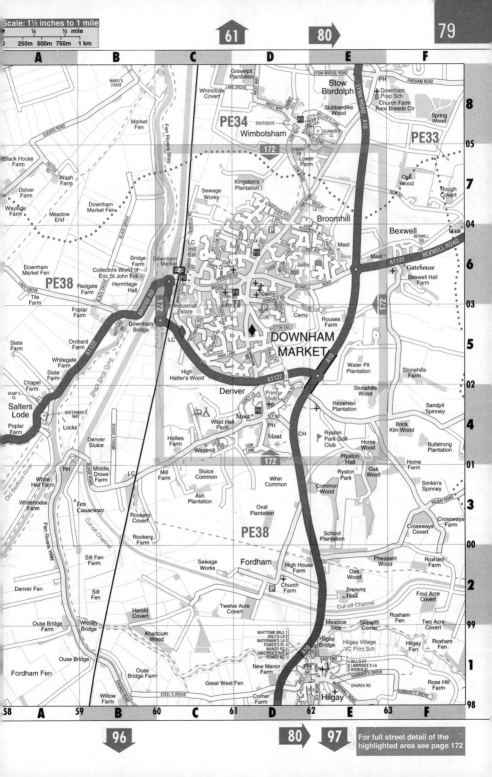

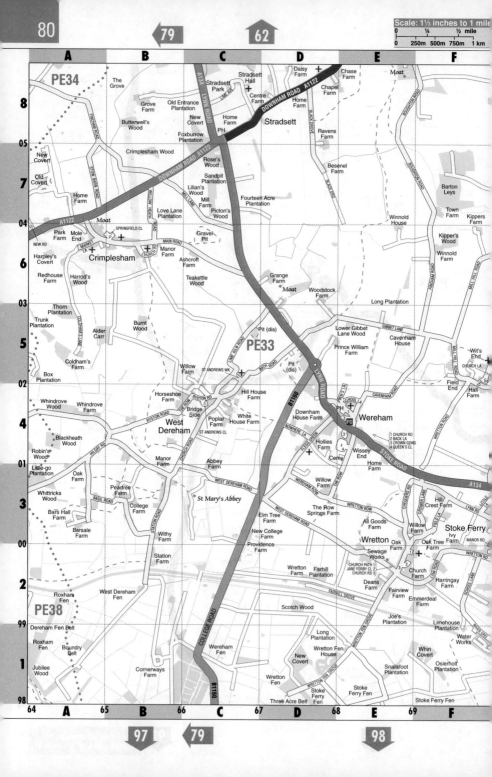

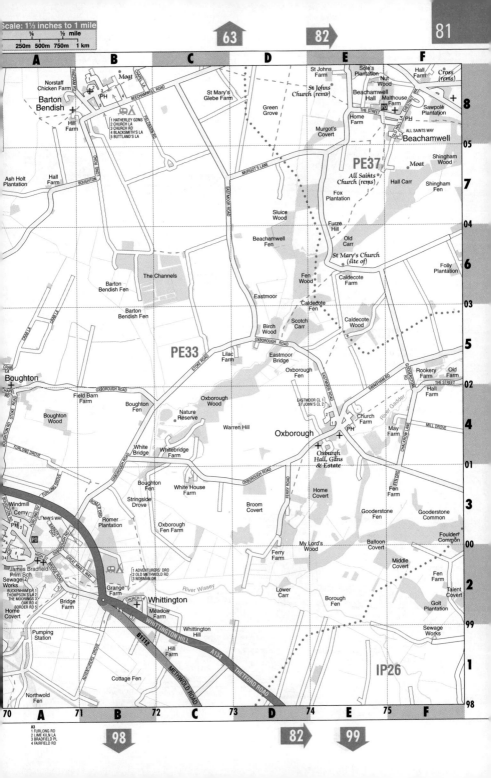

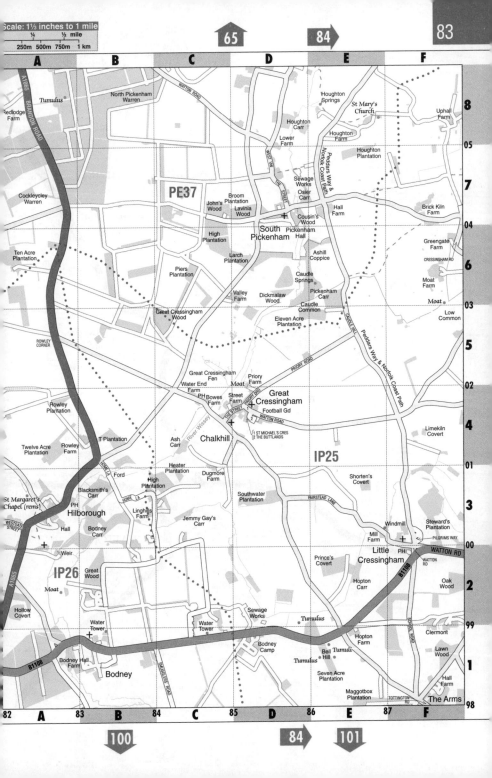

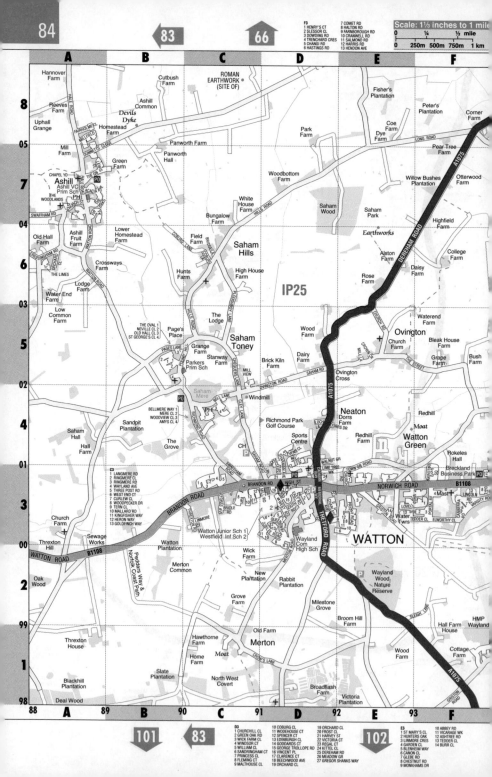

Scale: 1⅓ inches to 1 mile

0 ¼ ½ mile
0 250m 500m 750m 1 km

83
66

F3
1 HENRY'S CT
2 SLESSOR CL
3 DOWDING RD
4 TRENCHARD CRES
5 CHANGI RD
6 HASTINGS RD
7 COMET RD
8 HALTON RD
9 FARNBOROUGH RD
10 CRANWELL RD
11 SALMOND RD
12 HARRIS RD
13 HENDON AVE

IP25

ROMAN EARTHWORK (SITE OF)

Hannover Farm
Cutbush Farm
Reeves Farm
Ashill Common
Devils Dyke
Fisher's Plantation
Peter's Plantation
Corner Farm
Uphall Grange
Homestead Farm
Panworth Farm
Coe Dye Farm
Willow Bushes Plantation
Otterwood Farm
Mill Farm
Green Farm
Panworth Hall
Woodbottom Farm
Park Farm
Saham Wood
Saham Park
Pear Tree Farm
Ashill
Ashill VC Prim Sch
THE WOODLANDS
CHAPEL YD
PH
SWAFFHAM RD
Bungalow Farm
White House Farm
Highfield Farm
Old Hall Farm
Ashill Fruit Farm
Lower Homestead Farm
Field Barn
Saham Hills
Earthworks
Alston Farm
Daisy Farm
College Farm
Crossways Farm
Hunts Farm
High House Farm
Rose Farm
THE LIMES
Lodge Farm
Waterend Farm
Ovington
Bleak House Farm
Water End Farm
The Oval 1
NEVILLE CL 2
OLD HALL CL 3
ST GEORGE'S CL 4
The Lodge
Wood Farm
Church Farm
Grape Farm
Bush Farm
Low Common Farm
Page's Place
Saham Toney
Brick Kiln Farm
Dairy Farm
Ovington Cross
Redhill
Grange Farm
Parkers Prim Sch
Stanway Farm
MILL VIEW
Windmill
Neaton
Dorrs Farm
Moat
Sandpit Plantation
Saham Mere
PH
Richmond Park Golf Course
Sports Centre
Redhill Farm
Watton Green
Rokeles Hall
Saham Hall
Hall Farm
The Grove
CH
WALNUT GR
LIME TREE WK
Breckland Business Park
Mast
B1108
Church Farm
Sewage Works
Watton Plantation
Watton Junior Sch 1
Westfield Inf Sch 2
Wayland Com High Sch
Water Twrs
NORWICH ROAD
B1108
LINCOLN CL
Threxton Hill
WATTON ROAD B1108
Merton Common
Wick Farm
WATTON
Oak Wood
Peddars Way & Norfolk Coast Path
New Plantation
Rabbit Plantation
Wayland Wood, Nature Reserve
Grove Farm
Milestone Grove
Broom Hill Farm
HMP Wayland
Threxton House
Hawthorne Farm
Old Farm
Hall Farm House
Blackhill Plantation
Home Farm
Moat
Merton
Wood Farm
Cottage Farm
Deal Wood
Slate Plantation
North West Covert
Broadflash Farm
Victoria Plantation

101
83
102

C3
1 LANGMERE RD
2 RINGMERE CL
3 RINGMERE RD
4 WAYLAND AVE
5 WEST POST RD
6 THREE POST RD
7 CURLEW CL
8 WOODPECKER DR
9 TERN CL
10 MALLARD RD
11 KINGFISHER WAY
12 HERON WAY
13 GOLDFINCH WAY

D3
1 CHURCHILL CL
2 GREEN OAK RD
3 WICK FARM CL
4 WINDSOR CT
5 WILLIAM CL
6 SANDRINGHAM CT
7 PRINCESS CL
8 FLEMING CT
9 MALTHOUSE CL
10 COBURG CL
11 WODEHOUSE CT
12 SPENCER CT
13 EDINBURGH CL
14 GODDARDS CT
15 GEORGE TROLLOPE RD
16 VINCENT PL
17 CLARENCE CT
18 BEECHWOOD AVE
19 ORCHARD CL
19 ORCHARD CL
20 FROST CL
21 HARVEY ST
22 VICTORIA CT
23 REGAL CL
24 KITTEL CL
25 DEREHAM RD
26 MEADOW GR
27 GREGOR SHANKS WAY

E3
1 ST MARY'S CL
2 HUNTERS OAK
3 LINMORE CRES
4 GARDEN CL
5 BLENHEIM WAY
6 CANON CL
7 GLEBE RD
8 CHESTNUT RD
9 MONKHAMS DR
10 ABBEY RD
11 VICARAGE WK
12 ASHTREE RD
13 TEDDER CL
14 BURR CL

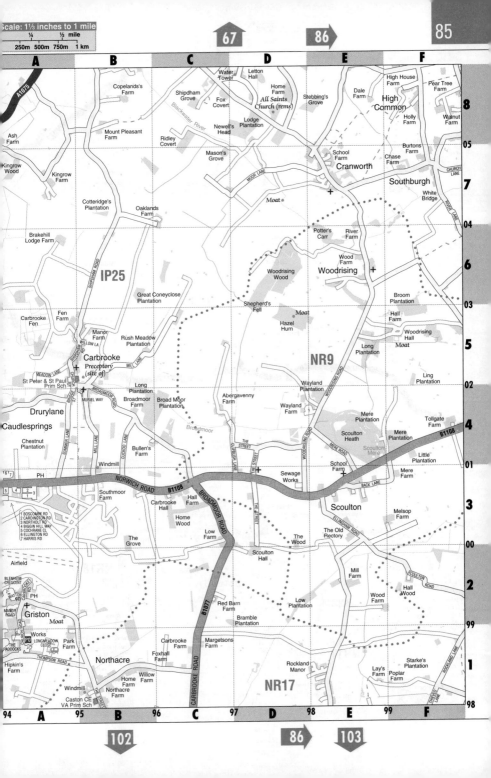

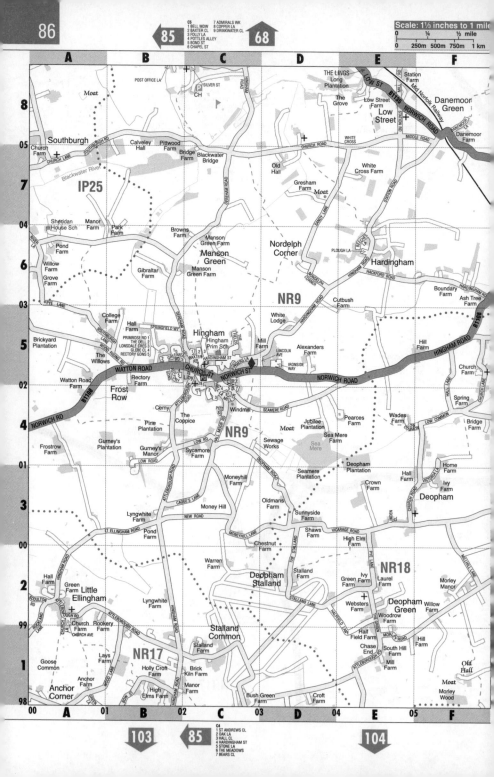

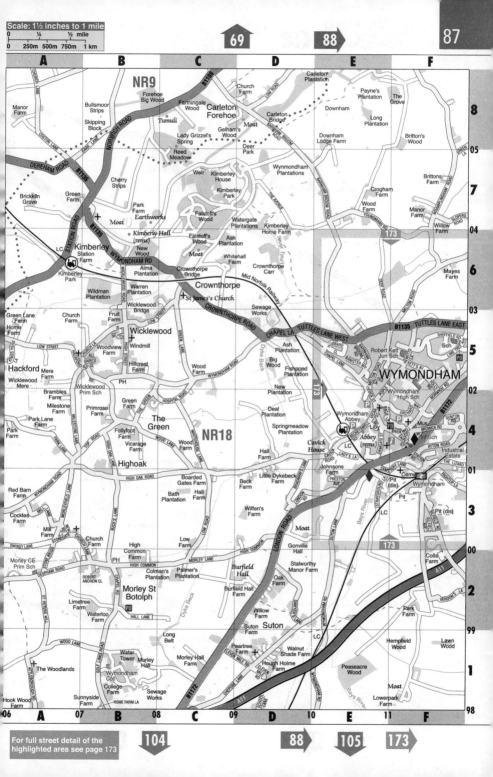

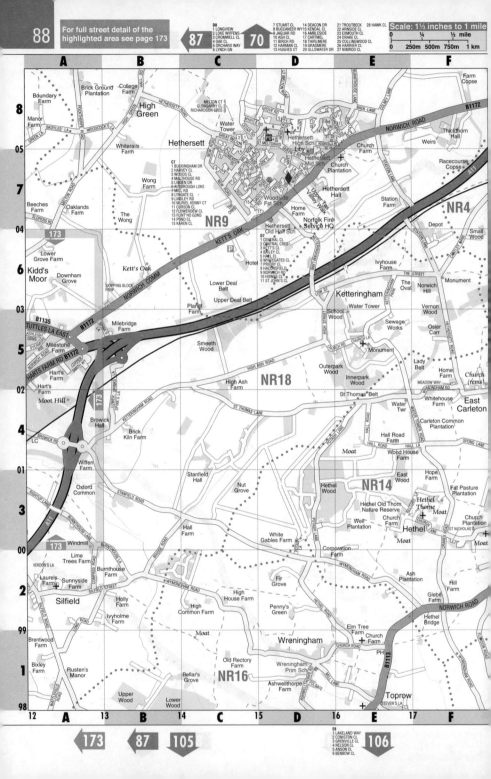

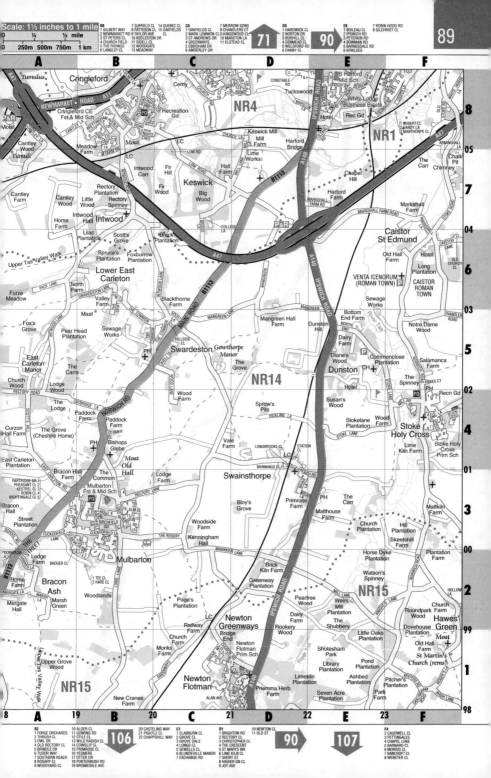

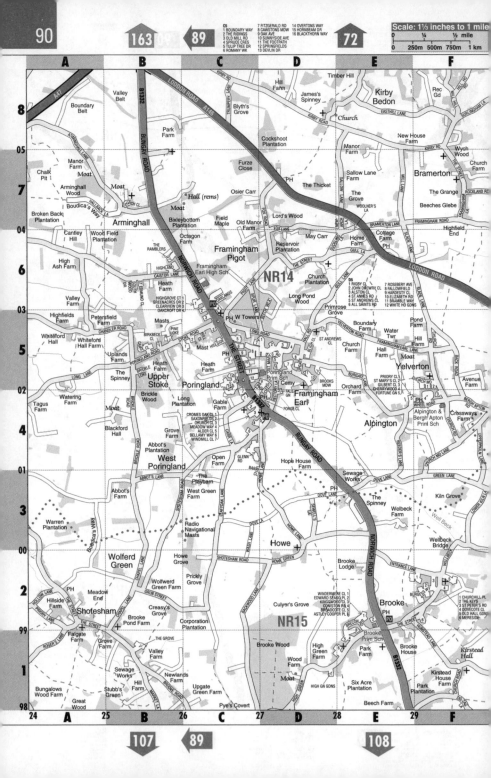

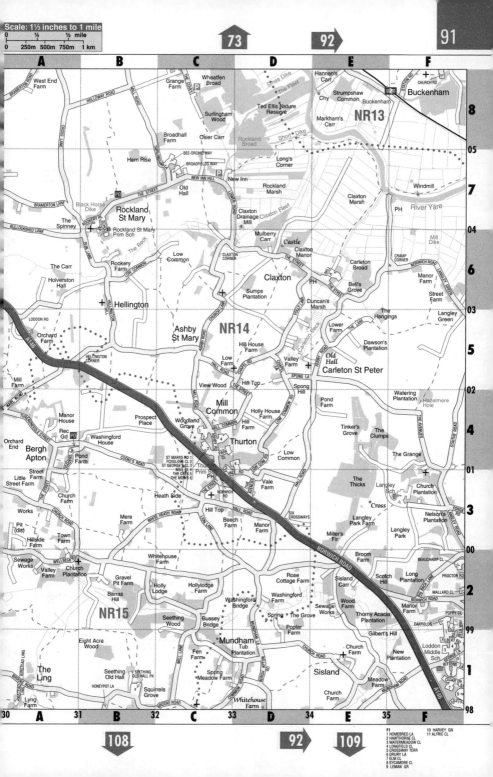

Scale: 1⅓ inches to 1 mile

0 ¼ ½ mile
0 250m 500m 750m 1 km

A B C D E F

8

Buckenham Carrs
Hassingham
Broad Farm
Cottage Carr
Earth Wall Carr
Goldie's Carr
Swill's Meadow
Thatch Farm
PH
Primrose Grove
SOUTHWOOD RD
Grove Farm
Hall Farm
Southwood
PORTER'S ROAD
REEDHAM RD
Lower Green Farm
Windmill
Lower Green
WHEELWRIGHTS CL
PALMER'S LA
CHURCH RD
PO
White House Farm
SUTTON CRES
LOW ROAD

05

Fleet Dike
River Yare
COW MOW ROAD
Manor Farm
Church
Oaks Farm
Freethorpe
Manor House
THE COMMON
GRANARY CL 1
PEARSONS CL 2
YOUNG'S CRES 3
BOWLERS CL 4
PRESTON CL 5
CRICKETER'S WLK 6
PH
Freethorpe Com Prim Sch

7

Barn End
Cantley First Sch
CHURCH CL
SCHOOL LANE
GRIMMER LANE
CARRS ROAD
MANOR RD
HIGH RD
LIMPENHOE ROAD
CANTLEY ROAD
SOUTHWOOD
NORWICH RD
DOBB'S LA
OLD CHAPEL RD
Mast

04

Cantley
LC
Cantley Grange
Sports Gd
STATION RD
GRANGE RD
Cantley View Farm
Wood Farm
Spong Carr
NR13
Limpenhoe
FREETHORPE RD
REEDHAM ROAD

6

Cantley
Marsh Farm
Red House
Chimney
Factory
LC
Chimney
Chimney
Chimney
Reservoir
Marsh Road
Marsh Farm
Low Farm
Hill Farm
SANDY LANE
HALL ROAD

Monks Plantation
Sewage Works
1 LANGLEY RD
2 HIGHLAND CL
3 WINDSOR RD
4 STATION RD
Settling Basins
LIMPENHOE ROAD

03

Moat
Langley Abbey
PH
The Wherry
Abbey Carr
Langley Dike
Round House
Limpenhoe Marshes
Settling Basins
LC
Limpenhoe Hill
John's Carr
Sprowston Wood
Gurney Wood
Wood Farm
1 STATION DR
2 WITTON CL
3 THE HAVAKER
POTTLE'S LA

5

Staithe Farm
STATHE ROAD
Poplars Farm
Langley Marshes
Hardley Drainage Mill
Reedham
NORTON LANE

02

Willow Farm
Langley Street
Hardley Street
Rustygate Farm
Limpenhoe Drainage Mill
Reedham Drainage Mill
FERRY ROAD
YARE VIEW CL 1
CLIFF CL 2
NEW RD 3
MIDDLE HILL 4
RISERSIDE 5
THE HILLS
PO

4

Chestnut Farm
Great Yard Farm
White House Farm
Westgate Farm
Hardley Marshes
Hardley Dike
Norton Staithe
PH
Reedham Ferry (V)

01

Ash Plantation
Church Farm
CHURCH ROAD
LOWER HARDLEY ROAD
HARDLEY HALL LA
Hardley Cross
River Chet
Norton Drainage Mill

3

Boundary Farm
FORGE ROAD
COCK ROAD
Avenue Farm
CROSS STONE ROAD
Broom Hill
Norton Marshes
Marshlands Farm
Nogdam End
Mill Dyke
Leys Farm
Boycot Dyke
Norton Marshes

00

GENTLEMAN'S WALK
LANGLEY STREET
Chedgrave Hills
LOWER HARDLEY ROAD
Hardley Wood
Hardley Hall
Hall Carr
NR14
Moat
Old Hall Carr
Hill House
Firs Farm
Ash Carr
Thatched House Farm
Walnut Tree Farm

2

LODDON QUAY
Chedgrave
RECTORY LA
Chedgrave Carr
COMM LINK
Loddon Common
Riverside Farm
Valley Farm
Little Church Farm
Church Farm
Hardley Flood Nature Reserve
Carr Farm
Willow Farm
Low Farm
Soc Dyke

99

Lib'y
P
P
Hall Green Farm
Beechgrove Farm
River Chet
LODDON ROAD
Heckingham
Reservoir
Beacon Hill
Highfield Farm
Elm Farm
Church Farm
Thurlton
LODDON ROAD
SCHOOL LANE
Thurlton Prim Sch

1

Hobart High Sch
PH
Loddon
Ind Est
STATION ROAD
SANDY LANE
Hill Farm
Hall
Avocet House Sch
FARM RD
BUTTER LA
High House Farm
BUCK LANE
BOUNDARY RD
Norton Subcourse
Norton Plantation
CHURCH RD
CROFT RD
PH

98

36 A 37 B 38 C 39 D 40 E 41 F

A1
1 GARDEN CT
2 GEORGE LA
3 OLD MARKET GN
4 MARKET PL
5 SALE CT
6 BEECH CL
7 DAVY PL
8 LEMAN CL
9 LEMAN GR
10 CEDAR DR
11 CANNELL RD
12 FOXES LOKE
13 Loddon Fst Sch

A2
1 BIG BACK LA
2 BEAUCHAMP RD
3 PROCTOR AV
4 PROCTOR CL
5 PROCTOR AVE
6 SNOW'S HILL
7 HILLCREST
8 HURST RD
9 MALLARD CL
10 THE RISE
11 FARM CL
12 NORWICH RD
13 CHURCH CL

F1
1 LOW RD
2 TITHEBARN LA
3 HAMPTON AVE
4 LINKS WAY
5 MEADOW CL
6 LINKS CL

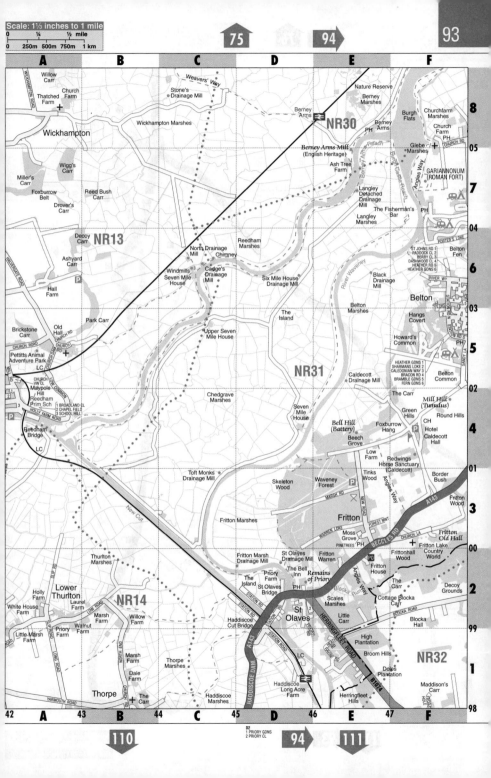

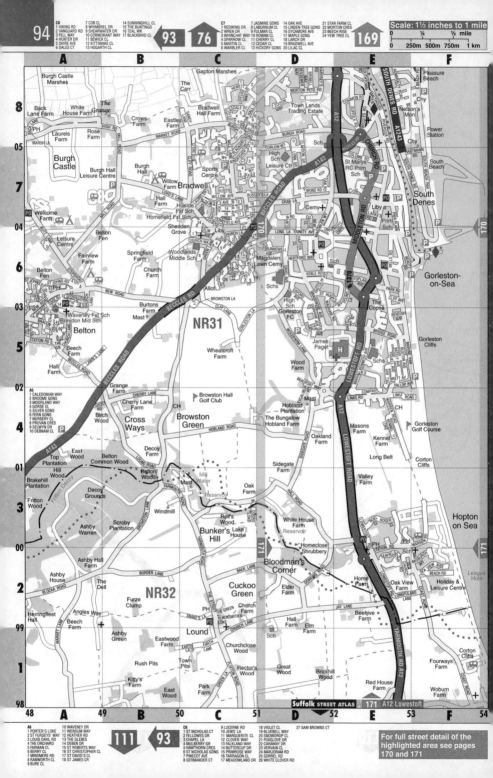

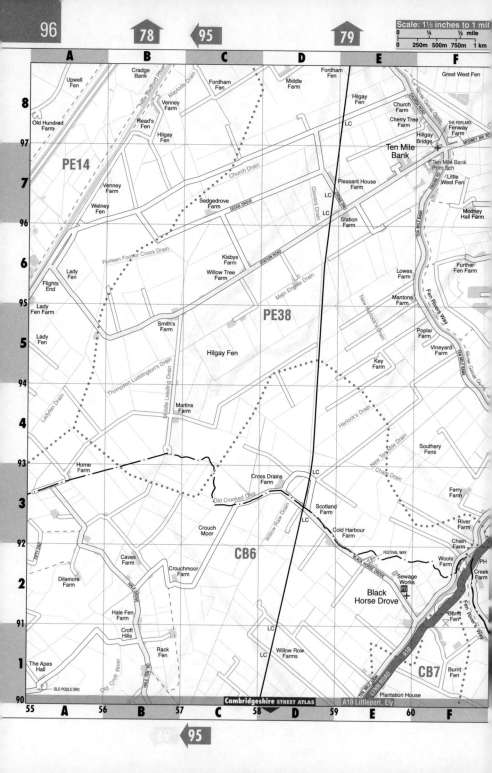

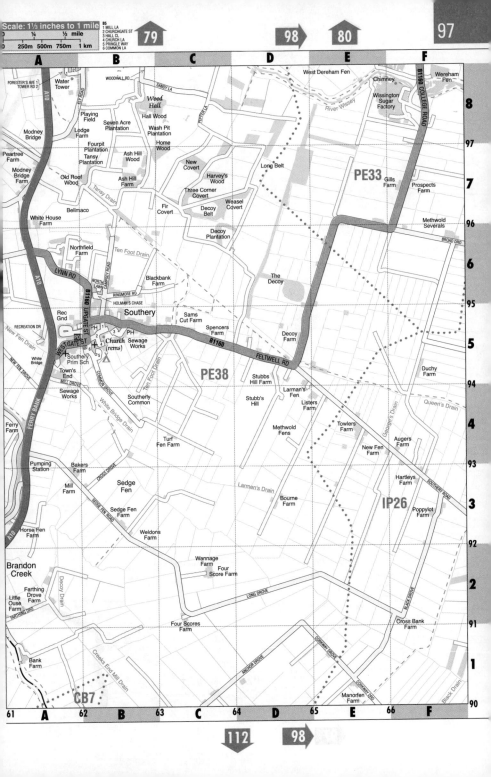

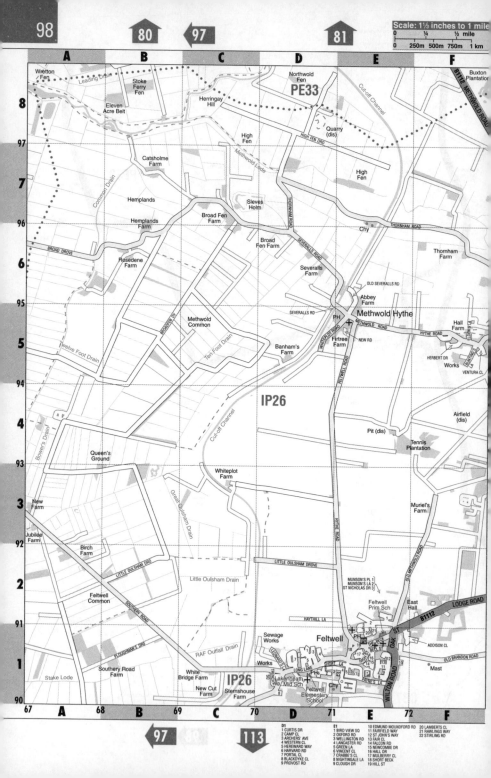

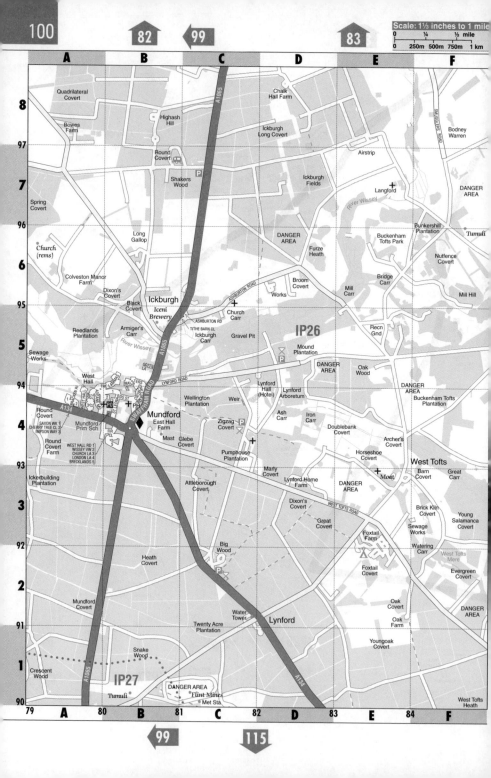

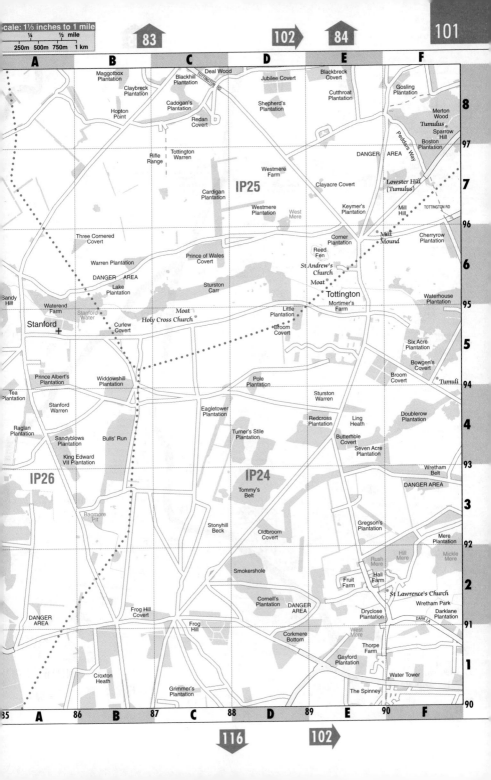

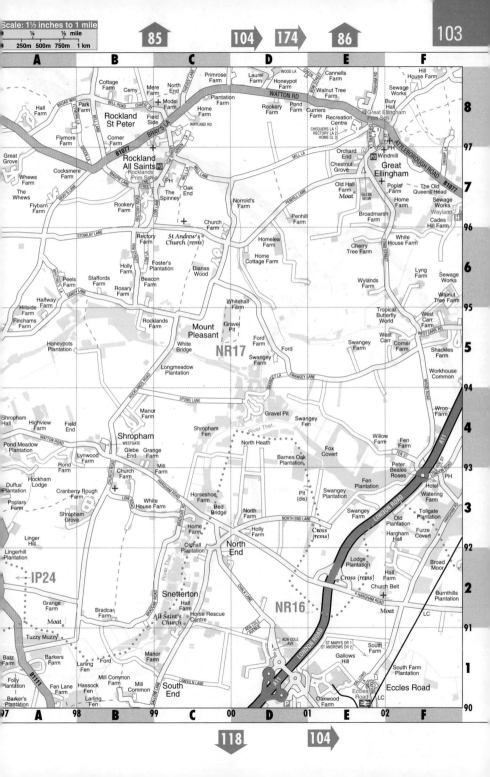

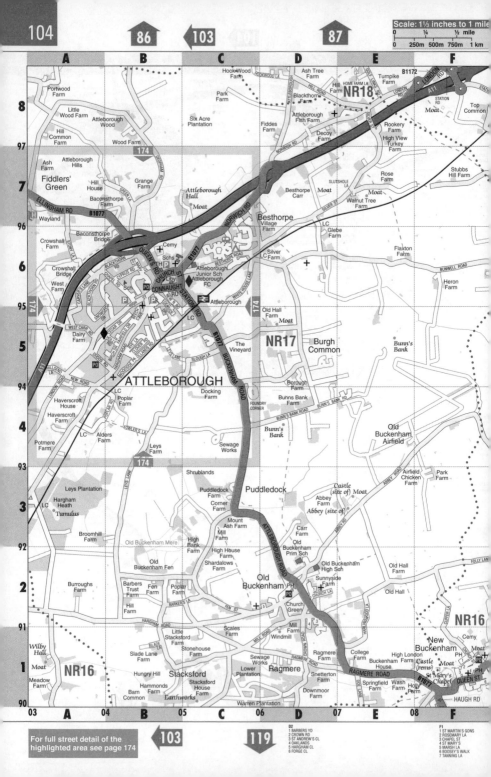

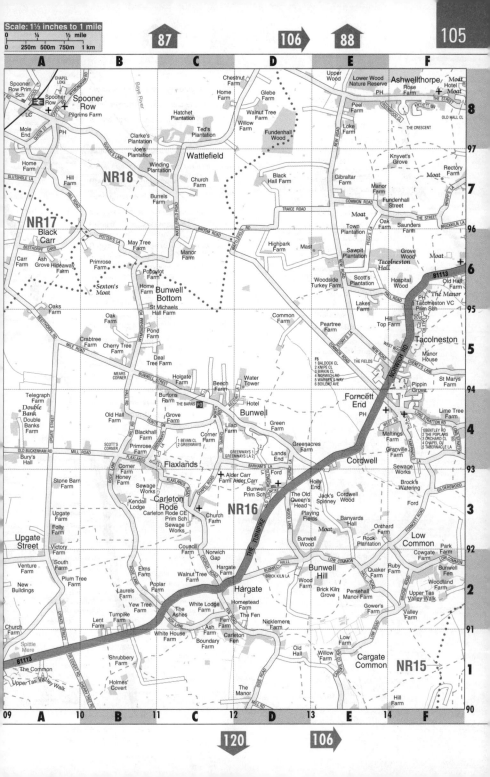

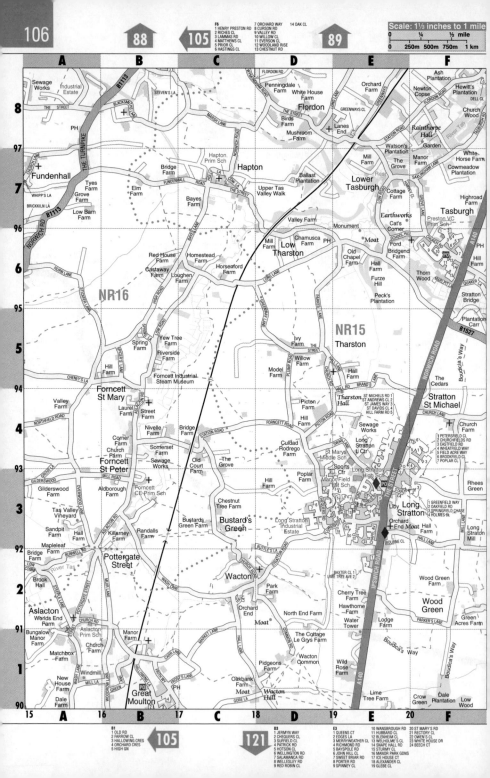

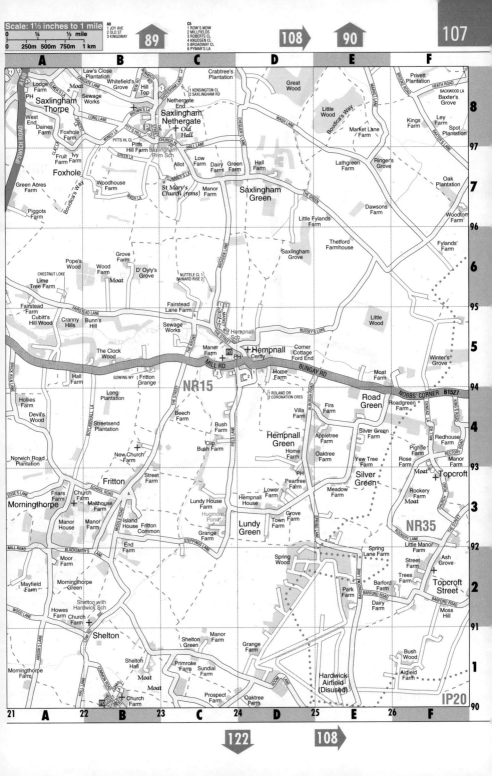

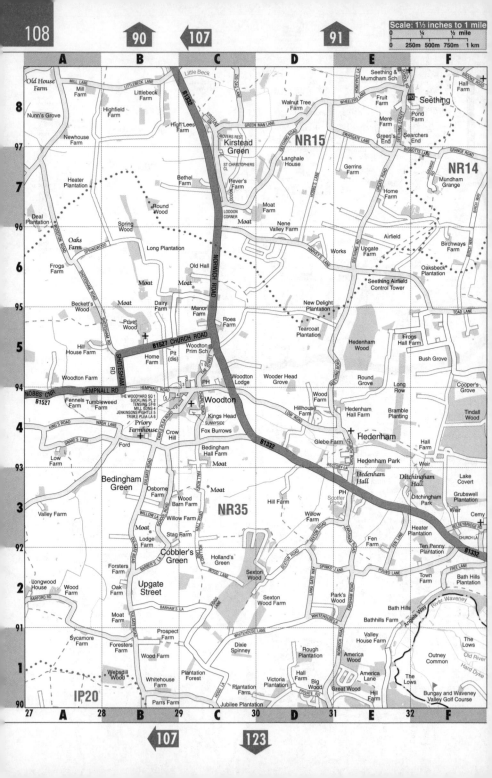

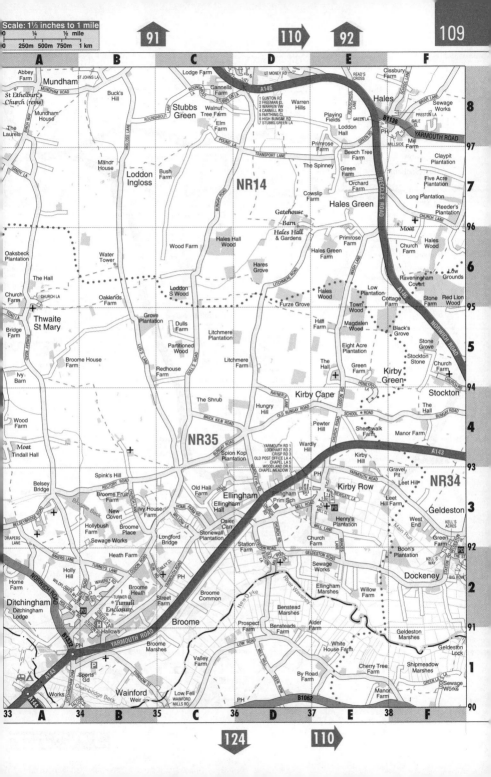

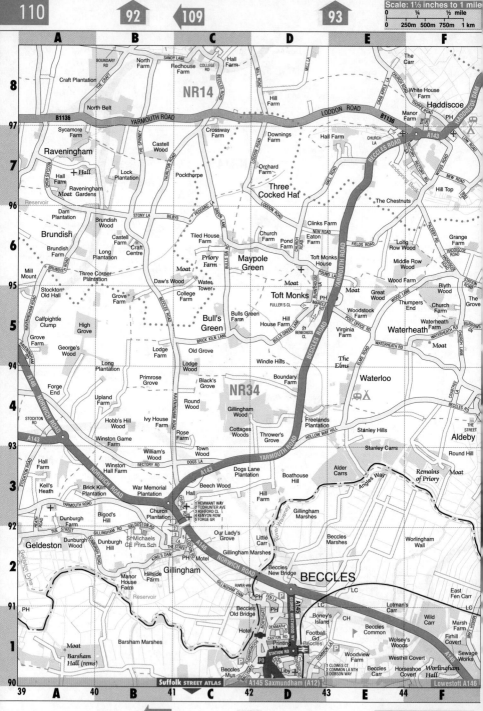

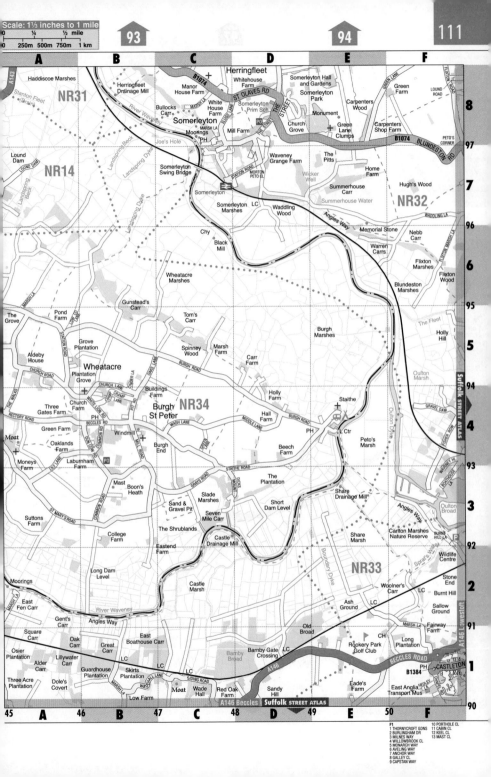

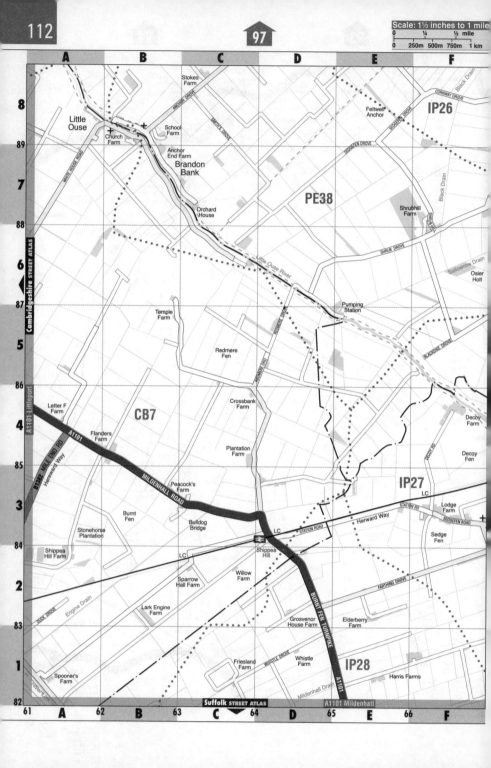

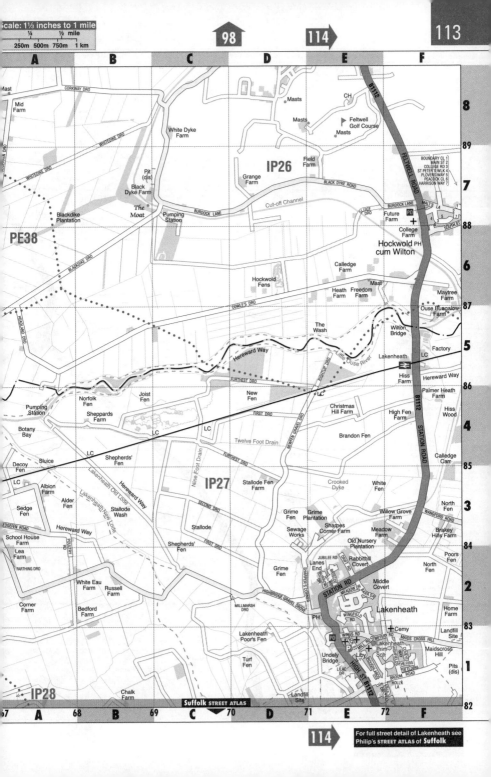

A   B   C   D   E   F

8

Mast
Mid Farm
CORKWAY DRO
WHITEDYKE DRO
White Dyke Farm
Masts
CH
Masts
Feltwell Golf Course
Masts
Masts

89

B1112
FELTWELL ROAD
BOUNDARY CL 1
MAIN ST 2
COLLEGE RD 3
ST PETER'S WLK 4
PLOVERS WAY 5
PEACOCK CL 6
HARRISON WAY 7

IP26
Field Farm
Grange Farm
BLACK DYKE ROAD
Cut-off Channel
BURDOCK LANE
Pumping Station
BURDOCK LANE
MALT
LA
SOUTH ST
Future Farm
College Farm

7

WHITEDYKE DRO
NORFOLK DRO
Black Dyke Farm
The Moat
BURDOCK LANE

88

PE38
Blackdike Plantation
BLACKDIKE DRO
Hockwold cum Wilton PH
PO

6
Calledge Farm
Hockwold Fens
Heath Farm
Freedom Farm
Mast
Maytree Farm

87

HEMP DRO
DOWNES DRO
The Wash
Ouse Bungalow Farm
Wilton Bridge
LC

Hereward Way
Little Ouse River
Lakenheath
Factory

5

FURTHEST DRO
RIGHTUP DRO
LC
Hiss Farm
Hereward Way

86

Pumping Station
Norfolk Fen
Joist Fen
New Fen
FIRST DRO
LC
Christmas Hill Farm
High Fen Farm
Palmer Heath Farm
Hiss Wood

4

Sheppards Farm
LC
LC
SEVEN GRAVEL DRO
B1112
STATION ROAD

Botany Bay
Twelve Foot Drain
Brandon Fen

Decoy Fen
Sluice
LC
Shepherds' Fen
Nine Foot Drain
FURTHEST DRO
Crooked Dyke
White Fen
Calledge Carr

85

Albion Farm
Alder Fen
LAKENHEATH NEW LODE
LAKENHEATH OLD LODE
Hereward Way

Sedge Fen
Stallode Wash
SECOND DRO
IP27
Stallode Fen Farm
Grime Fen
Grime Plantation
Willow Grove Farm
North Fen
WANGFORD ROAD

3

EDGEFEN ROAD
School House Farm
Hereward Way
POULTRY RD
Stallode
Sewage Works
Sharpes Corner Farm
Meadow Farm
Brakey Hills Farm

Lea Farm
FARTHING DRO
Shepherds' Fen
FIRST DRO
Old Nursery Plantation
Poors Fen

84

White Eau Farm
Russell Farm
Grime Fen
JUBILEE RD
Lanes End
Rabbithill Covert
Middle Covert
North Fen

2

Corner Farm
Bedford Farm
MILLMARSH DRO
HIGHBRIDGE GRAVEL DROVE
SHARPE'S CORNER
STATION RD
MEADOW DR
BAKER RD
PH
Lakenheath
Home Farm

Landfill Site

83

Lakenheath Poor's Fen
WINGS RD
PO
WINGFIELD
Cemy
Maidscross Hill
MAIDS CROSS HILL

Turf Fen
Undely Bridge
LILAC DR
Liby
Lakenheath Prim Sch
THE FIRS
HOLLY LA
BROOM RD
HIGH ST
B1112
SOUTH ST
LLOYDS ROAD
Pits (dis)

1

IP28
Chalk Farm
Landfill Site

82

A   68   B   69   C   70   D   71   E   72   F

114

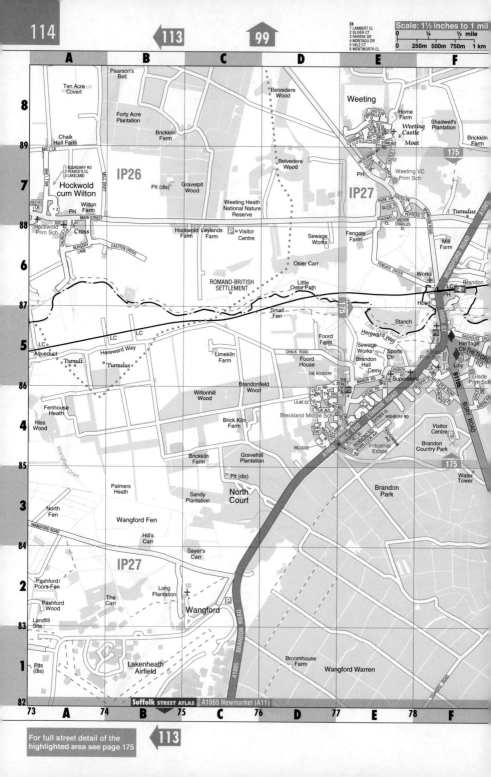

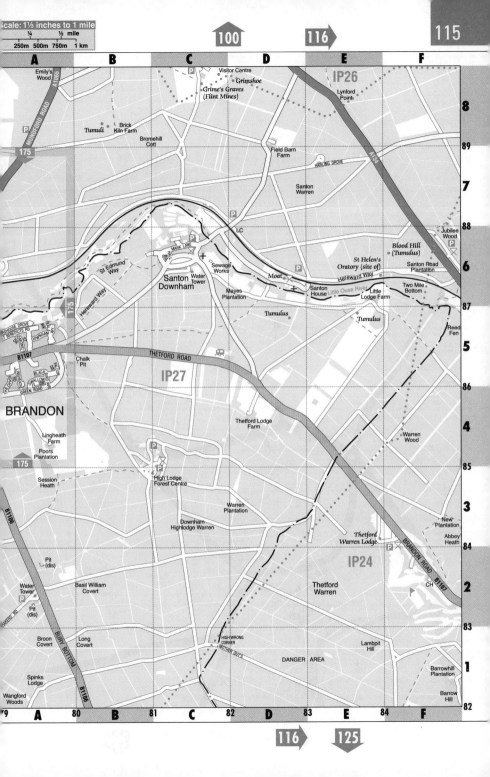

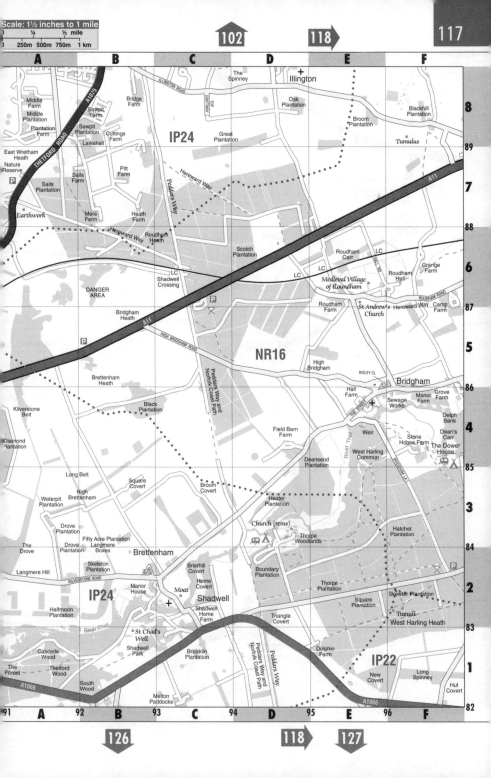

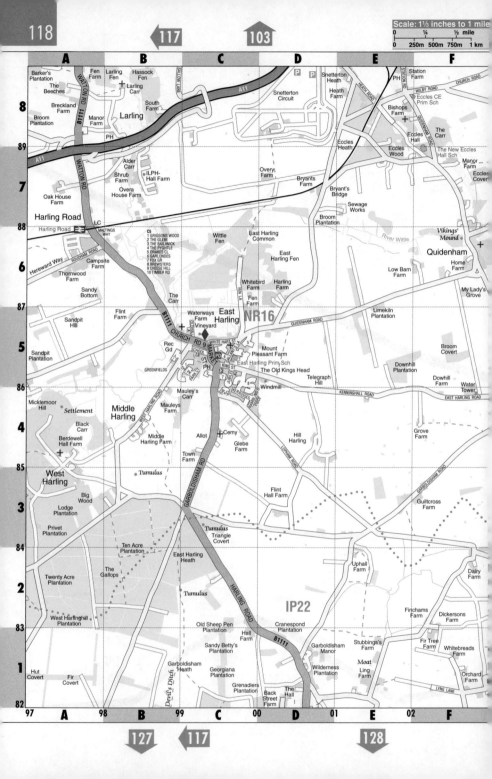

117
103

Scale: 1½ inches to 1 mile

0 ¼ ½ mile
0 250m 500m 750m 1 km

A **B** **C** **D** **E** **F**

Barker's Plantation
The Beeches
Breckland Farm
Broom Plantation
Fen Farm
Larling Fen
Hassock Fen
Larling Carr
South Farm
Larling
Manor Farm
PH
8

A11
Snetterton Heath
Heath Farm
Snetterton Circuit
Station Farm
PH
Wilby Road
Church Road
Bishops Farm
Eccles CE Prim Sch
Eccles Hall
The Carr
The New Eccles Hall Sch
Manor Farm

89
A11
Eccles Heath
Eccles Wood
Eccles Cover

Oak House Farm
Alder Carr
Shrub Farm
ILPH-Hall Farm
Overa House Farm
Overy Farm
Bryants Farm
Bryant's Bridge
Sewage Works
Vikings' Mound
7

Harling Road
LC
Harling Road
Maltings Way
Broom Plantation
River Wittle
Quidenham
88

Hereward Way
Rougham Road
Campsite Farm
Thornwood Farm
Sandy Bottom
CS
1 GRIGSONS WOOD
2 THE GLEBE
3 THE BAILIWICK
4 THE PYGHTLE
5 DRAKES CL
6 GARLONDES
7 FOX GR
8 BREWSTERS
9 CHEESE HILL
10 TIMBER RD
Wittle Fen
East Harling Common
East Harling Fen
Low Barn Farm
Home Farm
My Lady's Grove
6

Sandpit Hill
Flint Farm
The Carr
B1111
Church Rd
Waterways Farm
Vineyard
East Harling
Whitebird Farm
Harling Farm
Fen Farm
NR16
Limekiln Plantation
Broom Covert
87

Sandpit Plantation
Rec Gd
School
Greenfields
Mauley's Carr
White Hart St
Market St
PO
PH
King St
Kenrickes
Mount Pleasant Farm
East Harling Prim Sch
The Old Kings Head
Windmill
Telegraph Hill
Downhill Plantation
Dowhill Farm
Water Tower
5

Micklemoor Hill
Settlement
Black Carr
Berdewell Hall Farm
Middle Harling
Mauleys Farm
Allot
Cemy
Glebe Farm
Hill Harling
Quidenham Road
Kenninghall Road
East Harling Road
Grove Farm
86

West Harling
Tumulus
Middle Harling Farm
Town Farm
Flint Hall Farm
Lorham Road
4

Big Wood
Lodge Plantation
Privet Plantation
Ten Acre Plantation
East Harling Heath
Tumulus
Triangle Covert
Garboldisham Rd
Uphall Farm
Guiltcross Farm
Dairy Farm
85

Twenty Acre Plantation
The Gallops
Tumulus
Old Sheep Pen Plantation
Hall Farm
Cranespond Plantation
IP22
Finchams Farm
Dickersons Farm
3

84

West Harlinghill Plantation
Garboldisham Heath
Sandy Betty's Plantation
Georgiana Plantation
B1111
Garboldisham Manor
Stubbings's Farm
Moat
Wilderness Plantation
Ling Farm
Fir Tree Farm
Whitebreads Farm
2

Hut Covert
Fir Covert
Devil's Ditch
Grenadiers Plantation
Back Street Farm
The Hall
Lyng Lane
Orchard Farm
1

Harling Road

82
97 **A** 98 **B** 99 **C** 00 **D** 01 **E** 02 **F**

127
117
128

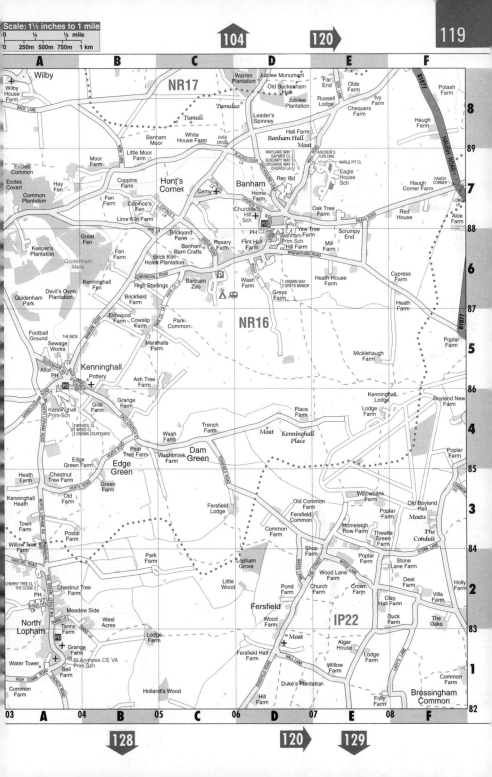

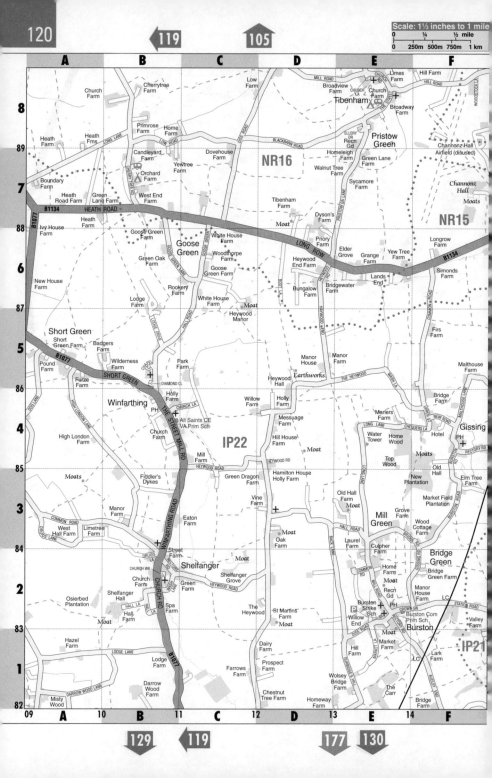

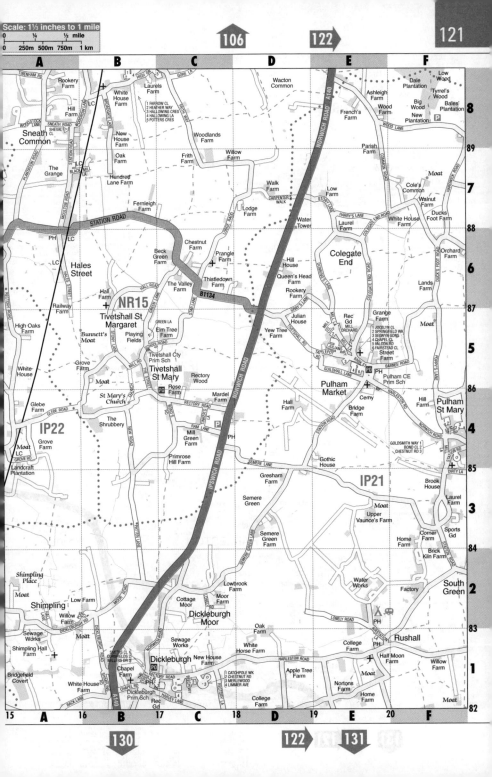

122

121

107

Scale: 1½ inches to 1 mile

0   ¼   ½ mile
0 250m 500m 750m 1 km

Map — Harleston and surrounding area

NR15 · IP21 · IP20

Grid labels (left): 8, 89, 7, 88, 6, 87, 5, 86, 4, 85, 3, 84, 2, 83, 1, 82

Grid labels (top): A, B, C, D, E, F

Grid labels (bottom): 21, A, 22, B, 23, C, 24, D, 25, E, 26, F

Selected place and feature names:

The Grove, Moat, Hardwick, Street Farm, Corner Farm, Willow End, Mill Farm, Harris Green Farm, Harris Green, Burlingham Lodge Farm, Barondole La, Darrow Green, Darrow Green Farm, Darrow Wood, Hangman's Hill, Misery Corner, Ivy Farm, Castle Hill (Motte & Bailey), Red House Farm, North Green, Cranes Farm, End Farm, Boughton Manor Farm, Hudson Farm, Nut Tree Farm, Grazing Ground Farm, Darrow Farm, Lammas Farm, Ford, Manor Farm, Elm Tree Farm, Rose Farm, Ash Tree Farm, Town Farm, Park Farm, Brook Farm, Oakley Grange Farm, Hundred Bound Farm, Sunny Side, Pied Bridge Farm, Pied Bridge, Mill Farm, Villa Farm, Shingle Farm, Kings Acre Farm, North Green Farm, Oaks Farm, Highland Farm, Clintergate Farm, Clintergate, Manor Farm, Hawthorn Farm, Abbey Farm, Alburgh Street, Friends Farm, Bush Green Farm, Bush Green, Sweeting's Green, Grange Farm, Gillows Farm, Willows Farm, Meadow Farm, Clintergate Road, Coldham Hall Moat, Alburgh, White House Farm, Astons Farm, Kemp's Corner, Kemps Farm, Park Farm, Wood Lane, Oaklands Farm, North Lodge Farm, North Farm, Church Farm, Ivy House Farm, IP21, Wood Farm, Starston Hall, Moat, Green La, New Grove, Low Ditch Farm, Bungalow Lane, Church Cl, 1 NORTH GREEN RD, 2 NORWICH RD, 3 STATION RD, 4 CHURCH CL, Glebe Farm, The Hall, Laurel Farm, Blake's Grove, Shadow Hill, Chestnut Grove, Abbey Yard, The Grange, Springfield Wood, The Maids Head, Moat, Colby's Farm, Ladies' Grove, Gawdy Grove, Gawdy Hall, Grange Farm, Jubilee Covert, Dairy Farm, Horse Wood, Little Hawker's Wood, Moat, Great Hawker's Wood, Earthworks, Railway Plantation, Starston, Home Farm, Coniferhill, Gawdyhall Big Wood, Lodge Farm, Church Farm, Crossingford Lodge, Crossingford Bridge, Ford, HARLESTON, Violet Plantation, Sewage Works, Pear Tree Farm, Garlic Street, Boundary Farm, White House Farm, Grove Hill House, Hill Farm, 1 HIGH CT, 2 ST MARY'S CL, 3 CHURCH VW, 4 MARTIN RD, 5 HOWARD CL, Redenhall, Ivy Wood Farm, Low Farm, Mill Farm, Jacksons Farm, Gable End, Poplars Farm, Yew Tree Farm, Pleasure Park, The Grove, Libry, Swan La, Harleston Prim Sch, Harleston Mus, Anthills, Rookery Farm, Furze Green, Brook Farm, Cranes Watering Farm, Archbishop Sancroft High Sch, Frestons Farm, Angles Way, Johnsons Farm, Barnaway Farm, Gunshaw Hall, Water Tower, Fuller Rd, Dairy Farm, Lodge Farm, Skeetsmere Farm, Doles Farm, Beacon Hill, Shotford Bridge, Pound Hill, Shotford Hill, A143, Wells Rd, B1116

Suffolk STREET ATLAS

Street index

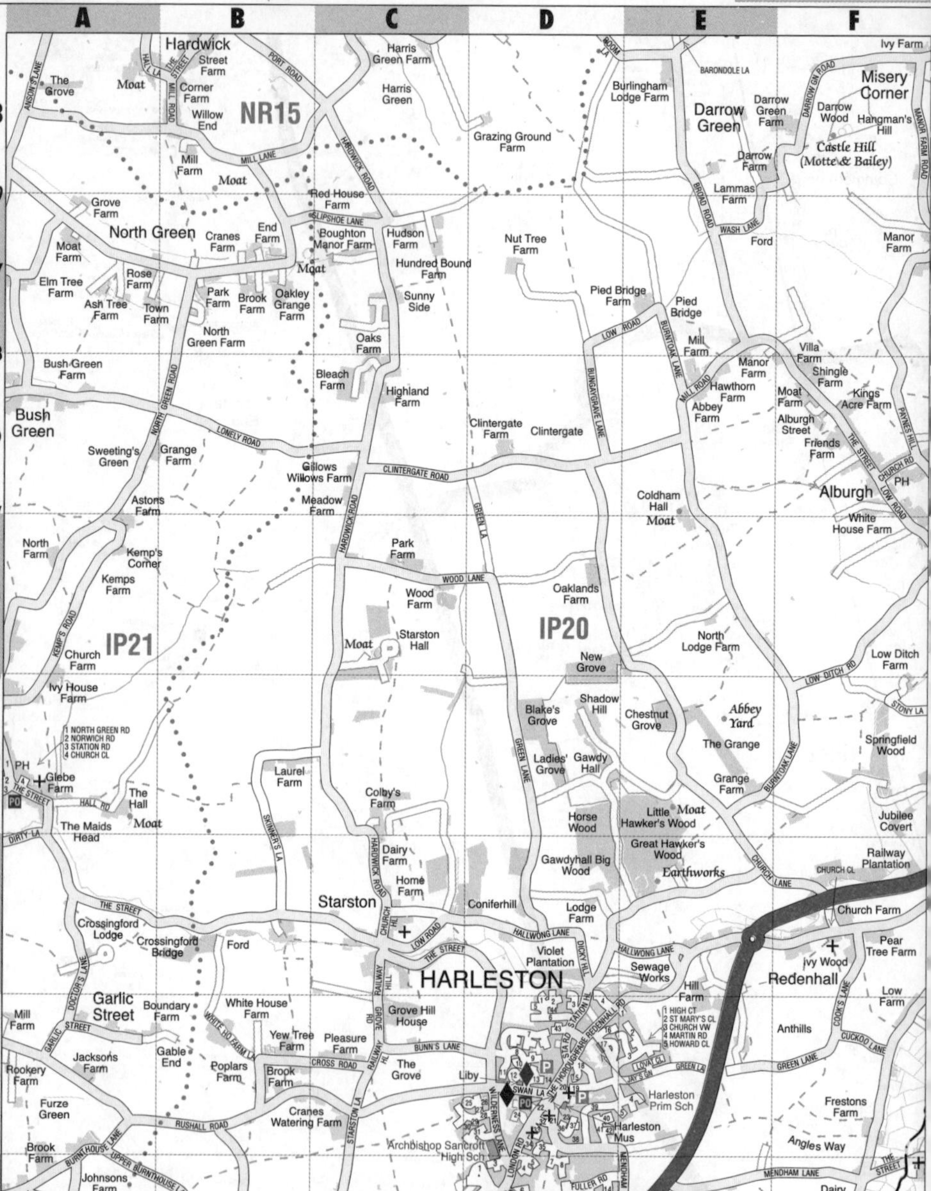

D1
1. THE COMMON
2. GOTHIC CL
3. WILDERNESS CL
4. PINE CL
5. WILLOW WLK
6. PEMBERTON RD
7. LIME CL
8. OAK TREE WAY
9. DOVE CL
10. CHERRYWOOD
11. NORTHGATE
12. SOUTHGATE
13. SPEEDWELL WAY
14. MAYFLOWER WAY

D2
1. HENRY WARD RD
2. GAWDY CL
3. BECK VW
4. POUND CL
5. HUNT CL
6. MALTINGS DR
7. PILGRIM'S WAY
8. WEAVERS CROFT
9. DOUNE WAY
10. CROFT CL
11. HEROLF WAY
12. ALLTHORPE RD
13. PADDOCK RD
14. BULLOCK FAIR CL
15. CONSTABLE CT
16. BRIDGE CL
17. SCHOOL LA
18. CANDLER'S LA
19. STRAIGHT LA
20. BROAD ST
21. OLD MARKET PL
22. MARKET PL
23. CHURCH ST
24. MALTHOUSE CT
25. TERENCE AIREY CT
26. GLAMIS CT
27. ELIZABETH WLK
28. TITLOW RD
29. KERRIDGE WAY
30. FRERE RD
31. CRANES MDW
32. EXCHANGE ST
33. MAGPIE CT
34. HOLLY CT
35. WOODLANDS
36. MENDHAM CL
37. RAINEY CT
38. MENDHAM LA
39. BRIAR RD
40. NEWLANDS CL
41. PARKLANDS WAY
42. GREEN PARK
43. MILLERS GN
44. GAWDY CL

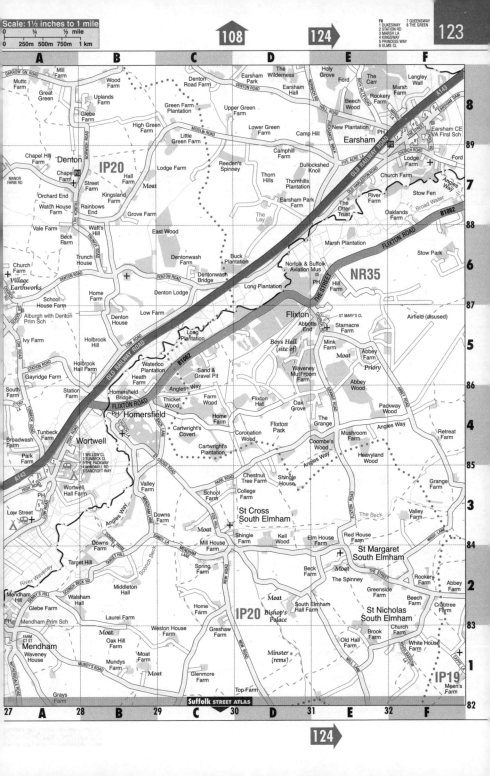

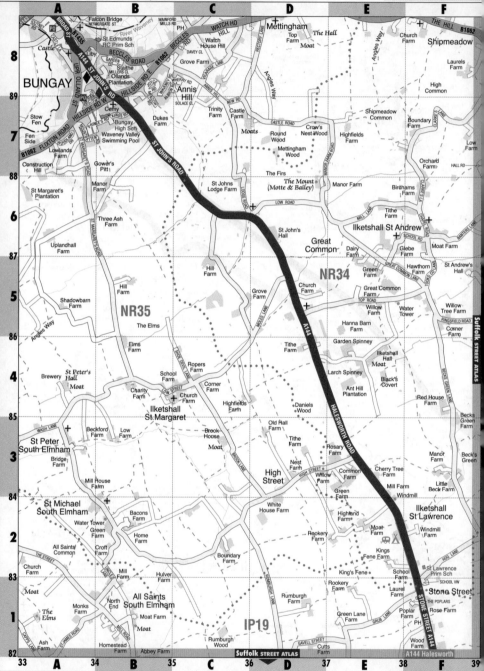

Scale: 1⅓ inches to 1 mile

0 ¼ ½ mile
0 250m 500m 750m 1 km

BUNGAY

Castle
PO
Falcon Bridge
NETHERGATE ST
WAINFORD MILLS RD
River Waveney
WATCH HO HILL

Mettingham
Top Farm
The Hall
Moat
The Hall
Church Farm

B1062
Shipmeadow

St Edmunds RC Prim Sch
Beccles Road
Watch House Hill
Davey Cl
Grove Farm

Libby
GARDEN CL
Staithe
MILLERS CL
Ollands Plantation

WHERRY RD
Annis Hill
SOLACE CL
Trinity Farm
Castle Farm
NEW RD

Laurels Farm
High Common

Stow Fen
Fen Side
B1062

Cemy
Dukes Farm

Moats
Castle Road
Round Wood
Craw's Nest Wood
Highfields Farm
Shipmeadow Common
Boundary Farm

Low Farm

Construction Hill
FLIXTON ROAD
Lowlands Farm
Gower's Pitt

Bungay High Sch
Waveney Valley Swimming Pool

The Firs
Mettingham Wood

Orchard Farm
HALL RD

Manor Farm

St Margaret's Plantation

Three Ash Farm

St Johns Lodge Farm
The Mount (Motte & Bailey)
LOW ROAD

Manor Farm
Ilketshall St Andrew
Tithe Farm
Birehams Farm
MILL LANE

Uplandhall Farm

Hill Farm

St John's Hall

Dairy Farm
Glebe Farm
Moat Farm
SCHOOL RD
St Andrew's Hall

Shadowbarn Farm
NR35
The Elms
Hill Farm

Great Common
NR34
Green Farm
Great Common Farm
Hawthorn Farm
GREAT COMMON LANE

Angles Way
Elms Farm
Ropers Farm

Hill Farm
Grove Farm
Church Farm
Willow Farm
Water Tower
Willow Tree Farm
RINGSFIELD ROAD
Corner Farm

Brewery
St Peter's Hall
Moat
School Farm
LOW STREET
Corner Farm
Highfields Farm

MILES LANE
Hanna Barn Farm
Garden Spinney
Ilketshall Hall
Moat

Charity Farm
Ilketshall St Margaret
Church Farm
Tithe Farm
Larch Spinney
Black's Covert
Red House Farm

Becks Green Farm

St Peter South Elmham
Beckford Farm
Low Farm
WASH LANE

Brook House
Moat
Old Hall Farm
Daniels Wood
Ant Hill Plantation

Bridge Farm
BROOK LANE
Tithe Farm
Nest Farm
Rosary Farm
Common Farm
Manor Farm
Beck's Green

Mill House Farm

St Michael South Elmham
Water Tower
Green Farm
Bacons Farm
High Street
HIGH STREET
Willow Farm
Cherry Tree Farm
Mill Farm
Windmill
Little Beck Farm

All Saints Common
Home Farm
White House Farm
Green Farm
Highland Farm
Moat Farm
Ilketshall St Lawrence
Windmill Farm

Croft Farm
THE STREET
Boundary Farm
Rookery Farm
Kings Fene Farm

Church Farm
Moat
Mill Farm
Hulver Farm
CEMETERY LANE
King's Fene
Rookery Farm
School Farm
SCHOOL VW
St Lawrence Prim Sch
Stone Street

The Elms
Monks Farm
North End
Moat Farm
All Saints South Elmham
Moat
Rumburgh Farm
Green Lane Farm
GRUB LANE
Laurel Farm
Poplar Farm
The Poplars
Rose Farm

Ash Farm
CAPPS LANE
Homestead Farm
Abbey Farm
Rumburgh Wood
IP19
GAVELL STREET
Cutts Farm
Wood Farm
A144

A144 Halesworth

Suffolk STREET ATLAS

For full street detail of Bungay see
Philip's STREET ATLAS of Suffolk

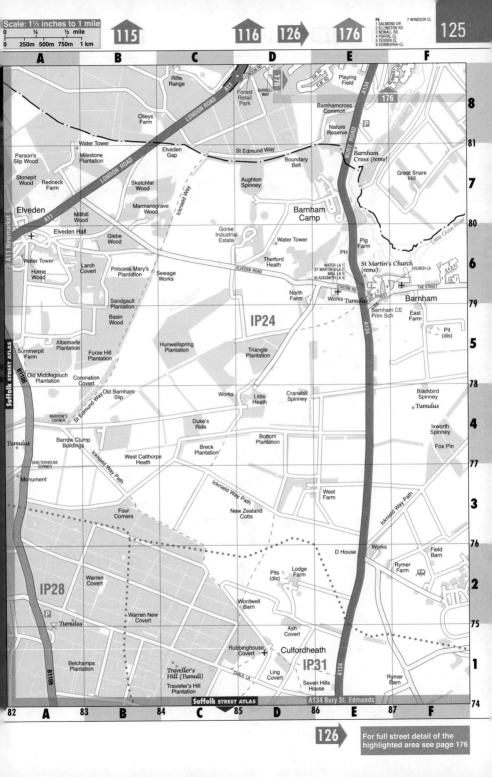

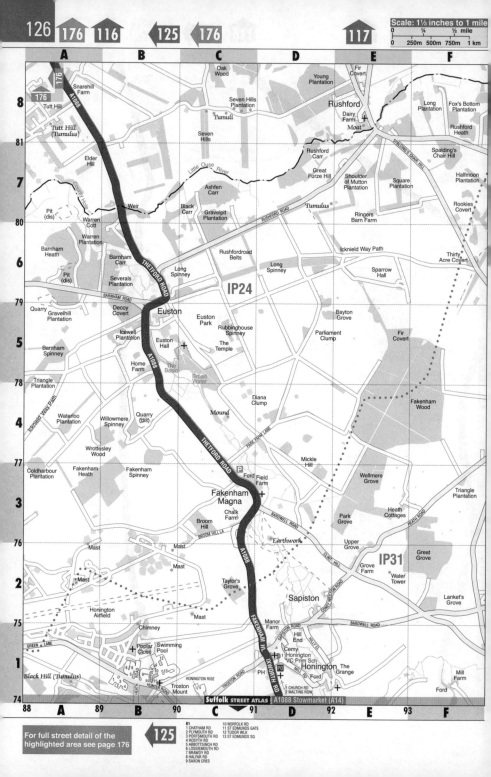

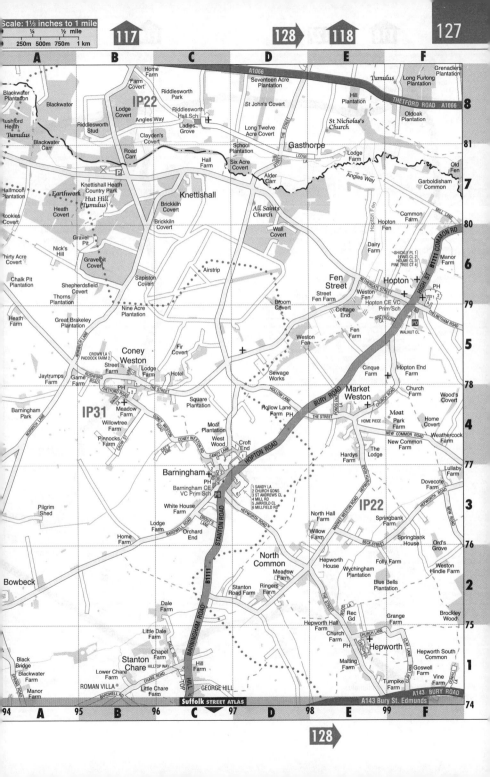

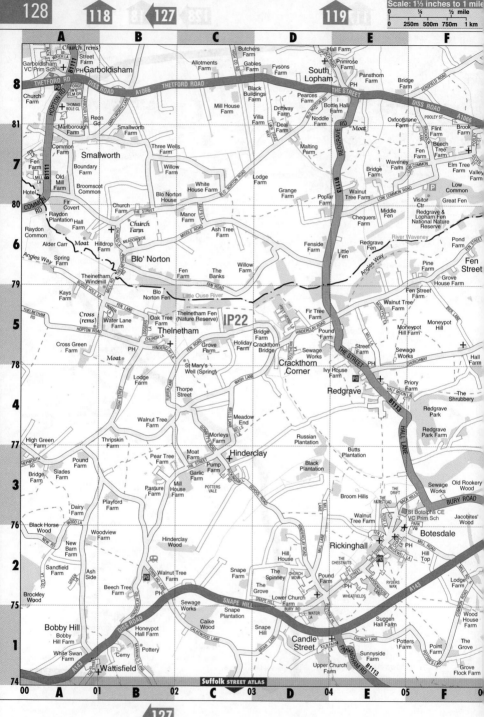

A   B   C   D   E   F

Church (rems)
Garboldisham VC Prim Sch
Street Farm
Garboldisham
Church Farm
Butchers Farm
Gables Farm
Allotments Farm
Fysons Farm
Hall Farm
Primrose Farm
South Lopham
Pansthorn Farm
Bridge Farm
THETFORD RD   DISS ROAD   THETFORD ROAD   A1066   THE STREET   DISS ROAD   A1066
Church Farm
Marlborough
Recn Gd
Smallworth Farm
Mill House Farm
Black Buildings Farm
Driftway Farm
Villa Farm
Pearces Farm
Bottle Hall Farm
Deal Farm
Noddle Farm
Moat
Oxfootstone Farm
Pooley St
Flint Farm
Brook Farm
Common Farm
Three Wells Farm
Beech Tree Farm
Elm Tree Farm
Valley Farm
Fen Farm
Smallworth
Boundary Farm
Willow Farm
Lodge Farm
Malting Farm
Waveney Farm
Bridge Farm
Low Common
Old Mill Farm
Broomscot Common
White House Farm
Blo Norton House
Grange Farm
Poplar Farm
Walnut Tree Farm
Chequers Farm
Redgrave Fen
Middle Fen
Great Fen
Visitor Ctr
Redgrave & Lopham Fen National Nature Reserve
Hotel
Fir Covert
Raydon Plantation
Church Farm
Manor Farm
Ash Tree Farm
Church Farm
Hall Farm
Fenside Farm
Little Fen
Redgrave Fen
River Waveney
Pond Farm
Raydon Common
Alder Carr
Spring Farm
Hilldrop Farm
Moat
Blo' Norton
Willow Farm
Angles Way
Pine Farm
Grove House Farm
Fen Street
Angles Way
Theinetham Windmill
Fen Farm
The Banks
Blo Norton Fen
Little Ouse River
Fen Street Farm
Walnut Tree Farm
Moneypot Hill
Kays Farm
Cross (rems)
Water Lane Farm
Oak Tree Farm
Thelnetham
Thelnetham Fen (Nature Reserve)
IP22
Fir Tree Farm
Moneypot Hill Farm
Sewage Works
Hall Farm
Cross Green Farm
Moat
PH
Grove Farm
Holiday Farm
Bridge Farm
Crackthorn Bridge
Pound Farm
Street Farm
Sewage Works
St Mary's Well (Spring)
Lodge Farm
Thorpe Street
Crackthorn Corner
Ivy House Farm
PH
Redgrave
Priory Farm
The Shrubbery
Walnut Tree Farm
Meadow End Farm
Wash Lane
Russian Plantation
Redgrave Park
Redgrave Park Farm
High Green Farm
Thripskin Farm
Pear Tree Farm
Morleys Farm
Hinderclay
Butts Plantation
Black Plantation
Sewage Works
Old Rookery Wood
Pound Farm
Moat Farm
Pump Lane Farm
Broom Hills
The Drift
BURY ROAD
Bridge Farm
Slades Farm
Pasture Farm
Mill House Farm
Garlic Farm
POTTERS VALE
Walnut Tree Farm
St Botolphs CE VC Prim Sch
Jacobites' Wood
Dairy Farm
Playford Farm
SCHOOL ROAD
The Fairstead
Botesdale
Black Horse Wood
Woodview Farm
Hinderclay Wood
Hill House
The Chestnuts
Rickinghall
Hill Top
New Barn Farm
Ash Side
Beech Tree Farm
PH
Walnut Tree Farm
Snape Farm
The Spinney
The Grove
CHURCH MDW
Pound Farm
PH
Ryders Way
WHEATFIELDS
Lodge Farm
Sandfield Farm
PO
SNAPE HILL
Sewage Works
Snape Plantation
Lower Church Farm
BURY RD
Brockley Wood
Bobby Hill
Bobby Hill Farm
White Swan Farm
Cemy
Pottery
Honeypot Hall Farm
Calke Wood
Snape Hill
Candle Street
WATER LA
Suggen Hall Farm
Potters Farm
Sunnyside Farm
Point Farm
Wood House Farm
The Grove
Wattisfield
A143
DISS ROAD
Upper Church Farm
CHURCH LANE
B1113
Grove Flock Farm

8 81 7 80 6 79 5 78 4 77 3 76 2 75 1 74

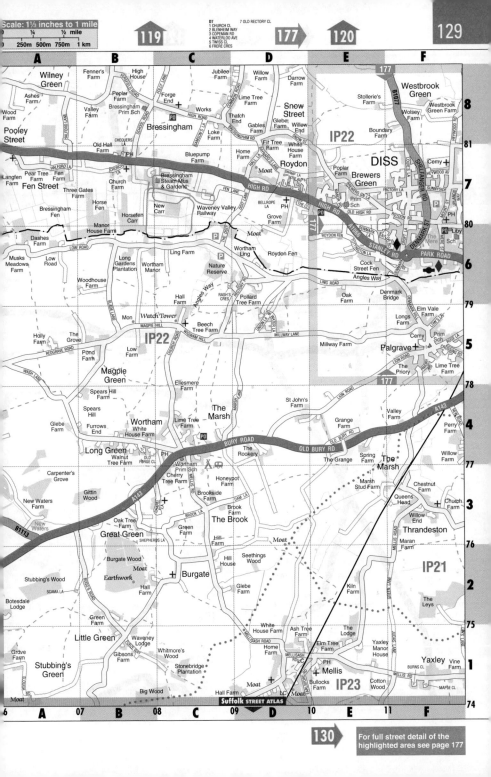

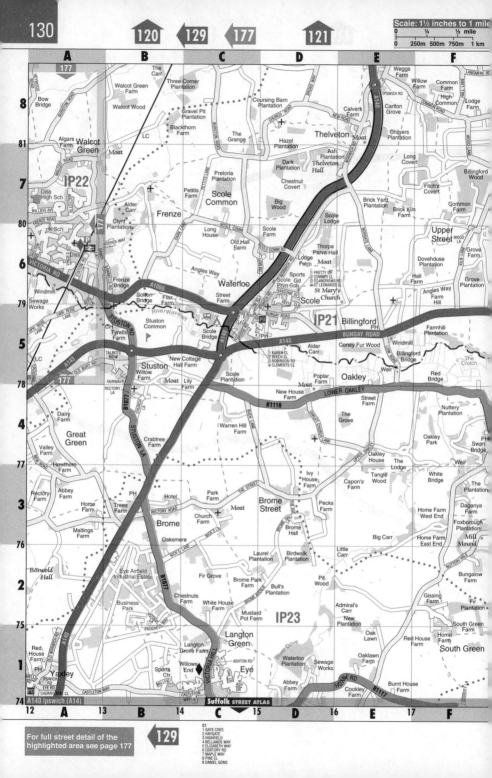

130
120
129
177
121
Scale: 1½ inches to 1 mile
0   ¼   ½ mile
0   250m 500m 750m 1 km

For full street detail of the highlighted area see page 177

129

C1
1 GAYE CRES
2 HAYGATE
3 HIGHFIELD
4 BELLANDS WAY
5 ELIZABETH WAY
6 CENTURY RD
7 MAPLE WAY
8 PINE CL
9 DANIEL GDNS

Suffolk STREET ATLAS

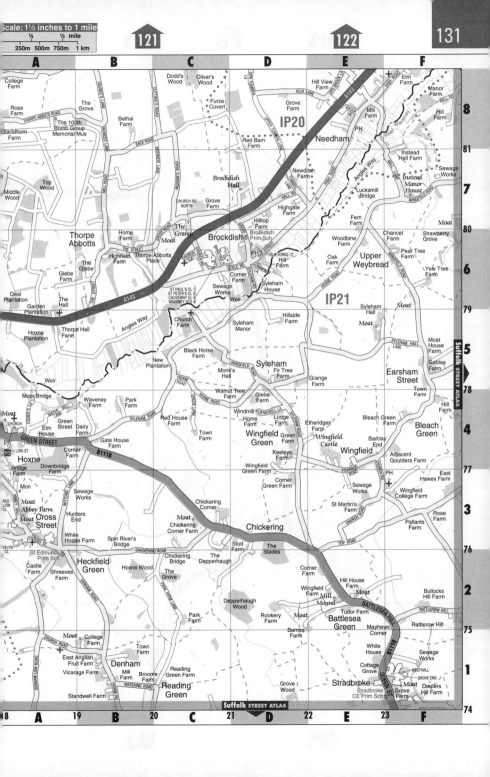

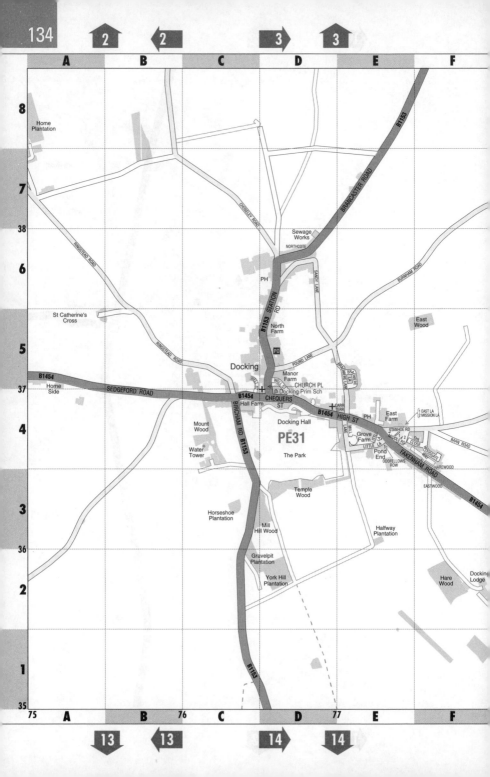

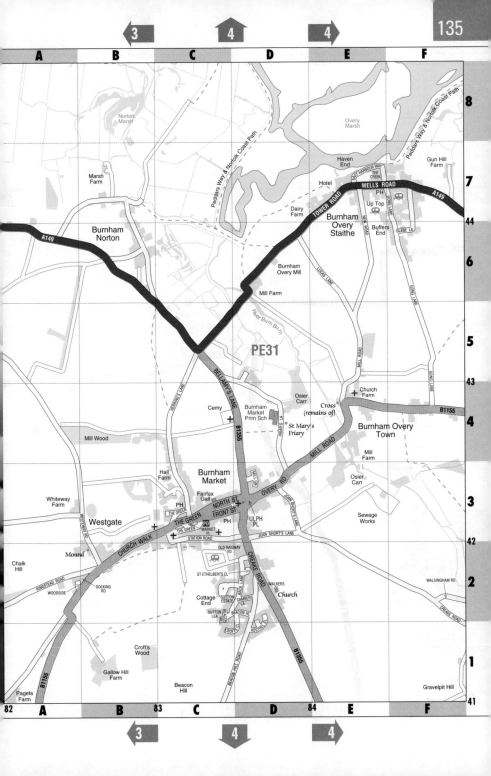

WELLS-NEXT-THE-SEA

NR23

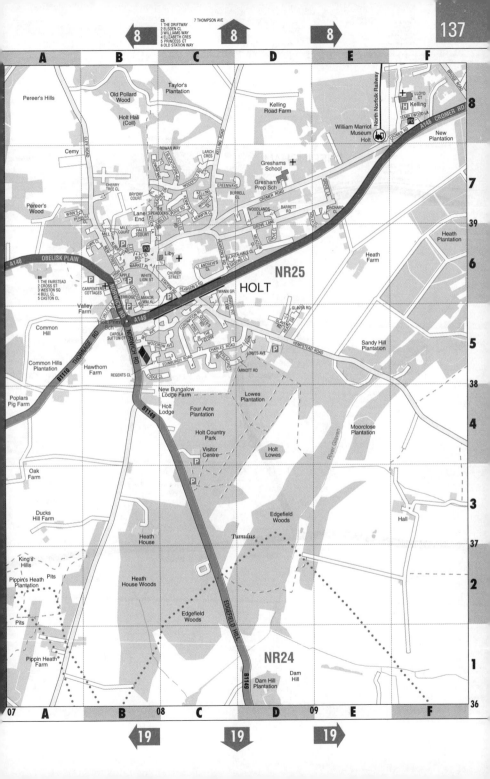

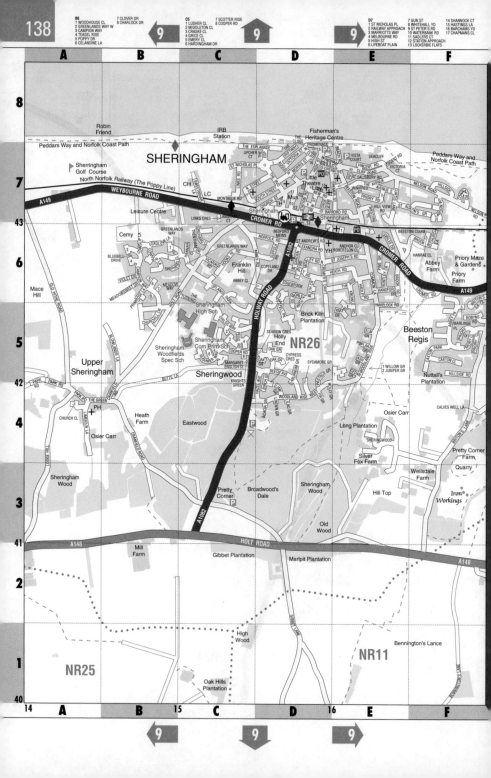

A7	B7	7 BOND ST	C6	7 WARREN CT
1 HOWARDS HILL W	1 JETTY ST	8 CROSS ST	1 ST MARGARET'S RD	
	2 CORNER ST	9 NORMAN TROLLER CT	2 ST MARGARET'S LA	
	3 HAMILTON RD	10 GOLDEN SQ	3 PRIOR BANK ORCH	
	4 CHURCH ST	11 CHESTERFIELD COTTS	4 WARNES CL	
	5 CHAPEL ST		5 OLIVER CT	
	6 HANS PL		6 CROMWELL CL	

139

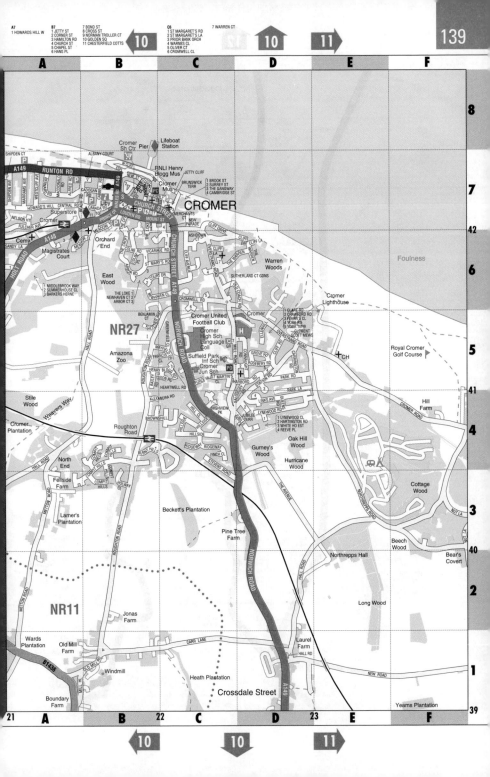

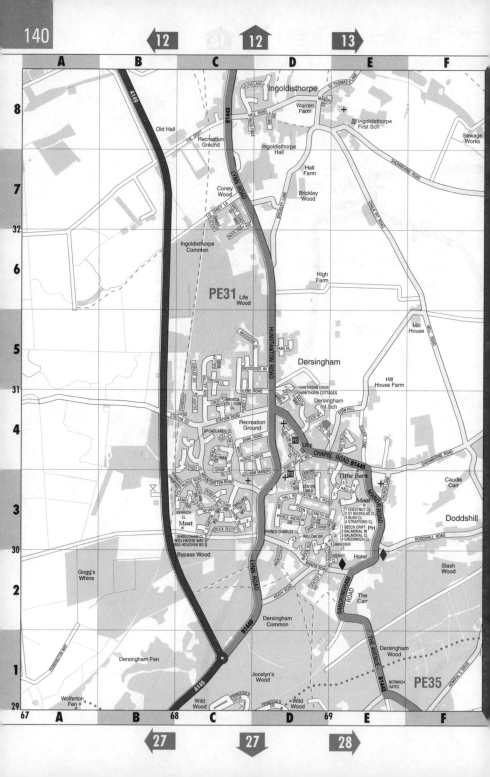

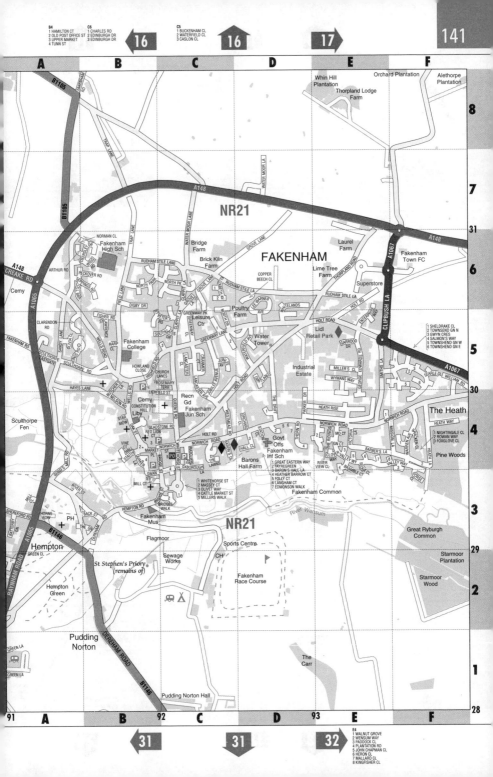

B4
1 HAMILTON CT
2 OLD POST OFFICE ST
3 UPPER MARKET
4 TUNN ST

C6
1 CHARLES RD
2 EDINBURGH DR
3 EDINBURGH DR

C5
1 BUCKENHAM CL
2 WATERFIELD CL
3 CASLON CL

16   16   17

NR21

FAKENHAM

Whin Hill Plantation
Orchard Plantation
Alethorpe Plantation
Thorpland Lodge Farm

Fakenham High Sch
NORMAN CL
Bridge Farm
Brick Kiln Farm
Laurel Farm
Lime Tree Farm

Fakenham Town FC
Superstore

B1105
A148
CREAKE RD
A1065
Cemy
ARTHUR RD
CLARENDON RD
PICKOVER RD
FISHER RD
HARP CT
RUDHAM STILE LANE
NORTH PK
DIGBY DR
COPPER BEECH CL
PETER'S

Fakenham College
GREENWAY PK
Leisure Ctr
GREENWIN LANE
Poultry Farm

Water Tower

1 SHELDRAKE CL
2 TOWNSEND GN N
3 GWYN CRES
4 SALMON'S WAY
5 TOWNSHEND GN W
6 TOWNSHEND GN E

Lidl Retail Park
HOLT ROAD
GARROOD DR
Industrial Estate
MILLER'S WAY
WYMANS WAY

The Heath
HEATH WAY
1 NIGHTINGALE CL
2 ROWAN WAY
3 FOXGLOVE CL
Pine Woods

Sculthorpe Fen
HAYES LANE
Cemy
Recn Gd
Fakenham Jun Sch
HEATH RISE
HOWLAND CLOSE
CHURCH LANES
ROSEMARY TERR
LICHFIELD ST

CONSTITUTION HILL
Liby
GLADSTONE RD
RED LION CT
Fakenham Inf Sch
Govt Offs
NORWICH ROAD
THORN RD
BARBER'S LA
VALLEY WAY

STAR MDW
VINE
MARKET ST
SWAN
MILL CT
PO
HOLT RD
NORWICH ROAD
Barons Hall Farm

1 GREAT EASTERN WAY
2 PAYREGREEN
3 BARON'S HALL LA
4 HEATHER BARROW CT
5 FOLLY CT
6 LANGHAM CT
7 EDMONSON WALK

1 WHITEHORSE ST
2 MASSEY CT
3 OLIVET WAY
4 CATTLE MARKET ST
5 MILLERS WALK

Fakenham Common
River Wensum

Fakenham Mus
Flagmoor
BRIDGES WALK
HEMPTON RD
BACK ST
THE GN
PH

Hempton
GREEN CL
B1146
HORNS LANE
BATTERY
A1065

NR21

St Stephen's Priory (remains of)
Sewage Works
Sports Centre
CH
Fakenham Race Course

Hempton Green

Great Ryburgh Common
Starmoor Plantation
Starmoor Wood

Pudding Norton
DEREHAM ROAD
B1146
RAYNHAM ROAD
GREEN LA

The Carr

Pudding Norton Hall

31   31   32

E4
1 WALNUT GROVE
2 WENSUM WAY
3 PADDOCK CL
4 PLANTATION RD
5 JOHN CHAPMAN CL
6 HERON CL
7 MALLARD CL
8 KINGFISHER CL

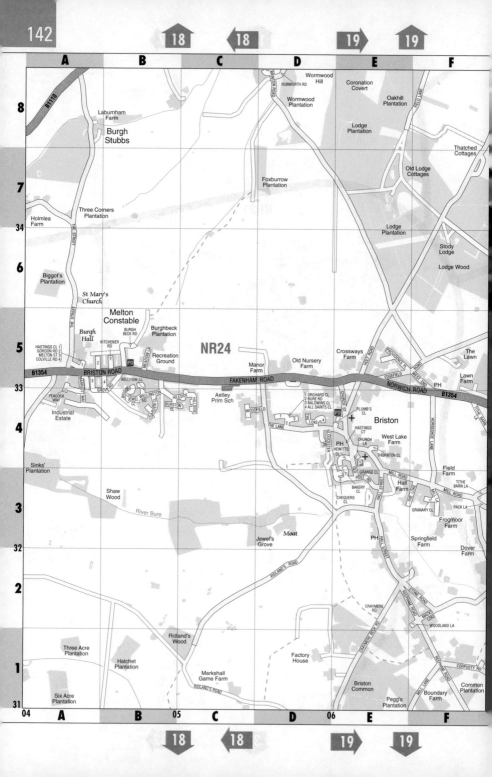

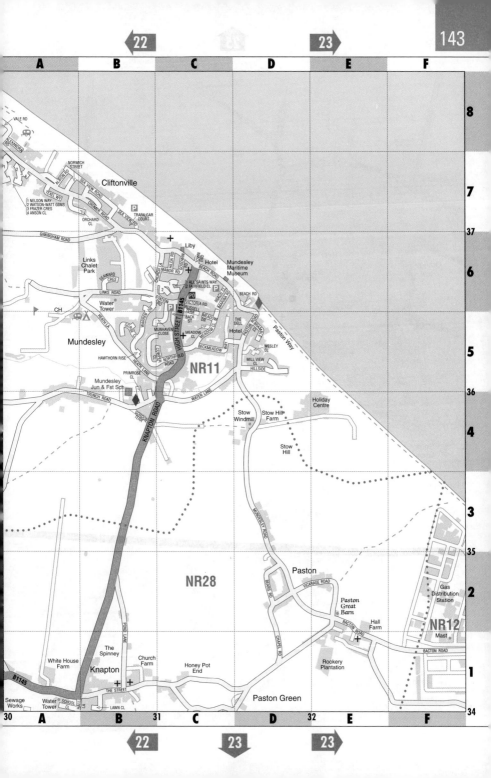

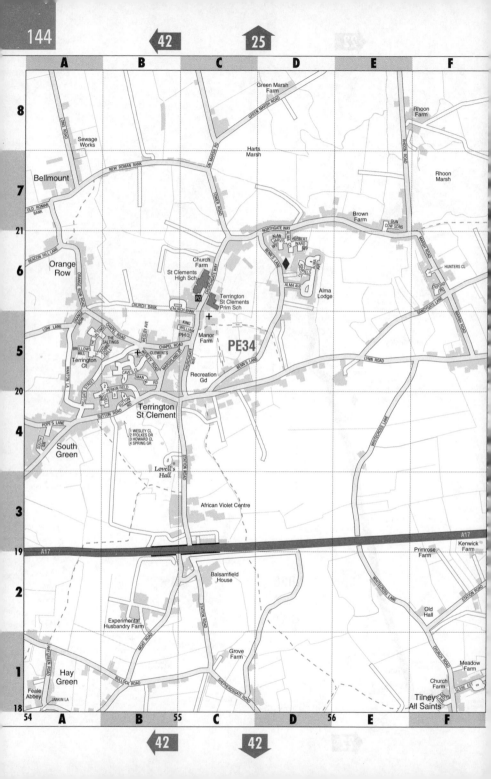

A B C D E F

8

7

21

6

5

20

4

3

19

2

1

18

54 A B 55 C D 56 E F

Bellmount

Orange Row

Terrington St Clement

South Green

Hay Green

Feale Abbey

Green Marsh Farm

Harts Marsh

Rhoon Farm

Rhoon Marsh

Brown Farm

Church Farm

St Clements High Sch

Terrington St Clements Prim Sch

Manor Farm

Recreation Gd

PE34

Alma Lodge

Hunters Cl

Sewage Works

Lovell's Hall

African Violet Centre

Balsamfield House

Experimental Husbandry Farm

Grove Farm

Primrose Farm

Kenwick Farm

Old Hall

Meadow Farm

Church Farm

Tilney All Saints

1 WESLEY CL
2 FFOLKES DR
3 HOWARD CL
4 SPRING GR

KING WILLIAM PH

A17

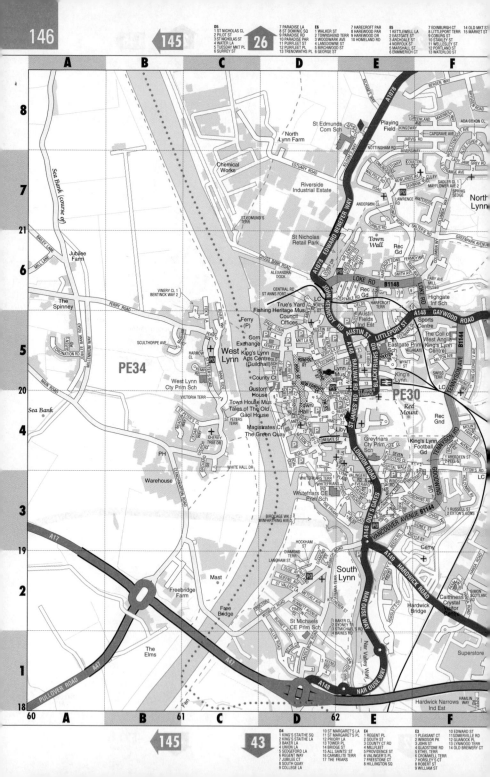

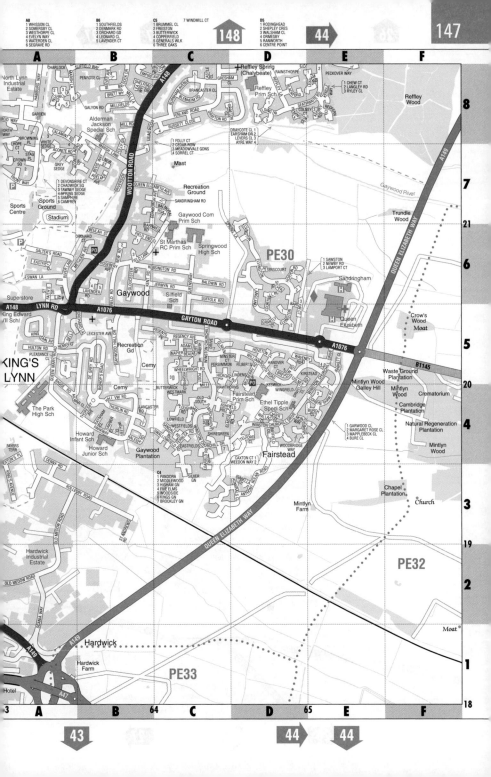

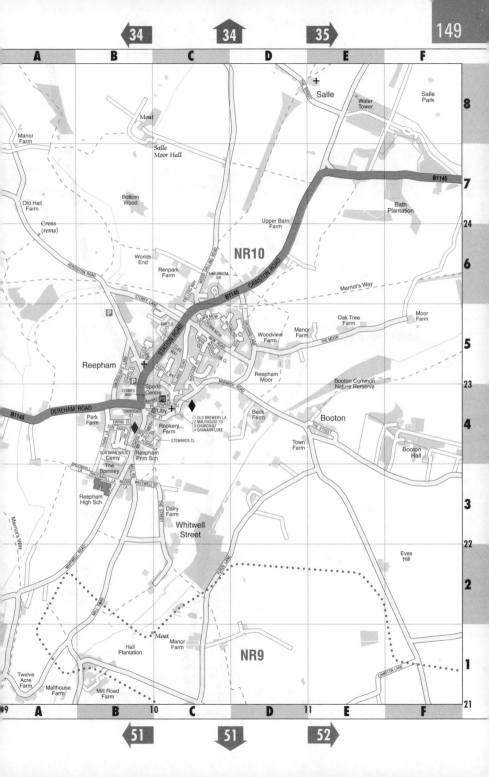

Salle

Salle Park

Water Tower

B1145

Bath Plantation

Manor Farm

Moat

Salle Moor Hall

Old Hall Farm

Bottom Wood

Cross (rems)

NR10

Upper Barn Farm

Kerdiston Road

Worlds End

Renpark Farm

Stoney Lane

Marriot's Way

Cawston Road

B1145

Moor Farm

Oak Tree Farm

The Moor

Woodview Farm

Manor Farm

Reepham

Station Road

New Road

Norwich Road

Reepham Moor

Booton Common Nature Reserve

Sports Centre

Dereham Road

B1145

Park Farm

Rookery Farm

Beck Farm

Booton

1 OLD BREWERY LA
2 MALTHOUSE YD
3 CHURCH ST
4 GRANARY LOKE

The Street

Town Farm

Booton Hall

Sun Barn Walk

Cemy

The Spinney

Reepham Prim Sch

Stewards Cl

Reepham High Sch

Broomhill La

Whitwell St

Rudds La

Dairy Farm

Whitwell Street

The Street

Eves Hill

Marriot's Way

Mill Road

Hall Plantation

Moat

Manor Farm

NR9

Twelve Acre Farm

Malthouse Farm

Mill Road Farm

Cawston Lane

34   34   35

51   51   52

24

7

6

5

23

4

3

22

2

1

21

A   B   C   D   E   F

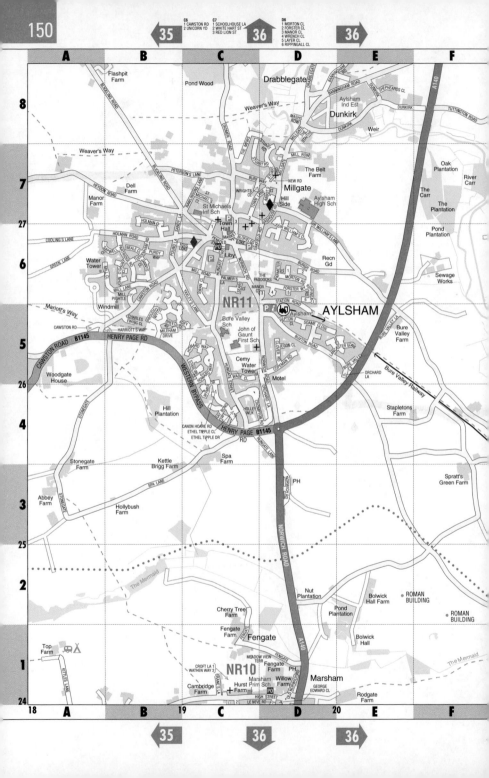

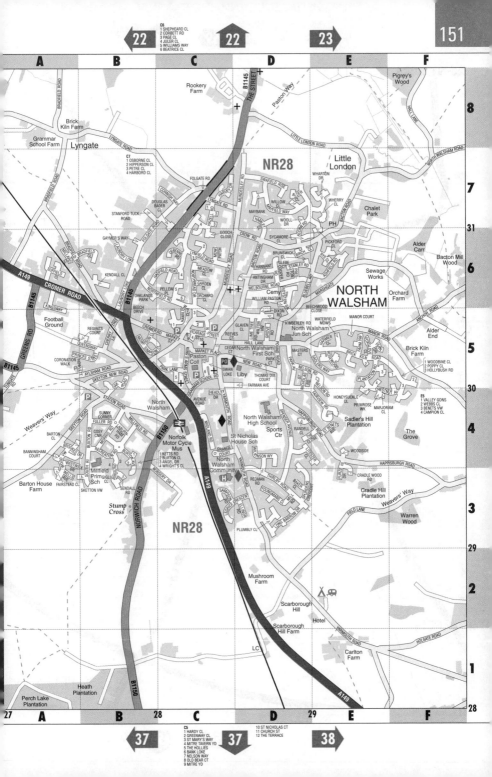

C6
1 SHEPHEARD CL
2 CORBETT RD
3 PAGE CL
4 JULER CL
5 WILLIAMS WAY
6 BEATRICE CL

← 22

↑ 22

23 →

C7
1 OSBORNE CL
2 HIPPERSON CL
3 PETRE CL
4 HARBORD CL

NR28

Little
London

Pigrey's
Wood

Grammar
School Farm

Lyngate

Brick
Kiln Farm

Rookery
Farm

Paston Way

Chalet
Park

Alder
Carr

Bacton Mill
Wood

Sewage
Works

Orchard
Farm

NORTH
WALSHAM

Alder
End

Brick Kiln
Farm

1 WOODBINE CL
2 POPPY CL
3 HOLLYBUSH RD

E5
1 VALLEY GDNS
2 WEBBS CL
3 BENETS VW
4 CAMPION CL

Football
Ground

Coronation
Walk

North
Walsham

Sadler's Hill
Plantation

The
Grove

Weavers' Way

Barton
CL

Banningham
Court

Millfield
Prim Sch

Barton House
Farm

North Walsham
Motor Cycle
Mus

Stump
Cross

St Nicholas
House Sch

North Walsham
High School

Sports
Ctr

North
Walsham
Community

Cradle Wood
Plantation

Cradle Hill
Plantation

Warren
Wood

Weavers' Way

Happisburgh Road

NR28

Mushroom
Farm

Scarborough
Hill

Hotel

Scarborough
Hill Farm

Carlton
Farm

Perch Lake
Plantation

Heath
Plantation

C5
1 HARDY CL
2 GREENWAY CL
3 ST MARY'S WAY
4 MITRE TAVERN YD
5 THE HOLLIES
6 BANK LOKE
7 NELSON WAY
8 OLD BEAR CT
9 MITRE YD

10 ST NICHOLAS CT
11 CHURCH ST
12 THE TERRACE

59

A1101 Holbeach (A17)

Little East Field

PE14

Osborne Park

Orchards Prim Sch

Gordon Fendick Sch

River Nene

Nene Way

CRAB MARSH

SUTTON ROAD

B1169

LEVERINGTON ROAD

Peckover Cty Prim Sch

Cemy

Superstore

Yacht Harbour

Windmill

WISBECH

Football Ground Sports Ground

The Clarkson Inf Sch

Walsoken

Hudson Leisure Centre

PE13

Peckover House

Wisbech Gram Sch

Octavia Hill Birthplace Mus

Castle

The Castle Mus

The Angles Theatre

Lib

St Peters CE Jun Sch

North Cambs

The Nene Sch

Ramnoth Cty Jun Sch

The Coll of West Anglia (Isle Campus)

Windpump Hall Field

PE13

Elm Rd Primary Sch

Meadowgate Sch

CROMWELL ROAD

The Bramley Line (Disused)

Superstore

The Queens Sch

Works

Industrial Estate

Great Bolepass Field

Cromwell Retail Park

PE14

B198

The Coll of West Anglia (Wisbech Campus)

The Peel Centre

West Meadowgate

Allotments

New Bridge LC

New Bridge Farm

Town Field

PE14

Oxburgh Hall

A47

A1122

59

Cambridgeshire STREET ATLAS

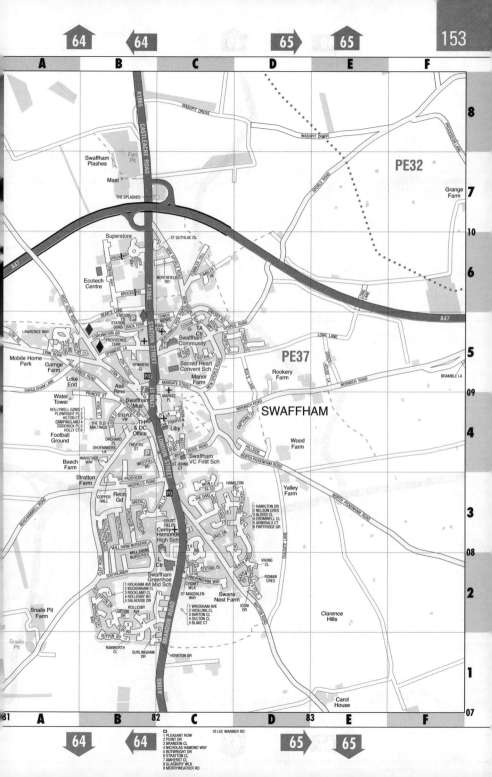

A   B   C   D   E   F

8
7
10
6
5
09
4
3
08
2
1
07

PE32

Grange Farm

Swaffham Plashes

Fen Pit

Mast

THE SPLASHES

Superstore

St GUTHLAC CL

Ecotech Centre

PE37

Rookery Farm

BRAMBLE LA

SWAFFHAM

Mobile Home Park

Garage Farm

Loke End

Water Tower

Football Ground

Beech Farm

Stratton Farm

Copper Hall

Snails Pit Farm

Snails Pit

Swaffham Mus

Swaffham Community

Sacred Heart Convent Sch

Manor Farm

Market Pl

Liby

Swaffham VC First Sch

Wood Farm

Yalley Farm

Clarence Hills

Carol House

Swaffham Greenhoe

Cerry Hamonds High Sch

Swans Nest Farm

HOLLYWELL GDNS 1
PLOWRIGHT PL 2
HILTON CT 3
CAMPINGLAND 4
GOODRICK PL 5
HOLLY CT 6

1 HOLKHAM AVE MID SCH
2 BUCKENHAM CL
3 ROCKLAND CL
4 ROLLESBY RD
5 SALHOUSE DR

1 HAMILTON DR
2 NELSON CRES
3 ALDISS CL
4 CROMWELL CL
5 ADMIRALS CT
6 PARTRIDGE GR

1 WROXHAM AVE
2 HICKLING CL
3 BARTON CL
4 OULTON CL
5 BLAKE CT

10 LEE WARNER RD

1 PLEASANT ROW
2 POINT DR
3 BRANDON CL
4 NICHOLAS HAMOND WAY
5 BOTWRIGHT DR
6 STRATTON CL
7 AMHERST CL
8 GLASBURY WLK
9 MERRYWEATHER RD

A   B   82   C   83   D   E   F

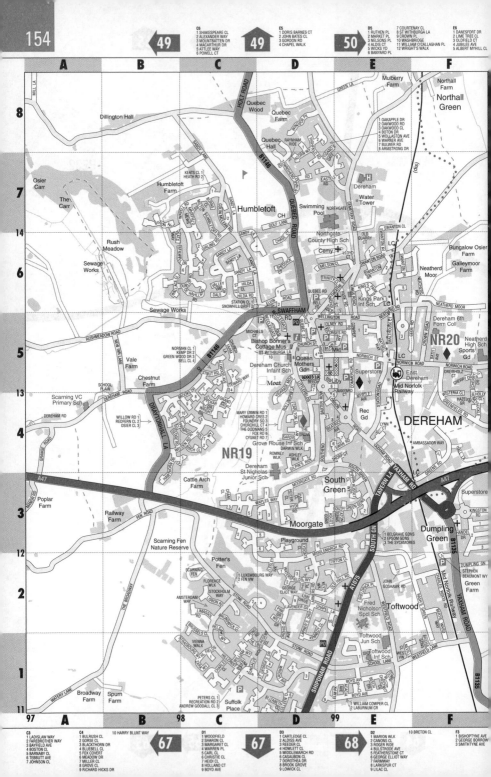

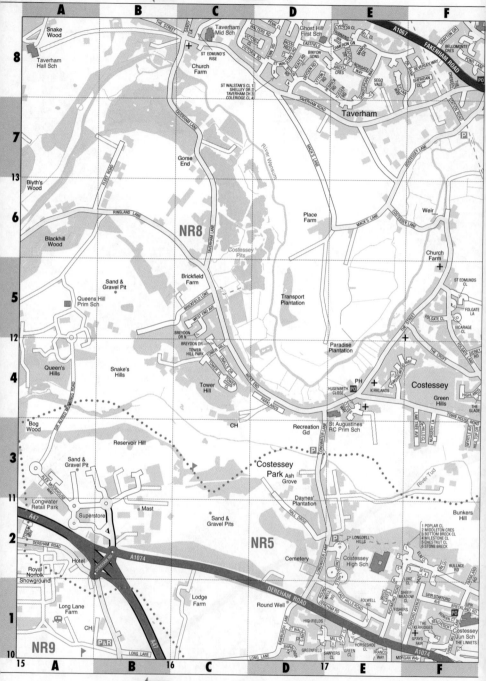

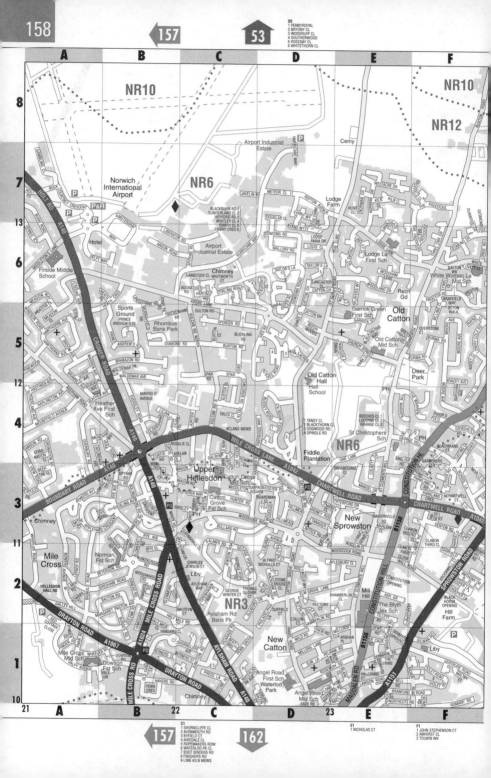

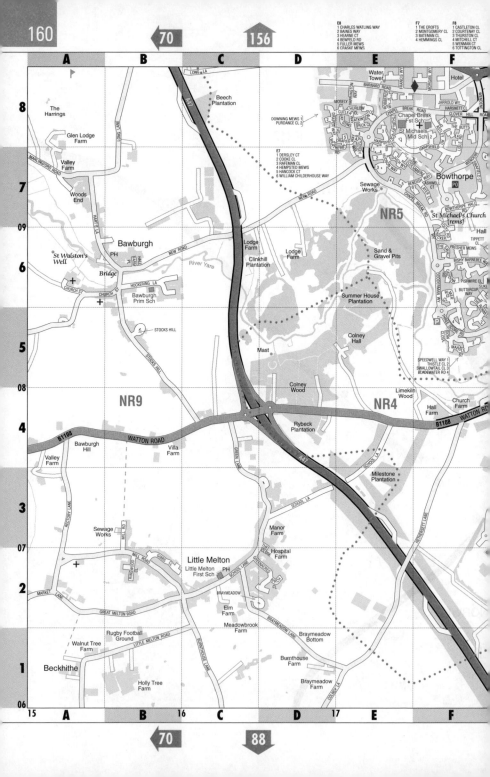

A	B	C	D	E	F

| 7 OFFLEY CT | B8 | 7 MAYES CL | C6 | B7 | 161 |

A
HARRY BARBER CL
WORTHAM CL
BRENNEWATER MEWS
BUMSTEDE CT
WALDEGRAVE

BRAITHWAIT CL

B8
1 DEREHAM RD
2 HOUGHTON CL
3 MORRIS CL
4 TOFTES PL
5 WEBSTER CL
6 JOE ELLIS CT

7 MAYES CL
8 FITZHENRY MEWS
9 LUSHINGTON CL
10 DRURY CL

C6
1 BRERETON CL
2 CONISTON CL
3 CRUMMOCK RD
4 BUTTERMERE RD
5 EARLHAM WEST CTR
6 EDGEWORTH RD

7 KEABLE CL

B7
1 GOODHALE RD
2 SMEAT ST
3 ST MILDREDS RD
4 ROGERS CL
5 LANGTON CL
6 NOOT ALLEY

157   162   161

F1
1 BRENTWOOD
2 ATMERE CL
3 CHESTNUT HILL
4 ELLCAR RISE
5 PENSHURST MEWS
6 WAKEHURST CL
7 NUTFIELD CL
8 BUCKLAND RISE

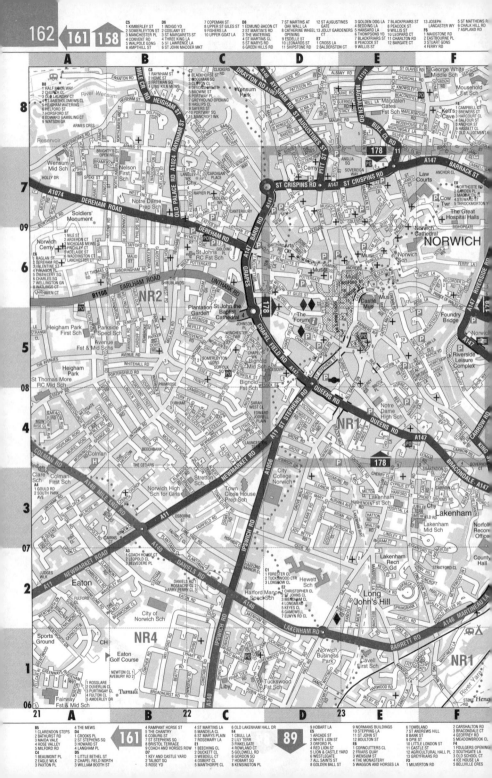

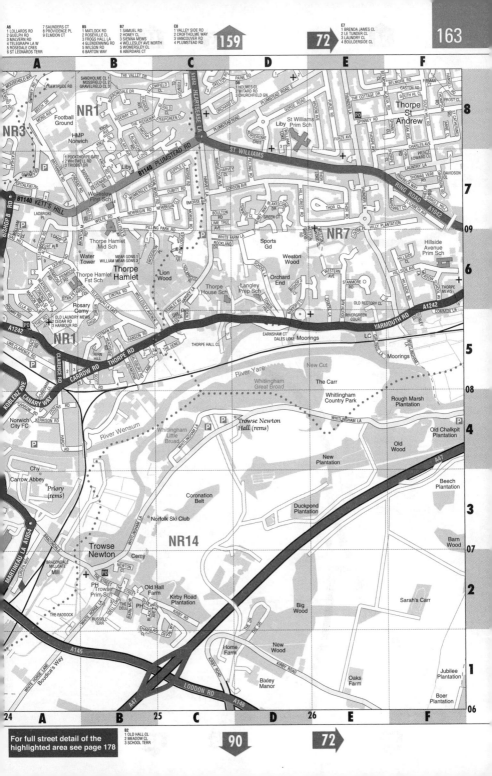

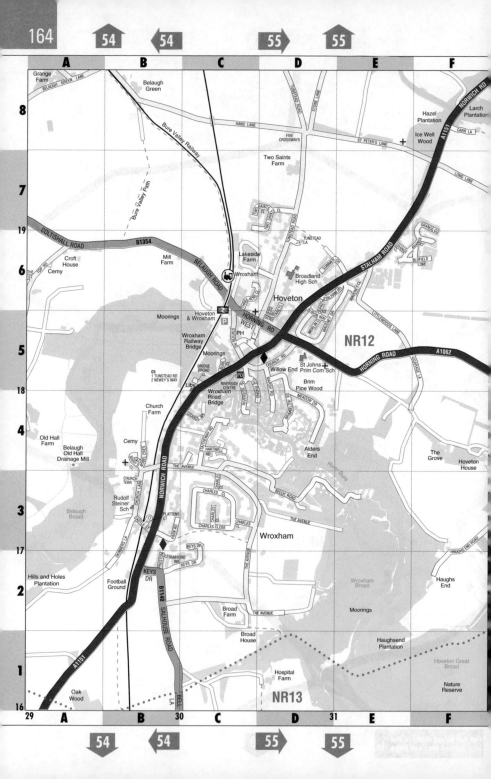

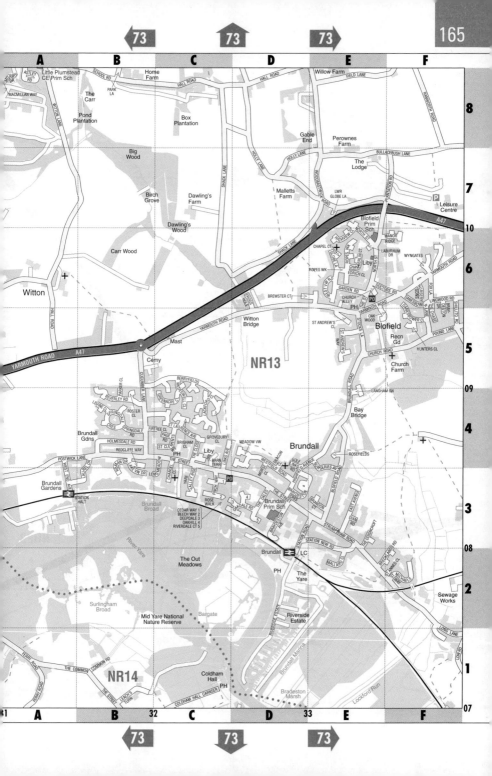

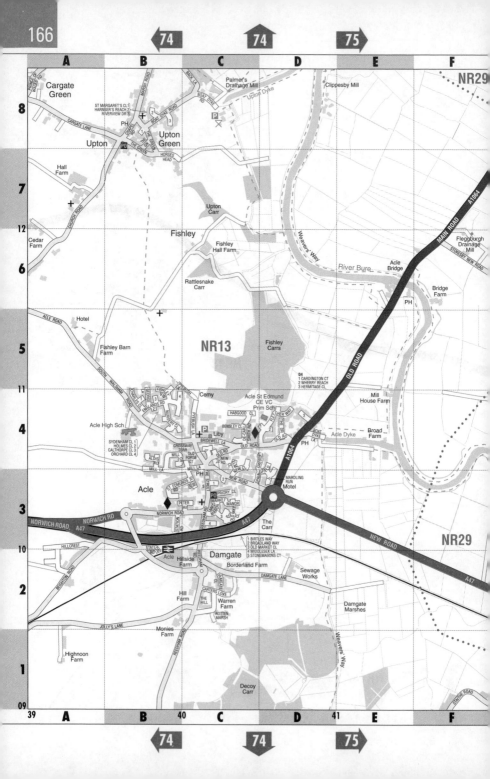

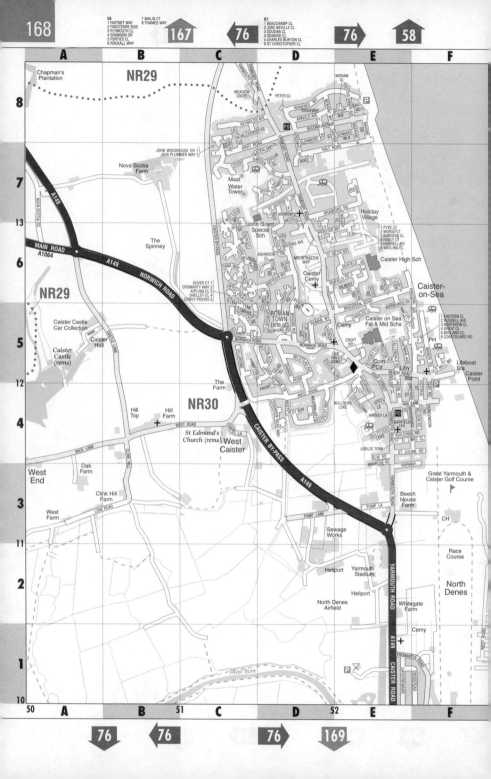

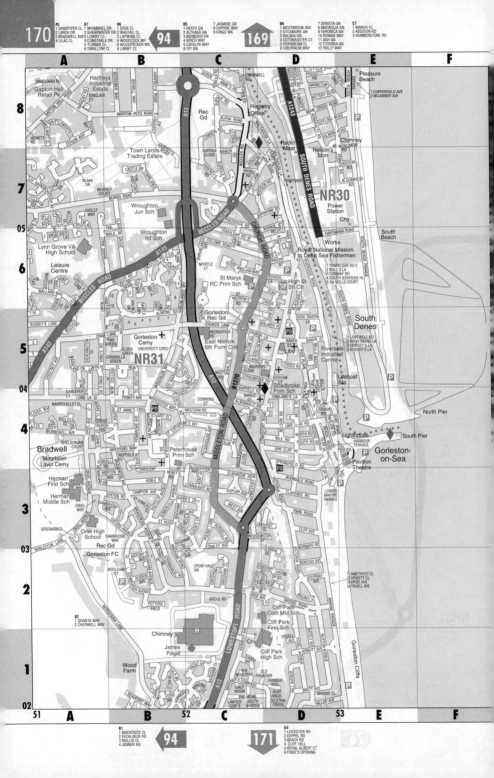

A B C D E F

8
7
01
6
5
00
4
3
99
2
1
98

Suffolk STREET ATLAS

NR31

NR32

Hobland
Plantation
Mast
The Bungalow
Hobland Farm
HOBLAND ROAD
Oakland
Farm
Sidegate
Farm
Sawmill
Reservoir
White House
Farm
HALL ROAD
Bloodman's
Corner
Homeclose
Shrubbery
BACK LANE
Cuckoo
Green
Cuckoo Green
Farm
Elder
Farm
DUNNING ROAD
CHURCH LANE
Hall
Farm
Elm
Farm
Lothingland
Middle Sch
Rector's
Wood
Great
Wood
Brickhill
Wood

HORSLEY DR
BEAUFELL WAY
CAMBER RD
SIDEGATE ROAD
DORKING ROAD

LINKS ROAD
QUAY OSTEND
MARINER'S COMP
MARINER'S CL
MARINE CL
LINKS
MARINE PARADE
CLIFF LA
MARINE
PARADE
CH
WARREN ROAD
KENNEL LANE
Masons
Farm
Kennel
Farm
Gorleston Golf Course
Corton
Cliffs
Long
Belt
Valley
Farm
LOWESTOFT ROAD
A12
RACKHAM CL
LOWESTOFT RD
WHITES
HALL RD
PO
PH
+
A12
IMPERIAL MEWS
STATION ROAD
YARMOUTH ROAD
Home
Farm
Home
Farm
JAY LANE
Beehive
Farm
Oak View
Farm
LONGFULANS LANE

Hopton
on Sea
FLOWERDAY
ROGER'S CL
ANGLIAN
MARINERS
WALK
ST VINCENT
WK
Holiday
Village
WARREN ROAD
1 ST ANDREW CL
2 BARN CL
JULIAN WAY
WATSON'S CL
Hopton First
Sch
+
St Margaret's
Church (rems)
SEAFIELDS DR
SEAFIELDS DRIVE
IVES
CADIZ WAY
OLD CHURCH RD
MANOR
GDNS
SEA VIEW RD
BEACH ROAD
PEBBLE VW WK
Holiday & Leisure
Centre
COAST ROAD
League
Hole

DS
1 RANDALL CL
2 ST MARGARET'S WAY
3 ANGLIAN WAY
4 GROOMES CL
5 BISHOPS WK
6 ST CLARE CT
7 ST CLEMENT MEWS

Red House
Farm
MARKET LANE
A12
YARMOUTH ROAD
Fourways
Farm
Corton
Cliffs
Mast
Woburn
Farm
STIRRUPS LANE
COAST ROAD
CHURCH LA
+

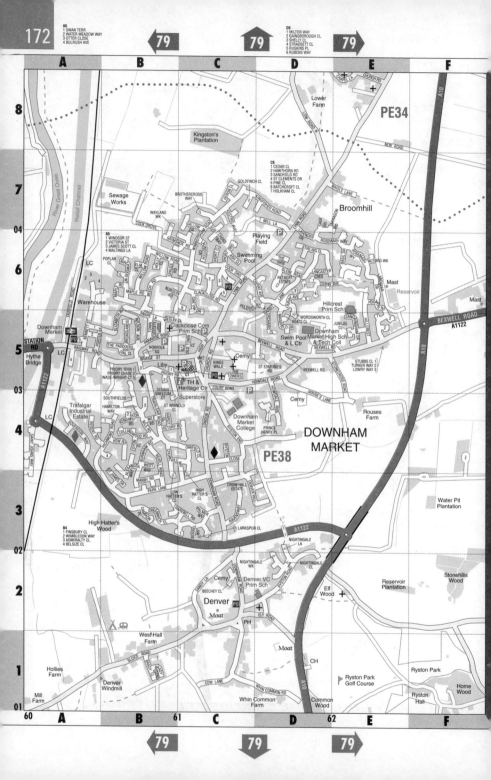

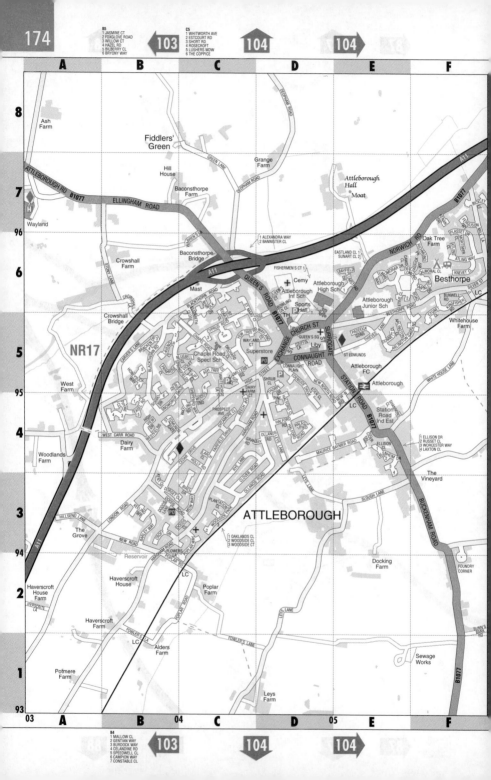

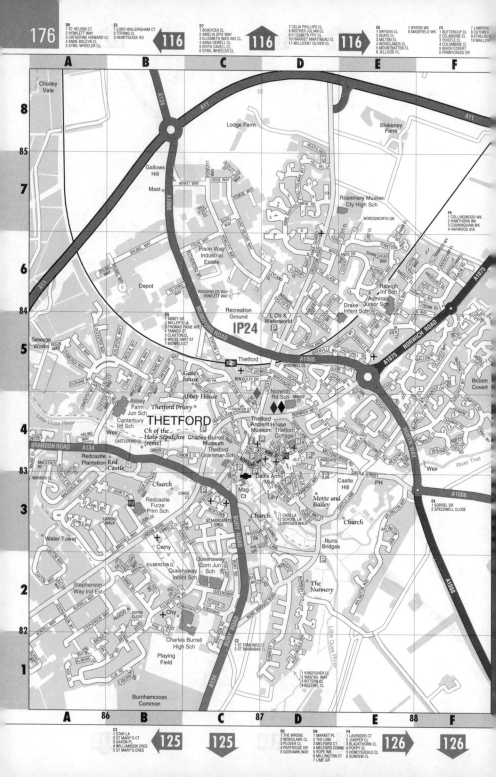

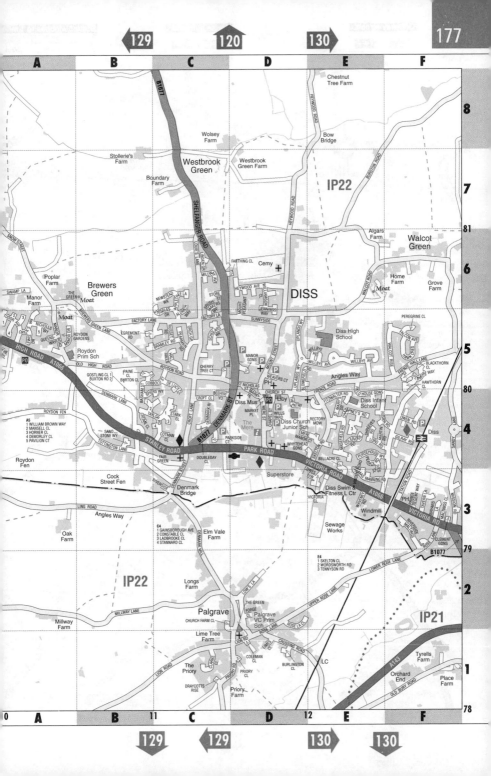

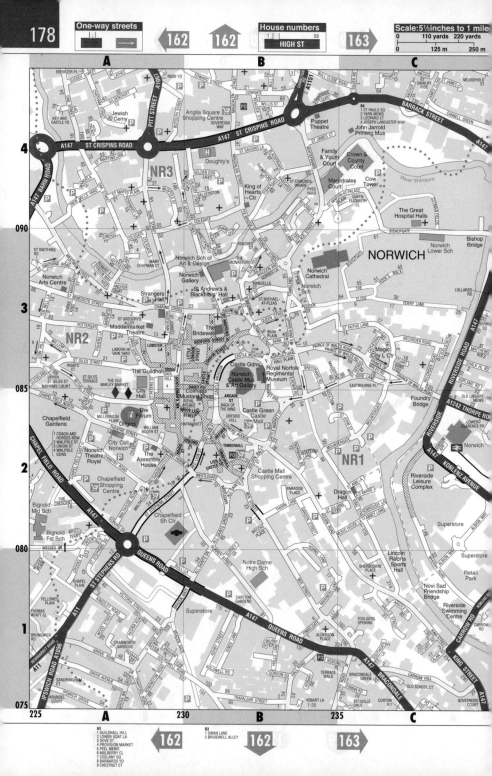

Index

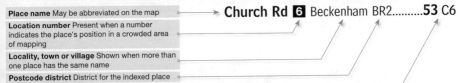

Place name May be abbreviated on the map

Location number Present when a number indicates the place's position in a crowded area of mapping

Locality, town or village Shown when more than one place has the same name

Postcode district District for the indexed place

Page and grid square Page number and grid reference for the standard mapping

Church Rd **6** Beckenham BR2.........**53** C6

Cities, towns and villages are listed in CAPITAL LETTERS

Public and commercial buildings are highlighted in magenta Places of interest are highlighted in blue with a star⋆

Abbreviations used in the index

Acad	Academy	Comm	Common	Gd	Ground	L	Leisure	Prom	Promenade
App	Approach	Cott	Cottage	Gdn	Garden	La	Lane	Rd	Road
Arc	Arcade	Cres	Crescent	Gn	Green	Liby	Library	Recn	Recreation
Ave	Avenue	Cswy	Causeway	Gr	Grove	Mdw	Meadow	Ret	Retail
Bglw	Bungalow	Ct	Court	H	Hall	Meml	Memorial	Sh	Shopping
Bldg	Building	Ctr	Centre	Ho	House	Mkt	Market	Sq	Square
Bsns, Bus	Business	Ctry	Country	Hospl	Hospital	Mus	Museum	St	Street
Bvd	Boulevard	Cty	County	HQ	Headquarters	Orch	Orchard	Sta	Station
Cath	Cathedral	Dr	Drive	Hts	Heights	Pal	Palace	Terr	Terrace
Cir	Circus	Dro	Drove	Ind	Industrial	Par	Parade	TH	Town Hall
Cl	Close	Ed	Education	Inst	Institute	Pas	Passage	Univ	University
Cnr	Corner	Emb	Embankment	Int	International	Pk	Park	Wk, Wlk	Walk
Coll	College	Est	Estate	Intc	Interchange	Pl	Place	Wr	Water
Com	Community	Ex	Exhibition	Junc	Junction	Prec	Precinct	Yd	Yard

Index of towns, villages, streets, hospitals, industrial estates, railway stations, schools, shopping centres, universities and places of interest

100th Bomb Group Memorial Mus, The⋆ IP21 ......131 A8

A

Abbey Cl
Horsham St Faith & Newton St
Faith NR10 ....53 D1
Sheringham NR26 ......138 D6
Wendling NR19 ......66 F7
Abbey Farm Mid Sch
IP24 ......176 B4
Abbeyfields PE32 ......29 D1
Abbeygate PE32 ......176 C5
Abbey Gn **1** IP24 ......176 C4
Abbey Hill IP21 ......131 A3
Abbey La
Haveringland NR10 ......52 D6
Norwich NR1 ......178 C2
Abbey Pk NR26 ......138 F5
Abbey Rd
Flitcham with Appleton
PE31 ......28 D5
Flixton NR35 ......123 F4
Great Massingham PE32 ......29 D1
Horsham St Faith NR10 ......53 D1
Old Buckenham NR17 ......104 D3
Pentney PE32 ......63 B8
Sheringham NR26 ......138 C6
Upton NR13 ......84 E3
Abbey St NR12 ......23 E4
Abbot Cl NR18 ......173 C5
Abbot Rd
Horning NR12 ......55 E4
Norwich NR1 ......162 D2
Abbot's Cl NR11 ......150 D7
Abbot's La NR14 ......90 B3
Abbots Way NR12 ......24 E4
Abbotsinch Rd **5** IP31 ......126 B1
Aberdare Ct **6** NR1 ......163 B7
Aberdeen St PE30 ......146 F4
Abinger Way NR4 ......89 D8
Abington Gr **4** PE14 ......59 A1
Abyssinia Rd NR30 ......169 D2
Acacia Ave
Ashill IP25 ......84 A7
East Dereham NR19 ......154 E1
2 Martham NR29 ......57 D4
Wisbech PE13 ......152 C8
Acacia Gr NR26 ......138 D4
Acacia Rd NR7 ......163 E8
Access Rd NR21 ......15 D2

Acer Rd PE34 ......43 D4
Ackland Cl **7** NR29 ......58 B6
Acland Mews NR6 ......158 C4
ACLE NR13 ......166 B3
Acle High Sch NR13 ......166 B4
Acle New Rd NR30 ......169 B5
Acle Rd
Beighton NR13 ......74 E2
South Walsham NR13 ......74 C7
Upton with Fishley NR13 ......166 A5
Acle St Edmund CE VC Prim Sch NR13 ......166 D2
Acle Sta NR13 ......166 B3
Aconite Rd NR26 ......147 B7
Acorn Dr PE32 ......45 B6
Acorn Rd NR28 ......151 D6
Acorn Way NR19 ......154 D7
Acres Way NR8 ......155 E2
Ada Cole Ave NR16 ......103 D1
Ada Coxon Cl PE30 ......146 F8
Adam Cl PE30 ......147 C5
Adams La **4** NR11 ......19 F1
Adams Rd NR7 ......159 A5
Adastral Pl PE37 ......153 C5
Addey Cl NR6 ......158 F5
Addison Cl
2 Coltishall NR12 ......54 C7
Feltwell IP26 ......98 F1
Addison Rd **2** NR31 ......170 C7
Adeane Mdw IP26 ......100 A4
Adelaide Ave PE30 ......147 B7
Adelaide St **5** NR2 ......162 B7
Adey Cl NR11 ......150 B5
Admirals Cl PE30 ......147 D3
Admirals Dr PE37 ......153 D3
Admirals Dr PE13 ......152 D8
Admiral's Dr PE35 ......140 F1
Admirals Jun Sch IP24 ......176 E6
Admirals Quay NR31 ......169 C1
Admirals Way
Hethersett NR9 ......88 D8
Thetford NR24 ......176 E5
Admirals Wlk **7** NR9 ......86 C5
Admiralty Cl **3** PE35 ......172 B4
Admiralty Rd NR30 ......169 D1
Adventurers' Dro PE33 ......81 B1
Aerodrome Est NR7 ......163 D8
Afghan Pl NR3 ......158 E1
Agricultural Hall Plain
NR1 ......178 B3
Ailmar Cl PE37 ......153 B6
Ainsworth Cl **7** NR20 ......50 B3
Airedale Cl **4** NR3 ......158 C1

Airfield Rd PE33 ......63 C4
Airport Ind Est NR6 ......158 C6
Airstation La IP21 ......121 E2
Akrotiri Sq IP25 ......84 F3
Alan Ave NR15 ......89 D1
Alan Jarvis Way PE34 ......144 D6
Alan Rd NR1 ......178 C1
Alban Rd PE30 ......148 C5
Albansfield **3** NR18 ......173 C5
Albany Cl NR31 ......169 C2
Albany Ct NR27 ......139 B7
Albany Rd
Great Yarmouth NR31 ......169 C2
Norwich NR3 ......162 D8
Wisbech PE13 ......152 C6
Albemarle Rd
Great Yarmouth NR30 ......169 D5
Norwich NR2 ......162 B3
Albert Ct **18** PE13 ......152 C4
Albert Gate Rd **22** NR30 ......169 D2
Albert Myhill Cl **5** NR20 ......154 E6
Albert Pl NR1 ......163 A6
Albert Rd **17** NR30 ......169 D2
Albert Sq **13** NR30 ......169 D2
Albert St
Holt NR25 ......137 B6
King's Lynn PE30 ......146 D5
Albert Terr NR2 ......162 C4
Albion Dr NR7 ......159 A3
Albion Rd
Bungay NR35 ......124 B8
Great Yarmouth NR30 ......169 D4
Mundesley NR11 ......143 A7
Trunch NR28 ......22 E5
Albion St PE30 ......146 E5
Albion Way
Norwich NR1 ......178 C1
Wroxham/Hoveton NR12 ......164 D6
Alborough Loke **6** NR9 ......88 C7
ALBURGH IP20 ......122 E6
Alburgh Rd NR15 ......107 D4
Alburgh with Denton Fst Sch
IP20 ......123 A5
Alby Craft Ctr⋆ NR11 ......21 C3
ALBY HILL NR11 ......21 B5
ALDBOROUGH NR11 ......21 A5
Aldborough Prim Sch
NR11 ......21 B5
Aldborough Rd NR11 ......21 A5
ALDEBY NR34 ......110 F4
Aldeby Rd NR34 ......110 F6
Alder Cl
Great Yarmouth NR31 ......94 C7

Alder Cl continued
10 Mulbarton NR14 ......89 B3
North Walsham NR28 ......151 D7
Poringland NR14 ......90 D4
Alder Covert IP24 ......116 D2
ALDERFORD NR9 ......52 A5
Alderman Jackson Specl Sch
PO30 ......147 B8
Alderman Peel High Sch
NR23 ......136 D4
Alderman Swindell Fst Sch
NR30 ......169 D8
Alderson Pl NR1 ......178 B1
Alderson Rd NR30 ......169 C5
Alder Way NR8 ......155 E1
Aldis Cl NR19 ......154 D5
Aldis Rd NR13 ......166 B4
Aldiss Ave NR19 ......154 D3
Aldiss Cl PE37 ......153 C3
Aldiss Ct PE13 ......154 D6
Aldrich Way IP22 ......177 C5
Aldryche Rd NR1 ......163 B8
Aldwick Rd **2** NR18 ......173 C6
Alexander Cl
Caister-on-Sea NR30 ......168 C8
18 Long Stratton NR15 ......106 E3
Alexander Rise NR11 ......22 F8
Alexander Way **1** NR9 ......154 C6
Alexandra Ave NR30 ......169 D7
Alexandra Cl PE31 ......140 C4
Alexandra Rd
Cromer NR27 ......139 B4
Great Yarmouth NR30 ......169 D4
Hunstanton PE36 ......132 C3
Mundesley NR11 ......143 A8
Norwich NR2 ......162 B6
Sheringham NR26 ......138 D6
Wisbech PE13 ......152 C5
Alexandra Way
Attleborough NR17 ......174 C6
Downham Market PE38 ......172 B3
Alex Moorhouse Way
NR5 ......156 A3
Alford Gr NR7 ......159 A3
Alfred Nicholls Ct NR3 ......158 D2
Alfred Rd NR7 ......139 A7
Alfric Cl **11** NR14 ......91 F1
Algores Way PE13 ......152 B2
Alice Fisher Cres PE30 ......146 F7
Alison Cl NR13 ......73 F3
Allanadale Rd NR4 ......162 C1
Allenbrooks Way NR18 ......173 C3
Allenby's Chase **10** PE12 ......41 B8

100–Alp 179

Allen Cl PE34 ......61 B8
Allendale Rd NR30 ......168 E5
Allen Meale Way **5** NR12 ......39 B4
Allen's Ave NR7 ......159 A4
Allens Cl **1** NR13 ......73 D6
Allens La NR2 ......162 C4
Allen's La NR7 ......159 A4
Allen's Cl NR7 ......159 B3
Allerton Rd NR7 ......159 B3
Alley The PE32 ......44 C1
All Hallows' Hospl NR35 ......109 B2
Allison St NR10 ......36 A2
Allotment La NR25 ......9 B3
All Saints IP27 ......175 B8
All Saints Ave PE13 ......152 F7
All Saints CE VA Prim Sch
Ryburgh NR21 ......32 C6
Winfarthing IP22 ......120 B4
All Saints Cl
Briston NR24 ......142 D4
Runhall NR20 ......69 A5
2 Weybourne NR25 ......8 E5
Wicklewood NR18 ......87 B5
1 Wisbech PE14 ......59 A1
All Saints Dr NR26 ......148 C4
All Saints Gn NR1 ......178 B1
All Saints La NR25 ......9 A5
All Saints Rd **6** NR14 ......90 D5
All Saints Sch NR12 ......24 D3
ALL SAINTS SOUTH ELMHAM
IP19 ......124 B1
All Saints Way
Beachamwell PE37 ......81 F8
Mundesley NR11 ......143 C4
All Saints Wlk **7** NR20 ......68 F6
Allthorpe Rd **12** IP20 ......122 D2
Allwood Ave NR19 ......154 C5
Alma Ave PE34 ......144 D6
Alma Chase PE34 ......144 D6
Alma Rd
Great Yarmouth NR30 ......169 D2
Snettisham PE31 ......12 E5
Alma Terr NR3 ......162 D8
Almond Cl **21** NR29 ......57 D4
Almond Gr IP24 ......176 A1
Almond Rd NR31 ......170 B6
Alpha Rd NR31 ......170 C8
ALPINGTON NR14 ......90 E4
Alpington & Bergh Apton
Prim Sch NR14 ......90 F4

Alston Cl 3 NR14 .... 90 D5
Alston Rd NR6 .... 157 E2
Althaea Gn 2 NR31 .... 170 B5
Altongate 1 NR13 .... 72 D6
Amazona Zoo* NR27 .... 139 B5
Amazonia World of
  Reptiles* NR30.... 169 E2
Ambassador Way NR20.. 154 F4
Ambleside
  10 Hethersett NR9 .... 88 D8
  5 Sculthorpe Airfield NR21 15 C2
Ambleside Cl NR5 .... 161 C6
Ambrose Cl 1 NR5 .... 161 A7
Ambrose Rd NR30.... 168 E3
Amderley Dr 6 NR4 .... 89 C8
Amelia Opie Way 2
  IP24 .... 176 D7
Ames Ct NR10 .... 35 B2
Amethyst Cl NR31 .... 170 D2
Amherst Cl 7 PE27 .... 153 C3
Amhirst Cl 2 NR6 .... 158 F1
Amhurst Gdns NR31 .... 94 A5
Ampthill St 3 NR2 .... 162 C5
Amsterdam NR6 .... 158 B6
Amsterdam Way PE13 .. 154 C2
Amys Cl IP25 .... 84 C4
Anchorage View PE31 ... 3 B6
Anchor Cl
  Norwich NR3 .... 178 C4
  Sheringham NR26 .... 138 E6
ANCHOR CORNER NR17.. 86 A1
Anchor Ct NR31 .... 169 C2
Anchor Dro PE38 .... 112 B8
Anchor Quay NR2 .... 178 A3
Anchor St
  North Walsham NR28 .. 151 F5
  Sutton Bridge PE34 .... 41 F8
Anchor St
  Coltishall NR12 .... 54 D6
  8 Norwich NR3 .... 162 F8
  Norwich NR3 .... 178 C4
  Tunstead NR12 .... 38 B2
ANCHOR STREET NR12 ... 38 B3
Anchor Way 1 NR31 .... 111 F1
Anderson Cl
  King's Lynn PE30 .... 146 E7
  Wisbech PE13 .... 152 A7
Andrew Goodall Cl NR19 154 C1
Andrew's Furlong NR16.. 119 E7
Andrews Pl PE36.... 132 D2
Angela Cl 2 NR10 .... 53 B3
Angela Cres 3 NR10 ... 53 B3
Angela Rd NR10 .... 53 B3
Angel Dr NR28 .... 151 B4
Angel Rd NR3 .... 158 D1
Angel Rd Fst Sch NR3 .. 158 D1
Angel Rd Mid Sch NR3 .. 158 D1
Angerstein Cl IP27 .... 114 E8
Angle Rd PE14 .... 78 A7
Anglian Way 3 NR31 .... 171 D5
Anglia Sq NR3 .... 178 A4
Anglia Way PE13 .... 152 B2
Anglo-Saxon Cath & Bishops
  Pal (remains of)* NR20. 49 F8
ANMER PE31 .... 28 E8
Anmer Cl NR3 .... 158 F3
Anmer Rd PE31 .... 28 C5
Anna Gurney Cl IP24.... 176 D6
Anna Sewell Cl 4 IP24.. 176 D7
Anne Bartholomew Rd
  IP24 .... 176 D7
Anne Boleyn Cl 4 IP24.. 176 D6
Anne Cl NR7 .... 163 F8
Anne Rd PE12 .... 41 B8
Annes Cl PE30 .... 148 D1
Annes Dr PE36 .... 132 D1
Anne Stannard Way NR12 23 F4
ANNIS HILL NR35 .... 124 C8
Annis Hill NR35 .... 124 C8
Anson Cl
  5 Hethersett NR9 .... 88 E8
  Mundesley NR11 .... 143 A7
Anson Rd
  Great Yarmouth NR31 .. 169 C2
  Norwich NR6 .... 158 B6
Anson's La NR15 .... 122 A8
Ant Broads & Marshes
  National Nature Reserve*
  NR12 .... 55 F8
Anthony Curton Prim Sch
  PE14 .... 41 E4
Anthony Dr NR3 .... 158 F2
Anthony Nolan Rd PE30 . 147 D3
ANTINGHAM NR28 .... 22 B4
Antingham Dr NR28 .... 151 D6
Antingham Hill NR28 .... 22 B3
Antingham Rd NR7 .... 159 D1
Antingham & Southrepps
  Com Prim Sch NR11 ... 22 B5
Apeldoorn Wlk PE13 .... 152 D7
Apollo Wlk NR30 .... 169 C6
Appleacres NR6 .... 158 D5
Appledore Cl PE30 .... 148 C2
Appledore La 4 NR21... 15 C2
Applegarth 1 NR18 .... 173 B4
Applegarth Ct 2 NR13 .. 173 B4
Appleton Dr NR29 .... 167 A3
Appleton Dro PE31.... 27 F5
Appletree Cl PE31 .... 133 C6
Appletree La IP22.... 177 C5
Appleyard Cres NR3.... 158 A3
Apple Yd NR35 .... 137 B6
Apsley Ct NR5 .... 161 F6
Apsley Rd NR30 .... 169 E3
Arbor Ct NR27 .... 139 B6

Arbor Rd NR27 .... 139 B6
Arcade St NR1 .... 178 B2
Archbishop Sancroft High
  Sch IP20 .... 122 D2
Archdale Cl PE33 .... 43 F3
Archdale St 3 PE30. .. 146 E5
Archer Cl NR6 .... 159 A5
Archer La PE32 .... 46 F2
Archers' Ave 3 IP26 .... 98 D1
Archer's Rd 2 NR30 .. 169 C5
Archibald Rd NR12.... 24 A7
Arden Cl NR27 .... 11 A3
Arden Gr NR10 .... 157 E7
Arden Gr Fst Sch NR10.. 157 E7
Arderon Ct 2 NR2 .... 162 B7
Ardleigh Cl 3 PE13 .... 152 E5
Ardney Rise NR3 .... 158 D3
Argyle St
  King's Lynn PE30 .... 146 E3
  Norwich NR1 .... 178 C1
Argyll Cres NR5 .... 156 E8
Arles Ave PE13.... 152 E3
Arlington Cl NR17 .... 174 E5
Arlington Gdns NR17... 174 E5
Arlington La NR2 .... 162 C4
Arlington Pk Rd PE32 ... 44 C3
Arlington Way IP24 .... 176 E3
Armada Cl NR12 .... 152 D8
Armes Cres NR2 .... 162 A8
Armes St NR2 .... 162 B7
ARMINGHALL NR14 .... 90 B7
Arminghall Cl NR3 .... 158 C3
Arminghall La NR14.... 89 F8
Armitage Cl NR4 .... 89 B8
Arms Pk Rd NR6 .... 158 B6
Armstrong Dr NR19 .... 154 E7
Armstrong Rd NR17 .... 159 E2
Army Rd NR21 .... 15 C2
Arnfield La NR5 .... 161 B8
Arnold Ave NR30 .... 168 D8
Arnold Miller Rd NR1 .. 162 F2
Arnott Ave NR31 .... 170 D1
Arnott Rd NR25 .... 137 D5
Arnside Cl 22 NR9.... 88 D8
Arthur Ave NR30 .... 168 E8
Arthur Rd NR21 .... 141 A6
Arthurton Rd NR10.... 54 A1
Artillery Sq 2 NR30.... 169 D4
Artillery St 12 PE13 .... 152 C4
Arundel Cl NR20 .... 49 C4
Arundel Ct NR2 .... 178 A1
Arundel Dr PE30 .... 148 C1
Arundel Rd
  Great Yarmouth NR30 .. 169 D7
  Wymondham NR18 .... 173 C6
Ascot Gdns NR19.... 154 D3
Ashbey Rd PE30.... 147 E8
Ashburton Rd IP26.... 100 C5
Ashby Rd
  Ashby St Mary NR14 .... 91 C5
  Repps with Bastwick NR29. 57 A3
  Thurton NR14 .... 91 C4
ASHBY ST MARY NR14... 91 C5
Ashby St NR1 .... 178 B1
Ash Cl
  Brandon IP27 .... 175 E3
  Downham Market PE38.. 172 C6
  10 Hethersett NR9 .... 88 D8
  Swaffham PE37 .... 153 B5
  Thetford IP24 .... 176 A1
  Wymondham NR18 .... 173 D6
Ashdale Pk
  Old Hunstanton PE36.. 132 F8
  Wisbech PE13 .... 152 A5
Ashdown NR1 .... 155 E1
Ashdown Ct NR27 .... 139 C6
Ash Dr IP23 .... 130 C1
Ashfield Ct PE34 .... 144 D6
Ashfield Hill PE30 .... 147 C4
Ashfield Rd NR28 .... 151 E6
Ashford Cl NR34 .... 110 C2
Ash Gn 11 NR31 .... 170 B6
Ash Gr
  King's Lynn PE30 .... 148 D2
  Norwich NR3 .... 158 E2
  Sheringham NR26 .... 138 E5
  4 West Winch PE33 .... 43 E2
Ashgrove 5 NR8 .... 155 E2
ASHILL IP25 .... 84 A7
Ashill VC Prim Sch IP25.. 84 A7
Ash La NR16 .... 105 C2
Ashleigh Gdns NR18.... 173 E6
Ashleigh Inf Sch NR18 .. 173 D6
Ashley Rd NR20 .... 49 D4
Ashley Wlk PE13 .... 154 D4
ASHMANHAUGH NR12.... 55 B8
Ash Rd PE33 .... 63 B4
Ash Tree Cl NR17 .... 174 C5
Ashtree Rd
  Norwich NR5 .... 157 B2
  12 Watton IP25 .... 84 E3
Ash Tree Rd NR13 .... 74 D1
Ashwell Ct NR5 .... 160 F7
ASHWELLTHORPE NR16... 105 F8
Ashwellthorpe Rd NR16.. 88 D1
ASHWICKEN PE32 .... 45 A6
Ashwicken CE Fst Sch
  PE32 .... 44 F6
Ashwicken Rd PE32 .... 45 A8
Ashwood Cl NR30 .... 168 D6
Ash Yd NR24 .... 18 D8
Aslack Way PE36 .... 2 A6
ASLACTON NR15.... 106 A2
Aslacton Prim Sch NR15 106 A1
Aslacton Rd NR16.... 106 B3
Aslake Cl NR47 .... 159 C5
Aspen Cl IP24 .... 176 B2
Aspen Way NR4 .... 89 B8

Aspland Rd NR1 .... 178 C3
Assembly House The
  NR2 .... 178 A2
Association Way 2 NR7.. 72 D4
Astell Rd NR1.... 89 F8
Astley Cooper Pl NR15 .. 90 E1
Astley Cres PE36 .... 132 D6
Astley Prim Sch NR24 .. 142 C4
Astley Rd
  Great & Little Plumstead
  NR13 .... 73 B6
  Little Plumstead NR13 .. 165 A8
  Norwich NR5 .... 160 F8
Astor Ct IP27 .... 175 D4
Atbara Terr PE30.... 146 E2
Atcherley Sq PE31 .... 30 B3
Atkinson Cl NR5 .... 160 E8
Atling Cl NR17 .... 174 F6
Atling Way 5 NR17 .... 174 F6
Atmere Cl 2 NR4 .... 161 F1
Attelsey Way NR5.... 160 E8
Atthill Rd NR2 .... 162 A7
ATTLEBOROUGH NR17.... 174 D3
Attleborough High Sch
  NR17.... 174 D6
Attleborough Inf Sch
  NR17.... 174 D6
Attleborough Jun Sch
  NR17.... 174 E6
Attleborough Rd
  Attleborough NR17.... 174 A7
  Caston NR17 .... 102 F8
  Deopham NR18 .... 86 E1
  Great Ellingham NR17 .. 103 F8
  Little Ellingham NR17 .. 86 A2
  Morley NR18 .... 87 A1
  Attleborough Sta NR17.. 174 E5
ATTLEBRIDGE NR9 .... 52 B3
Attlee Way 4 NR19 .... 154 C6
Audax Rd NR6 .... 158 C6
Audley Cl IP24.... 176 C7
Audley End IP21 .... 120 F1
Audley St NR30 .... 169 D5
Augusta St NR26 .... 138 D7
Augustus Hare Dr 1
  NR4 .... 161 C5
Aurania Ave NR1 .... 162 D3
Auster Cl NR6 .... 158 C4
Austin Fields PE30 .... 146 E5
Austin Fields Ind Est
  PE30 .... 146 E5
Austin Rd NR31 .... 169 B3
Austin St
  Hunstanton PE36.... 132 C5
  King's Lynn PE30 .... 146 D5
Autumn Cl IP24.... 176 E4
Autumn Dr NR5 .... 161 B8
Avebury Rd NR4 .... 162 B1
Aveling Way 6 NR33.... 111 F1
Avenue Cl PE38 .... 79 C1
Avenue Fst & Mid Schs
  NR2 .... 162 B5
Avenue Rd
  Great Yarmouth NR31 .. 170 D6
  High Kelling NR25 .... 8 E2
  Hunstanton PE36.... 132 C4
  King's Lynn PE30 .... 146 F4
  North Walsham NR28 .. 151 C4
  Norwich NR2 .... 162 B5
  Wymondham NR18 .... 173 C3
Avenue S NR26 .... 138 E7
Avenue The
  Brome & Oakley IP23 .. 130 D3
  Brookville IP26 .... 99 A7
  Brumstead NR12 .... 24 A1
  Dersingham PE35 .... 140 E1
  Hemsby NR29 .... 167 A7
  Holkham NR23 .... 5 A4
  Horning NR12 .... 55 E4
  4 Necton PE37.... 65 F3
  New Holkham NR23.... 5 A2
  Northrepps NR27 .... 139 D3
  Sheringham NR26 .... 138 E7
  Snettisham PE31 .... 12 D4
  Wiggenhall St Germans
  PE34 .... 61 A8
  Wroxham/Hoveton NR12 164 B4
  Wymondham NR18 .... 87 D7
Avian Way NR7 .... 159 C2
Avocet House Sch NR14 . 92 C1
Avondale Cl NR31.... 74 A2
Avondale Rd NR31 .... 170 D3
Avonmouth Rd 2 NR3 .. 158 C1
Avon Rd PE30 .... 148 C2
Aylesbury Cl NR31 .... 158 D2
Aylmer Dr PE34 .... 60 C8
AYLMERTON NR11.... 10 A2
AYLSHAM NR11.... 150 B5
Aylsham Cres NR3 .... 158 C3
Aylsham High Sch NR11 150 D8
Aylsham Ind Est NR11 .. 150 D8
Aylsham Rd
  Burgh & Tuttington NR11.. 36 C6
  Cawston NR10.... 35 B2
  Felmingham NR28 .... 37 A8
  North Walsham NR28 .. 22 C1
  Norwich NR3 .... 158 C1
  Oulton NR11 .... 35 E6
  Swanton Abbott NR10 .. 37 C4
Aylsham Rd Bsns Pk
  NR6 .... 158 C2
Aylsham Sta NR11 .... 150 D5
Ayre Way PE30.... 147 D8

Ayton Rd NR18.... 173 D3
Ayton Rd Ind Est NR18 .. 173 D3

B

BABINGLEY PE31 .... 27 D5
Babingley Cl 5 PE33.... 61 D6
Bachelor's La NR28 .... 23 E2
Back Chapel La NR31.... 170 D6
Back Dro
  Upwell PE14 .... 77 D4
  Welney PE14 .... 95 D4
Back Hills IP22 .... 128 E3
Back La
  Barford NR9.... 69 F2
  Beeston with Bittering PE32 48 C2
  Bircham PE31 .... 14 B3
  Blakeney NR25 .... 7 C7
  Burgh Castle NR31 .... 94 A8
  Burnham Market PE31... 135 D2
  Burnham Thorpe PE31... 4 D4
  Buxton with Lammas NR10 . 53 E8
  Castle Acre PE32 .... 46 F2
  Catfield NR29 .... 56 C8
  Cawston NR10.... 35 B2
  Dereham NR20 .... 68 A8
  Diss IP22 .... 120 D3
  East Rudham PE31.... 30 B7
  East Ruston NR12 .... 24 A3
  Elsing NR20 .... 50 E3
  Happisburgh NR12.... 23 F2
  Hempstead NR25.... 19 E7
  Hethersett NR9 .... 88 E8
  Kenninghall NR16 .... 119 A5
  Litcham PE32 .... 48 A4
  Lound NR32 .... 94 C2
  Lyng NR9 .... 51 A4
  Marthan NR29 .... 57 D5
  Mattishall NR20 .... 68 E6
  Mileham PE32 .... 48 C6
  North Elmham NR20 .... 49 E7
  Outwell PE14 .... 77 E7
  Potter Heigham NR29 .. 56 E7
  Quidenham NR16 .... 119 A8
  Rackheath NR13 .... 54 D1
  Ringland NR8.... 52 D2
  Rollesby NR29 .... 57 D3
  Roughton NR11 .... 21 D8
  Roydon PE32 .... 28 A1
  Scole IP21 .... 121 A1
  Scoulton NR9 .... 85 E3
  South Creake NR21 .... 15 E6
  Stanfield NR20.... 48 F8
  St Mary, South Elmham
  otherwise Homersfield
  IP20 .... 123 B4
  Upton with Fishley NR13 . 166 C8
  Walsingham NR22 .... 16 F7
  Wereham PE33 .... 80 E4
  West Beckham NR25 .... 9 B3
  West Caister NR30 .... 168 A4
  West Winch PE33 .... 43 E2
  Wymondham NR18 .... 173 C4
Back Mkt La NR29 .... 167 B7
Back Mundesley Rd NR11.. 22 F8
Back of the Inns NR1.... 178 B2
Back Path 11 NR29 .... 58 B6
Back Pier Plain NR31.... 170 D4
Back Rd
  Brockdish IP21 .... 131 B8
  East Ruston NR12 .... 38 F6
  Elm PE14 .... 77 A8
  Pentney PE32 .... 63 C8
  Somerton NR29 .... 57 F6
  Wisbech PE14 .... 77 A7
  Wood Dalling NR11 .... 34 D6
  Yelverton NR14 .... 90 F5
Back St
  Binham NR21.... 6 E2
  Fakenham NR21.... 141 B3
  Garboldisham IP22 .... 128 A8
  Gayton PE32 .... 45 C5
  Harpley PE31.... 29 D5
  Horsham St Faith NR10 .. 53 D1
  Lakenheath IP27 .... 113 E1
  Litcham PE32 .... 48 A4
  Mundesley NR11 .... 143 C5
  Reepham NR10 .... 149 B4
  South Creake NR21 .... 15 D6
  Tittleshall PE32 .... 48 B7
  Trunch NR28 .... 22 E5
  West Beckham NR25 .... 9 A3
Backwood La
  Howe NR15.... 90 C2
  Shotesham NR15.... 107 F8
Bacon Rd NR4 .... 161 F5
BACONSTHORPE NR25 .... 20 A8
Baconsthorpe Castle*
  NR25.... 9 A1
BACTON NR12.... 23 E5
Bacton Cl PE30 .... 148 D3
BACTON GREEN NR12 .... 23 D5
Bacton-on-Sea Fst Sch
  NR12.... 23 E4
Bacton Rd
  Bacton NR12 .... 23 E4
  North Walsham NR28 .. 151 D6
  Norwich NR3 .... 158 B2
  Paston NR28 .... 143 E2
  Witton NR28 .... 23 C6
Bader Cl PE30.... 147 D4
Badger Cl NR14 .... 89 A2
Badgers Brook Rd NR8.. 155 F2
Bagge Rd PE30 .... 147 A5
BAGTHORPE PE31 .... 14 D3
Bagthorpe Rd PE31 .... 30 A7

Bailey Cl
  4 Hethersett NR9 .... 88 D7
  6 Marthan NR29 .... 57 D5
Bailey La PE34 .... 145 E7
Bailey Rd NR27 .... 139 B5
Bailey St PE32 .... 46 F2
Bailiwick The 3 NR16... 118 C5
Baillie Cl 3 NR31 .... 170 B1
Bainard Rise NR15 .... 107 C6
Bainards Cl NR18 .... 173 B6
Baines Rd 4 NR30 .... 146 D1
Baines Way 2 NR5 .... 160 E8
Baird Way IP24 .... 176 C7
Baker Cl
  King's Lynn PE30 .... 146 D1
  North Walsham NR28 .. 151 D3
Baker La 3 PE30 .... 146 D4
Bakers La NR35 .... 109 A2
Bakers Rd NR3 .... 162 D8
Baker's Rd NR13 .... 75 A1
Baker St
  Great Yarmouth NR31 .. 170 D5
  14 Stalham NR12.... 39 B4
Bakery Rd NR23 .... 136 C6
Bakery Cl NR24 .... 142 E3
Bakery La NR9 .... 51 A5
Balderston Cl NR3 .... 178 B4
Baldock Cl 1 NR16 .... 105 F5
Baldock Dr PE30 .... 147 B8
Baldric Rd NR8 .... 155 D1
Baldwin Cl 3 PE13.... 152 D5
Baldwin Rd PE30.... 147 C6
Baldwins Cl NR24 .... 142 D4
Baldwins Dro 4 PE14... 77 F6
BALE NR21 .... 18 B7
Bale Rd
  Brinton NR24 .... 18 C7
  Hindringham NR21 .... 17 A5
Balfour Rd 4 NR27 .... 10 A5
Balfour St 3 NR3 .... 162 F8
Baliol Rd NR11.... 170 C5
Ball's La NR21 .... 17 D5
Ballygate NR34 .... 110 C1
Balmoral Ave NR30.... 169 C7
Balmoral Cl
  Attleborough NR17.... 174 F6
  Dersingham PE31.... 140 D3
Balmoral Cres PE31.... 133 C5
Balmoral Rd PE30.... 147 C7
Balmoral W PE31.... 140 D3
Bambers La PE14 .... 59 C2
Bancroft Cl 7 NR14.... 89 F4
BANHAM NR16 .... 119 D7
Banham Barn Craft*
  NR16.... 119 C6
Banham Dr NR20.... 50 B2
Banham Prim Sch NR16 119 D6
Banham Rd NR16 .... 119 B5
Banham's La NR35 .... 108 B2
Banister Way NR18.... 173 A5
Bank Dr PE13 .... 152 A7
Bank Loke 6 NR28.... 151 C5
Bank Plain NR3 .... 178 B3
Bank Rd PE31.... 140 C4
Bankside PE31.... 133 B6
Bank Side PE34 .... 146 C5
Bank St
  Norwich NR2 .... 178 B3
  Pulham Market IP21.... 121 E5
BANNINGHAM NR11.... 36 D8
Banningham Ct NR28.... 151 A4
Banningham Rd NR11... 150 D8
Bannister Cl NR17.... 174 C6
Bannister's Row PE13 .. 152 B7
Banters La PE14 .... 124 F6
Banting Cl NR31.... 170 C1
Banyard Ct PE13 .... 154 E5
Banyard Pl 6 NR19 .... 154 D5
Banyards Pl PE33 .... 61 D4
Baptist Rd PE14 .... 77 D4
Barberry Cl 5 NR8.... 155 B2
Barber's La
  Bedingham NR35.... 108 B2
  Fakenham NR21.... 141 E4
Barbers Yd 1 NR17.... 104 D2
Barchams Yd 10 NR26.. 138 D7
Barclay Rd NR7 .... 159 D1
Barclay Bd NR7.... 159 C1
Bard Hill NR25 .... 8 B6
Bardolph Pl PE34 .... 61 D1
Bardolphs Ct 1 NR8 .... 155 B2
Bardolph's Way PE33... 62 C6
Bar Dro PE14 .... 77 B8
Bardwell Rd
  Barningham IP31.... 127 C3
  Fakenham Magna IP24.. 126 D3
  Stanton IP31 .... 127 B1
Bardyke Bank PE14 .... 77 F4
BARFORD NR9 .... 69 F2
Barford Cty Prim Sch NR9 69 F2
Barford Rd
  Marlingford NR9 .... 69 E3
  Sheringham NR26 .... 138 D7
  Topcroft NR35 .... 107 E2
Bargate Cl NR3 .... 178 B4
Barham Ct NR31 .... 170 D5
Barham's La NR16 .... 105 C4
Barker's Dro PE33 .... 81 A3
Barkers Herne NR27 .... 139 A6
Barker's La
  Norwich NR7 .... 159 B5
  Old Buckenham NR17 .. 104 B2
Barker Sn NR2 .... 162 C8
Barker Way 3 NR13.... 72 C6
Barkis Rd NR30 .... 169 D1
Barleycroft NR29.... 167 B7
Barleyfield Rd 6 NR10.. 53 A3

Barley Way
Attleborough NR17 . . . . . . 174 B3
Thetford IP24 . . . . 176 D6
BARMER PE31. . . . . 14 F4
Barnaby CI 5 NR19 . . . . . 154 C3
Barnard Ave NR30 . . . . . 169 D7
Barnard CI
Great Yarmouth NR31 . . . 170 C1
5 Stoke Holy Cross NR14 . 89 F4
Barnard Cres NR30. . . . . 169 C7
Barnard Rd NR5 . . . . 160 E8
Barnards La 3 . . . . 61 D6
Barnards Rd NR28 . . . . . . 38 A5
Barnby Rd NR10 . . . . 37 B2
Barn CI
2 Hopton on Sea NR31 . . 171 E5
3 Lingwood NR13 . . . . . 74 A3
Barnes St . . . .
Brandon IP27 . . . . 175 A2
Norwich NR7 . . . . 159 D2
Barnesdale Rd 5 NR4 . . . 89 E8
Barnes' Rd IP21 . . . . 121 E5
BARNEY NR21 . . . . 17 F3
Barney Rd NR21 . . . . 17 F2
Barnfield CI NR12 . . . . . . 39 E2
BARNHAM IP24. . . . . 125 F6
BARNHAM BROOM NR9 . . 69 C2
Barnham Broom Prim Sch
NR9. . . . .
Barnham Broom Rd
East Tuddenham NR20 . . . 69 D5
Wymondham NR18 . . . . 173 A7
Barnham CE Prim Sch
IP24 . . . .
Barnham Rd IP24 . . . . . . 126 B6
Barn Hill NR13 . . . . 73 E2
BARNINGHAM IP31 . . . . . 127 C3
Barningham CE VC Prim Sch
IP31 . . . . 127 C3
BARNINGHAM GREEN
NR11. . . . . 20 A4
Barningham Rd NR11 . . . 20 C5
Barningham Rd
Gresham NR11 . . . . 20 D8
Stanton IP31 . . . . 127 C1
Barn La
Gressenhall NR19 . . . . . . 49 B2
Mautby NR29 . . . . 75 E6
Marsham NR14 . . . . 163 B2
Barn Rd
Docking PE31 . . . . 134 F4
Norwich NR2 . . . . 178 A4
Barns The NR16 . . . . 105 C4
Barn Terr NR13 . . . . 165 C4
Barnwell Rd PE30 . . . . . 147 B6
Barondole La
Alburgh IP20 . . . . 122 E8
Topcroft NR35 . . . . 107 E2
Baron's CI NR21 . . . . 141 C4
Baron's Hall La NR21 . . . 141 D4
Barrack Rd
Great Yarmouth NR30 . . 169 D1
Norwich NR1 . . . . 163 B7
Barrack St NR3 . . . . 178 C4
Barr Dr IP27 . . . . 113 E2
Barrett CI NR32 . . . . 147 E5
Barrett-Lennard Rd NR10 53 A4
Barrett Rd
Holt NR25 . . . . 137 D7
Norwich NR1 . . . . 162 E1
Barri CI NR14 . . . . 90 C3
Barroway Dro PE38 . . . . 78 E6
Barrow CI NR3 . . . . 157 F1
Barrow's Cnr IP24 . . . . . 125 A4
Barrows Hole La PE32. . . 65 E7
Barsham Dr PE30 . . . . . . 148 E1
Barsham Rd NR21 . . . . . . 17 A5
Bartle Ct NR10 . . . . 149 C5
BARTON BENDISH PE33 . . 81 A8
Barton CI
North Walsham NR28 . . . 151 A4
Swaffham PE37 . . . . . . 153 C2
Barton Ct PE30 . . . . 147 D5
Barton Rd
Ashmanhaugh NR12 . . . . 38 D1
Coltishall NR10 . . . . 37 B2
Wisbech PE13 . . . . 152 A4
BARTON TURF NR12. . . . . 38 F1
Barton Way
6 Norwich NR1 . . . . . . 163 B5
Ormesby St Margaret
NR29. . . . . 167 B3
Barwick Rd PE31. . . . . . . 14 E6
Bases La NR23 . . . . 136 C6
Basey Rd NR13. . . . . 72 E8
Basham St IP22 . . . . 177 B4
Basil Dr PE38 . . . . 172 E6
Basil Rd PE33 . . . . 80 A3
Bassingham Rd NR3. . . . . 158 B2
BASTWICK NR29. . . . . 57 A4
Batchcroft CI 6 PE38 . . . 172 C6
Batchelor Dr NR21 . . . . . 15 C2
Bately Ave NR13 . . . . 170 D1
Bateman CI 8 NR5. . . . . . 160 F7
Bates Gn NR5. . . . . 161 C8
Bates La IP22 . . . . 119 D2
Bate's Dro CB6 . . . . 95 D1
Bath Ave NR26 . . . . 154 F5
Bath Hill 7 NR30 . . . . . . 169 D3
Bath Hills Rd NR35 . . . . . 123 E8
Bath Hill Terr NR30 . . . . 169 D3
Bath Rd
West Dereham PE33 . . . . 80 D5
Wisbech PE13 . . . . 152 C7

Bathurst Rd 2 NR2 . . . . 162 B5
Batterby Gn . . . .
Fakenham NR21. . . . . . . 141 A3
Hempton NR21. . . . . 31 C8
Battery Rd NR30 . . . . 170 D8
BATTLESEA GREEN IP21. . 131 E2
Battlesea Hill IP21. . . . . 131 E2
BAWBURGH NR9. . . . . 160 B6
Bawburgh CI NR5. . . . . . . 156 D1
Bawburgh La NR5. . . . . . 156 D1
Bawburgh Prim Sch NR9 160 B6
Bawburgh Rd NR9 . . . . . . 70 B5
BAWDESWELL NR20. . . . . . 50 E8
Bawdeswell Prim Sch
NR20. . . . . 50 E7
Bawdeswell Rd NR20. . . . 50 C7
BAWSEY PE32. . . . . 44 D6
Bawsey Cntry Pk* PE32 . . 44 D6
Baxter CI . . . .
2 Hingham NR9 . . . . . . 86 C5
Long Stratton NR15. . . . . 106 E2
3 Wisbech PE13. . . . . . 152 E6
Baxter Ct NR3 . . . . 158 B3
Baxter Rd NR9. . . . . 86 C5
Baxter Row NR19 . . . . . . 154 D4
Baxter's La NR15. . . . . . . 107 F8
Bayes La NR16 . . . . 106 C6
Bayfield NR17 . . . . 174 E6
Bayfield Ave 3 NR19 . . . 154 C3
Bayfield CI . . . .
1 Ixworth NR9. . . . . . . 69 F2
King's Lynn PE30 . . . . . . 147 D4
Baynard's La IP22. . . . . . 129 D7
Bayse's La NR24 . . . . . . 18 C5
Bayspole Rd 5 NR15. . . . 106 E3
BEACHAMWELL PE37. . . . . 81 F8
Beachamwell Rd PE13. . . 153 A3
Beach CI . . . .
Hemsby NR29 . . . . 167 E3
Mundesley NR11 . . . . . 143 C6
Overstrand NR27. . . . . . . 11 A4
Beach Dr NR29 . . . . 167 E4
Beach La NR26 . . . . 8 E6
Beach Rd . . . .
Bacton NR12 . . . . 23 E5
Caister-on-Sea NR30. . . . 168 E5
Cley next the Sea NR25. . . 7 B8
Cromer NR27. . . . . 139 B7
Eccles on Sea NR12. . . . . 24 E4
3 Great Yarmouth NR31 170 D4
Hapisburgh NR12 . . . . . 24 C5
Hemsby NR29 . . . . 167 C7
Holme next the Sea PE36 . . 1 F6
Hopton on Sea NR31 . . . 171 E4
Lessingham NR12 . . . . . . 24 E3
Mundesley NR11 . . . . . 143 C6
Runton NR27 . . . . 10 C5
Salthouse NR25 . . . . 8 B6
Sea Palling NR12 . . . . . . 40 A6
Sheringham NR26 . . . . . 138 E7
Snettisham PE31 . . . . . . 12 A4
Wells-next-the-Sea NR23 . 136 C7
Winterton-on-Sea NR29. . . 58 B6
Beach Terr Rd PE36 . . . . 132 C4
Beacon Hill PE31. . . . . . 135 C2
Beacon Hill La PE34 . . . 144 A6
Beacon Hill Rd PE31 . . . 135 C1
Beacon Rd NR11 . . . . 11 F1
Beaconsfield Rd . . . .
Great Yarmouth NR30 . . 169 D6
Norwich NR3 . . . . 162 E8
Bears CI 7 NR9. . . . . 86 C4
Bears La NR9. . . . . 86 C4
Bear's La PE37. . . . . 153 B5
Bears Rd NR28. . . . . 143 D2
Beatrice Ave NR19 . . . . . 154 D4
Beatrice CI 6 NR28 . . . . 151 C6
Beatrice Rd . . . .
Norwich NR1 . . . . 163 A6
Wisbech PE13 . . . . 152 D7
Beatty CI . . . .
Great Yarmouth NR30 . . 169 D8
Thetford IP24 . . . . 176 E5
Beatty Rd . . . .
Great Yarmouth NR30 . . 169 D8
Norwich NR4 . . . . 162 B1
Beauchamp CI . . . .
1 Caister-on-Sea NR30. 168 D7
Chedgrave NR14 . . . . . . 91 F2
Beauchamp Rd 2 NR4 . . 92 A2
Beaufort CI NR6 . . . . . . 158 D6
Beaufort Way . . . .
Norwich NR31. . . . . 170 B1
Hopton on Sea NR31 . . . 171 B8
Beaumont PI 1 NR2 . . . . 162 C4
Beaumont Rd NR5 . . . . . 157 B1
Beaumont Way NR20 . . . 147 C5
Beaupre Ave PE14 . . . . . . 77 F7
Beavans CI 8 NR28 . . . . 151 B6
Beavens Ct 4 NR28 . . . . 169 B4
Beavor La PE37. . . . . 175 C4
BECCLES NR34. . . . . 110 D2
Becclesgate NR19. . . . . . 154 D6
Beccles Mus* NR34. . . . . 110 C1
Beccles Rds . . . .
Aldeby NR34. . . . . 110 F4
Aldeby, Wheatacre, Burgh St
Peter NR34. . . . . 111 B4
Belton with Browston NR31 94 A5
Bungay NR35. . . . . 124 B8
Carlton Colville NR33. . . . 111 F1
Fritton & St Olaves NR31 . 93 E3
Great Yarmouth NR31 . . . 170 A5
Haddiscoe NR14 . . . . . . 110 E7
Hales NR14 . . . . 109 F4
Loddon NR14. . . . . 92 A1
Ravenningham NR14 . . . . 110 A7
Thurlton NR14 . . . . 92 F1

Beccles Sta NR34 . . . . . . 110 D1
Beck Ave NR29. . . . . 167 A4
Beck CI 5 NR25 . . . . 8 F5
Becketswell Rd NR18. . . . 173 B3
Beckett CI 6 PE30 . . . . . 148 C4
Becketts Ct NR18 . . . . . . 173 B6
BECKHITHE NR9. . . . . . . 160 A1
Beck La . . . .
Burgh & Tuttington NR11 . . 36 E6
Horsham St Faith & Newton St
Faith NR10 . . . . 53 D2
Beckmeadow Way NR11. . 143 C5
Becks Fur 2 NR8 . . . . . . 155 E2
Becks Gn La NR34. . . . . . 124 F4
Beckside NR10. . . . . 53 A2
Beck St IP22. . . . . 127 E3
Beck The . . . .
Feltwell IP26 . . . . 98 E1
Kenninghall NR16 . . . . . 119 A5
Beck View 3 IP20 . . . . . . 122 D2
Beck Way NR14 . . . . 91 F1
Bedding La NR3. . . . . 178 A4
Bede CI PE30 . . . . 148 C4
Bedford Dr PE30. . . . . . . 148 B1
Bedford Mews NR26 . . . 138 D6
Bedford Row PE14 . . . . . . 41 A4
Bedford St . . . .
Norwich NR2 . . . . 178 B3
Wisbech PE13 . . . . 152 C7
Bedingfield Rd 6 NR20 . . 50 B3
BEDINGHAM GREEN
NR35 . . . . 108 B3
Bedingham Rd PE33. . . . . 81 A8
Beech Ave . . . .
Attleborough NR17 . . . . . 174 C4
King's Lynn PE30 . . . . . . 148 D2
7 Marham PE33 . . . . . . 63 B4
Sheringham NR26 . . . . . 138 D5
Taverham NR8 . . . . 155 B1
Beechbank NR21. . . . . . . 162 B4
Beechbank Dr 8 NR13 . . . 72 D6
Beech CI . . . .
1 Gresham NR11. . . . . . 9 E1
High Kelling NR25 . . . . . . 8 E2
6 Loddon NR14 . . . . . . 92 A1
Scole IP21 . . . . 130 C5
Swaffham PE37 . . . . . . 153 C4
Thetford IP24 . . . . 176 D3
Beech Cres 3 PE33. . . . . 43 E2
Beechcroft NR1 . . . . 156 F1
Beech Ct . . . .
24 Long Stratton NR15. . 106 E2
Swaffham PE37 . . . . . . 153 D5
Beech Dr . . . .
East Dereham NR19 . . . . 154 E1
North Walsham NR28 . . . 151 B6
Norwich NR6 . . . . 157 C4
Norwich NR7 . . . . 163 A8
Norwich NR6 . . . . 158 C4
Strumpshaw NR13 . . . . . 73 F3
Beech Drift PE31 . . . . . . 140 D3
Beecheno Rd NR5 . . . . . 161 C8
Beeches CI NR6. . . . . 158 E4
Beeches The 8 NR20 . . . 66 E6
Beechey CI PE38 . . . . . . 172 C2
Beechfields IP27 . . . . . . 175 F4
Beeching CI 1 NR1 . . . . 162 E1
Beeching Rd NR1 . . . . . . 162 E2
Beech La NR29. . . . . 75 C8
Beechlands NR8. . . . . . . 155 B1
Beechlands Pk NR11 . . . 22 B7
Beech Rd . . . .
Beetley NR20. . . . . 49 D4
Downham Market PE38. . . 172 B6
King's Lynn PE30 . . . . . . 148 D4
Wroxham/Hoveton NR12 . 164 D3
Beech Rise 23 NR14 . . . . 94 C7
Beech Way . . . .
Brundall NR13 . . . . 165 C3
Dickleburgh IP21 . . . . . . 121 C1
Beech Wlk NR14 . . . . 90 D5
Beechwood Ave . . . .
Aylmerton NR11. . . . . . . 10 A3
18 Watton IP25 . . . . . . 84 D3
Beechwood CI . . . .
North Walsham NR28 . . . 151 D6
Watlington PE33 . . . . . . 61 E5
Beechwood Ct NR18 . . . . 173 D1
Beechwood Dr NR7 . . . . 159 E1
Beechwood Rd . . . .
Hemsby NR29 . . . . 167 A8
Wisbech PE13 . . . . 152 D7
Beechwoods NR6 . . . . . . 158 D5
Beehive Yd IP22 . . . . 177 C4
Beeleigh Way NR30 . . . . 168 C7
Bee-Orchid Way NR14 . . . 91 C7
Beerlick's Loke NR14. . . . 73 B1
BEESTON PE32 . . . . 48 C7
Beeston Comm NR26 . . . 138 C4
Beeston Hall Sch NR27. . . 9 F5
Beeston La . . . .
Barton Turf NR12 . . . . . . 38 D1
Beeston St Andrew NR12 . 159 B8
Beeston Prim Sch PE32 . . 48 C2
Beeston Rd . . . .
Beeston with Bittering
PE32. . . . . 48 D1
Great Dunham PE32 . . . . 66 A8
Mileham PE32 . . . . 48 D5
Sheringham NR26 . . . . . 138 D5
BEESTON REGIS NR26 . . 138 F5
BEESTON ST LAWRENCE
NR12. . . . . 55 C8
BEETLEY NR20 . . . . 49 D4

Beetley Grange 1 NR20. . 49 D4
Beetley Mdws 3 NR20 . . . 49 D4
Beevor Rd NR30 . . . . 170 E7
Begdale Rd PE14. . . . . . . 59 A1
BEIGHTON NR13 . . . . 74 C2
Beighton Rd NR13 . . . . . 166 A2
Bek CI NR4 . . . . 161 E2
BELAUGH NR12. . . . . 54 E5
Belaugh Gn La NR12 . . . 164 A8
Belaugh La NR12 . . . . . . 55 A7
Belaugh Rd NR12 . . . . . . 164 C6
Belgrave Ave NR36. . . . . 132 C6
Belgrave Gdns NR19 . . . . 154 E3
Bellacre CI IP22 . . . . 177 E4
Bellamy's La . . . .
Burnham Norton PE31. . . 135 C5
West Walton PE14 . . . . . 59 A8
Bellamy Way NR14 . . . . . 90 C4
Bellands Way 4 IP23 . . . 130 C1
Bell CI . . . .
13 Bawdeswell NR20 . . . 50 E7
East Dereham NR19 . . . . 154 C5
Little Snoring NR21. . . . . 17 B3
Norwich NR6 . . . . 157 F6
Taverham NR8 . . . . 156 E8
Bell La . . . .
Rocklands NR17. . . . . . . 103 B8
Saham Toney IP25 . . . . . 84 C4
Salhouse NR13 . . . . 164 B1
Bell Mdw . . . .
1 Hingham NR9 . . . . . . 86 C5
3 Marthan NR29 . . . . . 57 D5
Bellmere Way IP25 . . . . . 84 C4
BELLMOUNT PE34 . . . . . . 144 A7
Bellomonte Cres 4 NR8 . 156 F8
Bell Rd . . . .
Barnham Broom NR9. . . . 69 B2
Grimston PE32 . . . . 28 C1
Norwich NR3 . . . . 158 E1
Rocklands NR17. . . . . . . 103 B8
Bellrope CI 8 NR18 . . . . . 173 D5
Bellrope La . . . .
Roydon IP22 . . . . 129 D7
Wymondham NR18 . . . . 173 D5
Bell's Dro . . . .
Littleport CB6 . . . . 95 E2
Runcton Holme PE33. . . . 61 C5
Bells La IP22 . . . . 128 C4
Bell's Marsh Rd NR31. . . 170 D5
Bells Mdw 2 PE37 . . . . . 66 A4
Bells Rd NR31 . . . . 170 D4
Bell St IP26. . . . . 98 E1
Bellview CI NR14. . . . . . . 142 B4
Bellville Cres NR1 . . . . . 178 C1
Belmore Rd NR7. . . . . . . 159 E1
Belmore Rd NR7. . . . . . . 163 F8
Beloe Ave 6 NR5 . . . . . . 161 A7
Belsey Cl NR14 . . . . 146 D1
Belseybridge Rd NR35. . . 108 F3
Belsize CI 4 PE38 . . . . . 172 B4
Belsize Rd NR1. . . . . 163 B7
Belstead Ave NR30 . . . . . 168 D5
BELTON NR31 . . . . 93 F6
Belt Rd NR13 . . . . 73 C7
Belvedere PI 1 NR4 . . . . 162 A3
Belvedere Rd NR5 . . . . . 157 B1
Belvoir St NR2. . . . . 162 B6
Benbow CI 6 NR9 . . . . . . 88 E8
Benbow Rd NR30. . . . . . . 170 B6
Ben Culey Dr IP24 . . . . . 176 C5
Bendish Ave NR1 . . . . . . 170 D2
Bendish Way NR5. . . . . . 160 E7
Bendon CI 8 NR3. . . . . . . 145 F5
Benedict Rd 8 NR7 . . . . . 159 E3
Benets View 3 NR28. . . . 151 E5
BENGATE NR28 . . . . 38 A6
Bengey's Rd 7 PE37. . . . . 65 F4
Benjamin CI NR27 . . . . . 139 B5
Bennett CI . . . .
Hunstanton PE36. . . . . . 132 D2
3 Watlington PE33 . . . . 61 D5
Bennett Rd NR20 . . . . . . 50 B2
Bennett St PE38 . . . . . . 172 A5
Bennington's La . . . .
Aylmerton NR11. . . . . . . 138 F1
East Beckham NR11 . . . . 9 D2
Ben's La PE34 . . . . 144 C5
Bensley CI NR13 . . . . . . 166 C4
Bensley Rd . . . .
Marthan NR29 . . . . 57 D5
Norwich NR2 . . . . 162 A4
Bentinck Way 2 NR24 . . 146 C5
Bentley Rd NR16 . . . . . . 105 F4
Bentley Way NR3 . . . . . . 158 C4
Bentons Way NR10 . . . . . 53 B8
Berberis Gn 3 NR31 . . . . 170 B5
Beresford Rd . . . .
Caister-on-Sea NR30. . . . 168 E4
Great Yarmouth NR30 . . 169 D7
Holt NR25 . . . . 137 C5
Bergamot CI IP24 . . . . . . 176 F4
Bergen Way PE30 . . . . . . 146 F8
Bergh Apton Rd . . . .
Alpington NR14 . . . . 90 F4
Bergh Apton NR15 . . . . . 91 D1
Bermondsey PI E 19
NR30. . . . . 169 D4
Bermondsey PI S 18
NR30. . . . . 169 D4
Bermondsey PI W 17
NR30. . . . . 169 D4
Bernard CI . . . .
High Kelling NR25 . . . . . . 8 E2
New Rackheath NR13. . . . 72 E7
Bernard Cres PE36. . . . . 132 D6

Bernard Rd . . . .
Cromer NR27. . . . . 139 A7
Great Yarmouth NR31. . . 170 D2
Berners CI NR3 . . . . 158 B1
Berners St NR3 . . . . 158 B1
Berners Arms Sta NR30. . 93 D8
Berney Arms Windmill*
NR30. . . . . 93 E7
Bernham Rd NR6 . . . . . . 157 F6
Berrington Rd NR6. . . . . 157 F6
Berry CI NR31. . . . . 93 F6
Berryfields NR13. . . . . . . 165 C5
Berry Hall Rd NR12 . . . . 38 E1
Berry's La NR9. . . . . 69 D6
Ber St NR1 . . . . 178 B1
Bertie Rd NR3 . . . . 158 C1
Bertie Ward Way NR19 . . 154 F2
Bessemer Rd NR4 . . . . . 162 D1
Bessemer Way NR31. . . . 169 B1
BESSINGHAM NR11 . . . . . 20 E7
Bessingham Rd NR25. . . . 20 E8
BESTHORPE NR17 . . . . . . 174 F6
Besthorpe Carr NR17 . . . 105 A6
Besthorpe Rd NR17 . . . . 174 E5
Besthorpe Rd NR16. . . . . 105 A5
Bethel St NR2. . . . . 178 A3
Betjeman Cl IP24 . . . . . . 176 C6
Beulah St PE30 . . . . 147 B6
Bevan CI . . . .
Carleton Rode NR16. . . . 105 C4
Norwich NR5 . . . . 161 B6
Beveridge Way PE33 . . . . 43 E4
Beverley CI NR5 . . . . 161 E4
Beverley Rd . . . .
Brundall NR13 . . . . 165 B4
Norwich NR5 . . . . 161 E4
Beverley Way . . . .
Clenchwarton PE34 . . . . 145 E5
Taverham NR8 . . . . 156 F8
Beverly Ct NR1. . . . . 170 A7
Bevis Way PE30 . . . . 147 B6
Bewfield Rd 4 NR5. . . . . 160 E8
Bewick CI . . . .
11 Great Yarmouth NR31 . 94 C8
5 Snettisham PE31 . . . . 12 E5
Bewick Rd NR7. . . . . 159 D4
Bexfield Rd NR20 . . . . . . 33 C4
BEXWELL PE38 . . . . 79 F6
Bexwell Rd . . . .
Bexwell PE38. . . . . 79 F6
Downham Market PE38. . . 172 D5
Bickley CI NR17. . . . . 174 F7
Bidewell Rd NR8 . . . . . . 157 B7
Bidwell Rd NR13 . . . . . . 72 E8
Bidwels ct IP24 . . . . 176 C4
Bier La IP22 . . . . 128 F5
Big Back La NR14 . . . . . . 92 A2
Biggin Hill Way IP25 . . . 85 A3
Biggotts La NR15 . . . . . . 108 D4
Biggs Rd PE14. . . . . 59 D4
Bignold Fst Sch NR2 . . . 178 A2
Bignold Mid Sch NR2 . . . 178 A2
Bignold Rd NR5 . . . . 158 A2
Big Row NR14 . . . . 109 F2
Big Yard PE36 . . . . 2 A3
Big Yard The PE26 . . . . . 132 E7
Bilberry CI 5 NR17 . . . . . 174 B5
Bilbys NR14 . . . . 110 B6
Billing CI NR6. . . . . 158 F5
BILLINGFORD . . . .
Billingford NR20 . . . . 50 B7
Dickleburgh and Rushall
IP21 . . . . 130 E5
Billingford Rd . . . .
1 Bawdeswell NR20 . . . 50 B7
Bintree NR20. . . . . 33 B1
BILLOCKBY NR29 . . . . 75 A7
Bill Todd Way NR8 . . . . . 155 C2
Billey La NR10. . . . . 155 E8
Bilney Rd . . . .
Beetley NR20. . . . . 49 B4
East Winch PE32 . . . . . . 45 B1
Pentney PE32. . . . . 63 C8
Bingles Turn NR10 . . . . . 53 B7
BINHAM NR21 . . . . 6 E2
Binham Rd . . . .
Field Dalling NR25. . . . . . 7 A1
Hindringham NR21. . . . . . 17 E8
4 King's Lynn PE30 . . . 148 C3
Langham NR25 . . . . 7 A4
Warham NR23 . . . . 6 A4
BINTREE NR20. . . . . 33 B2
Bintree Rd NR20 . . . . . . 50 B8
Binyon Gdns NR8 . . . . . . 156 D8
Birbeck Rd NR1 . . . . 162 E2
BIRCHAM NEWTON PE31. . 14 A4
Bircham Rd . . . .
Docking PE31 . . . . 134 C4
Reepham NR10 . . . . 149 C5
Snettisham PE31 . . . . . . 13 A4
Stanhoe PE31. . . . . 14 E7
BIRCHAM TOFTS PE31. . . 14 B3
Bircham Windmill* PE31. . 14 A4
Birch Ave 8 NR20 . . . . . . 49 C4
Birch CI . . . .
East Dereham NR19 . . . . 154 C4
Little Melton NR9 . . . . . 160 D2
North Walsham NR28 . . . 151 D6
6 Snettisham PE31 . . . . 12 E4
Birch Covert 5 IP24 . . . . 176 F5
Birch Ct . . . .
Erpingham NR11 . . . . . . 21 B2
Norwich NR7 . . . . 159 D4
Birch Dr . . . .
Attleborough NR17 . . . . . 174 C3

Birch Dr *continued*
Roydon PE32 . . . . 28 A2
Birches The PE30 . . . . 148 D4
Birchfield Gdns NR14 . . . . 89 B3
Birchfield La NR14 . . . . 89 B3
Birchfield Rd PE38 . . . . 78 F2
Birch Gr
Sheringham NR26 . . . . 138 D4
West Winch PE33 . . . . 43 E2
Wisbech PE14 . . . . 59 B1
Birchgrove Rd PE30 . . . . 147 C4
Birch Rd
Gayton PE32 . . . . 45 C6
🔟 Hethersett NR9 . . . . 88 D8
Birch Tree Cl PE33 . . . . . 146 E4
Birch Way
🔟 Great Yarmouth
NR31 . . . . 170 B5
Mundham NR14 . . . . 108 F6
Birchwood 🔟 NR7 . . . . . . 72 D3
Birchwood St 🔟 PE38 . . 146 E6
Birchwood Way PE38 . . 178 C8
Birdcage Wlk PE30 . . . . . 146 D3
Birds Cnr IP25 . . . . 67 E4
Birds Rd NR18 . . . . 55 B3
Bird View Sq 🔟 IP26 . . 98 E1
Birkbeck Cl
King's Lynn PE30 . . . . 148 B2
Norwich NR18 . . . . 89 C4
Stoke Holy Cross NR14 . . 90 B5
Birkbeck Way NR7 . . . . . 163 F7
Birkdale NR4 . . . . 162 A2
Birkin Cl 🔟 NR16 . . . . 105 F5
Birtles Way NR13 . . . . 166 C3
Biscay Gdns NR30 . . . . . . 168 C6
**Bishop Bonner's Cottage
Mus** ★ NR19 . . . . 154 D5
Bishop Bridge Rd NR1 . 163 A6
Bishopgate NR1 . . . . 178 C3
Bishop Herbert Cl NR20 . 69 B8
Bishop Rise 🔟 NR8 . . . . 155 E2
Bishop's Cl NR7 . . . . 163 D5
Bishop's Rd
Hunstanton PE36 . . . . 132 C2
King's Lynn PE30 . . . . 147 B4
Bishops Wlk 🔟 NR11 . . 171 D5
Bishopyne Ave 🔟 NR19 . 154 F3
Bisby Barnebee Way
NR5 . . . . 160 F6
BITTERING NR19 . . . . 48 F4
Bittering St
🔟 Beetley NR20 . . . . 49 C4
🔟 Gressenhall NR20 . . . . 49 C3
Bittern Cl
Necton PE37 . . . . 66 A3
Thetford IP24 . . . . 176 D1
Bittern Cres NR12 . . . . 38 F1
Bittern Rd NR29 . . . . 57 D3
Bixley Cl NR5 . . . . 161 D6
Blackbarn Rd NR16 . . . . . 120 D8
Black Bear La PE13 . . . . . 152 F7
Blackberry Ct NR6 . . . . . . 157 F2
Blackberry Cl NR27 . . . . . 10 C4
Blackberry Hall La NR11 . 11 D1
Blackbird Ave IP27 . . . . . 175 F3
Blackbird Cl 🔟 NR31 . . 94 C8
BLACKBOROUGH END
PE33 . . . . 44 C1
Blackburn Rd NR6 . . . . . . 158 C6
BLACK CARR NR17 . . . . . . 105 A6
Blackdale Mid Sch NR4 161 C4
Blackdike Dro IP27 . . . . . 112 F5
Black Drif PE37 . . . . 66 A4
Black Dro
Downham West PE38 . . . . 79 B6
Feltwell PE38 . . . . 97 F2
Fincham PE33 . . . . 80 D7
Marshland St James PE14 . 60 D4
Stow Bardolph PE34 . . . . . 78 E8
Blackdyke Cl 🔟 IP26 . . 98 D1
Black Dyke Rd IP26 . . . . 113 E7
Blackford PE30 . . . . 147 D8
Blackfriars Rd
King's Lynn PE30 . . . . 146 E5
🔟 Wisbech PE13 . . . . . . 152 C5
Blackfriars' Rd NR30 . . 169 D2
Blackfriars St
King's Lynn PE30 . . . . 146 D4
Norwich NR3 . . . . 178 A4
Blackhills Cnr NR13 . . . . . 73 C7
Blackhorse Cl 🔟 NR20 . 50 E7
Black Horse Cl NR19 . . . . 67 B7
Black Horse Dro CB6 . . . . 96 E2
Blackhorse Mdw 🔟 NR12 50 E7
Black Horse Opening
NR6 . . . . 158 F2
Black Horse Rd
Clenchwarton PE34 . . . . . 145 C4
Runhall NR9 . . . . 68 F1
Blackhorse St 🔟 NR2 . 162 C7
Blackhorse Yd NR13 . . . . 136 C6
Black Mill La NR15 . . . . . 121 A7
Black Moor Rd IP25 . . . . . 67 D2
Blackmoor Row IP25 . . . . 67 D1
Blacks Ave NR14 . . . . 163 B2
Blackslough La NR16 . . . 119 D7
Blacksmith La PE14 . . . . 125 E6
Blacksmiths Cl NR20 . . . . 33 B6
Blacksmiths La
Ashwellthorpe NR16 . . . . 106 B8
Happisburgh NR12 . . . . . . 24 B6
Hindringham NR21 . . . . . . 17 E7
Blacksmith's La
Barton Bendish PE33 . . . . 81 B8
Morning Thorpe NR15 . . . 107 A2

Blacksmith's Loke NR32 . . 94 C2
Blacksmith's Row 🔟 PE32 45 C6
Blacksmiths Way NR6 . . 158 E5
Black St
Hemsby NR29 . . . . 58 B6
Marthan NR29 . . . . 57 D5
Blackthorn Ave NR25 . . 137 C7
Blackthorn Cl
Diss IP22 . . . . 177 F5
Norwich NR6 . . . . 158 D4
🔟 Thetford IP24 . . . . . . 176 F4
Blackthorn Dr 🔟 NR19 . 154 C4
Blackthorn Rd
Attleborough NR17 . . . . . 174 B5
King's Lynn PE30 . . . . 148 C3
Wymondham NR18 . . . . . 173 D4
Blackthorn Way NR14 . . 90 C5
Blackwall Reach NR31 . . 170 D5
BLACKWATER NR11 . . . . . 36 F5
Blackwater La
Great Witchingham NR9 . . 51 C6
Heydon NR11 . . . . 34 D8
Blackwell Ave NR7 . . . . . 159 A3
Bladewater Rd NR5 . . . . . 160 F5
Blake Cl PE32 . . . . 28 A3
Blake Ct PE13 . . . . 153 C2
Blake St NR31 . . . . 170 A2
BLAKENEY NR25 . . . . 7 C6
Blakeney CE Prim Sch
NR25 . . . . 7 D6
Blakeney Cl NR4 . . . . 161 E2
Blakeney Long La NR25 . 7 C4
**Blakeney Point National
Nature Reserve** ★ NR25 . 7 C8
Blakeney Rd
Binham NR21 . . . . 6 D1
Letheringsett with Glandford
NR25 . . . . 7 F2
Morston NR25 . . . . 7 B6
Blakeney Short La NR25 . 7 C3
Blake Rd NR30 . . . . 169 D7
Blakes Cl NR3 . . . . 158 F3
Blakestone Dr NR7 . . . . . 163 D7
Bland Rd NR5 . . . . 161 B6
Blatchford Way PE31 . . . 133 B5
BLEACH GREEN NR21 . . . 131 F4
Blencowe Terr 🔟 PE13 . 152 C5
Blenheim Ave 🔟 NR29 . 57 D4
Blenheim Cl
🔟 Long Stratton NR15 . 106 E3
Norwich NR7 . . . . 159 B5
Blenheim Cres
Beeston with Bittering
PE32 . . . . 48 D2
Griston IP25 . . . . 85 A2
Norwich NR7 . . . . 159 B5
Tittleshall PE32 . . . . 48 A7
Blenheim Dr NR27 . . . . . . 174 E4
BLENHEIM PARK NR21 . . 15 C3
Blenheim Pk Sch NR21 . 15 C3
Blenheim Rd
King's Lynn PE30 . . . . 147 C8
Norwich NR7 . . . . 159 B5
Sculthorpe Airfield NR21 . 15 C3
Blenheim Way
Emneth PE14 . . . . 152 E2
🔟 Roydon IP22 . . . . . . 129 D7
🔟 Watton IP25 . . . . 84 E3
Blick Cl 🔟 PE33 . . . . 43 F2
BLICKLING NR11 . . . . 35 F7
Blickling Cl 🔟 PE30 . . . 148 F1
Blickling Hall ★ NR11 . . . 35 F7
Blickling Rd
Blickling NR11 . . . . 150 A8
Norwich NR6 . . . . 158 C5
Bligh Cl NR14 . . . . 90 D5
Blind Dick's La NR22 . . . 16 E7
Blind La
Castle Acre PE32 . . . . 46 F1
Hockering NR9 . . . . 51 A2
Honingham NR9 . . . . 69 F5
Horsham St Faith NR10 . . 53 D1
Mattishall NR20 . . . . 69 A7
Blithe Mdw Ct NR7 . . . . 159 C3
Blithemeadow Dr NR7 . 159 C3
Blithewood Gdns NR7 . 159 C3
Blocka Rd NR32 . . . . 93 F2
BLOFIELD NR13 . . . . 165 F5
Blofield Cnr Rd NR13 . . . 73 B6
BLOFIELD CORNER NR13 . 73 B7
BLOFIELD HEATH NR13 . 73 D6
Blofield Loke NR12 . . . . . 164 E6
Blofield Prim Sch NR13 165 E7
Blofield Rd
Brundall NR13 . . . . 165 E3
Lingwood & Burlingham
NR13 . . . . 73 F3
Blofields Loke NR11 . . . . 150 C6
Blomefield Rd
Diss IP22 . . . . 177 D4
Norwich NR3 . . . . 158 B2
BLO' NORTON IP22 . . . . . 128 B6
Blo' Norton Rd IP22 . . . . 128 C7
Bloodgate Hill NR21 . . . . 15 D6
Bloodhills Rd NR29 . . . . . 57 F5
BLOODMAN'S CORNER
NR32 . . . . 171 A4
Bloodslat La NR12 . . . . . . 23 D4
Bloomfield Rd NR30 . . . . 170 E7
Bloomstile La NR25 . . . . . 8 B6
Bloomstiles NR25 . . . . 8 B6
Blooms Turn NR28 . . . . . . 22 E5
Blowlands La NR26 . . . . . 138 B5
Bluebell Cl
Attleborough NR17 . . . . . 174 B5
🔟 East Dereham NR19 . 154 C4
Thetford IP24 . . . . 176 F4

Bluebell Cres NR4 . . . . . . 161 D2
Bluebell Dr NR26 . . . . 138 B6
Bluebell Gdns NR23 . . . . 136 E5
Bluebell Rd
Mulbarton NR14 . . . . 89 B3
North Walsham NR28 . . . 151 D6
Norwich NR4 . . . . 161 D3
Bluebell Way 🔟 NR31 . 94 C6
Bluebell Wlk IP27 . . . . . . 175 A2
Blue Boar La NR7 . . . . . . 159 D3
Blue Doors Loke NR31 . 94 C3
Blue Sky Cl NR31 . . . . 94 C7
Bluestone Cres NR21 . . . 15 D6
Bluestone La NR21 . . . . . 15 D7
Bluestone Rd NR21 . . . . . 15 D6
Blundeston Rd NR32 . . . 94 C4
Blundeville Manor 🔟
NR15 . . . . 89 C1
Blunt's Cnr NR13 . . . . 5 B2
Blyth Cres NR26 . . . . 138 D6
Blyth Jex Sch The NR3 . 158 E2
Blyth Rd NR3 . . . . 158 D2
Boadicea Cl 🔟 IP24 . . . 176 D7
Boal Quay NR30 . . . . 146 D4
Boal St PE30 . . . . 146 D4
Boardman Cl NR6 . . . . . . 158 D3
Boat Dyke La NR13 . . . . 166 D4
Boat Dyke Rd NR13 . . . . 166 B8
Boathouse La NR32 . . . . . 111 F3
Boatmans Row NR23 . . . 136 C6
BOBBY HILL IP22 . . . . 128 A1
Bob Carter Leisure Ctr
NR8 . . . . 157 A8
BODHAM NR25 . . . . 9 A3
Bodleian Ch NR14 . . . . . . 170 B2
BODNEY IP26 . . . . 83 B1
Boileau Ave 🔟 NR16 . . 105 F5
Boileau Cl 🔟 NR14 . . . . 89 E8
Boleness Rd PE13 . . . . . . 152 C2
Bolingbroke Rd NR3 . . . 158 B3
Boltons The PE30 . . . . . . 148 C1
Bolts Cl NR23 . . . . 136 D6
Bond Cl IP21 . . . . 121 F4
Bonds Rd NR13 . . . . 73 C7
Bond's Rd NR15 . . . . 121 C4
Bond St
🔟 Cromer NR27 . . . . . . 139 B7
🔟 Hingham NR9 . . . . . . 86 C5
Norwich NR2 . . . . 162 A7
Bone Rd NR8 . . . . 157 B8
Bonemill La NR13 . . . . 4 F7
Bone's Dro NR23 . . . . 4 F7
Boniface Cl NR4 . . . . 162 C1
Bonnetts La PE14 . . . . 60 B5
Boosey's Wlk 🔟 NR16 . 104 F1
Boot Binders Rd 🔟 NR6 158 C1
Boot La IP22 . . . . 120 D6
BOOTON NR10 . . . . 149 E4
**Booton Comm Nature
Reserve** ★ NR10 . . . . . . 149 E5
Booton Rd NR10 . . . . 35 B2
Booty Rd NR7 . . . . 159 F1
Borage Cl IP24 . . . . 176 F4
Border La NR32 . . . . 94 B2
Border Rd PE33 . . . . 81 A2
Borough Cl PE13 . . . . 152 D3
Borrowdale Dr NR1 . . . . 163 B8
Borton Rd NR13 . . . . 73 C6
Boscombe Rd IP25 . . . . . . 85 A3
Bosgate Rise 🔟 NR29 . 57 C4
Boston Cl 🔟 NR1 . . . . . 154 C3
Boston End 🔟 IP24 . . . . 116 A1
Boston Sq PE36 . . . . 132 C5
Boston St NR3 . . . . 158 D2
BOTESDALE IP22 . . . . 128 F2
Botolph St NR3 . . . . 178 A4
Boton Dr NR19 . . . . 154 D2
Bottom Breck NR5 . . . . . 156 F2
Botwright Dr 🔟 PE37 . 153 C3
Boudica's Way NR14 . . . 163 A1
Boughey Cl IP31 . . . . 3 B6
BOUGHTON PE33 . . . . 81 A5
Boughton Long Rd PE33 . 81 B7
Boughton Rd
Fincham PE33 . . . . 62 E1
Stoke Ferry PE33 . . . . 81 A3
Boulderside Cl 🔟 NR7 . 163 E7
Boulevard Rd 🔟 NR27 . 10 A5
Boulevard The
Sheringham NR26 . . . . . . 138 D7
Thorpe End NR13 . . . . 72 F6
Boulters The NR11 . . . . . . 170 C1
Boulton Rd NR7 . . . . 163 C7
Boulton St NR1 . . . . 178 B2
Boundary Ave NR6 . . . . . 158 A4
Boundary Cl IP26 . . . . 113 F7
Boundary La
Norwich NR7 . . . . 72 E3
Paston NR28 . . . . 23 B3
Boundary Rd
Ashby with Oby NR29 . . . 56 E2
Great Yarmouth NR31 . . . 169 B1
🔟 Hockwold cum Wilton
IP26 . . . . 114 A7
Marham PE33 . . . . 63 C3
Norton Subcourse NR14 . . 92 D1
Norwich NR6 . . . . 157 F3
Raveningham NR14 . . . . . 110 B8
Boundary Way 🔟 NR14 . 90 C5
Bourne Cl
King's Lynn PE30 . . . . 148 C2
Long Stratton NR15 . . . . . 106 E3
BOWBECK IP31 . . . . 127 A2
Bowers Ave NR3 . . . . 158 A2
Bowers Cl NR3 . . . . 158 A2
Bow Hill NR9 . . . . 70 A3
Bowlers Cl NR13 . . . . 92 E7

Bowling Gn Cl
Attleborough NR17 . . . . . 174 D6
Crostwick NR12 . . . . 54 B2
Bowling Gn The
Raynham NR21 . . . . 30 F4
Wells-next-the-Sea NR23 136 D5
Bowling Gn Wlk 🔟
NR30 . . . . 169 C4
Bowman Rd 🔟 NR4 . . . . 89 E8
Bow St NR9 . . . . 86 B1
BOWTHORPE NR5 . . . . . . 160 F7
Bowthorpe Hall Gdns ★
PE13 . . . . 152 D5
Bowthorpe Hall Rd NR5 . 160 F7
Bowthorpe Rd
Norwich NR5 . . . . 161 D6
Wisbech PE13 . . . . 152 D5
Box's La PE37 . . . . 153 D5
Boyces Rd PE13 . . . . 152 E5
Boyd Ave 🔟 NR19 . . . . . 154 D1
Boylandhall La NR15 . . . 107 B4
Brabazon Rd NR6 . . . . . . 158 B5
Bracecamp Cl NR29 . . . . 167 C2
Braces La NR35 . . . . 109 E3
Bracey Ave NR6 . . . . 158 F5
Bracken Ave
🔟 Beetley NR20 . . . . 49 C4
Norwich NR6 . . . . 158 A4
Overstrand NR27 . . . . 11 A3
Bracken Cl
Fakenham NR21 . . . . 141 F4
Horsford NR10 . . . . 53 A6
Stratton Strawless NR10 . 53 A6
Bracken Dr NR17 . . . . 174 B5
Bracken Rd
King's Lynn PE30 . . . . 148 C2
Thetford IP24 . . . . 176 C1
Bracken Rise
Brandon IP27 . . . . 175 E3
Mundford IP26 . . . . 100 A4
Bracken Way PE32 . . . . . . 28 B1
Brackenwoods PE37 . . . . 66 A4
BRACON ASH NR14 . . . . . 89 A2
Braconcombe NR1 . . . . . . 178 C1
Bracondale Cl 🔟 NR1 . 162 F3
Bracondale Gn NR1 . . . . 178 C1
Bracondale Millgate
NR14 . . . . 163 A2
Bracon Rd NR31 . . . . 93 F5
Bradcar Rd NR17 . . . . 103 B2
Braddock Rd NR30 . . . . . 168 E5
Bradeham Way NR14 . . . 162 A3
BRADENHAM IP25 . . . . . . 66 E4
**Bradenham Hall Gdn &
Arboretum** ★ IP25 . . . . 66 E4
Bradenham La NR19 . . . . 66 F6
Bradenham Rd IP25 . . . . . 67 A2
BRADFIELD NR28 . . . . 22 C4
Bradfield Cl NR28 . . . . . . 151 A6
Bradfield Pl 🔟 PE33 . . . 81 A3
Bradfield Rd
Antingham NR11 . . . . 22 C5
North Walsham NR28 . . . 151 A6
Swafield NR28 . . . . 22 E3
Bradman's La NR18 . . . . . 87 D3
Bradmere La PE31 . . . . . . 134 E5
Bradshaw Rd NR8 . . . . . . 157 C7
BRADWELL
Bradwell NR31 . . . . 94 C7
Great Yarmouth NR31 . . . 170 A4
Bradwell Ave 🔟 NR31 . 170 A5
Brady Cl PE38 . . . . 172 B1
Brady Gdns PE38 . . . . 172 B1
Braeburn Ave PE13 . . . . 152 C8
Braeford Cl NR6 . . . . 157 E2
Brailsford Cl NR20 . . . . . . 68 A7
Braithwait Cl 🔟 NR5 . . 161 A8
BRAKEFIELD GREEN
NR19 . . . . 68 D4
Brake La NR21 . . . . 16 C4
Bramble Ave NR6 . . . . . . 158 A5
Bramble Cl
Mundesley NR11 . . . . 143 D5
Sculthorpe Airfield NR21 . 15 C2
🔟 Taverham NR8 . . . . . 155 E2
Bramble Ct NR21 . . . . . . 141 E4
Bramble Dr PE30 . . . . 148 C2
Bramble Gdns NR13 . . . . 93 F5
Bramble La
Outwell PE14 . . . . 77 D7
Swaffham PE37 . . . . 153 F5
Brambles Cl 🔟 NR10 . . 54 A1
Bramble Way
🔟 Poringland NR14 . . . . 90 D5
Wymondham NR18 . . . . . 173 E4
BRAMERTON NR14 . . . . . 90 F7
Bramerton La
Framingham Pigot NR14 . 90 E7
Rockland St Mary NR14 . . 91 A7
Bramerton Rd NR14 . . . . 91 A8
Bramfield Cl NR17 . . . . . 174 F7
Bramford Cl NR7 . . . . 162 A7
Bramley Cl NR23 . . . . 136 D6
Bramley Dr NR21 . . . . 31 E5
Bramley Rd
Diss IP22 . . . . 177 C5
Wisbech PE13 . . . . 152 C7
BRAMPTON NR10 . . . . 36 E3
Brampton Cl PE13 . . . . . . 152 A4
Brampton Ct NR25 . . . . . 161 A7
Brampton St NR10 . . . . . . 36 E3
BRANCASTER PE31 . . . . 3 B6
Brancaster Cl
King's Lynn PE30 . . . . 147 C8
Taverham NR8 . . . . 155 F3
King's Lynn PE32 . . . . 148 C3
🔟 Leighton PE30 . . . . . . 74 A3
🔟 Necton PE37 . . . . 65 F4
BRANCASTER STAITHE
PE31 . . . . 3 D7

Brancaster Way PE37 . . 153 B2
Branch Rd NR13 . . . . 75 B2
BRANDISTON NR10 . . . . . . 52 B8
Brandiston Rd NR10 . . . . 35 B2
BRANDON IP27 . . . . 175 D3
BRANDON BANK PE38 . . 112 B7
Brandon Cl
Norwich NR6 . . . . 157 E4
🔟 Swaffham PE37 . . . . 153 C3
BRANDON CREEK PE38 . . 97 A2
Brandon Ct NR13 . . . . 165 E3
Brandon Her Ctr ★ IP27 175 D4
BRANDON PARVA NR9 . . 69 B2
Brandon Rd
Cockley Cley PE37 . . . . . . 83 A8
Methwold IP26 . . . . 99 B4
Saham Toney IP25 . . . . . . 84 B3
Swaffham PE37 . . . . 65 A1
Thetford IP24 . . . . 176 A4
Wangford IP27 . . . . 114 C1
Watton IP25 . . . . 84 C3
Weeting-with-Broomhill
IP27 . . . . 175 C5
Brandon Sports Ctr IP27 175 B3
Brandon Sta IP27 . . . . . . 175 C5
Brandon Terr NR30 . . . . . 169 E2
Brand's La
Felthorpe NR10 . . . . 155 D6
Tharston & Hapton NR15 . 106 E5
**Brandvnvm (Roman Fort)
(Branodunum)** ★ NR31 . . 3 C6
Branford Rd
Caister-on-Sea NR30 . . . 168 D7
Norwich NR3 . . . . 158 E1
Branksome Cl NR4 . . . . . 162 A2
Branksome Rd NR4 . . . . . 162 A2
Branodunum PE31 . . . . 3 B7
Bransby Cl PE30 . . . . 146 F4
Brasenose Ave NR31 . . . 170 B3
Brasier Rd NR3 . . . . 158 B2
Brawdy Rd 🔟 IP31 . . . . 126 B1
Braydeston Ave NR13 . . 165 D3
Braydeston Cres NR13 . 165 D3
Braydeston Dr NR13 . . . 165 F6
Braydeston Hall La NR13 . 73 E4
Brayfield Way NR6 . . . . . 158 F6
Braymeadow Cl NR9 . . . 160 D2
Braymeadow La NR9 . . . 160 D2
Bray's La
Guestwick NR20 . . . . 34 A6
Rocklands NR17 . . . . 103 A7
Brazen Gate NR1 . . . . 178 A1
Breck Farm Cl NR8 . . . . . 155 C2
Breck Farm La NR8 . . . . . 155 C2
Breckland Bsns Pk IP25 . 84 F3
**Breckland Leisure Ctr &
Waterworld** IP24 . . . . . 176 D5
Breckland Mid Sch IP27 175 D2
Breckland Rd NR5 . . . . . . 157 A1
Brecklands
Mundford IP26 . . . . 100 B4
🔟 Stalham NR12 . . . . . . 39 B4
Brecklands Rd NR13 . . . . 165 E2
BRECKLES NR17 . . . . 102 E5
Breck Rd
Norwich NR7 . . . . 72 C6
Weston Longville NR9 . . . 51 E1
Brecon Rd NR15 . . . . 90 E2
Breeze Ave NR1 . . . . 150 B5
Brellows Hill PE34 . . . . . . 144 A5
Brenda Collison Cl PE31 . 140 C4
Brenda James Cl 🔟 NR7 163 E7
Brennewater Mews 🔟
NR5 . . . . 161 A8
Brent Ave PE31 . . . . 12 E5
Brentwood 🔟 NR4 . . . . 161 F1
Brereton Cl NR5 . . . . 161 C6
BRESSINGHAM IP22 . . . . 129 C8
BRESSINGHAM COMMON
IP22 . . . . 119 F1
Bressingham Prim Sch
IP22 . . . . 129 B8
Bressingham Rd
🔟 Gresham NR11 . . . . . . 9 E1
Roydon IP22 . . . . 129 C8
**Bressingham Steam Mus &
Gdns** ★ IP22 . . . . 129 C7
Breton Cl 🔟 NR31 . . . . . 154 D2
Brett Ave NR31 . . . . 170 D1
BRETTENHAM IP24 . . . . . 117 B2
Brettingham Ave NR4 . . 89 B8
Brett Way PE30 . . . . 147 E6
Brewers Ct NR3 . . . . 178 C4
Brewers Gn La IP22 . . . . 177 B6
Brewery La NR18 . . . . 173 C3
Brewery Rd NR28 . . . . . . 22 D5
Brewery St NR30 . . . . 169 C4
Brewster Ct NR13 . . . . . . 165 D6
Brewsters 🔟 NR16 . . . . 118 C5
Breydon Dr NR8 . . . . 156 C4
Breydon Dr N NR8 . . . . . . 156 C5
Breydon Junc NR30 . . . . . 76 C3
Breydon Mid Sch NR31 . 94 A5
Breydon Rd
Great Yarmouth NR31 . . . 169 B4
King's Lynn PE30 . . . . 147 D5
Norwich NR7 . . . . 159 A4
Breydon Way NR30 . . . . 168 D6
Brian Ave NR1 . . . . 162 D3
Briar Ave NR31 . . . . 94 C7
Briar Cl
Dereham NR20 . . . . 68 A8
Grimston PE32 . . . . 28 B1
King's Lynn PE32 . . . . 148 C3
🔟 Leighton PE30 . . . . . . 74 A3
🔟 Necton PE37 . . . . 65 F4

Briar La
Heckingham NR14 109 F8
Rickinghall Inferior IP22 128 D1
Swainsthorpe NR14 89 D3
Briar Rd 39 IP20 122 D2
Briars Ct NR5 161 F7
Brickfield Loke NR8 156 C5
Brickfields NR13 73 F2
Brickfields Way IP24 176 C6
Brickkiln La
Ashwellthorpe NR16 105 F7
Mulbarton NR14 89 C2
South Lopham IP22 128 F7
Brick Kiln La
Bunwell NR16 105 D2
Gillingham NR34 110 C5
Long Stratton NR15 107 A5
Shipdham IP25 67 C2
Brick Kiln Rd
Ellingham NR35 109 C4
Hevingham NR10 53 A7
North Walsham NR28 151 E5
Thursford NR21 17 F4
Brick Kilns Rd NR13 73 B7
Brick La NR27 10 B5
Brickle Loke NR14 90 B5
Brickle Rd NR14 90 B4
Brickley La PE31 140 D7
Brickyard La PE31 29 C4
Brickyard Rd NR28 22 A2
Bridewell Alley 2 NR2 178 B3
Bridewell La
Acle NR13 166 C4
Botesdale IP22 128 E2
Bridewell Mus The★
NR2 178 B3
Bridewell St
1 Little Walsingham
NR22 16 F7
Wymondham NR18 173 C3
Bridge Broad Cl NR12 164 C5
Bridge Cl
16 Harleston IP20 122 D2
Heacham PE31 133 E5
Melton Constable NR24 142 B4
Bridgecourt NR29 58 A4
Bridge Farm La NR4 161 C6
Bridgefoot La NR25 7 F5
Bridge Gdns NR19 154 F1
BRIDGE GREEN IP22 120 F2
Bridge La IP25 84 C6
Bridge Mdw NR29 58 A4
Bridge Rd
Brome & Oakley IP21 130 C5
Bunwell NR16 105 F2
Burston & Shimpling IP22 120 E3
Colby NR11 36 D8
Downham West PE38 79 B5
Great Ryburgh NR21 32 C6
5 Great Yarmouth NR30 169 C5
High Kelling NR25 137 F8
North Elmham NR20 32 F3
Potter Heigham NR29 56 F5
Stoke Ferry PE33 81 A2
Sutton Bridge PE12 41 A8
Wymondham NR18 88 B2
Bridge St
Brandon IP27 175 C4
Carbrooke IP25 85 A4
Downham Market PE38 172 B5
Fakenham NR21 141 B3
Gressenhall NR20 49 C3
Hilgay PE38 79 E1
14 King's Lynn PE30 146 D4
Loddon NR14 92 A2
Stiffkey NR23 6 D5
Thetford IP24 176 C4
14 Wisbech PE13 152 C5
Bridges Wlk
Fakenham NR21 141 A3
Thetford IP24 176 D3
Bridgford Cl NR31 170 C2
BRIDGHAM NR16 117 F5
Bridgham La NR16 117 F4
Bridle La
Downham Market PE38 172 D7
Keswick NR4 89 C7
Bridle Rd IP25 84 C3
BRIGGATE NR28 38 B6
Briggs Loke NR11 36 D8
Brigg St NR1 178 A2
Brigham Cl NR13 165 C4
Brighton Rd 1 NR15 89 C1
Brightwell Rd NR3 158 D3
Brighty's Opening NR2 162 B7
Brig Sq NR23 136 C6
Brigstock Rd PE13 152 B7
Brimbelow Rd NR12 164 D4
Brindle Dr 5 NR14 89 B3
Brinell Way NR31 170 B8
BRININGHAM NR24 18 D4
BRINTON NR24 18 D6
Brinton Rd NR24 142 D8
Briscoe Way IP27 113 E2
BRISLEY NR20 49 A8
Brisley CE Prim Sch NR20 32 A1
Bristol Terr NR2 178 A2
BRISTON NR24 142 E4
Briston Rd
Briston NR24 142 A5
Corpusty NR11 19 F1
Edgefield NR24 19 C5
Wood Dalling NR11 34 C6
Britannia Pier Theatre
NR30 169 E4
Britannia Rd
Great Yarmouth NR30 169 E4
Norwich NR1 163 A7
Britannia Way PE13 152 C2
Britch La PE34 42 B4
Briton's La
Beeston Regis NR26 138 F4
Sheringham NR26 9 F5
Briton's La Cl
2 Beeston Regis NR27 9 F5
Sheringham NR26 138 F5
Briton Way NR18 173 B3
Britton Cl 9 PE33 61 D6
Broadacres 4 NR13 74 B8
Broadcote Cl NR15 90 E1
Broad Dro
Emneth PE14 59 C1
Grimston PE32 45 C8
Methwold IP26 97 F6
Upwell PE14 77 D4
Broad End La PE13 152 F4
Broad End Rd PE14 152 F4
Broaden La NR15 107 C6
Broadfen Dro IP26 98 B5
Broad Fen La NR28 38 D4
Broadfields Way NR14 91 C7
Broadgate NR8 155 B2
Broadgate Cl NR27 11 A2
Broadgate La
Great Moulton NR15 121 B8
Roydon PE32 28 A2
Broadhurst Rd NR4 162 B1
Broad La
Brancaster PE31 3 A7
Great & Little Plumstead
NR13 72 F6
South Walsham NR13 74 B8
Swannington NR9 52 B5
Broadland Cl NR13 93 A4
Broadland Dr NR13 72 D6
Broadland High Sch
NR12 164 D6
Broadlands PE38 172 B5
Broadlands Cl PE31 140 C4
Broadland Sports Club
NR29 75 D8
Broadlands Rd NR12 39 E1
Broadland Way
Acle NR13 166 C3
Postwick with Witton NR7 72 E3
Broadmead Gn NR13 72 E6
Broadmoor Rd IP25 85 B4
Broad Rd
Alburgh IP20 122 E8
Fleggburgh NR29 75 C8
Broad Reaches NR29 56 C5
Broad Row 17 NR30 169 C4
Broadsman Cl NR1 163 A4
Broad St
Bungay NR35 124 A8
20 Harleston IP20 122 D2
King's Lynn PE30 146 D5
Broad View 4 NR13 72 D6
Broadwater La PE32 45 B4
Broadwater Rd PE36 1 F7
Broadwater Way 1 NR12 55 E4
Broad Way
Dickleburgh & Rushall
IP21 130 D8
Rocklands NR17 103 A8
Broadway Cl 5 NR15 107 C5
Broadway The
Heacham PE31 133 D5
Honingham NR9 69 E8
Scarning NR19 154 B2
Broadwood Cl NR11 11 E1
BROCKDISH IP21 131 C6
Brockdish Prim Sch
IP21 131 D6
Brockley Gn 7 PE30 147 C4
Brocks Rd PE37 153 B6
Brockwell Ct NR3 158 F2
BROME IP23 130 B3
Brome Ave IP23 130 C2
Bromedale Ave 19 NR14 89 B3
Brome Hall La IP23 130 D3
BROME STREET IP23 130 D3
BROOKE NR15 90 E2
Brooke Ave NR30 168 D5
Brooke Prim Sch NR15 90 E1
Brooke Rd
Kirstead NR15 91 A1
Mundham NR14 108 F8
Seething NR15 91 C1
Shotesham NR15 107 F8
Brookes Dr NR28 151 A4
Brookfield Cl NR15 106 F4
Brook Gr 8 NR19 154 D3
Brook La
Brookville IP26 99 A7
Burgate IP22 129 C3
Needham IP20 131 E8
St Margaret, Ilketshall
NR35 124 C3
Brook Pl NR1 178 B2
Brook Rd
Dersingham PE31 140 D2
Sheringham NR26 138 E6
Brooks Dr NR19 154 B4
Brookside NR20 49 E8
Brooks Mdw NR14 90 D5
Brooks Rd NR10 53 B3
Brook St
Buxton with Lammas
NR10 36 E1
Cromer NR27 139 C7
Lamas NR10 53 E8
BROOKVILLE IP26 99 A6
Brookwell Springs 1
PE32 44 B3
Broom Ave
Norwich NR6 158 A5
Norwich NR7 163 E8
Broom Cl
15 Martham NR29 57 D4
Norwich NR1 162 F3
Taverham NR8 155 C3
BROOME NR35 109 C2
Broome Gdns 2 NR31 94 A5
Broom Gn Dr NR20 32 E4
Broom Gn Rd NR20 32 E2
BROOM GREEN NR20 32 E2
BROOMHILL PE38 172 E7
Broomhill 1 NR27 10 B5
Broomhill La NR10 149 B3
Broom Hill La IP24 126 C3
BROOMHOLM NR12 23 E4
Broom La
Easton NR9 70 B5
Witton NR28 38 C8
Broom Rd
Lakenheath IP27 113 F1
Wymondham NR18 105 C6
BROOMSTHORPE PE31 30 C7
Broomsthorpe Rd PE31 30 A7
Brothercross Way PE38 172 C7
Browick Rd NR18 173 C4
Browick Rd Inf Sch
NR18 173 C3
Browne St 5 NR2 162 C7
Browning Pl PE30 147 A8
Brownsfield NR11 21 D8
Brownshill NR27 139 B4
Brown's La
Holme Hale IP25 65 F2
Mautby NR29 76 B7
Necton PE37 65 F3
Saxlingham Nethergate
NR15 107 B8
Brow of the Hill PE32 44 E6
BROWSTON GREEN NR31 94 C4
Browston Hall Leisure Ctr
NR31 94 C4
Browston La NR32 94 B3
Brummel Cl 1 PE30 147 C5
Brumstead Rd
Brumstead NR12 24 A1
Stalham NR12 39 A4
BRUNDALL NR13 165 D4
Brundall Gdns Sta NR13 165 A3
Brundall Low Rd NR13 72 F3
Brundall Prim Sch NR13 165 D3
Brundall Rd NR13 165 E4
Brundall Sta NR13 165 D2
BRUNDISH NR14 110 A6
Brundish Rd NR14 110 A6
Brunel Way IP24 176 B6
Brunswick Cl
Dereham NR19 154 C2
North Walsham NR28 151 D6
Brunswick Rd NR2 178 A1
Brunswick Terr NR27 139 C7
Brush Hill NR20 33 A6
Brushmakers Way IP22 177 C6
Brush Mdw La PE34 42 B7
Brussels Cl NR19 154 C2
Bryars La IP22 177 F3
Bryggen Rd PE30 146 F8
Bryony Cl 2 NR6 158 D5
Bryony Cour NR25 137 B7
Bryony Ct PE30 148 C3
Bryony Way 6 NR17 174 B5
Buccaneer Way 8 NR9 88 D8
Buck Courtney Cres NR6 158 A7
BUCKENHAM NR13 91 F8
Buckenham Cl
1 Fakenham NR21 141 C5
Swaffham PE13 153 B2
Buckenham Dr PE33 81 A2
Buckenham La NR13 73 F2
Buckenham Rd
Attleborough NR17 174 F3
Lingwood & Burlingham
NR13 74 A2
Strumpshaw NR13 73 F2
Buckenham Sta NR13 91 F8
Bucket Rd NR21 15 D2
Buckingham Cl PE30 148 C5
Buckingham Ct PE36 132 C5
Buckingham Dr 1 NR9 88 C7
Buckingham Rd NR4 161 F3
Buckingham Wlk PE13 152 D8
Buck La IP21 130 C4
Buckland Rise 8 NR4 161 F1
Buck's Heath La NR11 11 D1
Bucksholt Rd PE14 59 B7
Buck's La NR18 87 B3
Buckthorn Cl 3 NR8 155 B2
Buddell's La NR23 5 F2
Buggs Hole La IP22 128 A6
Bugg's Rd IP22 129 B2
Buildings Rd NR30 168 E4
Bullacebush La NR13 165 E7
Bullace Rd NR5 156 F2
Bullard Rd NR3 158 C3
Bull Cl
East Tuddenham NR20 69 C6
4 Holt NR25 137 B6
Norwich NR3 178 B4
Bull Cl La NR21 17 B3
Bull Cl Rd NR3 178 B4
Bullemer Cl 3 NR12 39 B4
Bullfinch Way 4 PE14 77 A8
Bullies Way 3 NR13 73 D6
Bull La NR1 178 A1
Bullman's Cross La NR20 69 A6
Bullock Fair Cl 14 IP20 122 D2
Bullock Hill NR10 53 E1
Bullock Rd PE34 144 B1
Bullockshed La NR14 91 A7
Bullocks Loke NR30 168 E4
Bulls Gn La NR34 110 D5
Bulls Gn Rd NR34 110 C6
BULL'S GREEN NR14 110 C5
Bull's La NR31 170 D6
Bull's Row NR27 11 A2
Bull St NR25 137 B6
Bulmer La NR29 58 B6
Bulmer Rd NR3 158 A2
Bulrush Ave 4 PE38 172 A6
Bulrush Cl
1 East Dereham NR19 154 C4
4 Horsford NR10 53 A3
Bulstrode Ave 4 NR19 154 D2
Bultitudes Loke NR30 168 E4
Bulwer Rd
East Dereham NR19 154 E7
Lamas NR10 36 E1
Bumstede Ct 5 NR5 161 A8
BUMWELL HILL NR16 105 E2
Bungalow La NR7 72 D3
BUNGAY NR35 124 A8
Bungaygrave La IP20 122 D6
Bungay High Sch NR35 124 A7
Bungay Rd
Bixley NR14 90 B8
Dickleburgh & Rushall
IP21 130 E5
Ellingham NR35 109 C4
Hempnall NR15 107 D5
Loddon NR14 109 C7
Poringland NR14 90 D4
Scole IP21 130 D5
Stockton NR34 109 F4
Thwaite NR35 109 A5
Bunkel Rd NR13 72 E8
BUNKER'S HILL
Lound NR32 94 C3
Norwich NR5 161 B7
Bunnett Ave PE30 146 D2
Bunnewell Ave NR31 170 A4
Bunn's Bank Rd
Attleborough NR17 174 F2
Old Buckenham NR17 104 D4
Bunn's La
Great Yarmouth NR31 169 C3
Starston IP20 122 C2
Bunting's La IP26 98 F5
Buntings The 15 NR31 94 C8
BUNWELL NR16 105 D4
BUNWELL BOTTOM
NR16 105 C6
Bunwell Hill NR16 105 D2
Bunwell Prim Sch NR16 105 D3
Bunwell Rd
Aslacton NR16 106 A2
Attleborough NR17 174 F6
Besthorpe NR17 104 F6
Bunwell St NR16 105 B5
Bunyan Cl 3 NR13 72 E4
Burch Cl PE30 147 E4
Burcroft Rd PE13 152 B6
Burdett Rd PE13 152 B4
Burdock Cl NR18 173 E4
Burdock La
Hockwold cum Wilton
IP26 113 C7
8 Wramplingham NR9 69 F2
Burdock Way 3 NR17 174 B4
Bure Cl
9 Belton NR31 94 A6
Caister-on-Sea NR30 168 D6
Great Yarmouth NR30 169 C6
4 King's Lynn PE30 147 E5
1 Watlington PE33 61 D6
Wroxham/Hoveton NR12 164 C5
Bure Marshes National
Nature Reserve★ NR13 55 E3
Bure Rd
Briston NR24 142 D4
1 Great Yarmouth NR30 169 C5
Bure Valley La NR11 150 E5
Bure Valley Sch NR11 150 C5
Bure Way NR11 150 C7
BURGATE IP22 129 C2
Burgate La NR14 90 E5
Burgess Cl NR30 168 D6
Burgess Rd NR3 158 B2
Burgess Way NR15 90 E2
Burgh Beck Rd NR24 142 B5
BURGH CASTLE NR31 94 A7
BURGH COMMON NR17 104 D5
Burgh Hall Leisure Ctr
NR31 94 B7
Burgh La NR20 68 F6
Burghley Rd PE30 148 E1
BURGH NEXT AYLSHAM
NR11 36 D4
Burgh Rd
Aylsham NR11 150 D6
Burgh St Peter NR34 111 C5
Great Yarmouth NR31 170 B7
BURGH ST MARGARET
(FLEGGBURGH) NR29 57 C1
BURGH ST PETER NR34 111 C4
BURGH STUBBS NR24 142 B8
Burghwood Dr PE32 48 D6
Burgh Wood Rd NR29 57 E1
Burhill Cl 3 NR4 89 D8
Burkitt St PE30 146 E6
Burleigh Cl 1 NR30 169 D2
Burley Rd NR12 38 A3
Burlingham Dr 2 NR33 111 F1
BURLINGHAM GREEN
NR13 74 A5
Burlingham Rd NR13 73 F6
Burlington Cl IP22 177 D1
Burma Cl PE31 140 C4
Burma Rd NR6 158 E5
Burnet Rd
Great Yarmouth NR31 94 C6
Norwich NR3 157 F1
Burney Rd PE30 146 D2
Burnham Ave PE30 147 C8
BURNHAM DEEPDALE
PE31 3 E6
BURNHAM MARKET
PE31 135 C3
Burnham Mkt Prim Sch
PE31 135 D4
BURNHAM NORTON
PE31 135 B6
BURNHAM OVERY STAITHE
PE31 135 E6
BURNHAM OVERY TOWN
PE31 135 E4
Burnham Rd
Docking PE31 134 E6
Downham Market PE38 172 B4
North Creake NR21 4 D2
Ringstead PE36 2 C3
South Creake NR21 15 D7
BURNHAM THORPE PE31 4 D4
Burns Cl
East Dereham NR19 154 C7
Thetford IP24 176 E6
Yaxley IP23 129 F1
Burnside 3 PE37 66 A4
Burnt Fen Turnpike
IP28 112 D2
Burnt Hill La NR33 111 F3
Burnt Hills NR27 139 B4
Burnthouse Cres PE33 63 B4
Burnthouse Dro PE33 63 C5
Burnthouse La
Hethersett NR9 160 C1
Runhall NR20 69 A4
Scole IP20 122 A1
Toft Monks NR34 110 D5
Wymondham NR18 173 F1
Burnt House Rd NR13 92 B6
Burnt La
Great Yarmouth NR31 170 C7
Wiggenhall St Mary Magdalen
PE34 61 A4
Burntoak La IP20 122 E4
Burnt St NR23 136 D5
Burntwood La NR12 54 C4
Burr Cl 14 IP25 84 E3
Burrell Cl NR25 137 D7
Burrell Way IP24 176 A1
Burrettgate Rd PE13 152 F5
Burrett Gdns PE13 59 C5
Burrett Rd PE13 59 C5
Burroughs Way NR18 173 D4
Burrow Dr IP27 113 E2
Burrows Gn NR34 110 F5
BURSTON IP22 120 F2
Burston Cl NR24 142 B4
Burston Com Prim Sch
IP22 120 E2
Burston Rd
Dickleburgh & Rushall
IP21 130 C8
Diss IP22 177 E7
Gissing IP22 120 F3
Burston Strike Sch★
IP22 120 E2
Burton Ave NR28 151 B4
Burton Cl
North Walsham NR28 151 B4
Norwich NR6 158 C5
Roydon IP22 177 B5
Burton Dr 9 NR13 72 E7
Burton Rd NR6 158 C5
Burtontyne Ave NR19 68 A7
Bury Bottom IP27 115 A1
Bury Rd
Botesdale IP22 128 F3
Brandon IP27 175 D2
Hepworth IP22 127 F1
Market Weston IP22 127 E4
Rickinghall Inferior IP22 128 D1
Thetford IP24 176 C1
Wortham IP22 129 C4
Bury St NR2 162 B4
Bush Cl PE31 140 E3
Bush Dr NR12 24 E4
Bush Est NR12 24 D4
BUSH GREEN IP21 122 A6
Bush La
Dereham NR20 68 B8
Wisbech PE13 152 E5
Bush Rd
Hemsby NR29 58 B5
Norwich NR6 157 F7
BUSHY COMMON NR19 67 B8
Bussey Rd NR6 158 D4
Bussey's La NR31 170 D5
Bussey's Loke
Great Yarmouth NR31 170 A5
Hempnall NR15 107 D5
BUSTARD'S GREEN
NR16 106 C3
Bustards' La PE14 41 F3
Butchers La PE31 3 B7
Butcher's La NR21 141 B4
Buttercup Cl 1 IP24 176 F5
Buttercup Dr 14 NR31 94 C6
Buttercup Way NR5 160 F6
Butter La NR14 92 D1

Buttermere **1** NR29..... 167 B7
Buttermere Rd **4** NR5.... 161 C6
Butter's Hall La IP24...... 102 C7
Butterwick **3** PE30 ..... 147 C5
Butt La
　Belton NR31............ 94 A6
　Litcham PE32........... 48 A4
Buttlands Cl NR21......... 6 E2
Buttland's La PE33 ...... 81 B8
Buttlands The
　Great Cressingham IP25... 83 C4
　Wells-next-the-Sea NR23. 136 D5
Buttle's La NR15...... 106 D3
Butts La NR26........... 138 B5
Butts The NR5........ 160 F8
BUXTON NR10............. 36 E1
Buxton Ave NR31......... 170 D1
Buxton Cl
　4 Cromer NR27..... 10 B5
　Easton NR9............ 70 A6
Buxton Prim Sch NR10 .. 36 F1
Buxton Rd
　Aylsham NR11.......... 150 D5
　Cawston NR10......... 35 D2
　Diss IP22............. 177 B4
　Frettenham NR12....... 53 F3
　Hainford NR10......... 53 F3
　Horstead with Stanninghall
　NR12................ 54 B6
　North Walsham NR28... 151 B4
　Norwich NR3.......... 162 D8
　Spixworth NR10....... 158 F8
Buxton Sta NR10........ 36 F2
Byfield Cl **3** NR3.... 158 C1
Byron Ave PE13......... 154 B7
Byron Rd
　Great Yarmouth NR30.. 169 E8
　Taverham NR8......... 156 D8
Byron Way NR30........ 168 D6
Byron Wlk **7** IP24... 176 E6

C

Cabbell Rd NR27......... 139 B7
Cabin Cl **11** NR33.... 111 F1
Cadamys Yd NR23...... 136 D5
Cadge Cl NR5......... 161 D7
Cadge Rd NR5......... 161 D6
Cadge's La NR9......... 86 B3
Cadiz Way NR31........ 171 E4
Cadman Way IP25....... 84 D3
Cadogan Rd NR27...... 139 B7
Caernarvon Rd NR2.... 162 B6
Cage La IP24.......... 176 D3
Cains The NR8......... 155 C2
Cairns Ct NR4......... 162 A3
Caister By-pass NR30.. 168 C4
Caister Castle Car
　Collection★
　NR30................ 168 A5
Caister High Sch NR30 . 168 E6
CAISTER-ON-SEA NR30 . 168 F6
Caister on Sea Fst & Mid
　Schs NR30........... 168 E5
Caister Rd NR30........ 169 C7
Caister Sands Ave NR30 168 E8
Caistor La
　Caistor St Edmund NR14... 89 F6
　Poringland NR14...... 90 B6
Caistor Roman Town★
　NR14................ 89 F6
Caithness Crystal Visitor
　Ctr★ PE30........... 146 F2
Caius Cl PE31......... 133 C5
Calamint Rd PE30..... 147 A8
Caledonian Way **1** NR31 . 94 A5
Caley Cl NR3.......... 157 F2
Caley St PE31......... 133 B2
Calf La NR10.......... 53 E2
CALIFORNIA NR29..... 167 E3
California Ave NR29... 167 E4
California Cotts NR23. 136 E5
California Cres NR29.. 167 F2
California Rd NR29.... 167 E2
Callowell La IP22..... 128 C1
CALTHORPE NR11..... 21 A2
Calthorpe Cl
　Acle NR13............ 166 B4
　2 Stalham NR12... 39 B4
Calthorpe Rd
　Ingham NR12.......... 39 D4
　Norwich NR5......... 161 B6
CALTHORPE STREET
　NR12................ 39 D4
Calvert St NR3........ 178 B4
Calves Well La
　Beeston Regis NR26... 138 F4
　Sheringham NR27.... 10 A3
Camargue Pl **4** NR21 . 152 E3
Cambell Dr NR20..... 50 B5
Camberley Rd NR4..... 162 A2
Cambers La PE31..... 135 D2
Camborne Cl NR5.... 157 C1
Cambridge Ave NR31.. 170 A3
Cambridge Dr PE13... 152 A6
Cambridge Rd PE30... 148 D5
Cambridge St
　Cromer NR27.......... 139 C7
　Norwich NR2......... 162 C4
Cambridge Way NR31.. 170 B3
Camden Pl **21** NR30... 169 D2
Camden Rd NR30...... 169 D2

Camelot Rd NR31...... 171 B8
Cameron Cl PE31...... 133 C4
Cameron Cres **4** PE31... 12 D4
Cameron Gn NR8...... 156 E8
Camfrey **6** PE30.... 147 B7
Campbell Cl PE36..... 132 D4
Campbell Ct **1** NR3.. 162 F8
Camp Cl **2** IP26.... 98 D1
Camperdown **11** NR30... 169 D2
Camp Gr NR1.......... 163 A6
Camping Cl NR10...... 68 F6
Camping Field La NR11... 39 B4
Campingland PE13..... 153 C4
Campion Ave NR11.... 170 B3
Campion Cl **4** NR28.. 151 E5
Campion Pl PE38..... 172 B3
Campion Rd
　1 Dereham NR20... 68 A8
　Thetford IP24........ 176 F4
Campion Way
　6 Attleborough NR17... 174 B4
　3 Sheringham NR26.. 138 B6
Camp La NR27........ 10 A4
Camp Rd NR8......... 155 C1
Campsey Rd PE38..... 97 B6
Canada Cl **6** PE31... 12 E5
Canada Rd NR27...... 139 B7
Canal Farm La NR28.. 38 C6
Canal St **6** PE13.... 152 C5
Canary Way NR1...... 163 A4
Canberra Rd IP25..... 84 F3
Candlemaker Workshop★
　NR29................ 75 A5
Candler's La **8** IP20.. 122 D2
Candle Stick NR9..... 69 A3
Candlestick La PE32.. 45 C8
CANDLE STREET IP22.. 128 D1
Canfor Rd **2** NR13... 72 E7
CANGATE NR12........ 55 C6
Cangate Rd NR12..... 55 C6
Cannell Gn NR3...... 178 C4
Cannell Rd **11** NR14.. 92 A1
Cannerby La NR7..... 159 B3
Cannon St PE13...... 152 C4
Cannon Terr **9** PE13.. 152 C5
Cann's La NR9........ 88 D7
Canon Cl **6** IP25.... 84 E3
Canon Hoare Rd NR11.. 150 C4
Canon Pickering VC Jun Sch
　IP20................ 122 D2
Canon Pott Cl PE31... 133 D6
Canons Cl **2** NR19... 154 D2
Canon's Cl IP24....... 176 B4
Canon Wake Ct **4** NR29.. 56 C8
Canterbury Inf Sch IP24.. 176 B4
Canterbury Pl NR2.... 162 C7
Canterbury Way NR11.. 176 B5
CANTLEY NR13......... 92 D7
Cantley Cnr NR13..... 74 B1
Cantley Fst Sch NR13.. 92 B7
Cantley La
　Cringleford NR4...... 89 A8
　Ketteringham NR18... 88 F6
Cantley Rd NR13...... 92 D7
Cantley Sta NR13..... 92 B6
Cants Cl **4** NR9..... 69 F2
Capgrave Ave PE30... 146 F8
Capps La IP21....... 123 F1
Capstan Way **9** NR33.. 111 F1
Captains Cl PE13..... 153 D4
Caraway Dr **22** NR29.. 94 C6
Caraway Rd IP24..... 176 F4
CARBROOKE IP25..... 85 B5
Carbrooke Rd
　Caston NR17........ 85 C1
　Griston IP25........ 85 A2
Cardiff Rd NR2...... 162 B5
Cardigan Pl NR2.... 162 C7
Cardinal Cl NR9.... 70 B5
Cardington Ct **1** NR13 . 166 D4
Cardington Rd IP25... 85 A3
Cardun Cl **3** NR13... 73 C6
Carey House Con Ctr
　PE37................ 65 D1
CARGATE COMMON
　NR16................ 105 E1
Cargate Comm Rd NR16. 105 E1
CARGATE GREEN NR13.. 166 A8
Cargate La
　Saxlingham Nethergate
　NR15................ 107 A8
　Upton with Fishley NR13.. 166 A8
Carl Cl **8** NR19.... 154 D1
Carl Cres NR28..... 22 E5
Carleton Ct **11** NR13.. 173 C6
CARLETON FOREHOE
　NR9................ 87 C8
Carleton Rd NR7.... 159 B3
CARLETON RODE CE Prim Sch
　NR16................ 105 C3
CARLETON ST PETER
　NR14................ 91 E5
Carlton Cl NR19..... 154 D4
Carlton Dr PE30..... 148 D5
Carlton Gdns NR1... 178 B1
Carlton Marshes Nature
　Reserve★ NR33...... 111 F3
Carlyle Rd NR1..... 162 F3
Carmelite Terr **10** PE30. 146 D4
Carmen's La NR28... 38 B3
Carn Cl NR13....... 74 B2
Carnoustie NR4..... 162 A1
Carnoustie Ct PE31.. 41 C8
Carola Sutton Crt NR25.. 137 B5
Carol Cl NR14....... 90 B5
Caroline Ct NR4..... 161 F4

Carpenters Cotts NR25 . 137 B6
Carpenter's La NR15... 121 D7
Carrell Rd NR31...... 170 B1
Carrington Rd NR27... 139 C5
Carr La
　Great Moulton NR15... 106 B1
　Hoveton NR12........ 164 F8
　Northrepps NR27..... 139 C1
　Overstrand NR27..... 11 A3
　Poringland NR14..... 90 C4
　Wendling NR19....... 66 F7
Carrow Abbey NR1.... 163 A3
Carrow Cl NR1....... 162 F3
Carrow Hill NR1..... 178 C1
Carrow Rd NR1...... 178 C1
Carrs Hill Cl NR8.... 157 A4
Carrs Rd NR3........ 92 A8
Carr Terr PE31...... 134 E5
Carshalton Rd **2** NR1 . 162 F3
Carter Cl
　Caister-on-Sea NR30.. 168 D8
　Swaffham PE37....... 153 C2
Carterford Dr NR6... 158 E3
Carter Rd NR8....... 157 A8
Carter's Cl PE30.... 148 B1
Carter's La NR20.... 50 A6
Carters Loke NR13... 166 C2
Car Gap Rd NR21.... 22 C4
Cartledge Cl **1** NR19. 154 D3
Cartmel **17** NR9... 88 D8
Carver's La NR27.... 174 B5
Casaubon Cl **8** NR19.. 154 D3
Caslon Cl **3** NR21.. 141 C5
Castelins Way **20** NR14 . 89 B3
Castell Rd NR19..... 154 D7
CASTLE ACRE PE32... 46 F2
Castle Acre Castle★ PE32 47 A2
Castle Acre CE VC Fst Sch
　PE32................ 46 F1
Castle Acre Cl **2** NR20.. 148 C3
Castleacre Rd
　Great Massingham PE32.. 29 D1
　Swaffham PE37...... 153 B8
Castle Cl
　3 Gresham NR11... 9 E1
　King's Lynn PE30.... 147 C8
　Weeting IP27........ 175 B8
Castle Drift PE32.... 48 C6
Castleford Cl IP24... 176 B4
Castle Gn NR31..... 170 B7
Castle La
　Bungay NR35....... 124 A8
　Thetford IP24....... 176 E3
　West Caister NR30... 168 B5
Castle Mdw NR1..... 178 B2
Castle Mkt St NR1... 178 B2
Castle Rd
　Mettingham NR35.... 124 D7
　Wormegay PE33..... 62 C6
Castle Rise NR8..... 155 E3
CASTLE RISING PE31.. 27 C3
Castle Rising Castle★
　PE31............... 27 C3
Castle Rising Rd PE31.. 148 D3
Castle Sq **18** PE13.. 152 C5
Castle St
　Norwich NR2....... 178 B3
　Thetford IP24....... 176 B4
　Wroxham/Hoveton NR12. 164 B3
Castleton Ave NR3.. 111 F1
Castleton Cl **1** NR5. 160 F8
Castleton Way IP23.. 130 A1
CASTON NR17....... 102 E8
Caston CE VA Prim Sch
　NR17............... 85 D5
Caston Cl **5** NR5.. 137 B6
Caston Rd NR7..... 163 F8
Catalpa Way **5** NR31. 170 B5
Catbridge La NR14.. 89 A4
Catchpole Wlk IP21.. 121 C1
CATFIELD NR29..... 56 C8
Catfield CE Fst Sch NR29. 56 C8
Catfield Rd NR29... 56 D6
Cathedral Dr NR20.. 49 E8
Cathedral St NR1... 178 C3
Catherine Howard Cl **3**
　IP24............... 176 D6
Catherine Wheel Opening **8**
　NR3............... 162 D8
Catling's La PE11... 41 A3
Catmere Herne NR14.. 89 A3
Cator Rd NR8...... 155 F1
Catriona Ct NR19... 8 B6
Cats Cnr NR10..... 37 B7
Cattle Mkt St **4** NR21. 141 C4
Catton Chase NR6.. 158 D5
Catton Ct NR6..... 158 E6
Catton Gr Fst Sch NR3. 158 C3
Catton Gr Mid Sch NR3. 158 C3
Catton Gr Rd NR3.. 158 D3
Catton View Ct NR3. 158 D3
Caudle Hill IP25.... 83 E1
CAUDLESPRINGS IP25. 85 A4
Caudwell Cl **2** NR14. 89 F4
Causeway Cl
　Brockdish IP21..... 131 C6
　Norwich NR2...... 162 C8
Causeway Dr **4** NR13. 74 A5
Causeway The
　Heigham Bridge NR29.. 57 A5
　Hickling NR12....... 39 F2
　Stow Bardolph PE34.. 61 D1
Cavalier Ct **30** NR7. 72 D4
Cavell Cl NR14..... 89 C5
Cavell Fst Sch NR1.. 162 E2
Cavell Rd NR1...... 162 E2
Cavendish Cl PE32.. 44 C3

Cavenham Rd PE33 .... 80 E4
Cave's Cl PE34...... 144 B5
Cavick Rd NR18..... 173 A3
Cawdor Cl NR17..... 174 E6
CAWSTON NR10..... 35 B2
Cawston La
　Great Witchingham NR9.. 51 E7
　Little Witchingham NR9.. 149 E1
Cawston Rd
　Aylsham NR11...... 150 A5
　Reepham NR10..... 149 D6
Cawstons Mdw **8** NR4. 90 C5
Cawston VC Prim Sch
　NR10............... 35 B2
Caxton Cl NR26..... 138 F5
Caxton Ct PE30..... 147 D4
Caxton Pk NR26..... 138 F5
Caxton Rd NR34.... 110 D1
Caxton Way IP24.... 176 A2
Caysteward NR10.... 168 E1
Cecil Cl **7** PE31... 61 D6
Cecil Gowing Ct NR27. 159 B4
Cecil Gowing Fst Sch
　NR7................ 159 C3
Cecil Rd
　East Dereham NR20.. 154 F5
　Norwich NR1....... 162 D3
Cedar Ave **4** NR10.. 54 A2
Cedar Cl
　1 Downham Market
　PE38............... 172 C6
　12 Great Yarmouth NR31.. 94 C7
　19 Martham NR29.. 57 D4
　12 Mattishall NR20.. 68 E6
　North Elmham NR20.. 49 E7
Cedar Ct
　North Walsham NR28.. 151 C5
　Wymondham NR18.. 173 D6
Cedar Dr
　Attleborough NR17.. 174 C4
　10 London NR14.. 92 A1
Cedar Gr
　North Runcton PE33.. 44 A3
　Sheringham NR26... 138 E5
Cedar Rd
　Hethersett NR9..... 88 C8
　Marham PE33...... 63 B4
　Norwich NR1...... 163 A5
Cedar Rise NR10.... 68 E6
Cedar Row PE30.... 147 B7
Cedar Springs PE31.. 133 B6
Cedars The
　Keswick NR12...... 23 F3
　Norwich NR2...... 162 B4
　Shepherd's Port PE31.. 12 B4
Cedar Way
　Brandon IP27...... 175 D2
　Brundall NR13..... 165 C3
　4 Gayton PE32.. 45 C6
　King's Lynn PE30.. 148 C4
Celandine Cl **2** IP24. 176 F5
Celandine La NR26.. 138 B6
Celandine Rd **4** NR17. 174 B4
Celia Phillips Cl **7** IP24.. 176 D7
Cemetery La NR18.. 173 B3
Cemetery Rd
　East Dereham NR19.. 154 E7
　Lakenheath IP27.... 113 E1
　Outwell PE14...... 78 A6
Centenary Way PE12.. 41 C6
Central Ave NR7.... 72 D3
Central Cl **1** NR9.. 88 D7
Central Cres **2** NR9. 88 D7
Central Dr NR20.... 50 A5
Central Rd
　Cromer NR27...... 139 A7
　King's Lynn PE30.. 146 D6
Centre Cres PE31.. 140 D3
Centre Point **6** PE30. 147 D5
Centre Vale PE31.. 140 D3
Centre Vale Rd PE31. 140 D3
Century Rd
　6 Eye IP23...... 130 C1
　Great Yarmouth NR31.. 169 B3
Century Way NR31.. 155 F3
Cere Rd NR7...... 159 C4
CESS NR29........ 57 C5
Cess Rd NR29..... 57 C5
Chadwick Sq **2** PE30. 147 A7
Chalfont Wlk NR4.. 161 E2
Chalfont Wlk **2** NR4. 83 C4
Chalk Hill Rd NR1.. 178 C3
Chalk La
　Culford IP31...... 125 C1
　Narborough PE32.. 63 E5
　North End NR16... 106 D2
　Sutton Bridge PE12. 41 C7
Chalkpit Rd PE31.. 3 A6
Chalk Pit Rd PE31. 140 E7
Chalk Rd
　Brandon IP27..... 114 D5
　8 Walpole St Andrew PE14 41 E4
Chalkrow La PE33.. 81 F4
Chamberlin Cl NR13. 158 E2
Chamberlin Ct NR13. 165 E6
Chamberlin Rd NR3. 158 B3
Chameryhall La NR11. 21 E6
Champney's Rd IP22. 177 E4
Chancel Ct NR13.. 165 C3
Chancellors Dr NR4. 161 C4
Chandler Rd NR14.. 89 F5
Chandlers Cl **2** NR18. 173 B3
Chandlers Ct NR8.. 89 C8
Chandlers Hill **4** NR18. 173 B3
Chandler's Hill La **1**
　NR18............. 173 B3
Changi Rd **5** IP25. 84 F3

Chantry Ct **8** PE37.. 65 F4
Chantry La PE37..... 66 A4
Chantry Rd NR2..... 178 A2
Chantry The NR2.... 178 A2
Chapel Ave NR15.... 106 E3
Chapel Bank PE36... 132 E6
Chapel Break Fst Sch
　NR5................ 160 F8
Chapel Break Rd NR5. 160 E7
Chapel Cl
　Barnham Broom NR9.. 69 C2
　Pulham Market IP21.. 121 E5
　Reepham NR10..... 149 B5
　Tacolneston NR16.. 105 F4
　Winfarthing IP22.. 120 B5
Chapel Cnr NR12.... 55 D6
Chapel Ct
　Blofield NR13...... 165 E6
　Norwich NR1...... 157 F5
CHAPEL FIELD NR22.. 39 A3
Chapel Field N NR2.. 93 A4
Chapelfield Cl **1** NR29.. 56 C8
Chapel Field E NR2.. 178 A2
Chapel Field N NR2. 178 A2
Chapel Field Rd
　Norwich NR2...... 178 A2
　Stalham NR12..... 39 A3
Chapel La
　Aldborough NR11.. 21 A5
　Ashby St Mary NR14.. 91 D5
　Barton Bendish PE33. 81 B8
　Beeston with Bittering PE32 48 C2
　Beetley NR20..... 49 C4
　Botesdale IP22.... 128 E2
　Burgate IP22..... 129 C3
　Coltishall NR12.. 54 D7
　East Dereham NR19. 154 D2
　Emneth PE14..... 59 B2
　Felthorpe NR10... 155 C8
　Fincham PE33.... 62 E1
　Foulsham NR20... 33 D3
　3 Great Yarmouth NR31. 94 C6
　Hempstead NR25.. 19 E8
　Hockering NR20.. 69 B8
　Hunstanton PE36. 132 C4
　Kirby Row NR35.. 109 E3
　Methwold IP26... 99 A5
　Necton PE37..... 66 A4
　Norwich NR7.... 163 E6
　Potter Heigham NR29.. 56 F7
　Ringstead PE36.. 2 E2
　Scarning NR19... 67 B7
　Sculthorpe NR21.. 16 B1
　Shelton NR15.... 107 B1
　Shotesham NR15.. 90 B2
　Skeyton NR10.... 37 B6
　West Caister NR30. 168 C4
　West Winch PE33. 43 E3
　Wimbotsham PE34.. 172 E8
　Wiveton NR25.... 7 E6
　Wymondham NR18. 173 A5
Chapel Loke
　Lessingham NR12.. 24 C2
　Salhouse NR13... 55 B1
　4 Stoke Holy Cross NR14. 89 F4
　Surlingham NR14. 73 B1
　Wymondham NR18. 105 A8
Chapel Mdw NR35. 109 E3
Chapel Rd
　Alby with Thwaite NR11.. 21 B3
　Ashby St Mary NR14.. 91 D5
　Attleborough NR17. 174 C5
　Beighton NR13.... 74 C2
　Boughton PE33... 81 A4
　Carleton Rode NR16. 105 C3
　Dersingham PE31.. 140 D4
　Dilham NR28..... 38 B3
　East Ruston NR12.. 38 E6
　Foxley NR20..... 50 D8
　Grimston PE32... 28 A5
　Guestwick NR20.. 33 F6
　Hainford NR10... 53 E5
　Halvergate NR13.. 75 A2
　Lingwood NR13... 73 F3
　Longham NR19... 49 A2
　Lowestoft NR33.. 111 F1
　Morley NR18..... 87 B2
　Neatishead NR12.. 55 E6
　Necton PE37..... 66 B4
　Norwich NR5.... 157 A2
　Paston NR28.... 143 D1
　Roughton NR11... 21 D8
　Roydon PE32.... 45 A8
　Scole IP21...... 121 B1
　Sea Palling NR12.. 40 A6
　Southrepps NR11.. 22 B6
　St Andrew, Ilketshall NR34 124 C1
　Swafield NR28... 22 D3
　Terrington St Clement
　PE34............ 144 B5
　Upton with Fishley NR13.. 166 B8
　Wisbech PE13... 152 B5
　Woodton NR35... 108 C4
　Wymondham NR18. 105 A8
Chapel Rd Specl Sch
　NR17............ 174 C5
Chapel Rise **11** PE33.. 63 B4
Chapel St
　Barford NR5..... 70 A3
　Cawston NR10... 35 B3
　3 Cromer NR27. 139 B7
　Diss IP22....... 177 D4
　6 Hingham NR9. 86 C5
　Ixworth NR9.... 69 F2
　King's Lynn PE30. 146 D5
　3 Old Buckenham NR16.. 104 F1
　Rocklands NR17.. 103 B8
　Shipdham IP25... 67 C2

Chapel St continued
Warham NR23 . . . . 6 A4
14 Wisbech PE13 . . . . 152 C4
Chapel Terr PE30 . . . . . . 148 B1
Chapel Wlk 4 NR19 . . . 154 E5
Chapel Yd
Ashill IP25 . . . . 84 A7
Wells-next-the-Sea NR23 . 136 C6
Chapman Ave NR30 . . . . 168 E5
Chapmans Cl 17 NR26 . 138 D7
Chapnall Cl PE13 . . . . . . 152 F6
Chapnall Rd PE13 . . . . . 152 F6
Chappshill Way 22 NR14 . . 89 B3
Chare Rd IP31 . . . . 127 B1
Charing Cross NR2 . . . . 178 A3
Charles Ave
Norwich NR7 . . . . 163 F8
Watton IP25 . . . . 84 D3
Charles Burrell High Sch
IP24 . . . . 176 C1
Charles Burrell Mus★
IP24 . . . . 176 C1
Charles Burton Cl 5
NR30 . . . . 168 D7
Charles Cl
Acle NR13 . . . . 166 B4
Caister-on-Sea NR30 . . 168 E5
Cromer NR27 . . . . 10 C4
Dereham NR19 . . . . 154 C1
Wroxham/Hoveton NR12 . 164 C3
Charles Ewing Cl NR11 . 150 B5
Charles Jewson Ct NR6 . 158 B2
Charles Rash Cl NR28 . . 37 B8
Charles Rd
Fakenham NR21 . . . . 141 C6
Holt NR25 . . . . 137 C5
Hunstanton PE36 . . . . . 132 C4
5 Sutton Bridge PE12 . . 41 B8
Charles Sq 6 NR2 . . . . . 162 C6
Charles St
Great Yarmouth NR30 . 169 D2
King's Lynn PE30 . . . . . . 146 E4
11 Wisbech PE13 . . . . . . 152 C4
Charles Watling Way 1
NR5 . . . . 160 E8
Charles Wood Rd NR19 . 154 F2
Charlock PE30 . . . . 147 A8
Charlock Dr 8 NR26 . . . 138 B6
Charlotte's Cl 1 NR27 . . 9 F5
Charlton Rd NR1 . . . . . . 178 B4
Charmbeck Pk NR10 . . . 52 D8
Charolais Cl NR14 . . . . . 163 B2
Charter Cl NR31 . . . . . . 170 B4
Chartwell Ct NR7 . . . . . 158 F3
Chartwell Rd NR6 . . . . . 158 F3
Chase Ave PE30 . . . . 146 E3
Chase Cl NR6 . . . . 158 D5
Chase Ct
East Dereham NR19 . . . 154 D6
Thetford IP24 . . . . 176 B3
Chase St PE13 . . . . 152 C6
Chase The
Brandon IP27 . . . . 175 E2
Brundall NR13 . . . . 165 F6
Stow Bardolph PE34 . . 78 E7
Upwell PE14 . . . . 77 D3
Walpole St Andrew PE14 . . 41 E4
Wisbech PE13 . . . . 152 C5
Chatham Rd 1 IP31 . . . 126 B1
Chatham St NR3 . . . . 178 A4
Chatsworth Rd PE36 . . 132 C3
Chaucer Cl 14 NR20 . . . 50 E7
Chaucer Rd NR30 . . . . . . 169 D8
Checker St PE30 . . . . 146 E3
CHEDGRAVE NR14 . . . . . 92 A2
Cheese Hill 9 NR16 . . . 118 C5
Chenery Dr NR7 . . . . 133 D4
Chenery Cres PE31 . . . . 133 D4
Cheney Hill PE31 . . . . . . 133 D4
Cheney's La NR16 . . . . . 105 F5
Chepore La NR18 . . . . . . 87 C1
Chequers Cl
Briston NR24 . . . . 142 E3
2 Long Stratton NR15 . 106 D3
1 Roydon PE22 . . . . 28 A1
Chequers La
Bressingham IP22 . . . . . 129 B7
Burston & Shimpling IP22 . 120 E4
Great Ellingham NR17 . . 103 E8
Gressenhall NR20 . . . . . 49 B4
North Runcton PE33 . . . 44 A2
Saham Toney IP25 . . . . . 84 C5
West Winch PE33 . . . . . . 43 F3
Chequer's La NR15 . . . . 107 D8
Chequers Rd
Roydon PE32 . . . . 28 A1
Tharston & Hapton NR15 . 106 D3
Wroxham PE33 . . . . 80 E3
Chequers St
Docking PE31 . . . . 134 D4
East Ruston NR12 . . . . . 38 F5
Gresham NR11 . . . . 9 E1
Cherry Cl
11 Great Yarmouth NR31 . . 94 C7
Marham PE33 . . . . 63 A4
Norwich NR1 . . . . 162 E3
Cherry Dr NR19 . . . . 154 F5
Cherry Drift NR19 . . . . 154 E6
Cherry La
Belton with Browston
NR31 . . . . 94 A4
Dereham NR20 . . . . 68 B7
Cherry Orch NR20 . . . . 154 F5
Cherry Rd
Great Yarmouth NR31 . 170 B6
Wisbech PE13 . . . . 152 C8
Cherry Tree Ave 22 NR5 . . 57 D4
Cherrytree Cl PE31 . . . 133 D6

Cherry Tree Cl
Holt NR25 . . . . 137 B7
Mundford IP26 . . . . 100 A4
North Lopham IP22 . . . . 119 A2
Wretham IP24 . . . . 102 B1
Cherry Tree Ct IP22 . . 177 C5
Cherry Tree Dr PE34 . . 146 C4
Cherry Tree La NR18 . . 151 B5
Cherry Tree Rd
Carleton Rode NR16 . . . 105 A1
Plumstead NR11 . . . . . . 20 A8
Snettisham PE31 . . . . . . 12 C5
Tibenham NR16 . . . . 120 B7
Cherrywood
Alpington NR14 . . . . 90 F4
16 Redenhall with Harleston
IP20 . . . . 122 D1
Cherrywood Ave NR11 . . 15 C2
Chervil Wlk IP24 . . . . . . 116 D2
Cherwell Way 2 NR1 . . 170 B2
Chesterfield Cotts 11
NR27 . . . . 139 B7
Chester Pl NR2 . . . . 162 C6
Chester St NR2 . . . . 162 C4
Chester Way IP24 . . . . . 176 A4
Chestnut Ave
Great Yarmouth NR31 . 170 A5
North Walsham NR28 . 151 E4
Sculthorpe Airfield NR21 . . 15 C2
1 Spixworth NR10 . . . . 54 A2
Welney PE14 . . . . 95 D5
West Winch PE33 . . . . . 43 E1
Chestnut Cl
Brandon IP27 . . . . 175 E2
Dersingham PE31 . . . . . 140 E3
East Dereham NR19 . . . 154 E1
Norwich NR5 . . . . 156 E2
5 Watlington PE33 . . . 61 D5
Chestnut Ct 9 NR2 . . . 178 A3
Chestnut Gr NR26 . . . . 138 D4
Chestnut Hill 3 NR4 . . 161 F1
Chestnut Loke NR15 . . 107 A6
Chestnut Rd
Dickleburgh IP21 . . . . . 121 C1
East Dereham NR19 . . . 154 C5
Pulham St Mary IP21 . . 121 F4
5 Snettisham PE31 . . . 12 E4
13 Tasburgh NR15 . . . . 106 F6
8 Watton IP25 . . . . 84 E3
8 Wisbech PE13 . . . . . . 152 A5
Chestnuts The IP22 . . . 128 E2
Chestnut Terr PE12 . . . 41 B8
Chestnut Wlk PE37 . . . 81 F8
Chew Ct NR30 . . . . 147 E8
Cheyham Mount NR4 . . 161 F1
Cheyney Ave 1 NR13 . . 55 A1
CHICKERING IP21 . . . . . 131 D3
Chickering Rd IP21 . . . 131 B2
Childs Rd NR9 . . . . 168 A8
Childs Way NR26 . . . . . . 138 C5
Chiltern Cres PE14 . . . 152 D7
Chilver House La PE32 . . 44 E7
Chilvers Pl IP31 . . . . 133 D5
Chimes Way NR10 . . . . . 149 B4
Chimney Springs NR9 . . 167 A3
Chimney St PE32 . . . . . . 46 F1
Chipperfield Rd NR7 . . 159 E1
Chittock Cl 5 NR10 . . . 54 A1
Cholmondeley Way 3
PE33 . . . . 43 F2
Choseley Ct NR18 . . . . 173 C4
Choseley Rd
Docking PE31 . . . . 134 C7
Thornham PE36 . . . . 2 D6
CHRISTCHURCH PE14 . . 95 A7
Christchurch Rd NR2 . . 162 A4
Christ Church Rd NR1 . . 170 A4
Christie Cl 8 NR19 . . . . 154 D1
Christine Ave NR13 . . . 74 A2
Christine Rd 1 NR10 . . 54 A1
Christopher Cl
3 Newton Flotman NR15 . . 89 D1
8 Norwich NR1 . . . . 162 E2
Christopher Dr PE13 . . 152 A7
Church Alley NR13 . . . . 165 E6
Church Ave
Croxton IP24 . . . . 116 C5
Halvergate NR13 . . . . . . 74 F1
Little Ellingham NR17 . . 86 A1
Norwich NR4 . . . . 162 B3
Norwich NR4 E NR2 . . 162 B3
Church Bank
Marshland St James PE14 . 60 C2
Terrington St Clement
PE34 . . . . 144 B6
Church Cl
Antingham NR28 . . . . . 22 B3
5 Bawdeswell NR20 . . 50 E7
Beeston Regis NR27 . . . 9 F5
Bixley NR14 . . . . 90 B7
Brandon IP27 . . . . 175 B3
Caister-on-Sea NR30 . . 168 D5
Cantley NR13 . . . . 92 C7
Colby NR11 . . . . 36 D8
6 Coltishall NR12 . . . . 54 C6
Grimston PE32 . . . . 28 B8
Hepworth IP22 . . . . 127 E1
1 Horstead with Stanninghall
NR12 . . . . 54 C6
King's Lynn PE34 . . . . . 146 C4
Lamas NR10 . . . . 36 F1
13 Loddon NR14 . . . . . 92 A2
2 Norwich NR2 . . . . . . 162 B8
Overstrand NR27 . . . . . 11 A3
Pentney PE32 . . . . 63 C8
Poringland NR14 . . . . . 90 C4
Pulham St Mary IP21 . . 122 A4
1 Roydon IP22 . . . . 129 D7

Church Cl continued
Sea Palling NR12 . . . . . 40 B5
Shipdham IP25 . . . . 67 B2
South Walsham NR13 . . 74 A8
Upper Sheringham NR26 . 138 A4
Walpole St Andrew PE14 . . 41 E4
Whissonsett NR20 . . . . 31 D2
Wiggenhall St Mary Magdalen
PE34 . . . . 61 B6
Wortwell IP20 . . . . 122 F3
Church Cotts NR19 . . . 48 E3
Church Crofts PE31 . . . 27 C3
Church Dam NR13 . . . . 93 A5
Church Dro PE14 . . . . . . 77 F6
CHURCH END PE14 . . . . 41 F2
Church End IP27 . . . . . . 175 B3
Church Farm Cl
Palgrave NR22 . . . . 177 C2
1 Weybourne NR25 . . . 8 F5
Church Farm Cres NR29 . 167 B6
Church Farm La NR19 . 154 C5
Church Farm Rare Breeds
Ctr★ NR18 . . . . 79 F8
Church Farm Rd PE31 . 133 F7
Churchfarm Wlk PE33 . 62 E1
Church Field 4 NR4 . . . 89 B8
Churchfield Gn 3 NR7 . . 163 D8
Churchfield Rd 8 PE14 . . 77 F6
Churchfields NR8 . . . . . 188 D8
Churchfields Rd NR15 . 106 F4
Church Gate 16 PE12 . . 41 B8
Churchgate St 2 PE38 . 97 B5
Churchgate Way PE34 . 144 C5
Church Gdns IP31 . . . . 127 C3
Church Gn
Norwich NR7 . . . . 159 B5
West Acre PE32 . . . . 46 B2
Church Hill
Banham NR16 . . . . 119 D7
Beighton NR13 . . . . 74 C3
Hoxne IP21 . . . . 131 A4
Reepham NR10 . . . . 149 C3
Saxlingham Nethergate
NR15 . . . . 107 B8
Starston IP20 . . . . 122 C3
Church Hill Fst Sch PE32 . . 45 C8
Church Hill Sch NR16 . 119 D7
Churchill Cl
Hevingham NR10 . . . . . 53 B8
1 Watton IP25 . . . . 84 D3
Churchill Cres
Fincham PE33 . . . . 62 E1
Sheringham NR26 . . . . 138 B5
Churchill Ct NR19 . . . . 154 D4
Churchill Pl NR15 . . . . 90 F2
Churchill Rd
Great Yarmouth NR30 . 169 D6
Norwich NR3 . . . . 162 E8
Thetford IP24 . . . . 176 E5
Wisbech PE13 . . . . 152 D4
Churchill Way PE38 . . 172 B4
Church La
Aldeby NR34 . . . . 110 F5
Aldeby, Wheatacre, Burgh St
Peter NR34 . . . . 111 B3
Antingham NR28 . . . . . 22 B3
Ashwellthorpe NR16 . . 106 A7
Baconsthorpe NR25 . . . 19 F7
Bacton NR28 . . . . 23 C3
Barford NR9 . . . . 69 F3
Barnham IP24 . . . . 125 F6
Barton Bendish PE33 . . 81 A5
Belaugh NR12 . . . . 54 E5
Billith with Browston NR31 94 A5
Billingford NR20 . . . . . 50 B7
Bintree NR20 . . . . 33 B2
Bircham PE31 . . . . 14 B3
Blo' Norton IP22 . . . . . . 128 B6
Boughton PE33 . . . . . . 80 F5
Bracon Ash NR14 . . . . 88 F3
Bradenham IP25 . . . . . 66 D4
Bressingham IP22 . . . . 129 B7
Briningham NR24 . . . . 18 D5
Briston NR24 . . . . 142 E4
Brockdish IP21 . . . . 131 C6
Broome NR35 . . . . 109 B3
Bunwell NR16 . . . . 105 D3
Burgh & Tuttington NR11 . . 36 D4
Claxton NR14 . . . . 91 C5
Cley next the Sea NR25 . . 7 E6
Corton NR32 . . . . 171 F1
Cranworth IP25 . . . . . . 85 F7
Deopham NR18 . . . . . . 86 F4
Dersingham PE31 . . . . . 140 E3
Ditchingham NR35 . . . 108 F3
Easton NR9 . . . . 70 B6
East Tuddenham NR20 . . 69 C6
East Walton PE32 . . . . 45 E3
East Winch PE32 . . . . . 44 F2
Felthorpe NR10 . . . . . . 155 D7
Filby NR29 . . . . 75 E8
Fleggburgh NR29 . . . . 57 A1
Frettenham NR12 . . . . 54 A5
Fritton & St Olaves NR31 . . 93 F3
Great Massingham PE32 . . 29 D1
Great Yarmouth NR31 . 170 C5
Gresham NR11 . . . . 9 E1
Gressenhall NR20 . . . . 49 C2
Guestwick NR20 . . . . . 33 F6
Haddiscoe NR14 . . . . . . 110 E7
Hales NR14 . . . . 109 F7
Harpley PE31 . . . . 29 C5
Heacham PE31 . . . . 133 E6
Heckingham NR14 . . . . 92 E1
Hemblington NR13 . . . 73 F6
Hepworth IP22 . . . . 127 E1
Hevingham NR10 . . . . 36 B1
Hindolveston NR20 . . 33 C8

Church La continued
Hockwold cum Wilton
IP26 . . . . 114 A6
Holme NR6 . . . . 15 F2
Holme Hale PE37 . . . . 65 F2
Ilworth NR9 . . . . 69 E2
Ketteringham NR18 . . 88 E5
King's Lynn PE30 . . . . . 146 E4
Langley with Hardley NR14 . 92 C3
Lessingham NR12 . . . . 24 E3
Leziate PE32 . . . . 44 F4
Little Ellingham NR17 . . 86 A1
Little Massingham PE32 . . 29 C2
Long Stratton NR15 . . 106 F4
Lound NR32 . . . . 171 A3
Marham PE33 . . . . 63 A4
Marlingford NR9 . . . . . 69 E4
Marsham NR10 . . . . . . 36 B2
Mattishall NR20 . . . . . 68 F6
Mautby NR29 . . . . 75 D5
Morley NR18 . . . . 87 A3
Mundesley NR11 . . . . . 143 C6
Mundford IP26 . . . . . . 100 B4
Neatishead NR12 . . . . 55 E6
North Elmham NR20 . 49 E8
Northwold PE33 . . . . . 81 B2
Norwich NR4 . . . . 161 E1
Norwich NR7 . . . . 159 C5
Old Buckenham NR17 . . 104 D2
Oulton NR11 . . . . 35 C7
Potter Heigham NR29 . . 56 F7
Redenhall with Harleston
IP20 . . . . 122 E3
Rickinghall Superior IP22 . 128 E1
Roydon PE32 . . . . 27 F2
Runcton Holme PE33 . 61 D4
Runhall NR9 . . . . 87 A8
Runhall NR20 . . . . 69 A6
Sheringham NR26 . . . . 138 F6
Shipdham IP25 . . . . 67 B2
Shouldham Thorpe PE33 . . 62 B3
South Creake NR21 . . 14 D7
4 Southery PE38 . . . . . 97 B5
Sparham NR9 . . . . 51 B6
Spixworth NR10 . . . . . 53 F2
Sprowston NR7 . . . . . . 159 E5
Stanfield NR20 . . . . . . 48 F8
Stanhoe PE31 . . . . 14 E7
St Mary, South Elmham
otherwise Homersfield
IP20 . . . . 123 B4
Stuston IP21 . . . . 130 B4
Surlingham NR14 . . . . 73 A1
Sustead NR11 . . . . 21 B8
Swannington NR9 . . . . 52 B6
Swanton Abbott NR10 . . 37 C5
Terrington St John PE14 . . 42 B2
Thelnetham IP22 . . . . . 128 B5
Thompson IP24 . . . . . . 102 C7
Thwaite NR35 . . . . 109 A6
Tibenham NR16 . . . . . . 120 E8
Tilney All Saints PE34 . 42 E4
Tittleshall PE32 . . . . . . 48 B8
Tivetshall St Mary NR15 . . 121 B4
Tunstead NR12 . . . . . . 37 F1
Watlington PE33 . . . . . 61 C6
Weasenham All Saints PE32 47 C8
Wicklewood NR18 . . . 87 B5
Winfarthing IP22 . . . . . 120 B4
Wood Dalling NR11 . . 34 B5
Wormegay PE33 . . . . . 62 D6
Wroxham/Hoveton NR12 . 164 B3
Yaxham NR19 . . . . 68 A5
Church Lanes NR21 . . 141 B5
Church Loke NR11 . . . 21 D7
Churchman Rd NR7 . . 159 C2
Church Marsh Nature
Reserve★ NR14 . . . . . . 73 A1
Church Mdw
Rickinghall Inferior IP22 . 128 D2
Yelverton NR14 . . . . . . 90 E5
Church Mdw La NR14 . . 90 F4
Church Mews PE13 . . 152 C5
Church of the Holy
Sepulchre (rems)★
IP20 . . . . 176 B4
Church Path PE33 . . . 80 E2
Church Pl PE13 . . . . . . 134 D5
Church Plain
14 Great Yarmouth
NR30 . . . . 169 C4
Wells-next-the-Sea NR23 . 136 C5
Church Rd
Alburgh IP20 . . . . 122 F6
Alpington NR14 . . . . . . 90 F4
Aslacton NR15 . . . . 106 A2
Aylmerton NR11 . . . . . 10 A3
Bacton NR12 . . . . 23 D4
Barningham IP31 . . . . . 127 C3
Barton Bendish PE33 . . 81 B8
Barton Turf NR12 . . . . 55 E8
Beeston with Bittering PE32 48 B2
Beetley NR20 . . . . 49 B4
Bergh Apton NR15 . . . 91 A3
Bintree NR20 . . . . 33 B2
Brandon IP27 . . . . 175 B3
Bridgham NR16 . . . . . . 118 B5
Brockdish IP21 . . . . 131 C6
Brundall NR13 . . . . 165 E5
Burgh Castle NR31 . . 93 F8
Catfield NR29 . . . . 56 C8
Christchurch PE14 . . . 95 A7
Clenchwarton PE34 . 145 D5
Colby NR11 . . . . 36 D8
Colkirk NR21 . . . . 31 D5
Crimplesham PE33 . . 80 B6
Denham IP21 . . . . 131 A1

Church Rd continued
Deopham NR18 . . . . . . 86 E3
Dickleburgh & Rushall
IP21 . . . . 130 D8
Dilham NR28 . . . . 38 C4
Downham Market PE38 . 172 C5
Earsham NR35 . . . . 123 F7
Ellingham NR35 . . . . . . 109 D3
Elm PE14 . . . . 77 B7
Elsing NR20 . . . . 50 E2
Felmingham NR28 . . . 37 B7
Flitcham PE31 . . . . 28 C5
Flixton NR35 . . . . 123 E5
Fordham PE38 . . . . 79 B1
Freethorpe NR13 . . . . 92 F8
Frettenham NR10 . . . 53 F4
Garboldisham IP22 . . 128 A8
Gillingham NR34 . . . . . 110 C3
Great & Little Plumstead
NR13 . . . . 73 A4
Great Yarmouth NR31 . 170 C7
Griston IP25 . . . . 85 A1
Haddiscoe NR14 . . . . . 110 E8
Hardingham NR9 . . . . 86 D7
Hedenham NR35 . . . . . 108 E4
Hilgay PE38 . . . . 79 E1
Hoe NR20 . . . . 49 F6
Holme Hale PE31 . . . . 66 A2
Honington IP31 . . . . . . 126 D1
Horning NR12 . . . . 55 F3
Hunstanton PE36 . . . . 132 F7
Itteringham NR11 . . . 20 C2
Ketteringham NR18 . . 88 D5
Kirby Cane NR35 . . . . 110 D5
Kirstead NR15 . . . . 90 F1
Leverington PE13 . . . . 152 F7
Lingwood & Burlingham
NR13 . . . . 73 F3
Little Barningham NR11 . . 20 C4
Market Weston IP22 . 127 E4
Marlingford NR9 . . . . 70 A3
Neatishead NR12 . . . . 55 E6
Newton Flotman NR15 . . 89 C1
North Lopham IP22 . . 119 A1
Norton Subcourse NR14 . . 92 E1
Ovington IP25 . . . . 84 E5
Postwick with Witton NR13 . 72 F3
Potter Heigham NR29 . . 56 F6
Quidenham NR16 . . . . 118 F8
Reedham NR13 . . . . . . 92 F3
Repps with Bastwick NR29 . . 57 A4
Runhall NR9 . . . . 69 A1
Sea Palling NR12 . . . . 40 A5
Shelfanger IP22 . . . . . . 120 B2
Shouldham PE33 . . . . 62 E3
Shropham NR17 . . . . . 103 B3
Sisland NR14 . . . . 91 D1
Somerton NR29 . . . . . 57 F6
South Lopham IP22 . . 128 D8
Stockton NR34 . . . . 109 F5
Stoke Ferry PE33 . . . . 80 E2
Strumpshaw NR13 . . 91 F8
Sutton NR12 . . . . 39 C3
Swafield NR28 . . . . . . 22 C4
Swainsthorpe NR14 . . 89 D5
Tasburgh NR15 . . . . . . 106 F6
Terrington St John PE14 . . 42 B1
Tharston & Hapton NR15 . . 106 D3
Thompson IP24 . . . . . . 102 B7
Thurlton NR14 . . . . 92 F1
Thurne NR29 . . . . 56 E2
Tibenham NR16 . . . . . . 120 E8
Tilney All Saints PE34 . 144 F1
Tilney St Lawrence PE34 . . 42 D2
Toft Monks NR34 . . . . 110 D6
Topcroft NR35 . . . . 107 F3
Tunstead NR12 . . . . . . 55 B8
Upton with Fishley NR13 . 166 A6
Wacton NR15 . . . . 106 C2
Walpole St Andrew PE14 . . 41 E3
Walsingham NR22 . . . 16 F8
Watlington PE34 . . . . 61 C6
Watton IP25 . . . . 84 E3
Wellingham PE32 . . . 30 E1
Wereham PE33 . . . . . . 80 E4
West Beckham NR25 . . 9 C2
West Dereham PE33 . 80 B4
Wheatacre NR34 . . . . . 111 A5
Whinburgh & Westfield
NR19 . . . . 68 A3
Wiggenhall St Germans
PE34 . . . . 61 A8
Wimbotsham PE34 . . 172 E8
Wingfield IP21 . . . . 131 E3
Woodton NR35 . . . . . . 108 B5
Wortham IP22 . . . . 129 C5
Wreningham NR16 . . 88 E1
Wroxham/Hoveton NR12 . 164 D5
Yelverton NR14 . . . . . . 90 F5
Church Rd N IP21 . . . . 131 C7
Church St
Ashill IP25 . . . . 84 A7
Attleborough NR17 . . 174 D5
Bawburgh NR9 . . . . . . 160 A6
Barnham IP25 . . . . 66 D4
Brisley NR20 . . . . 49 A8
Briston NR24 . . . . 142 E4
Carbrooke IP25 . . . . . 85 A5
Carleton Rode NR16 . . 54 C6
Cromer NR27 . . . . 139 C6
Diss IP22 . . . . 177 D4
East Dereham NR19 . 154 D5
Elsing NR20 . . . . 50 F3
Gimingham NR11 . . . 22 E7

Church St continued
Great Ellingham NR17....103 E7
29 Harleston IP20.......122 D2
Hingham NR9.............86 C5
Holt NR25...............137 C6
Horsford NR10...........53 B2
Hunstanton PE36.........132 C4
Kenninghall NR16........119 B4
King's Lynn PE30........146 D4
Litcham PE32............45 A4
Little Walsingham NR22...16 F7
New Buckenham NR16....104 F1
North Creake NR21.......15 DB
Northrepps NR27.........11 A2
11 North Walsham NR28..151 D5
Norwich NR6.............158 E5
Plumstead NR11..........149 C4
Reepham NR10...........149 C4
Sheringham NR26.........138 D7
Southrepps NR11.........22 B7
Stiffkey NR23.............6 D6
15 Sutton Bridge PE12...41 B8
Thornham PE36............2 D6
Trimingham NR11.........11 D1
Wells-next-the-Sea NR23.136 D5
Wymondham NR18........173 B4
Church Terr
5 Outwell PE14..........77 F6
21 Wisbech PE13.........152 C5
Wroxham NR12...........164 B3
Church View
Harleston IP20...........122 E2
Marham PE33............63 B4
Ormesby St Margaret
  NR29.................167 B2
Pentney PE32............63 CB
Church View Cl
Norwich NR7.............159 B5
Reedham NR13...........93 A5
Church View Ct NR7.....159 B5
Churchway IP22..........128 F5
Church Wlk
Burnham Market PE31....135 B2
Great Yarmouth NR31.....94 C6
Shelfanger IP22.........120 B2
Cider Cl NR17...........174 E4
Cinder La..............111 B4
Cintra Rd NR1...........163 B6
Cirrus Way NR7..........159 C2
City Coll Norwich NR2...178 A2
City of Norwich Aviation
  Mus★ NR6.............53 D1
City of Norwich Sch NR4 162 B2
City View Rd NR6........158 A4
Civic Gdns NR3..........158 B3
Civray Ave PE36.........172 C6
Clabburn Cl 8 NR15......99 C1
Clabon Fst Cl NR3.......158 F2
Clabon Rd NR3...........158 F2
Clabon Second Cl NR3...158 F3
Clabon Third Cl NR3.....158 F3
Clackclose Com Prim Sch
  PE38.................172 B5
Clackclose Rd PE38......172 C6
Clancy Rd NR7...........159 C1
Clapper La PE34..........49 E5
Clare Ave NR31..........170 B2
Clare Cl NR3............158 E1
Claremont Rd
Norwich NR4.............162 A2
Wisbech PE13...........152 C5
Clarence Ct
Hunstanton PE36.........132 C6
14 Watton IP25..........84 D3
Clarence Rd
14 Great Yarmouth
  NR30.................169 D2
Hunstanton PE36.........132 D6
Norwich NR1.............163 A5
Wisbech PE13...........152 D6
Clarendon Ct 8 NR29....169 D2
Clarendon Dr **10** NR29...57 D4
Clarendon Rd
Norwich NR2.............162 C5
Sculthorpe NR21.........141 A5
Clarendon Stps **1** NR2..162 B5
Clare Rd
Cromer NR27............139 C6
King's Lynn PE30........148 C3
Clare Sch NR4...........162 A3
Clarke Cl IP22...........177 C1
Clarke Rd NR3...........162 DB
Clarke's Cl 2 NR9.......69 F2
Clarke's La
Barsham NR34...........124 F7
Gooderstone PE33........82 A5
Clarkes Rd NR30.........169 B5
Clarke's Yd NR31........170 C5
Clark Rd NR35...........109 B2
Clark's La NR21..........17 E5
Clark's Loke **7** NR13...73 D6
Clarkson Ave NR13......152 D5
Clarkson Ct PE13........152 D6
Clarkson Inf Sch The
  PE13.................152 E6
Clarkson Rd
16 Harleigh NR13........74 A3
Norwich NR5.............161 C7
CLAXTON NR14...........91 D6
Claxton Cl
Mileham PE32............48 D6
6 Thetford IP24........176 C4
Claxton Cnr NR14........91 C6
Claydon Gr NR31.........170 B7

Clay Hill PE32...........48 B7
Clay La
Bacton NR28.............23 B3
Bradwell NR31...........94 C5
Hepworth IP22...........127 F1
Saxlingham Nethergate
  NR15.................107 A7
Swannington NR9.........52 C7
Claymore Gdns NR29.....167 B2
Claypit La NR21.........141 C5
Claypit Rd NR20.........33 D3
Clay Rd NR30............168 F5
Clayton Cl
Dersingham PE31........140 D4
Wisbech PE13...........152 T5
Clearview Dr NR14......90 C5
Cleaves Dr NR22.........16 F8
Clement Gdns IP22......177 C3
Clements Cl IP21........130 C5
Clement Scott Mews
  NR27.................139 D5
Clements Ct PE34.......144 B5
CLENCHWARTON PE34....145 E5
Clenchwarton Prim Sch
  PE34.................145 E5
Clenchwarton Rd PE34..146 B4
Clere Cl NR18...........173 C5
Cleveland Rd NR3.......178 A3
Cleves Way NR8.........156 E4
Cley La IP25............84 C4
Cley Marshes Nature
  Reserve★ NR25........7 F7
CLEY NEXT THE SEA NR25..7 E6
Cley Rd
Blakeney NR25...........7 D6
Bradwell NR31...........94 C7
Cockley Cley PE37.......82 E8
Holt NR25..............137 B8
Swaffham PE37..........153 B2
Clickers Rd NR3.........162 C8
Cliff Ave
Cromer NR27............139 C6
Great Yarmouth NR31....170 D3
Cliff Cl NR13...........92 F4
Cliff Ct NR36...........132 C6
Cliff Dr NR27...........139 C7
Cliffe-en-Howe Rd PE32..44 F8
Cliff Hill 4 NR31.......170 D4
Cliff La
Cromer NR27............139 C6
Great Yarmouth NR31....170 D3
Clifford Ave NR30.......168 D5
Clifford Burman Cl PE30.148 A1
Clifford Pye Cl NR10....35 B2
Cliff Par PE36..........132 C5
Cliff Pk Com Mid Sch
  NR31.................170 D2
Cliff Pk Fst Sch NR31...170 D2
Cliff Pk High Sch NR31..170 D1
Cliff Rd
Cromer NR27............139 D5
Overstrand NR27........11 A3
Sheringham NR26........138 E7
Cliff Terr PE36..........132 C5
Clifton Cl 8 NR2........162 C7
Clifton Pk NR27.........10 C5
Clifton Rd
King's Lynn PE30........148 B1
Wymondham NR18........173 C6
Clifton St NR2..........162 B7
CLIFTONVILLE NR11......143 B7
Clifton Way NR27........11 B3
Clink Hill NR30..........168 B4
Clink Rd NR12...........40 A6
Clintergate Rd IP20.....122 C6
CLINT GREEN NR19.......68 E8
Clint Hill IP31..........126 D2
Clintock Pl 8 NR30......169 C5
Clint St NR29...........56 B5
Clipbush La
Banham NR16...........119 C7
Fakenham NR21.........141 E4
Scoulton NR9...........85 C4
Clipped Hedge La NR11..22 B7
CLIPPESBY NR29.........57 A1
CLIPPINGS GREEN NR20...68 E7
Clipstreet La NR21......18 B8
Close The
Brancaster PE31..........3 D7
Brundall NR13..........165 C4
Docking PE31...........134 E4
Great Yarmouth NR31....170 A5
Hemsby NR29...........167 B2
Holt NR25..............137 C5
Little Melton NR9.......160 D2
North Lopham IP22......119 A2
North Walsham NR28....151 D4
Norwich NR1.............178 C3
Rackheath NR13.........72 DB
Roydon IP22............177 A5
Sheringham NR26........138 DB
Stow Bedon NR17.......102 D7
Clough Dr 9 IP26.......98 E1
Clough La PE30..........146 D4
Clovelly Dr NR6.........157 E2
Clover Dr 2 NR26.......138 B6
Clover Hill Fst Sch NR5.161 B8
Clover Hill Rd NR5......160 F8
Cloverland Dr 8 NR29...167 B7
Clover Rd
Attleborough NR17......174 C3
Aylsham NR11...........150 D5
Norwich NR7.............158 F3
Clover Way
Fakenham NR21.........141 E4
Great Yarmouth NR31....170 A4
Thetford IP24...........176 D5
Clover Wlk PE34.........61 B8

Clowes Ct NR34..........110 D1
Clubbs La NR23..........136 D6
Clydesdale Rise NR31....94 C8
Coach & Horses Row
  NR2..................178 A2
Coach House Ct 1 NR4..162 A3
Coach La NR19...........67 C6
Coachmans Ct NR7......158 F4
Coal Shed Gall, The★
  PE36.................132 C4
Coalwharf Rd PE13......152 B4
Coastguard Rd NR30....168 F5
Coast Rd
Bacton NR12............23 F4
Cley next the Sea NR25...7 F7
Corton NR32............171 F1
Happisburgh NR12.......23 F3
Hopton on Sea NR31....171 D4
Overstrand NR27........11 B3
Salthouse NR25..........8 A5
Wiveton NR25............7 D6
Coates Ct 5 PE14.......59 D2
COBBLER'S GREEN NR35..108 B2
Cobblers La PE14........41 C2
Cobbleways The 9 NR29..58 B6
Cobbold St IP22.........177 B5
Cobbs Hill PE34.........163 D4
Cobb's Pl 8 NR30.......169 D4
Cob Cl 7 NR31..........94 C8
Cobham Way NR7........159 C2
Cobholm Cl 14 NR31....169 B4
Cobholm Fst Sch NR31..169 B4
COBHOLM ISLAND NR31..169 A4
Cobholm Rd 6 NR31.....169 B4
Coburg Cl 10 IP25......83 D3
Coburg La IP25..........84 B6
Coburg St
9 King's Lynn PE30......146 E5
Norwich NR2.............178 A2
Cochrane Cl IP25........85 A3
Cock Dro PE38..........172 B7
Cocketts Dr PE13.......152 E5
Cock Fen Rd PE14.......95 F7
Cocklehole Rd PE34.....41 F8
COCKLEY CLEY PE37......82 D7
Cock Rd NR14...........92 A3
Cock St
Ixworth NR9............69 F2
Wymondham NR18........173 B5
COCKTHORPE NR23........6 E5
Codling's La NR11.......150 A6
Coigncroft The NR13....165 C3
Coke Rd NR1............162 E1
Coker's Hill NR22........16 F7
COLBY NR11.............21 E2
Colby Prim Sch NR11....36 B8
Coldershaw Rd NR6......158 B4
Coldham Cl NR4.........167 B3
Coldham Hall Carnser
  NR14.................165 C1
Coldham Rd NR11.......17 D7
Coldham's La PE33.......80 A5
Cold Harbour Rd NR29..56 D4
Coldhorn Cres PE13.....152 D7
Coleburn Rd NR1........89 E8
Colegate NR3............178 A3
COLEGATE END IP21......121 E6
Colegate End Rd IP21...121 E6
Coleman Cl
Palgrave IP22...........177 D1
Taverham NR8...........155 F2
Coleridge Cl NR8........156 DB
Coleridge Rd IP22.......177 E4
Coles Way NR10.........149 C5
Colindeep La NR7.......159 A4
Colin Mclean Rd NR19..154 C7
Colkett Dr NR6..........158 E3
COLKIRK NR21...........31 D5
Colkirk CE VA Prim Sch
  NR21.................31 D5
Collectors World of Eric St
  John Foti★ PE38......79 B6
Colleen Cl
Dereham NR19..........67 E5
East Dereham NR19.....154 D1
College Cl NR12.........54 D7
College Ct 1 NR31......169 B4
College Dr PE31.........133 C4
College La
Keswick NR4............89 C7
9 King's Lynn PE30......146 D4
Runcton Holme PE33....61 F3
College Rd
Hockwold cum Wilton
  IP26.................113 F7
Norwich NR2.............162 A5
Thompson IP24.........102 C7
Thurlton NR14..........110 C8
Wereham PE33..........97 F8
Collen's Gn NR9.........51 B3
Colliers Way NR10......149 C6
Collett's Bridge La PE14.59 C1
Colley Hill Drift PE32....48 D4
Collingwood Cl
Heacham PE31..........133 D3
25 Hethersett NR9.......88 D7
Collingwood Dr NR11....22 F8
Collingwood Way IP24...176 F6
Collingwood Wlk [1]
  IP24.................176 F6
Collins Cl NR6..........158 D2
Collins La PE31.........133 D5
Collin's Lea PE33........63 C5
Collis La NR29..........57 F5

Coll of W Anglia (Hunstanton
  Learning Ctr) The
  PE36.................132 D4
Coll of W Anglia (Isle
  Campus) The PE13.....152 E2
Coll of W Anglia (King's Lynn
  Ctr) The PE30........146 F5
Coll of W Anglia (Wisbech
  Campus) The PE13.....152 E2
Colls Rd NR7...........159 D1
Colman Ave 11 NR14.....89 F4
Colman Fst Sch NR4.....162 A3
Colman Hospl NR2.......162 A4
Colman Mid Sch NR4....161 F3
Colman Rd NR4..........161 F5
Colmans Mustard Shop★
  NR1..................178 B2
Colne Pl NR27..........139 B6
Colne Rd NR27..........139 B6
COLNEY NR4.............161 A4
Colney La
Colney NR4.............161 A3
Hethersett NR9.........160 D1
Colney Rd PE30.........147 D5
Colomb Rd NR31........170 C6
COLTISHALL NR12........54 E2
Coltishall La NR10......53 E2
Coltishall Prim Sch NR12.54 D7
Coltishall Rd
Belaugh NR12...........164 A6
Buxton with Lammas NR10..53 F8
Coltishall Sta NR12.....54 C7
COLTON NR9.............69 E4
Colton Rd NR9..........69 E6
Coltsfoot Rd NR10......53 A7
Coltsfoot Way IP24......176 F5
Columbia Way NR4......146 F6
Columbine Cl 4 IP24....176 F5
Columbine Rd NR10.....53 B2
Columbine The NR5.....160 E7
Colville Rd PE13........142 B5
Colville Rd NR14........142 B5
Comber Cl IP21.........130 D6
Comet Rd 7 IP25.......84 F3
Comfrey Way IP24......116 D2
Commercial Rd NR19...154 E5
Common Drift NR20.....49 C4
Common La
Beccles NR34...........110 D1
Beetley NR20...........49 E5
Brancaster PE31..........3 D6
Brockdish IP21.........131 D6
Burgh & Tuttington NR11..36 E6
East Walton PE32........7 B1
Field Dalling NR25.......7 D1
Filby NR29.............75 E8
Gayton PE32............45 C4
Great Witchingham NR9..51 D4
King's Lynn PE30........148 C2
North Runcton PE33.....44 A2
Norwich NR7.............162 B8
Runcton Holme PE33....61 C6
6 Southery PE38........97 B5
Thorpe Market NR11....22 A6
Common La N NR14.....110 D1
Common Loke NR14.....92 A2
Common Pl 8 NR22.....16 F7
Common Rd
Aldeby NR34............111 B3
Ashwellthorpe NR16.....105 E7
Botesdale IP22..........128 F1
Bressingham IP22.......129 C8
Brumstead NR12.........24 A1
Burston & Shimpling IP22 120 E2
Castle Acre PE32........46 E1
Forncett NR16..........105 E5
Foxley NR20............33 D1
Gissing NR15...........120 F5
Great Yarmouth NR31....170 C8
Hemsby NR29...........57 F4
Hopton IP22............127 F6
Lessingham NR12........24 E2
Martham NR29..........57 B4
Mundham NR14.........57 B4
Neatishead NR12........55 E6
Pulham Market IP21.....121 E7
Runcton Holme PE33....61 D4
Runhall NR20...........68 F4
Scole IP21.............130 F8
Shelfanger IP22.........119 F3
Shelton NR15...........107 B1
Skeyton NR10...........37 A6
Smallburgh NR12........24 D4
Somerton NR29.........57 E6
Surlingham NR14........165 B1
Swafield NR28..........22 D4
Thurne NR29...........56 E3
Wacton NR15...........106 D2
West Walton PE14......59 D7
Wiggenhall St Germans
  PE34.................60 F7
Commonside NR10......35 A2
Common The
Freethorpe NR13........92 E7
1 Harleston IP20........122 D1
Lyng NR9..............51 A4
Surlingham NR14........165 A1
Swardeston NR14........88 B6
Commonwealth Way 12
  NR7..................72 D4
Compass Rd NR18.......173 F1

Compit Hills NR27.......139 B3
Concorde Rd NR6........158 C5
Conesford Dr NR1.......162 F3
CONEY WESTON IP31.....127 B5
Coney Weston Rd
Barningham IP31........127 C4
Sapiston IP31...........126 D2
Conference Way
Colkirk NR21............31 E5
Wisbech PE13...........152 C8
Conge The NR30.........169 C4
CONGHAM PE32..........28 B2
Congham Rd PE32.......28 B1
Conifer Cl NR29.........167 A3
Coniston Cl
2 Hethersett NR9........88 E8
King's Lynn PE30........148 F1
8 Norwich NR5..........161 C6
Coniston Rd NR15.......90 E1
Coniston Sq 1 NR30....169 E4
Connaught Ave NR31....170 C3
Connaught Plain NR17..174 D5
Connaught Rd
Attleborough NR17......174 D5
Cromer NR27............139 D5
Norwich NR2.............162 B7
Constable Cl
7 Attleborough NR17....174 B4
2 Diss IP22.............177 C4
Constable Ct 15 IP20...122 D2
Constable Dr 4 NR31...170 A7
Constable Rd NR4.......162 C1
Constitution Hill
Fakenham NR21.........141 B4
North Runcton PE33.....43 F4
Norwich NR6.............158 E3
Constitution Opening
  NR3..................158 E2
Convent Rd 4 NR2......162 C5
Convy Priors NR30......138 C6
Conway Rd
Great Yarmouth NR31....170 D6
Sheringham NR26........138 F7
Conyers NR18...........173 C6
Cooke Cl 2 NR5........160 E7
Cooke's Rd NR15........91 B4
Cookley La IP23.........130 F1
Cook Rd IP25...........66 A3
Cook's La IP20..........122 F2
Co-operative St NR26...138 D7
Cooper La NR1..........89 F8
Cooper Rd
North Walsham NR28....151 B6
8 Sheringham NR26.....138 C5
Coopers Cl NR8.........155 E3
Coopers La PE33........62 B2
Copeland Dr NR26......138 C6
Copeman Rd
Aylsham NR11..........150 D5
Great & Little Plumstead
  NR13.................73 A6
3 Roydon IP22..........129 D7
Copenhagen Way NR6..158 C2
Copince's La NR16......119 C7
Copper Beech Cl NR21..141 D6
Copperfield 4 PE30.....147 C5
Copperfield Ave
  NR30.................170 DB
Copper Hall PE37.......153 B3
Copper La 8 NR5.......160 E7
Copper Smith Way NR18.173 F5
Coppice Ave NR6.......157 E5
Coppice The 6 NR17....174 C5
Coppins Ct PE14........154 E2
COPY'S GREEN NR23......6 A2
Corbet Ave NR7.........159 B2
Corbett Rd 2 NR28.....151 C6
Corbyn Shaw Rd PE30..147 E4
Cordon St PE13.........152 C4
CORDWELL NR16.........105 E4
Coriander Dr IP24.......176 F4
Corie Rd NR4...........161 F4
Corkway Dro PE38.......97 E1
Cormorant Way 10 NR31..94 C8
Corncutters Cl NR3......178 B3
Corner Comm Rd NR28..38 B7
Corner La NR10.........53 B3
Corner St 2 NR27.......139 B7
Cornfields IP21..........121 B1
Cornfield The NR25.......7 A3
Cornish Ave NR28.......22 E5
Cornish Way NR28......151 C7
Cornwallis Cl 7 NR5....161 A7
Coronation Ave
2 Marthan NR29........57 D4
Nordelph PE38..........78 D3
1 Rollesby NR29........57 D2
West Winch PE33........43 F3
Coronation Cl NR6......158 A4
Coronation Cots PE32...47 F4
Coronation Cres NR31...107 D5
Coronation Gn NR31....94 C8
Coronation Gr PE37.....153 B5
Coronation La
Blakeney NR25...........7 D7
Somerton NR29.........57 F5
Coronation Pl IP27......175 B2
Coronation Rd
Clenchwarton PE34.....146 A5
Great Yarmouth NR31....169 B3
Holt NR25..............137 C5
Norwich NR6.............158 A4
Coronation Terr
Caston NR17............102 F8
Great Yarmouth NR30...169 C4
Coronation Wlk NR28...151 A5
Coronilla Gn NR31.......170 B5
Corporation Rd PE13....152 D3

CORPUSTY NR11 . . . . 19 E1
Corpusty Prim Sch NR11 . . 19 F1
Corpusty Rd
 Briston NR24 . . . . 142 F1
 Thurning NR24 . . . . 19 B2
 Wood Dalling NR11 . . . . . . 34 D7
Corton Rd NR1 . . . . 178 C1
Coslany Sq 7 NR3 . . . . 178 A3
Coslany St NR3 . . . . 178 A3
COSTESSEY NR8 . . . . 156 F4
Costessey High Sch NR5 156 E2
Costessey Inf Sch NR5 . . 157 B1
Costessey Jun Sch NR5 . 156 F1
Costessey La
 Drayton NR8 . . . . 156 E6
 Ringland NR8 . . . . 70 B8
 Taverham NR8 . . . . 157 A7
COSTESSEY PARK NR5 . . 156 D4
COSTON NR9 . . . . 69 A1
Coston La NR18 . . . . 87 A8
Cosy Cnr NR28 . . . . 151 B4
Cotman Cl IP22 . . . . 177 C4
Cotman Dr NR31 . . . . 170 A7
Cotman Fields NR1 . . . . . 178 C4
Cotman Rd NR1 . . . . 163 B5
Cotoneaster Ct 4 NR31 170 B6
Cottage Dr The NR7 . . . . 163 E8
Cottage Farm Abbey
 PE32 . . . . 46 C2
Cottage Rd NR29 . . . . 57 E6
Cotterall Ct NR8 . . . . 55 A2
Cottinghams Dr NR10 . . 157 E7
Cotton Rd NR9 . . . . 70 A4
Cotton's Cnr PE14 . . . . 77 D2
Cottons Head PE14 . . . . . . 77 E7
Cotts La PE34 . . . . 144 F1
Coughtrey Cl NR7 . . . . . . 159 B5
Couhe Cl NR7 . . . . 153 C5
Coulson La IP27 . . . . 175 C4
Coulton Cl PE30 . . . . 146 E7
Council Rd 3 PE13 . . . . . . 152 E6
County Ct Rd 3 PE30 . . 146 E4
Court Cl 6 NR29 . . . . 57 D2
Court Dr NR27 . . . . 139 B6
Courtenay Cl
 4 East Dereham NR19 . . 154 D5
 2 Norwich NR5 . . . . 160 F8
Courtfields PE37 . . . . 153 B3
Court Gdns PE38 . . . . 172 C5
Court Hill NR12 . . . . 54 A4
Courtnell Pl PE30 . . . . . . 147 D5
Courtney Cl 7 NR1 . . . . . 154 D5
Court Rd
 Great Snoring NR21 . . . . . 17 B5
 Rollesby NR29 . . . . 57 D2
Covent Gdn Rd NR30 . . 168 C7
Coventry St 8 NR21 . . . . . 15 C2
Coventry Way IP24 . . . . . 176 A4
Covert Sycamore IP24 . . 176 A4
Covert The IP24 . . . . 176 E6
Covey The
 Surlingham NR14 . . . . 91 C8
 Taverham NR8 . . . . 155 D2
Covey Way IP27 . . . . 113 F1
Cowdrewell Mews 7
 NR8 . . . . 155 D1
Cowgate NR3 . . . . 178 B4
Cow Hill NR2 . . . . 178 A3
Cow La
 Denver PE38 . . . . 172 C1
 Tharston & Hapton NR15 . 106 D7
Cow Lake Dro PE14 . . . . . 59 D5
Cowle's Dro IP26 . . . . . . 113 D5
Cowper Cl NR11 . . . . 143 C5
Cowper Rd NR1 . . . . 154 E5
Cowslip Cl 14 NR14 . . . . . 89 B3
Cowslip La NR26 . . . . 138 B6
Cowslip Wlk PE34 . . . . 61 B8
Cow Tro NR29 . . . . 57 D3
Cow Twr* NR3 . . . . 178 C4
COXFORD PE31 . . . . 30 C8
Cox's La PE13 . . . . 152 A3
Coxswain Read Way
 NR30 . . . . 168 D4
Cozens-Hardy Rd NR7 . . 159 B4
Crabapple Cl 12 NR31 . . 171 D3
Crabapple La NR9 . . . . 68 D1
Crab Apple La NR14 . . . . 110 E8
Crabbe's Cl 7 IP26 . . . . . . 98 E1
Crabb La PE34 . . . . 42 E1
Crabb's Abbey PE34 . . . . . 61 B2
CRABGATE NR11 . . . . 34 D6
Crabgate La N NR11 . . . . . 34 D6
Crabgate La S NR11 . . . . . 34 D5
Crab La
 Boughton PE33 . . . . 81 A5
 Great Yarmouth NR31 . . 170 A5
Crab Marsh PE13 . . . . . . 152 B8
Crabtree La NR34 . . . . . . 110 D1
Crabtree Rise IP21 . . . . . 131 C6
CRACKTHORN CORNER
 IP22 . . . . 128 D5
Cradle Wood Rd NR28 . 151 E3
Cradock Ave NR30 . . . . . 169 D8
Craft La NR27 . . . . 11 A1
Craft The
 Raveningham NR14 . . . . . 110 B8
 Winterton-on-Sea NR29 . . 58 B6
Cramp Cnr NR14 . . . . 91 F6
Cranage Rd NR1 . . . . 162 E1
Crane Cl NR19 . . . . 154 C3
Crane's La NR10 . . . . 150 C1
Cranes Mdw 31 IP20 . . . 122 D2
Cranes Rd NR14 . . . . 88 F3
Cranfield Rd NR26 . . . . . 138 A4

Cranleigh Rise NR4 . . . . . 161 F1
Cranley Rd NR7 . . . . 72 E4
Cranmer Ave PE30 . . . . . 148 C4
Cranmer Ct NR11 . . . . . . 141 C5
Cranny Field Chase PE14 . 41 E1
Cranwell Rd 10 IP25 . . . . . 84 F3
CRANWICH IP26 . . . . 99 F6
Cranworth Rd NR1 . . . . . . 85 E7
Cranworth Gdns NR1 . . 178 A1
Craske Cl 3 NR26 . . . . . . 138 C5
Craske Dr NR18 . . . . 72 E7
Craske La PE34 . . . . 42 A7
Craske Mews 6 NR5 . . . 160 E8
Craven La PE33 . . . . 62 B6
Crawford Rd NR27 . . . . . 139 D5
CRAYMERE BECK NR24 . . 18 F1
Craymere Beck Rd
 Briston NR24 . . . . 142 E1
 Hindolveston NR24 . . . . . . 18 F1
Craymere Rd NR24 . . . . . . 18 E1
Creake Rd
 Burnham Market PE31 . . 135 D2
 Sculthorpe Airfield PE31 . . 15 B3
 Sculthorpe NR21 . . . . . . 141 A6
Creance Rd NR7 . . . . 159 C4
Crecen La PE36 . . . . 132 C4
Creek The PE31 . . . . 135 E7
Cremer Cl 14 PE31 . . . . . . 12 E4
Cremer's Drift NR26 . . . 138 D6
Cremer St NR26 . . . . 138 D7
Cremorne La NR1 . . . . . . 163 B5
Crescent Pas PE13 . . . . . 152 C5
Crescent Rd PE36 . . . . . . 132 C3
Crescent The
 Ashwellthorpe NR16 . . . . 105 F8
 Bacton/Walcott NR12 . . . . 24 A7
 East Dereham NR19 . . . . 154 C1
 East Harling NR16 . . . . . 118 C4
 Hemsby NR29 . . . . 167 D2
 Hethersett NR9 . . . . 88 C7
 4 Newton Flotman NR15 . 89 D1
 Norwich NR2 . . . . 178 A2
 Taverham NR8 . . . . 156 F8
 Thurton NR14 . . . . 91 C4
 Wisbech PE13 . . . . 152 C4
Cressener Cl NR6 . . . . . . 157 E5
Cressingham Rd IP25 . . . 83 F6
Cresswell Cl NR5 . . . . . . 161 B6
Cresswell St PE30 . . . . . . 146 E6
Crest Rd PE31 . . . . 140 C4
Cricket Cl NR8 . . . . 155 E3
Cricketers Way PE11 . . . 152 A6
Cricketer's Wlk NR13 . . . 92 E7
Cricket Gd Rd NR1 . . . . . 162 E3
Cricket Pasture The PE31 . 3 E7
Crick's Wlk IP22 . . . . 177 A5
Crimp Cramp La NR34 . . 111 B4
CRIMPLESHAM PE33 . . . . 80 B6
CRINGLEFORD NR4 . . . . . . 89 B8
Cringleford CE Fst & Mid Sch
 NR4 . . . . 161 C1
Cringleford Chase NR4 . 161 C1
Crinoline La NR20 . . . . . . 69 C5
Crisp Cl PE31 . . . . 140 C3
Crisp Rd NR35 . . . . 109 E3
Critten's Rd NR31 . . . . . . 169 B4
Croft Cl
 Diss IP22 . . . . 177 C4
 10 Harleston IP20 . . . . . 122 D2
Croft Gn NR17 . . . . 174 B3
Crofthole Way 2 NR7 . . 163 E8
Croft La
 Corpusty NR11 . . . . 19 F2
 Diss IP22 . . . . 177 C4
 Marsham NR10 . . . . 150 C1
Croft Rd
 Caister-on-Sea NR30 . . . 168 E5
 Norton Subcourse NR14 . . 92 E1
 Upwell PE14 . . . . 77 D3
Crofts Cl IP25 . . . . 135 C1
Crofts The 1 NR5 . . . . . . 160 F7
Croft The
 Costessey NR8 . . . . 156 F4
 Cromer NR27 . . . . 139 B6
 Little Snoring NR21 . . . . . 17 C3
 Swanton Novers NR24 . . . 18 B3
 Croft Yd NR23 . . . . 136 D6
Cromarty Way NR30 . . . 168 D5
Crome Cl IP22 . . . . 177 B4
CROMER NR27 . . . . 139 C7
Crome Rd NR3 . . . . 162 F8
Cromer High Sch Language
 Coll NR27 . . . . 139 C5
Cromer Hospl NR27 . . . . 139 C6
Cromer Jun Sch NR27 . . 139 C5
Cromer Mus* NR27 . . . . 139 C7
Cromer Rd
 Aylsham NR11 . . . . 150 C8
 Blickling NR11 . . . . 36 B7
 Hevingham NR10 . . . . 36 B1
 Holt NR25 . . . . 137 D7
 Hunstanton PE36 . . . . . . 132 D5
 Mundesley NR11 . . . . . . 143 B7
 North Walsham NR28 . . 151 A6
 Norwich NR6 . . . . 158 A5
 Ormesby St Margaret with
  Scratby NR29 . . . . 167 A2
 Overstrand NR27 . . . . . . 139 F4
 Runton NR27 . . . . 10 A5
 Sheringham NR26 . . . . . 138 E6
 Southrepps NR11 . . . . 22 C8
 Trimingham NR11 . . . . . . 11 C2
Cromer Sta NR27 . . . . . . 139 A7
Cromes Oak Cl NR14 . . . . 90 C4
Cromes PI NR10 . . . . 37 B2
Crompton Rd NR11 . . . . 150 C4

Cromwell Cl
 6 Cromer NR27 . . . . 139 C6
 3 Hethersett NR9 . . . . . . 88 D8
 7 Marthan NR29 . . . . 57 D4
 Swaffham PE37 . . . . 153 D3
Cromwell Rd
 Cromer NR27 . . . . 139 C6
 Great Yarmouth NR31 . . 169 C1
 Norwich NR7 . . . . 159 B3
 Weeting-with-Broomhill
  IP27 . . . . 114 E8
 Wisbech PE13 . . . . 152 A2
Cromwell Terr 6 PE30 . . 146 E3
Crooks PI NR1 . . . . 178 A1
Crosby Row PE21 . . . . 41 A8
Cross Bank Rd PE30 . . . 146 C6
CROSSDALE STREET
 NR27 . . . . 139 D1
Cross Dro
 Hilgay PE38 . . . . 96 D7
 Southery PE38 . . . . 97 B3
Crossing Rd
 Great Green IP21 . . . . . . 130 A5
 Palgrave IP22 . . . . 177 D1
Cross Keys Cl 2 NR10 . . . 53 D2
Crosskeys Way 3 NR20 . 68 F6
Cross La
 Brancaster PE31 . . . . 3 B7
 Lessingham NR12 . . . . . . 24 E4
 Northwold IP26 . . . . 99 C7
 Norwich NR3 . . . . 178 A4
 Runton NR27 . . . . 10 B4
 Stanhoe PE31 . . . . 14 E7
 Surlingham NR14 . . . . 91 A8
Cross Rd
 Ashby with Oby NR29 . . . 56 F1
 Great Yarmouth NR31 . . 170 D6
 Starston IP20 . . . . 122 C2
Crossroad NR10 . . . . 37 C4
Cross's Grave PE31 . . . . . 29 E4
Cross St
 6 Cromer NR27 . . . . 139 B6
 Harpley PE31 . . . . 29 C5
 2 Holt NR25 . . . . 137 B6
 Hoxne IP21 . . . . 131 A3
 Salthouse NR25 . . . . 8 B6
Cross Stone Rd NR14 . . . 92 B3
CROSS STREET IP21 . . . 131 A3
Crosstead NR20 . . . . 169 D8
Cross Way PE31 . . . . 133 C5
CROSS WAYS NR31 . . . . . 94 B4
Crossways 4 NR29 . . . . 167 A2
Crossway Terr
 Acle NR13 . . . . 166 B4
 5 Loddon NR14 . . . . 91 F1
CROSTWICK NR12 . . . . 54 B3
Crostwick La NR10 . . . . . . 54 A2
CROSTWIGHT NR28 . . . . . 38 B5
Crostwight Rd NR28 . . . . 38 D7
Croughton La PE31 . . . . . . 30 B8
Crowden Rd NR12 . . . . . . 24 D4
Crowes Loke NR13 . . . . . . 73 B7
CROWGATE STREET NR12 . 55 A8
Crowhall La NR12 . . . . 55 B8
Crow Hall Est PE38 . . . . 172 C3
Crow Hall Rd NR12 . . . . 170 C2
Crow Hill NR11 . . . . 34 C7
Crow La
 Bircham PE31 . . . . 14 A2
 Elsing NR20 . . . . 50 F4
 Great Dunham PE32 . . . . 47 E1
Crown Ave PE14 . . . . 95 A7
Crown Cres IP25 . . . . 84 E5
Crown Ctyd NR16 . . . . . 119 A4
Crown Gdns PE33 . . . . . . 80 E4
Crown Gn PE20 . . . . 120 E2
Crown La
 Coney Weston IP31 . . . . 127 B4
 Fransham NR19 . . . . 66 D6
Crown Mdw NR10 . . . . . 149 C5
Crown PI 9 NR10 . . . . . . 149 D5
Crown Rd
 Christchurch PE14 . . . . . . 95 A7
 Colkirk NR21 . . . . 31 D5
 East Dereham NR20 . . . . 154 F5
 Great Yarmouth NR30 . . 169 D3
 Marsham IP24 . . . . 36 E1
 Mundford IP26 . . . . 100 B4
 Norwich NR1 . . . . 178 B3
 2 Old Buckenham NR17 . 104 D2
Crown Sq PE30 . . . . 147 A7
Crown St
 Banham NR16 . . . . 119 D7
 Methwold IP26 . . . . 99 A5
CROWNTHORPE NR18 . . . 87 C6
Crownthorpe Rd NR18 . . 87 C6
Crow Way NR16 . . . . 119 D6
Crow Rd NR28 . . . . 151 D6
Crowshall La PE37 . . . . . 174 B5
CROWSHILL IP25 . . . . 67 A1
Crow's La IP25 . . . . 84 C1
Crow St IP31 . . . . 127 B4
CROXTON
 Croxton IP24 . . . . 116 C5
 Fulmodeston NR21 . . . . . 17 E2
Croxton Rd
 Fulmodeston NR21 . . . . . 17 E2
 Thetford IP24 . . . . 116 D5
Crummock Rd 3 NR5 . . 161 C6
Cubitt Rd NR13 . . . . 163 C7
Cubitts Cl NR20 . . . . 33 B2
Cuckoofield La NR14 . . . 89 A3
CUCKOO GREEN NR32 . . 171 A4
Cuckoo Hill Rd PE31 . . . . 14 B3

Cuckoo La
 Brundall NR13 . . . . 73 E3
Carbrooke IP25 . . . . 85 B4
Redenhall with Harleston
 IP20 . . . . 122 F2
Cuckoo Rd PE14 . . . . 79 A8
Cuck Stool La 8 PE32 . . . 46 F2
Cucumber La NR13 . . . . 165 B5
Cuddle Dike Bank PE14 . 78 A5
Cuffer La NR18 . . . . 104 F2
Culey Cl PE30 . . . . 147 A8
CULFORDHEATH IP31 . . . 125 D1
Culley's Pit Rd NR12 . . . . 38 A2
Culling's Hill NR13 . . . . . . 72 F7
Cullum Cl NR20 . . . . 50 B3
Culverin Cl 3 NR29 . . . . . 72 D4
Cummings Bvd NR21 . . . . 15 C2
Cunningham Ave 2
 NR30 . . . . 169 D8
Cunningham Cl IP24 . . . 176 F6
Cunningham Rd 6 NR5 . 161 C5
Cunningham Wlk 3
 IP24 . . . . 176 F6
Curd's Hall NR19 . . . . 66 A7
Curie Dr NR31 . . . . 170 B1
Curlew Cl 7 IP25 . . . . 84 C3
Curlew Way NR31 . . . . . . 170 A6
Curson Cl 11 NR9 . . . . 88 C7
Curson Rd 8 NR15 . . . . . 106 F6
Cursons Mews NR18 . . . 173 B6
Curtis Dr 1 IP26 . . . . 98 D1
Curtis La NR26 . . . . 138 E7
Curtis Rd NR3 . . . . 158 B4
Cushing Cl 1 IP25 . . . . . . 67 B2
Cushing Dr 3 NR21 . . . . . 17 B3
Custance Ct NR4 . . . . . . 161 E3
Customhouse St PE12 . . . 41 C8
Cuthbert Cl
 4 King's Lynn PE30 . . . 148 C5
 Norwich NR7 . . . . 159 B4
 8 Thetford IP24 . . . . 176 F5
Cutler Way
 Bowthorpe NR5 . . . . 160 F6
 Norwich NR5 . . . . 160 E8
Cut Loke NR14 . . . . 73 C1
Cutthroat La NR19 . . . . . . 68 A6
Cutting's Rd IP21 . . . . . . 131 C8
Cuttons Cnr NR13 . . . . . . 73 C6
Cydonia Gn 12 NR31 . . . 170 B6
Cygnet Cl NR17 . . . . 174 F6
Cygnet Rd NR19 . . . . 154 E4
Cygnet Wlk PE13 . . . . . . 153 C2
Cypress Cl NR8 . . . . 156 E8
Cypress Cres NR26 . . . . 138 D5
Cypress PI PE36 . . . . 132 D4
Cyprus Rd NR17 . . . . 174 C5
Cyprus St NR1 . . . . 162 E3
Cyril Rd NR7 . . . . 163 F7

D

Dacre Cl NR4 . . . . 161 E1
Dades La PE14 . . . . 60 B6
Dad's Army Mus* IP24 . 176 D4
Daffodil Way NR20 . . . . . . 68 E6
DAFFY GREEN NR19 . . . . . 67 C4
Dagmar Mews 12 NR30 . 169 D2
Dairy Drift PE32 . . . . 48 C2
Dairy Dro CB6 . . . . 95 F2
Dairy Farm Cl NR21 . . . 141 C6
Dairy Farm Ct NR17 . . . 174 C5
Dairy La NR11 . . . . 9 E1
Dakenham Cl NR13 . . . . . 72 F8
Dakin Rd NR3 . . . . 158 D1
Dalbier Cl 2 NR13 . . . . . . 72 E4
Dale End PE31 . . . . 3 D7
Dale La NR29 . . . . 56 C8
Dale Rd
 East Dereham NR19 . . . . 154 C6
 Scarning NR19 . . . . 67 A7
 Stanton IP31 . . . . 127 C1
Dales Cl 6 NR31 . . . . 94 C8
Dales Loke NR14 . . . . . . 163 C6
Dales The NR14 . . . . 163 C6
Dalrymple Way NR3 . . . . 158 C4
DAMGATE
 Acle NR13 . . . . 166 C2
 Martham NR29 . . . . 57 E5
Damgate Back La NR29 . . 57 D6
Damgate Cl NR13 . . . . . . 166 C2
Damgate La
 Acle NR13 . . . . 166 D2
 Martham NR29 . . . . 57 D6
Damgate St NR18 . . . . . . 173 B3
Dam Gdns NR17 . . . . 119 C4
Dam La IP22 . . . . 129 D3
Danby Cl 6 NR4 . . . . 89 D8
Danby Rd NR3 . . . . 170 C6
Dane Cl IP24 . . . . 176 B3
DANEMOOR GREEN NR9 . 86 F8
Danemoor La NR9 . . . . . . 86 F8
Danesbower Cl NR13 . . . 165 F6
Danesbower La NR13 . . . 165 F6
Danesfort Dr 1 NR19 . . . 154 E6
Daniels Rd NR4 . . . . 162 B2
Danish House Gdns NR21 . 11 A4
Daphne Way 8 NR31 . . . 170 B5
Dark La
 Ashmanhaugh NR12 . . . . 38 C1
 Dickleburgh & Rushall
  IP21 . . . . 130 B6
 Erpingham NR11 . . . . 21 A1
 Kimberley NR18 . . . . 87 B7
 Smallburgh NR12 . . . . . . 38 D3
 Somerton NR29 . . . . 57 F6
 Wretham IP24 . . . . 101 F2
Darrell PI NR5 . . . . 161 D7

Darrow Gn Rd IP20 . . . . 122 F8
DARROW GREEN IP20 . . 122 E8
Darrow Wood 2 IP20 . . 122 E8
Darrow Wood La IP22 . . 120 A1
Darwin Cl 3 PE12 . . . . 41 B8
Darwin Way NR19 . . . . . 154 D4
Dashwood Cl NR31 . . . . . 93 F6
Daseley's Cl PE30 . . . . . . 148 A1
Dashwood Cl NR31 . . . . . 93 F6
Dauber's La NR13 . . . . . . 74 C2
Davey CI NR21 . . . . 17 B3
Davey PI NR2 . . . . 178 B3
Davidson Cl NR7 . . . . . . 163 F7
Davidson Rd NR7 . . . . . . 163 F7
Da Vols Ct NR31 . . . . 170 D6
Davy PI
 Heacham PE31 . . . . 133 C5
 7 Loddon NR14 . . . . 92 A1
Dawber Cl PE30 . . . . 147 B4
Dawes La 2 PE13 . . . . 12 E4
Dawnay Ave PE30 . . . . . 148 B1
Dawsons La NR20 . . . . . . 33 C3
Day's La IP31 . . . . 127 C4
Day's Lode Rd PE14 . . . . 95 A4
Deacon Cl NR13 . . . . 165 D4
Deacon Dr 14 NR9 . . . . . . 88 D8
Deben Dr 14 NR31 . . . . . . 94 A6
Debenne Rd NR28 . . . . . 151 C6
Debnam Cl 10 NR13 . . . . 73 C6
Deborah Rd NR11 . . . . . . 170 C2
De-Carle Smith Rd
 NR13 . . . . 166 C4
Decoy Rd
 Lakenheath IP27 . . . . . . 112 F4
 Ormesby St Margaret with
  Scratby NR29 . . . . 167 A4
 Ormesby St Michael NR29 . 57 F7
 Potter Heigham NR29 . . . 56 F7
Deepdale NR13 . . . . 165 D3
Deepdale Ave 1 NR29 . . . 57 C4
Deep Rd NR18 . . . . 173 B8
Deer Row NR35 . . . . 109 D1
De Grey Rd PE30 . . . . . . 147 B5
De Hague Rd NR4 . . . . . 161 F4
De Havilland Rd
 Dereham NR19 . . . . 154 C6
 Wisbech PE13 . . . . 152 C6
Delane Rd NR18 . . . . 157 C7
Delft Way NR6 . . . . 158 A6
Delgate La PE31 . . . . 3 E7
Dell Cl NR15 . . . . 106 F8
Dell Cnr La NR13 . . . . 73 F5
Dell Cres NR5 . . . . 161 C7
Dell Loke NR14 . . . . 163 B2
Dell The
 Bodham NR25 . . . . 9 A3
 Hingham NR9 . . . . 86 B5
 Mundesley NR11 . . . . . . 143 D5
 Trowse Newton NR14 . . 163 B2
Denby Ind NR7 . . . . 159 C2
Delta Cl NR6 . . . . 158 C4
De Lucy Cl IP22 . . . . 177 C5
De Morley Cl 4 IP27 . . . 177 A5
De Morley Garth NR26 . . 138 C6
De-Narde Rd NR19 . . . . 154 D7
Denbigh Rd NR2 . . . . 162 B5
Dene Ave NR29 . . . . 167 A3
Deneside 20 NR30 . . . . . 169 D3
Dene Side 1 NR30 . . . . . 169 D3
Denes The NR1 . . . . 163 C5
DENHAM IP21 . . . . 131 B1
Denham Low Rd IP21 . . 131 A1
Denham Rd IP21 . . . . 131 B2
Denmark Hill IP27 . . . . . 177 C3
Denmark La IP22 . . . . . . 177 B4
Denmark Opening NR3 . 158 E1
Denmark Rd
 Beccles NR34 . . . . 110 D1
 2 King's Lynn PE30 . . . 147 B6
 Norwich NR3 . . . . 158 E1
Denmark Rise IP22 . . . . 177 C4
Denmead Cl 4 NR4 . . . . . 89 D8
Dennis Rd NR6 . . . . 157 F7
Dennis Sneezum Ct
 PE38 . . . . 172 B4
Denny Rd PE30 . . . . 147 A4
Denny's Hill IP20 . . . . . . 123 A2
Denny's Wlk PE32 . . . . . . 63 F7
DENTON IP20 . . . . 123 A7
Denton Rd
 Denton IP20 . . . . 123 C6
 Norwich NR3 . . . . 158 F3
DENVER PE38 . . . . 172 C2
Denver Hill PE38 . . . . . . 172 C3
Denver VC Prim Sch
 PE38 . . . . 172 B1
Denver Windmill* PE38 . 172 B1
DEOPHAM NR18 . . . . 86 E3
DEOPHAM GREEN NR18 . 86 E2
Deopham Rd
 Attleborough NR17 . . . . 174 C7
 Hingham NR9 . . . . 86 C4
 Morley NR18 . . . . 87 A2
DEOPHAM STALLAND
 NR9 . . . . 86 D2
Derby St NR2 . . . . 162 C7
DEREHAM NR20 . . . . 154 D5
Dereham 6th Form Coll
 NR20 . . . . 154 F5
Dereham Church Inf Sch
 NR19 . . . . 154 D5
Dereham Hospl NR19 . . 154 E7
Dereham La NR19 . . . . . . 66 C8

Dereham Rd
🖪 Bawdeswell NR20 . . . . . . 50 E7
Beeston with Bittering PE32 48 D2
Briningham NR24 . . . . 18 D5
Bylaugh NR20 . . . . 50 C5
Colkirk NR21 . . . . 31 E5
Costessey NR5 . . . . 156 D1
Dereham NR20 . . . . 50 B2
East Dereham NR19 . . . . 154 B5
Easton NR9 . . . . 70 C5
Garvestone NR9 . . . . 68 C1
Gressenhall NR19 . . . . 49 C2
Hempton NR21 . . . . 141 B2
Hingham NR9 . . . . 86 B5
Honingham NR9 . . . . 69 D7
Kimberley NR18 . . . . 87 A7
Litcham PE32 . . . . 48 A4
Mattishall NR20 . . . . 68 F6
North Elmham NR20 . . . . . 49 E6
🖪 Norwich NR5 . . . . 161 B8
Ovington IP25 . . . . 84 E6
Pudding Norton NR21 . . . 141 B1
Reepham NR10 . . . . 149 A4
Scarning NR19 . . . . 154 A4
Shipdham IP25 . . . . 67 A1
🖪 Watton IP25 . . . . 84 D3
Whinburgh & Westfield
NR19 . . . . 67 F5
Whissonsett NR20 . . . . . . 31 E2
Yaxham NR19 . . . . 68 A5
Dereham St Nicholas Jun
Sch NR19 . . . . 154 D4
DERSINGHAM PE31 . . . . 140 D5
Dersingham Bog National
Nature Reserve★ PE31 . . 27 D7
Dersingham Inf Sch
PE31 . . . . 140 D4
Dersley Cl 🖪 NR5 . . . . . 160 E7
Derwent Ave PE30 . . . . 148 F2
Desborough Way NR13 . . 72 D4
Desmond Dr NR6 . . . . . 158 F6
Devlin Dr 🖪 NR14 . . . . . 90 C5
Devon Ave NR6 . . . . . . 157 E4
Devon Cres PE30 . . . . . 148 D5
Devonshire Cl 🖪 PE30 . 147 A7
Devonshire Rd NR30 . . . 169 D2
Devonshire St 🖪 NR2 . . 162 C7
Devon Way NR14 . . . . . 163 C1
Dewarrene Dr IP27 . . . . 175 B7
De Warrene Pl PE32 . . . 47 A2
Dewdrop Cl PE31 . . . . . 133 D6
Dewing Rd NR13 . . . . . . 72 E8
Dexter Rd PE34 . . . . 79 A7
Dial Cl PE38 . . . . 172 B5
Diamond Cl IP22 . . . . . . 120 B5
Diamond Rd NR6 . . . . . 158 B5
Diamond St PE30 . . . . . 146 D2
Diamond Terr PE30 . . . . 146 D2
Dianas Dro IP26 . . . . . . 132 C2
Diana Way NR30 . . . . . . 168 C6
Dian Rd NR13 . . . . 165 E3
Dibden Rd NR13 . . . . . . 165 F2
Dickens Ave NR30 . . . . . 169 D1
Dickens Ct 🖪 NR30 . . . . 169 D1
Dickfool's La NR19 . . . . . 66 F8
DICKLEBURGH IP21 . . . 121 C1
DICKLEBURGH MOOR
IP21 . . . . 121 C2
Dickleburgh Prim Sch
IP21 . . . . 121 B1
Dickleburgh Rd IP21 . . . 121 A3
Dicks Mount NR34 . . . . 111 D3
Dicky Hill IP20 . . . . 122 D3
DIDLINGTON IP26 . . . . . . 99 E8
Digby Dr NR21 . . . . 141 B6
DILHAM NR28 . . . . 38 D4
Dilham Arts Ctr★ NR28 . 38 C4
Dilham Rd
Honing NR28 . . . . 38 C6
Worstead NR28 . . . . 38 A4
Dilldash La NR21 . . . . . . 17 A5
Dinosaur Adventure Pk★
NR9 . . . . 51 E4
Dirty La
North Tuddenham NR20 . . 50 E1
Pulham St Mary IP21 . . . . 121 F3
DISS IP22 . . . . 177 D6
Diss Church Jun Sch
IP22 . . . . 177 D4
Diss High Sch IP22 . . . . 177 E5
Diss Inf Sch IP22 . . . . . 177 E4
Diss Mus★ IP22 . . . . . . 177 D4
Diss Rd
Burston & Shimpling
IP22 . . . . 120 E1
Garboldisham IP22 . . . . . 128 A8
Scole IP21 . . . . 130 C5
South Lopham IP22 . . . . 128 F6
Tibenham NR16 . . . . 120 C8
Wattisfield IP22 . . . . 128 B1
Diss Sta IP22 . . . . 177 F4
Diss Swimming & Fitness Ctr
IP22 . . . . 177 E3
Distillery Sq 🖪 NR2 . . . 162 C6
DITCHINGHAM NR35 . . . 109 A1
Ditchingham Dam NR35 . 109 A1
Dixon Rd
Cromer NR27 . . . . 139 B5
North Walsham NR28 . . . 151 D5
Norwich NR7 . . . . 159 A4
Dixon's Dro PE14 . . . . . . 59 C8
Dixon's Fold NR6 . . . . . 158 F4
Dobbs' La NR13 . . . . 54 D2

Dobby Dr PE30 . . . . 146 D6
Dobson Way NR34 . . . . 110 D1
DOCKENEY NR34 . . . . . 109 F2
DOCKING PE31 . . . . 134 C4
Docking Prim Sch PE31 . 134 C4
Docking Rd
Burnham Westgate PE31 . 135 B2
Ringstead PE36 . . . . 2 B2
Sedgeford PE36 . . . . 13 B7
Stanhoe PE31 . . . . 14 D7
Syderstone PE31 . . . . 15 A3
Dock Tavern La NR31 . . 170 D5
Doctor's La IP21 . . . . . . 122 A2
Doctors Mdw 🖪 NR10 . . 53 D2
Doctors Rd NR11 . . . . . 165 E6
Dodd Cl NR10 . . . . 149 C2
Dodderman Way NR5 . . 160 F6
Dodds Cl NR17 . . . . 174 B3
DODDSHILL PE31 . . . . . 140 F3
Doddshill Rd PE31 . . . . 140 F3
Dodds La NR17 . . . . 174 B3
Dodd's La PE32 . . . . 45 B2
Dodds Rd NR17 . . . . . . 174 B3
Dodgers La NR15 . . . . . . 91 A3
Dodmans Cl PE30 . . . . . 146 E5
Dodman's La NR21 . . . . 31 F2
Dodmans The NR19 . . . 154 D4
Dodma Rd PE32 . . . . . . 47 C8
Dodson Dr
🖪 Beetley NR19 . . . . . . 49 C3
🖪 Gressenhall NR20 . . . 49 C3
Doe La
Banham NR16 . . . . 119 E8
Old Buckenham NR17 . . . 104 E1
Dog Cnr NR11 . . . . 35 A5
Dogger La NR23 . . . . . . 136 C6
Doggetts La NR22 . . . . . . 24 D4
Dog La
Easton NR9 . . . . 70 B6
Horsford NR10 . . . . 155 F4
Shelfanger IP22 . . . . 120 A4
Dogs La NR34 . . . . 110 C3
Dogwood Cl 🖪 NR18 . . . 173 E4
Dogwood Rd NR6 . . . . . 158 D4
Dohamero La 🖪 PE33 . . 43 F7
Doit La NR22 . . . . 129 D7
Doit The IP22 . . . . 129 C6
Dolman Cl 🖪 NR31 . . . . 169 B4
Dolphin Gr NR2 . . . . . . 162 B8
Doman Rd NR1 . . . . 178 C3
Donchurch Cl 🖪 NR5 . . 161 A7
Doris Barnes Ct 🖪 NR19 154 E5
Doris Rd NR2 . . . . 162 B5
Dorking Rd NR11 . . . . . 171 B4
Dorothea Dr 🖪 NR19 . . 154 D3
Dorothy Ave NR31 . . . . . 94 C7
Dorrs Dr IP25 . . . . 84 D4
Dorset Cl
Attleborough NR17 . . . . . 174 B3
🖪 Great Yarmouth NR30 169 D3
Doubleday Cl IP27 . . . . . 177 C4
Doughty's Hospl NR1 . . 178 B4
Douglas Bader Cl NR28 . 151 C7
Douglas Bader Sch The
NR10 . . . . 37 B2
Douglas Cl
Croxton IP24 . . . . 116 C5
Norwich NR6 . . . . 158 D7
Douglas Haig Rd NR5 . . 161 D6
Doune Way 🖪 IP20 . . . . 122 D2
Douro PE31 . . . . 162 C6
Dove Cl
🖪 Great Yarmouth
NR31 . . . . 170 A6
🖪 Harleston IP20 . . . . . 122 D1
Dovecote Cl NR15 . . . . . . 90 F2
Dovecote Rd PE14 . . . . . 77 D3
Dovedale Rd NR18 . . . . 105 F5
Dovedales Fold NR7 . . . 158 F4
Dovehouse La NR11 . . . . 21 B4
Dove House La 🖪 NR19 . . 56 F6
Dove La NR15 . . . . 90 C3
Dover Ct NR30 . . . . 168 C5
Dover St NR2 . . . . 162 B5
Dove St 🖪 NR3 . . . . 178 A3
Dow Cl NR5 . . . . 160 F5
Dowding Rd
Norwich NR6 . . . . 158 D6
🖪 Watton IP25 . . . . 84 F3
DOWE HILL NR29 . . . . . 167 C5
Dow La NR12 . . . . 54 C3
Downham Cres NR18 . . 173 B6
Downham Dro PE32 . . . . 63 F7
DOWNHAM MARKET
PE38 . . . . 172 C4
Downham Mkt Coll PE38 172 C4
Downham Mkt High Sch &
Tech Coll PE38 . . . . 172 D5
Downham Mkt Sta PE38 172 D5
Downham Prep Sch PE34 . 79 B8
Downham Rd
Crimplesham PE33 . . . . . . 80 B7
Denver PE38 . . . . 172 C2
Fincham PE33 . . . . 62 E1
Nordelph PE38 . . . . 78 D3
Outwell PE14 . . . . 77 F6
Runcton Holme PE33 . . . . 61 D4
Stradsett PE33 . . . . 80 D8
Downham Way IP27 . . . 175 F4
Downing Cl NR31 . . . . . 170 C4
Downing News NR5 . . . 160 D8
Downing Rd NR31 . . . . . 170 C4
Downs Cl PE36 . . . . 132 D4
Downs Farm La IP20 . . . 123 B3
Downs Rd NR3 . . . . 132 D4
Dowsing Cl 🖪 NR13 . . . . 72 D5
Dowson Fst Sch NR3 . . 158 A1
Dowson Rd NR3 . . . . . . 158 B1

DRABBLEGATE NR11 . . 150 D8
Drabblegate NR11 . . . . . 150 D8
Drabbs La NR12 . . . . 38 E6
Dragon Hall★ NR1 . . . . 178 C2
Dragoon Cl 🖪 NR7 . . . . . 72 D4
Drake Ave NR30 . . . . . . 169 D7
Drake Cl 🖪 NR9 . . . . 88 D8
Drake Inf Sch IP24 . . . . 176 E6
Drake Rd IP24 . . . . 176 E5
Drakes Cl 🖪 NR16 . . . . 118 C5
Drakes Loke NR10 . . . . . 36 F1
Drapers La NR35 . . . . . . 109 A3
Draper Way NR5 . . . . . . 160 D8
Draycote Cl IP20 . . . . . . 122 E4
Draycotts Rise IP22 . . . . 177 C1
DRAYTON NR8 . . . . 157 A8
Drayton Com Fst Sch
NR8 . . . . 155 F1
Drayton Gr NR8 . . . . 156 F8
Draytonhall La NR9 . . . . 154 B3
Drayton High Rd NR8 . . 157 A8
Drayton La NR10 . . . . . . 53 B1
Drayton Lodge Pk NR8 . 157 B7
Drayton Rd NR3 . . . . . . 157 F2
Drayton Wood Rd NR8 . 157 D6
Dreibholz Ct NR20 . . . . 154 F5
Drewray Dr NR8 . . . . . . 155 E2
Dried Flower Ctr★ NR12 . 55 C7
Drift La IP25 . . . . 85 F1
Driftlands NR21 . . . . . . 141 D5
Drift Rd
Caister-on-Sea NR30 . . . 168 C7
Lakenheath IP27 . . . . . . 113 E2
DRIFTBLEACH
Bawdeswell NR20 . . . . . . 50 E6
Beetley NR20 . . . . 49 A6
Botesdale IP22 . . . . 128 E3
Fakenham NR21 . . . . 141 D4
Fulmodeston NR21 . . . . . 17 F3
Heacham PE31 . . . . 133 D6
Ingoldisthorpe PE31 . . . 140 C8
Swardeston NR14 . . . . . . 89 B5
Driftway PE30 . . . . 148 C1
Driftway The
🖪 Holt NR25 . . . . 137 C5
Sheringham NR26 . . . . . 138 D8
Drill Sch NR21 . . . . 15 C3
Drinkwater Cl 🖪 NR9 . . . 86 C5
Drive The
Acle NR13 . . . . 166 D4
East Winch PE32 . . . . 45 A2
Norwich NR5 . . . . 161 B8
Trowse with Newton NR14 163 D1
Drout's La IP31 . . . . 127 C3
Drovers Rest NR15 . . . . 108 C8
Drove The
Brandon IP27 . . . . 114 D4
Raynham NR21 . . . . 30 E4
Taverham NR8 . . . . 155 C2
Drudge Rd NR30 . . . . . . 170 D4
Druids La
Litcham PE32 . . . . 48 A4
Shelfanger IP22 . . . . 120 B2
Druids' La IP22 . . . . 120 A3
Drunken Dro PE32 . . . . . 46 C8
Drury Cl 🖪 NR5 . . . . . . 161 B8
Drury La
🖪 Castle Acre PE32 . . . 46 F2
🖪 Loddon NR14 . . . . 91 F1
DRURYLANE IP25 . . . . . . 85 A4
Dryden Cl 🖪 IP24 . . . . . 176 E6
Dryden Rd NR8 . . . . 156 D8
DRYMERE PE37 . . . . 64 C1
Duck Decoy Cl PE31 . . . 140 C3
Duck Dro CB7 . . . . 112 A2
Duckett Cl 🖪 NR1 . . . . . 162 E1
Duck's Foot Rd IP21 . . . 121 F6
Duffield Cres NR2 . . . . . 51 A4
Duff Rd NR3 . . . . 158 D2
Dugard Ave NR1 . . . . . . 163 B8
Duke Rd NR31 . . . . 170 D6
Duke's La NR17 . . . . 102 E8
Duke St
Norwich NR3 . . . . 178 A4
Wisbech PE13 . . . . 152 D4
Dukesway 🖪 NR35 . . . . 123 F8
Dulgate La PE37 . . . . 64 C3
Dulgate Rd NR35 . . . . . 108 B3
Dull's Rd NR35 . . . . 109 C5
Dumbs La NR10 . . . . 53 E5
Dumpling Gn
Dereham NR19 . . . . 68 A6
East Dereham NR19 . . . . 154 F2
DUMPLING GREEN NR19 154 F3
Dunburgh Rd NR34 . . . . 110 A2
Duncan Cl IP24 . . . . 176 F6
Duncan Rd 🖪 NR30 . . . . 169 D2
Dun Cow Gdns NR34 . . . 144 E7
Dun Cow Rd NR34 . . . . . 111 B4
Dunford La IP24 . . . . . . 102 A2
Dunham Rd
Litcham PE32 . . . . 48 A4
Necton PE37 . . . . 65 F6
Dunhill La IP22 . . . . 127 F1
DUNKIRK NR11 . . . . 150 E8
Dunkirk Rd NR11 . . . . . 150 E8
Dunlop Rd NR19 . . . . . . 154 B6
Dunnett Cl NR17 . . . . . . 174 E5
Dunnetts Cl IP25 . . . . . . 84 D2
Dunning's La IP21 . . . . . 121 E6
Dunns La NR21 . . . . 49 C1
DUNSTON NR14 . . . . 89 D1
Dunston Dro PE31 . . . . . 133 B1
DUNTON NR21 . . . . 15 F1
Dunwood Dr NR6 . . . . . 158 F7
Durbidge's Hill IP22 . . . 120 E1
Durham Ave NR31 . . . . . 170 B2
Durham Rd NR31 . . . . . 162 B4

Durham Way IP24 . . . . . 176 A5
Dussindale 🖪 NR18 . . . 173 C6
Dussindale Dr 🖪 NR7 . . 72 D4
DUSSINDALE PARK NR13 . 72 E4
Duverlin Cl NR4 . . . . 162 A1
Dyball's La NR12 . . . . . . 38 F8
Dyers Yd NR3 . . . . 178 A3
Dye's Rd NR13 . . . . 73 C7
Dyes The NR20 . . . . 33 E8**

E

Eade Rd NR3 . . . . 162 D8
Eagle Cl NR11 . . . . 21 B2
Eagle House Sch NR16 . . 119 E7
Eagle Rd NR11 . . . . 21 B2
Eagles Ct NR23 . . . . 136 E4
Eagles The 🖪 NR30 . . . . 169 D4
Eagle Wlk 🖪 NR2 . . . . . 162 C4
Earl Cl NR11 . . . . 140 C3
EARLHAM NR4 . . . . 161 D5
Earlham Gn La NR5 . . . . 161 B7
Earlham Gr NR5 . . . . 161 D6
Earlham High Sch NR4 . . 161 D5
Earlham Rd NR4 . . . . . . 161 C5
Earlham W Gdns NR5 . . 161 C6
Earl of Brandon Ave NR31 30 B3
Earl Rd NR13 . . . . 72 E8
Earlsford Rd IP23 . . . . . 129 D1
Earls' St IP24 . . . . 176 D4
Earl Warren IP24 . . . . . . 116 C5
Earnshaw Ct NR1 . . . . . 163 D5
EARSHAM NR35 . . . . . . 123 E8
Earsham CE VA Fst Sch
NR35 . . . . 123 F8
Earsham Dam NR35 . . . 123 F8
Earsham Dr PE30 . . . . . 148 D8
Earsham Rd NR35 . . . . . 108 C8
EARSHAM STREET IP21 . 131 F5
Earth La NR32 . . . . 94 C1
East Anglian Way NR31 . 170 C6
East Ave NR13 . . . . 165 E3
East Bank PE12 . . . . 41 C8
EAST BARSHAM NR21 . . 16 C5
EAST BILNEY NR20 . . . . . 49 A6
East Bilney Hall NR20 . . 49 A6
Eastbourne Pl NR1 . . . . 178 C3
East Carleton NR14 . . . . 88 F4
East Carleton Rd NR14 . . 89 A4
East Cres NR20 . . . . 50 B5
East Dereham Sta NR20 . 154 E5
East End PE38 . . . . 79 E1
East End Cl NR30 . . . . . . 168 E8
Easterley Way NR29 . . . 167 A7
Eastern Ave
Caister-on-Sea NR30 . . . 168 D6
Norwich NR7 . . . . 72 D4
Eastern Cl
Caister-on-Sea NR30 . . . 168 D6
Norwich NR7 . . . . 72 D4
Eastern Cres NR7 . . . . . . 72 D4
Eastern Rd NR7 . . . . 72 D4
East Farm La NR10 . . . . . 53 B1
Eastfen Dro IP26 . . . . . . 114 B6
Eastfield NR8 . . . . 156 D8
Eastfield Cl PE30 . . . . . . 147 A6
Eastfield Rd
Hickling NR12 . . . . 39 F2
Long Stratton NR15 . . . . 106 F4
🖪 Wisbech PE13 . . . . . . 152 E7
Eastfields
King's Lynn PE30 . . . . . . 147 C4
Narborough PE32 . . . . . . 63 F7
Eastfield Way NR13 . . . . 152 C6
EASTGATE NR10 . . . . 35 C2
Eastgate IP25 . . . . 67 D3
Eastgate Dro
Congham PE31 . . . . 28 D2
Grimston PE32 . . . . 45 D8
Hillington PE31 . . . . 28 C3
Eastgate Prim Sch PE30 146 E5
Eastgate Rd PE36 . . . . . . 2 A6
Eastgate St
🖪 King's Lynn PE30 . . . 146 E5
North Elmham NR20 . . . . 49 E7
Shouldham PE33 . . . . 62 D4
East Gn NR9 . . . . 68 F2
East Gr NR27 . . . . 139 C5
East Harbour Way PE31 . 135 E2
EAST HARLING NR16 . . . 118 C5
East Harling Prim Sch
NR16 . . . . 118 C5
East Harling Rd NR16 . . 118 F4
EASTHAUGH NR9 . . . . . . 51 C4
Easthaugh Rd NR9 . . . . . 51 D4
Easthill La NR14 . . . . 90 E8
East Hills Rd NR5 . . . . . 156 E1
East La PE31 . . . . 134 E4
Eastland Ct NR17 . . . . . 174 E6
Eastlands Bank PE14 . . . 41 E5
Eastleigh Gdns 🖪 NR9 . . 69 F2
EAST LEXHAM PE32 . . . . 47 D3
Eastmans La PE32 . . . . . 28 D8
Eastmoor Cl PE33 . . . . . 81 E4
Eastmoor Rd PE33 . . . . . 81 C7
East Norfolk 6th Form Coll
NR31 . . . . 170 A6
EASTON NR9 . . . . 70 B5
Easton Coll NR9 . . . . 70 C4
Easton Way NR10 . . . . . . 35 C1
EAST RAYNHAM NR21 . . 31 A4
East Rd
Great Yarmouth NR30 . . . 169 D5
Watton IP25 . . . . 84 D3
EAST RUDHAM PE31 . . . 30 A7

EAST RUNTON NR27 . . . . 10 B5
EAST RUSTON NR12 . . . . 38 E6
East Ruston Area Com Sch
NR12 . . . . 38 F7
East Ruston Old Vicarage
Gdn★ NR12 . . . . 24 A3
East Ruston Rd NR28 . . . 38 D6
EAST SOMERTON NR29 . . 58 A6
EAST TUDDENHAM NR20 . 69 C6
EAST WALTON PE32 . . . . 45 E3
East WINCH NR20 . . . . . 44 F3
East WINCH CE Prim Sch
PE32 . . . . 44 F3
East Winchcommon (Nature
Reserve)★ PE32 . . . . . . 45 A2
East Winch Rd
Leziate PE32 . . . . 44 F5
Middleton PE32 . . . . 44 C2
Eastwood PE31 . . . . 134 F3
EAST WRETHAM IP24 . . 102 A1
EATON NR4 . . . . 161 F2
Eaton Chase NR4 . . . . . 161 E2
Eaton Dro
Sedgeford PE36 . . . . 13 A7
Snettisham PE31 . . . . 12 F5
Eaton Gdns NR19 . . . . . 154 E3
Eaton Hall Specl Sch
NR4 . . . . 161 F3
Eaton Rd NR4 . . . . 162 B2
Eaton St
Cringleford NR4 . . . . 89 B8
Norwich NR4 . . . . 161 E1
EAU BRINK PE34 . . . . . . 43 A3
Eau Brink Rd PE34 . . . . . 43 A2
Ebbisham Dr NR4 . . . . . 161 F1
Ebble Cl PE30 . . . . 148 C2
Ebenezer Pl NR3 . . . . . . 178 A4
Eccles CE Prim Sch
NR16 . . . . 118 F8
ECCLES ON SEA NR12 . . . 24 E4
Eccles Rd NR25 . . . . 137 C7
Eccles Rd Sta NR16 . . . . 103 E1
ECCLES ROAD NR16 . . . 103 F1
Ecclestone Cl NR31 . . . . 170 A4
Eckersley Dr NR21 . . . . . 141 A6
Ecotech Ctr★ PE37 . . . . 153 B6
Ecton Gr 🖪 PE14 . . . . . . 59 A1
Ecton Wlk NR5 . . . . 158 F5
Eddington Way NR9 . . . . 70 B5

Eden Cl
Bacton/Walcott NR12 . . . 23 E4
Norwich NR7 . . . . 163 C6
Edenhurst Cl NR4 . . . . . 161 F3
Eden La NR17 . . . . 174 D5
Edenside Dr NR17 . . . . . 174 D5
Edge Bank PE14 . . . . 77 F8
Edgebrook NR26 . . . . . . 138 D6
EDGEFIELD NR29 . . . . . . 19 D5
Edgefield Cl NR6 . . . . . . 158 F7
Edgefield Hill NR25 . . . . 137 C2
Edgefield Rd NR24 . . . . . 142 E5
EDGEFIELD STREET NR24 . 19 D4
Edgehill Rd NR16 . . . . . . 119 B4
Edgehill 🖪 PE37 . . . . . . 153 B6
Edges La 🖪 NR15 . . . . . 106 E3
Edge's La NR15 . . . . 107 A3
Edgeworth Rd 🖪 NR5 . . 161 C6
Edinburgh Ave
Great Yarmouth NR31 . . . 170 B2
King's Lynn PE30 . . . . . . 147 C7
Edinburgh Cl
🖪 Barnham IP24 . . . . . . 125 E2
Caister-on-Sea NR30 . . . 168 E5
🖪 Watton IP25 . . . . 84 D3
Edinburgh Ct 🖪 NR30 . . 146 E5
Edinburgh Dr
Fakenham NR21 . . . . 141 C6
Wisbech PE13 . . . . 152 C8
Edinburgh Pl
Great Yarmouth NR30 . . . 169 B3
🖪 Wiggenhall St Germans
PE34 . . . . 43 B1
Edinburgh Rd
Holt NR25 . . . . 137 C5
Norwich NR2 . . . . 162 A6
Edinburgh Way
Dersingham PE31 . . . . . . 140 D3
Thetford IP24 . . . . 176 A5
EDINGTHORPE NR28 . . . . 23 C3
EDINGTHORPE GREEN
NR28 . . . . 23 A2
Edison Way NR31 . . . . . . 170 A8
Edith Cavell Cl 🖪 IP24 . . 176 D7
Edma St PE30 . . . . 146 E6
Edmondson Wlk NR21 . . 141 D4
Edmund Bacon Ct 🖪
NR3 . . . . 162 D8
Edmund Moundford Rd 🖪
PE30 . . . . 98 E1
Edmund Rd IP27 . . . . . . 175 A2
Edrich Cl NR13 . . . . 165 E6
Edrich Way NR5 . . . . . . 160 E7
Edward Benefer Way
King's Lynn PE30 . . . . . . 146 D6
North Wootton PE30 . . . . 26 E1
Edward Gambling Ct 🖪
NR2 . . . . 162 B8
Edward Rd NR29 . . . . 58 B5
Edwards Cl NR20 . . . . . . 50 B2
Edward Seago Pl NR15 . . 90 E2
Edward St NR1 . . . . 159 A5
Edward St
🖪 King's Lynn PE30 . . . 146 E3
Norwich NR1 . . . . 178 B4
Edward Worlledge Mid Sch
NR31 . . . . 169 C2
Edwin Cl NR18 . . . . 173 B5
Eels Foot Rd NR29 . . . . . 57 E1

Egmere Medieval Village of★ NR22 16 B8
Egmere Rd NR22 16 F8
Egremont Rd IP22 177 B5
Eighth Ave PE13 152 E4
El Alamein Way NR31 94 C8
Elan Cl NR18 173 D3
Elden's La IP26 98 F5
Elderberry Dr 5 NR20 68 A8
Elderbush La NR29 56 C7
Elder Gn NR31 170 B5
Elder La PE32 45 C8
Elders The IP27 113 F1
Elderton La NR28 22 B5
Eleanor Rd NR1 162 D3
Eleven Mile Rd NR18 87 C1
Elgin IP24 176 A5
Elgood's Brewery & Gdn★ PE13 152 A4
Eliot Cl IP24 176 E6
Elise Way NR18 173 D2
Elizabethan House Mus★ NR30 169 C3
Elizabeth Ave
  Downham Market PE38 172 B5
  Fakenham NR21 141 C6
  Norwich NR7 163 F7
Elizabeth Cl
  Attleborough NR17 174 C6
  East Dereham NR19 154 D1
  Hunstanton PE36 132 C3
  Norwich NR7 159 A5
  Reepham NR10 149 B4
Elizabeth Cres
  Caister-on-Sea NR30 168 E6
  4 Holt NR25 137 C5
Elizabeth Dr PE37 65 F3
Elizabeth Fry Cl 9 IP24 176 D7
Elizabeth Fry Rd NR2 161 F4
Elizabeth Rd
  Brandon IP27 175 C3
  10 Poringland NR14 90 D5
Elizabeth Terr PE13 152 D4
Elizabeth Watling Cl 3 IP24 176 D7
Elizabeth Way 5 IP23 130 C1
Elizabeth Wlk 27 IP20 122 D2
Elkins Rd NR18 173 B5
Ella Rd NR1 163 A6
Ellcar Rise 4 NR4 161 F1
Ellenhill NR27 139 D5
Eller Dr PE33 43 E2
ELLINGHAM NR35 109 D3
Ellingham Prim Sch NR35 109 D3
Ellingham Rd
  Attleborough NR17 174 B7
  Scoulton NR9 85 E3
Ellington Rd
  2 Barnham IP24 125 F6
  Watton IP25 85 A3
Ellinor Rd NR28 151 D3
Ellis Cl 4 NR12 39 B4
Ellison Cl NR17 174 E4
Ellison Dr NR17 174 E4
ELM PE14 59 B1
Elm Ave NR31 170 C4
Elm CE Jun Sch PE14 59 B1
Elm Cl
  Acle NR13 166 C4
  Brandon IP27 175 E3
  Downham Market PE38 172 B6
  King's Lynn PE30 148 D2
  5 Lingwood NR13 74 A3
  7 Loddon NR14 91 F1
  Mulbarton NR14 89 B3
  North Elmham NR20 49 E8
  Norwich NR5 156 F2
  Yaxham NR19 68 A5
Elmdon Ct 9 NR1 163 A6
Elmer's La NR15 107 A8
Elmfield Dr PE14 152 E1
Elm Gr
  Garboldisham IP22 128 A8
  Sheringham NR26 138 E5
Elm Gr La NR3 158 D2
Elmgrove Rd NR31 170 C3
Elmham Rd
  Beetley NR20 49 D4
  North Elmham NR20 50 A7
Elm High Rd PE14 152 E1
Elm Hill NR3 178 B3
Elmhurst Ave NR12 39 C2
Elmhurst Cl NR31 170 C3
Elmhurst Dr PE30 148 C2
Elm La PE31 30 D8
Elm Low Rd PE14 152 D2
Elm Pk NR19 154 E1
Elm Rd
  Caister-on-Sea NR30 168 E4
  Lingwood NR13 74 A3
  Marham PE33 63 B4
  Thetford IP24 176 B1
  Wisbech PE13 152 D3
Elm Rd Prim Sch PE13 152 D4
Elms Cl 6 NR35 123 F8
Elmside PE14 59 D1
Elms Rd NR34 110 E5
Elmstead Rd PE30 147 C4
Elms The
  Hindringham NR21 17 E6
  Norwich NR6 158 E6
Elm Terr 2 NR18 173 C4
Elmtree Gr PE33 43 E1
Elsden Cl 2 NR25 137 C5
Elsie Rd NR31 169 B3
ELSING NR20 50 F3
Elsing Dr PE30 147 D8
Elsing La
  Bawdeswell NR20 50 E6
  Dereham NR20 50 C1
Elsing Rd
  Lyng NR9 51 A5
  North Tuddenham NR20 50 E2
  Swanton Morley NR20 50 C4
Elstead Cl 11 NR4 89 C8
ELVEDEN IP24 125 A7
Elveden Cl NR4 161 F1
Elveden Rd IP24 125 D6
Elvina Rd 10 NR10 54 A2
Elvington PE30 147 D5
Elvin Rd NR19 154 D6
Elvin Way 3 NR3 157 F1
Elworthy Cl IP25 84 F3
Elwyn Rd 7 NR1 162 E2
Ely Pl 19 PE13 152 C5
Ely Rd
  Denver PE38 172 D2
  Hilgay PE38 97 B8
Ely Row PE14 42 B1
Ely St NR2 162 C7
Ely Way IP24 176 A5
Embry Cl NR6 158 D6
Embry Cres NR6 158 C6
Emelson Cl NR19 154 D6
Emery Cl 5 NR26 138 C5
Emery's La NR11 21 B6
Emmanuel Ave NR31 170 B2
Emmas Way NR13 73 B6
Emmerich Ct 6 PE30 146 E5
Emms's La NR21 17 E7
EMNETH PE14 59 D2
EMNETH HUNGATE PE14 59 F2
Emneth Prim Sch PE14 59 D2
EMORSGATE PE34 42 B7
Emorsgate PE34 42 B7
Empire Ave PE30 147 B8
Empress Rd NR31 169 B3
Empsons Loke NR29 58 B6
End Lodge PE31 133 C5
Enfield Rd NR5 161 C6
Engine Rd
  Hilgay PE38 96 F7
  Sculthorpe Airfield NR21 15 D2
England's La NR31 170 D4
Englands Rd NR13 166 B4
English Rd NR6 158 E4
Ennerdale Dr PE30 148 F2
Enterprise Way
  Fakenham NR21 141 E5
  King's Lynn PE33 43 E4
  Wisbech PE13 152 A2
Entrance La NR15 90 E2
Entry The IP22 177 D4
Enue 13 PE33 63 B4
Eppingham Cl IP24 176 F6
Epsom Gdns NR19 154 E3
Erica Way NR31 170 B6
Erins The 1 NR6 158 E1
Eriswell Dr IP27 113 E1
ERPINGHAM NR11 21 B2
Erpingham Ct PE36 132 E7
Erpingham Prim Sch NR11 21 B2
Esdelle St 9 NR3 162 D8
Esplanade NR27 139 B7
Esplanade The
  Hemsby NR29 167 E5
  Sheringham NR26 138 C7
Esprit Cl NR18 173 D2
Essex St NR2 162 C5
Estcourt Rd
  2 Attleborough NR17 174 C5
  Great Yarmouth NR30 169 D6
Estelle Way NR18 173 E6
Estuary Cl PE30 146 E7
Estuary Rd PE30 146 D7
Ethel Colman Way IP24 176 D7
Ethel Gooch Rd NR18 173 B5
Ethel Rd NR1 163 A5
Ethel Terr 5 PE30 146 E3
Ethel Tipple Cl NR11 150 C4
Ethel Tipple Dr NR11 150 C4
Ethel Tipple Specl Sch PO30 147 D4
ETLING GREEN NR20 68 B8
Eurocentre Ind Est NR30 169 B7
Europa Way
  Norwich NR1 163 A2
  Wisbech PE13 152 B2
EUSTON IP24 126 B5
Euston Hall★ IP24 126 B5
Euston Rd NR30 169 D4
Euston Way PE30 148 D1
Euximoor Dro PE14 77 B1
Eva Cl 4 IP25 67 B2
Evans Gdns PE36 132 D3
Evans Lombe Cl NR29 57 A4
Evans Way NR6 158 D6
Eva Rd NR13 72 E7
Evelyn Cl IP21 131 A3
Evelyn Way 4 PE30 147 A8
Eversley Rd NR6 158 B4
Everson Cl
  Norwich NR5 157 C1
  11 Tasburgh NR15 106 F6
Ewing Cl NR10 149 B4
Excalibur Rd 2 NR31 170 B1
Exchange Rd 7 NR15 89 C1
Exchange Sq PE13 152 B5
Exchange St
  Attleborough NR17 174 D5
  32 Harleston IP20 122 D2
  Norwich NR2 178 A3
Exeter Cres PE30 148 D5
Exeter Rd NR31 170 B4
Exeter St NR2 162 C7
Exeter Way 9 IP24 176 F5
Exmouth Cl 23 NR9 88 D8
Exmouth Pl 11 NR30 169 D4
Exmouth Rd NR30 169 D1
Exton's Gdns PE30 146 F3
Exton's Pl PE30 147 A3
Exton's Rd PE30 146 F4
EYE IP23 130 C1
Eye Airfield Ind Est IP23 130 B2
Eye La PE31 30 B7
Eye Rd IP23 130 A1

F

Factory La IP22 177 B5
Factory Rd NR30 169 D5
Faeroes Dr NR30 168 C6
Fair Cl
  Beccles NR34 110 D1
  13 Feltwell IP26 98 E1
Fairfax Dr
  6 Norwich NR7 72 D4
  3 Weeting IP27 114 E1
Fairfax Gall★ PE31 135 C3
Fairfax Rd NR4 161 F4
Fairfield Cl
  Great & Little Plumstead NR13 73 B7
  Mundesley NR11 143 C6
Fairfield Dr NR17 174 C4
Fairfield La 10 PE33 61 D6
Fairfield Rd
  Downham Market PE38 172 A5
  5 Middleton PE32 44 B3
  Norwich NR2 162 C3
  4 Stoke Ferry PE33 81 A3
Fairfields
  Cawston NR10 35 B2
  Thetford IP24 176 D5
Fairfields Way NR11 36 D4
Fairfield Way 11 IP26 98 E1
Fair Gn IP22 177 C4
FAIR GREEN PE32 44 B4
Fairhaven CE VA Prim Sch NR13 74 B8
Fairhaven Ct NR2 162 A6
Fairhaven Woodland & Water Gdn★ NR13 74 A8
Fairhill Dro PE33 80 E2
Fairholme Cl IP25 84 A8
Fairholme Rd NR10 53 E4
Fairisle Dr NR30 168 C5
Fairland St NR18 173 C3
Fairmile Cl NR2 162 B3
FAIRSTEAD PE30 147 D4
Fairstead Cl
  North Walsham NR28 151 A3
  Pulham Market IP21 121 E5
Fairstead Ct NR7 159 A3
Fairstead Dro PE33 62 D4
Fairstead La
  Hempnall NR15 107 A5
  Little Cressingham IP25 83 D3
Fairstead Prim Sch PE30 147 D4
Fairstead Rd NR7 159 A3
Fairstead The
  Botesdale IP22 128 E3
  2 Cley next the Sea NR25 7 E6
  1 Holt NR25 137 B6
  Scottow NR10 37 D2
Fairview Cl NR8 157 A7
Fairview Dr NR21 31 E5
Fairview Rd NR28 151 E4
Fairway NR30 168 E3
Fairway Fst Sch NR4 162 A1
Fairway Mid Sch NR4 162 A1
Fairways
  Norwich NR6 157 D5
  Stuston IP21 130 B5
Fairway The NR31 171 D8
FAKENHAM NR21 141 D6
Fakenham Coll NR21 141 B5
Fakenham High Sch NR21 141 B6
Fakenham Hill IP31 126 C2
Fakenham Jun Sch NR21 141 C4
FAKENHAM MAGNA IP24 126 C3
Fakenham Mus★ NR21 141 B3
Fakenham Race Course NR21 141 D2
Fakenham Rd
  Attlebridge NR9 52 C2
  Beetley NR20 49 C5
  Briston NR24 142 C5
  Docking PE31 134 E4
  East Rudham PE31 30 A7
  Foxley NR20 33 C1
  Great Snoring NR21 17 A5
  Ryburgh NR21 32 A6
  Sculthorpe NR21 141 A5
  South Creake NR21 15 E6
  Sparham NR9 51 A6
  Taverham NR8 155 B2
  Tittleshall PE32 48 A7
Fakenham View NR21 31 E5
Fakes Rd NR29 167 D6
Falcon Ave IP22 177 F5
Falcon Ct 15 NR30 169 C4
Falcon Dr IP27 175 F3
Falconers Chase NR18 173 F5
Falcon La
  Bungay NR35 109 A1
  24 Wisbech PE13 152 C5
Falcon Mews NR7 159 C4
Falcon Mid Sch NR7 159 C3
Falcon Rd
  14 Feltwell IP26 98 E1
  Norwich NR7 159 C3
  Pulham Market IP21 121 E5
  7 Wisbech PE13 152 C5
Falcon Rd E NR7 159 C2
Falcon Rd W NR7 159 C4
Falgate NR10 35 C2
Falkland Cl NR6 157 D5
Falklands Dr PE13 152 E3
Falklands Rd PE12 41 A8
Falkland Way 13 NR31 94 C6
Fall Gn NR14 90 D4
Fallowfield
  4 Hemsby NR29 167 B7
  8 Poringland NR14 90 D5
Fallowfield Cl NR1 163 B8
Fallow Pipe Rd PE34 43 B2
Fallows The 3 NR8 155 D2
Faraday Pl IP24 176 B2
Faraday Rd NR31 170 A8
Fardell Rd 7 PE13 152 C4
Farebrother Way 2 NR19 154 C3
Farman Ave NR28 151 D5
Farman Cl
  5 Belton NR31 94 A6
  Lyng NR9 51 A5
  7 Salhouse NR13 55 A1
Farm Cl
  Lingwood NR13 74 A2
  11 Loddon NR14 92 A2
Farm Ct St IP20 123 A1
Farmers Ave NR1 178 B2
Farm La NR13 56 A1
Farmland Rd NR5 156 F1
Farm Rd
  Heckingham NR14 92 D1
  Worstead NR28 38 A7
Farm View NR28 151 E5
Farmway 7 NR19 154 D2
Farm Wlk
  Marham PE33 63 C5
  6 Necton PE37 65 F4
Farnborough Rd 9 IP25 84 F3
Farrow Cl
  2 Great Moulton NR15 106 B1
  7 Mattishall NR20 68 E6
  2 Swanton Morley NR20 50 B3
Farthing Cl
  Diss IP22 177 D6
  Loddon NR14 109 D8
Farthing Dro
  Beck Row, Holywell Row & Kenny Hill IP27 112 E2
  Lakenheath IP27 113 A2
  Southery PE38 97 A2
Farthing Rd PE38 79 B5
Fastnet Way 1 NR30 168 C6
Fastolf Cl NR6 157 E5
Fastolff Ave NR31 170 B3
Fayers Terr PE30 147 A4
Fayregreen NR21 141 D4
Feale Abbey PE34 144 A1
Fearn's Cl NR27 139 D5
Featherstone Ct 5 NR19 154 D2
FELBRIGG NR11 10 C2
Felbrigg Cl PE30 148 F1
Felbrigg Hall Garden & Park★ NR11 10 B2
Felbrigg Rd
  Downham Market PE38 172 C6
  Roughton NR11 21 D8
Fellowes Dr 2 NR31 94 C6
Fellowes Rd NR9 69 E6
Fellows Cl NR5 161 D6
Fell Way 3 NR31 94 C8
FELMINGHAM NR28 37 A8
Felmingham Rd NR28 37 C7
Felsham Way NR8 155 E2
Felsted Ave PE13 152 E5
FELTHORPE NR10 155 C8
Felthorpe Rd NR9 52 B3
FELTWELL IP26 98 D1
Feltwell Elementary Sch IP26 98 D1
Feltwell Prim Sch IP26 98 E2
Feltwell Rd
  Hockwold cum Wilton IP26 113 F7
  Methwold IP26 98 E5
  Southery PE38 97 D5
Fence Bank PE14 42 A1
Fences Farm Rd PE34 78 E8
Fen Cl PE13 152 E6
Fen Dro PE33 81 F3
Fendyke Rd PE14 59 E1
Fen Folgate 6 IP25 67 B2
FENGATE NR10 150 C1
Fengate
  Heacham PE31 133 C4
  Marsham NR10 150 D1
Fengate Dro IP27 175 B6
Fengate Rd PE14 59 C5
Fen La
  Banham NR16 119 B6
  Beccles NR34 110 D2
  Ditchingham NR35 108 E3
  Garboldisham IP22 128 A7
  Grimston PE32 45 A7
  Harling NR16 118 C6
  Leziate PE32 45 A6
  Marham PE33 63 A5
  Rickinghall Inferior IP22 128 E2
  Roydon IP22 129 C7
Fen La *continued*
  Thelnetham IP22 128 B5
Fenland Rd
  King's Lynn PE30 147 C8
  Wisbech PE13 152 E6
Fenland & W Norfolk Aviation Mus★ PE14 59 C7
Fenn Cres NR3 158 B1
Fennel Way IP24 176 F4
Fenner Rd NR30 170 E7
Fen Rd
  Blo' Norton IP22 128 C6
  Carleton Rode NR16 105 C2
  Hinderclay IP22 128 C5
  Marham PE33 63 B4
  Scarning NR19 154 B3
  Watlington PE33 61 D5
FENSIDE NR29 56 B8
Fenside PE31 133 C4
Fen St
  Attleborough NR17 103 F3
  Old Buckenham NR17 104 C2
  Redgrave IP22 128 F6
  Rocklands NR17 103 B6
FEN STREET
  Hopton IP22 127 E6
  Redgrave IP22 128 F6
Fen View
  Christchurch PE14 95 A7
  East Dereham NR19 154 C2
Fenway PE31 133 B3
Fen Way 2 PE14 59 A1
Ferguson Way NR17 174 F7
Fermoy Ave PE30 146 E6
Fern Ct 3 NR18 173 B4
Ferndale Cl NR6 157 E4
Fern Dr NR28 151 E5
Fern Gdns NR31 93 F5
Fern Hill
  Dersingham PE31 140 E4
  Norwich NR1 163 B5
Fernlea Rd PE30 147 C4
Ferrier Cl 7 NR30 169 D5
Ferrier Ct NR29 167 B6
Ferrier Rd NR30 169 C5
Ferry Bank PE38 97 A4
Ferryboat La NR31 170 D7
Ferry Ct NR29 75 A5
Ferrygate La NR29 57 D5
Ferry Hill NR31 170 D7
Ferry La
  Great Yarmouth NR31 169 C2
  Norwich NR1 178 C3
  Postwick with Witton NR13 73 A2
  Stokesby with Herringby NR29 75 B5
Ferry Rd
  Carleton St Peter NR14 91 E5
  Clenchwarton PE34 145 F5
  Horning NR12 55 E3
  King's Lynn PE34 146 B6
  Norton Subcourse NR14 92 D2
  Norwich NR1 178 C3
  Oxborough PE33 81 D3
  Reedham NR13 92 E4
  Surlingham NR14 165 A1
  Woodbastwick NR13 55 D2
Ferry Sq PE34 146 C5
Ferry St PE30 146 D5
Ferry View Rd NR12 55 E3
FERSFIELD IP22 119 D2
Fersfield Rd
  Bressingham IP22 129 B8
  Kenninghall NR16 119 C4
  South Lopham IP22 128 F8
Festival Cl PE30 148 B1
Festival Rd NR20 50 B7
Festival Way CB6 96 E2
Ffolkes Dr
  King's Lynn PE30 148 C1
  Terrington St Clement PE34 144 B5
Ffolkes Pl 1 PE33 61 D3
FIDDLERS' GREEN NR17 174 B8
Fiddle Wood Rd NR6 158 D4
Field Acre Way NR15 106 E4
Field Barn Cotts PE32 46 E3
Fieldbarn Dro PE33 82 A4
Field Barn La PE33 61 F3
Fieldbarn Rd PE33 81 B8
FIELD DALLING NR25 7 B1
Field Dalling Rd
  Field Dalling NR25 7 A3
  Gunthorpe NR21 18 B8
Field End Cl PE30 147 B6
Fieldfare Cl 6 NR12 54 A1
Field House Gdns IP22 177 E5
Field La
  Beetley NR20 49 C5
  10 Blofield NR13 73 D6
  Blofield NR13 165 E8
  Fakenham NR21 141 B6
  Hempnall NR15 107 C4
  King's Lynn PE30 147 B6
  Marsham NR10 36 B2
  North Walsham NR28 151 E3
  Stody NR24 142 F8
  Whinburgh & Westfield NR19 67 F4
  Wretton PE33 80 F3
Field Rd
  Brandon IP27 114 D4
  King's Lynn PE30 147 B5
  Ringland NR8 70 B8
  South Walsham NR13 74 B8

Field Rd continued
Stalham NR12 . . . . 39 C3
Fields Rd NR34 . . . . 110 E6
Fields The
Forncett NR16 . . . . 105 E5
Hingham NR9 . . . . 86 C5
Fieldview NR5 . . . . 161 E6
Fiennes Rd 4 NR7 . . . . 72 D5
Fifers La NR6 . . . . 158 C6
Fifth Ave PE13 . . . . 152 E4
Fifty Dro CB6 . . . . 95 F3
Fifty Rd PE14 . . . . 95 A3
Filbert Rd NR14 . . . . 91 F1
Filberts PE30 . . . . 147 D5
FILBY NR29 . . . . 75 F8
Filby Cl NR29 . . . . 75 F8
Filby Fst Sch NR29 . . . . . . 75 E8
FILBY HEATH NR29 . . . . . . 76 B8
Filby La NR29 . . . . 167 A1
Filby Rd
Coltishall NR10 . . . . 37 B2
Stokesby with Herringby
NR29 . . . . 75 C6
Swaffham PE37 . . . . 153 B2
FINCHAM PE33 . . . . 62 F1
Fincham Dro PE32 . . . . 64 B5
Fincham Rd
Barton Bendish PE33 . . . . . 81 A8
Crimplesham PE33 . . . . 80 A8
Fincham PE33 . . . . 63 A1
Shouldham Thorpe PE33 . . 62 C2
Stow Bardolph PE34 . . . . . . 79 F8
Wereham PE33 . . . . 80 F6
Finch Cl
Cromer NR27 . . . . 139 C4
Norwich NR7 . . . . 159 D2
Finchdale Cl 5 NR30 . . . . . 148 C4
Finchley Cl 4 NR21 . . . . . 162 B7
Finch Way NR13 . . . . 165 C3
Finderne Dr NR18 . . . . 173 D6
Finishers Rd 8 NR6 . . . . . . 158 C1
Finisterre Rise 2 NR30 . . 168 C6
Finkelgate NR1 . . . . 178 B1
Finningham Rd IP22 . . . . . 128 E1
Finsbury Cl 1 PE38 . . . . . 172 B4
Fiona Cl NR18 . . . . 173 E6
Fir Cl
Heacham PE31 . . . . 133 C6
Mundford IP26 . . . . 100 B4
Fir Covert Rd
Carleton Rode NR16 . . . . . 105 A1
Taverham NR10 . . . . 155 B4
Firethorn Cl NR8 . . . . 155 B2
Fir Gr NR20 . . . . 138 D4
Fir La NR10 . . . . 34 A1
Firman Ct NR7 . . . . 163 F8
Fir Pk IP25 . . . . 84 A7
Fir Rd IP24 . . . . 176 B1
Firs Ave NR29 . . . . 167 A3
Firside Mid Sch NR6 . . . . 158 A6
Fir La NR12 . . . . 39 C2
Firs Rd
Hethersett NR9 . . . . 88 D7
Norwich NR6 . . . . 157 F6
First Ave PE13 . . . . 152 D5
First Dro IP27 . . . . 113 C3
Firs The
Downham Market PE38 . . . 172 D6
Lakenheath IP27 . . . . 113 F1
First Marsh Rd PE13 . . . . . 59 A6
Firs Way IP27 . . . . 175 C2
Firtree Cl NR13 . . . . 165 B4
Fir Tree Dr 7 PE33 . . . . . . 43 E2
Firtree Rd NR7 . . . . 159 E1
Firwood Cl NR13 . . . . 163 C8
Fisher Ave NR30 . . . . 169 D8
Fishergate NR3 . . . . 178 B4
Fisherman's Her Ctr★
NR26 . . . . 138 D8
Fishermen's Ct NR17 . . . . 174 D6
Fisher Rd
Diss IP22 . . . . 177 C4
Fakenham NR21 . . . . 141 B5
Fisher Row NR32 . . . . 111 F4
Fishers Cl NR5 . . . . 156 E1
Fishers La
Beetley NR20 . . . . 49 D6
Norwich NR2 . . . . 178 A3
Fisher's La IP21 . . . . 131 A4
Fishers' Quay NR30 . . . . . 169 C4
Fisher Way IP24 . . . . 176 E5
FISHLEY NR13 . . . . 166 C6
Fishley View NR13 . . . . . 166 B4
Fish Wharf 2 NR30 . . . . . 169 D1
Fiskes Ct NR14 . . . . 89 F5
Fiske's Opening 6 NR31 170 D4
Fison Way IP24 . . . . 176 C6
Fison Way Ind Est IP24 . . 176 C6
Fitton Rd NR24 . . . . 61 B8
Fitzalan Cl 8 NR30 . . . . . 169 C4
Fitzgerald Rd
Norwich NR1 . . . . 162 E1
7 Poringland NR14 . . . . . . 90 C5
Fitzhenry Mews 5 NR5 . . 161 B8
Fitzwalter Rd IP22 . . . . . . 177 E4
Five Acre La NR35 . . . . . . 123 E7
Five Acres NR14 . . . . 89 F4
Five Alls Rd PE14 . . . . 41 F1
Five Crossways NR12 . . . 164 D8
Five Elms 4 PE30 . . . . . . 147 C4
Flag St NR12 . . . . 15 C2
FLAXLANDS NR16 . . . . . . 105 C4
Flaxlands NR16 . . . . 105 B4
Flaxlands Rd NR16 . . . . . . 105 C3
Fleet La NR13 . . . . 56 B1

Fleet Rd NR8 . . . . 156 B6
Fleetwood Dr 4 NR13 . . . 72 D4
Fleggburgh Prim Sch
NR29 . . . . 75 C8
Fleggburgh Rd NR29 . . . . . 57 C2
Flegg Gn PE33 . . . . 80 D4
Flegg High Sch NR29 . . . . . 57 E6
Fleming Cl 3 IP25 . . . . . . 84 D3
Fletcher Cl NR12 . . . . 55 A8
Fletcher Way
Acle NR13 . . . . 166 D4
Cromer NR27 . . . . 139 B5
Norwich NR3 . . . . 158 C3
Flint Dr NR23 . . . . 136 D5
Flint Gate 17 PE12 . . . . . . 41 B8
Flint House Gdns 6 NR9 . 88 C7
Flint House Rd PE14 . . . . . 77 F1
Flint Way 2 PE14 . . . . 77 A8
FLITCHAM PE31 . . . . 28 C5
Flitcham Abbey PE31 . . . . 28 D5
Flitcham CE Prim Sch
PE31 . . . . 28 C5
FLIXTON NR35 . . . . 123 D5
Flixton Marsh La NR32 . . 111 F6
Flixton Rd
Bungay NR35 . . . . 124 A7
Flixton NR35 . . . . 123 E6
Lound NR32 . . . . 94 C1
Somerleyton, Ashby &
Herringfleet NR32 . . . . . 111 F8
St Margaret, South Elmham
IP20 . . . . 123 E3
FLORDON NR15 . . . . 106 D8
Flordon Rd
Bracon Ash NR14 . . . . 88 F1
Flordon NR15 . . . . 106 D8
Florence Barclay Cl
IP24 . . . . 176 D6
Florence Rd NR1 . . . . 163 A6
Florence Wlk NR15 . . . . . 154 D2
Florida Bvd NR21 . . . . 15 C2
Flowerday Cl NR31 . . . . . 171 D5
Flowerdew Cl 12 NR9 . . . 88 C7
Flowerdew's La NR13 . . . . 74 B7
Flowerpot La NR15 . . . . . 106 D3
Flowers La NR17 . . . . 174 B3
Fludge's La NR20 . . . . 49 B6
Flymore La NR17 . . . . 103 A8
Fodderfen Dro PE38 . . . . 113 A7
FODDERSTONE GAP PE33 . . 62 C4
Foldgate La PE34 . . . . 61 A5
Folgate NR16 . . . . 88 D1
Folgate Cl
Costessey NR8 . . . . 156 F5
Thornham PE36 . . . . 2 D6
Folgate La
Costessey NR8 . . . . 156 F4
Walpole PE14 . . . . 41 D3
Folgate Rd
Heacham PE31 . . . . 133 C4
North Walsham NR28 . . . . 151 B6
Folland Ct 8 NR20 . . . . . . 50 E7
Follies The PE37 . . . . 65 F4
Folly Cl NR18 . . . . 173 C5
Folly Gr PE30 . . . . 147 B7
Folly La
Beetley NR20 . . . . 49 B6
Bressingham IP22 . . . . . . 129 C8
Claxton NR14 . . . . 91 D5
3 Hingham NR9 . . . . 86 C5
Old Buckenham NR17 . . . 104 F2
Folly Rd NR18 . . . . 173 C5
Folly View 5 PE37 . . . . . . 65 F4
Folly Yd PE32 . . . . 46 B7
Folwell Rd NR5 . . . . 156 E1
Footpath The 11 NR14 . . . 90 C5
Ford Ave PE30 . . . . 148 D5
FORDHAM PE38 . . . . 79 D2
Ford St IP24 . . . . 176 D3
Foregate Cl 2 NR8 . . . . . 155 D2
Forest Cl IP27 . . . . 175 C2
Forest Dr PE31 . . . . 133 C6
Forester Cl 1 NR14 . . . . . 162 C1
Forester's Ave PE38 . . . . . 97 A8
Forest Mount NR31 . . . . . . 93 E3
Forest Prim Sch IP27 . . . 175 C3
Forest Ret Pk IP24 . . . . . 125 D8
Forge Cl
Old Buckenham NR17 . . . 104 D2
Palgrave IP22 . . . . 177 D2
Poringland NR14 . . . . 90 D4
Forge Gr NR14 . . . . 110 C2
Forge Orchards 1 NR14 . . 89 B3
Forge Rd NR14 . . . . 91 F3
Forget-Me-Not Rd 3
PE31 . . . . 12 D4
Forge Way IP22 . . . . 128 A8
Forncett CE Prim Sch
NR16 . . . . 106 B3
FORNCETT END NR16 . . . . 105 E4
Forncett Ind Steam Mus★
NR16 . . . . 106 B5
Forncett Rd
Bunwell NR16 . . . . 105 F3
Tharston & Hapton NR15 . 106 C4
FORNCETT ST MARY
NR16 . . . . 106 B4
FORNCETT ST PETER
NR16 . . . . 106 B4
Forster Cl 2 NR11 . . . . . . 150 D6
Forster Way NR11 . . . . . . 150 D6
Forsythia Rd NR31 . . . . . . 170 B5
Forth Cl NR35 . . . . 168 C5

Forties Cl 8 NR30 . . . . . 168 C6
Fortune Gn NR14 . . . . 90 D4
Forum The★ NR2 . . . . . . 178 A2
Forwater Rd NR10 . . . . . . 34 B3
Foster Cl
Brundall NR13 . . . . 165 B4
Ormesby St Margaret
NR29 . . . . 167 C2
Foster Rd NR3 . . . . 158 D3
FOUL ANCHOR PE13 . . . . . 41 A4
FOULDEN IP26 . . . . 82 A2
Foulgers Opening NR1 . . 178 C1
FOULSHAM NR20 . . . . 33 D3
Foulsham Prim Sch NR20 33 D3
Foulsham Rd
Bintree NR20 . . . . 33 C2
Guestwick NR20 . . . . 33 F4
Guist NR20 . . . . 33 A4
Hindolveston NR20 . . . . . . 33 D7
Wood Norton NR20 . . . . . . 33 B6
Foundry Cl
Bodham NR25 . . . . 9 A3
Foulsham NR20 . . . . 33 D3
Northrepps NR27 . . . . 11 A2
Sculthorpe NR21 . . . . 16 C2
Foundry Cnr NR14 . . . . . 174 F2
Foundry La PE36 . . . . 2 A3
Foundry Sq NR19 . . . . . . 154 D4
Fountaine Gr PE30 . . . . . 148 C4
Fountains Rd NR4 . . . . 89 E8
Four Acres Est NR29 . . . . 167 C8
Fourth Ave PE13 . . . . 152 E4
Fowell Cl NR5 . . . . 161 B6
Fowler's La NR17 . . . . 174 B2
Foxburrow Rd NR7 . . . . . 159 A5
Foxcotte Cl NR6 . . . . 157 E7
Fox Covert 5 NR19 . . . . . 154 C4
Foxes Loke 12 NR14 . . . . . 92 A1
Foxes Mdw 2 PE32 . . . . . . 46 F2
Foxglove Cl
Fakenham NR21 . . . . 141 F4
North Walsham NR28 . . . . 151 E5
Thurton NR14 . . . . 91 C4
Foxglove Dr 21 NR31 . . . . 94 C6
Foxglove La NR26 . . . . . . 138 B6
Foxglove Rd
2 Attleborough NR17 . . . 174 B5
Thetford IP24 . . . . 176 F4
Fox Gr 4 NR16 . . . . 118 C5
Fox Hill IP20 . . . . 123 C3
Fox Hill NR14 . . . . 38 E7
FOXHOLE NR15 . . . . 107 A7
Foxley Cl NR5 . . . . 161 D6
Foxley Rd
Bawdeswell NR20 . . . . 50 D8
Foulsham NR20 . . . . 33 C2
Foxley Wood National Nature
Reserve★ NR10 . . . . 33 F1
Fox Rd
Dereham NR19 . . . . 154 D4
Framingham Pigot NR14 . . 90 D7
Fox's La PE14 . . . . 146 C6
Foxs Loke NR11 . . . . 150 B6
Foxwood 9 NR31 . . . . 73 D6
Foxwood Cl NR8 . . . . 155 E3
FRAMINGHAM EARL
NR14 . . . . 90 D4
Framingham Earl High Sch
NR14 . . . . 90 C6
Framingham Earl La
NR14 . . . . 90 F7
FRAMINGHAM PIGOT
NR14 . . . . 90 C6
Framingham Rd NR14 . . . . 90 F7
Framlingham Cl NR17 . . . 174 D6
Francis Cl NR27 . . . . 139 C5
Francis La NR13 . . . . 73 C6
Francis Rd NR15 . . . . 106 E3
Francis Stone Ct NR7 . . . . 72 D3
Francis Way NR5 . . . . 160 E8
FRANKFORT NR12 . . . . 38 A3
Franklin Cl PE34 . . . . 145 E6
Frank Stone Ct NR30 . . . 169 E1
FRANS GREEN NR20 . . . . . 51 A7
Fransham Rd NR19 . . . . . . 66 D8
Fransham Rd PE32 . . . . . . 48 B1
Frazer Cres NR11 . . . . . . 143 A7
Frederick Cl PE30 . . . . . . 148 D6
Frederick Rd NR30 . . . . . 169 C5
Fred Nicholson Sch NR20
. . . . 154 E2
Freebridge Haven PE13 . . 43 F3
Freedom Bridge PE13 . . 152 B6
Free La NR35 . . . . 108 F2
Freeland Cl NR18 . . . . . . 155 E3
Freeland Cnr NR10 . . . . . 155 C6
Freeman Cl NR14 . . . . . . 109 D8
Freeman Sq NR2 . . . . . . 162 C8
Freeman St NR14 . . . . . . 134 C6
Freestone Ct 8 PE30 . . . 146 E4
FREETHORPE NR13 . . . . . . 92 E8
Freethorpe Com Prim Sch
NR13 . . . . 92 F7
Freethorpe Rd
Cantley NR13 . . . . 92 D6
Freethorpe NR13 . . . . 74 F1
Frensham Rd NR30 . . . . . 168 E5
French's Rd PE14 . . . . 41 C4
Frensham Rd NR3 . . . . . . 157 F2
FRENZE IP21 . . . . 130 B7

Frenze Hall La IP22 . . . . 177 F5
Frenze Rd IP22 . . . . 177 E4
Frere Cnr 6 IP22 . . . . . . 129 D7
Frere Rd
30 Harleston IP20 . . . . . 122 D2
Norwich NR7 . . . . 159 D1
Fresher Mews NR5 . . . . . 160 F6
Freshfield Cl NR5 . . . . . . 161 C7
Freshgap La NR20 . . . . . . 33 E6
Freshwater Way NR8 . . . 156 F3
FRETTENHAM NR12 . . . . . . 54 A4
Frettenham Fst Sch NR12 54 A4
Frettenham Rd
Hainford NR10 . . . . 53 F5
Horstead with Stanninghall
NR12 . . . . 54 B5
Freydon Way NR12 . . . . . . 54 A4
Friarscroft La NR18 . . . . 173 B3
Friar's La PE31 . . . . 135 D4
Friars' La NR30 . . . . 169 D2
Friars Quay NR3 . . . . 178 B3
Friars St PE30 . . . . 146 E3
Friars The 17 PE30 . . . . . 146 D4
Friar Tuck Rd NR4 . . . . . . 162 C1
FRIDAY BRIDGE PE14 . . . . . 77 A7
Friday Bridge Prim Sch
PE14 . . . . 77 A7
Fridaybridge Rd
Elm PE14 . . . . 77 A8
Wisbech PE14 . . . . 59 A1
Friday Mkt 4 NR22 . . . . . . 16 F7
Friends Cl NR5 . . . . 161 D6
Friends Rd NR4 . . . . 161 C5
FRING PE31 . . . . 13 D5
Fring Rd
Bircham PE31 . . . . 14 A3
Snettisham PE31 . . . . 13 A5
Frinton Way 4 PE13 . . . . 152 E5
Frith Way NR15 . . . . 106 B1
Fritillary Dr NR18 . . . . . . 173 E4
FRITTON
Fritton and St Olaves
NR31 . . . . 93 E3
Ludham NR29 . . . . 56 E5
Morning Thorpe NR15 . . . 107 B3
Fritton Rd NR29 . . . . 167 B3
Fritton Rd NR29 . . . . 56 E6
Frobisher Cl IP24 . . . . . . 176 F6
Frobisher Cres PE36 . . . . 132 D3
Frogge La
Coltishall NR12 . . . . 54 C8
Scottow NR12 . . . . 37 C1
FROGSHALL NR27 . . . . 11 B1
Frogshall La NR18 . . . . . 173 A5
Frogs Hall La 3 NR31 . . . 163 B5
Frog's Hall La NR20 . . . . . 50 C2
Frogge La
Blofield NR13 . . . . 165 D6
Somerleyton, Ashby &
Herringfleet NR32 . . . . . . 93 F1
Front Rd
Tydd St Giles PE13 . . . . . . 41 A4
Wood Dalling NR11 . . . . . . 34 D6
Front St
Binham NR21 . . . . 6 E2
Burnham Market PE31 . . . 135 C3
Trunch NR28 . . . . 22 E5
Front Way PE30 . . . . 147 A7
Frost Cl
Norwich NR7 . . . . 163 F8
20 Watton IP25 . . . . 84 D3
FROST ROW NR9 . . . . 86 B4
Frost's La NR15 . . . . 106 B1
Fugill Rd NR7 . . . . 159 D1
Fulcher Ave NR27 . . . . . . 139 A7
Fulford Cl NR4 . . . . 162 A2
Fuller Cl
2 Rackheath NR13 . . . . . 72 E7
7 West Winch PE33 . . . . . 43 F2
Fuller Mews 5 NR5 . . . . . 160 E8
Fuller Rd
North Walsham NR28 . . . . 151 B4
Redenhall with Harleston
IP20 . . . . 122 D1
Fuller's Cl NR34 . . . . 110 D5
Fuller's Hill 10 NR30 . . . 169 C4
Fuller's La NR31 . . . . 94 C7
Fulmar La PE32 . . . . 46 E2
Fulmerston Cl IP24 . . . . . 176 B2
Fulmerston Rd IP24 . . . . 176 B2
FULMODESTON NR21 . . . . . 17 F1
Fulmodeston Rd
Fulmodeston NR21 . . . . . . 18 B1
Hindolveston NR20 . . . . . . 33 C8
Stibbard NR21 . . . . 32 E7
Fulton Cl NR4 . . . . 162 A1
FUNDENHALL NR16 . . . . . 106 A7
Fundenhall Rd NR15 . . . . 106 B7
Fundrey Rd PE13 . . . . . . 152 F6
Furlong Dro PE33 . . . . 81 A3
Furlong Rd 1 PE33 . . . . . . 81 A3
Furness Cl PE30 . . . . 148 F1
Furthest Dro IP27 . . . . . . 113 C4
Furze Ave NR7 . . . . 163 E8
Furze Hill NR27 . . . . 139 C5
Furze Hill Dr NR28 . . . . . 151 E3
Furze La
Great Witchingham NR9 . . 149 C2
Guist NR20 . . . . 33 A6
Furze Rd NR7 . . . . 163 E8
Furze Way NR21 . . . . 129 B1
Fye Bridge St NR3 . . . . . 178 B4

G

Gablehurst Cl NR31 . . . . . 170 A4
Gables Ave NR11 . . . . 22 B7
Gage Rd NR7 . . . . 159 C4
Gagman's La NR19 . . . . . . 68 A5
Gainsborough Ave
1 Diss IP22 . . . . 177 C4
Gainsborough Cl 2
PE38 . . . . 172 D6
Gale Cl NR14 . . . . 109 F8
Gales Ct NR23 . . . . 136 D6
Gales Rd NR23 . . . . 136 C6
Gallant's La NR16 . . . . . . 118 C5
Galley Cl 8 NR33 . . . . . . 111 F1
Galley Hill NR3 . . . . 158 A2
Galloway Cl 1 NR20 . . . . . 68 A8
Gallow Dr PE38 . . . . 172 C7
Gallowhill La NR24 . . . . . . 18 C3
Gallow Hill (Tumulus)★
NR25 . . . . 8 B5
Gallow La PE33 . . . . 62 D2
Gallows La NR16 . . . . . . 103 E1
Galpon Rd PE30 . . . . 147 B8
Gambling Cl NR6 . . . . . . 158 A7
Gamecock Cl NR6 . . . . . . 158 C6
Gamewell Cl 5 NR1 . . . . 162 E2
Gangway The NR27 . . . . . 139 C7
Ganners Hill NR8 . . . . . . 155 E3
Gannet Rd NR29 . . . . 167 E4
Gant Cl 9 NR20 . . . . 68 F6
Gaol Hill NR2 . . . . 178 A3
Gaol St 3 PE13 . . . . 152 C4
Gapton Hall Ind Est
NR31 . . . . 170 A8
Gapton Hall Rd NR31 . . . 170 A8
Gapton Hall Ret Pk
NR31 . . . . 169 A1
GARBOLDISHAM IP22 . . . 128 A8
Garboldisham Rd
Harling NR16 . . . . 118 C3
Kenninghall NR16 . . . . . . 118 F3
Garboldisham VC Prim Sch
IP22 . . . . 128 A8
Garden Cl
Briston NR24 . . . . 142 B4
Bungay NR35 . . . . 124 B8
North Walsham NR28 . . . . 151 C6
4 Watton IP25 . . . . 84 E3
Garden Ct
King's Lynn PE30 . . . . 147 A8
1 Loddon NR14 . . . . 92 A1
Gardeners Terr NR7 . . . . 158 F4
Gardenhouse La IP22 . . . 128 E2
Garden La NR25 . . . . 8 A1
Garden Pl 2 NR3 . . . . . . 162 E8
Garden Rd
Brundall NR13 . . . . 165 E6
Hemsby NR29 . . . . 167 D7
Sheringham NR26 . . . . . . 138 D6
3 Wiggenhall St Germans
PE34 . . . . 43 B1
Garden Row PE30 . . . . . . 146 E3
Garden St
Cromer NR27 . . . . 139 B7
Norwich NR1 . . . . 178 B2
Gardyn Croft 5 NR8 . . . . 155 D2
Garfield Rd NR30 . . . . . . 169 D7
Garfield Terr NR30 . . . . . 168 E4
Gargle Hill NR7 . . . . 163 F7
Gariannonum (Roman Fort)★
NR31 . . . . 93 F7
Garlic St IP21 . . . . 122 A2
GARLIC STREET IP21 . . . . 122 A2
Garlondes 6 NR16 . . . . . 118 C5
Garner's La PE34 . . . . 41 C8
Garnham Rd NR1 . . . . . . 170 C7
Garrett Cl NR3 . . . . 158 F1
Garrick Gn NR6 . . . . 158 E5
Garrick Gn Fst Sch NR6 . 158 E5
Garrison Rd NR30 . . . . . . 169 C5
Garrood Dr NR21 . . . . . . 141 E5
GARVESTONE NR9 . . . . 68 C2
Garvestone Prim Sch NR9 68 C2
Garvestone Rd NR9 . . . . . 68 E4
Garwood Cl PE30 . . . . . . 147 E4
Gas Hill NR1 . . . . 163 A6
Gashouse Dro IP27 . . . . . 175 E4
Gashouse Hill NR11 . . . . 150 D6
Gas House La PE12 . . . . . . 41 B8
Gaskell Way NR30 . . . . . 148 C1
GASTHORPE IP22 . . . . . . 127 D7
Gatacre Rd NR31 . . . . . . 169 B3
Gatehouse La PE30 . . . . . 148 C6
Gatekeeper Cl NR18 . . . . 173 E4
GATELEY NR20 . . . . 32 C3
Gateley Gdns NR5 . . . . . 158 B3
Gateley Rd NR20 . . . . 49 B8
Gaultree Sq PE14 . . . . 59 D2
Gavell St IP19 . . . . 124 D1
Gawdy Cl 2 NR20 . . . . . . 122 D2
Gawdy Rd NR7 . . . . 159 D1
Gaye Cres 1 IP23 . . . . . . 130 C1
Gayford Rd NR10 . . . . 35 B2
Gaymer Cl NR16 . . . . 119 D7
Gaymer's Way NR28 . . . . 151 B6
Gaynor Cl NR18 . . . . 173 B5
GAYTON PE32 . . . . 45 C5
Gayton Fst Sch PE32 . . . . 45 C4
Gayton Rd
East Winch PE32 . . . . 45 A4
Grimston PE32 . . . . 28 B2
Norwich NR10 . . . . 147 C5
GAYTON THORPE PE32 . . . . 45 E5
Gayton Wlk NR6 . . . . 158 F6
GAYWOOD PE30 . . . . 147 B6

Gaywood Cl NR30 . . . . 168 D5
Gaywood Com Prim Sch
  PE30 . . . . 147 C7
Gaywood Hall Dr PE30 . . 147 B5
Gaywood Rd PE30 . . . . . . 146 F5
Geddes Way 5 NR20 . . . . 68 F6
Gedge Rd NR30 . . . . 168 E6
GELDESTON NR34 . . . . . . 109 F3
Geldeston Hill NR34 . . . . 109 F2
Geldeston Rd
  Ellingham NR35 . . . . 109 D2
  Geldeston NR34 . . . . 110 B2
Gelham Manor PE31 . . . . 140 C3
Generals Wlk 5 PE30 . . . 147 C5
Geneva Gdns NR31 . . . . . 171 E4
Genista Gn 7 NR21 . . . . . 170 B6
Gentian Way 2 NR17 . . . . 174 B4
Gentlemans Wlk NR14 . . . 92 A3
Gentleman's Wlk NR2 . . . 178 A3
Gentry Pl NR5 . . . . 161 C8
Geoffrey Rd 4 NR1 . . . . . 162 E3
George Beck Rd 6 NR29 . 58 B6
George Borrow Rd
  2 East Dereham NR19 . . 154 F3
  Norwich NR4 . . . . 161 E5
George Cl NR8 . . . . 157 B8
George Dance Pl NR3 . . . 161 C7
George Dr NR8 . . . . 157 B7
George Edwards Rd
  NR21 . . . . 141 E5
George Elliot Way 6
  NR19 . . . . 154 D2
George Fox Way NR5 . . . . 161 B5
George Hill
  Norwich NR6 . . . . 158 E4
  Stanton IP31 . . . . 127 C1
George La
  Acle NR13 . . . . 166 B4
  2 Loddon NR14 . . . . 92 A1
George Pope Cl NR3 . . . . 158 C2
George Pope Rd NR3 . . . . 158 C2
George Rd IP24 . . . . 176 F5
Georges Rd NR19 . . . . . . 154 D5
George St
  Brandon IP27 . . . . 175 D3
  Great Yarmouth NR30 . . 169 C4
  6 King's Lynn PE30 . . . . 146 E6
  Sheringham NR26 . . . . . 138 D7
George Trollope Rd 15
  IP25 . . . . 84 D3
George Westwood Way
  NR33 . . . . 110 D2
George White Mid Sch
  NR3 . . . . 162 F8
Georgia Rd NR1 . . . . 15 C2
Gerald Cl NR1 . . . . 163 C8
Germander Ct 8 NR31 . . . 94 C6
German's La PE34 . . . . . . 42 A6
Gertrude Rd NR5 . . . . 158 F1
Ghost Hill Fst Sch NR8 . 156 D8
Gibbet La
  East Beckham NR11 . . . . 138 D2
  Wereham PE33 . . . . 80 E5
Gibbs Cl NR9 . . . . 160 B2
Gibson Rd 5 IP25 . . . . . . 67 B2
Gidney Dr PE31 . . . . 133 C5
Gigli Cl NR23 . . . . 151 B3
Gilbard Rd NR5 . . . . 161 C7
Gilbert Cl NR14 . . . . 90 F4
Gilbert Rd NR30 . . . . 168 E6
Gilbert Way NR4 . . . . 161 D1
Gilchrist Cl 8 NR4 . . . . . . 89 C8
Gildencroft NR3 . . . . 178 A4
Gilderswood NR16 . . . . . . 105 F3
Giles Rd NR10 . . . . 54 A1
GILLINGHAM NR14 . . . . . 110 C2
Gillingham Rd NR34 . . . . 110 C3
Gillingham Dam NR34 . . 110 C2
Gilman Rd NR5 . . . . 158 F1
Gilpin's Ride NR19 . . . . . 154 D4
Gilray Rd IP22 . . . . 177 F4
GIMINGHAM NR11 . . . . . 22 E7
Gimingham Rd
  Mundesley NR11 . . . . . . 143 A6
  Southrepps NR11 . . . . . . 22 C7
Gipsies La NR29 . . . . 56 D6
Gipsies' La NR25 . . . . 9 A3
Gipsy Cl NR5 . . . . 161 D6
Gipsy La
  Norwich NR5 . . . . 161 E6
  Watlington PE33 . . . . . . 61 D5
Girling Rd NR19 . . . . 154 C6
Girlings La NR7 . . . . 163 E5
Girton Rd
  Great Yarmouth NR31 . . 170 A3
  Norwich NR2 . . . . 162 B4
GISSING IP22 . . . . 120 F4
Gissing Rd IP22 . . . . 120 F2
Glade Prim Sch IP27 . . . 175 D3
Glade The
  Costessey NR8 . . . . 156 F4
  Overstrand NR27 . . . . . . 11 A3
  Thetford IP24 . . . . 176 D6
Gladstone Rd
  Fakenham NR21 . . . . 141 B4
  4 King's Lynn PE30 . . . . 146 E3
Gladstone St NR2 . . . . . . 162 B6
Glamis Ct 2 IP20 . . . . . . 122 D2
GLANDFORD NR25 . . . . . 7 E4
Glandford Rd NR25 . . . . . 7 E5
Glasbury Wlk PE13 . . . . . 153 C3
Glaven PE30 . . . . 147 C5
Glaven Cl NR28 . . . . 151 D5
Glaven Hale NR25 . . . . . . 137 C6
Glaven Rd NR25 . . . . 137 D5
Glebe Ave
  Hunstanton PE36 . . . . . . 132 D5

Glebe Ave *continued*
  Watlington PE33 . . . . . . 61 E5
Glebe Cl
  Fransham NR19 . . . . 66 C7
  Hingham NR9 . . . . 86 B5
  19 Long Stratton NR15 . 106 E3
  Northwold IP26 . . . . 99 C8
  2 Potter Heigham NR29 . 56 F6
  Taverham NR8 . . . . 155 F1
  Thetford IP24 . . . . 176 D5
Glebe Est PE34 . . . . 144 F1
Glebe House Sch PE36 . 132 D5
Glebe La PE31 . . . . 135 F6
Glebe Mdw NR17 . . . . . . 103 E7
Glebe Rd
  Acle NR13 . . . . 166 C3
  Dersingham PE31 . . . . . 140 C4
  Downham Market PE38 . 172 D6
  Gissing IP21 . . . . 121 A4
  Norwich NR2 . . . . 162 A4
  7 Watton IP25 . . . . 84 E3
  Weeting IP27 . . . . 175 B7
Glebes The 13 NR31 . . . . 94 A5
Glebe The
  2 Harling NR16 . . . . 118 C5
  Hemsby NR29 . . . . 167 C8
  Honing NR28 . . . . 38 C6
  Stibbard NR21 . . . . 32 E7
  Wells-next-the-Sea NR23 . 136 D6
Glebe Way 6 NR12 . . . . . 54 C6
Glenalmond NR4 . . . . 162 A1
Glenburn Cl NR7 . . . . 159 A3
Glenburn Ct NR7 . . . . 159 A3
Glenda Cl NR5 . . . . 157 C1
Glenda Cres NR5 . . . . 157 B1
Glenda Ct NR5 . . . . 157 B1
Glenda Rd NR5 . . . . 157 C1
Glendenning Rd 4 NR1 . 163 B5
Glenfield Cl IP20 . . . . 78 A5
Glengarry Cl NR9 . . . . 88 C8
Glenham Ct IP21 . . . . 140 C4
Glenmore Ave NR30 . . . . 168 D7
Glenmore Gdns NR3 . . . . 158 B2
Glenn Rd NR14 . . . . 90 C4
Globe La NR13 . . . . 165 E6
Globe Pl NR2 . . . . 162 C5
Globe St IP26 . . . . 99 A5
Glosthorpe Manor PE32 . 44 F5
Gloucester Ave NR31 . . . 170 C4
Gloucester Ct PE13 . . . . . 152 D7
Gloucester Pl NR24 . . . . . 142 D4
Gloucester Rd PE30 . . . . 147 B6
Gloucester St NR1 . . . . . 162 E4
Gloucester Way IP24 . . . 176 A5
Gobbett's Rd IP22 . . . . . . 128 C4
Goddard Cres 1 PE13 . . . 152 D7
Goddards Ct 14 NR17 . . . 174 B5
Godfrey Rd 5 NR10 . . . . . 54 A2
Godric Pl NR2 . . . . 161 F6
Godwick Medieval Village
  of * PE32 . . . . 31 C1
Godwin Rd PE13 . . . . 152 D7
Goffe Cl IP25 . . . . 84 D4
Goffins La NR19 . . . . 56 C6
Goggles La NR19 . . . . 66 C6
Gogg's Mill Rd NR21 . . . . 141 A3
Golden Cl 8 NR20 . . . . . . 68 F6
Golden Ball St NR1 . . . . . 178 B2
Golden Dog La NR3 . . . . . 178 A4
Golden Gates NR23 . . . . . 136 B2
Golden Gates Dr NR23 . . 136 A2
Golden Pightle 7 NR9 . . . 69 F2
Golden Sq 10 NR27 . . . . . 139 B7
Goldfinch Cl PE38 . . . . . . 172 C7
Golding Pl
  Norwich NR2 . . . . 162 C6
  16 Wisbech PE13 . . . . . 152 C4
Goldsmith St NR2 . . . . . . 162 C7
Goldsmith Way IP21 . . . . 121 F4
Golds Pightle PE36 . . . . . 2 B3
Goldwell Rd NR1 . . . . 178 B1
Golf Cl
  King's Lynn PE30 . . . . . . 148 D1
  Runton NR27 . . . . 10 A5
Golf Course Rd PE36 . . . 132 E8
Golf La NR19 . . . . 154 D7
Golf Links Rd
  Brundall NR13 . . . . 165 D4
  Wymondham College
    NR18 . . . . 104 E8
Gong La PE31 . . . . 135 F6
Gonville Ct PE31 . . . . 133 C5
Gonville Rd NR31 . . . . . . 170 A4
Gooch Cl NR28 . . . . 151 C6
GOODERSTONE PE33 . . . 82 A4
Gooderstone CE Prim Sch
  PE33 . . . . 81 F5
Gooderstone Water Gdns *
  PE33 . . . . 82 A5
Goodhale Rd NR5 . . . . . . 161 B7
Goodman Sq 2 NR2 . . . . 162 C7
Goodmins PE36 . . . . 13 A7
Goodrick Pl PE13 . . . . . . 153 C4
Goodwins Rd PE30 . . . . . 146 E4
Goodwood IP24 . . . . 176 A5
Goosander Cl 4 PE31 . . . 12 E5
Goosecare La PE25 . . . . . 67 D3
Gooseberry Hill PE30 . . . 50 B3
Goose Gn
  8 Sutton Bridge PE12 . . 41 B8
  Winfarthing IP22 . . . . . . 120 C6
Goose Gn La IP22 . . . . . . 120 B6
Goose Gn Rd IP22 . . . . . . 120 E4
GOOSE GREEN IP22 . . . . 120 C6

Goose La
  Alby with Thwaite NR11 . 21 B3
  Stalham NR12 . . . . 39 C4
Goose's La PE14 . . . . 41 D5
Gordon Ave NR7 . . . . 163 C7
Gordon Ct PE13 . . . . 152 C3
Gordon Fendick Sch
  PE13 . . . . 152 D8
Gordon Godfrey Way
  NR10 . . . . 53 A3
Gordon Rd
  Briston NR24 . . . . 142 A5
  3 East Dereham NR19 . . 154 E5
  Great Yarmouth NR31 . . 169 C2
Gordon Sq NR1 . . . . 178 B1
Gordon Terr NR11 . . . . . . 143 B4
Gore La NR15 . . . . 121 C8
Gorgate Rd NR20 . . . . . . 49 E3
Gorleston La NR31 . . . . . 170 A2
GORLESTON-ON-SEA
  NR31 . . . . 170 E4
Gormans La NR21 . . . . . . 31 D5
Gorse Ave NR6 . . . . 158 A5
Gorse Cl
  4 Belton NR31 . . . . 94 A5
  2 East Dereham NR19 . . 154 C4
  Fakenham NR21 . . . . 141 F3
  Norwich NR6 . . . . 143 B5
Gorse Ind Est NR20 . . . . 125 C6
Gorse Rd NR7 . . . . 163 D8
Gorse View 4 NR20 . . . . 49 D4
Gorse Vw 4 NR20 . . . . . . 49 D4
Goshawk Way 5 IP24 . . . 176 D2
Gosmoor La PE14 . . . . . . 59 B1
Gostling Cl IP27 . . . . 177 B4
Gothic Cl 1 IP20 . . . . 122 D1
Goulburn Rd NR7 . . . . . . 159 D1
Gould Rd 1 NR2 . . . . 162 A4
Gournay Ave NR1 . . . . . . 170 D2
Governors Ct NR1 . . . . . . 178 C1
Gowing Cl NR6 . . . . 157 F7
Gowing Ct NR3 . . . . 158 B3
Gowing Rd
  11 Mulbarton NR14 . . . . 89 B3
  Norwich NR6 . . . . 157 F6
Gowing Way NR15 . . . . . 107 B5
Grace Edwards Cl NR8 . . 155 F2
Grafton Cl PE30 . . . . 147 C8
Grafton Rd PE30 . . . . 147 C8
Graham Dr 2 PE32 . . . . . 44 B3
Graham Sq NR7 . . . . 159 D1
Graham St PE30 . . . . 146 E3
Grammar Sch Rd NR28 . 151 C4
Granary Cl
  Briston NR24 . . . . 142 F3
  Freethorpe NR13 . . . . . . 92 F7
  9 Lingwood NR13 . . . . . 74 A3
Granary Ct PE30 . . . . 146 D4
Granary Loke NR10 . . . . . 149 C4
Granary Rd NR17 . . . . . . 174 C4
Grand Cl NR11 . . . . 154 C4
Grange Ave NR27 . . . . . . 11 B3
Grange Cl
  Briston NR24 . . . . 142 E3
  Ludham NR29 . . . . 56 D5
  Norwich NR6 . . . . 158 E4
  10 Snettisham PE31 . . . 12 E4
  Wroxham/Hoveton NR12 . 164 E6
Grange Cres PE33 . . . . . 43 E5
Grange Ct NR31 . . . . 151 C4
Grange La
  Honingham NR9 . . . . 69 F5
  West Winch PE33 . . . . . 61 E8
Grange Rd
  Caister-on-Sea NR30 . . 168 D5
  Cantley NR13 . . . . 92 C6
  Flixton NR35 . . . . 123 E4
  Hainford NR10 . . . . 53 F5
  Ludham NR29 . . . . 56 D5
  Mundham NR14 . . . . 108 F7
  Norwich NR2 . . . . 162 B4
  Scarning NR19 . . . . 154 A4
  Sutton Bridge PE34 . . . . 41 E8
  Wending NR19 . . . . 66 F8
  Wisbech PE13 . . . . 152 A7
Grange Wlk NR14 . . . . . . 164 C4
Granny Bard's La NR12 . . 54 C3
Granta Way 1 NR31 . . . . 170 B2
Grantly Ct PE30 . . . . 147 D5
Grant Rd NR10 . . . . 54 A2
Grant St NR2 . . . . 162 A7
Granville Rd 2 PE12 . . . . 39 B4
Granville Rd NR31 . . . . . 169 B4
Granville Terr PE12 . . . . . 41 A8
Grapes Hill NR2 . . . . 162 C6
Grasmere Rd NR5 . . . . . . 88 D8
Grasmere Cl NR5 . . . . . . 161 C6
Grassgate La PE14 . . . . . 59 B7
Gravel Bank PE14 . . . . . . 60 D6
Gravel Dam NR32 . . . . . . 111 C4
Gravelfield Cl NR7 . . . . . 163 B8
Gravel Hill NR14 . . . . 89 F4
Gravelhill La PE33 . . . . . 43 F1
Gravelpit Hill NR17 . . . . 102 F6
Gravel Pit La NR25 . . . . . 137 C5
Gray Dr NR20 . . . . 50 B4
Grays Fair NR5 . . . . 156 F1
Grays La PE14 . . . . 59 C2
Gray's La
  Barsham NR22 . . . . 16 E6
  Pulham Market IP21 . . . 121 D5
Grays Rd NR34 . . . . 111 C3
Great Barn Rd NR23 . . . . 5 A4
GREAT BARWICK PE31 . . 14 E6
Great Barwick Medieval
  Village of * PE31 . . . . . . 14 E6
GREAT BIRCHAM PE31 . . 14 B3
Great Cl NR30 . . . . 168 F5

Great Comm La NR34 . . . 124 E5
GREAT COMMON NR34 . . 124 D6
GREAT CRESSINGHAM
  IP25 . . . . 83 D4
GREAT DUNHAM PE32 . . 47 E1
Great Dunham Prim Sch
  PE32 . . . . 47 F1
Great Eastern Rd PE13 . 152 B4
Great Eastern Way
  Fakenham NR21 . . . . 141 D4
  Wells-next-the-Sea NR23 . 136 C5
GREAT ELLINGHAM
  NR17 . . . . 103 E8
Great Ellingham Prim Sch
  NR17 . . . . 103 E8
GREAT FRANSHAM
  NR19 . . . . 66 B8
GREAT GREEN
  Burgate IP22 . . . . 129 B3
  Thrandeston IP21 . . . . . 130 A4
GREAT HAUTBOIS NR12 . 54 C7
Great Hautbois Rd NR12 . 54 C7
Greatheath Rd NR20 . . . 32 D1
GREAT HOCKHAM IP24 . 102 C3
Great Hockham Prim Sch
  IP24 . . . . 102 C4
Great Hospl NR1 . . . . 178 C3
Great Man's Way PE33 . . 81 A2
GREAT MASSINGHAM
  PE32 . . . . 29 D2
Great Massingham VC Prim
  Sch PE32 . . . . 29 E1
GREAT MELTON NR9 . . . 70 B1
Great Melton Rd
  Hethersett NR9 . . . . 88 C8
  Little Melton NR9 . . . . . . 160 A2
GREAT MOULTON NR15 . 106 B1
Great Northern Cl NR30 . 169 D6
Great Palgrave Medieval
  Village of * PE32 . . . . . . 65 B6
GREAT PLUMSTEAD NR13 . 72 F5
GREAT RYBURGH NR21 . . 32 B6
GREAT SNORING NR21 . . 17 A5
Great Snoring Rd NR21 . . 17 A8
GREAT WALSINGHAM
  NR22 . . . . 17 A8
GREAT WITCHINGHAM
  NR9 . . . . 178 C1
Great Witchingham Prim Sch
  NR9 . . . . 51 E5
GREAT YARMOUTH
  NR30 . . . . 169 A5
Great Yarmouth Coll
  NR31 . . . . 169 C1
Great Yarmouth High Sch
  NR30 . . . . 169 E6
Great Yarmouth Race Course
  NR30 . . . . 168 F2
Great Yarmouth Sea Life
  Ctr * NR30 . . . . 169 E2
Great Yarmouth Sta
  NR30 . . . . 169 B5
Grebe Cl
  Great Yarmouth NR31 . . 170 A7
  7 Rollesby NR29 . . . . . . 57 D2
Greenacre Cl
  Brundall NR13 . . . . 165 C4
  King's Lynn PE30 . . . . . . 148 B2
Greenacre Fst & Mid Sch
  NR30 . . . . 169 C1
Greenacre Rd NR9 . . . . . . 86 B5
Greenacres
  Bradwell NR31 . . . . 170 A3
  Little Melton NR9 . . . . . . 160 C2
Greenacres Dr NR14 . . . . 90 C5
Green Bank PE36 . . . . . . 2 C3
Greenborough Cl NR7 . . 159 D2
Greenborough Rd NR7 . . 159 E2
Green Cl
  Hempton NR21 . . . . 141 A2
  Norwich NR5 . . . . 156 E1
Green Court La PE31 . . . . 3 C6
Greencourts 10 NR29 . . . 58 B6
Green Ct
  Fakenham NR21 . . . . 141 E4
  Norwich NR7 . . . . 163 D7
Green Dragon La NR23 . . 136 D5
Green Dro PE14 . . . . 77 D6
Greenfield NR5 . . . . 156 D1
Greenfield Cl NR27 . . . . . 139 C5
Greenfields NR16 . . . . . . 118 B5
Greenfields Rd NR20 . . . 154 F4
GREENGATE NR20 . . . . . 50 B3
Greengate NR20 . . . . 50 B2
Greengate La
  Bircham PE31 . . . . 14 B3
  Great Massingham PE32 . 29 C1
Greenhill Ave NR30 . . . . 168 D8
Green Hill La PE31 . . . . . 14 B3
Greenhill Rd NR27 . . . . . 139 C5
Green Hills Cl NR8 . . . . . 156 F3
Green Hills Rd 8 NR13 . . 162 D8
Greenhoe PE37 . . . . 153 B3
Green House La PE37 . . . 153 E5
Green La
  Alpington NR14 . . . . 90 F3
  Attleborough NR17 . . . . 174 F3
  Aylsham NR11 . . . . 150 A6
  Bawburgh NR9 . . . . 160 B4
  Beetley NR20 . . . . 49 D4
  Billingford NR20 . . . . . . 49 F8
  Burgh St Peter NR34 . . . 111 C4
  Burnham Thorpe PE31 . . 4 A5
  Caister-on-Sea NR30 . . 168 A4
  Christchurch PE14 . . . . . 95 A7
  Coltishall NR12 . . . . 54 C6
  Dereham NR19 . . . . 154 E4
  Ditchingham NR35 . . . . 109 B3

Green La *continued*
  Earsham NR35 . . . . 108 E2
  5 Feltwell IP26 . . . . 98 E1
  Filby NR29 . . . . 75 F8
  Foulsham NR20 . . . . 33 E3
  Great Ellingham NR17 . . 103 E8
Great & Little Plumstead
  NR13 . . . . 72 E5
  Great Moulton NR15 . . . 106 B1
  Great Yarmouth NR31 . . 94 C6
  Guist NR20 . . . . 33 A5
  Hales NR14 . . . . 109 E8
  Haveringland NR10 . . . . 52 E7
  Horsford NR10 . . . . 53 B4
  King's Lynn PE30 . . . . . . 148 E2
  Little Ellingham NR17 . . 86 A1
  Methwold IP26 . . . . 99 A7
  Mundford IP26 . . . . 100 B5
  Postwick with Witton NR7 . 72 E4
  Potter Heigham NR29 . . 56 F6
  Pudding Norton NR21 . . 141 A1
  Redenhall with Harleston
    IP20 . . . . 122 C2
  Rocklands NR17 . . . . . . 103 C7
  Saxlingham Nethergate
    NR15 . . . . 107 B7
  Shipdham IP25 . . . . 67 D4
  Shipmeadow NR34 . . . . 109 F1
  Somerleyton, Ashby &
    Herringfleet NR32 . . . 111 E8
  South Walsham NR13 . . 74 B6
  Starston IP20 . . . . 122 D4
  Stow Bedon NR17 . . . . . 103 B8
  Syleham IP21 . . . . 131 C4
  Thelnetham IP22 . . . . . . 128 A2
  Thetford IP24 . . . . 176 E4
  Thornham PE36 . . . . 2 D6
  Thrandeston IP21 . . . . . 129 F2
  Tivetshall St Margaret
    NR15 . . . . 121 B5
  Toft Monks NR34 . . . . . . 110 C6
  Tottenhill PE33 . . . . 61 F5
  Troston IP31 . . . . 126 A1
  Upwell PE14 . . . . 95 B6
  Walsoken PE14 . . . . 152 F4
  Wicklewood NR18 . . . . . 87 C5
  Wramplingham NR18 . . . 87 F7
  Wymondham NR18 . . . . 173 D1
  Yaxham NR19 . . . . 68 B6
Green La E NR13 . . . . 72 E7
Green La N NR13 . . . . 72 D5
Greenland Ave
  King's Lynn PE30 . . . . . . 146 E8
  Wymondham NR18 . . . . 173 E6
Greenlands Way NR26 . . 138 C6
Greenlands Way 2
  NR26 . . . . 138 B6
Green La W
  Horsham St Faith NR13 . . 53 D1
  Rackheath NR13 . . . . . . 72 D8
Green Man La NR15 . . . . 108 C8
Green Marsh Rd PE34 . . 144 C7
Greenpark Ave PE30 . . . 146 F6
Green Pk PE30 . . . . 122 D2
Green Pk Rd NR10 . . . . . 53 B3
Green Quay The * NR30 . 146 D4
Green Rd
  Brandon IP27 . . . . 175 E2
  Hales NR14 . . . . 109 E8
  Upwell PE14 . . . . 77 E4
GREENSGATE NR9 . . . . . 51 E2
Green's La NR27 . . . . 10 C4
Greens Rd
  East Dereham NR20 . . . 154 F3
  North Walsham NR28 . . 151 A5
Green St IP21 . . . . 131 A4
Green The
  Ashill IP25 . . . . 84 A7
  Belton with Browston NR31 . 94 A5
  Boughton PE33 . . . . 80 C4
  Brisley NR20 . . . . 49 B8
  Burnham Market PE31 . . 135 C3
  Deopham NR18 . . . . 86 E2
  Dersingham PE31 . . . . . 140 D4
  Diss IP22 . . . . 177 A6
  8 Earsham NR35 . . . . . . 123 F8
  Fakenham NR21 . . . . 141 A3
  Freethorpe NR13 . . . . . . 92 E3
  Hickling NR12 . . . . 39 E2
  Hockham IP24 . . . . 102 E3
  Hunstanton PE36 . . . . . . 132 C4
  Lound NR32 . . . . 94 C2
  North Lopham IP22 . . . . 119 A2
  North Wootton PE30 . . . 148 C5
  Norwich NR2 . . . . 178 D2
  Ormesby St Margaret
    NR29 . . . . 167 A2
  Runhall NR9 . . . . 68 F2
  Saxlingham Nethergate
    NR15 . . . . 107 D7
  South Wootton PE30 . . . 149 C2
  Surlingham NR14 . . . . . 73 B1
  Thornham PE36 . . . . 2 D6
  Upton with Fishley NR13 . 166 B8
  Wicklewood NR18 . . . . . 87 B4
Green Way
  Barsham NR22 . . . . 16 C6
  Stiffkey NR23 . . . . 6 C6
  Swaffham PE37 . . . . 153 B6
Greenway Cl
  Fakenham NR21 . . . . 141 C5
  2 North Walsham NR28 . 151 C5
Greenway La
  Fakenham NR21 . . . . 141 C5

Greenway La continued
Tharston & Hapton NR15. . 106 D6
Greenway Pk NR21. . . . . . 141 C6
Greenways
Bunwell NR16 . . . . 105 D4
Flordon NR15. . . . . 106 E8
Holt NR25 . . . . 137 C7
Newton Flotman NR15. . . . 89 C1
Norwich NR4 . . . . 161 F1
Greenways CI NR15 . . . . . 106 E8
Greenways La
Bunwell NR16 . . . . 105 D4
Carleton Rode NR16 . . . . . 105 B4
Greenwich CI
Dersingham PE31 . . . . 140 E3
Downham Market PE38. . . 172 B3
Greenwood CI NR16. . . . 105 E8
Greenwood Dr NR9 . . . . 154 C5
Greenwood Rd NR4 . . . . 162 C1
Greenwood Way
5 Shipdham IP25. . . . . . . 67 C2
Thorpe St Andrew NR7 . . . 159 F2
Greevegate PE36. . . . . . . 132 C4
Gregor Shanks Way **27**
IP25. . . . . 84 D3
Gregory CI **1** PE30. . . . . 148 C5
Gregs CI NR1. . . . . 68 F5
Grenville CI **3** NR9 . . . . . 88 E8
Grenville PI **1** NR30 . . . 169 D8
Grenville Way IP24 . . . . . 176 D5
GRESHAM NR11 . . . . 9 E1
Gresham CI
Great Yarmouth NR31 . . . 170 C2
King's Lynn PE30 . . . . 147 C8
Gresham Rd
Baconsthorpe NR25. . . . . . . 20 B8
Norwich NR3 . . . . 158 B2
Greshams Prep Sch
NR25. . . . . 137 D7
Greshams Sch NR25. . . . . 137 D7
Gresham Village Sch NR11. . 9 E1
Gresley CI NR20. . . . . 16 F6
GRESSENHALL NR20 . . . . . 49 B3
Gressenhall Farm &
Workhouse★ NR20. . . . . . . 49 D4
Gressenhall Rd NR20 . . . . 49 D4
Greyfriars CI NR6 . . . . . . 158 E5
Greyfriars Cty Prim Sch
PE30 . . . . 146 E4
Greyfriars Rd NR1 . . . . . . 178 B3
Greyfriars Way NR30 . . . 169 C3
Greyhound La
Banham NR16 . . . . 119 D7
Hopton IP22 . . . . 127 E5
Greyhound Opening **7**
NR2 . . . . 178 A3
Greylag CI **8** NR13. . . . . . 55 A1
Grey Sedge PE30. . . . . . . 147 A7
Greys Manor NR16 . . . . . 119 D6
Grice CI **4** NR26. . . . . . . 138 C5
Griffin La
Attleborough NR17 . . . . . 174 D5
Thorpe St Andrew NR7 . . . 72 D3
Grigsons Wood **1** NR13. . . 73 D5
Grime's Graves★ IP27. . . 115 C8
Grimmer La NR13 . . . . 92 B7
Grimmer's Rd **6** PE31. . . 152 E7
Grimshoe Rd PE38 . . . . . 172 B6
GRIMSTON IP22. . . . . 28 B1
Grimston Jun Sch PE32. . 28 B1
Grimston Pott Row Fst Sch
PE32. . . . . 45 A8
Grimston Rd
Gayton PE32 . . . . 45 C6
King's Lynn PE30 . . . . 148 E1
Gristock PI NR5. . . . . 161 C8
GRISTON IP25. . . . . 85 A2
Griston Rd
Thompson IP24 . . . . 102 B8
Watton IP25 . . . . 84 E3
Groomes CI **3** NR31 . . . . 171 D5
Grosvenor Rd
Norwich NR2 . . . . 162 B5
Wisbech PE13 . . . . 152 D7
Grouts La NR25 . . . . 8 B6
Grove Ave
Norwich NR1 . . . . 178 A1
Norwich NR5 . . . . 157 A1
Grovebury CI NR13. . . . . . 165 C4
Grove CI
8 East Dereham NR19. . . 154 C4
Holt NR25 . . . . 137 D6
2 Newton Flotman NR15. . 89 C1
Grove Dale **3** NR15. . . . . . 89 C1
Grovedale CI NR5 . . . . . . 157 A1
Grove End IP21 . . . . 131 F1
Grove Gdns **7** PE32. . . . . 45 C6
Grove House Inf Sch
NR19. . . . . 154 D4
Grove La
Booton NR10 . . . . 52 A8
Fakenham NR21. . . . . 141 C6
Forncett NR16. . . . . 106 A3
Holt NR25 . . . . 137 D6
Sparham NR9 . . . . 51 B6
Tasburgh NR15 . . . . 106 F7
Thetford IP24 . . . . 176 D4
Grovelands PE31. . . . . . . 140 D8
Grove Rd
Banham NR16 . . . . 119 C6
Barsham NR16. . . . . 16 C4
Brockdish IP21 . . . . 131 C6
Cantley NR13. . . . . 92 D8
Cromer NR27. . . . . 139 D5
Gissing IP21 . . . . 121 A4

Grove Rd continued
Hethersett NR9 . . . . 88 D8
Ingham NR12. . . . . 24 C1
4 Marthan NR29 . . . . 57 D5
Melton Constable NR24. . . 142 A4
North Walsham NR28 . . . . 151 D5
Norwich NR1 . . . . 178 A1
Repps with Bastwick NR29 . 57 A4
Starston IP20 . . . . 122 C2
Wells-next-the-Sea NR23 . 136 E4
Groveside PE31. . . . . 30 A7
Grove The
Coltishall NR12 . . . . 54 D6
East Dereham NR19 . . . . . 154 D4
Fleggburgh NR29. . . . . 57 A1
2 Necton PE37. . . . . 65 F4
Roydon PE32 . . . . 28 A1
Shotesham NR15. . . . . 90 B1
Grove Way NR15. . . . . 89 C1
Grove Wlk NR1 . . . . 178 A1
Growle Abbey NR24 . . . . . 19 B2
Grubb's La NR12 . . . . 24 C1
Grub La IP19 . . . . 124 E1
Grub St
Happisburgh NR12. . . . . . . 24 B4
Shotesham NR15. . . . . 90 B2
Guanock PI **12** PE30 . . . . 146 E3
Guanock Terr PE30 . . . . . 146 F3
Guardian Rd NR5 . . . . . . 161 F7
Guelph Rd **2** NR1. . . . . . 163 A6
Guernsey Rd NR3 . . . . . . 162 E8
GUESTWICK NR20. . . . . . . 34 A6
GUESTWICK GREEN NR20. . 33 F5
Guestwick Rd
Foulsham NR20 . . . . 33 E4
Hindolveston NR20 . . . . . . 33 F7
Wood Norton NR20 . . . . . . 33 C6
Guildford Way IP24 . . . . 176 B5
Guildhall Hill **1** NR2 . . . 178 A3
Guildhall La IP21 . . . . . . 121 E5
Guildhall St IP24. . . . . . . 176 D3
Guild Rd PE13 . . . . 152 E6
Guildhall St NR22. . . . . . . 16 F8
Guiler's La NR18 . . . . 105 B8
Guilt Cross Way PE38 . . . 172 C6
GUIST NR20 . . . . 32 F4
Guist Bottom Rd NR21. . . 32 E6
Guist Rd NR20 . . . . 33 C4
Gulgate La NR11 . . . . 21 A1
Gull La NR14. . . . . 90 E6
Gullpit Dro PE14 . . . . 61 D1
Gunn CI **3** NR7 . . . . 72 D5
Gunn Rd NR7 . . . . 159 D1
Gunn's Cnr NR12 . . . . 38 D2
Gunn St NR20. . . . . 33 C3
Gun St **7** NR29 . . . . 138 D7
GUNTHORPE NR24 . . . . 18 B5
Gunthorpe Rd PE14 . . . . . 41 B5
Gunton La NR5 . . . . 157 B2
Gunton Rd
Loddon NR14 . . . . 109 C8
Norwich NR2 . . . . 161 F5
Wymondham NR18 . . . . . 173 D4
Gunton Sta NR11 . . . . 22 B6
Gurney CI NR5. . . . . 161 B8
Gurney CI NR5. . . . . 161 B8
Gurney Dr NR7. . . . . 159 D3
Gurney La NR7. . . . . 161 C2
Gurney Rd
Norwich NR1 . . . . 163 A7
Norwich NR5 . . . . 157 A1
Gwyn Cres NR21 . . . . 141 F5
Gymkhana Way PE31. . . . 133 B5

H

Habgood CI NR13 . . . . . . 166 C4
HACKFORD NR18 . . . . 87 A5
Hackford Rd
Hardingham NR9 . . . . 86 E6
Wicklewood NR18 . . . . 87 A5
Haconsfield NR9 . . . . 88 D7
HADDISCOE NR14. . . . . . . 110 F8
Haddiscoe Dam NR14 . . . 110 F6
Haddiscoe Rd NR14 . . . . 110 F6
Haddiscoe Sta NR31 . . . . . 93 D1
Hadfield Rd NR28 . . . . . . 151 B6
Hadley Cres PE31 . . . . . . 133 C5
Hadley Dr NR21. . . . . 161 F6
Hadley Rd NR26. . . . . 138 E6
Hagbech Hall CI **2** PE14 . . 59 D2
Haggard's CI IP25 . . . . 66 E3
Haig CI NR19 . . . . 154 D3
HAINFORD NR10 . . . . 53 E5
Hainford Fst Sch NR10 . . . 53 E6
Hainford Rd NR10 . . . . . . 53 E7
Halcombe Ct NR3. . . . . . . 158 E1
Halden Ave NR6 . . . . 158 C4
Hale Ct NR13 . . . . 73 A4
Hale Dro
Littleport CB6 . . . . 96 B2
Welney PE14 . . . . 95 E6
Hale Fen Rd CB6. . . . . 96 B1
Hale Rd
Ashill IP25. . . . . 84 A7
Bradenham IP25 . . . . 66 D3
Necton PE37 . . . . 65 F4
HALES NR14 . . . . 109 F8
Hales CI NR30 . . . . 168 D5
Hales Ct NR25 . . . . 137 B6
HALES GREEN NR14 . . . . . 109 E7
Hales Hall & Gdns★
NR14. . . . . 109 D6
Hales St NR15 . . . . 121 A6
HALES STREET NR15. . . . . 121 A6
Halesworth Rd NR34 . . . . 124 E4
Haley CI **4** IP13 . . . . 152 C8

Half Acre CI NR27. . . . . . . 10 B4
Halfar Rd **8** IP31 . . . . . . 126 B1
Halfield La NR18 . . . . 86 D2
Half Mile CI NR63 . . . . . . 147 A7
Halfmile Drift IP25. . . . . . 66 D3
Half Mile Rd NR3 . . . . . . 158 B2
Half Moon NR31 . . . . 170 C1
Half Moon La IP22 . . . . . 128 E4
Half Moon Way **1** NR2. . 162 B8
Halford CI NR17 . . . . 174 D4
Halford La IP22. . . . . 129 A7
Halford PI NR17 . . . . 174 D4
Halford Rd NR17. . . . . . . 174 D4
Halfpenny La
Beetley NR20. . . . . 49 C5
Elm PE14 . . . . 59 A2
Wisbech PE14 . . . . 152 D1
Halfpenny Toll Rd PE14 . . 95 B8
Hall Year CI **7** NR27 . . . . 10 B5
Halifax Cres NR21 . . . . . . 15 C3
Haling Way IP24 . . . . 176 A4
Hallback La NR14 . . . . 90 A7
Hall Bridge Rd PE14. . . . . 77 D5
Hall CI
Fakenham NR21. . . . . 141 D4
Heacham PE31. . . . . 133 D7
4 Hemsby NR29. . . . . . . 167 A7
Hethersett NR9 . . . . 88 D7
3 Hingham NR9 . . . . 86 C4
3 Southery PE38 . . . . 97 B5
Hall Comm Rd NR29. . . . . 56 C4
Hall Cres PE33. . . . . 63 C5
Hall Dike 77 F7
Hall Dr
Costessey NR5. . . . . 156 D2
10 Feltwell IP26 . . . . 98 E1
Honingham NR9 . . . . 69 E6
North Runcton PE33 . . . . . 44 A3
Santon Downham IP27 . . . 115 C6
Hall Farm Gdns PE32. . . . 44 F3
Hall Farm PI NR9 . . . . . . 160 B6
Hallfield Rd IP24. . . . . . . 102 A7
Hallfields 63 D4
Hallgate **2** NR13. . . . . 72 D6
Hall Hills IP22 . . . . 177 C5
Hall La
Baconsthorpe NR25. . . . . . 19 F8
Bressingham IP22. . . . . . . 119 D1
Burston & Shimpling IP21 121 A2
Colkirk NR21 . . . . 31 E5
Deopham NR18 . . . . 86 F4
East Carleton NR14. . . . . . 88 E4
East Dereham NR20 . . . . . 154 F4
East Tuddenham NR20 . . . 69 B6
Felthorpe NR10 . . . . 52 E5
Frettenham NR12 . . . . 54 B3
Gunthorpe NR24 . . . . 18 A5
Hingham NR9 . . . . 86 C5
Horsford NR10. . . . . 53 B1
King's Lynn PE30. . . . . . . 148 B1
Knapton NR28 . . . . 143 B1
Long Stratton NR15. . . . . 106 F3
Morley NR18 . . . . 87 B2
North Tuddenham NR20 . . 68 F8
North Walsham NR28 . . . . 151 D5
Northwold IP26 . . . . 99 C7
Postwick with Witton NR13 . 72 F2
Redgrave IP22. . . . . 128 D4
Ringstead PE36 . . . . 2 A3
Roydon IP22 . . . . 129 D7
Saxlingham Nethergate
NR15. . . . . 107 C2
Scole IP21. . . . . 130 F8
Shelfanger IP22. . . . . 120 B2
Shelton NR15 . . . . 122 A8
Tacolneston NR16 . . . . . . 105 B3
Taverham NR8 . . . . 157 B8
Tharston & Hapton NR15. 106 D5
Thompson IP24 . . . . 102 B7
Thornham PE36. . . . . 2 D6
Thursford NR21 . . . . 17 F5
Wacton NR15. . . . . 106 C1
West Winch PE33 . . . . 43 E2
Whissonsett NR20. . . . . . . 31 D2
Wiveton NR25 . . . . 7 F6
Wood Norton NR20 . . . . . . 33 B6
Hall Loke NR28 . . . . 38 C8
Hall Moor Rd NR9 . . . . 86 C4
Hall Orchards PE32 . . . . . . 44 C3
Hallowing Cres **3** NR15. . 106 B1
Hallowing La NR15. . . . . . 121 B8
Hall Plain NR30 . . . . 169 C3
Hall Rd
Alderford NR9 . . . . 52 A5
Barsham NR34. . . . . 124 F7
Barton Turf NR12 . . . . 55 E8
12 Bawdeswell NR20 . . . . 50 E7
Bedingham NR35. . . . . . . 108 C3
Beetley NR20. . . . . 49 D5
Blofield NR13. . . . . 165 C8
Bracon Ash NR14. . . . . 88 E4
Brockdish IP21 . . . . 131 D7
Bunwell NR16 . . . . 105 E2
Burston & Shimpling IP22 120 E3
Cantley NR13. . . . . 92 C8
Carleton Rode NR16 . . . . 105 B4
Catfield NR29 . . . . 56 B8
Clenchwarton PE34 . . . . . 145 D6
Cromer NR27 . . . . 139 B5
Earsham NR35 . . . . 123 B8
Easton NR9 . . . . 70 B5
Ellingham NR35 . . . . 109 C3
Elsing NR20 . . . . 50 D2
Felbrigg NR27 . . . . 139 A4
Fleggburgh NR29. . . . . 57 A1
Framingham Earl NR14 . . . 90 D5
Gimingham NR11. . . . . 22 D7
Great Melton NR9 . . . . 88 B8

Hall Rd continued
Great Witchingham NR9 . . . 51 F5
Hainford NR10. . . . . 53 E5
Hemsby NR29 . . . . 167 A7
Hoe NR20. . . . . 49 F3
Honing NR28 . . . . 38 D8
Hopton on Sea NR31 . . . . 171 B6
King's Lynn PE30 . . . . 148 C1
Ludham NR29 . . . . 56 B4
Marthan NR29 . . . . 57 D4
Mautby NR29. . . . . 76 A6
Northrepps NR27. . . . . . . 139 D2
Norwich NR1 . . . . 178 B1
Oulton NR11 . . . . 35 B7
Outwell PE14 . . . . 77 F7
Postwick with Witton
NR13. . . . . 165 A5
Pulham St Mary IP21. . . . 122 A4
Reedham NR13 . . . . 92 F6
Roudham NR16 . . . . 117 E6
Runhall NR20. . . . . 69 A4
Smallburgh NR12. . . . . 38 D2
9 Snettisham PE31 . . . . . 12 E5
Sutton NR12 . . . . 39 D3
Swafield NR28 . . . . 22 C5
Tacolneston NR16 . . . . . . 105 E6
Tharston & Hapton NR15 . 106 E5
Thurton NR14 . . . . 91 C3
Tivetshall St Margaret
NR15. . . . . 121 B6
Toft Monks NR14 . . . . . . 110 D7
Walpole Highway PE14 . . . 59 F8
Winfarthing IP22 . . . . 120 C5
Wood Dalling NR11 . . . . . . 34 C6
Hall Sch NR6 . . . . 158 D5
Halls Cnr NR10 . . . . 53 B8
Halls Cnr Rd NR10 . . . . . . 53 B8
Hall St NR24 . . . . 142 E3
Hall Staithe NR21 . . . . . . 141 B4
Hall View Rd PE30 . . . . . . 147 B4
Hall Wlk NR9 . . . . 51 D5
Hallwong La IP20 . . . . . . 122 D3
Halstead CI **2** PE13. . . . . 152 E5
Halton Rd **8** IP25. . . . . . . 84 F3
Halt Rd NR30 . . . . 168 D7
HALVERGATE NR13 . . . . . . 74 F1
Halvergate Rd
Beighton NR13. . . . . 74 E1
Reedham NR13 . . . . 93 A6
Hambling's Piece NR16 . . 118 C4
Hamburg Way PE30 . . . . . 147 A8
Hamilton CI
North Walsham NR28 . . . . 151 C5
South Walsham NR13 . . . . 74 A8
Hamilton Ct **1** NR21 . . . . 141 B4
Hamilton Dr PE37 . . . . . . 153 D3
Hamilton Rd
3 Cromer NR27 . . . . 139 B7
Great Yarmouth NR30 . . . 169 D7
Pulham Market PE36. . . . 132 E7
Hamilton Rd W PE36 . . . . 132 E7
Hamilton Way PE38 . . . . 172 B5
Hamilton Wlk **9** NR29. . . 57 D4
Hamlet CI NR28 . . . . 151 D7
Hamlet Way PE30 . . . . . . 146 F1
Hammond CI NR7 . . . . . . 158 B3
Hammond Ct **2** NR30. . . 169 D5
Hammond Way NR7. . . . . 159 E3
Hamon CI PE36 . . . . 132 E7
Hamond Rd NR6 . . . . 157 E6
Hamonds High Sch PE37 153 C3
Hampden Dr **19** NR7 . . . . 72 D4
Hampden Rd **2** PE13. . . . 152 D5
Hampton Ave **3** NR40 . . . 87 A8
Hampton CI NR10 . . . . . . 168 C5
HAMROW NR20 . . . . 31 D3
Hanbury CI NR5. . . . . 161 D5
Hancock CI **3** NR12 . . . . . 54 C7
Hancock Ct **5** NR5. . . . . . 160 E7
Handel Dr NR19. . . . . 154 F3
Handford Dr NR26 . . . . . . 138 E6
Hand La
Basham NR21. . . . . 16 C5
Hoveton NR12 . . . . 164 C8
Hanginghill NR13 . . . . 74 C6
Hankin Ct **3** NR4 . . . . . . 161 C5
Hankinson's Est PE34 . . . . 42 A5
Hanly CI NR7 . . . . 159 C2
Hanly Ct NR30 . . . . 168 D6
Hannah CI NR26 . . . . 138 C6
Hannah Rd NR20 . . . . 50 B4
Hannant Rd NR28 . . . . . . 151 D6
Hanover Ct
Dersingham PE31 . . . . 140 E3
King's Lynn PE30 . . . . 147 D5
Hanover Gdns PE36 . . . . 132 D3
Hanover Rd NR2 . . . . 162 C4
Hanrae CI NR26 . . . . 138 F6
Hansa Rd NR30. . . . . 168 C4
Hansard CI NR3 . . . . 158 B1
Hansard La NR3 . . . . 178 B4
Hansell Rd NR7 . . . . 163 F8
Hans PI **4** NR27 . . . . 139 B7
Hantons Loke NR13 . . . . . 74 B2
HANWORTH NR11. . . . . 21 B6
Hanworth Cross NR11. . . . 21 D5
Hanworth Rd NR11. . . . . . . 21 B6
HAPPISBURGH NR12 . . . . . 24 C6
HAPPISBURGH COMMON
NR12 . . . . 24 B4
Happisburgh Fst Sch
NR12. . . . . 24 C5
Happisburgh Rd
East Ruston NR12 . . . . 24 A3
Lessingham NR12 . . . . 24 D4
North Walsham NR28 . . . . 151 D4

Happisburgh Rd continued
Witton NR28 . . . . 23 E2
HAPTON NR15. . . . . 106 C7
Hapton Prim Sch NR15 . . 106 C7
Harbord CI **3** NR28. . . . . 151 C7
Harbord Cres NR30 . . . . . 170 D8
Harbord Rd
Cromer NR27. . . . . 139 C5
Norwich NR4 . . . . 161 F5
Overstrand NR27 . . . . 11 A3
Harbour La IP22 . . . . 128 A7
Harbour Rd
1 Frettenham NR12. . . . . 54 A4
Norwich NR1 . . . . 163 A5
Harbour Terr NR11. . . . . . 150 F7
Harcourt CI **3** NR3 . . . . . 162 F8
Hardesty CI **9** NR14. . . . . 90 D5
HARDINGHAM NR9. . . . . . . 86 E6
Hardingham Dr NR20 . . . 138 C5
Hardingham Rd NR9 . . . . . 86 D5
Hardingham St **4** NR9 . . . 86 C4
Hardley Cross★ NR14 . . . . 92 E4
Hardley Hall La NR14. . . . 92 C3
Hardley Rd NR14. . . . . 92 A2
Hardley St NR14 . . . . 92 B3
HARDLEY STREET NR14 . . . 92 C3
HARDWICK
North Runcton PE30 . . . . . 147 B1
Shelton NR15. . . . . 122 C8
Hardwick CI **1** NR4. . . . . . 89 D8
Hardwick Ind Est PE30 . . 147 A2
Hardwick Narrows Ind Est
PE30 . . . . 146 F1
Hardwick Rd
King's Lynn PE30 . . . . 146 E3
Pulham Market IP21 . . . . 121 F7
Shelton NR15. . . . . 122 C8
Hardy CI
Downham Market PE38. . . 172 B4
1 North Walsham NR28. . 151 C5
Thetford IP24 . . . . 176 D6
Hardy Rd NR1 . . . . 163 A4
Hardy's La PE32. . . . . 46 C2
Hare CI **8** NR14 . . . . 89 B2
Harecroft Gdns PE30 . . . . 146 E6
Harecroft Par **7** PE30. . . . 146 E6
Harecroft Rd PE13 . . . . . . 152 E5
Harecroft Terr PE30. . . . . 146 E6
Harefen La NR13 . . . . 74 B7
Harefield Rd IP24. . . . . . . 116 C5
Hares CI NR21. . . . . 72 F5
Hares Ct NR21 . . . . 17 C3
Harewood PE31 . . . . 134 F4
Harewood Dr
9 King's Lynn PE30 . . . . 146 E6
Taverham NR8 . . . . 155 E3
Harewood Par **8** PE30 . . 146 E6
Harford Manor CI NR2 . . 162 C2
Harford Manor Specl Sch
NR4. . . . . 162 C3
Harford St NR1 . . . . 162 E3
Harfreys Ind Est
Gorleston-on-Sea NR31. . 170 A8
Great Yarmouth NR31 . . . 169 B1
HARGATE NR16 . . . . 105 D2
Hargate La PE34 . . . . 42 B7
Hargham CI NR17 . . . . . . 104 D2
Hargham Rd
Attleborough NR17 . . . . . 174 B2
Old Buckenham NR17 . . . 104 D8
Shropham NR17. . . . . 103 C3
Harker Way **8** NR13 . . . . . 73 D6
HARLESTON IP20 . . . . 122 D3
Harleston Mus★ IP20 . . . 122 D2
Harleston Prim Sch
IP20 . . . . 122 E2
Harleston Rd
Pulham Market IP21 . . . . 121 E4
Scole IP21. . . . . 121 D1
Harley Rd NR30 . . . . 169 D6
Harling Dro IP27. . . . . 115 E7
Harling Rd
Garboldisham IP22 . . . . . 118 C2
Hockham IP24 . . . . 102 E3
North Lopham IP22 . . . . . 119 A2
Harling Rd Sta NR16 . . . . 118 A6
Harlington Ave NR6 . . . . 158 A4
Harlingwood La NR17 . . . 104 E1
Harman CI **12** NR9 . . . . . . 88 D8
Harman's La IP20 . . . . . . 122 C1
Harmer CI NR28. . . . . 151 E5
Harmer Rd NR3 . . . . 158 D3
Harmer's La NR11. . . . . . . 21 A5
Harnser's Reach NR13. . . 166 B8
Harold Rd NR28 . . . . 141 B5
HARPER'S GREEN NR20. . . 32 A1
Harper's La NR20 . . . . 32 A1
HARPLEY PE31 . . . . 29 D4
Harpley CE VC Prim Sch
PE31. . . . . 29 C4
Harpsfield NR5 . . . . 160 E8
Harp's Hall Rd PE14 . . . . . 59 E5
Harrier CI **18** NR9 . . . . 88 D8
Harriet CI PE12 . . . . 41 A8
Harriet Martineau CI **10**
IP24. . . . . 176 D7
Harriott's Way NR11 . . . . 150 B5
Harris Mews **2** NR5. . . . . 161 A7
Harrisons Dr NR7 . . . . . . 159 E3
Harris Rd
11 Swanton Morley NR20 . 50 B3
12 Watton IP25 . . . . 84 F3

Harrold Cl
 1 South Walsham NR13... 74 B8
 Taverham NR8 . . . . 155 E2
Harrolds Cl PE13. . . . . 59 C5
Harrow Cl PE34. . . . . 146 C5
Harry Barber Cl **2** NR5. . 161 A8
Harry Blunt Way **10**
 NR19 . . . . 154 C4
Harry Miller Ct **7** NR30 169 D1
Harry Perry Cl NR4. . . . . . 162 C2
Harry's La IP21 . . . . 121 E7
Harrys Way
 Hunstanton PE36. . . . . . . 132 D1
 Wisbech PE13 . . . . 152 C2
Harry Watson Ct NR6. . . . 158 C3
Harsnett Ct NR5 . . . . 160 F8
Hartbee Rd NR6 . . . . 158 C6
Hartington Rd NR27 . . . . . 139 D4
Hart La NR25 . . . . 9 A2
Hartley Cl **3** PE36. . . . . . 132 D4
Hartmann Rd NR30. . . . . . 170 E6
Harts Farm Rd NR18 . . . . 173 E5
Harts La NR4 . . . . 161 C1
Hart's La NR9 . . . . 160 A7
Hartwell Rd NR12 . . . . . . 164 C4
Harvard Rd **6** IP26 . . . . . 98 D1
Harvest Cl **1** NR10. . . . . . 53 E5
Harvest La NR21 . . . . 17 D6
Harvey Cl
 2 Hethersett NR9 . . . . . . 88 C7
 Norwich NR7 . . . . 163 C7
 Tasburgh NR15 . . . . 106 E2
Harvey Dr NR30. . . . . 151 C7
Harvey Est NR11 . . . . 22 E7
Harvey Gn **10** NR14. . . . . . 91 F1
Harvey La
 Caister-on-Sea NR30. . . . 168 E4
 Dickleburgh IP21. . . . . . . 121 C1
 Norwich NR7 . . . . 163 C6
Harvey's La NR15 . . . . 108 D6
Harwood Ave **2** IP24 . . . 176 E6
Harwood Rd NR1 . . . . 162 E1
Hase's La NR9 . . . . 51 C4
Haslips Cl **8** NR2 . . . . . . 162 C7
Haspalls Rd PE37 . . . . 153 B3
Hassett Cl **6** NR3. . . . . . . 162 F8
HASSINGHAM NR13. . . . . . 92 B8
Hastings Ave NR6. . . . . . . 158 A4
Hastings Cl
 Briston NR24 . . . . 142 A5
 6 Tasburgh NR15 . . . . . . 106 F6
Hastings Ct NR24 . . . . 142 E4
Hastings Dr **7** NR26. . . . 132 D6
Hastings La
 15 Sheringham NR26 . . . 138 D7
 Wiggenhall St Germans
  PE34. . . . . 61 C8
Hastings Rd **6** IP25. . . . . 84 F3
Hastings Way **10** NR19 . . 39 C3
Hatherley Gdns PE33. . . . . 81 B8
Hatton Rd NR1 . . . . 162 E3
Haugh Cnr NR16 . . . . 119 F7
Haugh Rd NR16. . . . . 119 F8
Haughs End Rd NR12 . . . . 164 F2
Hautbois Rd NR10. . . . . . . 37 B2
Hauteyn Ct NR6. . . . . 158 C2
Havaker The NR13 . . . . 92 F5
Havant Cl NR4 . . . . 161 E1
Havelock Pl **10** NR30 . . . 169 D2
Havelock Rd
 Great Yarmouth NR30 . . 169 D2
 Norwich NR2 . . . . 162 B6
 Sheringham NR26 . . . . . 138 C5
Havergate **2** NR31 . . . . . . 94 C6
Haveringland Rd NR10 . . . 52 E6
Haverscroft Cl NR8. . . . . . 155 D2
Havers Rd NR3. . . . . 158 B1
HAWES' GREEN NR15. . . . . 89 F2
Hawk Cl **28** NR7 . . . . 88 D8
Hawk Cres IP22. . . . . 177 F5
Hawkins Ave NR30 . . . . . . 169 C8
Hawkins Cl NR30. . . . . 169 C8
Hawkins Dr **1** PE13. . . . . 152 E5
Hawthorn Ave **6** PE33 . . . 63 B4
Hawthorn Cl
 Diss IP22. . . . . 177 F5
 3 Spixworth NR10. . . . . . 54 A1
 2 Watlington PE34. . . . . . 61 D5
Hawthorn Cotts PE31. . . . 140 D4
Hawthorn Cres NR31 . . . . . 94 C6
Hawthorn Dr
 Dersingham PE31 . . . . . 140 D5
 East Dereham NR19 . . . . 154 B3
Hawthorne Ave
 Grimston PE32. . . . . 28 B1
 Hellesdon NR6. . . . . 158 A5
 Wisbech PE13 . . . . 152 C8
Hawthorne Cl
 2 Loddon NR14 . . . . 91 F1
 Wymondham NR18 . . . . . 173 D6
Hawthorn Rd
 2 Downham Market
  PE38. . . . . 172 C6
 Emneth PE14 . . . . 59 D1
 6 Gayton PE32. . . . . 45 C5
 Great Yarmouth NR31. . . 170 B6
 Norwich NR5 . . . . 157 A2
Hawthorn Rise NR11 . . . . 143 B5
Hawthorns PE30 . . . . 147 C4
Hawthorn Way IP24 . . . . . 176 E6
Hawthorn Wlk **2** IP24 . . . 176 F6
Haycroft **3** NR29 . . . . 167 B7
Hayes La NR21 . . . . 141 A5
Hayfield Rd PE30 . . . . 148 C4
Haygate **2** IP23 . . . . 130 C1
Hay Gn Rd PE34. . . . . 144 A1

Hay Gn Rd N PE34. . . . . . . 42 B6
Hay Gn Rd S PE34. . . . . . . 42 A6
HAY GREEN PE34 . . . . 144 A1
Haylett Cl NR30. . . . . 168 E5
Haymarket NR2 . . . . 178 B2
Haythill La IP26. . . . . 98 D2
Hayward Cl **3** NR25. . . . . . 7 C6
Haywood End IP22. . . . . . 120 D6
Hazel Ave NR16 . . . . 138 D4
Hazel Cl
 Grimston PE32. . . . . 28 B1
 5 King's Lynn PE30 . . . 148 C3
 Taverham NR8 . . . . 155 E1
 West Winch PE33 . . . . . . 43 E1
 Wymondham NR18 . . . . . 173 D4
Hazel Covert IP24. . . . . . . 176 F5
Hazel Cres **4** PE33. . . . . . 63 B4
Hazel Gdns **1** PE13. . . . . 152 D4
Hazel Gr NR19 . . . . 154 F4
Hazell Rd NR28 . . . . 151 C7
Hazel Rd
 4 Attleborough NR17. . . . 174 B5
 Norwich NR5 . . . . 156 F1
Hazel Way NR31 . . . . 170 B6
HEACHAM PE31 . . . . 133 E5
 Heacham Fst Sch PE31. . 133 D5
 Heacham Jun Sch PE31. . 133 C4
Heacham Rd PE36 . . . . 13 A7
Headington Cl NR31 . . . . 170 A5
Headland Dro IP26. . . . . . 113 A5
Headley Dr NR28. . . . . . . 151 C4
Hearne Ct **3** NR5. . . . . . . 160 E8
Heartsease Fst & Mid Sch
 NR7 . . . . 159 C1
Heartsease High Sch
 NR7. . . . . 159 B1
Heartsease La NR7. . . . . . 159 B1
Heartsease Mid Sch
 NR7. . . . . 159 C1
Heartsease Rd **3** IP24 . . 176 E5
Heartwell Rd NR7 . . . . . . 139 C5
Heater La NR13 . . . . 73 F4
Heath Cl
 10 Horsford NR10. . . . . . 53 A3
 Lenwade NR9 . . . . 51 D5
 Norwich NR8 . . . . 158 A6
Heath Cres NR6. . . . . 158 B5
Heath Dr NR25 . . . . 137 D5
Heather Ave
 Hemsby NR29 . . . . 167 D4
 Norwich NR6 . . . . 158 B4
Heather Ave Fst Sch
 NR6. . . . . 158 B4
Heather Barrow Ct NR21 141 D4
Heather Cl PE30 . . . . 148 C5
Heather Dr NR25. . . . . . . 137 B7
Heather Gdns NR31. . . . . . 93 F6
Heather Rd **12** NR31. . . . . 94 A6
Heather Way
 Brandon IP27 . . . . 175 E3
 Great Moulton NR15 . . . 121 B8
Heatherwood Cl **7** NR13 . 72 D6
Heath Farm La NR11 . . . . . 36 C6
Heathfield Cl NR25. . . . . . . 8 E3
Heathfield Rd NR25 . . . . . . 8 A7
Heathgate NR3 . . . . 163 A8
Heath Gn **1** NR13. . . . . . . 72 E7
Heath La
 Fakenham NR21. . . . . . . 141 F4
 Gimingham NR11. . . . . . . 22 D8
 Great Witchingham NR9 . . 51 E6
 Gunthorpe NR24 . . . . 18 B5
 Lenwade NR9. . . . . 51 D5
 Mundesley NR11 . . . . . . 143 B5
 Roughton NR11 . . . . 21 E8
 Thursford NR21. . . . . 17 E4
 Tittleshall PE32. . . . . 47 F7
Heathlands PE37. . . . . . . 153 D2
Heathlands Dr IP24 . . . . . 176 D8
Heath Rd
 Banham NR16 . . . . 119 E7
 2 Brandon IP27 . . . . 175 D3
 Catfield NR29. . . . . 56 D8
 Corpusty NR11. . . . . 19 D1
 Dersingham PE31 . . . . . 140 D2
 East Dereham NR19 . . . . 154 C7
 Felmingham NR28 . . . . . . 37 B8
 Fritton & St Olaves NR31 . 93 E1
 6 Geldeston NR34 . . . . . 110 A3
 Gunthorpe NR24 . . . . 18 B5
 Heydon NR11. . . . . 34 D8
 Hickling NR12 . . . . 39 E1
 Hockering NR20. . . . . 69 B8
 Honing NR28 . . . . 23 C1
 Kenninghall NR16 . . . . . 119 A3
 Lessingham NR12 . . . . . . 24 F2
 Lyng NR9 . . . . 51 A4
 Norwich NR3 . . . . 162 D8
 Quidenham NR16 . . . . . 118 E8
 Rollesby NR29. . . . . 57 B2
 Sapiston IP31. . . . . 126 A1
 Sheringham NR26 . . . . . 138 D6
 Shotesham NR15. . . . . . 107 F8
 9 Thorpe End NR13 . . . . 72 D6
 Troston IP31. . . . . 126 A1
 Winfarthing IP22. . . . . . 120 A7
Heath Rise
 Fakenham NR21. . . . . . . 141 E4
 Sculthorpe Airfield PE31. . 15 B3
Heathside Rd NR1 . . . . . . 163 B5
Heath The NR10 . . . . 52 F8
Heath Way
 Blofield NR13. . . . . 73 C6
 Fakenham NR21. . . . . . . 141 F4
Hebrides Way NR30. . . . . 168 C6
HECKFIELD GREEN IP21. . 131 B2
HECKINGHAM NR14. . . . . . 92 C1

Heckingham Holes NR14 . . 92 B1
HEDENHAM NR35. . . . . . . 108 C4
Hedgehog Wlk NR12 . . . . . 24 E4
Hedgelands **1** PE13 . . . . 152 C8
Hedgemere **1** NR8 . . . . . 155 D2
Hedgerows The **8** NR5 . 161 A7
Hedley La NR33. . . . . 111 F1
Heffer Cl NR19. . . . . 154 D3
Heggatt Rd NR12 . . . . 54 C5
Heidi Cl **9** NR19 . . . . 154 D1
Heigham Gr NR2 . . . . 162 C6
Heigham Pk Fst Sch
 NR2. . . . . 162 A5
Heigham Rd NR2. . . . . . . 162 B6
Heigham St NR2 . . . . 162 B6
Heigham Watering **5**
 NR2. . . . . 162 B8
Helena Rd
 Norwich NR2 . . . . 162 B6
 Witton NR12 . . . . 23 F3
Helen Ave **7** NR29. . . . . . 57 C4
Helford St **6** NR2. . . . . . 162 B8
HELHOUGHTON NR21 . . . . 30 E5
HELLESDON NR6. . . . . 157 F5
Hellesdon Cl NR5. . . . . . . 160 F8
Hellesdon Hall Rd NR6 . . 157 E1
Hellesdon High Sch NR6 157 E2
Hellesdon Hospl NR6. . . . 157 D4
Hellesdon Mill La NR6. . . 157 D1
Hellesdon Pk Rd NR6. . . . 157 E3
Hellesdon Rd NR6 . . . . . . 161 D8
Hellgate La NR11 . . . . 20 F8
HELLINGTON NR14 . . . . . . 91 B6
Hellington Cnr NR14 . . . . . 91 B5
Hellington Hill NR14 . . . . . 91 B6
Helpit La NR24 . . . . 19 B2
Helsinki Way NR19 . . . . . 154 C2
Helska Leisure Ctr NR12. . 55 E3
HEMBLINGTON NR13 . . . . . 73 E6
HEMBLINGTON CORNER
 NR13 . . . . 73 D6
Hemblington Hall Rd
 NR13 . . . . 73 D6
Hemblington Prim Sch
 NR13 . . . . 73 C6
Hemington Cl PE30 . . . . . 147 D8
Hemington Cl PE30 . . . . . 147 D8
Hemlin Cl NR5. . . . . 161 C6
Hemmant Way NR34 . . . . 110 B3
Hemmings Cl **4** NR5. . . . 160 F7
HEMPNALL NR15. . . . . . . 107 D5
HEMPNALL GREEN
 NR15 . . . . 107 D4
Hempnall Rd NR35. . . . . . 108 A4
Hempnall St NR15. . . . . . 107 C5
HEMPSTEAD
 Hempstead NR25. . . . . . . 19 E8
 Lessingham NR12 . . . . . . 24 E3
Hempstead Rd
 Holt NR25 . . . . 137 D5
 Lessingham NR12 . . . . . . 24 E3
Hempton Rd NR21 . . . . . . 141 A3
Hempsby Fst Sch NR29 . . 167 A7
Hemsby Rd
 13 Martham NR29 . . . . . . 57 D4
 Winterton-on-Sea NR29. . 58 B5
Henby Way NR7. . . . . 163 D7
Henderson Rd NR4. . . . . . 161 F5
Hendon Ave **12** IP25. . . . . 84 F3
Hendon Cl NR5 . . . . 157 B1
Hendred Rd NR25 . . . . . . 137 C7
HENGRAVE NR9 . . . . 52 A6
Henley Rd NR2 . . . . 162 A4
Hennessey's Loke NR28 . . 23 A3
Henry Bell Cl **3** NR30. . . 147 A5
Henry Blogg Rd NR27 . . . 139 B5
Henry Cross Cl **1** IP25. . . 67 C2
Henry Page Rd NR31 . . . . . 94 A5
Henry Preston Rd NR11. . 150 B6

Heron Cl
 Downham Market PE38. . 172 C7
 6 Fakenham NR21. . . . . . 141 E4
 Great Yarmouth NR31 . . 170 A7
 Salhouse NR13 . . . . 55 B1
Heron Gdns NR12. . . . . . . 39 B3
Heron Rd PE13. . . . . 152 D2
Heron Way
 Hickling NR12 . . . . 39 E1
 12 Watton IP25. . . . . 84 C3
Herrick Rd NR8 . . . . 156 E8
Herries **7** NR30. . . . . . . 169 C4
HERRINGFLEET NR32. . . . 111 D8
Herringfleet Rd NR31 . . . . 93 E2
Herring La NR9 . . . . 69 A1
Herring's La PE31. . . . . . . 135 C4
Hertford Way NR31 . . . . . 170 B4
HETHEL NR14 . . . . 88 F3
Hethel Old Thorn Nature
 Reserve* NR14. . . . . 88 E3
Hethel Rd NR16. . . . . 88 D2
HETHERSETT NR9. . . . . . . 88 D7
Hethersett High Sch NR9 88 C7
Hethersett La NR4 . . . . . . 161 D6
Hethersett Old Hall Sch
 NR9. . . . . 88 D7
Hethersett Rd
 East Carleton NR14. . . . . 88 F5
 Great Melton NR9 . . . . . . 88 B8
HEVINGHAM NR10 . . . . . . 53 B7
Hevingham Prim Sch
 NR10. . . . . 53 B8
Hewett Cl NR31. . . . . 170 D2
Hewett Rd NR31 . . . . 170 D2
Hewett Sch NR1. . . . . 162 D8
Hewitts Cl NR24 . . . . 142 E4
Hewitts La NR18 . . . . 173 C5
Hextable Rd PE30 . . . . . . 146 E6
HEYDON NR11. . . . . 34 F6
Heydon Hall* NR11. . . . . . 34 F6
Heydon La NR11 . . . . 34 E7
Heydon Rd
 Aylsham NR11. . . . . 150 A7
 Corpusty NR11. . . . . 34 F8
 Wood Dalling NR11 . . . . . 34 D6
Heyford Rd NR6. . . . . 158 C6
Heywood Ave IP22 . . . . . 177 D6
Heywood Rd
 Diss IP22 . . . . 177 E8
 Shelfanger IP22 . . . . . . 120 C2
 Tibenham NR16. . . . . . . 120 D6
 Winfarthing IP22 . . . . . . 120 C4
Heywood The IP22. . . . . . 120 E5
Hickathrift Field PE14 . . . . 61 A4
HICKLING NR12. . . . . 39 F3
Hickling Broad National
 Nature Reserve* NR12. . . 57 A8
Hickling Broad Visitor Ctr*
 NR12. . . . . 39 F3
Hickling Cl **7** NR3 . . . . . 153 C2
Hickling Fst Sch NR12. . . . 39 F2
HICKLING GREEN NR12. . . 39 F2
HICKLING HEATH NR12 . . . 39 E1
Hickling La NR14 . . . . 89 D4
Hickling Rd
 Sea Palling NR12. . . . . . . 24 F1
 Sutton NR12 . . . . 39 C2
Hickling Way NR29. . . . . . 167 B3
Hickory Gdns **18** NR31. . . 94 C7
Hickory Rd PE30 . . . . 147 C5
Higham Cl NR7 . . . . 159 A3
Higham Gn **3** PE30 . . . . 147 C4
High Ash Rd NR18 . . . . 88 C5
High Banks NR18 . . . . 173 C4
Highbridge Gravel Dro
 IP27 . . . . 113 D2
Highbridge Rd PE34. . . . . . 78 F8
High Bridgham Rd NR16. . 117 C5
High Bungay Rd NR14. . . 109 D8
Highbury Rd IP27 . . . . . . 175 A2
High Comm NR18 . . . . 87 D2
HIGH COMMON IP25 . . . . . 85 F8
High Comm Rd IP22 . . . . 128 D8
High Cross NR20 . . . . 33 A2
High Ct IP20. . . . . 122 E8
Higher Gn Cl **11** NR15. . . 89 D1
High Fen Dro IP26. . . . . . . 98 D8
Highfield
 3 Eye IP23 . . . . 130 C1
 Field Dalling NR25 . . . . . . 7 B2
 Great & Little Plumstead
  NR13. . . . . 73 B7
 King's Lynn PE30 . . . . . . 147 C5
Highfield Ave NR13 . . . . . 165 D3
Highfield Cl
 Foulsham NR20 . . . . 33 C4
 1 Norwich NR7 . . . . 72 D3
 Ryburgh NR21 . . . . 32 A6
Highfield La NR5 . . . . 156 D1
Highfield Rd
 East Dereham NR19 . . . . 154 D8
 Fakenham NR21. . . . . . . 141 B5
 Great Yarmouth NR31 . . 170 C7
 Taverham NR8 . . . . 155 F1
Highfields
 Felmingham NR28 . . . . . . 37 A8
 Lakenheath IP27 . . . . . . 113 F1
 Norwich NR5 . . . . 156 D1
Highfield Way **4** NR12. . . 54 C7
Highgate PE30 . . . . 146 E5
Highgate Inf Sch PE30 . . 146 F6
High Gn
 Brooke NR15 . . . . 90 D1
 Great Melton NR9 . . . . . . 88 B8
 8 Great Moulton NR15 . . 121 B8
 Norwich NR1. . . . . 163 B5
High Gn Gdns NR15 . . . . . 90 D1

Har–HIL 193

HIGH GREEN
 Bradenham IP25 . . . . 66 E2
 Fransham NR19 . . . . 48 E1
 Great Melton NR9 . . . . . . 88 B8
Highgrove Ct NR14. . . . . . 90 C6
High Hatter's Cl PE38 . . . 172 C3
High Hill Rd NR21 . . . . 38 F6
High House Ave
 7 Wymondham NR18. . . 173 D5
 3 Wymondham NR18 . . . 173 D5
High House Cotts PE32. . . 47 E5
High House La **8** NR13. . . 72 E6
High House Rd NR20. . . . . 49 C4
HIGH KELLING NR25 . . . . . . 8 E3
Highland NR14. . . . . 90 B6
Highland Ave NR2. . . . . . 162 A4
Highland Cl NR13 . . . . 92 C6
Highland Cres NR14. . . . . 163 B2
Highland Rd
 Norwich NR2 . . . . 162 A4
 Taverham NR8 . . . . 155 D1
Highlands
 Costessey NR8. . . . . 156 F4
 Thetford IP24 . . . . 176 D5
High Lodge Forest Ctr*
 IP27 . . . . 115 C3
High London La IP22. . . . 120 A4
Highlow Rd NR5 . . . . 157 A1
High Mill Rd NR31 . . . . . . 169 B3
Highmoor Dro IP26 . . . . . . 99 D8
High Noon La NR13 . . . . . . 73 A4
High Noon Rd NR13. . . . . . 21 D2
HIGHOAK NR18. . . . . 87 B4
High Oak La NR18. . . . . . . 87 B4
High Oak Rd NR18. . . . . . . 87 B3
High Rd
 Beighton NR13. . . . . 74 B1
 Bressingham IP22. . . . . . 129 C8
 Burgh Castle NR31 . . . . . 94 B8
 Cantley NR13 . . . . 92 B8
 Forncett NR16. . . . . 106 B6
 Great Yarmouth NR31 . . 170 D7
 Lessingham NR12 . . . . . . 24 C2
 Needham IP20 . . . . 122 C1
 Repps with Bastwick NR29 57 A4
 Roydon IP22 . . . . 129 D3
 Tilney St Lawrence PE34. . 60 F8
 Wiggenhall St Germans
  PE34. . . . . 42 F1
 Wortwell IP20 . . . . 123 A3
High St
 Attleborough NR17 . . . . 174 D5
 Blakeney NR25 . . . . 7 C6
 Brandon IP27 . . . . 175 C5
 Caister-on-Sea NR30 . . . 168 E5
 Castle Acre PE32. . . . . . . 46 F2
 Cawston NR10 . . . . 35 B3
 Cley next the Sea NR25. . . 7 E6
 Coltishall NR12 . . . . 54 C7
 Cromer NR27 . . . . 139 B7
 Docking PE31. . . . . 134 E4
 Downham Market PE38. . 172 C5
 East Dereham NR19 . . . . 154 D5
 Feltwell IP26 . . . . 98 E1
 Fincham PE33 . . . . 62 E1
 Foulsham NR20 . . . . 33 D3
 Great Yarmouth NR31 . . 170 D6
 Heacham PE31. . . . . 133 D5
 Hilgay PE38 . . . . 79 E1
 Holt NR25 . . . . 137 B6
 Hopton IP22 . . . . 127 F6
 Hunstanton PE36. . . . . . 132 C4
 Ketteringham NR18 . . . . . 88 D5
 King's Lynn PE30 . . . . . . 146 D5
 Loddon NR14 . . . . 92 A1
 Ludham NR29 . . . . 56 C5
 Marsham NR10 . . . . 150 C1
 Methwold IP26 . . . . 99 A5
 Mundesley NR11 . . . . . . 143 C5
 North Elmham NR20 . . . . 49 E8
 Northwold IP26 . . . . 99 C7
 Overstrand NR27 . . . . 11 A3
 Ringstead PE36 . . . . 2 A3
 5 Sheringham NR26 . . . 138 D7
 Shipdham IP25 . . . . 67 B2
 Southrepps NR11. . . . . . . 22 B7
 Stalham NR12 . . . . 39 B4
 St Margaret, Ilketshall
  NR35. . . . . 124 D3
 Stoke Ferry PE33. . . . . . . 81 A2
 Sutton Bridge PE12 . . . . . 41 C8
 Thelnetham IP22. . . . . . 128 B4
 Thornham PE36 . . . . 2 D6
 Thursford NR21. . . . . 17 D5
 Tittleshall PE32. . . . . 48 B8
 Walsingham NR22 . . . . . . 16 F7
 Watton IP25 . . . . 84 D3
 Wells-next-the-Sea NR23 . 136 D5
 Whissonsett NR20. . . . . . 31 D2
 Wicklewood NR18 . . . . . . 87 B5
 Wighton NR23 . . . . 5 F2
 Wisbech PE13 . . . . 152 C5
HIGH STREET NR35 . . . . . 124 D3
Highview Cl NR13 . . . . . . 165 E6
High View Dr NR12 . . . . . 174 B4
Highview Pk NR27 . . . . . . 139 C4
High Way **10** NR13 . . . . . 74 A3
High Wrong Cnr IP24. . . . 115 C3
Hilary Ave NR1. . . . . 163 B8
Hilary Cl **6** NR13 . . . . . . 74 A3
HILBOROUGH PE33 . . . . . . 83 A3
Hilda Rd NR11 . . . . 143 C6
HILGAY PE38 . . . . 79 E1

Hilgay Rd
Ryston PE38. . . . . 79 F3
West Dereham PE33 . . . . . . 80 A4
Hilgay Village Prim Sch
PE38 . . . . 79 E1
Hilary Rd IP24 . . . . 176 C2
Hill Ave NR31 . . . . 170 D1
Hillburn Rd PE13 . . . . 152 B4
Hill Cl NR27 . . . . 139 C4
Hill Comm NR12 . . . . 39 F1
HILL COMMON NR12 . . . . . 39 F1
Hillcrest
Acle NR13 . . . . 166 A3
Downham Market PE38 . . 172 E5
Great Ryburgh NR21 . . . . . 32 B6
7 Loddon NR14 . . . . 92 A2
Hillcrest Ave NR11 . . . . . . 150 C4
Hillcrest Prim Sch PE38 . . 172 E6
Hill Crest Rd NR7 . . . . 163 D7
Hill Rd PE30 . . . . 146 D2
Hill Est The PE33 . . . . 62 B6
Hill Farm Rd NR15 . . . . . . 106 F3
Hillfield NR12 . . . . 38 D3
Hill Fields NR10 . . . . 154 C1
Hill Fort Cl IP24 . . . . 176 C7
Hillgate St PE34 . . . . 144 A4
Hill House La IP24 . . . . . . 176 D7
Hill House Rd
Bramerton NR14 . . . . 90 F8
Norwich NR1 . . . . 163 A5
Hillington Pk NR27 . . . . . . 11 A4
Hillings Way PE32 . . . . 28 A1
HILLINGTON PE31 . . . . 28 B4
Hillington Sq PE30 . . . . . . 146 E4
Hill La
Runhall NR20 . . . . 69 A4
Sculthorpe Airfield NR21 . . 15 C2
Hillmead NR3 . . . . 158 D3
Hill Rd
Ingoldisthorpe PE31 . . . . 140 C8
King's Lynn PE30 . . . . 147 B8
Middleton PE33 . . . . 44 B3
Morley NR18 . . . . 104 D8
Norwich NR5 . . . . 157 A2
Tibenham NR16 . . . . 120 F8
Wymondham NR18 . . . . . 105 A7
Hill's Cl
3 Corpusty NR11 . . . . 19 F1
Sporle PE32 . . . . 65 C6
Hill's Ct PE38 . . . . 79 E1
Hillsend La NR17 . . . . 114 E4
Hillside
Barnham Broom NR9 . . . . . 69 B2
Barsham NR21 . . . . 16 D5
Brandon IP27 . . . . 114 D4
Briston NR24 . . . . 142 B4
Cromer NR27 . . . . 139 C4
Loddon NR14 . . . . 92 A2
Marham PE33 . . . . 63 B5
Mundesley NR11 . . . . 143 D5
North Pickenham PE37 . . . 65 E2
Poringland NR14 . . . . 90 C5
Roughton NR11 . . . . 10 D1
Sheringham NR26 . . . . . . 138 F7
Swaffham PE37 . . . . 153 D4
Hillside Animal Sanctuary *
NR12. . . . . 54 B4
Hillside Ave NR7 . . . . 163 F6
Hillside Ave Prim Sch
NR7 . . . . 163 F6
Hillside Cl
Norwich NR7 . . . . 163 F6
Ormesby St Margaret
NR29 . . . . 167 B2
Swardeston NR14 . . . . 89 C5
Hill Side Cl **3** PE32 . . . . . . 44 B3
Hillside Cres NR18 . . . . . . 87 B5
Hillside Fst Sch NR31 . . . . 94 C7
Hillside Rd
Horning NR12 . . . . 55 E3
Norwich NR7 . . . . 163 F6
Sheringham NR26 . . . . . . 138 F5
Hillside Rd E NR35 . . . . . . 124 B7
Hillside Rd W NR35 . . . . . . 124 A7
Hills Rd IP25 . . . . 84 C5
Hill St
10 Feltwell IP26 . . . . 98 E1
Hunstanton PE36. . . . . . . 132 C4
Norwich NR2 . . . . 162 C4
5 Wisbech PE13. . . . . . . 152 C5
Hills The NR13 . . . . 92 F4
Hill Top
Brandon IP27 . . . . 175 A2
Coltishall NR12 . . . . 54 D7
Damgate NR13 . . . . 166 C2
Horsham St Faith NR10 . . . 53 D1
Little Snoring NR21 . . . . . . 17 B3
Shipmeadow NR34. . . . . . 124 F8
Westwick NR10 . . . . 37 C5
Woodbastwick NR13 . . . . . 55 F1
Hill Top
Cley next the Sea NR25 . . . . 7 E7
Stanton IP31 . . . . 127 C1
Hill Top Dr NR8 . . . . 156 F3
Hilltop Way IP31 . . . . 127 C1
Hillview PE37 . . . . 65 E2
Hillview Dr NR29 . . . . 58 B6
Hill View Rd PE30 . . . . . . 138 E7
Hillvue Cl NR5 . . . . 157 A2
Hilly Cl IP31 . . . . 126 D1
Hilly Plantation NR7 . . . . 163 E7
Hilton Cl PE37 . . . . 153 C4
Hilton Ct PE13 . . . . 153 D4
Hiltons La **5** PE34 . . . . . . 43 B1
Hinchingbrook Cl PE30. . . 148 E1

HINDERCLAY IP22 . . . . . . 128 C3
Hinderclay La IP22. . . . . . . 128 B5
Hinderclay Rd
Redgrave IP22. . . . . 128 C3
Rickinghall Inferior IP22. . 128 C3
Wattisfield IP22. . . . . 128 B1
HINDOLVESTON NR20 . . . . 33 D8
Hindolveston Rd
Foulsham NR20 . . . . 33 D4
Fulmodeston NR21 . . . . . . 17 F1
Guestwick NR20 . . . . 33 F6
Thurning NR20 . . . . 34 A8
HINDRINGHAM NR21 . . . . . 17 E7
Hindringham Prim Sch
NR21. . . . . 17 D7
Hindringham Rd
Binham NR21. . . . . 6 E2
Gunthorpe NR21 . . . . 18 A7
Hindringham NR21 . . . . . . 17 F7
Walsingham NR22 . . . . 17 A8
HINGHAM NR9. . . . . 86 C5
Hingham Prim Sch NR9 . . . 86 C5
Hingham Rd
Deopham NR18 . . . . 86 F5
Garvestone NR9 . . . . 86 C8
Great Ellingham NR17 . . . 103 E8
Hardingham NR9 . . . . 86 F6
Little Ellingham NR17 . . . . 86 A2
Hingley Cl NR31 . . . . 170 C8
Hinks Cl NR10 . . . . 155 C3
Hinshalwood Way NR8 . . . 156 E4
Hipkin Rd PE31. . . . . 140 C3
Hipperson Cl **2** NR28. . . . 151 C7
Hippodrome * NR30. . . . . . 169 E3
Hobart Cl NR18 . . . . 173 C6
Hobart High Sch NR14 . . . 92 A1
Hobart La NR11 . . . . 178 B1
Hobart Sq NR11 . . . . 178 B1
Hobb's La NR13. . . . . 92 D7
Hobbs's La NR15. . . . . 108 D7
Hobland Rd
Belton with Browston
NR31. . . . . 94 C4
Bradwell NR31. . . . . 171 A4
Hobrough La NR1 . . . . 178 C2
HOCKERING NR20. . . . . 69 B8
HOCKERING HEATH NR20. . 51 C6
Hockering La NR9 . . . . 160 B6
Hockering Prim Sch NR20 69 B8
Hockham St PE30 . . . . 146 D2
HOCKWOLD CUM WILTON
IP26. . . . . 114 A7
Hockwold Prim Sch
IP26. . . . . 114 A6
Hockwold Rd NR4. . . . . . . 161 F5
Hodgson Rd NR4. . . . . 161 F5
HOE NR20. . . . . 49 F3
Hoe Hall NR20 . . . . 49 F3
Hoe Rd
Hoe NR20. . . . . 49 F5
Longham NR19. . . . . 49 A3
Hoe Rd E NR20. . . . . 50 A4
Hoe Rd N NR20 . . . . 50 A3
Hoe Rd S NR20. . . . . 50 A4
Hoe Rough Nature Reserve *
NR20. . . . . 49 E4
Hogarth Cl **13** NR31 . . . . . . 94 C8
Hogarth Rd PE38. . . . . 172 E6
Hog Bog La NR10 . . . . 53 F3
Hogg La NR35 . . . . 108 C1
Hogherd's La **9** PE13 . . . . 152 C5
Hog La NR34 . . . . 124 F2
Hogsty La IP21 . . . . 122 A1
Holbrigg La NR21 . . . . 17 C1
Holcombe Ave PE30 . . . . . 146 F3
Holders La IP26. . . . . 99 A7
Holgate Hill NR25 . . . . 8 D4
Holgate La NR27 . . . . 10 B5
Holgate Rd
North Walsham NR28 . . . . 151 F1
South Creake NR21 . . . . . . 15 C7
HOLKHAM NR23 . . . . 5 B6
Holkham Ave PE37 . . . . . . 153 B2
Holkham Hall & Bygones
Mus * 5 A5
**Holkham National Nature
Reserve** * NR23 . . . . 5 B8
Holkham Rd NR23 . . . . 136 B6
Holland Ct **8** NR19 . . . . . . 154 D1
Holland's La NR35 . . . . . . 108 C3
Holley Wlk NR11 . . . . 150 C4
Hollies The
Clenchwarton PE34 . . . . . 145 D5
5 North Walsham NR28. . . 151 C5
Holl La
Billingford NR20 . . . . 50 B7
Garvestone NR9 . . . . 68 B1
Holloway Rd NR14 . . . . 91 B8
Hollow Hill Rd NR35. . . . . 109 A2
Hollow La
Barningham IP31. . . . . . . 127 D4
4 Haddiscoe PE35 . . . . 7 A4
Raynham NR21 . . . . 30 F3
Shotesham NR15. . . . . 89 F2
Hollow Way Hill NR34 . . . 110 D4
Holl Rd NR11 . . . . 21 B4
Holls La NR21 . . . . 178 B1
Hollway La NR14 . . . . 33 A4
Holly Ave NR31 . . . . 94 C7
Holly Bank NR7 . . . . 159 A2
Holly Blue Rd NR18 . . . . . 173 E4
Hollybush Rd NR28. . . . . . 151 F5
Holly Cl
Dereham NR19 . . . . 154 F4
Downham Market PE38. . . 172 B6
Holt NR25 . . . . 137 D7

Holly Cl *continued*
King's Lynn PE30 . . . . 148 D2
14 Marthan NR29 . . . . 57 D4
Mattishall NR20. . . . . 68 E6
Rougham PE32. . . . . 47 B7
1 West Winch PE33 . . . . . . 43 E2
Hollycroft Cl PE14 . . . . 59 D1
Hollycroft Rd PE14 . . . . . . 77 D8
Holly Ct
34 Harleston IP20. . . . . . . 122 D2
Swaffham PE13 . . . . 153 C4
Wymondham NR18 . . . . . 173 E6
Holly Dr NR2 . . . . 162 A7
HOLLY END PE14 . . . . 59 D1
Holly Farm Rd NR13. . . . . . 93 A4
Holly Gr NR26. . . . . 138 D5
Holly La
Blofield NR13. . . . . 165 D7
Lackenheath IP27 . . . . . . 113 E1
9 Tharston & Hapton
NR15. . . . . 106 D3
Wood Dalling NR11 . . . . . . 34 D5
Holly Rd NR17 . . . . 174 C4
Holly Way **13** NR31 . . . . . 170 B6
Hollywell Gdns PE13 . . . . 153 B4
Holman Cl NR11 . . . . 150 B7
Holman Rd NR11 . . . . 150 B6
Holman's Chase PE38 . . . . 97 B6
Holme Cl
Hopton IP22 . . . . 127 F6
Runcton Holme PE33. . . . . 61 D4
**Holme Dunes National
Nature Reserve** * PE36. . 2 A8
HOLME HALE IP25. . . . . 66 B2
HOLME NEXT THE SEA
PE36. . . . . 2 A6
Holme Rd PE36 . . . . 2 A4
Holmes Cl
Acle NR13 . . . . 166 B4
Norwich NR7 . . . . 163 D8
Holmesdale Rd NR13. . . . . 165 B4
Holmes Dr PE13 . . . . 152 E5
Holmes Rd
East Ruston NR12 . . . . 38 F5
Somerton NR29 . . . . 57 F7
Holmwood Rise NR7 . . . . . 163 C6
HOLT NR25 . . . . 137 C6
Holt Cl PE14 . . . . 41 E3
Holt Ctry Pk * NR25 . . . . . 137 C4
Holt House La PE32 . . . . . . 44 D5
Holt Prim Sch NR25 . . . . . 137 B5
Holt Rd
Aylmerton NR11. . . . . 10 B3
Briston NR24 . . . . 142 E5
Cawston NR10. . . . . 35 D2
Cley next the Sea NR25. . . . 7 F6
Cromer NR27. . . . . 139 A6
Fakenham NR21. . . . . 141 C4
Felthorpe NR10 . . . . 52 F6
Field Dalling NR25 . . . . 7 B2
Gresham NR11. . . . . 9 E1
Guist NR20. . . . . 32 F4
Hoe NR19. . . . . 154 C8
Langham NR25. . . . . 7 A4
Letheringsett with Glandford
NR25. . . . . 8 A1
Little Snoring NR21 . . . . . . 17 C3
North Elmham NR20 . . . . . 49 E7
Norwich NR10 . . . . 157 F8
Sheringham NR26 . . . . . . 138 B5
Thornage NR25 . . . . 18 F7
Upper Sheringham NR26. . 138 C3
Walsingham NR22 . . . . 17 A8
Weybourne NR25. . . . . 8 E5
Holt's La PE38 . . . . 79 D1
Holt Sta NR25 . . . . 137 E8
Holway Cl NR27 . . . . 139 B3
Holway Rd NR26 . . . . 138 D5
Holway The NR29 . . . . 58 B6
Holworthy Rd NR5 . . . . . . 161 B8
Holy Rd NR24 . . . . 18 D5
Holyrood Dr PE31. . . . . . . 140 D3
Homebred La **11** NR14. . . . 91 F1
Home Cl
Great Ellingham NR17 . . . 103 E8
Lyng NR9 . . . . 51 A4
5 Sheringham NR27 . . . . . 10 A5
Home Farm La NR18 . . . . . 104 E8
Home Farm Rd NR15 . . . . 109 C3
Home Farm Rise NR25 . . . . 8 E6
Homefield Fst Sch NR31. . . 94 C7
Homefields La PE36. . . . . 132 D4
Home La
Hilborough IP25 . . . . 83 B4
Hindringham NR21 . . . . . . 17 E7
Homeland Rd **10** PE30 . . . 146 E6
Homelea Cres **18** NR13 . . . . 74 A3
Home Piece IP22 . . . . 127 E4
HOMERSFIELD IP20. . . . . . 123 B4
Home St NR2 . . . . 162 C8
Homestead Cl NR13 . . . . . . 74 A3
Homestead Gdns NR29 . . . 167 B7
Honey Cl **3** NR1 . . . . 163 B7
Honeycombe Rd NR13. . . . 73 B6
Honey Dro PE33 . . . . 80 B1
Honey Hill PE34. . . . . 79 D8
Honey Hills PE31. . . . . 14 A5
Honeymoon Loke NR30. . . 168 F4
Honeymoon Row NR30. . . 136 D5
Honeypot Dro PE32 . . . . . . 46 C5
Honeypot La
Kirby Cane NR35 . . . . 109 C5
Longham NR19 . . . . 48 F2
Seething NR15. . . . . 108 E8
Honeysuckle Cl
North Walsham NR28 . . . . 151 E4
5 Thetford IP24 . . . . 176 F4

Honeysuckle Dr NR20. . . . 154 F4
Honeysuckle Way NR17 . . 174 B5
HONING NR28 . . . . 38 C6
HONINGHAM NR9 . . . . 69 E7
Honingham La NR8 . . . . . . 70 A8
Honingham Rd NR9 . . . . . . 69 C3
Honing Long La NR28 . . . . 38 C7
Honing Rd NR28 . . . . 38 B5
Honing Row NR28. . . . . . . 38 A5
HONINGTON IP31. . . . . 126 D1
Honington Airfield IP31 . . 126 A2
Honington Rise IP31 . . . . . 126 C1
Honington VC Prim Sch
IP31. . . . . 126 D1
Hood Way IP24 . . . . 176 E5
Hooker Rd NR7 . . . . 159 D1
Hooks Hill Rd NR26 . . . . . 138 C6
Hook's Wlk NR1 . . . . 178 C3
Hookwood La NR18 . . . . . 104 C8
Hooper La NR3 . . . . 158 F2
Hooton's Row PE36 . . . . . . 78 F6
Hope Ct PE30 . . . . 147 A8
Hope La PE14. . . . . 60 A4
HOPTON IP22 . . . . 127 F5
Hopton CE VC Prim Sch
IP22. . . . . 127 F5
Hopton Cl **8** NR5 . . . . 72 D4
Hopton Fst Sch NR31 . . . . 171 E4
Hopton Gdns NR31 . . . . . . 171 D5
HOPTON ON SEA NR31 . . . 171 D6
Hopton Rd
Barningham IP31. . . . . . . 127 D4
Garboldisham IP22 . . . . . 128 A8
Thelnetham IP22. . . . . . . 128 A3
Horizon Views NR12 . . . . . 24 A7
Hornbeam Cl
5 Great Yarmouth
NR31. . . . . 170 B6
Norwich NR7 . . . . 159 D4
Hornbeam Dr **18** NR14. . . . 90 C5
Horner Cl **3** IP22. . . . . 177 A5
HORNING NR12. . . . . 55 E4
Horning Cl NR5. . . . . 161 D7
Horning Fst Sch NR12. . . . 55 F3
Horning Rd
Hoveton NR12 . . . . 164 E5
Neatishead NR12. . . . . 55 D6
Woodbastwick NR13 . . . . . 55 D2
Horning Rd W NR12. . . . . . 164 C5
HORNINGTOFT NR20 . . . . . 31 F1
Hornor Cl NR12 . . . . 162 C3
Horns La NR1. . . . . 178 B2
Horns Row NR21. . . . . 141 A3
Horsbeck Way NR10. . . . . . 53 A3
Horse Fair **2** PE13 . . . . . . 152 C5
Horsefen Rd NR29 . . . . 56 F6
Horsehead Dro PE14 . . . . . 95 C8
Horse Rescue Ctr *
NR16. . . . . 103 C2
Horses Head NR13 . . . . . . 166 B7
Horseshoe Cl NR5 . . . . . . 156 E1
Horseshoe La NR24 . . . . . 142 F4
Horse Shoe Rd NR20 . . . . . 50 A2
Horseshoe Terr PE13. . . . . 152 B7
HORSEY NR29 . . . . 40 D2
HORSEY CORNER NR29 . . . 40 D2
Horsey Rd NR29. . . . . 57 E7
Horsey's La NR31. . . . . . . 170 D5
Horsey Windpump *
NR29. . . . . 40 D1
HORSFORD NR10 . . . . 53 B4
Horsford All Saints Mid Sch
NR10. . . . . 53 B4
Horsford St **2** NR2 . . . . . . 162 B8
Horsford VC Fst Sch
NR10. . . . . 53 A3
HORSHAM ST FAITH
NR10 . . . . 53 E1
Horsham St Faith VC Fst Sch
NR10. . . . . 53 E2
Horsley Dr
Great Yarmouth NR31 . . . 170 B1
Hopton on Sea NR31. . . . 171 D4
Horsley's Chase PE30 . . . . 146 E2
Horsley's Ct **7** PE30 . . . . . 146 E3
Horsley's Field PE30 . . . . . 146 E2
HORSTEAD NR12 . . . . 54 C6
Horton Rd PE30. . . . . 147 D6
Hospital La
Heilesdon NR6 . . . . 157 D3
Norwich NR1 . . . . 162 E3
Hospital Rd
Great & Little Plumstead
NR13. . . . . 73 A5
Sutton Bridge PE12. . . . . . 41 E8
Wicklewood NR18 . . . . 87 C4
Hospital Wlk PE30 . . . . . . 146 E4
Hotblack Rd NR2 . . . . 162 A8
Hotch La PE14 . . . . 60 B8
Hotson Cl **5** NR15 . . . . . . 106 D3
Houghton Ave PE30. . . . . . 148 D1
Houghton Cl **2** NR5. . . . . . 161 B8
Houghton Hall * **8** IP31. . . 29 C7
Houghton La PE37 . . . . 65 E1
HOUGHTON ST GILES
NR22 . . . . 16 E6
House Gdns NR10 . . . . 53 E5
Hovell's La IP26 . . . . 99 C7
HOVETON NR12. . . . . 164 D6
Hoveton Cl PE30 . . . . 147 D5
Hoveton Dr PE37. . . . . 153 C1
Hoveton Hall Gdns *
NR12. . . . . 55 B7
Hoveton Pl NR10 . . . . 37 B2
Hoveton & Wroxham Sta
NR12. . . . . 164 C5

Howard Cl
Harleston IP20 . . . . 122 E2
Norwich NR7 . . . . 163 D7
4 Swanton Morley NR20 . . 50 B3
Terrington St Clement
PE34. . . . . 144 B4
Howard Cres NR19 . . . . . . 154 D4
Howard Dr NR28 . . . . 147 B4
Howard Jun Sch PE30. . . . 147 B4
Howard Mews NR3. . . . . . . 158 E1
Howard St N **9** NR30. . . . . 169 C4
Howard St S NR30 . . . . . . 169 C4
Howards Cl PE36. . . . . 132 E7
Howard's Hill NR27 . . . . . 139 A7
Howards Hill Cl NR27 . . . . 10 C5
Howard's Hill Rd NR28 . . . . 151 C5
Howard's Hill W **1** NR27 . . 139 A7
Howard St NR1 . . . . 178 A1
Howards The PE30 . . . . . . 148 D4
Howard's Way NR10. . . . . . 35 B2
Howdale Rd PE38 . . . . 172 C5
Howdale Rise PE38. . . . . . 172 D5
HOWE NR15 . . . . 90 D3
Howe Gn NR15. . . . . 90 D2
Howe La NR15 . . . . 90 D3
Howell Rd NR8 . . . . 157 C6
Howe Rd NR30 . . . . 169 D7
Howes La NR20 . . . . 68 D6
Howes Yd **1** NR25 . . . . 7 F6
HOW HILL NR29 . . . . 56 B6
How Hill Nature Reserve *
NR29. . . . . 56 A6
How Hill Rd NR29. . . . . 56 B6
Howland Ct NR21 . . . . 141 B5
Howlett Cl
4 East Dereham NR19. . . . 154 D3
North Walsham NR28 . . . . 151 A5
Howlett Dr NR5 . . . . 161 A8
Howletts Hill PE13 . . . . . . 152 C4
Howlett Way **2** IP24 . . . . . 176 D6
HOXNE IP21 . . . . 131 A4
Hoxne Rd
Denham IP21. . . . . 131 B1
Eye IP23 . . . . 130 E1
Syleham IP21. . . . . 131 C4
Upper Weybread IP21. . . . 131 E6
Hubbard Cl
11 Long Stratton NR15 . . . 106 E3
Wymondham NR18 . . . . . 173 A6
Hubbard's Dro PE38. . . . . . 79 E1
Hudson Leisure Ctr
PE13. . . . . 152 A5
Hudson Way NR5 . . . . 160 E7
Hugh Cl PE30 . . . . 148 C5
Hughenden Rd NR1 . . . . . . 162 E3
Hughes Cl **8** NR9. . . . . 88 D8
Huiton Rd PE30 . . . . 147 A5
Hulver Rd NR13 . . . . 73 E8
Hulver St NR19 . . . . 66 F6
Humber Cl NR30 . . . . 168 C5
Humber Keel NR31. . . . . . . 170 D1
Humberstone Rd **3**
NR31. . . . . 170 C7
HUMBLETOFT NR19 . . . . . . 154 C7
Humbletoft Rd NR19 . . . . . 154 C7
Humbleyard NR5. . . . . 161 A7
Hungate La NR11 . . . . 150 C4
Hungate Rd PE14 . . . . 59 E2
Hungate St NR11. . . . . 150 C5
Hungry Hill NR27 . . . . 11 B2
HUNSTANTON PE36 . . . . . 132 D5
Hunstanton Commercial Pk
PE36. . . . . 132 D4
Hunstanton Inf Sch
PE36. . . . . 132 D4
Hunstanton Rd
Dersingham PE31 . . . . . . 140 D5
Heacham PE31. . . . . 133 D5
**Hunstanton Sea Life
Sanctuary** * **9** PE36. . . . 132 B3
Hunstead La NR15 . . . . 90 F2
Hunt Cl
Old Catton NR6 . . . . 158 F2
5 Redenhall with Harleston
IP20. . . . . 122 D2
Hunter Ave NR20. . . . . 68 F5
Hunter Dr **4** NR31. . . . . . . 94 C8
Hunter Rd
Norwich NR3 . . . . 158 C3
Troston IP31 . . . . 126 B1
Hunters Cl
Brundall NR13 . . . . 165 F5
Terrington St Clement
PE34. . . . . 144 F6
Hunter's Dro PE14 . . . . 60 B6
Hunters Oak **2** IP25 . . . . . 84 E3
Huntley Cres NR26 . . . . . . 138 E6
HUNT'S CORNER NR16. . . . 119 C7
Hunts Gn NR16 . . . . 105 B4
HUNWORTH NR24. . . . . 19 A6
Hunworth Rd NR24. . . . . . 142 D8
Hurdle La NR25 . . . . 7 E4
Hurd Rd NR4 . . . . 161 E3
Hurn La NR16 . . . . 106 A6
Hurn Rd
Dereham NR20 . . . . 68 A7
Taverham NR8 . . . . 157 C7
Hurrell Rd NR30 . . . . 168 D6
Hurricane Way NR6 . . . . . 158 C6
Hurst Rd **8** NR14 . . . . 92 A2
Hurth Way NR6 . . . . 174 E4
Husenbeth Cl NR8 . . . . . . 156 E4
Hutchinson Rd NR5 . . . . . 161 D6
Huxley Cl NR1 . . . . 162 F2
Huxley Rd NR1 . . . . 162 F2
Hyde Cl PE31. . . . . 14 D4

Hyde Ct NR13 . . . . 72 E5
Hyde Rd NR19 . . . . 154 D3
HYLTONS CROSSWAYS
NR28 . . . . 36 F8
Hypocrite La NR17 . . . . . 174 A2
Hyrn Cl NR29 . . . . 57 D4
Hythe Rd
Feltwell IP26 . . . . 98 E3
Foulden IP26 . . . . 82 A1
Methwold IP26 . . . . 98 F5

I

Ice House Ct **17** NR15 . . 106 E5
Ice House La NR1 . . . . . . 178 C1
Iceni Dr PE37 . . . . 153 C2
ICKBURGH PE26 . . . . 100 B6
Icknield Cl IP24 . . . . 176 B3
Icknield Way IP24 . . . . . . 176 B3
Ickworth Cl PE30 . . . . . . 148 C1
Ilex Ct NR7 . . . . 159 D4
ILKETSHALL ST ANDREW
NR34 . . . . 124 E6
ILKETSHALL ST LAWRENCE
NR34 . . . . 124 F2
ILKETSHALL ST MARGARET
NR35 . . . . 124 B4
ILLINGTON IP24 . . . . 117 D8
Illington Rd IP24 . . . . 117 C8
ILPH Hall Farm* NR16 . . 118 B7
Impala Cl NR6 . . . . 159 A6
Imperial Mews NR31 . . . 171 C4
Impson Way IP26 . . . . . . 100 A4
Incleborough Cl **2** NR27 . 10 B5
Independent Way **14** NR27 . 72 E8
Indigo Yd NR3 . . . . 178 A3
INGHAM NR12 . . . . 39 D4
Ingham Cnr NR12 . . . . . . 24 D1
INGHAM CORNER NR12 . . 24 D2
Ingham Rd
Lessingham NR12 . . . . . . 24 D2
Stalham NR12 . . . . 39 C5
INGLEBOROUGH PE14 . . 41 B1
Ingleby Cl
Heacham PE31 . . . . 133 E6
King's Lynn PE30 . . . . . . 147 B4
Ingle Rd PE14 . . . . 59 B7
Ingloss La NR14 . . . . 109 B7
Ingoldale PE31 . . . . 140 D8
INGOLDISTHORPE PE31 . 140 D8
INGOLDISTHORPE
PE31 . . . . 140 E8
Ingoldsby Ave PE31 . . . . 140 C6
Ingolside PE31 . . . . 140 D8
Ingram's Cl NR12 . . . . . . 162 E3
Ingram's Rd IP21 . . . . . . 131 C7
INGWORTH NR11 . . . . . . 36 B8
Inman Rd NR7 . . . . 159 D4
INTWOOD NR4 . . . . 89 B7
Intwood La
East Carleton NR14 . . . . 89 A5
Swardeston NR14 . . . . . 89 C6
Intwood Rd NR4 . . . . 89 E8
Invaders Ct NR23 . . . . . . 136 D6
Ipswich Gr NR2 . . . . 178 A1
Ipswich Rd
Norwich NR2 . . . . 178 A1
2 Norwich NR4 . . . . 89 E8
Pulham Market NR15 . . . 121 E8
Saxlingham Nethergate
NR15 . . . . 107 A7
Scole IP21 . . . . 130 D5
Yaxley IP23 . . . . 130 A1
Ireton Cl **15** NR7 . . . . . . 72 D4
Iris Cl NR17 . . . . 174 B5
Irmingland Rd NR11 . . . . 34 F8
Ironside Way NR9 . . . . . . 86 D5
IRSTEAD NR12 . . . . 56 A7
Irstead Rd
Barton Turf NR12 . . . . . . 55 F7
Norwich NR5 . . . . 161 E6
IRSTEAD STREET NR12 . 55 F6
Irving Rd NR4 . . . . 162 C1
Irwin Cl NR10 . . . . 149 C5
Isaac's Rd NR31 . . . . 169 B4
Isabella Cl IP24 . . . . 147 D3
Isabella Sq **2** NR30 . . . 169 D3
Isbets Dale NR8 . . . . 155 D2
Isis Cl NR31 . . . . 170 B3
Isle Bridge Rd PE14 . . . . 77 E6
Isle Rd PE14 . . . . 77 F7
ITTERINGHAM NR11 . . . . 20 C1
ITTERINGHAM COMMON
NR11 . . . . 35 D8
Iveagh Cl IP31 . . . . 140 E2
Iveson Cl IP22 . . . . 177 E4
Ives Rd NR6 . . . . 158 D5
Ivory Rd NR4 . . . . 161 E4
Ivy Gn **6** NR31 . . . . 170 B5
Ivy Rd
Earlham NR5 . . . . 161 E7
3 Spixworth NR10 . . . . 54 A2
Ivy TODD Rd PE37 . . . . . 66 B4
Ivy Way NR19 . . . . 68 E6
Ixworth Rd IP31 . . . . 126 D1

J

Jack Plummer Way
NR30 . . . . 168 C7
Jaguar Rd **8** NR9 . . . . . 88 D8
James Bradfield Prim Sch
PE33 . . . . 81 A2
James Cl PE30 . . . . 148 B1
James Gn **14** NR10 . . . . 54 A2

James Jackson Rd PE31 . 140 C3
James Paget Hospl
NR31 . . . . 170 B1
James Rd **7** NR32 . . . . . 55 E4
James Scott Cl **3** PE38 . 172 A5
James St PE36 . . . . 132 D4
James Watt Cl NR11 . . . . 170 A8
Jamieson Pl NR5 . . . . 161 C8
Jane Forby Cl PE33 . . . . . 80 E2
Jankin La PE34 . . . . 144 A1
Jannys Cl NR11 . . . . 150 B6
Jarrold Cl IP31 . . . . 127 D3
Jarrold Way NR5 . . . . 160 F8
Jarvie Cl PE36 . . . . 13 A7
Jarvis Dr NR31 . . . . 171 C5
Jarvis Rd PE30 . . . . 146 E8
Jasmin Cl PE13 . . . . 152 F7
Jasmine Cl
Earlham NR4 . . . . 161 E5
Thetford IP24 . . . . 176 F4
Jasmine Ct **1** NR17 . . . 174 B5
Jasmine Gdns **7** NR1 . . 94 C7
Jasmine Gn **7** NR31 . . . 170 B5
Javelin Rd NR6 . . . . 158 E8
Jay Gdns NR5 . . . . 160 E8
Jay La NR32 . . . . 171 C3
Jay's Gn IP20 . . . . 122 E2
Jefferey Ave **4** PE13 . . 152 E7
Jeffery Cl PE30 . . . . 146 E8
Jegon Cl NR11 . . . . 150 D5
Jellicoe Pl **6** IP24 . . . . . 176 E5
Jellicoe Rd NR30 . . . . . . 169 C8
Jenkinsons Pightle
NR35 . . . . 108 A4
Jenner Rd **4** NR31 . . . . 170 B1
Jennings Cl PE31 . . . . . . 133 C5
Jennings Way IP22 . . . . . 177 D5
Jenny Rd **8** NR10 . . . . . 54 A2
Jermyn Rd PE30 . . . . 147 C6
Jermyn Way **1** NR15 . . 106 D3
Jerningham Rd NR5 . . . . 157 A1
Jessopp Cl
Norwich NR2 . . . . 161 F4
Scarning NR19 . . . . 67 B7
Jessopp Rd NR4 . . . . 161 F4
Jetty Cl NR27 . . . . 139 B7
Jetty Cliff NR27 . . . . 139 B7
Jetty St **2** NR27 . . . . . . 139 B7
Jewel Cl NR24 . . . . 142 B4
Jews' La **10** NR31 . . . . . 94 C6
Jewson Rd NR3 . . . . 158 C2
Jex Ave NR5 . . . . 161 D8
Jex Rd NR5 . . . . 161 D8
Jickling Rd NR23 . . . . 136 B6
Joan Short's La PE31 . . . 135 D3
Jocelyn Cl IP21 . . . . 121 E5
Joe Ellis Ct **6** NR5 . . . . 161 B8
John Bates Cl **2** NR19 . 154 E5
John Chapman Cl **5**
NR21 . . . . 141 E4
John Davis Way PE33 . . . 61 D5
John Drewry Cl **2** NR14 . 90 D5
John F Kennedy Ct **2**
PE13 . . . . 152 D4
John Gale Ct NR8 . . . . . . 155 E3
John Goshawk Rd NR19 . 154 E2
John Grant Specl Sch
NR30 . . . . 168 D6
John Hill Cl **6** NR15 . . . 106 E3
John Jarrod Printing Mus
NR1 . . . . 178 C4
John Kennedy Rd PE30 . . 146 D6
John Morton Cres PE32 . 29 D1
John of Gaunt Fst Sch
NR11 . . . . 150 C5
John O'Gaunt Cl NR11 . . 150 B6
John Rd
Caister-on-Sea NR30 . . . 168 E7
Great Yarmouth NR30 . . 170 D5
Johnson Cl **7** NR19 . . . 154 C3
Johnson Cres PE31 . . . . 133 C4
Johnson Pl NR22 . . . . . . 162 C5
JOHNSON STREET NR29 . 56 B4
John St **3** PE30 . . . . 146 E3
John Stephenson Ct **1**
NR6 . . . . 158 F1
John Thompson Rd **8**
PE13 . . . . 152 D4
John Woodhouse Dr
NR30 . . . . 168 C7
Jolly Gardeners Ct **13**
NR3 . . . . 162 D8
Jolly Sailor Yd NR23 . . . 136 C6
Jolly's La NR13 . . . . 166 A2
Jones (GC) Way NR31 . . 169 B2
Jones's Dro PE14 . . . . . . 95 E8
Jordan Cl
Norwich NR5 . . . . 161 B6
Taverham NR8 . . . . 155 E4
JORDAN GREEN NR10 . . 51 A8
Jordan La NR10 . . . . 51 A8
Jordan Rd NR30 . . . . 168 E6
Jose Neville Cl **2** NR30 . 168 F7
Josephine Cl NR1 . . . . . . 162 D3
Joseph Lancaster Way **4**
NR3 . . . . 178 B4
Joshua Ct NR31 . . . . 171 D8
Joy Ave **1** NR15 . . . . . . 107 A8
Joyce La
Heacham PE31 . . . . 133 D5
Walpole PE14 . . . . 41 F3
Joyce Rd NR35 . . . . 124 B8
Joyce Way **9** NR7 . . . . 72 D5
Joyland* NR30 . . . . 169 E4
Jubilee Ave
4 East Dereham NR20 . . 154 E6
East Harling NR16 . . . . . 118 C5

Jubilee Ave continued
Fakenham NR21 . . . . . . 141 C4
Heacham PE31 . . . . 133 B5
Jubilee Bank Rd PE34 . . 146 A5
Jubilee Cl
Cawston NR10 . . . . 35 B2
Downham Market PE38 . . 172 E5
Erpingham NR11 . . . . . . 21 B2
Hunstanton PE36 . . . . . . 132 C3
Repps with Bastwick NR29 . 57 A4
Thetford IP24 . . . . 176 B3
Weeting IP27 . . . . 175 B7
Jubilee Ct **3** PE30 . . . . . 146 D4
Jubilee Dr
Dersingham PE31 . . . . . 140 C5
Sheringham NR26 . . . . . 138 B6
Jubilee Gdns **2** PE31 . . 12 E4
Jubilee Hall La **2** PE32 . 45 C6
Jubilee La NR27 . . . . 139 C4
Jubilee Rd
Heacham PE31 . . . . 133 A5
Holt NR25 . . . . 137 B6
Lackenheath IP27 . . . . . 113 E2
Watton IP25 . . . . 84 D3
Jubilee Rise PE33 . . . . . . 61 D3
Jubilee Terr
Caister-on-Sea NR30 . . . 168 E4
Cromer NR27 . . . . 139 D4
Norwich NR1 . . . . 162 F3
Jubilee Way **11** PE37 . . 65 F4
Jubilee Wlk PE13 . . . . . . 152 D8
Judas La IP23 . . . . 129 F1
Judges Dr NR4 . . . . 161 F2
Judges Gdns NR4 . . . . . . 155 E2
Judges Wlk NR4 . . . . 161 F2
Juler Cl **4** NR28 . . . . . . 151 C6
Julian Hospl NR7 . . . . 161 F6
Julian Rd
King's Lynn PE30 . . . . . . 148 C5
3 Spixworth NR10 . . . . 54 A2
Julians Way IP21 . . . . . . 121 E5
Julian Way NR1 . . . . 171 D5
Junction Rd NR3 . . . . 158 C1
Juniper Cl **2** IP24 . . . . . 176 F4
Juniper Gr NR26 . . . . 138 E5
Juniper Way NR8 . . . . . . 155 B2
Jupiter Rd NR6 . . . . 158 C4
Jury St NR30 . . . . 169 D4

K

Kabin Rd NR5 . . . . 157 B2
Kalmia Gn **2** NR31 . . . . 170 B6
Karen Cl
8 Hethersett NR9 . . . . 88 C7
Scole IP21 . . . . 130 C5
Keable Cl **7** NR5 . . . . . . 161 C6
Keats Cl
Downham Market PE38 . . 172 D5
East Dereham NR19 . . . . 154 C7
2 Thetford IP24 . . . . . . 176 E6
Keats Rd NR8 . . . . 156 D8
Keble Cl PE30 . . . . 148 B4
Keble Rd NR31 . . . . 170 B3
Kedleston Dr **10** NR4 . . 89 B8
Keelan Cl NR16 . . . . 158 B4
Keel Cl **12** NR33 . . . . . . 111 F1
Keeling Hall La NR20 . . . 33 E3
Keeling Way NR17 . . . . . 174 B3
Keene Rd NR30 . . . . 146 D1
Keepers Rd NR15 . . . . . . 89 F1
Keepham Rd NR20 . . . . . 33 E1
Keillers Cl PE13 . . . . 152 A7
Keith Rd **9** NR20 . . . . . 50 B3
KELLING NR25 . . . . 8 D5
Kelling Cl NR25 . . . . 137 C7
Kelling Heath Pk Sta NR25 . 8 E4
Kelling Prim Sch NR25 . . 8 D6
Kelling Rd NR25 . . . . 137 C7
Kell's Acres NR4 . . . . 109 F3
Kell's Way NR34 . . . . 109 F2
Kelsey Cl PE36 . . . . 132 D7
Kelvin Pl IP24 . . . . 176 A1
Kemp Dr NR19 . . . . 154 C5
Kempe Cl NR7 . . . . 159 C1
Kempe Rd PE14 . . . . 146 C5
Kemp's Cl PE38 . . . . 79 A4
Kemp's Rd IP21 . . . . 122 A5
Kenan Dr NR17 . . . . 174 F7
Kendal Cl **15** NR9 . . . . . 88 D8
Kendall Cl NR28 . . . . 151 B6
Kendle Way PE30 . . . . . . 147 E8
Kenhill Cl **3** PE31 . . . . . 12 E5
Kenlan Rd PE13 . . . . 152 D6
Kennedy Ave NR31 . . . . 170 C1
Kennedy Cl
East Dereham NR19 . . . . 154 D1
Easton NR9 . . . . 70 A2
Kennel Loke NR31 . . . . . 171 D8
Kennett Cl NR31 . . . . 161 F4
KENNINGHALL NR16 . . . 119 B5
Kenninghall Prim Sch
NR16 . . . . 119 A4
Kenninghall Rd
Banham NR16 . . . . 119 B6
Harling NR16 . . . . 118 C4
Kenninghall NR16 . . . . . 119 A3
Kenside Rd **1** PE31 . . . 12 E5
Kensington Cl NR15 . . . . 107 C8
Kensington Rd **1** NR31 . 178 B1
Kensington Rd
Downham Market PE38 . . 172 B4
King's Lynn PE30 . . . . . . 147 B6
Kent Ave NR31 . . . . 170 C3
Kent Cl
Attleborough NR17 . . . . 174 B3

Kent Cl continued
2 Sutton Bridge PE12 . . 41 B8
Kent Rd PE30 . . . . 147 B6
Kent Sq NR30 . . . . 169 D3
Kenwood Rd PE31 . . . . . 133 D5
Kenwood Rd S PE31 . . . 133 D5
Kenwyn Cl NR25 . . . . . . 137 C7
Kenyon Row NR34 . . . . . 110 C2
Keppel Cl PE32 . . . . 48 A5
Keppel Rd **2** NR31 . . . . 170 D4
KERDISTON NR10 . . . . . . 34 C3
Kerdiston Rd
Reepham NR10 . . . . 149 A6
Themelthorpe NR20 . . . . 33 F2
Kered Cl NR6 . . . . 157 F6
Kered Rd NR6 . . . . 157 F6
Kerrich Cl PE30 . . . . 140 C3
Kerridge Ct NR25 . . . . . . 137 B6
Kerridges NR16 . . . . 118 C4
Kerridges The NR5 . . . . 156 F1
Kerridge Way
20 Harleston IP20 . . . . 122 D2
Reedham NR20 . . . . 137 B6
Kerridge Rd NR31 . . . . . 163 A4
Kerville St **3** NR5 . . . . . 161 A7
Kestrel Ave PE38 . . . . . . 172 C7
Kestrel Cl
Burnham Market PE31 . . 135 D1
Great Yarmouth NR31 . . 170 A7
Mulbarton NR14 . . . . . . 89 A3
Swaffham PE37 . . . . 153 D2
Thetford IP24 . . . . 176 D1
Kestrel Dr
Brandon IP27 . . . . 175 F3
2 Wisbech PE14 . . . . . 152 D2
Kestrel Rd NR7 . . . . 159 C4
Kett's Ave NR18 . . . . 173 C5
Kett's Cl
3 Hethersett NR9 . . . . 88 D7
Wymondham NR18 . . . . 173 C5
Ketts Hill PE37 . . . . 66 A4
Kett's Hill NR1 . . . . 163 A7
Kett Sixth Form Ctr NR7 . 159 C2
Kett's La NR9 . . . . 52 A6
Kett's Oak NR9 . . . . 88 C6
Ketts Rd NR28 . . . . 151 B4
Kevill Davies Dr NR13 . . 73 A4
Kevin Davison Cl **2** NR30 . 169 D7
Kew Rd PE38 . . . . 172 B4
Key & Castle Yd NR3 . . . 178 A4
Keyes Ave NR30 . . . . 169 D7
Keyes Cl **5** NR1 . . . . . . 162 E2
Keyes Farm **4** NR20 . . . 68 F6
Keys The NR15 . . . . 90 F2
KIDD'S MOOR NR18 . . . . 173 D8
Kilderkin Cl PE14 . . . . . . 77 A7
Kilham's Way
King's Lynn PE30 . . . . . . 146 E7
North Wootton PE30 . . . 26 E1
Kiln Cl NR6 . . . . 158 E7
Kiln Farm La IP22 . . . . . . 128 E1
Kiln La
Dickleburgh & Rushall
IP21 . . . . 130 F6
Needham IP20 . . . . 131 D8
Kiln Rd **5** NR10 . . . . . . 53 A3
Kilverstone Rd IP24 . . . . 117 A2
KIMBERLEY NR18 . . . . . . 87 B6
Kimberley Pk Rd NR18 . . 87 A6
Kimberley Rd NR28 . . . . 151 D5
Kimberley St
1 Norwich NR2 . . . . . . 162 C5
Wymondham NR18 . . . . 173 C4
Kimberley Terr NR30 . . . 169 E2
Kimms Belt PE31 . . . . . . 176 B2
Kinderley Rd PE13 . . . . . 152 C8
Kingcup PE30 . . . . 148 A1
King Edward VII Sch
PE30 . . . . 147 A5
Kingfisher Cl
8 Fakenham NR21 . . . 141 E4
7 Fakenham NR21 . . . 141 E4
Great Yarmouth NR31 . . 94 C7
2 Thetford IP24 . . . . . . 176 D1
Kingfisher Dr
Norwich NR12 . . . . 175 E3
Necton PE37 . . . . 66 A3
6 Wisbech PE14 . . . . . 152 D2
Kingfisher Rd
Attleborough NR17 . . . . 174 F6
Downham Market PE38 . . 172 C7
Kingfisher Way **17** PE31 . 84 C3
King George Cl NR29 . . . 57 D2
King George Rd NR21 . . 31 C7
King George's Ave **2**
NR29 . . . . 57 D2
King George V Ave PE30 . 146 F5
King George VI Sch PE31 . 14 A3
Kinghorn Rd NR2 . . . . . . 161 F4
King John Ave PE30 . . . . 147 A5
King John Bank PE14 . . . 41 C5

Hyd–Kit **195**

King of Hearts Ctr★
NR1 . . . . 178 B4
King's Arms St NR28 . . . 151 C5
King's Ave
Anmer PE31 . . . . 28 C8
King's Lynn PE30 . . . . . . 147 A3
Kings Croft PE31 . . . . 140 E4
Kings Ct NR29 . . . . 167 A8
Kingsdale **16** NR13 . . . . 74 A3
King's Dam NR34 . . . . . . 110 B2
Kings Gn **3** PE30 . . . . . . 147 C4
Kings Head La
Deopham NR18 . . . . 87 A5
North Lopham IP22 . . . . 119 A2
Kings La NR1 . . . . 178 B1
Kingsleigh Cl NR28 . . . . 22 E5
Kingsley Ave PE13 . . . . . 152 B4
Kingsley Rd NR1 . . . . 178 A1
Kings Loke NR29 . . . . . . 167 B8
KING'S LYNN PE30 . . . . . 147 A5
King's Lynn Arts Ctr
(Guildhall)★ PE30 . . . . 146 D5
King's Lynn PE36 . . . . . . 132 C4
King's Lynn Sports Ctr
PE30 . . . . 146 F5
King's Lynn Sta PE30 . . . 146 E5
King's Pk NR19 . . . . 154 E6
Kings Pk Fst Sch NR19 . . 154 E6
Kings Rd
Bungay NR35 . . . . 124 B7
East Dereham NR19 . . . . 154 E6
Fakenham NR21 . . . . . . 141 A5
Hunstanton PE36 . . . . . . 132 D6
Wisbech PE13 . . . . 152 C4
King's Rd
Great Yarmouth NR30 . . 169 D2
Holt NR25 . . . . 137 C5
Topcroft NR35 . . . . 108 A4
Kings Rd NR24 . . . . 19 A6
King's Staithe La PE30 **2**
PE30 . . . . 146 D4
King's Staithe Sq **1**
PE30 . . . . 146 D4
King St
East Harling NR16 . . . . . 118 C5
Great Yarmouth NR30 . . 169 C4
King's Lynn PE30 . . . . . . 146 D4
Neatishead NR12 . . . . . . 55 E7
Norwich NR1 . . . . 178 C1
13 Sutton Bridge PE12 . 41 B8
Swaffham PE37 . . . . 153 B4
Thetford IP24 . . . . 176 C4
Winterton-on-Sea NR29 . 58 B6
Wisbech PE13 . . . . 152 C5
Kingston Ave NR30 . . . . 168 E5
Kingston Rd NR19 . . . . . 154 F3
Kingston Sq NR4 . . . . . . 162 A3
Kingsway
7 Blakeney NR25 . . . . . 7 C6
4 Earsham NR35 . . . . . 123 F8
King's Lynn PE30 . . . . . . 146 E8
Leverington PE13 . . . . . 152 F7
3 Newton Flotman NR15 . 107 A8
North Walsham NR28 . . 151 A6
Norwich NR2 . . . . 162 A5
Thetford IP24 . . . . 176 C2
Kings Way NR29 . . . . 167 B7
King's Wlk **4** PE13 . . . . 152 C5
Kings Wlk
Downham Market PE38 . . 172 C5
9 Great Yarmouth NR31 . 170 B5
Kingswood Ave NR8 . . . 155 C2
Kingswood Cl
Brooke NR15 . . . . 90 E1
9 Norwich NR4 . . . . . . 89 C8
Kingswood Ct NR8 . . . . . 155 D2
Kingswood Pk PE13 . . . . 152 D3
King William Cl PE34 . . . 144 C5
Kinsale Ave NR6 . . . . 157 E5
Kinsale Ave Fst & Mid Sch
NR6 . . . . 157 E4
Kinver Cl NR4 . . . . 162 B3
Kipling Cl NR30 . . . . 168 D6
KIRBY BEDON NR14 . . . . 90 E8
KIRBY CANE NR35 . . . . . 109 E4
Kirby Cl **5** NR29 . . . . . . 57 D5
KIRBY GREEN NR35 . . . . 109 F5
Kirby Rd
Bixley NR14 . . . . 90 C8
Norwich NR14 . . . . 163 C2
KIRBY ROW NR35 . . . . . . 109 E3
Kirby St PE30 . . . . 146 E5
Kirkgate La NR23 . . . . . . 6 A2
Kirkgate St
Holme next the Sea PE36 . 2 A2
Wisbech PE13 . . . . 152 E7
Kirkham's La PE14 . . . . . 77 C8
Kirkhams Mdw NR19 . . . 66 C7
Kirklands NR8 . . . . 156 E4
Kirklands **8** NR4 . . . . . . 89 E8
Kirkpatrick Rd NR3 . . . . 158 B2
Kirk Rd **2** PE14 . . . . 41 D4
Kirkstone Gr **2** PE30 . . 148 F1
Kirstead PE30 . . . . 147 D5
Kirstead Gn NR15 . . . . . 108 C8
KIRSTEAD GREEN NR15 . 108 C8
Kirstead Ling NR15 . . . . 91 A1
Kirtons Cl **1** PE14 . . . . . 41 E4
Kitchener Rd
Great Yarmouth NR30 . . 169 D5
Melton Constable NR24 . 142 B5
Kitchener St PE30 . . . . . . 146 D2
Kitlings Beck Rd NR28 . . 38 A7
Kittel Cl **24** IP25 . . . . . . 84 D3
Kittens La NR14 . . . . 91 F1

Kittiwake Cl 12 NR31 . . . . . 94 C8
Kittles La NR10 . . . . . . 150 A1
Kittles Rd NR13 . . . . . . 74 D1
Knappers Way IP27 . . . . 175 D3
KNAPTON NR28 . . . . . . 143 B1
KNAPTON GREEN NR28 . . . 22 F5
Knapton Rd
  Knapton NR28 . . . . . . 22 F3
  Mundesley NR11 . . . . . 143 B4
  Trunch NR28 . . . . . . 22 E5
KNETTISHALL IP22 . . . . 127 C7
Knevet Cl NR17 . . . . . . 174 F6
Knights Gn NR26 . . . . . 138 C5
Knight's La NR15 . . . . . 89 E2
Knights Rd NR3 . . . . . . 158 B2
Knight St NR22 . . . . . . 16 F7
Knipe Cl 2 NR18 . . . . . . 105 F5
Knitting Needle La NR23 136 E6
Knowland Gr NR5 . . . . . 161 C8
Knowland Gr Fst Sch
  NR5 . . . . 161 C8
Knowle Cres NR26 . . . . 138 E5
Knowle Rd NR26 . . . . . 138 E6
Knowles' La NR12 . . . . . 38 C2
Knowsley Rd NR3 . . . . . 162 E8
Knox Ave NR1 . . . . 163 B8
Knox Cl NR1 . . . . 163 B8
Knox Rd NR1 . . . . 163 B7
Knudsen Cl 4 NR15 . . . 107 C5
Knyvett Gn NR15 . . . . . 105 F8
Koblenz Ave NR1 . . . . . 178 C1
Kooreman Ave PE13 . . . 152 D7
Krons The NR15 . . . . . . 107 C5

L

Laburnham Rd NR28 . . . 151 B4
Laburnum Ave
  2 Marham PE33 . . . . . . 63 B4
  Taverham NR8 . . . . . . 155 B1
Laburnum Cl
  6 Great Yarmouth NR31 . . 94 C7
  2 Horsford NR10 . . . . . 53 A3
  5 Wisbech PE13 . . . . . 152 C6
Laburnum Cres NR19 . . . 154 E1
Laburnum Dr NR13 . . . . 165 F6
Laburnum Gr
  Reepham NR10 . . . . . . 149 C6
  Sheringham NR26 . . . . 138 D4
  Thetford IP24 . . . . . . 176 B1
Laburnum Wlk IP27 . . . 175 E2
Lacey Cl 2 PE33 . . . . . . 61 D6
Lacey Rd NR8 . . . . 155 D1
Lackford Cl NR13 . . . . . 165 C4
Lacon Rd NR30 . . . . . . 168 E5
Ladbroke Pl NR1 . . . . . . 163 A7
Ladbrooke Cl 3 IP22 . . . 177 C4
Laddus Bank PE14 . . . . . 77 A6
Laddus Dro PE14 . . . . . . 77 B6
Ladislaw Way 3 NR13 . . 154 C3
Lady Ann's Rd NR5 . . . . . 5 B7
Lady Betty Rd NR1 . . . . 162 D3
Lady Dro PE38 . . . . 79 A6
Lady Hamilton La NR29 . 167 C6
Lady Haven Mews 12
  NR1 . . . . 169 C5
Lady Haven Rd 6 NR31 . 169 B4
Lady Jane Grey Rd PE30 . 146 F7
Lady La NR10 . . . . 53 E5
Lady Margaret's Ave
  NR1 . . . . 170 B4
Lady Mary Rd NR1 . . . . 162 D3
Lady's Dro 1 PE14 . . . . . 59 D2
Lady's La
  Bressingham IP22 . . . . 119 F1
  Wymondham NR18 . . . . 173 A3
Ladywood Cl 9 PE33 . . . . 63 B4
Ladywood Rd PE33 . . . . . 63 B4
Lake Ave PE14 . . . . 95 C7
Lake Ct PE13 . . . . 152 D4
Lake Dro PE34 . . . . 61 C1
Lakeland 3 IP26 . . . . . 114 A7
Lakeland Way 1 NR9 . . . 88 E8
Lakenfields NR1 . . . . . . 162 F2
LAKENHAM NR1 . . . . . . 162 F3
Lakenham Fst Sch NR1 . 162 E3
Lakenham Mid Sch NR1 . 162 E3
Lakenham Rd NR4 . . . . . 162 C2
Lakenham Way NR1 . . . . 162 E3
LAKENHEATH IP27 . . . . 113 E2
Lakenheath Airfield
  IP27 . . . . 114 B1
Lakenheath Prim Sch
  IP27 . . . . 113 E1
Lakenheath Sta IP27 . . . 113 F5
Lakes Ave NR14 . . . . . . 89 B3
LAKES END PE14 . . . . . . 95 C7
Lake View Dr NR19 . . . . 51 D5
Lake View Dr NR13 . . . . 165 B4
LAMAS NR10 . . . . 37 A2
Lambert Cl 1 IP27 . . . . . 114 E1
Lambert Rd NR7 . . . . . . 159 A3
Lamberts Cl 20 IP26 . . . . 98 E1
Lambert's La PE32 . . . . . 30 D1
Lamb La NR21 . . . . 31 C7
Lammas Rd 3 NR15 . . . 106 F6
Lammas The IP26 . . . . . 100 A4
Lamport Cl 3 PE30 . . . . 147 D6
Lamsey La PE31 . . . . . . 133 D3
Lancaster Ave NR21 . . . 141 C5
Lancaster Cl
  Fakenham NR21 . . . . . 141 C5
  Methwold IP26 . . . . . . 99 A5
  Norwich NR6 . . . . 158 D6

Lancaster Cl continued
  7 Stalham NR12 . . . . . . 39 B4
Lancaster Cres PE38 . . . 172 D6
Lancaster Gdns NR11 . . . 150 D5
Lancaster Pl 11 PE31 . . . 12 E5
Lancaster Rd
  4 Feltwell IP26 . . . . . . 98 E1
  Great Yarmouth NR30 . 169 D3
  King's Lynn PE30 . . . . 147 B4
  Sculthorpe Airfield NR21 . 15 C3
Lancaster Rise NR11 . . . 22 F8
Lancaster Sq 18 NR30 . . 169 D3
Lancaster Way PE32 . . . . 44 F3
Lanchester Ct 7 NR2 . . 162 B7
Landlow La NR9 . . . . 70 B1
Lane The
  Briston NR24 . . . . 142 D4
  Carleton St Peter NR14 . . 91 E5
  Little Barningham NR11 . 20 C4
  Winterton-on-Sea NR29 . 58 B6
Lang Gate Way NR35 . . . 108 D2
LANGHAM NR25 . . . . 7 B3
Langham Ct
  Fakenham NR21 . . . . . 141 D4
  Sheringham NR26 . . . . 138 C7
Langham Glass & Rural
  Crafts* NR25 . . . . 7 A4
Langham Gn NR13 . . . . 165 E4
Langham La NR25 . . . . . . 7 C3
Langham Pl NR1 . . . . . . 178 A1
Langham Rd
  Binham NR21 . . . . 6 E2
  Blakeney NR25 . . . . 7 C6
  Field Dalling NR25 . . . . . 7 A2
  Morston NR25 . . . . 7 A6
Langham St PE30 . . . . . 146 D2
Langhorn's La PE14 . . . . 78 A7
Langland PE30 . . . . 147 D6
Langley Abbey NR14 . . . . 92 A6
Langley Cl 1 NR4 . . . . . . 89 B8
Langley Gn NR14 . . . . . . 91 F6
Langley Prep Sch NR7 . . 163 D6
Langley Rd
  Cantley NR14 . . . . 92 C6
  Chedgrave NR14 . . . . . 91 F3
  King's Lynn PE30 . . . . 147 E8
  Loddon NR14 . . . . 92 A2
Langley Sch NR14 . . . . . 91 F3
Langley St NR14 . . . . . . 92 A4
LANGLEY STREET NR14 . . 92 B4
Langley Wlk NR2 . . . . . 162 C7
Langmere Rd
  Scole IP21 . . . . 130 F8
  1 Watton IP25 . . . . . . 84 C3
Langton Cl 3 NR5 . . . . 161 B7
LANGTON GREEN IP21 . . 130 C1
Lansdowne Cl 10 PE32 . . 45 C6
Lansdowne Rd NR6 . . . . 158 B6
Lansdowne St 4 PE30 . . 146 E6
Lantern La NR12 . . . . . . 24 B5
Lapwing Cl 3 NR31 . . . 170 A6
Larch Cl
  Attleborough NR17 . . . 174 C4
  King's Lynn PE30 . . . . 148 D2
  Norwich NR7 . . . . 159 D4
Larch Cres NR25 . . . . . 137 C7
Larch Dr
  18 Great Yarmouth NR31 . 94 C7
  2 Great Yarmouth NR31 . 170 A5
Larch Gr NR20 . . . . 49 E7
Larch Rd PE34 . . . . 43 D8
Lark Cl IP27 . . . . 175 F3
Larkey's La NR14 . . . . . . 38 F7
Larkman Fst Sch NR5 . . 161 D7
Larkman La NR5 . . . . . . 161 C7
Larkman Mid Sch NR5 . . 161 D7
Lark Rd 2 PE33 . . . . 61 D6
Lark Rise NR14 . . . . 89 A3
Larksfield PE13 . . . . . . 152 C3
Larkspur Cl PE38 . . . . . 172 C3
Larkspur Ct 8 NR19 . . . 154 D2
Lark Way NR31 . . . . 94 C7
LARLING NR16 . . . . 118 B8
Larner's Drift NR19 . . . . 154 D1
Larners Rd NR19 . . . . . 154 D2
Larwood Cl 1 PE32 . . . . 66 A4
Larwood Way 8 IP25 . . . 67 C2
Latchmoor La NR29 . . . . 56 D5
Latchmoor Pk NR29 . . . . 56 D5
Lathes The NR3 . . . . . . 178 A4
Latimer Rd NR1 . . . . . . 162 E1
Latimer Way PE37. . . . . . 65 E1
Laud Cl 24 NR7 . . . . 72 D4
Laughing Image Cnr 6
  NR30 . . . . 169 C5
Launditch Cres PE38 . . . 172 C6
Laundry Cl 3 NR27 . . . . 163 F7
Laundry La
  Blofield NR13 . . . . 73 B6
  Norwich NR7 . . . . 163 F7
Laundry Loke NR28 . . . . 151 B6
Laurel Dr
  Brundall NR13 . . . . . . 165 B3
  Great Yarmouth NR31 . . 94 C7
Laurel Gr 3 PE33 . . . . . . 43 E2
Laurel Rd NR7 . . . . 159 E1
Laurels Cres 1 NR29 . . . 56 C5
Laurels Rd NR29 . . . . . . 56 D7
Laurels The NR31 . . . . . 171 D5
Lavender Cl
  Attleborough NR17 . . . 174 B5
  2 Brandon IP27 . . . . . 175 A2
  Heacham PE31 . . . . . . 133 C5
  Horsford NR10 . . . . . . 53 A4
Lavender Ct
  12 Hemsby NR29 . . . . . 167 B7
  5 King's Lynn PE30 . . . 147 B6
  1 Thetford IP24 . . . . . 176 F4

Lavender Dr PE38 . . . . . 172 D6
Lavender Gr NR19 . . . . 154 D2
Lavender Rd PE30 . . . . . 147 B6
Lavengro Rd NR3 . . . . . 163 A8
Lawn Ave NR30 . . . . . . 169 C6
Lawn Cl
  1 Horsford NR10 . . . . . 53 B3
  Knapton NR28 . . . . . . 143 B1
Lawn Cres 6 NR13 . . . . . 72 E6
Lawn's La
  Belton with Browston
    NR31 . . . . 94 A5
  Fleggburgh NR29 . . . . . 57 B2
Lawns The
  Fakenham NR21 . . . . . 141 C4
  Great Yarmouth NR30 . 169 C7
  Wisbech PE13 . . . . . . 152 B6
Lawnswood Dr NR30 . . . 168 D6
Lawrence Cl
  Fakenham NR21 . . . . . 141 B5
  Harpley PE31 . . . . 29 D4
Lawrence Pl NR20 . . . . . 50 D8
Lawrence Rd
  King's Lynn PE30 . . . . 146 E7
  7 Thetford IP24 . . . . . 176 F5
Lawrence's La PE38 . . . . 79 E1
Lawrence Way PE37. . . . 153 A5
Lawson Rd
  Croxton IP24 . . . . 116 C5
  Norwich NR3 . . . . 158 E1
Lawson Way NR26 . . . . 138 F7
Lawyer Corys NR31 . . . . 170 C1
Laxfield Rd NR12 . . . . . . 39 C3
Laxton Cl NR17 . . . . . . 174 E4
Layer Cl
  5 Aylsham NR11 . . . . . 150 D6
  Norwich NR5 . . . . 160 F7
Laylands Yd NR23 . . . . 136 C6
Layton Cl NR8 . . . . 157 B7
Leach Cl
  Great Yarmouth NR31 . 170 A4
  Wisbech PE13 . . . . . . 152 C2
Leach's Turn NR14 . . . . 165 B1
Leafield Rd PE30 . . . . . 147 C3
Leafyoak La NR14 . . . . . 90 C3
Leamon Ct IP27. . . . . . 175 D4
Lea Rd 2 NR29 . . . . 56 C8
Leaside PE31 . . . . 133 B6
Lea The NR30 . . . . 169 C6
Leatherpool La NR25 . . . . 7 E6
Leathway NR29 . . . . . . 167 B2
Lea Way PE30 . . . . 147 B8
Lebanon Dr PE13 . . . . . 152 F7
Leeder Hill NR13 . . . . . . 72 F2
Leeds Way 8 NR12 . . . . 55 E4
Lees Yd NR25 . . . . 137 B6
Leete Way PE31 . . . . . . 43 E2
Lee Warner Ave NR21 . . 141 D6
Lee Warner Rd 10 PE13. . 153 C3
Leewood Cres NR5 . . . . 157 C1
Lefevre Way NR31 . . . . . 94 C8
Lefroy Rd NR3 . . . . 158 A2
Legge-Bourke Cl PE13 . . 152 F6
Legge Pl 7 PE34 . . . . . . 43 B1
Legrice Cres NR28 . . . . 151 C3
Leicester Ave PE30 . . . . 147 B5
Leicester Rd 1 NR1 . . . 170 D4
Leicester St NR2 . . . . . 162 C4
Leigh Cl NR17 . . . . 174 C5
Leman Cl 1 NR14 . . . . . 92 A1
Leman Gr 9 NR14 . . . . . 91 F1
Leman Rd NR31 . . . . . . 170 D2
Le Neve Rd NR10 . . . . . 150 D1
Leng Cres NR4 . . . . 161 E2
Lenthall Cl 18 NR7 . . . . . 72 D4
LENWADE NR9 . . . . 51 D5
Leonard Cl 4 PE34 . . . . 147 B6
Leonard Medler Way
  NR10 . . . . 53 B8
Leonard's La IP26 . . . . . 98 D1
Leonards St 10 NR3 . . . 162 D8
Leopard Ct 3 NR3 . . . . 178 A4
Leopold Cl 2 NR4 . . . . . 162 A3
Leopold Rd NR4 . . . . . . 162 A3
Lerowe Rd PE13 . . . . . . 152 E7
Les Baux Pl 9 PE13 . . . . 152 E3
Lesley Wlk NR19 . . . . . 154 D2
LESSINGHAM NR12 . . . . 24 D3
Lestrange PE36 . . . . . . 132 C4
Le Strange Ave PE30 . . . 146 F7
Le Strange Cl 2 NR12 . . 161 F5
LETHERINGSETT NR25. . . . 8 A1
Letheringsett Rd NR25 . . 137 A1
Letherington's La NR12 . . 55 D5
LETTON GREEN IP25 . . . . 67 E1
Leven Cl 8 NR7 . . . . 72 D4
Leverington Rd PE13 . . . 152 A6
Levers Cl 2 PE30 . . . . . 147 D8
Leveson Rd NR7 . . . . . . 159 B3
Levine Cl NR11 . . . . . . 165 B4
Levishaw Cl NR10 . . . . . 36 E1
Lewis Cl
  Ashill IP25 . . . . 84 A7
  Hopton IP22 . . . . 127 F6
Lewis Dro
  Roydon IP22 . . . . 177 A5
  Wiggenhall St Germans
    PE34 . . . . 61 A8
Lexham Rd
  Great Dunham PE32 . . . 47 E2
  Litcham PE32 . . . . 47 F4
Lexington Cl NR29 . . . . 167 A7
Leyland Cl IP24 . . . . . . 176 D6
Leys Cl NR31. . . . . 169 C1

Leys La
  Attleborough NR17 . . . 174 D2
  Old Buckenham NR17 . . 104 B3
  Yaxley IP23 . . . . 129 F1
Ley's La NR20 . . . . 51 C1
LEZIATE PE32 . . . . 44 D6
Leziate Dro
  Grimston PE32 . . . . . . 45 A8
  Leziate PE32 . . . . 44 F6
Leziate Heath Nature
  Reserve* PE32 . . . . . . 44 E6
Liberator Cl 3 NR13 . . . 72 E8
Liberator Rd NR6 . . . . . 158 B6
Libra Ct NR7. . . . . 159 C4
Lichfield Rd NR31. . . . . 169 B3
Lichfield St NR1 . . . . . . 162 D4
Licking's Dro PE13. . . . . 152 A2
Lidl Retail Park NR21 . . 141 C5
Lifeboat Plain 6 NR26 . 138 D7
Lighthouse Cl
  Happisburgh NR12. . . . 24 C5
  Hunstanton PE36. . . . 132 D7
Lighthouse La PE36 . . . 132 D6
Lilac Cl
  Brandon IP27 . . . . . . 114 D4
  Lee Warner Way NR19 . . 154 D2
  20 Great Yarmouth NR31 . 94 C7
  4 Great Yarmouth NR31 . 170 A5
Lilac Dr NR26 . . . . 138 D4
Lilac Wood PE30 . . . . . 147 B8
Lilburne Ave NR3 . . . . . 158 D2
Lilian Cl NR6 . . . . 158 B4
Lilian Rd NR10 . . . . 54 A2
Lily Ave NR20 . . . . 69 B8
Lily La NR34 . . . . 111 A3
Lily Terr NR1 . . . . 178 B1
Limasol Rd NR19 . . . . . 154 C2
Lime Ave
  Stradsett PE33 . . . . . . 80 C8
  Wisbech PE13 . . . . . . 152 C7
Lime Cl
  7 Harleston IP20 . . . . 122 D1
  Mattishall NR20 . . . . . 68 E6
  Dn Dr NR19 . . . . 154 D2
Lime Gr
  Gayton PE32 . . . . 45 C6
  Sheringham NR26 . . . . 138 D4
  7 Thetford IP24 . . . . . 176 D4
Lime Kiln Cl
  5 Cley next the Sea NR25. . 7 E6
  6 Newton Flotman NR15. . 89 D1
Limekiln La
  Houghton PE31 . . . . . . 29 D6
  South End NR16. . . . . 106 C1
  Upper Sheringham NR26. 138 A4
Lime Kiln La
  2 Stoke Ferry PE33 . . . 81 A3
  Thetford IP24 . . . . . . 176 D4
Lime Kiln Mews
  6 New Catton NR6. . . . 158 C1
  Norwich NR3 . . . . 162 C8
Lime Kiln Rd
  Gayton PE32 . . . . 45 C6
  Sparham NR9. . . . . . . 50 F5
  West Dereham PE33 . . . 80 C5
Limekiln Wlk 1 NR30. . 169 C4
Limes Ave NR1 . . . . 59 A1
Limes Cl IP22. . . . . . . 177 D1
Limes Rd 3 NR29 . . . . . 56 C8
Limes Rd PE32 . . . . 81 C8
Limes The IP25 . . . . . . 84 A6
Lime Tree Ave
  Costessey NR8. . . . . . 156 F4
  Long Gratston NR15. . . 106 E2
  Norwich NR7 . . . . 163 C7
  Wymondham NR18 . . . . 173 D6
Limetree Cl 10 NR10 . . . 53 B3
Lime Tree Cl
  Great Yarmouth NR31 . 169 C2
  Taverham NR8 . . . . . . 155 B2
Lime Tree Rd
  North Walsham NR28 . . 151 D5
  Norwich NR7 . . . . 162 B3
Lime Tree Wlk IP25 . . . . 84 D3
Lime Way NR31 . . . . . . 170 B5
Limmer Ave IP21 . . . . . 121 C1
Limmer Rd NR31 . . . . . 170 D4
LIMPENHOE NR13. . . . . . 92 D6
Limpenhoe Rd
  Cantley NR13 . . . . 92 C7
  Reedham NR13 . . . . . . 92 E6
Linacre Ave NR19 . . . . 154 C4
Linacre Cl NR7 . . . . 159 C3
Linalls Dr NR8 . . . . 156 C4
Lincoln Ave
  Great Yarmouth NR31 . 170 C3
  Hingham NR9 . . . . 86 D5
Lincoln Cl 12 NR20 . . . . 50 B3
Lincoln Ralphs Sports Hall
  NR1 . . . . 178 C1
Lincoln Rd IP25. . . . . . . 84 F3
Lincoln Sq N PE36 . . . . 132 C5
Lincoln Sq S PE36 . . . . 132 C5
Lincoln St
  Hunstanton PE36. . . . 132 D5
  Norwich NR2 . . . . 162 B5
Lincoln Way IP24 . . . . . 176 B5
Linden Cl NR18 . . . . 86 E3
Linden Dr 5 NR9 . . . . . . 88 C7

Linden Gr
  Diss IP22. . . . . 177 C6
  Sheringham NR26 . . . . 138 D4
Linden Rd
  Clenchwarton PE34 . . . 145 E5
  Norwich NR5 . . . . 157 C1
Linden Tree Gdns 15
  NR31 . . . . 94 C7
Lindford Dr NR4 . . . . . . 89 C8
Lindley Cl NR6. . . . . . . 158 E6
Lindley Rd 9 NR9. . . . . . 88 C7
Lindley St NR1 . . . . . . 162 E3
Lindsay Rd NR7 . . . . . . 159 C4
Linford PE34. . . . . 145 D6
Linford Clapper La PE34. 145 E6
Linford Cl PE34 . . . . . . 145 E5
Ling Cl 1 NR12. . . . . . . 54 C7
Ling Comm Rd PE30 . . . 148 D6
Lingheath Rd IP27 . . . . 175 E3
Ling House Rd PE31. . . . 13 B1
Ling Rd IP22. . . . . 177 B3
Lings Cl 1 NR10. . . . . . . 53 B3
Lings The NR9 . . . . 86 D8
Ling Way NR12 . . . . 54 C7
LINGWOOD NR13 . . . . . . 73 F3
Lingwood Fst Sch NR13 . 73 F3
Lingwood Gdns 2 NR13 . 74 A3
Lingwood Jun Sch NR13 . 74 A3
Lingwood Rd
  Blofield NR13. . . . . . . 73 E4
  Brundall NR13 . . . . . . 165 F6
Lingwood Sta NR13 . . . . 74 A3
Links Ave
  Brundall NR13 . . . . . . 165 C4
  Cromer NR27. . . . . . . 139 D4
  Norwich NR6 . . . . 157 F4
Links Cl
  Caister-on-Sea NR30. . 168 E4
  Norwich NR5 . . . . 157 F5
  6 Thurlton NR14 . . . . . 92 F1
Links Cres NR26 . . . . . 138 C7
Links Rd
  Great Yarmouth NR31 . 171 D8
  Mundesley NR11. . . . . 143 B6
  Sheringham NR26 . . . . 138 C7
Links Way
  Sheringham NR27 . . . . 10 A5
  4 Thurlton NR14 . . . . . 92 F1
Link The 8 IP24 . . . . . 176 D4
Linmore Cres 3 IP25. . . 84 E3
Linmore Ct IP25 . . . . . . 84 C3
Linn Chilvers Dr PE31 . . 133 B5
Linnet Cl 6 NR31 . . . . . 170 A6
Linnet Cres IP27 . . . . . 175 E3
Linnets The NR5 . . . . . 156 F1
Lintock Rd NR3 . . . . . . 158 D3
Linton Cl NR7. . . . . . . 159 B3
Linton Cres NR7 . . . . . 159 B4
Lion & Castle Yd NR1 . . 178 B2
Lion La NR14 . . . . 91 C3
Lion Rd
  Buxton with Lammas
    NR10 . . . . 36 E1
  Palgrave IP22 . . . . . . 177 C1
Lion's Mouth NR11. . . . 10 A3
Lion Wood Rd NR1. . . . 163 B7
Lisbon Rd NR19 . . . . . . 154 C2
Lishman Rd NR7 . . . . . 159 B4
Lisle Rd NR5 . . . . 160 F7
Lister Cl NR31 . . . . 170 B1
Lister's Rd PE14 . . . . . . 77 E5
LITCHAM PE32 . . . . 48 A4
Litcham Hall PE32 . . . . 48 A4
Litcham High Sch PE32 . 48 A4
Litcham Prim Sch PE32 . 48 A4
Litcham Rd
  Beeston with Bittering
    PE32 . . . . 48 D4
  Great Dunham PE32 . . . 47 F2
  Gressenhall NR20 . . . . 49 C3
  Dunham PE32 . . . . . . 65 F8
  Mileham PE32 . . . . . . 48 C5
  Tittleshall PE32 . . . . . 48 A4
Litcham Village Mus*
  PE32 . . . . 48 A4
Litchmere Rd NR14 . . . 109 D6
Litester Cl NR28 . . . . . 151 D4
Little Armes St NR2 . . . 162 A8
Little Barney La NR21 . . 17 F3
LITTLE BARNINGHAM
  NR11 . . . . 20 C4
LITTLE BARWICK PE31 . . 14 E6
Littlebeck La NR15 . . . . 108 B8
Little Bethel St NR2 . . . 178 A2
Little Bittering Medieval
  Village of* NR19 . . . . 48 F4
Little Carr Rd PE30 . . . 148 D5
Little Church St PE13 . . 152 C5
LITTLE CRESSINGHAM
  IP25 . . . . 83 E2
Little Dowgate PE13 . . . 152 A7
LITTLE DUNHAM PE32 . . 65 E8
LITTLE ELLINGHAM NR17 . 86 A2
Little Ellingham Rd NR9 . 86 A3
Little Fendike La PE14. . 77 E8
Littlefields NR19 . . . . . 154 D5
LITTLE FRANSHAM NR19. . 66 A2
LITTLE GREEN IP22 . . . . 129 B1
LITTLE HALE IP25 . . . . . 67 A1
LITTLE HAUTBOIS NR12. . 54 A8
Little Hockham La IP24 . 102 E2
Little Holme Rd PE34. . . 41 F6
Little La
  1 Castle Acre PE32. . . . 46 F2
  Docking PE31. . . . . . . 134 E4
  9 Horsford NR10 . . . . . 53 B3
  Roydon PE32 . . . . 28 A1

Little La continued
Stoke Ferry PE33 . . . . 80 F3
LITTLE LONDON
Corpusty NR11 . . . . 19 E1
Marsham NR10 . . . . 36 A2
North Walsham NR28 . . . . . 151 E7
Northwold IP26 . . . . 99 D7
Little London Rd
North Walsham NR28 . . . . . 151 D8
Northwold IP26 . . . . 99 C7
Little London St NR3 . . . . . . 178 B3
Little Man's Way PE33 . . . . 81 A3
LITTLE MARSH NR25 . . . . . . 7 A1
LITTLE MASSINGHAM
PE32 . . . . 29 C3
LITTLE MELTON NR9 . . . . . 160 C2
Little Melton Fst Sch
NR9 . . . . 160 C2
Little Melton Rd NR9 . . . . 160 B1
Little Money Rd NR14 . . . . 109 D8
Little Oulsham Dro IP26 . . 98 B2
LITTLE OUSE CB7 . . . . 112 A8
LITTLE PLUMSTEAD NR13 . . 73 B6
Little Plumstead CE Prim Sch
NR13 . . . . 165 A8
Littleport St PE30 . . . . . . 146 E5
Littleport Terr 8 PE30 . . 146 E5
Little Rybburgh NR21 . . . . 32 C7
Little Scratby Cres NR29 167 E4
LITTLE SNORING NR21 . . . . 17 B3
Little Snoring Prim Sch
NR21 . . . . 17 A3
Little Snoring Rd NR21 . . 17 A5
LITTLE THORNAGE NR25 . . . . 7 F1
LITTLE WALSINGHAM
NR22 . . . . 16 F7
Little Walsingham Cl
PE30 . . . . 148 C3
Littlewoods La NR12 . . . . 164 E5
Livingstone Rise NR11 . . 22 F8
Livingstone St NR2 . . . . . 162 A7
Lizard The NR18 . . . . 173 D3
Lloyd Ct NR25 . . . . 137 F8
Lloyd Rd
Norwich NR1 . . . . 163 B7
Taverham NR8 . . . . 155 B2
Loanin The NR1 . . . . 162 F3
Lobster La NR2 . . . . 178 A3
Loch La IP25 . . . . 84 D4
Lockerbie Flats 9 NR26 138 D7
Lockhart Rd NR35 . . . . . . 109 D3
Lock Rd NR28 . . . . 38 D6
Lock's La NR34 . . . . 109 F1
Locksley Rd NR4 . . . . 89 E8
LODDON NR14 . . . . 92 A1
Loddon Cnr NR15 . . . . 108 C2
Loddon Cnr NR15 . . . . 108 C2
Loddon Fst Sch 13 NR14 . 92 A1
LODDON INGLOSS NR14 . . 109 B7
Loddon Sch NR14 . . . . 91 F1
Loddon Rd
Ditchingham NR35 . . . . . . 109 B2
Gillingham NR34 . . . . 110 C3
Haddiscoe NR14 . . . . 110 D8
Heckingham NR14 . . . . . . 92 D1
Holverston NR14 . . . . 91 A5
Kirby Cane NR35 . . . . 109 E4
Norton Subcourse NR14 . 92 E1
Toft Monks NR34 . . . . 110 D7
Trowse with Newton NR14 163 C1
Yelverton NR14 . . . . 90 E6
Lode Ave PE14 . . . . 77 F5
Lode St IP27 . . . . 175 C4
Lodge Breck NR8 . . . . 157 A7
Lodge Cl NR25 . . . . 137 B5
Lodge Dr IP22 . . . . 120 B5
Lodge Farm Dr NR6 . . . . 158 D6
Lodge Farm Mdws NR20 . 49 C4
Lodge Hill NR4 . . . . 138 C3
Lodge La
Norwich NR6 . . . . 158 E6
Riddlesworth IP22 . . . . . . 127 D7
Shelfanger IP22 . . . . 120 B1
13 Snettisham PE31 . . . . 12 E4
Lodge La Fst Sch NR6 . . . 158 E6
Lodge Pl NR7 . . . . 163 E6
Lodge Rd
Catfield NR29 . . . . 56 B8
Feltwell IP26 . . . . 98 F2
Heacham PE31 . . . . 133 C5
Lingwood & Burlingham
NR13 . . . . 74 A3
St John, Ilketshall NR34 . 124 C6
Tivetshall St Margaret
NR15 . . . . 121 C8
Lodge Way IP24 . . . . 176 C7
Lodore Ave NR6 . . . . 158 A6
Loggers La IP22 . . . . 128 B5
Loke PE30 . . . . 146 E6
Loke The
Belton with Browston
NR31 . . . . 93 B6
Briston NR24 . . . . 142 D4
Brumstead NR12 . . . . 24 A2
Cringleford NR4 . . . . 89 C8
Cromer NR27 . . . . 139 B6
East Beckham NR11 . . . . . 9 D2
Felmingham NR28 . . . . . . 37 B8
Plumstead NR25 . . . . 8 E6
Freethorpe NR13 . . . . 92 E7
2 Gresham NR11 . . . . 9 E1
Haddiscoe NR14 . . . . 110 F8
4 Hemsby NR29 . . . . 58 B6
Salhouse NR13 . . . . 55 B2
Strumpshaw NR13 . . . . . . 73 F2
Loke Wiffens 2 NR9 . . . . 88 D8
Lollards Rd
1 Norwich NR1 . . . . 163 A6

Lollards Rd continued
Norwich NR1 . . . . 178 C3
Lolly Moor Nature Reserve★
NR19 . . . . 67 F5
Lomond Rd NR17 . . . . 174 F6
London La
Mundford IP26 . . . . 100 B4
South Creake NR21 . . . . . 15 E5
London Rd
Attleborough NR17 . . . . . 174 B3
Brandon IP27 . . . . 175 B3
Downham Market PE38 . . 172 C4
East Dereham NR19 . . . . 154 E4
Elveden IP24 . . . . 125 B7
Harleston IP20 . . . . 122 D1
King's Lynn PE30 . . . . . . 146 E4
Snetterton NR16 . . . . 103 D1
Thetford IP24 . . . . 176 B3
Wymondham NR18 . . . . . 173 A2
London St
Brancaster PE31 . . . . 3 B7
Norwich NR2 . . . . 178 B3
Swaffham PE37 . . . . 153 C4
Whissonsett NR20 . . . . . . 31 D2
Londs The NR27 . . . . 11 A3
Lone Barn Rd NR7 . . . . . 159 B2
Lonely Rd
Pulham St Mary IP21 . . . 122 B6
Scole IP21 . . . . 121 C2
Long Barrow Dr NR28 . . 151 D3
Long Beach Est NR29 . . 167 C8
Longbow Cl NR4 . . . . 162 C1
Longbrooke Cl NR14 . . . . 89 D4
Long Comm La NR10 . . . . 37 D4
Long Dale NR8 . . . . 155 E2
Longdell Hills NR5 . . . . . 156 E2
Longdon Cl 4 PE12 . . . . . 41 B8
Long Dro PE38 . . . . 97 D2
Longe Rd NR6 . . . . 158 F6
Longfellow Rd NR30 . . . . 168 D5
Longfield Cl 4 NR14 . . . . 91 F1
Longfields PE37 . . . . 153 C5
Longfields Rd NR7 . . . . . . 72 D5
Longfulans La NR31 . . . . 171 D3
LONG GREEN IP22 . . . . . . 129 B4
LONGHAM NR19 . . . . 49 A2
Longham La NR20 . . . . 49 A3
Longham Rd NR19 . . . . . . 49 A2
Longhead La PE14 . . . . . . 59 A6
Long John Hill NR1 . . . . 162 E2
LONG JOHN'S HILL NR1 . . 162 E2
Long La
Baconsthorpe NR25 . . . . . 20 A7
Bawburgh NR9 . . . . 160 B8
Burston & Shimpling IP22 120 E4
Catfield NR29 . . . . 56 D7
Feltwell IP26 . . . . 98 D1
Flordon NR15 . . . . 106 E8
Great Yarmouth NR31 . . 170 A4
Hoveton NR12 . . . . 164 F7
Mulbarton NR14 . . . . 89 B2
Saxlingham Nethergate
NR15 . . . . 107 B8
Southrepps NR11 . . . . 22 B7
Stoke Holy Cross NR14 . . 89 F4
Strumpshaw NR13 . . . . . 165 F2
Swaffham PE37 . . . . 153 E5
West Winch PE33 . . . . . . 43 E2
Winfarthing IP22 . . . . . . 119 F7
Longlands Dr NR18 . . . . . 173 A6
Long Lots PE14 . . . . 59 F3
Longmead 4 NR1 . . . . . . 162 E2
Longmeadow NR13 . . . . . 165 B3
Longmeadow Cl IP25 . . . . 85 A1
Long Rd
Barton Turf NR12 . . . . 55 F7
Poringland NR14 . . . . 90 C5
Saham Toney IP25 . . . . . . 84 F8
Terrington St Clement
PE34 . . . . 144 A8
Thurlton NR14 . . . . 93 A1
Wymondham NR18 . . . . . 88 A1
Long Row
Norwich NR3 . . . . 158 D1
Tibenham NR16 . . . . 120 D6
Longs Cl 4 NR15 . . . . 89 C1
Long's Cres NR13 . . . . 72 D7
Long St NR17 . . . . 103 E6
Long Straton Mill★
NR15 . . . . 106 E7
LONG STRATTON NR15 . . 106 C3
Long Stratton High Sch
NR15 . . . . 106 C3
Long Stratton Ind Est
NR15 . . . . 106 D3
Long Stratton Leisure Ctr
NR15 . . . . 106 C3
Long Stratton Rd NR16 . 105 F4
Longview 1 NR9 . . . . 88 D8
Longview Cl 4 PE31 . . . . . 12 E4
Longwater La NR8 . . . . . 156 D3
Longwater Ret Pk NR5 . 156 A2
Lonsdale Cres NR6 . . . . . . 86 B5
Lonsdale Rd NR13 . . . . 72 E7
Lonsdale Terr PE13 . . . . 152 C3
Loombe Cl NR20 . . . . 50 B3
Loop Rd NR11 . . . . 11 D1
Lopham Rd NR16 . . . . 118 D6
Lord Cres NR20 . . . . 50 B5
Lord Rd IP22 . . . . 177 E4
LORDSBRIDGE PE34 . . . . . 60 E7
Lords La PE31 . . . . 133 D5
Lord's La NR11 . . . . 94 B7
Lord Walsingham Ct 1
PE24 . . . . 176 E5
Lorraine Gdns NR3 . . . . . 158 E3
Losinga Cres NR3 . . . . . . 158 B3

Losinga Rd PE30 . . . . 146 E7
Lossiemouth Rd 6 IP31 . 126 B1
Lothian St NR2 . . . . 162 C6
Lothingland Mid Sch
NR32 . . . . 171 A3
Louden Rd NR27 . . . . 139 B7
Louie's La IP22 . . . . 177 C6
Louis Cl NR6 . . . . 158 D6
Louis Dahl Rd 3 NR31 . . 94 A6
Louise Cl 15 NR30 . . . . . 169 D2
LOUND NR32 . . . . 94 C1
Lound Dam NR14 . . . . . . 111 A7
Lound Rd
Belton with Browston
NR31 . . . . 94 B4
Norwich NR4 . . . . 161 F5
Somerleyton, Ashby &
Herringfleet NR32 . . . . . 111 F8
Lovat Cl IP20 . . . . 122 E2
Love La
Fransham NR19 . . . . 66 D7
Sporle with Palgrave PE32 65 C6
Wisbech PE13 . . . . 152 C4
Lovelace Rd NR4 . . . . 161 E4
Lovell Gdns IP25 . . . . 84 E3
Lovells The 6 PE14 . . . . . 59 D7
Lovell Way NR4 . . . . 144 B4
Lovelstaithe NR1 . . . . 178 C3
Lovers' La NR29 . . . . 56 C4
Lovett Cl NR5 . . . . 158 F6
Lovewell Rd NR31 . . . . . 170 D5
Low Bungay Rd NR14 . . . 92 A1
Low Comm
Aslacton NR16 . . . . 106 A2
Bunwell NR16 . . . . 105 E2
Deopham NR18 . . . . 86 E4
Hellington NR14 . . . . 91 B6
Reedham NR13 . . . . 93 A5
South Lopham IP22 . . . . 128 F7
Swardeston NR14 . . . . . . 89 B6
Low Comm La NR34 . . . . 111 A5
LOW COMMON NR16 . . . . 105 F3
Low Comm Rd
South Lopham IP22 . . . . 128 E7
Thurlton NR14 . . . . 91 D3
Low Ditch Rd IP20 . . . . . 122 F4
Lower Clarence Rd NR1 . 178 C2
Lower Cliff Rd NR31 . . . . 170 D4
Lower Drag Way IP22 . . 128 D8
LOWER EAST CARLETON
NR14 . . . . 89 B6
LOW THARSTON NR15 . . 106 D6
Lower Espl NR31 . . . . 170 D3
Lower Globe La NR13 . . 165 E7
Lower Gn NR19 . . . . 92 E8
Lower Goat La 2 NR2 . . 178 A3
LOWER GRESHAM NR11 . . . 9 F1
Lower Hall La NR24 . . . . . 18 D7
Lower Hardley Rd NR14 . 92 C2
Lower Kiln La NR15 . . . . 90 F3
Lower Lincoln St PE34 . 132 C5
Lower Marine Par NR31 . 170 D3
Lower Oakley IP21 . . . . . 130 D4
Lower Rd
Holme Hale IP25 . . . . 66 B3
Rockland St Mary NR14 . . 91 C7
Lower Rose La IP21 . . . . 177 C2
Lower Spink's La NR18 . . 88 B4
Lower St
Horning NR12 . . . . 55 E4
Salhouse NR13 . . . . 55 A1
LOWER STOW BEDON
NR17 . . . . 102 F5
LOWER STREET
Southrepps NR11 . . . . 22 C6
Wickmere NR11 . . . . 20 C5
LOWER TASBURGH
NR15 . . . . 106 E7
LOWER THURLTON NR14 . 93 A2
Lower Wood Nature
Reserve★ NR16 . . . . . . 105 E8
Lowes Ave NR25 . . . . 137 D5
Lowe's La PE31 . . . . 4 D4
Lowestoft Rd NR31 . . . . . 170 C1
Lowes View IP22 . . . . . . 177 E3
Low Farm Rd NR13 . . . . . 75 A3
Lowfield PE30 . . . . 147 C4
Lowhatter's Cl PE38 . . . 172 B3
Lowick Cl 9 NR19 . . . . . . 154 D3
Low La
Hevingham NR10 . . . . 53 C7
Rocklands NR17 . . . . 103 B6
Terrington St Clement
PE34 . . . . 144 A5
Low Rd
Alburgh IP20 . . . . 122 F6
Bunwell NR16 . . . . 105 E1
Denton IP20 . . . . 123 B5
Dickleburgh & Rushall
IP21 . . . . 130 C5
Forncett NR16 . . . . 106 B5
Freethorpe NR13 . . . . 92 F7
Great & Little Plumstead
NR13 . . . . 72 C5
Grimston PE32 . . . . 28 B1
Haddiscoe NR14 . . . . 110 F7
Hedenham NR35 . . . . . . 108 D4
Hellesdon NR6 . . . . 157 C5
Hingham NR9 . . . . 86 B4
Keswick NR4 . . . . 89 C7
Kimberley NR9 . . . . 87 D8
King's Lynn PE30 . . . . . . 148 C1
Mautby NR29 . . . . 75 E5
Mettingham NR35 . . . . . . 109 D1
Narborough PE32 . . . . . . 63 F7
North Tuddenham NR20 . 68 E8
Norton Subcourse NR14 . 92 E2
Pentney PE32 . . . . 63 C8

Low Rd continued
Redenhall with Harleston
IP20 . . . . 122 F1
Repps with Bastwick NR29 . 57 A4
Rollesby NR29 . . . . 57 D2
Roydon PE32 . . . . 28 A1
Scole IP21 . . . . 130 C5
Shelton NR15 . . . . 107 B1
Shropham NR17 . . . . 103 B3
Skeyton Corner NR10 . . . 37 B6
South Walsham NR13 . . . 74 B8
Starston IP20 . . . . 122 C3
St John, Ilketshall NR34 . 124 D6
St John's Fen End PE14 . . 60 B6
Stoke Ferry PE33 . . . . 80 F2
Stow Bardolph PE34 . . . . 61 C2
Stow Bedon NR17 . . . . . 102 E5
Strumpshaw NR13 . . . . . 165 F1
Swaffham PE37 . . . . 153 A5
Tasburgh NR15 . . . . 106 F7
1 Thurlton NR14 . . . . 92 F1
Thurlton NR14 . . . . 93 B2
Tibenham NR16 . . . . 120 B8
Walpole Cross Keys PE34 . 42 A7
West Acre PE32 . . . . 46 C2
West Caister NR30 . . . . . 168 A3
Wicklewood NR18 . . . . . . 87 C3
Wimbotsham PE34 . . . . . 43 D3
Winterton-on-Sea NR29 . 58 B6
Wisbech PE14 . . . . 152 E1
Woodbastwick NR13 . . . . 55 C1
Wortham IP22 . . . . 129 A6
Wortwell IP20 . . . . 123 A3
Lowry Cl 3 NR31 . . . . 170 A7
Lowry Cole Rd NR6 . . . . 158 E5
Low Side PE14 . . . . 77 F6
Lows La IP22 . . . . 177 D2
Low St
Hardingham NR9 . . . . 86 E8
Hoxne IP21 . . . . 131 A4
Ketteringham NR18 . . . . . 88 D6
Macks Loke NR22 . . . . 32 E3
Smallburgh NR12 . . . . . . 38 E3
St Margaret, Ilketshall
NR35 . . . . 124 B4
Weasenham St Peter PE32 . 30 D2
Wicklewood NR18 . . . . . . 87 A5
Low Street La PE38 . . . . . 79 C3
LOW STREET NR9 . . . . 86 E8
Lowther Rd NR4 . . . . 162 B1
Low Wr La IP22 . . . . 129 D5
Loxwood NR6 . . . . 157 E6
Lubbock Cl NR2 . . . . 161 F5
Lucas Ct 2 NR7 . . . . 72 D5
Lucas La NR13 . . . . 135 E6
Lucas Rd 9 NR31 . . . . 169 B4
Lucerne Cl NR6 . . . . 158 F4
Lucerne Rd 8 NR31 . . . . . 94 C6
Lucombe Dr PE13 . . . . . . 152 F7
Luddenham Rd NR20 . . . . 50 B2
LUDHAM NR29 . . . . 56 C6
Ludham Airstrip NR29 . . . 56 D6
Ludham Fst Sch NR29 . . . 56 C6
Ludham Rd
Catfield NR29 . . . . 56 C6
Potter Heigham NR29 . . . 56 F5
Ludkin Sq 8 NR30 . . . . . 169 C5
Lugger Yd NR23 . . . . 136 D6
Lug's La NR35 . . . . 109 B5
Luke Cl NR5 . . . . 156 F2
LUNDY GREEN NR15 . . . . 107 D3
Luscombe Way 6 NR13 . . 72 E7
Lusher Cl 1 NR6 . . . . 138 C5
Lusher Rd NR6 . . . . 158 E6
Lusher's Loke NR7 . . . . . 158 F4
Lushers Mdw 5 NR17 . . 174 C5
Lushington Cl 9 NR5 . . . 161 A8
Luxembourg Way NR14 . 154 C2
Lydgate Cl NR19 . . . . 154 D3
Lyhart Rd NR4 . . . . 162 B1
Lynch Gn 6 NR9 . . . . 88 D8
Lyndford Rd NR12 . . . . . . 39 B4
Lyndhurst Ct PE36 . . . . . 132 D3
Lynewood Cl NR27 . . . . . 139 D4
Lynewood Rd NR27 . . . . 139 D4
Lynfield Rd NR28 . . . . . . 151 C6

Lynn Rd continued
King's Lynn PE30 . . . . . . 147 A5
Littleport CB7 . . . . 96 E1
Middleton PE32 . . . . 44 D2
Roydon PE32 . . . . 28 A1
Runcton Holme PE33 . . . 61 F4
Shouldham PE33 . . . . 62 D3
Shouldham Thorpe PE33 . 62 B2
Southery PE38 . . . . 97 A6
Stow Bardolph PE34 . . . . 79 E8
Stradsett PE33 . . . . 80 C8
Swaffham PE37 . . . . 153 A5
Terrington St Clement PE34 42 A6
Tilney St Lawrence PE34 . 42 D2
Walpole Cross Keys PE34 . 41 F6
Walsoken PE14 . . . . 59 B6
Watlington PE33 . . . . 61 E6
Weeting IP27 . . . . 175 A8
Wereham PE33 . . . . 80 D5
West Rudham PE31 . . . . . 29 F6
West Walton PE14 . . . . . . 59 D8
West Winch PE33 . . . . 61 F8
Wiggenhall St Mary Magdalen
PE34 . . . . 60 F3
Wisbech PE13 . . . . 152 C6
Wretton PE33 . . . . 80 F3
Lynn Rd Terr PE14 . . . . . . 59 D8
Lynn St PE37 . . . . 153 B4
Lynton Rd NR12 . . . . 24 A7
Lynwood Terr 1 PE30 . . 146 E3
Lytton Rd NR8 . . . . 156 D8

M

MacArthur Dr 3 NR19 . . 154 C6
MacDonald Rd NR27 . . . 139 A7
Mackenzie Cl 1 NR31 . . 170 B1
Mackenzie Rd IP24 . . . . 176 A3
Mackintosh Rd NR13 . . . 72 E8
Mack's La NR8 . . . . 156 D7
Macks Loke NR22 . . . . . . 142 F2
Macmillan Way NR13 . . 165 A8
Madden Ave NR30 . . . . . 169 D8
Maddermarket Theatre★
NR2 . . . . 178 A3
Mad Dog La PE32 . . . . 29 C2
Maden Cl NR18 . . . . 173 B5
Magazine Cl PE13 . . . . . . 152 A4
Magazine La PE13 . . . . . 152 A4
Magdalen Cl 3 NR31 . . . 169 B3
Magdalen Gates Fst Sch
NR3 . . . . 162 E8
Magdalen High Rd PE34 . 61 A6
Magdalen Rd
Norwich NR3 . . . . 162 E8
Tilney St Lawrence PE34 . 60 D8
Wiggenhall St Germans
PE34 . . . . 61 C7
Magdalen Sq NR31 . . . . . 170 B4
Magdalen St
Norwich NR3 . . . . 178 B4
Thetford IP24 . . . . 176 D4
Magdalen Way NR31 . . . 170 B4
Magic City Leisure Ctr
NR1 . . . . 178 C3
Magnay Rd NR1 . . . . 157 C7
Magnolia Cl NR10 . . . . . . 53 A4
Magnolia Gn 8 NR31 . . . 170 B6
Magpie Cl 33 IP20 . . . . . 122 D2
MAGPIE GREEN IP22 . . . . 129 B5
Magpie Hill IP22 . . . . 129 B5
Magpie La NR17 . . . . 103 B7
Maida Vale 1 NR2 . . . . . 162 B5
Maidens Cl 1 NR13 . . . . . 72 E4
Maid Marian Rd NR4 . . . 162 C1
Maids Cross Hill IP27 . . 113 F1
Maidstone Rd NR1 . . . . . 178 B3
Main Cross Rd NR30 . . . 170 D8
Main Dereham Rd NR21 . 31 F4
Main Dr NR20 . . . . 32 E4
Maine St
1 Thetford IP24 . . . . 116 A1
Thetford IP24 . . . . 176 A4
Main Rd
Clenchwarton PE34 . . . . 145 B5
Crimplesham PE33 . . . . . 80 B6
Filby NR29 . . . . 76 A8
Fleggburgh NR29 . . . . 57 B5
Holme next the Sea PE36 . 2 A5
Lingwood & Burlingham
NR13 . . . . 74 A5
Methwold IP26 . . . . 99 A7
Narborough PE32 . . . . . . 63 E8
Ormesby St Michael NR29 58 A1
Rollesby NR29 . . . . 57 D2
Swardeston NR14 . . . . . . 89 C5
Tilney All Saints PE34 . . . 42 C4
Upwell PE14 . . . . 77 E3
Walpole Highway PE14 . . 59 E8
Weeting IP27 . . . . 175 B7
West Caister NR30 . . . . . 168 A6
West Winch PE33 . . . . 61 F8
Wisbech PE14 . . . . 77 A7
Main St
Hockwold cum Wilton
IP26 . . . . 113 F7
Honing NR28 . . . . 38 C6
Welney PE14 . . . . 95 D4
Makaloff Cl 9 NR30 . . . . 169 D2
Makaloff Rd 4 NR30 . . . 169 D2
Malborough Gn Cres
NR29 . . . . 57 D4
Malbrook Rd NR5 . . . . . . 161 B7

Maldon Rd PE13 . . . . 152 E5
Malin Ct **7** NR30 . . . . 168 C6
Mallard Cl
　Brundall NR13 . . . . 165 E2
　Chedgrave NR14 . . . . 91 F2
　7 Fakenham NR21 . . . . . . 141 E4
　9 Loddon NR14 . . . . 92 A2
　4 Salhouse NR13 . . . . 55 A1
　1 Snettisham PE31 . . . . . . 12 E4
Mallard Rd **10** IP25 . . . . . 84 C3
Mallard Way
　Brandon IP27 . . . . 175 E2
　Great Yarmouth NR31 . . . 170 A6
　Hickling NR12 . . . . 39 F1
Mallory Rd NR6 . . . . 158 D6
Mallow Cl **8** NR17 . . . . . 174 B4
Mallow Rd IP24 . . . . 176 F5
Mallow Way NR18 . . . . . . 173 D4
Malsters Cl IP26 . . . . 100 B5
Malt Dr PE13 . . . . 112 B5
Malthouse Cl **9** IP25 . . . 84 D2
Malthouse Cres PE31 . . . . 133 D5
Malthouse Ct
　East Dereham NR20 . . . . . 154 E5
　24 Redenhall with Harleston
　IP20 . . . . 122 D2
　8 Snettisham PE31 . . . . . 12 E5
　Thornham PE36 . . . . 2 D6
Malthouse La
　Cantley NR13 . . . . 92 B6
　Gissing IP22 . . . . 120 F4
　Great Yarmouth NR31 . . . 170 C8
　Guist NR20 . . . . 32 F4
　Ludham NR29 . . . . 56 D5
Malthouse Pl NR23 . . . . . 136 D6
Malthouse Rd
　4 Hethersett NR9 . . . . . . 88 C7
　Norwich NR2 . . . . 178 A2
Malthouse Yd NR10 . . . . . 149 C4
Malting Way IP31 . . . . . . 126 D1
Maltings Cl IP22 . . . . 177 F3
Maltings Dr **9** IP20 . . . . 122 D2
Maltings La **4** PE38 . . . . 172 A5
Maltings Way NR16 . . . . . 119 B6
Maltmas Dro PE14 . . . . 77 A7
Malt's La IP24 . . . . 113 F7
Malvern Cl IP30 . . . . 148 D3
Malvern Rd **3** NR31 . . . . 163 A6
Manby Rd
　Downham Market PE38 . . 172 B3
　Great Yarmouth NR30 . . . 169 D4
　Norwich NR7 . . . . 159 C1
Manchester Pl **8** NR2 . . 162 C5
Mancroft Wlk **11** NR2 . . 162 C7
Mandela Cl NR3 . . . . 178 A4
Mandells Ct NR3 . . . . 178 B3
Mangate St PE37 . . . . 153 C5
Mangreen NR14 . . . . 89 C6
Mangreen La NR14 . . . . . . 89 C5
Manning's La IP22 . . . . . . 128 B1
Mannington Hall★ NR11 . . 20 C3
Mannington Dr IP20 . . . . . 148 E1
Mann's La NR20 . . . . 50 B4
Manor Chase NR6 . . . . . . 156 E8
Manor Cl
　8 Aylsham NR11 . . . . . . 150 D6
　1 Great Walsingham NR22 . 170 C7
　Hockering NR20 . . . . 69 B8
　Horsham St Faith & Newton St
　Faith NR10 . . . . 53 D2
　Ingoldisthorpe PE31 . . . . 140 D8
　Lamas NR10 . . . . 36 E1
　4 Little Snoring NR21 . . . 17 B3
　Tunstead NR12 . . . . 37 F1
Manor Ct
　Aylsham NR11 . . . . 150 C6
　North Walsham NR28 . . . 151 E5
Manor Dr
　Litcham PE32 . . . . 48 A4
　Roydon IP22 . . . . 177 A5
　Terrington St John PE14 . . 42 B1
Manor Farm Barn IP18 . . . 157 A8
Manor Farm Rd
　Denton IP20 . . . . 122 F8
　Somerton NR29 . . . . 58 A6
　St John, Ilketshall NR34 . 124 D7
Manorfield Cl **1** NR29 . . 167 A2
Manor Field Fst Sch
　NR15 . . . . 106 E3
Manor Gdns
　Diss IP22 . . . . 177 D5
　Hopton on Sea NR31 . . . . 171 E4
　3 Lingwood NR13 . . . . . . 74 A3
　Wisbech PE13 . . . . 152 A4
MANOR HOUSE PE32 . . . . 46 E2
Manor House Cl
　Brandon IP27 . . . . 175 B3
　Mautby NR29 . . . . 75 E6
Manor La PE31 . . . . 12 E5
Manor Pk Gdns **18** NR15 . 106 E3
Manor Rd
　Brandon IP27 . . . . 175 A3
　Caister-on-Sea NR30 . . . 168 F5
　Cantley NR13 . . . . 92 B8
　Great Yarmouth NR31 . . . 170 C7
　Griston IP25 . . . . 85 A2
　Heacham PE31 . . . . 133 D8
　Hilgay PE38 . . . . 79 D1
　Hopton on Sea NR31 . . . . 171 D4
　Horsham St Faith & Newton St
　Faith NR10 . . . . 53 D3
　Hunstanton PE36 . . . . . . 132 C2
　King's Lynn PE30 . . . . . . 148 C5
　Long Stratton NR15 . . . . 106 E3

Manor Rd continued
　Mundesley NR11 . . . . 143 C6
　Newton St Faith NR10 . . . 53 D4
　North Walsham NR28 . . . 151 E5
　Roydon IP22 . . . . 177 A5
　Scarning NR19 . . . . 154 A3
　Stoke Ferry PE33 . . . . 80 F2
　Terrington St Clement
　PE34 . . . . 144 B5
Manor Ridge NR13 . . . . . . 165 E6
Manorside PE31 . . . . 140 D2
Manor Way
　Ormesby St Margaret
　NR29 . . . . 167 A2
　Swaffham PE37 . . . . 153 C5
Manor Wlk NR25 . . . . 137 B6
Manse Ct IP24 . . . . 176 D4
Mansel Dr NR6 . . . . 158 E3
Mansell Cl **2** IP22 . . . . . 177 A5
Mansell Rd PE13 . . . . 152 D3
Mansfield La NR1 . . . . 162 E1
MANSON GREEN NR9 . . . . 86 C6
Manthorpe Cl **5** NR1 . . . 162 E1
Mantle Cl NR7 . . . . 159 D4
Maple Ave PE13 . . . . 152 C7
Maple Cl
　16 Beetley NR20 . . . . 49 D4
　10 Beetley NR20 . . . . 49 D4
　5 Gayton PE32 . . . . 45 C6
　20 Marham NR29 . . . . 57 D4
　Wymondham NR18 . . . . . 173 D6
　Yaxley IP23 . . . . 129 F1
Maple Dr
　King's Lynn PE30 . . . . . . 148 D3
　Norwich NR2 . . . . 161 F7
　Sculthorpe Airfield NR21 . 15 C3
　Taverham NR8 . . . . 155 B1
Maple Gdns **17** NR31 . . . 94 C7
Maple Rd
　Downham Market PE38 . . 172 B6
　King's Lynn PE34 . . . . . . 43 D4
Maple Way
　7 Eye IP23 . . . . 130 C1
　Great Yarmouth NR31 . . . 170 B6
Mapplebeck Cl PE30 . . . . 147 E4
Marauder Rd NR6 . . . . . . 158 D6
March La PE14 . . . . 59 E8
March Rd
　Elm PE14 . . . . 77 A7
　Welney PE14 . . . . 95 C5
March Riverside PE14 . . . . 77 B4
Mardle Rd NR34 . . . . 110 D5
Mardle St NR5 . . . . 160 F5
Mardling Run NR13 . . . . . 166 D3
Marea Mdws PE31 . . . . . . 133 D5
Margaret Cl
　3 East Dereham NR19 . . . 154 D1
　Norwich NR6 . . . . 157 D5
Margaret Cres NR7 . . . . . 163 F7
Margaret English Cl
　PE30 . . . . 138 C5
Margaret Lilly Way **1**
　NR11 . . . . 21 A5
Margaret Paston Ave
　NR3 . . . . 158 A2
Margaret Rd NR5 . . . . 157 B2
Margaret Reeve Cl **6**
　NR18 . . . . 173 D5
Margaret Rose Cl PE30 . . 147 E4
Margarets Cl PE36 . . . . . 132 D2
Margaretta Cl PE14 . . . . . 145 F5
Margetson Ave NR7 . . . . . 163 C7
Marguerite Cl **11** NR11 . . 94 C6
MARHAM PE33 . . . . 63 B4
Marham Airfield PE33 . . . . 63 C3
Marham Airfield Fst Sch
　PE33 . . . . 63 B4
Marham Cl PE34 . . . . 146 B5
Marham Mid Sch PE33 . . . 63 B5
Marham Rd PE33 . . . . 62 E2
Marie Cl NR13 . . . . 92 B6
Marigold Cl **6** NR10 . . . . 53 A3
Marina Leisure Ctr NR30 . 169 E3
Marina La NR11 . . . . 143 C6
Marina Ct NR31 . . . . 170 D1
Marine Cres
　Great Yarmouth NR30 . . . 169 E6
　6 Hemsby NR29 . . . . 58 B6
Marine Dr NR30 . . . . 168 E8
Marine Par NR31 . . . . . . 170 D2
Mariner's Cl NR31 . . . . . . 171 D8
Mariner's Compass
　NR31 . . . . 171 C8
Mariners La NR1 . . . . 178 B1
Mariners Pk Cl NR31 . . . . 171 D5
Mariners' Rd NR30 . . . . . 169 D2
Mariners Way PE30 . . . . . 146 F8
Marion Cl NR18 . . . . 173 C5
Marion Rd NR1 . . . . 163 A6
Marionville Rd NR3 . . . . . 158 E3
Marion Wlk **8** NR1 . . . . 154 D2
Marjoram Cl NR28 . . . . . . 151 E4
Marjoram Rd **24** NR31 . . 94 C6
Market Ave NR1 . . . . 178 B3
Marketfield La NR10 . . . . . 53 E2
Market Gates **8** NR30 . . 169 D4
Market Hill
　Brandon IP27 . . . . 175 C3
　Coltishall NR12 . . . . 54 D8
　Diss IP22 . . . . 177 D4
Market La
　Blundeston NR32 . . . . . . 171 D1
　Brancaster PE31 . . . . 3 B6
　Burston & Shimpling IP22 . 120 E1
　Crimplesham PE33 . . . . . . 80 A6
　Filby NR29 . . . . 76 B7
　Great Melton NR9 . . . . . . 70 C1
　Great Moulton NR15 . . . . 106 C1

Market La continued
　King's Lynn PE30 . . . . . . 146 D5
　Little Melton NR9 . . . . . . 160 A2
　Salthouse NR25 . . . . 8 B6
　Shotesham NR15 . . . . . . 107 E8
　Somerleyton, Ashby &
　Herringfleet NR32 . . . . . . 94 A1
　Terrington St Clement NR34 42 B6
　Walpole Cross Keys PE14 . . 41 F5
　Wells-next-the-Sea NR23 . 136 D4
Market Mews PE13 . . . . . 152 C5
Market Pl
　Aylsham NR11 . . . . 150 C6
　Burnham Westgate PE31 . 135 C3
　Diss IP22 . . . . 177 D4
　Downham Market PE38 . . 172 C5
　2 East Dereham NR19 . . . 154 D5
　Fakenham NR21 . . . . . . 141 B4
　Great Yarmouth NR30 . . . 169 C4
　22 Harleston IP20 . . . . . 122 D2
　Holt NR25 . . . . 137 B6
　4 Loddon NR14 . . . . 92 A1
　North Walsham NR28 . . . 151 C5
　Reepham NR10 . . . . 149 B4
　Swaffham PE37 . . . . 153 C4
　1 Thetford IP24 . . . . . . 176 C4
　14 Winterton-on-Sea NR39 58 B6
　Wisbech PE13 . . . . 152 C5
　1 Wymondham NR18 . . . 173 C4
Market Rd
　Burgh Castle NR31 . . . . . . 94 B8
　Potter Heigham NR29 . . . . 56 E6
Market Rd Pl **27** NR30 . . 169 D4
Market Row **11** NR30 . . . 169 C4
Market St
　East Harling NR16 . . . . . 118 C5
　15 King's Lynn PE30 . . . . 146 E5
　North Walsham NR28 . . . 151 C5
　Shipdham IP25 . . . . 67 C2
　Tunstead NR12 . . . . 37 F1
　18 Wisbech PE13 . . . . . . 152 C5
Market Way NR18 . . . . . . 173 B4
MARKET WESTON IP22 . . 127 E4
Market Weston Rd IP22 . . 127 E3
Mark La IP27 . . . . 115 C6
Mark Lemmon Cl **2** NR4 . 89 C8
Mark's Cl La NR9 . . . . 52 A7
Markshall Farm Rd NR14 . 89 E7
Markshall La NR14 . . . . . . 89 F7
Marland Rd **4** NR8 . . . . 155 D2
Marlborough Ct PE13 . . . 152 A4
Marlborough Rd NR3 . . . . 162 E8
Marlborough Sq NR30 . . . 169 E4
Marlborough Terr NR30 . . 169 E4
Marle Ct NR31 . . . . 170 C4
Marle Pit Cl NR16 . . . . . . 119 E7
Marl Hill Rd NR9 . . . . 51 F3
Marlinge Pl NR26 . . . . . . 138 F5
MARLINGFORD PE30 . . . . 70 A4
Marlingford Rd
　Easton NR9 . . . . 160 A2
　Marlingford NR9 . . . . 69 F4
Marlingford Sports Club
　NR9 . . . . 70 B4
Marlingford Way NR9 . . . . 70 B5
Marlow Cl NR3 . . . . 158 E3
Marlpit La NR15 . . . . 106 F6
Marl Pit La NR5 . . . . 161 C8
Marlpit Rd
　Hempstead NR25 . . . . 19 E7
　Thompson IP24 . . . . 102 A7
Marram Dr NR30 . . . . 168 E8
Marrams Ave NR27 . . . . . 139 A7
Marram Way NR11 . . . . . 133 B6
Marriott Cl NR2 . . . . 162 C7
Marriott Chase NR8 . . . . 155 E1
Marriotts Way **3** NR26 . 138 D7
Marriott Way NR4 . . . . . . 142 A5
Marryat Rd NR7 . . . . 159 C1
Marryats Loke **3** NR25 . . 7 A4
Marshall Cl
　Norwich NR5 . . . . 161 B8
　13 Spixworth NR10 . . . . . 54 A2
Marshall Rd NR3 . . . . 158 B3
Marshall St **8** PE30 . . . 146 E5
MARSHAM NR10 . . . . 150 D1
Marsham Prim Sch
　NR10 . . . . 150 C1
Marsh Cl **7** NR29 . . . . . . 57 D5
Marshgate NR28 . . . . 151 E6
Marsh La
　Aldeby NR34 . . . . 111 A6
　Bracon Ash NR14 . . . . 89 A2
　Burgh Castle NR31 . . . . . . 94 A8
　Carlton Colville NR33 . . . 111 F2
　3 Earsham NR35 . . . . . . 123 F8
　King's Lynn PE30 . . . . . . 146 D5
　5 New Buckenham NR16 . 104 F1
　North Cove NR34 . . . . . . 111 B1
　Somerleyton, Ashby &
　Herringfleet NR32 . . . . . . 111 C8
　Tharston & Hapton NR15 . 106 C8
　Wells-next-the-Sea NR23 . 136 D5
　Wiveton NR25 . . . . 7 E6
　Worlingham NR34 . . . . . 110 F1
　Wortham IP22 . . . . 129 C3
Marshland High Sch PE14 59 B8
MARSHLAND ST JAMES
　PE14 . . . . 60 A4
Marshland St James VC Prim
　Sch PE14 . . . . 60 A4
Marshland Smeeth & Fen
　Mus★ PE14 . . . . 60 C6
Marsh Loke NR28 . . . . 23 D1
Marsh Rd
　Cantley NR13 . . . . 92 D6

Marsh Rd continued
　Fleggburgh NR29 . . . . 75 C8
　Fritton & St Olaves NR31 . . 93 E3
　Great Yarmouth NR31 . . . 169 B3
　Halvergate NR13 . . . . 75 A1
　North Wootton PE30 . . . . 148 A6
　Outwell PE14 . . . . 77 F8
　Potter Heigham NR29 . . . . 57 A6
　Repps with Bastwick NR29 . 56 F4
　South Walsham NR13 . . . . 74 B8
　Terrington St Clement
　PE34 . . . . 144 F6
　Thurne NR29 . . . . 56 E3
　Upton with Fishley NR13 . 166 B8
　Walpole PE14 . . . . 41 C4
　Wroxham/Hoveton NR12 . 164 D5
MARSH SIDE PE31 . . . . 3 C7
Marsh Side PE31 . . . . 3 B7
Marsh The PE14 . . . . 41 C4
Marsh Wlk PE13 . . . . 152 D5
Marston Cl **3** NR4 . . . . . 89 C8
Marston La **10** NR4 . . . . . 89 C8
Marston Moor **7** NR7 . . . 72 D4
MARTHAM NR29 . . . . 57 D5
Martham Broad National
　Nature Resrve★ NR29 . . . 57 D7
Martham Fst Sch NR29 . . . 57 D5
Martham Rd
　Martham NR29 . . . . 57 F4
　Rollesby NR29 . . . . 57 D3
　Somerton NR29 . . . . 57 E6
Martin Cl
　Brandon IP27 . . . . 175 E3
　1 Great Yarmouth NR31 . . 94 C7
　Norwich NR7 . . . . 159 B4
　3 Weybourne NR25 . . . . . 8 F5
Martineau La NR1 . . . . . . 162 F1
Martin Rd
　Diss IP22 . . . . 177 E4
　Harleston IP20 . . . . 122 E2
Marvell Gn **10** NR7 . . . . 72 D5
Marwood Cl NR18 . . . . . . 173 B3
Mary Chapman Cl **31** NR7 . 72 D4
Mary Chapman Ct NR3 . . 178 A3
Maryland NR21 . . . . 136 D5
Mary Unwin Rd NR19 . . . 154 D4
Masefield Dr PE38 . . . . . 172 D5
Masefield Mews NR19 . . . 154 C7
Masefield Rd IP22 . . . . . . 177 E4
Masefield Wlk **8** IP24 . . 176 E6
Mashs Row NR11 . . . . . . 150 D8
Mason Cl **11** PE33 . . . . . 43 F2
Mason Rd
　Norwich NR6 . . . . 158 B3
　5 Swanton Morley NR20 . . 50 B3
Masons Dr PE37 . . . . 65 F4
Masquers Cl NR31 . . . . . . 170 C2
Massey Ct **2** NR21 . . . . 141 C3
Massingham Rd
　Castle Acre PE32 . . . . . . 46 F2
　Grimston PE31 . . . . 28 C1
　Norwich NR3 . . . . 158 E1
Mast Cl **18** NR33 . . . . . 111 F1
Masters Ct NR28 . . . . . . 151 D5
Mather La IP20 . . . . 122 B1
MATLASKE NR11 . . . . 20 D5
Matlock Rd **1** NR1 . . . . 163 B5
Matthews Cl **4** NR15 . . 106 F6
Matthews Ct PE34 . . . . . . 68 E5
MATTISHALL NR20 . . . . . . 68 F7
MATTISHALL BURGH
　NR20 . . . . 68 F7
Mattishall La
　Hockering NR20 . . . . 69 A7
　Mattishall NR20 . . . . 69 A7
Mattishall Prim Sch NR20 68 F5
Mattishall Rd
　Dereham NR20 . . . . 68 B8
　East Tuddenham NR20 . . . 69 B6
　Garvestone NR9 . . . . 68 D2
　Honingham NR9 . . . . 69 D6
　Runhall NR9 . . . . 69 A3
Maud St NR2 . . . . 162 B6
Maud Terr NR30 . . . . 169 D6
Maurice Gaymer Rd
　NR17 . . . . 174 D4
MAUTBY NR29 . . . . 75 F7
Mautby La NR29 . . . . 75 F6
Mavish Cl NR5 . . . . 161 A6
Max Carter Cl NR28 . . . . . 38 A4
Maybank NR28 . . . . 151 D7
May Cl **17** NR5 . . . . 161 B8
Mayes Cl **7** NR5 . . . . . . 161 B8
Mayfield Ave NR6 . . . . . . 158 B4
Mayfield Dr NR27 . . . . . . 139 B5
Mayfield Way NR28 . . . . . 151 D7
Mayflower Ave PE30 . . . . 146 F7
Mayflower Rd **1** PE13 . . 152 E3
Mayflower Way **14** IP20 . 122 D1
Maygrove Rd **5** NR30 . . 169 D5
MAYPOLE GREEN NR34 . . 110 C6
Mayton Ave **2** NR12 . . . 54 A4
Mdws The **2** PE31 . . . . . 12 D4
Mead Cl NR10 . . . . 36 E1
Meadow Way PE14 . . . . . 146 B4
Meadowbrook Cl **5** NR1 162 F3
Meadow Brown Way **9**
　NR18 . . . . 173 E4

Meadow Cl continued
　2 Norwich NR14 . . . . . . 163 B2
　Shipdham IP25 . . . . 67 D2
　Thurlton NR14 . . . . 92 F1
Meadow Cotts PE32 . . . . . 48 B6
Meadowcroft NR29 . . . . . 168 C8
Meadow Ct
　Fakenham NR21 . . . . . . 141 C4
　Great Yarmouth NR31 . . . 171 C8
Meadow Dr
　11 Beetley NR19 . . . . 49 C3
　Norwich NR9 . . . . 154 C4
　1 Gressenhall NR20 . . . . 49 C3
　Lackenheath IP27 . . . . . 113 E2
　Mundesley NR11 . . . . . . 143 C5
　Wroxham/Hoveton NR12 . 164 D4
Meadow Farm Dr NR4 . . . 89 B7
Meadow Farm La NR10 . . . 53 E2
Meadowgate La PE14 . . . 152 E2
Meadowgate Sch PE13 . . 152 E3
Meadow Gdns NR6 . . . . . 158 F4
Meadow Gr
　North Runcton PE33 . . . . . 44 A2
　26 Watton IP25 . . . . 84 D3
Meadow La
　Briston NR24 . . . . 142 B5
　Carbrooke IP25 . . . . 85 A5
　Kelling NR25 . . . . 8 D5
　Norwich NR12 . . . . 163 F6
　5 Snettisham PE31 . . . . . 12 D4
Meadowland Dr **17** NR31 . 94 C6
Meadow Loke **2** NR20 . . 50 E7
Meadow Patch NR28 . . . . 151 C6
Meadow Rd
　Bungay NR35 . . . . 124 B8
　Cromer NR27 . . . . 139 B6
　Heacham PE31 . . . . 133 D5
　King's Lynn PE30 . . . . . . 148 C2
　Narborough PE32 . . . . . . 63 E7
　Norwich NR5 . . . . 157 A2
Meadowrise NR21 . . . . 15 E6
Meadow Rise NR29 . . . . . 167 A8
Meadow Rise Ave NR12 . . 162 A4
Meadow Rise Cl NR12 . . . 162 A4
Meadow Rise Rd NR12 . . . 162 A4
Meadowside IP22 . . . . . . 128 B6
Meadows The
　Aylsham NR11 . . . . 150 C7
　6 Hingham NR9 . . . . 86 C4
　South Wootton PE30 . . . . 148 B2
　Thetford IP24 . . . . 176 E4
　Thurton NR14 . . . . 91 D4
Meadowsweet **13** NR10 . . 53 A3
Meadowsweet Dr NR26 . . 138 B6
Meadowsweet Rd **2**
　NR18 . . . . 173 E4
Meadow Vale NR5 . . . . . . 157 A3
Meadow View NR13 . . . . . 165 D4
Meadow View Terr NR11 . 150 B5
Meadway Cl
　East Carleton NR14 . . . . . 88 F5
　Horsford NR10 . . . . 53 B3
　Norwich NR6 . . . . 157 F5
　Poringland NR14 . . . . 90 C4
　Sheringham NR26 . . . . . 138 C6
Meadway **13** NR4 . . . . . . 89 B8
Mear Gdns NR11 . . . . 163 B6
Mears Cnr NR1 . . . . 105 B5
Medeswell **2** NR29 . . . . 167 B7
Medeswell Cl NR13 . . . . . 165 C5
Medway Cl PE13 . . . . 152 C5
Meer Dyke La PE14 . . . . . . 59 D5
Meeting Hill Rd NR28 . . . . 38 A7
MEETING HOUSE HILL
　NR28 . . . . 38 B7
Meeting House Hill Rd
　NR28 . . . . 38 B6
Melbourne Rd
　North Walsham NR28 . . . 151 D6
　4 Sheringham NR26 . . . 138 D7
Melford Bride Rd IP24 . . . 176 D4
Melford Cl PE30 . . . . 148 E1
Melford Comm **4** IP24 . . 176 D4
Melford Ct **3** IP24 . . . . . 176 D4
MELLIS IP23 . . . . 129 E1
Mellisash Rd IP23 . . . . . . 129 D1
Mellis Rd
　Thrandeston IP21 . . . . . . 129 F2
　Wortham IP22 . . . . 129 C3
　Yaxley IP23 . . . . 130 A1
Melrose Dr NR11 . . . . 11 A2
Melrose Rd NR4 . . . . 162 A3
Melrose Terr **8** NR30 . . 169 D2
Melton Cl NR18 . . . . 173 B6
MELTON CONSTABLE
　NR24 . . . . 142 B5
Melton Constable Hall★
　NR24 . . . . 18 D2
Melton Ct NR9 . . . . 88 C8
Melton Dr
　Hunstanton PE36 . . . . . . 132 C3
　Taverham NR8 . . . . 155 C1
Melton Gate NR18 . . . . . . 173 B5
Melton Rd
　Hindolveston NR20 . . . . . 33 D8
　Wymondham NR18 . . . . . 173 B5
Melton St NR24 . . . . 142 A5
Melville Rd IP24 . . . . 116 C5
Memorial Way
　Thorpe St Andrew NR7 . . . 72 E4
　Watton IP25 . . . . 84 D4
MENDHAM IP20 . . . . 123 A1
Mendham Cl
　10 Harleston IP20 . . . . . 122 D2
　3 Norwich NR1 . . . . . . 162 E2

Mendham La
30 Harleston IP20......122 D2
St Mary, South Elmham
  otherwise Homersfield
  IP20...............123 B3
Mendham Prim Sch
  IP20...............123 A2
Mercedes Ave PE36....132 D2
Merchants Ct NR27...139 C7
Merchant Way NR6....158 A4
Mere CI IP25..........84 C4
Meredith Rd NR6.....157 E6
Mere Manor Ct IP22..177 E4
Mere Plot Dro PE33....62 E5
Mere Rd
  Scoulton NR9.........85 E4
  Stow Bedon NR17....102 E7
Mereside NR15.........90 F2
Mere St IP22..........177 D4
Mergate La NR14.......89 A2
Meridian Way NR7......72 E3
Merlewood IP21......121 C1
Merlin Ave NR7......159 B4
Merlin CI NR10......158 D7
Merlin Mews NR7....159 C4
Merriman Rd 13 NR29...57 C4
Merrivale Model Village*
  NR30..............169 E2
Merrow Gdns 7 NR4...89 C8
Merryweather CI 3
  NR15..............170 E3
Merryweather Rd 9
  PE13..............153 C3
MERTON IP25..........84 C1
Merton Ave NR31....170 A3
Merton Rd
  Norwich NR2........162 A7
  Watton IP25..........84 D2
Metcalf Ave PE30....146 D2
Metcalf CI 4 NR3....157 F1
Meteor CI NR14......158 D7
Methuen Ave PE30...147 A6
METHWOLD IP26.......99 A5
Methwold High Sch IP26..99 A4
METHWOLD HYTHE IP26..98 E5
Methwold Prim Sch IP26..99 A5
Methwold Rd
  Methwold IP26........98 E5
  Northwold IP26........99 C7
METTINGHAM NR35...124 E8
METTON NR11.........21 C8
Metton Rd
  Felbrigg NR11........139 A2
  Roughton NR11........21 D8
Mews Ct 7 IP25........67 C2
Mews The
  Great Yarmouth NR31..170 C1
  2 Norwich NR2......162 C4
Micawber Ave 2 NR30..170 D8
Michaels Ct NR13....154 C5
Midden Sta The NR23..136 F4
Middlebrook Way
  Cromer NR27.........139 A6
  Runton NR27..........10 C4
Middle Dro
  Denver PE38..........79 B4
  Marshland St James PE14..60 C2
  Stow Bardolph PE14....78 D8
Middlegate NR30......169 D2
Middle Gates Dro PE14..60 B8
MIDDLE HARLING NR16..118 B4
Middle Hill
  Alby with Thwaite NR11..21 A5
  Reedham NR13........92 F4
Middle La NR34......111 D4
Middlemarch Rd 5
  NR19..............154 D3
Middle Mkt Rd NR30..169 D4
Middle Rd
  Blo' Norton IP22....128 C6
  Docking PE31........134 E4
  Earsham IP20........123 C8
  Great & Little Plumstead
  NR13..............72 F5
  Hardingham NR9......86 E8
  Morning Thorpe NR15..107 B8
  Shouldham Thorpe PE33..62 C2
  Terrington St Clement PE34..42 B8
Middle Rd W 3 NR30..169 D1
Middle Rd E 3 NR30..169 D1
Middlesex La NR13....166 C3
Middle St NR11.......11 E1
Middlestone CI NR31..170 C4
MIDDLETON PE32.......44 C3
Middleton Ave NR20....50 B4
Middleton CI
  Norwich NR3.........158 C3
  2 Sheringham NR26..138 C5
Middleton Cres NR5..156 E2
Middleton CI 4 NR18..173 B4
Middleton Gdns NR3..170 C5
Middleton Prim Sch PE32..44 C2
Middleton Rd NR31....170 C4
Middleton's Ct NR6...157 E4
Middleton's La NR6...157 F5
Middleton St NR18....173 B4
Middle Wall NR29.....167 A6
Middlewood 2 PE30...147 C4
Midland CI
  Caister-on-Sea NR30..168 F5
  1 Great Yarmouth NR30..169 D5
Midland Rd NR28....151 C4
Midland St NR2......162 C7
Midland Wlk NR2....162 C7
Mid Norfolk Rly* NR19..154 C6
Mid Yare National Nature
  Reserve* NR13....165 D1
Mikanda CI PE14.....152 C2

Mildenhall Rd CB7....112 B3
MILE CROSS NR3.....158 A2
Mile Cross La NR6...158 C4
Mile Cross Mid Sch NR3..158 B1
Mile Cross Rd NR3...162 B8
Mile End IP27.......175 A1
Mile End CI NR4......162 A3
Mile End Rd
  Littleport CB7........112 A3
  Norwich NR4.........162 A3
MILEHAM PE32.........48 D6
Mileham Prim Sch PE32..48 D6
Mileham Rd
  Beeston with Bittering
  PE32..............48 C3
  Litcham PE32.........48 A4
Mile Rd
  Carleton Rode NR16..105 A5
  Garvestone NR9.......68 A1
Milestone CI NR5....156 F2
Milestone La NR18....87 A4
Milford Rd 5 NR2...162 B5
Millard CI NR28.....151 A6
Mill Bank PE14........59 F7
Mill CI
  Aylsham NR11.......150 A6
  2 Blofield Heath NR13..73 D6
  Hempton NR21.......141 A3
  Hethersett NR9.......88 C7
  Hickling NR12........39 F2
  Kirby Row NR35......109 E3
  Mattishall NR20.......68 F5
  Norwich NR1.........162 E3
  Poringland NR14......90 C5
  Pulham Market IP21..121 E5
  8 Salhouse NR13......55 A1
  Thurton NR14.........91 C4
  Wisbech PE13........152 C6
Mill Cnr NR9..........86 C4
Mill Comm NR14.......91 C4
MILL COMMON NR14....91 C4
Mill Comm Rd NR28..23 E2
Mill Cres NR13......166 B4
Millcroft NR13......158 E1
Mill Croft CI NR5...156 E1
Mill Ct
  Fakenham NR21.......141 B3
  Holt NR25...........137 B6
  Wells-next-the-Sea NR23..136 D5
Mill Drift
  Beeston with Bittering
  PE32..............48 C3
  Hockwold cum Wilton
  IP26..............114 A7
Mill Dro
  Gooderstone PE33.....81 F4
  Middleton PE32.......44 D2
  Southery PE38........97 A5
Millennium Plain NR2..178 A2
Millennium Way PE34..146 A5
Miller CI 7 NR19....154 C4
Miller's Breck NR8...155 D1
Millers CI NR35.....124 B8
Millers Dr IP21......121 B1
Millers Gn 43 IP20..122 D2
Millers La
  Harpley PE31.........29 D4
  Norwich NR3........158 D1
Miller's La
  2 Thetford IP24....176 C4
  Wimbotsham PE34......79 E8
Millers Sq NR17.....174 C5
Millers Way 1 NR10...53 B3
Millers Wlk NR11...141 C3
Mill Farm Nurseries
  PE37..............153 B2
Millfield
  Ashill IP25...........84 A8
  Eye IP23............130 B1
Millfield CI 5 NR13...73 D6
Mill Field CI PE14....42 C1
Millfield La PE33......43 F3
Millfield Prim Sch NR28..151 B3
Millfield Rd
  Barningham IP31......127 D3
  North Walsham NR28..151 B4
Millfields 2 NR15...107 C5
Millfleet 4 PE30....146 E4
MILLGATE NR11......150 D7
Millgate NR11.......150 D7
Millgate St IP26......99 A5
Mill Gdns
  Bedingham NR35.....108 B4
  Horsford NR10........53 B3
Mill Gn
  Burnham Market PE31..135 D3
  Stoke Holy Cross NR14..89 F4
MILL GREEN IP22....120 E3
Mill Hill
  Bradenham IP25.......66 E3
  Bramerton NR14.......90 F8
  Brancaster PE31.......3 B6
  Brandon IP27.......175 D3
  2 Horning NR12......55 E4
  Mettingham NR35...109 D1
  Norwich NR3........158 C2
  Roughton NR11......139 A1
  Salhouse NR13........55 B1
  Strumpshaw NR13.....73 F2
Millhill La NR18.......86 F2
Mill Hill Rd
  Boughton PE33........80 F5
  Norwich NR2........162 B5
Mill Houses PE30....146 F6
Millicent Oliver CI 11
  IP24..............176 D7
Millington Ct 6 IP24..176 D4

Mill La
  Acle NR13...........166 C3
  All Saints & St Nicholas, South
  Elmham IP20.........123 E1
  Aslacton NR15.......106 A1
  Attleborough NR17...174 F7
  Aylsham NR11.......150 B6
  Bacton/Walcott NR12...23 E4
  Barnham IP24.......125 E6
  Bircham PE31.........13 F3
  Blackborough End PE32...44 C1
  Briston NR24........142 F3
  Brooke NR15........108 A8
  Burnham Thorpe PE31...4 D4
  Carbrooke IP25.......85 B4
  Catfield NR29.........56 C7
  Claxton NR14.........91 E6
  Clenchwarton PE34..145 F6
  Crimplesham PE33.....80 B7
  Cromer NR27..........10 B5
  Dereham NR19......154 A8
  Docking PE31........134 E4
  Downham Market PE38..172 D7
  Ellingham NR35......109 E3
  Felthorpe NR10.....155 C8
  Fleggburgh NR29......57 B1
  Foulsham NR20.......33 D4
  Garboldisham IP22...128 A7
  Great Ellingham NR17..103 D7
  Great Massingham PE32...29 D2
  Great Yarmouth NR31..94 C7
  Haddiscoe NR14......110 D3
  Hindringham NR21....17 E8
  Hockering NR20.......69 B7
  Hockwold cum Wilton
  IP26..............114 A7
  Hoe NR20............49 D3
  Honingham NR9.......69 E6
  Hopton IP22.........127 F7
  Horsford NR10........53 B3
  Horsham St Faith & Newton St
  Faith NR10..........53 E2
  Keswick NR4..........89 D7
  King's Lynn PE30....147 B8
  Kirby Bedon NR14.....90 E7
  Long Stratton NR15..106 F3
  Morley NR18..........87 A3
  Newton Flotman NR15...89 E2
  Norwich NR3........158 D1
  Ormesby St Margaret with
  Scratby NR29.........58 A1
  Ovington IP25........84 E5
  Postwick with Witton NR13..73 A3
  Pulham Market IP21..121 E5
  Redgrave IP22.......128 C5
  Repps with Bastwick NR29..57 B3
  Rickinghall Inferior IP22..128 D2
  Rocklands NR17......103 C7
  Seething NR15........91 C1
  Shelton NR15........122 B8
  1 Southery PE38......97 B5
  St John, Ilketshall NR34..124 C6
  14 Sutton Bridge PE12...41 B8
  Swaffham PE37.......153 C2
  Syderstone PE31......15 B3
  Thetford IP24.......176 D3
  Tilney St Lawrence PE14..42 C2
  Tunstead NR12........38 A3
  Walpole Highway PE14..59 F7
  Walsingham NR22.....16 F7
  West Walton PE14.....59 C8
  Weybread IP21......131 F7
  Wreningham NR16.....88 D1
  Yaxham NR19.........68 B5
Mill Loke 8 NR12......55 E4
Millmarsh Dro PE27..113 D2
Mill Orch IP21......121 E5
Mill Pightle NR11...150 B6
Mill Pool La NR35..109 D2
Mill Rd
  Alburgh IP20.........122 E6
  Aldborough NR11.......21 A6
  All Saints South Elmham
  IP19..............123 E1
  Ashby St Mary NR14...91 C4
  Aylsham NR11.......150 C6
  Bacton NR28.........23 A1
  Banham NR16.......119 D7
  Barnham Broom NR9....69 B2
  Barningham IP31.....127 C3
  Barton Turf NR12......38 E1
  Bergh Apton NR14.....91 A4
  Bintree NR20.........33 C3
  Blofield Heath NR13...73 D6
  Botesdale IP22.......128 F2
  Brancaster PE31.......3 B6
  Briston NR24........142 F3
  Brockdish IP21......131 B7
  Burgh Castle NR31....94 A7
  Burgh St Peter NR34..111 B4
  Burnham Market PE31..135 E4
  Burston & Shimpling IP22..120 E2
  Carleton Rode NR16..105 A4
  Colby NR11...........36 F7
  Coltishall NR12.......54 C6
  Cromer NR27.........139 C5
  Dersingham PE31.....140 F5
  Dilham NR28.........38 D4
  East Ruston NR12......24 A4
  Emneth PE14..........59 D2
  Forncett NR16.......106 B3
  Foxley NR20..........50 D8
  Freethorpe NR13......92 F8
  Frettenham NR12......54 A4
  Great Yarmouth NR31..169 B8
  Gresham NR11.........9 D1
  Halvergate NR13......74 F1
  Hardingham NR9......86 E8

Mill Rd continued

  Harpley PE31..........29 D4
  Hempnall NR15.......107 C5
  Hemsby NR29.........58 A4
  7 Hethersett NR9.....88 C7
  Honington IP31......126 D1
  Kirby Row NR35......109 D3
  Lakenheath IP27.....113 E1
  Little Melton NR9....160 B2
  Loddon NR14..........92 A1
  Long Stratton NR15..107 A2
  Marlingford NR9......70 A3
  Marsham NR10........36 C2
  Mattishall NR20.......68 E6
  Mautby NR29.........75 E7
  North Walsham NR28..151 D3
  Old Buckenham NR17..104 C1
  Potter Heigham NR29...56 F5
  Reepham NR10.......149 B3
  Reepham NR10.......149 B2
  Repps with Bastwick NR29..57 A4
  Ryburgh NR21.........32 C6
  Salhouse NR13........55 A1
  Shelton NR15........122 B8
  Shipdham IP25........67 B2
  Shouldham Thorpe PE33..62 C2
  Stalham NR12.........39 A3
  Stoke Holy Cross NR14..89 F4
  Stokesby with Herringby
  NR29..............75 A6
  Surlingham NR14......91 B8
  Sutton NR12..........39 C3
  Terrington St John PE14..42 B1
  Thelnetham IP22.....128 B5
  Thompson IP24.......102 A7
  Thurlton NR14.......110 D8
  Tibenham NR16......120 D8
  Tivetshall St Mary NR15..121 B5
  Topcroft NR35.......107 F4
  Walpole St Andrew PE14..41 E3
  Watlington PE34......61 D8
  Watton IP25..........84 D3
  Wells-next-the-Sea NR23..136 B5
  West Walton PE14.....59 B8
  Weybread IP21......131 F8
  Whissonsett NR20.....31 D2
  Wiggenhall St Germans
  PE34..............43 C1
  Wiggenhall St Mary Magdalen
  PE34..............61 B5
  Winfarthing IP22....120 B8
Mill Rd S IP22......128 F2
Mill Reach NR10......36 F1
Mill Row NR11......150 D7
Mills CI NR8.........155 C1
Millside
  Hales NR14.........109 F8
  Stalham NR12.........39 B3
Mill St
  Bradenham IP25.......66 E3
  Elsing NR20..........50 F4
  Gimingham NR11......22 E7
  Holt NR25...........137 B6
  Horsham St Faith NR10..53 E2
  Lamas NR10..........36 F1
  Mattishall NR20.......68 F5
  1 Necton IP25........84 D3
  Swanton Morley NR20..50 B4
MILL STREET NR20.....50 E4
Millview NR29......167 A3
Mill View
  Barnham Broom NR9....69 B2
  Saham Toney IP25.....84 C5
  Sedgeford PE36........13 A7
Mill View CI NR11...143 D5
Mill View Mid Sch NR5..161 C8
Millway NR13.......173 B6
Mill Way PE14.........77 B8
Millway Ave IP22....177 C6
Millway La
  Palgrave IP22........177 B2
  Wortham IP22.......129 D5
Milne Rd PE13.......152 C4
Milnes Way 3 NR33..111 F1
Milton Ave NR20....146 F5
Milton CI
  East Dereham NR19..154 C7
  Norwich NR1........162 E3
  3 Thetford IP24.....176 E6
Milton Rd
  Great Yarmouth NR30..169 D8
  3 Swanton Morley NR20..50 B3
Milton Way 1 PE38..172 D6
Milverton Rd 1 NR1..162 F3
Mindhams Yd NR23..136 C6
Mingay Rd PE14......176 B2
Minion CI 8 NR7......72 D4
Minsmere Rd 7 NR8..94 A6
Minster CI PE30.....147 C5
Mintergate IP24....176 C4
Miriam CI NR29.....168 E8
Misburgh Way NR31..171 E4
MISERY CORNER IP20..122 F8
Mission La
  Docking PE31........134 E4
  Fakenham NR21......141 E4
Mission Pl NR30....169 D6
Mission Rd
  Diss IP22............177 F3
  3 Great Yarmouth NR31..169 B4
  Rackheath NR13.......72 E8
Mitchell Ct 4 NR5...160 F8
Mitre Ct NR3........158 A3
Mitre Tavern Yd 4
  NR28..............151 C5
Mitre Yd 9 NR28....151 C5

Moat Rd
  3 Great Yarmouth
  NR30..............169 C5
  Terrington St Clement
  PE34..............144 B1
Modney Bridge Rd PE38..96 F8
Mokyll Croft NR8...155 D2
Moles La NR34......124 D5
Molls Dro PE14........77 C7
Monastery The NR3...178 B3
Money Bank PE13....152 E4
Moneyhill La NR9......86 C3
Moneypot La IP22...128 E5
Monkhams Dr 9 IP25...84 E3
Monks CI PE31........14 D5
Monksgate IP24.....176 B4
Mons Ave NR1.......163 A8
Montagu CI PE37....153 C3
Montagu Dr 4 IP27..114 E1
Montague Rd NR26..138 C7
Montcalm Rd NR1...163 B6
Mont Cross 8 NR8...155 D2
Montgomery CI 2 NR5..160 F7
Montgomery Way PE30..147 D4
Montpelier Dr 1 IP24..116 A1
Montrose Ct 1 NR47...72 D4
Monument Rd NR30..170 E7
Moorditch La PE34....42 E2
Moore Ave NR6......158 F5
Moorend La NR21......32 D7
Moorfield Rd 3 NR20..68 E6
MOORGATE NR19....154 D3
Moorgate Rd
  East Dereham NR19..154 D3
  Hindringham NR21....17 E8
Moorhouse CI NR10..149 C5
Moorings The PE33....81 A2
Moor La
  Cranworth IP25.......85 D7
  Elsing NR20..........50 F3
  Fransham NR19......66 A7
  Scalthorpe NR21.....16 B2
  Stalham NR12........39 C3
Moorland Ct NR7....159 A2
Moorland Way 3 NR31..94 A5
Moor Rd
  Burston & Shimpling
  IP21..............121 B2
  Stalham NR12.........39 C3
Moors The NR8.......155 F2
Moor The NR10......149 E5
Morar Dr NR17......174 E6
Morello CI NR4......161 E5
Morgans Way NR10....53 C8
Morgan Way NR5....160 F8
Morgrove La NR29....57 D6
Morley CE Prim Sch NR18..87 A2
Morleyfield La NR18..87 A3
Morley La NR18.......87 C2
Morley Rd
  Beighton NR13........74 D2
  Deopham NR18........86 E1
  Sheringham NR26...138 D6
Morley Rd N NR26...138 D6
MORLEY ST BOTOLPH
  NR18..............87 B2
Morley St NR3......162 F8
Mormor La IP21.....131 C8
MORNINGTHORPE NR15..107 A3
Mornington Rd NR2..162 A4
Morris CI
  3 Norwich NR5......161 B8
  8 Stoke Holy Cross NR14..89 F4
Morris Dr NR13......165 A8
Morrison CI NR28...151 B5
Morris Rd NR28.....151 B4
Morris St NR26......138 D7
Morse Ave NR1......163 A8
Morse CI
  Brundall NR13......165 D3
  Great Witchingham NR9..51 D5
Morse CI NR30.......168 D6
Morse Rd NR1......163 C7
MORSTON NR25........7 B6
Morston Chase NR25....6 F6
Morston Rd
  Blakeney NR25........7 C6
  Stiffkey NR23........6 C2
Mortimer CI NR17...174 F6
MORTON NR9.........52 A4
Morton CI 1 NR11...150 D6
Morton Cres 22 NR31...94 C7
Morton La NR9.......51 F3
Morton Peto CI NR32..111 D7
Morton Peto Rd NR31..170 B8
Morton Rd NR11.....150 C6
Mosely Ct NR5.......160 E8
Mossfield CI NR1....163 B8
Mother Julian CI 8
  IP24..............176 D7
Mother Quy's IP24..115 C1
Mottram CI NR5.....161 D6
Motum Rd NR5......161 C7
Moulton Rd
  Halvergate NR13......74 F1
  Tivetshall St Margaret
  NR15..............121 A7
MOULTON ST MARY
  NR13..............74 D2
Mountain's Rd IP24...19 F1
Mountbatten CI 8 IP24..176 E6
Mountbatten Dr
  2 East Dereham NR19..154 C6
  Old Catton NR6.....159 A6
  Wisbech PE13.......152 A7

Mountbatten Rd
 Bungay NR35 . . . . .124 A7
 Dersingham PE31 . . . . . .140 C3
Mountbatten Way NR30 .168 B6
Mount Cl
 Brandon IP27 . . . . .175 D2
 Swaffham PE37 . . . . .153 A5
Mount Dr PE13 . . . . .152 E4
Monteney Cl NR7 . . . . . . .159 A4
Mountergate NR1 . . . . . . .178 B2
Mountfield Ave
 Hellesdon NR6 . . . . .157 F4
 Norwich NR6 . . . . .158 A4
Mount Pk Cl PE32 . . . . . . .44 C3
MOUNT PLEASANT
 NR17 . . . . .103 C5
Mount Pleasant
 Diss IP22 . . . . .177 D5
 Little Walsingham NR22 . .16 F8
 Norwich NR2 . . . . .162 B4
Mount Pleasant Rd PE13 .152 C7
Mount Rd IP27 . . . . .175 D2
Mount St
 Cromer NR27 . . . . .139 B7
 Diss IP22 . . . . .177 D5
 King's Lynn PE30 . . . . . . .146 F4
Mount Surrey **4** NR18 .173 C6
Mount Tumbledown Cl **7**
 PE12 . . . . .41 B8
Mousehold Ave NR3 . . . . .163 A8
Mousehold St NR3 . . . . . .162 F8
Mousehold La NR7 . . . . . .159 A3
Mousehold St NR13 . . . . .178 C4
Mowles Rd NR20 . . . . .68 C8
Moyse's Bank
 Emneth Hungate PE14 . . .59 F2
 Marshland St James PE14 .60 A2
Muck La NR13 . . . . .72 F8
Mucklebrough Collection
 The ★ NR25 . . . . .8 E6
MUCKLETON PE31 . . . . . . .3 F2
Mudd's Dro PE14 . . . . . . .77 F2
Mud Rd NR21 . . . . .15 D2
Muir La NR15 . . . . .106 B2
MULBARTON NR14 . . . . . .89 B3
Mulbarton Fst Sch NR14 . .89 A3
Mulbarton Mid Sch NR14 .89 B3
Mulberry Cl
 7 Feltwell IP26 . . . . . . .98 E1
 6 Norwich NR3 . . . . . .178 A3
Mulberry Ct **2** NR8 . . . .155 B2
Mulberry Gr **4** NR31 . . . .94 C6
Mulberry La NR15 . . . . . .107 A3
Mulberry Rd PE30 . . . . . .147 D4
Mullicourt Rd PE14 . . . . . .78 B6
Mumby's Dro PE14 . . . . . .77 E1
MUNDESLEY NR11 . . . . . .143 B5
Mundesley Hospl NR11 . . .22 F7
Mundesley Jun & Fst Sch
 NR11 . . . . .143 B5
Mundesley Maritime Mus★
 NR11 . . . . .143 C6
Mundesley Rd
 Gimingham NR11 . . . . . . .22 E7
 North Walsham NR28 . . . .151 C6
 Overstrand NR27 . . . . . . .11 A3
 Paston NR28 . . . . .143 D3
 Trimingham NR11 . . . . . . .11 E1
 Trunch NR28 . . . . .22 F5
MUNDFORD IP26 . . . . . . .100 B4
Mundford Prim Sch
 IP26 . . . . .100 B4
Mundford Rd
 Thetford IP24 . . . . .176 C6
 Weeting-with-Broomhill
 IP27 . . . . .175 D7
MUNDHAM NR14 . . . . .91 C1
Mundham La NR14 . . . . . .91 D2
Mundham Rd
 Loddon NR14 . . . . .91 E1
 Mundham NR14 . . . . .109 A8
Mundy's Rd IP20 . . . . . . .123 A4
Munhaven Cl NR11 . . . . . .143 C5
Munnings Cl NR14 . . . . . . .89 D4
Munnings Rd NR7 . . . . . . .159 D1
Munson's La IP26 . . . . . . .98 E2
Munson's Pl IP26 . . . . . . .98 E1
Murgot's La PE33 . . . . . . .81 D7
Muriel Kenny Ct 10 NR9 . .88 C7
Muriel Rd NR2 . . . . .162 A4
Muriel Way IP25 . . . . .85 B4
Murrayfield Rd NR6 . . . . .158 B5
Museum Sq PE13 . . . . . . .152 C5
Music House La NR1 . . . . .178 B2
Musketeer Way **22** NR7 . .72 D4
Mus of the Broads The★
 NR12 . . . . .39 B3
Muspole St NR3 . . . . .178 A4
MUSTARD HYRN NR29 . . . .57 C5
Musticott Pl PE13 . . . . . .152 F6
Myles Way PE13 . . . . .152 C8
Myrtle Ave
 Costessey NR8 . . . . .156 F3
 East Dereham NR19 . . . . .154 E4
Myrtle Cl NR31 . . . . .170 C6
Myrtle Rd NR9 . . . . .88 C8

N

Naber Furlong **1** NR8 . .155 E2
Napier Cl PE30 . . . . .147 C5
Napier Pl
 Norwich NR2 . . . . .162 C7
 Thetford IP24 . . . . .176 A1

Naples Cl NR31 . . . . .171 E4
Napoleon Pl **9** NR30 . . .169 D3
NARBOROUGH PE32 . . . . . .63 E7
Narborough Hill PE32 . . . .63 E2
Narborough Rd PE32 . . . . .63 D8
Narborough VC Fst Sch
 PE32 . . . . .63 E7
Narford La PE32 . . . . .45 F2
Narford Rd PE32 . . . . .63 F7
NARROWGATE CORNER
 NR29 . . . . .57 C2
Narrows Trading Est The
 PE30 . . . . .147 A1
Naseby Way **23** NR7 . . . .72 D4
Nash Rd NR10 . . . . .155 C8
Nash's La NR28 . . . . .23 E1
Nasmith Rd NR4 . . . . .161 D1
Naylor Rd **1** NR3 . . . . . .157 F1
Neale Cl NR11 . . . . .150 B6
Neatherd High Sch NR20 .154 F5
Neatherd Moor NR20 . . . .154 F6
Neatherd Rd NR19 . . . . . .154 E5
NEATISHEAD NR12 . . . . . . .55 E7
Neatishead Prim Sch
 NR12 . . . . .55 D7
Neatishead Rd NR12 . . . . .55 E5
NEATON IP25 . . . . .84 E4
Necton CE Fst Sch PE37 . .66 A4
Necton Mid Sch PE37 . . . .66 A4
Necton Rd PE32 . . . . .65 E2
NEEDHAM IP20 . . . . .131 D8
Needham Bank PE14 . . . . .77 C8
Needham Rd IP20 . . . . . . .122 C1
Neil Ave NR5 . . . . .137 B5
Neilsen Cl NR13 . . . . .136 E6
Nelonde Dr **1** NR18 . . . .173 C5
Nelson Ave PE38 . . . . . . .172 B5
Nelson Cl
 Bradenham IP25 . . . . .66 E3
 4 Hethersett NR9 . . . . .88 E8
Nelson Cres PE37 . . . . . . .153 D3
Nelson Ct PE36 . . . . .132 D3
Nelson Fst Sch NR12 . . . .162 B7
Nelson Gdns PE13 . . . . . .152 D6
Nelson Hts NR27 . . . . . . .139 A7
Nelson Pl **3** NR19 . . . . .154 D5
Nelson Rd
 Caister-on-Sea NR30 . . . .168 F4
 Fakenham NR21 . . . . .141 B4
 Great Yarmouth NR31 . . .170 D4
 North Walsham NR28 . . . .151 D5
 Sheringham NR26 . . . . . .138 F7
Nelson Rd Central NR30 .169 D3
Nelson Rd N NR30 . . . . . .169 D5
Nelson Rd S NR30 . . . . . .169 D2
Nelson St
 King's Lynn PE30 . . . . . . .146 D4
 Norwich NR2 . . . . .162 B7
Nelson Way
 Hevingham NR10 . . . . . . .53 B8
 Mundesley NR11 . . . . . . .143 A7
 7 North Walsham NR28 .151 C5
Nenelands PE12 . . . . .41 C8
Nene Mdws PE12 . . . . . . .41 C8
Nene Par PE13 . . . . .152 B6
Nene Quay PE13 . . . . .152 C5
Nene Rd
 Hunstanton PE36 . . . . . . .132 C4
 4 Watlington PE33 . . . . .61 D6
Nene Sch The PE13 . . . . .152 C4
Nethergate St
 Ditchingham NR35 . . . . . .124 A8
 Harpley PE31 . . . . .29 C4
 Hopton IP22 . . . . .127 E6
Nether Row IP24 . . . . . . .176 D3
Netherwood Gn NR1 . . . .162 F2
Nettle Hill E **15** NR30 . . .169 D4
Nettle Hill W NR30 . . . . . .169 D4
Neve's Cl NR13 . . . . .73 F3
Neville Cl
 East Dereham NR19 . . . . .154 E1
 Norwich NR7 . . . . .158 F3
 Saham Toney IP25 . . . . . .84 B5
Neville La PE31 . . . . .133 C6
Neville Rd
 Heacham PE31 . . . . .133 C6
 Norwich NR7 . . . . .159 A3
 Stalham NR12 . . . . .39 C3
Neville St NR2 . . . . .162 C5
Newall Rd **4** IP24 . . . . . .125 F6
Newarch La NR14 . . . . . . .90 E7
Newark Cl NR7 . . . . .72 D4
Newarp Way NR30 . . . . . .168 D8
Newbegin Cl NR1 . . . . . . .163 C7
Newbegin Rd NR1 . . . . . .163 B7
New Bridge La
 Elm PE14 . . . . .59 A1
 Wisbech PE14 . . . . .152 A1
New Bridge Rd PE14 . . . . .77 D5
NEW BUCKENHAM NR16 . .104 F8
Newbury Way NR7 . . . . . .72 D4
Newby Rd **2** PE30 . . . . .147 D6
Newcastle Cl **3** NR7 . . . .72 D4
Newcastle Rd NR30 . . . . .169 D1
NEW CATTON NR3 . . . . . .158 C1
New Cl NR13 . . . . .166 C3
New Coll Cl NR13 . . . . . . .170 B5
Newcombe Cl PE14 . . . . . .42 B1
Newcombe Dr **16** IP26 . .98 E1
New Comm Rd IP22 . . . . .127 F4
NEW COSTESSEY NR5 . . . .157 A1
New Dro **3** NR13 . . . . . .152 D2
New Eccles Hall Sch The
 NR16 . . . . .118 F7
Newell Cresent NR27 . . . .10 A6

New England Way **2**
 IP24 . . . . .116 A1
Newey's Way **2** NR12 . .164 C5
New Fen Dro PE38 . . . . . . .97 A5
Newfen Gravel Dro IP27 .113 D4
Newfields PE32 . . . . .65 C5
Newfound Dr NR4 . . . . . .161 C1
NEWGATE NR25 . . . . .7 E5
Newgate NR35 . . . . .109 C3
NEWGATE CORNER NR29 . .75 C8
Newgate La
 Kirby Cane NR35 . . . . . . .109 C3
 Wells-next-the-Sea NR23 .136 D6
New HAINFORD NR10 . . . .53 D5
New Hampshire Way **5**
 IP24 . . . . .116 A1
Newhaven Cl NR27 . . . . . .139 B6
Newhaven Ct NR27 . . . . . .139 B6
NEW HOLKHAM NR23 . . . . .5 A2
NEW HOUGHTON PE31 . . . .29 C6
New Inn Hill NR14 . . . . . . .91 C7
New Inn La NR19 . . . . . . .154 B5
New La
 Banham NR16 . . . . .119 B8
 Bradenham IP25 . . . . .66 F4
 Mattishall NR20 . . . . .68 F5
Newlands Ave PE30 . . . . .146 E2
Newlands Cl **40** IP20 . . . .122 D2
Newman Rd IP22 . . . . . . .177 D7
Newmarket Rd
 2 Cringleford NR4 . . . . .89 B8
 Norwich NR2 . . . . .178 A1
Newmarket St NR2 . . . . . .162 C4
New Mills Yd NR3 . . . . . . .178 A4
Newnham Gn NR31 . . . . . .70 A4
New N Rd NR17 . . . . .174 D5
New Par NR27 . . . . .139 C7
Newport NR29 . . . . .167 D6
Newport Rd
 Hemsby NR29 . . . . .167 C6
 South Walsham NR13 . . . .74 A6
NEW RACKHEATH NR13 . . .72 E7
New Rd
 Acle NR13 . . . . .166 C3
 Attleborough NR17 . . . . .174 B3
 Aylsham NR11 . . . . .150 D7
 Baconsthorpe NR25 . . . . .20 A8
 Bawburgh NR9 . . . . .160 B6
 Belton NR31 . . . . .94 A5
 Blakeney NR25 . . . . .7 C6
 Bodham NR25 . . . . .9 B1
 Brettenham IP24 . . . . . . .117 B2
 Brinton NR24 . . . . .18 D8
 Burnham Overy Staithe
 PE31 . . . . .135 E7
 Catfield NR29 . . . . .56 C8
 Crimplesham PE33 . . . . . .80 A6
 Dickleburgh & Rushall
 IP21 . . . . .130 D8
 Dunton NR21 . . . . .16 A2
 Fritton & St Olaves NR31 . .93 E3
 Gissing IP22 . . . . .120 D7
 Great Yarmouth NR30 . . .169 A6
 Haddiscoe NR14 . . . . . . .110 F7
 Halvergate NR13 . . . . . . .75 B4
 Hethersett NR9 . . . . .88 C7
 Hingham NR9 . . . . .86 C3
 Itteringham NR11 . . . . . . .35 D8
 King's Lynn PE30 . . . . . . .147 B6
 12 Lingwood NR13 . . . . .74 A3
 Longham NR19 . . . . .48 F2
 Methwold IP26 . . . . .98 E5
 Mettingham NR35 . . . . . .124 C7
 Morley NR18 . . . . .87 A3
 Northrepps NR27 . . . . . . .139 E1
 North Runcton PE33 . . . . .44 A3
 North Walsham NR28 . . . .151 D5
 Norton Subcourse NR14 . .92 E1
 Oulton NR11 . . . . .35 D7
 Outwell PE14 . . . . .77 E5
 Palgrave IP22 . . . . .129 F4
 Reedham NR13 . . . . .92 F4
 Reepham NR10 . . . . .149 C5
 Saxlingham Nethergate
 NR15 . . . . .107 B8
 Sculthorpe NR21 . . . . . . .16 A2
 Sheringham NR26 . . . . . .138 D7
 Shipdham IP25 . . . . .67 B2
 Shouldham PE33 . . . . . . .62 D4
 Skeyton NR10 . . . . .37 A5
 South Creake NR21 . . . . .15 D7
 Stanfield NR20 . . . . .48 F7
 St Cross, South Elmham
 IP20 . . . . .123 D1
 Stokesby with Herringby
 NR29 . . . . .75 A6
 Surlingham NR14 . . . . . . .73 B1
 Sutton Bridge PE12 . . . . .41 B8
 Sutton NR12 . . . . .39 D2
 Tacolneston NR16 . . . . . .105 E5
 Thelnetham IP22 . . . . . . .127 F3
 Thetford IP24 . . . . .176 C4
 Thrandeston IP21 . . . . . .129 D4
 Tilney St Lawrence PE34 . .42 C1
 Tivetshall St Mary NR15 . .121 B4
 Toft Monks NR34 . . . . . . .110 D6
 Welney PE14 . . . . .95 D5
 Whissonsett NR20 . . . . . .31 D2
 Wimbotsham PE34 . . . . . .172 E8
 Wiveton NR25 . . . . .7 E6
 Wormegay PE33 . . . . .62 C8
New Roman Bank PE34. .144 B7
New Row PE31 . . . . .133 D6
New Sporle Rd PE37 . . . . .153 C5
NEW SPROWSTON NR3 . . .158 E3
New St
 Cawston NR10 . . . . .35 B2

New St continued
 Cromer NR27 . . . . .139 B7
 Holt NR25 . . . . .137 B6
 King's Lynn PE30 . . . . . . .147 B7
 Sheringham NR26 . . . . . .138 D7
Newstead's La NR27 . . . . .10 C4
Newstead Wlk IP22 . . . . .177 C6
NEWTON PE32 . . . . .47 B2
Newton Cl
 Horsham St Faith & Newton St
 Faith NR10 . . . . .53 D4
 10 Newton Flotman NR15 . .89 D1
 Norwich NR4 . . . . .162 B1
Newton Cross NR31 . . . . .170 D1
NEWTON FLOTMAN NR15 . .89 C1
Newton Flotman Prim Sch
 NR15 . . . . .89 D1
NEWTON GREENWAYS
 NR15 . . . . .89 D2
Newton Rd
 Hainford NR10 . . . . .53 E5
 Newton by Castle Acre
 PE32 . . . . .47 A2
 Sporle with Palgrave PE32 .65 C7
NEWTON ST FAITH NR10. . .53 D4
NEWTOWN NR30 . . . . . . .169 D7
Newtown IP24 . . . . .176 C3
New Wellington Pl **23**
 NR30 . . . . .169 D2
Neylond Cres NR6 . . . . . .157 E6
Nicholas Ave PE34 . . . . . .145 E6
Nicholas Hamond Way **4**
 PE37 . . . . .153 C3
Nicholas Mews **3** NR2 . .162 B7
Nicholls Way IP22 . . . . . .177 A5
Nick's La IP23 . . . . .130 B2
Nicolson Ave NR20 . . . . . .50 B5
Nightingale Cl
 Denver PE38 . . . . .172 D2
 Fakenham NR21 . . . . .141 F4
 Hemsby NR29 . . . . .167 E4
 Mulbarton NR14 . . . . .89 A3
Nightingale Dr NR8 . . . . .155 B1
Nightingale Fst Sch NR8 .155 B1
Nightingale La
 Denver PE38 . . . . .172 D3
 3 Feltwell IP26 . . . . . . .98 E1
 3 Feltwell IP26 . . . . . . .98 E1
 Norwich NR3 . . . . .162 E8
Nightingale Wlk PE38 . . .172 C2
Nightmarsh La PE31. . . . . .27 C4
Nile Rd
 Downham Market PE38. . .172 B4
 Great Yarmouth NR31 . . .170 D4
Nile St **1** NR2 . . . . .162 B7
Nimrod Cl **22** NR9 . . . . . .88 D8
Nine Acre La NR24 . . . . . . .19 C4
Ninhams Ct NR2 . . . . .178 A3
Ninham St NR1 . . . . .162 E3
Nobb's Loke NR12 . . . . . . .38 F4
Nobbs' Cnr NR35 . . . . . . .108 A4
Nobel Cres NR12 . . . . . . .164 B4
Noble Cl NR7 . . . . .159 D2
Noel Cl NR13 . . . . .171 C5
Nogdam End NR14 . . . . . . .92 D3
Noot Alley **6** NR5 . . . . .161 B7
NORDELPH PE38 . . . . .78 D3
Nordelph Cnr NR9 . . . . . . .86 D6
NORDELPH CORNER NR9 . .86 D6
Norfolk Dr NR17 . . . . .174 C6
Norfolk Lavender Visitor
 Ctr★ PE31 . . . . .133 E6
Norfolk Motor Cycle Mus★
 NR28 . . . . .151 C4
Norfolk Nelson Mus★
 NR30 . . . . .169 C3
Norfolk & Norwich Univ
 Hospl NR4 . . . . .161 A3
Norfolk Rd
 10 Honington IP31 . . . . .126 B1
 10 Marham PE33 . . . . . . .63 B4
 Norwich NR4 . . . . .161 B3
 Sheringham NR26 . . . . . .138 D6
 Thetford IP24 . . . . .176 E4
Norfolk Record Office
 NR1 . . . . .162 F3
Norfolk Shire Horse Ctr★
 NR27 . . . . .9 F5
Norfolk Sq
 Downham Market PE38. . .172 B5
 Great Yarmouth NR30 . . .169 C5
Norfolk St
 4 King's Lynn PE30 . . . .146 E5
 Norwich NR2 . . . . .162 C5
 Wisbech PE13 . . . . .152 C4
Norfolk & Suffolk Aviation
 Mus★ NR35 . . . . .123 C6
Norfolk Wildlife Ctr &
 Country Pk★ NR9 . . . . . .51 C6
Norfolk Wildlife Hospl
 (RSPCA)★ PE32 . . . . .44 F3
Norgate La IP21 . . . . .130 E6
Norgate Rd NR4 . . . . .161 E3
Norgate Way NR8 . . . . . . .156 E8
Norman CE Prim Sch
 IP26 . . . . .99 C7
Norman Cl
 East Dereham NR19 . . . . .154 C5
 Fakenham NR21 . . . . .141 B6
Norman Dr
 Methwold PE33 . . . . .81 B2
 Norwich NR6 . . . . .158 E7
Normandy Cl IP26 . . . . . . .99 C7
Norman Fst Sch NR3 . . . .158 B2

Norman La **10** NR31 . . . .169 B4
Norman Rd
 Flitcham with Appleton
 PE31 . . . . .28 E7
 Norwich NR3 . . . . .158 E1
Normans Bldgs NR1 . . . . .178 B2
Norman's Burrow Rd
 NR21 . . . . .31 B3
Normans La NR21 . . . . .4 D1
Norman Troller Ct **9**
 NR27 . . . . .139 B7
Norman Way PE31 . . . . . .15 B3
NORTHACRE NR17 . . . . . . .85 B1
NORTHALL GREEN
 Dereham NR20 . . . . .154 F8
 Hoe NR20 . . . . .49 F2
North Barningham Rd
 NR25 . . . . .20 D7
NORTH BARSHAM NR22 . . .16 D6
North Beach PE36 . . . . . .132 B1
North Brink PE13 . . . . . . .152 A4
NORTH BURLINGHAM
 NR13 . . . . .74 A5
North Cambridgeshire Hospl
 PE13 . . . . .152 D5
NORTH COMMON IP22 . . .127 D2
Northcote PE31 . . . . .134 D6
Northcote Rd **1** NR3 . . .162 E8
NORTH COURT PE27 . . . . .114 C3
NORTH CREAKE NR21 . . . . .4 D1
NORTH DENES NR30 . . . . .168 F2
North Denes Airfield
 NR30 . . . . .168 D2
North Denes Mid Sch
 NR30 . . . . .169 D8
North Denes Rd NR30 . . .169 D8
North Dr
 Fakenham NR21 . . . . .141 C5
 Great Yarmouth NR30 . . .169 E4
NORTH ELMHAM NR20 . . . .49 E8
North Elmham Chapel★
 NR20 . . . . .49 F8
North Elmham Prim Sch
 NR20 . . . . .49 E8
NORTH END NR16 . . . . . . .103 C3
North End
 Haddiscoe NR14 . . . . .93 B1
 Stoke Holy Cross NR14 . . .89 E5
 Wisbech PE13 . . . . .152 B6
North End La NR16 . . . . . .106 D3
Northern Cl NR30 . . . . . . .168 F5
North Everard St PE30. . . .146 E3
Northfield Ave NR23 . . . . .136 D6
Northfield Cl NR18 . . . . . .173 B6
Northfield Cres NR23 . . . .136 E5
Northfield Gdns NR18 . . .173 B5
Northfield La
 Plumstead NR11 . . . . .20 B6
 Wells-next-the-Sea NR23 .136 C6
Northfield Loke NR18 . . . .173 B6
Northfield Rd
 Forncett NR16 . . . . .106 A4
 Mundesley NR11 . . . . . . .143 C5
 North Walsham NR28 . . . .151 B6
 Swaffham PE37 . . . . .153 C6
Northfields NR4 . . . . .161 E4
Northfields Fst Sch NR4 . .161 E4
Northfield Way NR23 . . . .136 E6
North Gage Cl NR7 . . . . . .159 C4
Northgate
 Beccles NR34 . . . . .110 D1
 Dereham NR19 . . . . .154 C7
 11 Harleston IP20 . . . . .122 D1
 Hunstanton PE36 . . . . . . .132 C5
 Norwich NR6 . . . . .157 F5
 3 Thorpe End NR13 . . . .72 D6
Northgate Cty High Sch
 NR19 . . . . .154 D6
Northgate Hospl NR30 . . .169 D6
Northgate Prec NR30 . . . .132 C6
Northgate St Andrews Fst
 Sch NR30 . . . . .169 D6
Northgate St NR30 . . . . . .169 C5
Northgate Way PE34 . . . .144 D7
North Gn Rd IP21 . . . . . . .122 A4
NORTH GREEN
 Garvestone NR9 . . . . .68 C1
 Pulham St Mary IP21. . . .122 A7
North La NR21 . . . . .17 E5
North Lawn PE38 . . . . .97 B6
NORTH LOPHAM IP22 . . . .119 A2
North Lopham Rd NR16 . .119 A3
NORTH LYNN PE30 . . . . . .146 F7
North Lynn Ind Est PE30 .147 A8
Northmead Dr NR28 . . . . .151 C6
North Mkt Rd
 14 Great Yarmouth
 NR30 . . . . .169 D4
 Winterton-on-Sea NR29 . .58 B6
North Norfolk Rly★ NR26 . .9 B6
Northolt Rd IP25 . . . . .85 A3
NORTH PICKENHAM PE37. .65 E1
North Pickenham Rd
 PE37 . . . . .153 C4
North Pk NR11 . . . . .141 B6
North Pk Ave NR4 . . . . . . .161 E4
North Pk Dr NR4 . . . . .161 F4
North Quay NR30 . . . . . . .169 C4
North Rd
 Bunwell NR16 . . . . .105 C5
 4 Great Yarmouth NR30 .169 D5
 Great Yarmouth NR31 . . .170 D4
 Hemsby NR29 . . . . .167 A7
 Ormesby St Margaret with
 Scratby NR29 . . . . .167 A4
 Watton IP25 . . . . .84 D3

NORTHREPPS NR27 ...... 11 A2

Northrepps Prim Sch
NR27.............. 11 A2
Northrepps Rd NR27 ..... 139 E3
North River Rd NR30 .... 169 C6
NORTH RUNCTON PE33.... 44 A2
Northside NR7......... 72 E3
North St
Brundall NR13 .... 165 E6
Burnham Market PE31... 135 C3
6 Castle Acre PE32..... 46 F2
Great Dunham PE32 .... 47 E2
King's Lynn PE30 ...... 146 D6
Langham NR25......... 7 A4
North Walsham NR28 ... 151 C5
Sheringham NR26 ..... 138 C7
Wisbech PE13 .... 152 C5
NORTH TUDDENHAM
NR20 .... 50 D1
Northumberland St NR2. 162 B7
North View NR21....... 17 F3
Northview Rd NR5 ..... 157 C1
NORTH WALSHAM 151 E6
North Walsham Com Hospl
NR28............... 151 C4
North Walsham Fst Sch
NR28............... 151 D5
North Walsham High Sch
NR28............... 151 D4
North Walsham Jun Sch
NR28............... 151 D4
North Walsham Rd
Bacton NR28 .... 23 C3
Coltishall NR12 .... 54 B2
Crostwick NR12........ 54 B2
Felmingham NR28 ..... 37 B8
Happisburgh NR12..... 23 F2
Northrepps NR27...... 10 E1
Norwich NR6 .... 159 A5
Paston NR28 .... 151 F7
Sprowston NR6 .... 159 B6
Swafield NR28......... 22 E4
Thorpe Market NR11 ... 22 A7
Witton NR28 .... 38 B8
North Walsham Sta
NR28............... 151 C4
North Way PE30 ...... 147 A8
Northwell Pool Rd PE37. 153 C5
North-West Twr* NR30. 169 C5
NORTHWOLD IP26 ..... 99 C8
Northwold Rd IP26..... 99 A6
NORTH WOOTTON PE30. 148 C5
North Wootton Prim Sch
PE30 .... 148 D4
NORTON CORNER NR11... 34 C7
Norton Dr
2 Norwich NR4 .... 89 D8
Norwich NR4 .... 162 A1
Norton Hill NR13....... 74 A8
Norton Rd NR14 ...... 92 B1
NORTON SUBCOURSE
NR14 .... 92 E1
Nortridge Rd NR5...... 161 A7
Norvic Dr NR4 .... 161 E1
Norway Cl PE31....... 133 C6
NORWICH NR2 .... 178 A3
Norwich Arts Ctr* NR2. 178 A3
Norwich Bsns Pk NR4.. 162 D1
Norwich Castle Mus & Art
Gall* NR1........... 178 B3
Norwich Cath* NR1 ... 178 B3
Norwich City FC NR1.. 163 A4
Norwich Com Hospl NR2 161 F7
Norwich Comm NR18 .. 173 F6
Norwich Dr NR20 ..... 32 E4
Norwich Gall* NR1.... 178 B3
Norwich Gates NR1 ... 140 E1
Norwich High Sch for Girls
NR2................ 162 B3
Norwich Int Airport NR6 158 B7
Norwich La IP31...... 127 A4
Norwich Lower Sch NR1 178 C3
Norwich Puppet Theatre
NR1................ 178 B4
Norwich Rd
Acle NR13 .... 166 A3
Ashmanhaugh NR12 ... 55 C7
Attleborough NR17 .... 174 C6
Aylsham NR11 .... 150 C6
Barnham Broom NR9.. 69 D2
Bawdeswell NR20 .... 50 E7
Bracon Ash NR14..... 88 F2
Briston NR24 .... 142 E5
Brooke NR15 .... 90 E3
Burgh & Tuttington NR11. 36 E6
Caister-on-Sea NR30.. 168 C5
Cantley NR13........ 92 D7
Carbrooke IP25 ...... 85 B3
Cawston NR10 .... 35 B2
Chedgrave NR14 ..... 91 F2
Cromer NR27........ 139 C5
Denton IP20 .... 123 B7
Dickleburgh & Rushall
IP21 .... 130 D6
Ditchingham NR35.... 109 A2
Earsham NR35 ...... 108 E1
East Dereham NR20 .. 154 F5
East Tuddenham NR20.. 69 C6
Edgefield NR24 ...... 19 D6
Fakenham NR21...... 141 C4
Foxley NR20......... 50 D8
Gillingham NR34 ..... 110 C2
Great & Little Plumstead
NR13.............. 73 A7
Guist NR20.......... 33 A4
Hardingham NR9 ..... 86 E8
9 Hethersett NR9 .... 88 D7
Hingham NR9........ 86 D5

Norwich Rd *continued*
Holt NR25 .... 137 B5
Horning NR12 .... 55 E4
Horsham St Faith NR10 .. 53 D2
Horstead with Stanninghall
NR12.............. 54 C4
Ingworth NR11 .... 36 B8
Kimberley NR18....... 87 B7
Langley with Hardley NR14. 91 F6
Lingwood & Burlingham
NR13.............. 74 A2
Long Stratton NR15.... 106 F5
Ludham NR29 .... 56 C5
Marlingford NR9 ..... 69 F4
Mattishall NR20...... 68 F6
Mulbarton NR14 ..... 89 B4
Neatishead NR12..... 164 F8
North Walsham NR28 . 151 B3
Norwich NR5 .... 157 B2
Poringland NR14 ..... 90 B6
Pulham St Mary IP21.. 121 F4
Rackheath NR13 ..... 72 F8
Reepham NR10 ...... 149 C5
Roughton NR11...... 21 D8
Salhouse NR13 ...... 55 B1
Saxlingham Nethergate
NR15.............. 107 B8
Scole IP21 .... 121 B1
Shotesham NR15..... 89 F2
Shouldham PE33 ..... 62 F3
Smallburgh NR12..... 38 D2
Stockton NR34....... 109 F5
Strumpshaw NR13.... 73 F2
Swaffham PE37 ..... 153 D4
Swanton Morley NR20. 50 B2
4 Tacolneston NR16... 105 F5
Tacolneston NR16 .... 106 A6
Tharston & Hapton NR15. 106 C7
Thetford IP24 .... 176 D4
Thurton NR14 .... 91 C3
Tivetshall St Mary NR15.. 121 D4
West Caister NR30 ... 168 B6
Weston Longville NR9 .. 51 E5
Wisbech PE13 ...... 152 E5
Woodton NR35....... 108 C6
Wroxham/Hoveton NR12. 164 B3
Wymondham NR18 ... 173 D5
Yaxham NR19........ 68 A5
Norwich Rd Sch IP24... 176 D4
Norwich Research Pk
NR4................ 161 A4
Norwich Riverside NR1. 178 C2
Norwich Sch NR1 .... 178 B3
Norwich Sch of Art & Design
NR3................ 178 B3
Norwich St
East Dereham NR19 ... 154 E5
Fakenham NR21...... 141 B4
Hingham NR9........ 86 C5
Mundesley NR11..... 143 A7
Norwich Sta NR1 ..... 178 C2
Norwich Theatre Royal
NR2................ 178 A2
Norwood Rd IP27 .... 175 A1
Notre Dame High Sch
NR1................ 178 B1
Notre Dame Prep Sch
NR2................ 162 B7
Nottingham Rd PE30 .. 146 E8
Nottingham Way NR30. 169 C3
Notykin St NR5 ...... 161 A8
Nourse Dr PE31....... 133 C5
Nova Scotia Rd
Filby NR30 .... 168 A7
Ormesby St Margaret with
Scratby NR29 ...... 167 B1
Nowhere La PE33 .... 80 D4
Nuffield Cl NR31...... 170 B4
Nuffield Cres NR31.... 170 B4
Nunnery Dr IP24...... 176 D1
Nunnery Pl IP24 ..... 176 D2
Nunnery The* IP24 ... 176 D2
Nunn's Way NR19 .... 154 D5
Nuns' Bridges Rd IP24. 176 C2
Nunsgate IP24........ 175 A1
Nurseries Ave NR13... 165 E4
Nursery Cl
Acle NR13 .... 166 B4
2 Beetley NR19 ...... 49 C3
5 Belton NR31 .... 94 A5
2 Gressenhall NR20 ... 49 C3
King's Lynn PE30 .... 148 C2
8 Marthan NR29 ..... 57 D5
Norwich NR6 .... 157 E5
2 Roydon PE32 ..... 28 A1
Nursery Dr
Hunstanton PE36...... 132 D4
North Walsham NR28. 151 B3
Wisbech PE13 ...... 152 E8
Nursery Gdns NR13 ... 165 F6
Nursery La
Brancaster PE31...... 3 E6
Costessey NR8....... 156 F3
Hockwold cum Wilton
IP26 .... 114 A6
King's Lynn PE30 .... 148 C3
Nursery Rd PE38 .... 172 C6
Nursery Terr NR30.... 169 C6
Nursery Way PE32 ... 28 A1
Nursey Cl NR35 ..... 109 D3
Nutfield Cl **7** NR4 ... 161 F1
Nuthall Cres PE30..... 147 A8
Nut La NR27 .... 139 F3
Nutmeg Wlk PE38 ... 172 E6
Nuttele Ct NR15...... 107 C6
Nuttery Vale IP23.... 130 F2
Nutwood Cl NR8 ..... 155 D2

O

Oakapple Dr NR19 .... 154 D8
Oak Ave
14 Great Yarmouth NR31 .. 94 C7
King's Lynn PE30..... 148 D2
Marham PE33 .... 63 B4
North Elmham NR20 .. 49 E7
Norwich NR7........ 163 F8
2 Poringland NR14 ... 90 C5
West Winch PE33 .... 43 F2
Oak Cl
4 Hethersett NR9 .... 88 D8
Norwich NR5 .... 156 F2
14 Tasburgh NR15.... 106 F6
Thetford IP24 .... 176 A1
Oak Cres IP23 .... 130 C1
Oakcroft Dr NR14 .... 90 C5
Oakdale Rd NR13 .... 165 D3
Oakdene NR21........ 15 C2
Oak Dr PE14 .... 77 F7
Oakfield Cl PE38 ..... 172 C4
Oakfield Dr **3** NR13... 74 B8
Oakfield Rd
Aylsham NR11 .... 150 C6
Long Stratton NR15... 106 F3
Oakfields NR14 ...... 91 F2
Oakfields Cl **1** NR4 .. 89 C8
Oakfields Rd NR4 .... 89 B8
Oak Gr
7 Horsford NR10..... 53 B3
Sheringham NR26 .... 138 D5
Oakhill NR13......... 165 D3
Oak La
East Ruston NR12 .... 38 E7
2 Hingham NR9 ..... 86 C4
Norwich NR3........ 158 D3
Oakland Dr **5** NR20.. 49 D4
Oaklands
Little Snoring NR21 ... 17 C3
Old Buckenham NR17. 104 D2
Poringland NR14 ..... 90 C6
6 Taverham NR8 .... 155 B2
Oaklands Cl
Attleborough NR17 ... 174 C3
Halvergate NR13..... 74 F2
Oaklands Dr
Brandon IP27........ 114 D4
Cringleford NR4 ..... 161 C1
Walsoken PE13 ...... 152 F7
Oaklands La **2** PE33 .. 61 D3
Oaklands Pk NR28 ... 151 B6
Oaklands The PE37.... 153 C3
Oakleigh Dr PE13 .... 153 A5
OAKLEY IP21......... 130 E5
Oakley Church La IP21.. 130 D4
Oakley Ct PE13....... 152 E4
Oak Lodge NR7 ...... 163 C5
Oak Rd
Dilham NR28 .... 38 C4
Great Yarmouth NR31.. 170 B6
North Walsham NR28 . 151 B4
Stoke Ferry PE33 .... 81 A2
Oakroyd Cres PE13.... 152 C6
Oaks Dr
Necton PE37........ 65 F4
Swaffham PE37 ..... 153 C3
Oaks La NR34........ 111 B5
Oak's La NR13 .... 72 F2
Oak St
Fakenham NR21...... 141 B4
Feltwell IP26........ 98 E1
Norwich NR3........ 178 A4
Oaks The
Ashill IP25.......... 84 A7
3 Beetley NR19 ..... 49 C3
3 Gressenhall NR20 .. 49 C3
Mattishall NR20...... 68 F5
Oak Tree Bsns Pk NR13.. 72 E8
Oak Tree Cl **3** NR29.. 57 D5
Oaktree Dr NR7...... 159 B2
Oak Tree Way **3** IP20.. 122 D1
Oak View Dr PE38..... 172 C6
Oak Wood NR13 ..... 165 E5
Oakwood Cl NR13 ... 154 D8
Oakwood Dr NR18 ... 173 E6
Oakwood Rd NR19 ... 154 D8
Oasis Leisure Ctr PE36. 132 C4
Oasis Sport & Leisure Club
NR7................ 72 D5
Oasis Way PE36..... 132 C2
Oatfield Cl **7** NR10 .. 53 A3
Obelisk La NR28 .... 38 F5
Obelisk Plain NR25.... 137 A6
Occupation Rd **1** NR20.. 68 F6
Octagon Dr **4** PE13 .. 152 A6
Octavia Cl PE13...... 152 F4
Octavia Hill Birthplace Mus*
PE13............... 152 C5
Oddfellows Field **4** NR25. 7 C6
Oddfellows Row NR11. 134 E4
Offley Ct **7** NR5 ..... 161 A8
Ogden Cl NR18....... 173 C4
Oil Mill La PE13 ...... 152 B5
Old Allotment Ct **7** NR3. 162 F8
Old Bakery Ct PE31... 133 C5
Old Barge Yd NR1.... 178 C2
Old Barley Mkt The NR2. 178 A3
Old Bear Ct NR28 .... 151 C5
Old Becclesgate NR19.. 154 D5
OLD BEETLEY NR20 ... 49 D5
Old Brandon Rd IP26.. 98 F1
Old Brewery Cl **4** NR17.. 174 D4
Old Brewery La NR14.. 149 C4
OLD BUCKENHAM NR17.. 104 D2

Old Buckenham Airfield*
NR17.............. 104 E4
Old Buckenham High Sch
NR17.............. 104 D2
Old Buckenham Prim Sch
NR17.............. 104 D3
Old Bungay Rd NR35.. 109 D4
Old Bury Rd
Palgrave IP22 .... 129 E4
Stuston IP21 .... 177 F1
Thetford IP24 .... 176 C4
Wortham IP22 .... 129 D4
OLD CATTON NR6 .... 158 E5
Old Catton Mid Sch NR6 158 E5
Old Chapel Rd
Cantley NR13........ 92 E7
3 Hemsby NR29..... 58 B6
Old Chapel Way NR7 .. 72 E3
Old Church Cl NR14 .. 89 F6
Old Church Rd
Hainford NR10 ...... 53 E6
Hopton on Sea NR31.. 171 D4
Snettisham PE31..... 12 E5
Old Coach Rd NR27 .. 139 C6
Old Coast Rd NR29 .. 167 E2
Old Fakenham Rd
Attlebridge NR9...... 52 B3
Foxley NR20......... 50 D8
Old Farm La NR3..... 158 E1
Old Feltwell Rd IP26... 99 A5
Oldfield Ave PE14 .... 59 B1
Oldfield Ct **8** NR19 .. 154 E6
Oldfield La PE13 ..... 152 B3
Old Forge Cl IP22 .... 129 B4
Old Forge Ct
Acle NR13 .... 166 C4
Brockdish IP21 ...... 131 D6
Old Fountain NR11.... 150 C4
Old Friendship La NR10. 35 C2
Old Gr Ct NR3 .... 158 D2
Old Hall Cl
Ashwellthorpe NR16.. 105 F8
1 Norwich NR14 .... 163 B2
Saham Toney IP25.... 84 B5
Old Hall Dr PE31..... 140 E3
Old Hall Gdns
Brooke NR15........ 90 F2
Buxton with Lammas NR10. 37 A2
Old Hall Gdns NR20 .. 32 A5
Oldhall La NR16 ..... 118 C5
Old Hall La PE37 ..... 81 F8
Oldhall Rd NR4 ...... 89 B6
Old Hall Rd
East Dereham NR19 .. 154 D2
Mattishall NR20...... 68 D5
Norwich NR28 .... 38 B8
OLD HALL STREET NR28. 23 A4
Old Harleston Rd NR35.. 123 E7
Old High Rd IP22 .... 177 A5
Old Hithe Rd NR25 ... 8 E3
Old La
East Ruston NR12 ... 24 A5
Happisburgh NR12.... 23 F1
Reepham NR10 ..... 34 B1
Thelnetham IP22 .... 128 A2
Old Lakenham Hall Dr **6**
NR1................ 162 E1
Old Laundry Ct **3** NR2. 162 B8
Old Laundry Mews NR1. 163 A5
Old Liby Mews NR7 .. 72 C8
Old Lynn Rd PE13 ... 152 E7
Old Maltings The PE13. 153 B4
Old Manor Cl NR20 .. 148 C1
Old Methwold Rd
Feltwell IP26........ 98 E2
Northwold PE33...... 81 B2
Old Mill Dr IP21...... 121 F4
Old Mill Rd
Caister-on-Sea NR30. 168 F5
3 Poringland NR14 .. 90 C5
Roughton NR11...... 139 B1
Old Mkt PE13 .... 152 C5
Old Mkt Cl NR13 .... 166 C3
Old Mkt Gn **5** NR14.. 92 A1
Old Mkt Pl **2** IP20 .. 122 D2
Old Mkt St
14 King's Lynn PE30 . 146 E5
Thetford IP24 .... 176 D3
Old Mkt Way NR15 .. 107 C5
Old Norwich Rd
Horsham St Faith & Newton St
Faith NR10 .... 53 D1
Yaxley IP23 .... 130 A1
Old Pal Rd NR2 ..... 162 B7
Old Pools Dro CB6 ... 95 F1
Old Post Office La NR35. 109 E3
Old Post Office St
2 Fakenham NR21... 141 B4
2 Shipdham IP25 ... 67 B2
Old Post Rd NR24 ... 142 E4
Old Quarry Ct NR19 .. 154 E6
Old Rd
Acle NR13 .... 166 C5
1 Great Moulton NR15. 106 B1
Old Rectory Cl
King's Lynn PE30 ... 148 D5
Norwich NR14...... 90 B3
4 Mulbarton NR14... 89 B3
9 Roydon IP22..... 129 D7
South Wootton PE30.. 148 B1
Old Rectory Rd NR12.. 24 A1

NOR–Orc 201

Old Reepham Rd **4** NR20. 50 E7
Old Rly Rd IP20...... 123 B5
Old Rly Yd PE31..... 135 C2
Old Roman Bank PE34.. 144 A7
Old Sch Cl NR5 ...... 161 E6
Old Sch Ct NR1 ..... 178 C1
Old Sch Rd
East Ruston NR12 ... 38 E7
Guestwick NR20 .... 33 F5
Old Severalls Rd IP26. 98 E6
Old South PE30...... 147 C4
Old Southwood Rd NR13. 74 B2
Old St **2** NR15...... 107 A8
Old Sta La NR35..... 109 D2
Old Sta Way **8** NR25.. 137 C5
Old Stoke Rd NR14... 89 F8
Oldsunway PE30 .... 146 D5
Old Town Way PE36.. 132 D6
Old Turnpike Rd NR11. 21 D7
Old Vicarage Pk PE32.. 63 E7
Old Warren NR8 .... 155 D2
Oldwash La NR14 ... 105 D3
Old Watton Rd NR4 .. 161 A5
Old Wellington Pl **15**
NR30.............. 169 D3
Old Wells Rd
Sculthorpe NR21..... 16 A2
Walsingham NR22 ... 16 E8
Old Woman's La NR25.. 7 F6
Old Yarmouth Rd NR12. 39 C2
Olive Ave NR15 ..... 89 D1
Olive Cl NR5 .... 157 C1
Olive Cres NR10..... 53 A4
Oliver Ct
5 Cromer NR27 .... 139 C6
2 Weeting IP27 .... 114 E1
Olive Rd
Great Yarmouth NR31. 169 B3
Norwich NR5........ 161 B3
Oliver Mews **4** NR30. 169 D4
Olivet Way NR11 .... 143 C3
Olivia Cl NR21...... 141 A5
Ollands Rd
Attleborough NR17 .. 174 C3
Reepham NR10 ..... 149 C4
Ollard Ave PE13...... 152 D7
Olley Rd **6** NR27.... 10 A5
Omey Rd NR31 ..... 154 D5
Onedin Cl PE13 ..... 140 C5
Onley St NR2 .... 162 B4
Onslow Ave NR30 ... 169 D7
Onyx Ct **10** PE13 .. 152 C4
Opie St NR2 .... 178 B3
Opportune Rd PE13 .. 152 C6
Orange Gr **3** PE13 .. 152 C4
ORANGE ROW PE34 .. 144 A6
Orange Row PE34.... 144 A5
Orange Row Rd PE34. 144 A6
Orchard Bank NR8 .. 156 E8
Orchard Cl
Acle NR13 .... 166 B4
Ashill IP25.......... 84 A6
Attleborough NR17 .. 174 C5
Biofield Heath NR13 .. 73 C6
Brancaster Staithe PE31. 3 D7
Briston NR24 .... 142 D4
Caister-on-Sea NR30. 168 E4
Dersingham PE31.... 140 D4
Downham Market PE38. 172 D5
Fakenham NR21..... 141 D4
Holt NR25 .... 137 E7
8 Ixworth NR9..... 86 C8
Mundesley NR11..... 143 B7
North Elmham NR20 . 49 E7
North Walsham NR28. 151 C6
Norwich NR7........ 163 C8
Roughton NR11...... 21 D7
Sheringham NR26 ... 138 C6
Tacolneston NR16 ... 105 F4
Watlington PE33..... 61 E5
Wisbech PE13 ...... 152 C6
Orchard Cres **15** NR15... 106 B1
Orchard Ct
King's Lynn PE30 ... 147 B6
Ormesby St Margaret
NR29.............. 167 A3
Orchard Dr
Hellesdon NR6...... 157 D3
3 Potter Heigham NR29. 56 F6
West Walton PE14... 59 C8
Wisbech PE13 ...... 152 E4
Orchard Gdns **3** PE38. 147 B6
Orchard Gr
Diss IP22........... 177 C5
Kettlestone NR21.... 17 C2
King's Lynn PE34.... 146 C3
Orchard La
Aylsham NR11 ...... 150 D4
Castle Acre PE32.... 46 F2
King's Lynn PE30.... 147 B5
Reepham NR10 ..... 149 C5
Shouldham PE33 .... 62 D4
Orchard Pl
Swaffham PE37 ..... 153 B4
Thompson IP24 ..... 102 A7
Orchard Rd
8 Gayton PE32..... 45 C6
Lingwood NR13...... 73 F3
5 Mattishall NR20... 68 E6
2 Spixworth NR10 .. 54 A2
4 Wiggenhall St Germans
PE34............. 43 B1
Orchards Prim Ssh NR13 152 D8
Orchard St NR2...... 162 C7

Orchard The
- **4** Belton NR31. . . . . 94 A6
- Brandon IP27 . . . . 175 C3

Orchard Way
- Banham NR16 . . . . 119 D7
- **4** Burgh St Margaret (Fleggburgh) NR29 . . . . 57 C1
- **5** Hethersett NR9 . . . . . . 88 D8
- **7** Tasburgh NR15 . . . . . . 106 F6
- Terrington St John PE14 . . 42 B1
- Thetford IP24 . . . . 176 D5
- Wymondham NR18 . . . . 173 C4
Orchid Ave NR19 . . . . 154 D1
Orde Ave NR31 . . . . 170 C2
Ordnance Rd NR30 . . . . . . 169 D1
Orford CI 5 NR30 . . . . . . 169 D3
Orford Hill NR1 . . . . 178 B2
Orford PI
- Norwich NR1 . . . . 178 B2
- **7** West Winch PE33 . . . . 43 F2
Orford Rd PE37 . . . . 153 C6
Orford St NR1 . . . . 178 B2
Orhard Gr PE33 . . . . 43 E2
Oriel Ave NR31. . . . . 170 A3
Oriel High Sch NR31 . . . . 170 A3
- Origins* NR22. . . . . 178 A2
Ormesby 4 PE30 . . . . . . 147 D5
Ormesby Fst Sch NR29 . . 167 A2
Ormesby La NR29 . . . . 76 A8
Ormesby Mid Sch NR29 . . 167 A3
Ormesby Rd
- Caister-on-Sea NR30 . . . . 168 D7
- Hemsby NR29 . . . . 167 A6
- Ormesby St Margaret with Scratby NR29 . . . . 168 C8
- Scottow NR10 . . . . 37 B2
ORMESBY ST MARGARET NR29 . . . . 167 B3
ORMESBY ST MICHAEL NR29 . . . . 58 A1
Ormond Rd NR30 . . . . 169 C5
Orwell CI
- King's Lynn PE30 . . . . . . 147 D4
- **2** Wymondham NR18. . 173 D5
Orwell Cres NR31 . . . . 94 A6
Orwell Rd NR2 . . . . 162 C3
Osbert CI 4 NR1 . . . . 162 E1
Osborne Ave NR3 . . . . 169 C7
Osborne CI 3 NR28 . . . . . 151 C7
Osborne Ct NR4 . . . . 162 B3
Osborne Pk PE13 . . . . . . 152 C8
Osborne Rd
- Norwich NR4 . . . . 161 D2
- Wisbech PE13 . . . . 152 B7
Osier CI NR19. . . . . 154 B4
Osier La NR25 . . . . 9 C1
Osprey CI NR12 . . . . 164 D5
OSTEND NR12. . . . . 24 A7
Ostend Gap NR12 . . . . 24 A7
Ostend PI NR12 . . . . 24 A7
Ostend Rd NR12 . . . . 24 A6
Ostrich La NR19. . . . . 49 A3
Otter CI
- **3** Downham Market PE38. . . . . 172 A6
- **5** Salhouse NR13 . . . . . . 55 A1
Otter Dr 7 NR14 . . . . 89 B3
Otter Trust The* NR35. . . . 123 E7
OULTON NR11. . . . . 35 B7
Oulton CI PE37. . . . . 153 C2
Oulton Rd NR6 . . . . 158 C5
OULTON STREET NR11. . . . 35 D6
Ouse Ave NR30 . . . . 146 D2
Ouse Ave The IP24 . . . . . 176 C3
Ouse La NR12. . . . . 39 F1
Outney Rd NR35 . . . . 124 A8
Out S Gates PE30 . . . . . . 146 E3
OUTWELL PE14. . . . . 77 F6
Outwell Rd
- Emneth PE14 . . . . 59 B2
- Stow Bardolph PE34 . . . . 78 E8
Overbury Rd NR6 . . . . . . 158 A4
Over Cross NR16 . . . . 119 C8
Overstone Ct NR6 . . . . . . 158 F5
OVERSTRAND NR27 . . . . . . 11 A4
Overstrand Belfry VA Prim Sch NR27 . . . . 11 A3
Overstrand Rd NR27. . . . . 139 C6
Overstrand Sports Club NR27 . . . . 11 A3
Overtons Way 14 NR14 . . . 90 C5
Overwood La NR3 . . . . . . 106 A3
Overy Rd PE31 . . . . 135 D3
OVINGTON IP25 . . . . 84 E5
Ovington Rd IP25 . . . . 84 C4
Owen Rd
- Diss IP22 . . . . 177 F4
- Great Yarmouth NR31 . . 169 B1
Owen's CI 22 NR15 . . . . . 106 E3
Owl Dr 3 NR14 . . . . 89 B3
OXBOROUGH PE33 . . . . . . 81 D4
Oxborough Dr PE30 . . . . . 148 E1
Oxborough La NR21 . . . . . 141 C4
Oxborough Rd
- Oxborough PE33 . . . . . . 81 D3
- Stoke Ferry PE33 . . . . . . 81 A2
Oxburgh CI 1 PE13 . . . . . 152 A7
Oxburgh Hall Gdns & Estate* PE33. . . . . 81 E4
Oxcroft NR13 . . . . 166 C4
Oxford Ave NR31. . . . . . . 170 B3
Oxford PI PE34. . . . . 144 F6

Oxford Rd
- **2** Feltwell IP26 . . . . 98 E1
- **2** Feltwell IP26 . . . . 98 E1
Oxford St NR2 . . . . 162 C5
Oxford Way 11 NR29 . . . . 57 D4
OXNEAD NR10. . . . . 36 E2
Oxnead Dr NR30 . . . . 168 C7
Oxnead La NR35 . . . . 107 F4
Oxnead Rd NR3 . . . . 158 B2
OXWICK NR21 . . . . 31 D4

P

Pack La
- Briston NR24 . . . . 142 F3
- East Carleton NR14 . . . . . 89 A6
- Strumpshaw NR13 . . . . . . 73 F3
Packway The IP20 . . . . . . 123 A3
Paddock CI
- Belton NR31. . . . . 93 F6
- **3** Fakenham NR21. . . . . 141 B4
Paddock Farm IP31 . . . . . 127 B4
Paddock Farm Dr NR29. . . 75 F8
Paddock Gdns NR17. . . . . 174 E5
Paddock Rd 18 IP20. . . . . 122 D2
Paddock St NR29 . . . . 162 C8
Paddocks The
- **3** Cromer NR27 . . . . 10 B5
- Hemsby NR29 . . . . 167 A8
- Trowse with Newton NR14 163 A2
Paddy's La NR7 . . . . 51 E1
Paddys Loke NR30 . . . . . . 169 A7
Padgate NR13 . . . . 72 D6
Padgett's Rd PE14 . . . . . . 95 A6
Page CI
- **3** North Walsham NR28. . . . . 151 C6
- Poringland NR14 . . . . 90 C5
Page Rd
- Brundall NR13 . . . . 165 C4
- Norwich NR13 . . . . 157 F1
Pages CI 8 NR18 . . . . . . 173 B3
Pages La IP25 . . . . 84 B5
Page Stair La PE30 . . . . . 146 D5
Paget Adams Dr 4 NR20 . . 68 A8
Paget Cres NR31 . . . . 170 C1
Paget Rd NR30. . . . . 169 D4
Paige CI 1 PE31 . . . . 61 D5
Paine CI IP22 . . . . 177 B5
Paine Rd NR7 . . . . 163 D8
Painter St IP24 . . . . 176 C4
Pakenham Dr PE31. . . . . . 140 C3
Palace St NR1 . . . . 178 B3
Pales Gn 4 PE32 . . . . 46 F2
PALGRAVE IP22 . . . . 177 C2
Palgrave CI NR8 . . . . 155 B1
Palgrave Rd
- Great Dunham PE32 . . . . . 47 E1
- Great Yarmouth NR30 . . 169 C5
- Little Dunham PE32 . . . . . 65 D8
Palgrave VC Prim Sch IP22 . . . . 177 D2
Palling Rd NR12 . . . . 24 D1
Palm CI NR18. . . . . 173 B5
Palmer Rd
- Great Yarmouth NR31 . . 170 D1
- **8** New Rackheath NR13. . 72 E7
- Norwich NR3 . . . . 158 C3
Palmers La NR12. . . . . 55 C5
Palmer's La
- Aylsham NR11 . . . . 150 C6
- Freethorpe NR13 . . . . 92 F8
Palmer Way PE38 . . . . . . 172 C3
Pandora 1 PE30. . . . . . . 147 C4
Pansey Dr PE31 . . . . 140 C4
Panton CI PE30 . . . . 146 D2
PANXWORTH NR13 . . . . . . 73 E7
Panxworth Church Rd NR13 . . . . 73 E8
Panxworth Rd NR13 . . . . . 73 C7
Paper St NR19 . . . . 68 C7
Papillon Rd NR18. . . . . . 173 D4
Paradise La
- **8** Bawdeswell NR20 . . . . 50 E7
- **7** King's Lynn PE30 . . . 146 D5
Paradise Par 10 PE30. . . . 146 D5
Paradise PI NR1 . . . . 178 B2
Paradise Rd
- **7** Bawdeswell NR20 . . . . 50 E7
- Downham Market PE38 . . 172 B5
- **8** King's Lynn PE30 . . . 146 D5
Paragon PI 2 NR2 . . . . . . 162 C6
Parana CI NR7 . . . . 159 C5
Parana Ct NR7 . . . . 159 C5
Parana Rd NR7 . . . . 159 C5
Parish Rd NR10 . . . . 53 D7

Park Ave
- **5** Barford NR9 . . . . 69 F2
- King's Lynn PE30 . . . . . 146 F4
- North Walsham NR28 . . . 151 D5
- Scottow NR10 . . . . 37 D2
- Wisbech PE13 . . . . 152 C6
Park CI
- Hethersett NR9 . . . . 88 D7
- Holt NR25 . . . . 137 D5
- Norwich NR8 . . . . 158 E5
- Thurton NR14 . . . . 91 C4
- Wymondham NR18 . . . . 173 D1

Park Comm La NR16 . . . . 119 B5
Park Cres PE34 . . . . 61 B5
Park Ct
- Harling NR16 . . . . 118 C5
- North Walsham NR28 . . . 151 D5
Park Dr NR9 . . . . 88 C7
Parker CI NR13 . . . . 165 B4
Parker Dr NR21 . . . . 141 D4
Parker Rd NR2. . . . . 162 B5
Parkers CI NR18 . . . . 173 B6
Parker's CI NR9 . . . . 70 C5
Parker's La NR15 . . . . . . 106 F2
Parkers Prim Sch IP25 . . . 84 C5
Parker's Rd 10 NR20 . . . . 68 F6
Parkes La NR15 . . . . 106 D6
Park Est 3 IP25 . . . . 67 B2
Park Farm La
- Euston IP24 . . . . 126 C4
- Hoxne IP21 . . . . 131 C2
Park Highatt Dr 2 IP25 . . 67 C2
Park High Sch PE30 . . . . . 147 A4
Parkhill 4 PE32 . . . . 44 B3
Park Hill PE31 . . . . 140 D5
Park La
- Blofield NR13 . . . . 165 B8
- Cromer NR27 . . . . 139 D4
- Deopham NR18 . . . . 87 A4
- Downham Market PE38. . . 172 B3
- Helhoughton NR21. . . . . . 30 E5
- Hockering NR20 . . . . 69 C8
- North Walsham NR28 . . . 151 C5
- Norwich NR2 . . . . 162 B5
- Reepham NR10 . . . . . . 149 B4
- Scarning NR19 . . . . 67 B6
- Snettisham PE31 . . . . 12 E4
- Wymondham NR18 . . . . 173 C2
Parkland CI 8 NR12 . . . . . 55 E4
Parkland Cres
- **9** Horning NR12. . . . . . . 55 E4
- Norwich NR6 . . . . 158 F3
Parkland Dr NR31. . . . . . 170 A5
Parkland Est NR6 . . . . . . 167 A8
Parkland Rd NR6. . . . . . . 158 F3
Parklands NR8. . . . . 156 D4
Parklands Ave IP25 . . . . . . 67 B2
Parklands Way IP20 . . . . . 122 D2
Park Rd
- Cromer NR27 . . . . 139 D5
- Diss IP22 . . . . 177 D4
- East Dereham NR19 . . . . 154 E6
- Great Yarmouth NR31 . . 170 D3
- Gressenhall NR20 . . . . . . 49 C3
- Hunstanton PE36 . . . . . . 132 C4
- Spixworth NR10 . . . . 54 A1
- St Cross, South Elmham IP20 . . . . 123 C3
- Upper Sheringham NR26 . 138 A4
- Warham NR23 . . . . 6 A4
- Wells-next-the-Sea NR23 . 136 C6
- Wisbech PE13 . . . . 152 D5
- Wroxham/Hoveton NR12 . 164 B3
Parkside PE36 . . . . 13 A7
Parkside CI IP22 . . . . 177 C4
Parkside Dr NR6 . . . . 158 E5
Parkside Specl Sch NR7 . . 162 A5
Park St 4 IP25 . . . . 152 D5
Park The NR16. . . . . 118 B5
Parkview IP24 . . . . 176 E4
Park View
- Botesdale IP22 . . . . 128 F3
- Brandon IP27 . . . . 175 B2
- Weeting IP27 . . . . 175 A7
Park View Ave NR29. . . . . 57 D3
Parkway PE30 . . . . 147 B4
Park Way NR6 . . . . 157 E5
Parliament Ct 5 NR7 . . . . . 72 D7
Parliament La IP24 . . . . . . 102 E3
Parmenter Rd NR4 . . . . . . 161 F3
Parmeter CI NR11. . . . . . 150 D6
Parrow La NR11. . . . . 21 C6
Parr Rd NR3 . . . . 158 A1
Parsons CI IP27. . . . . 175 B2
Parsons La NR31. . . . . 14 D8
Parsons Mead NR4 . . . . . 161 F1
Partridge Dr
- Mulbarton NR14 . . . . 89 A3
- **4** Thetford IP24 . . . . . . 176 D2
Partridge Gr PE37. . . . . . 153 D3
Partridge Rd NR11 . . . . . 150 B6
Partridge Way NR6. . . . . 158 D4
Partridge Wlk IP27 . . . . . 175 F5
Parva CI NR12 . . . . 20 B4
Pasteur Rd NR31. . . . . . . 169 B2
PASTON NR28 . . . . 143 D2
Paston CI 4 NR11 . . . . 9 E1
Paston Coll NR28 . . . . . . 151 C5
Paston Dr NR30 . . . . 168 C8
Paston Great Barn* NR28. . . . . 143 D2
PASTON GREEN NR28 . . . . 143 D1
Paston Rd
- Great Yarmouth NR31 . . 170 C5
- Mundesley NR11 . . . . . . 143 D5
Paston Way NR7 . . . . 159 E2
Pasture CI NR31. . . . . 28 B4
Pastures The
- **3** Blakeney NR25 . . . . 7 C5
- Great Yarmouth NR31 . . 170 B7
- Hemsby NR29 . . . . 167 A8
- Little Snoring NR21. . . . . . 17 B3
Patricia Ave NR12. . . . . . . 54 C6
Patricia Rd NR12 . . . . . . 162 D3
Patrick Rd 4 NR15. . . . . . 106 D3
Patten La NR15 . . . . 121 B3
Patterson CI 4 NR30. . . . . 169 C4
Patteson CI 8 NR4. . . . . . 89 B8
Patteson Rd NR3. . . . . . . 162 D8
Paul Dr PE32 . . . . 44 B3

Pauls La NR27 . . . . 11 A3
Pavilion Ct 5 IP22. . . . . . 177 A5
Pavilion Rd NR31 . . . . . . 170 D4
Pavilion Theatre NR31. . . . 170 E4
Paxman Rd PE30. . . . . . . 146 F2
Paxton PI 3 NR2 . . . . 162 C4
Paxton Terr NR4 . . . . 146 E5
Payne Ave PE13 . . . . 152 D7
Paynes Hill IP20 . . . . 122 F6
Payne's La IP26. . . . . 98 E1
Peachman Way 6 NR7 . . . . 72 E4
Peachtree St NR1 . . . . 15 C2
Peacock Chase NR18 . . . . 173 D4
Peacock CI
- Easton NR9 . . . . 70 B5
- Hockwold cum Wilton IP26 113 F6
Peacock La
- Beetley NR20. . . . . 49 C5
- Holt NR25 . . . . 137 B7
Peacock St NR3. . . . . 178 B4
Peacock Way NR24 . . . . . 142 A4
Peakhall Rd PE32 . . . . 48 B8
Peakwell CI NR8 . . . . 155 C2
Pearcefield NR3 . . . . 158 E2
Pearce Rd IP22 . . . . 177 E4
Pearce's CI 2 IP26 . . . . . 114 A7
Pearmain Rd IP22 . . . . . . 177 C5
Pearsons CI
- Freethorpe NR13. . . . . . . 92 E7
- Holt NR25 . . . . 137 C6
Pearson's Rd NR25. . . . . . 137 C6
Peartree Ave 2 NR29 . . . . 57 C4
Pear Tree CI NR20 . . . . 68 E6
Pear Tree Cnr NR21 . . . . . . 31 C2
Peartree Way 9 PE14. . . . . 59 A1
PEASELAND GREEN NR20 . . 50 F3
Peatlings La PE13. . . . . . . 152 A7
Pebble CI 3 PE32 . . . . 41 B8
Pebble View Wlk NR31. . . 171 E4
Peck CI NR5 . . . . 160 E8
Peckover Cty Prim Sch PE13 . . . . 152 B6
Peckover Dr PE13 . . . . . . 152 E4
Peckover House* PE13 . . . 152 B5
Peckover Rd
- Fakenham NR21. . . . . . . 141 A6
- Norwich NR21. . . . . 161 B3
Peckover Way PE30 . . . . . 147 E8
Peddars CI PE36 . . . . 132 D6
Peddars Dr NR8 . . . . 155 D2
Peddars' La NR34 . . . . . . 110 C6
Peddars Way NR8. . . . . . 155 D2
Peddars Way N PE36 . . . . . 2 A4
Peddlars Turnpike NR20. . . 33 F3
PEDHAM NR13 . . . . 73 D7
Pedham Rd NR13 . . . . 73 E7
Pedlars Croft 2 NR29 . . . 167 A8
Pedlar's Gr PE27 . . . . 153 C5
Pedlar's La NR21. . . . . 17 F1
Pedley La PE13 . . . . 152 A6
Peel Mews 5 NR3 . . . . . . 178 A3
Peel St NR20 . . . . 146 F4
Pegasus CI NR30. . . . . . . 168 D7
Pegg CI NR9 . . . . 70 B5
Peggotty Rd NR30. . . . . . 170 D8
Pegg Rd NR26 . . . . 138 C5
Pegg's La NR10. . . . . 105 E6
Peldon Dr PE13 . . . . 152 E5
Pelham Rd NR3 . . . . 158 D1
Pellew PI NR28 . . . . 151 C6
Pell PI 2 PE33. . . . . 43 F2
Pell Rd NR5 . . . . 160 D4
Pemberton Rd 8 IP20 . . . 122 D2
Pembrey CI NR3 . . . . 158 D3
Pembroke Ave NR31 . . . . 170 B4
Pembroke Rd NR2 . . . . . . 162 B5
Pendlesham Rise NR8. . . . 155 E2
Pendula Rd PE13. . . . . . . 152 E7
Penfold Dr NR18 . . . . 173 E5
Penfold St NR11 . . . . 150 C6
Penguin Rd NR29 . . . . . . 167 D4
Penhill La NR17. . . . . 103 D7
Penn CI NR8 . . . . 156 D8
Penn Gr NR3 . . . . 158 C1
Pennington Way PE31. . . . 140 A1
Pennon Rd NR8 . . . . 156 D8
Pennycress Dr
- **6** Thetford IP24. . . . . . 176 F5
- Wymondham NR18 . . . . 173 E4
Penny Croft 8 NR21 . . . . . 15 C2
PENNYGATE NR12 . . . . 38 E2
Pennygate La NR12 . . . . . . 38 F1
Pennyroyal 1 NR6 . . . . . . 158 D5
Penrose CI PE30 . . . . 147 B8
Penrose Gdns PE13 . . . . . 152 E4
Penryn CI NR4 . . . . 161 E5
Penshurst Mews 5 NR4. . . 161 F1
Penshorpe Nature Reserve & Gdns* NR21 . . . . 32 B8
PENTNEY PE32 . . . . 63 C8
Pentney Abbey Leisure Ctr PE32 . . . . 63 A7
Pentney Dro PE33. . . . . . . 62 E6
Pentney La PE32 . . . . 63 D8
Pepper La PE38 . . . . 97 C8
Peppers CI IP27 . . . . 175 D7
Peppers' Gn PE30 . . . . . . 148 B1
Percival CI NR4 . . . . 161 E4
Perebrown Ave NR30. . . . 169 D7
Pereers CI NR25 . . . . 137 A7
Peregrine CI
- Diss IP22 . . . . 177 F5
- Norwich NR7 . . . . 159 C4
Peregrine Mews NR7. . . . 159 C4
Peregrine Rd NR7. . . . . . 159 C4
Perkin Field PE34 . . . . . . 144 B4
Perrings NR18 . . . . 173 B6

Perrys La NR10 . . . . 35 C2
Persimmon PE30. . . . . . . 147 C5
Peter Ave NR13 . . . . 166 B3
Peter Beales Roses* NR17. . . . . 103 F3
Peter CI NR29. . . . . 168 D8
Peter Dr IP24 . . . . 176 F5
Peterhouse Ave NR13 . . . 170 C4
Peterhouse Prim Sch NR13. . . . . 170 B4
Peterkin Rd 8 NR4 . . . . . . 89 E8
Peters CI NR19. . . . . 154 C1
Peterscourt PE30 . . . . . . 147 D6
Peter's Dro PE34. . . . . 61 A7
Petersfield CI NR15 . . . . . 106 F4
Peterson Rd NR3 . . . . . . 158 A2
Peterson's La NR11 . . . . . 150 B7
Peterspoint PE12 . . . . 41 A7
Peto Ct NR5 . . . . 161 C7
Peto's Cnr NR32 . . . . 111 F8
Petre CI 3 NR28. . . . . . . 151 C7
Petticoat Dro PE32. . . . . . 64 E8
Petticoat La PE33 . . . . 62 D6
Pettingales 3 NR14. . . . . . 89 F4
Pettits La IP21 . . . . 130 C7
Pettits Animal Adventure Pk* NR13 . . . . 93 A5
Petts CI 3 PE13 . . . . 152 E7
Pettus Rd NR4 . . . . 161 E3
Petty Spurge Sq 8 NR18 . . . . 173 E4
PETTYWELL NR10. . . . . 34 C2
Petunia Way IP27 . . . . . . 175 A2
Peverell Rd NR14 . . . . . . 161 B7
Pheasant CI NR14 . . . . 89 A3
Pheasants Wlk NR35 . . . . 123 E8
Pheasant Way IP27 . . . . . 175 F4
Pheasant Wlk 2 NR13 . . . 74 B8
Phelps Rd NR7. . . . . 163 F7
Philadelphia La NR3 . . . . 158 C2
Philip Ford Way NR18 . . . 173 C2
Philip Nurse Rd PE31. . . . 140 B3
Philip PI NR19 . . . . 154 D2
Philip Rudd Ct PE32 . . . . . 45 A8
Philips' Chase PE36 . . . . . 132 D2
Phillippo CI 2 NR32 . . . . . 28 A1
Pickards Way NR13 . . . . . 152 A6
Pickford CI NR28. . . . . . . 151 E6
Picton Rd NR15 . . . . 106 D4
Pier Gdns NR31 . . . . 170 E4
Pier Plain NR31. . . . . 170 D2
Pier Plain NR31 . . . . 170 D2
Pier Rd NR31 . . . . 170 E4
Pier Wlk NR31 . . . . 170 D4
Pigeon St PE14 . . . . 41 D3
Pigg La NR3 . . . . 178 B4
Pightle CI 5 NR14 . . . . . . 89 B3
Pightle The PE37. . . . . . . 153 C4
Pightle Way
- Lyng NR9 . . . . 51 A4
- Reepham NR10 . . . . 149 C5
Pigot La NR14 . . . . 90 C6
Pike La IP24 . . . . 176 D3
Pikeman PI NR13 . . . . 72 E5
Pikes Nursery NR29 . . . . . 56 C5
Pilgrims Way
- Little Cressingham IP25 . . . 83 F3
- Weeting IP27. . . . . 175 A2
Pilgrim's Way 7 IP20. . . . 122 D2
Pilling Pk Rd NR1. . . . . . . 163 B7
Pilling Rd NR7 . . . . 163 D7
Pilot St 2 PE30. . . . . 146 D5
PILSON GREEN NR13 . . . . . 74 B8
Pimpernel Rd NR10 . . . . . 53 B2
Pincushion Dro PE14. . . . . 78 B5
Pinder CI NR3 . . . . 158 A1
Pinder Rd NR3 . . . . 158 A1
Pine Ave
- Cockley Cley PE37 . . . . . . 82 D7
- Marham NR3 . . . . 63 B4
Pine CI
- **5** Downham Market PE38. . . . . 172 C6
- **8** Eye IP23. . . . . 130 C1
- **4** Harleston IP20. . . . . . 122 D1
- Hunstanton PE36. . . . . . 132 D4
- **17** Marthan NR29 . . . . . . 57 D4
- Norwich NR4 . . . . 162 A3
- Ormesby St Margaret NR29. . . . . 167 A3
- **3** Snettisham PE31 . . . . . 12 E4
- Thetford IP24 . . . . 176 B1
Pine Coombe 1 NR21. . . . . 15 C2
Pinecot Ave 7 NR31. . . . . 94 C6
Pine Ct NR17 . . . . 174 D4
Pine Gn NR31. . . . . 170 B5
Pine Gr
- East Dereham NR19 . . . . 154 D2
- Sheringham NR26 . . . . . 138 E6
Pineheath Rd NR25 . . . . 8 E3
Pinelodges Th NR7 . . . . . 163 C6
Pine Loke NR14. . . . . 90 B5
Pine Mall PE31 . . . . 133 C6
Pine Rd
- King's Lynn PE30 . . . . . . 148 D2
- Norwich NR7 . . . . 159 C2
Pine Tree Chase PE33 . . . . 43 F1
Pine Tree Ct IP22 . . . . . . 127 F5
Pinetrees NR31 . . . . 170 B4
Pinetrees Rd NR7 . . . . . . 159 D3
Pine Wlk 6 NR25 . . . . 8 F5
Pinewood CI NR6 . . . . . . 157 F4
Pinewood Dr
- Brandon IP27 . . . . 175 C2
- **8** Horning NR12. . . . . . . 55 E4
Pinewood Leisure Ctr NR25. . . . . 9 B3

Pinfold La
Hindolveston NR20 . . . . 33 D8
Northwold IP26 . . . . 99 B8
Pinfold Rd PE14 . . . . 77 E5
Pingle Rd PE14 . . . . 78 A4
Pingles Rd PE30 . . . . 148 C4
Pinkney La NR24 . . . . 19 B5
Pintail Dr
 2 Blakeney NR25 . . . . 7 C6
 Great Yarmouth NR31 . . . 170 A6
Pioneer Rd NR6 . . . . 159 A6
Piper Rd
 King's Lynn PE30 . . . . 146 F1
 Norwich NR7 . . . . 159 E1
Pipit's Mdw NR11 . . . . 21 A5
Pippin Cl
 Dereham NR19 . . . . 154 C3
 Ormesby St Margaret
 NR29 . . . . 167 A2
Pippin Gdns PE13 . . . . 152 F7
Pippin Gn NR4 . . . . 161 E5
Pippin Pl PE13 . . . . 152 E2
Pirnhow St NR35 . . . . 109 B1
Pishmire Cl NR5 . . . . 160 F6
Pitchford Rd NR5 . . . . 161 C6
Pit La PE37 . . . . 153 C4
Pit Rd
 Aldeby, Wheatacre, Burgh St
 Peter NR34 . . . . 111 B4
 Hemsby NR29 . . . . 167 A7
 Northrepps NR27 . . . . 11 A1
 Woodbastwick NR13 . . . . . 55 D1
Pit St NR11 . . . . 22 C6
Pitt's Hill NR15 . . . . 107 B8
Pitts Hill Cl NR15 . . . . 107 B8
Pitt Sq NR9 . . . . 86 C4
Pitt St NR3 . . . . 178 A4
Pius Dro PE14 . . . . 77 F6
Plaford Rd NR7 . . . . 159 A2
Plane Rd NR31 . . . . 170 B6
Plantation Cl NR13 . . . . . . 174 C3
Plantation Dr NR7 . . . . 159 D3
Plantation Gdn The ★
 NR2 . . . . 162 C5
Plantation Rd
 Aslacton NR15 . . . . 121 A7
 Blofield NR13 . . . . 165 F7
 4 Fakenham NR21 . . . . 141 E4
 North Walsham NR28 . . . 151 E5
 Norwich NR6 . . . . 157 E6
Plantation The NR2 . . . . . 162 B4
Plantsman Cl NR2 . . . . 162 B3
Plasset Dr NR17 . . . . 174 F7
Platten's Cl 8 NR11 . . . . . 19 F1
Platten's Cl 8 NR12 . . . . . 164 B3
Playbarn The ★ NR15 . . . . 90 C3
Players Rd NR6 . . . . 158 A4
Playing Field La 12 NR29 . 57 D4
Pleasance Cl PE30 . . . . 147 A5
Pleasant Cl NR6 . . . . 157 D5
Pleasant Cl 8 PE30 . . . . . 146 E3
Pleasant Pl PE31 . . . . 133 C8
Pleasant Row NR37 . . . . . 153 C3
Pleasure Beach ★ NR30 . 169 E1
Plevna Terr NR31 . . . . 169 B3
Ploughboy La IP25 . . . . 84 C6
Plough La
 Hardingham NR9 . . . . 86 D6
 Watlington PE33 . . . . 61 E5
Ploughman Rd PE30 . . . . . 147 C4
Ploughman's Dro IP26 . . . 98 B1
Ploughman's La NR21 . . . . 17 E6
Ploughman's Piece PE36 . . 2 B1
Plover Cl
 Great Yarmouth NR31 . . . 170 A7
 3 Thetford IP24 . . . . . . 176 D2
Plovers Ct IP27 . . . . 175 F3
Plovers Way IP26 . . . . 113 E7
Plowright Pl PE13 . . . . 153 B4
Plumbly Cl NR28 . . . . 151 D3
Plumb's Cl NR4 . . . . 142 E4
Plum La NR11 . . . . 20 C8
Plummers Hill NR23 . . . . . 136 D5
Plummer's La NR15 . . . . . 107 C2
Plump Rd NR15 . . . . 106 D5
Plumsgate Rd NR12 . . . . . . 39 C1
Plumstead Dr NR17 . . . . . 174 E6
PLUMSTEAD GREEN
 Great and Little Plumstead
 NR13 . . . . 73 B6
 Plumstead NR11 . . . . 20 B6
Plumstead Rd
 Baconsthorpe NR25 . . . . . 20 A7
 Edgefield NR24 . . . . 19 E5
 Great & Little Plumstead
 NR13 . . . . 72 E6
 4 Norwich NR1 . . . . 163 C8
 Thorpe End NR13 . . . . 72 E6
 Woodbastwick NR13 . . . . . 73 D7
Plumstead Rd E NR7 . . . 163 D8
Plymouth Cl 3 NR30 . . . 168 C6
Plymouth Rd 2 IP31 . . . . 126 B1
Pocahontas Way PE31 . . 133 E5
POCKTHORPE
 Sparham NR9 . . . . 51 B5
 Thompson IP24 . . . . 102 A7
 West Rudham PE31 . . . . . . 29 F6
Pockthorpe Gate NR3 . . . 163 A7
Pockthorpe La IP24 . . . . . 102 A7
Pockthorpe Loke
 Barnham Broom NR9 . . . . . 69 D2
 Hickling NR12 . . . . 39 F2
Pockthorpe Rd NR9 . . . . . . 88 A8
PODMORE NR19 . . . . 67 B7
Podmore La NR19 . . . . 67 C8
Point Dr 2 PE37 . . . . 153 C3
Police Rd PE14 . . . . 41 D4
Polka Rd NR23 . . . . 136 D5

Pollard Rd NR10 . . . . 53 E6
POLLARD STREET NR12 . . 23 D3
Pollywiggle Cl NR5 . . . . . . 161 A6
Pommer's La NR30 . . . . . . 170 D8
Pond Cl 14 NR9 . . . . 88 C7
Pond Hills Rd NR25 . . . . . . 19 E7
Pond La
 Brandon IP27 . . . . 175 A2
 Knapton NR28 . . . . 143 B2
 Surlingham NR14 . . . . 73 B1
 Taverham NR8 . . . . 156 F8
Pond Rd
 Antingham NR28 . . . . 22 B4
 East Dereham NR19 . . . . 154 C2
 8 Horsford NR10 . . . . . . 53 A3
 Swafield NR28 . . . . 22 C3
Ponds End La IP22 . . . . . . 127 E4
Pooley St IP22 . . . . 128 F7
POOLEY STREET IP22 . . . 129 A8
Poorhouse La NR14 . . . . . . 89 A2
Pope's La PE34 . . . . 144 A4
Poplar Ave
 Great Yarmouth NR31 . . . 170 C3
 Heacham PE31 . . . . 133 C5
 King's Lynn PE34 . . . . 43 D4
 5 Marham PE33 . . . . . . 63 B4
 Norwich NR4 . . . . 161 E1
Poplar Cl
 Downham Market PE38 . . 172 B6
 Honington IP31 . . . . 126 B3
 12 Horsford NR10 . . . . . . 53 A3
 Long Stratton NR15 . . . . . 106 F4
 Norwich NR5 . . . . 156 F2
Poplar Dr
 Filby NR29 . . . . 75 F8
 Happisburgh NR12 . . . . . . 23 F3
 King's Lynn PE30 . . . . 148 D2
 Loddon NR14 . . . . 109 C8
Poplar Gr NR26 . . . . 138 E5
Poplar Rd
 Attleborough NR17 . . . . . 174 B2
 West Winch PE33 . . . . 43 F1
Poplars The
 Hilgay PE38 . . . . 96 F8
 Spexhall IP19 . . . . 124 F1
 Swanton Abbott NR10 . . . . 37 C4
 Tacolneston NR16 . . . . . . 105 F4
Poplar Way NR17 . . . . 174 C2
Pople St NR18 . . . . 173 B4
Poppy Cl
 Chedgrave NR14 . . . . 91 F2
 North Walsham NR28 . . . 151 F5
 4 Thetford IP24 . . . . . . 176 F4
Poppy Dr 5 NR26 . . . . . . 138 B6
Poppyfields 14 NR10 . . . . . 53 A3
Poppy's La IP27 . . . . 121 F5
PORINGLAND NR14 . . . . . . 90 C5
Poringland Prim Sch
 NR14 . . . . 90 D5
Poringland Rd NR14 . . . . . 90 B5
Porson Rd NR7 . . . . 159 C1
Portal Ave IP25 . . . . 84 F3
Portal Cl
 8 Barnham IP24 . . . . . . 125 F6
 7 Feltwell IP26 . . . . 98 D1
Portalfield 10 NR12 . . . . . . 39 B4
Porterbush Rd 18 NR14 . . 89 B3
Porter Rd 8 NR15 . . . . . . 106 E3
Portersfield Rd NR2 . . . . . 162 B5
Porter's La NR9 . . . . 51 E5
Porter's Loke
 1 Belton NR31 . . . . 94 A6
 Burgh Castle NR31 . . . . . . 93 F6
 Norwich NR7 . . . . 159 A3
Porter's Rd
 Beighton NR13 . . . . 74 E1
 Freethorpe NR13 . . . . 92 E8
Porter St PE38 . . . . 172 A5
Porthole Cl 10 NR13 . . . . 111 F1
Portland Cl NR31 . . . . 169 C3
Portland Pl
 Great Yarmouth NR30 . . . 169 E3
 King's Lynn PE30 . . . . 146 D2
 3 Thetford IP24 . . . . . . 116 A1
Portland St
 12 King's Lynn PE30 . . . 146 E5
 Norwich NR2 . . . . 162 B5
Port Rd NR15 . . . . 122 B8
Port Row NR9 . . . . 51 B4
Portsmouth Rd 3 IP31 . . 126 B1
Portway Pl 2 NR2 . . . . . . 162 C7
Portway Sq 10 NR2 . . . . . 162 C7
Post Mill Dr NR7 . . . . 147 C5
Postmill Cl NR18 . . . . 173 C4
Post Mill Cl NR7 . . . . 159 A3
Post Office Cl 8 NR13 . . . 74 A3
Post Office La
 Corpusty NR11 . . . . 34 F8
 Garvestone NR9 . . . . 86 B8
 Weston Longville NR9 . . . . 51 E2
 12 Wisbech PE13 . . . . . 152 C5
Post Office Rd
 Dersingham PE31 . . . . . . 140 D3
 Frettenham NR12 . . . . 54 A4
 Great & Little Plumstead
 NR13 . . . . 73 B7
 Lingwood & Burlingham
 NR13 . . . . 74 A3
 Lingwood NR13 . . . . 74 A3
 Toft Monks NR34 . . . . 110 E5
POSTWICK NR13 . . . . 72 F2
Postwick La NR13 . . . . 165 A4
Postwick Sta NR13 . . . . . . 72 E3
Potash La
 Bracon Ash NR16 . . . . 88 D2
 Eye IP23 . . . . 130 A2
Potato Dro PE14 . . . . 60 B4
Potspoon Hole
 Coltishall NR12 . . . . 54 D8

Potspoon Hole continued
 Tunstead NR12 . . . . 37 D1
Pottergate NR2 . . . . 178 A3
Pottergate St NR15 . . . . . . 106 A2
POTTERGATE STREET
 NR15 . . . . 106 B2
POTTER HEIGHAM NR29 . . 56 F6
Potter Heigham Rd NR29 . 56 D8
Potteries ★ NR30 . . . . 169 D2
Potters Cres NR15 . . . . . . 121 C8
Potters Dr NR31 . . . . 171 D5
Potter's La
 Rickinghall Superior
 IP22 . . . . 128 F1
 Wymondham NR18 . . . . . 105 B6
Potters Vale IP22 . . . . 128 C3
POTTHORPE NR20 . . . . 49 A8
Pottles Alley 4 NR9 . . . . . 86 C5
Pottle's La NR13 . . . . 92 F5
Poulter's Dro PE14 . . . . 77 D1
Poultry Rd IP27 . . . . 113 A3
Pound Cl
 4 Harleston IP20 . . . . . 122 D2
 Hevingham NR10 . . . . 53 C8
Pound Gn La IP25 . . . . 67 C2
Pound Hill IP25 . . . . 84 B5
Pound La
 Aylsham NR11 . . . . 150 B6
 Brundall NR13 . . . . 165 F5
 Burgh St Margaret (Fleggburgh)
 NR29 . . . . 75 C8
 Ditchingham NR35 . . . . . 108 C2
 Docking PE31 . . . . 134 D5
 Filby NR29 . . . . 75 F8
 Great Yarmouth NR31 . . . 170 C3
 Heacham PE31 . . . . 133 D6
 Litcham PE32 . . . . 48 A4
 Loddon NR14 . . . . 109 C8
 North Tuddenham NR20 . . 50 D2
 Norwich NR7 . . . . 72 D4
 Runhall NR20 . . . . 69 A4
 Sloley NR12 . . . . 37 F2
 Toft Monks NR34 . . . . 110 D6
Pound Rd
 East Ruston NR12 . . . . 38 F7
 Hevingham NR10 . . . . 53 C8
 Ludham NR29 . . . . 56 C5
 North Walsham NR28 . . . 151 D5
Powell Ct 5 NR19 . . . . . . 154 C6
Power's Pl PE38 . . . . 79 D1
Poynt Cl NR13 . . . . 173 B5
Pratts Hill NR14 . . . . 73 A1
Press La NR3 . . . . 158 C1
Preston Ave NR18 . . . . 173 A2
Preston Cl
 Freethorpe NR13 . . . . 92 E7
 Wroxham/Hoveton NR12 . 164 B2
Preston La NR18 . . . . 109 F8
Preston Rd NR28 . . . . 151 D6
Preston VC Prim Sch
 NR15 . . . . 106 F7
Pride Way NR11 . . . . 72 E5
Primrose Cl
 Attleborough NR17 . . . . . 174 B5
 East Dereham NR19 . . . . 154 B4
 15 Mulbarton NR14 . . . . . 89 B3
 Mundesley NR11 . . . . 143 B5
 Thetford IP24 . . . . 176 F4
PRIMROSE CORNER NR13 . 55 C1
Primrose Cres 2 NR7 . . . . 72 D3
Primrose Ct 3 NR7 . . . . . . 72 D3
Primrose Dr IP27 . . . . 175 A2
PRIMROSE GREEN NR9 . . . 51 A3
Primrose Hill NR20 . . . . . . 50 B4
Primrose La
 Crostwick NR12 . . . . 54 C3
 Sheringham NR26 . . . . . . 138 B5
 Swanton Morley NR20 . . . 50 B4
Primrose Pl NR2 . . . . 162 B5
Primrose Rd
 Hingham NR9 . . . . 86 B5
 Norwich NR1 . . . . 163 A6
Primrose Sq NR20 . . . . 50 B4
Primrose Way
 15 Great Yarmouth NR31 . . 94 C6
 10 Horsford NR10 . . . . . . 53 A3
Primrose Wlk NR4 . . . . . . 151 E4
Primula Dr NR4 . . . . 161 D5
Prince Andrew's Cl
 2 Attleborough NR11 . . . 21 A5
 Norwich NR6 . . . . 158 B5
Prince Andrew's Rd NR6 158 B5
Prince Charles Cl PE31 . . 140 D3
Prince Edward Cl NR7 . . . 163 F7
Prince Henry Pl IP38 . . . . 122 D4
Prince of Wales Cl PE13 152 D8
Prince of Wales Rd
 Caister-on-Sea NR30 . . . 168 C6
 Cromer NR27 . . . . 139 B7
 Norwich NR1 . . . . 178 B3
 Upton with Fishley NR13 . 166 A8
Prince Regent Way IP22 . 177 F3
Prince Rupert Way NR13 . 72 C5
Princes Cl IP27 . . . . 175 A2
Princes Rd PE13 . . . . 152 C4
Prince's Rd
 Bungay NR35 . . . . 124 A7
 Great Yarmouth NR30 . . . 169 D4
Princess Beatrice Cl
 NR6 . . . . 157 D2
Princess Cl 7 IP25 . . . . . . 84 D3
Princess Ct 5 NR25 . . . . . 137 C5
Princess Dr PE36 . . . . 132 D2
Princess's Dr
 Dersingham PE35 . . . . . . 140 C1

Princess's Dr continued
 Sandringham PE35 . . . . . . 27 D7
Princes St
 North Walsham NR28 . . . 151 A5
 Norwich NR3 . . . . 178 B3
 Swaffham PE37 . . . . 153 B4
Prince's St PE12 . . . . 41 B8
Princess Theatre PE36 . . 132 C4
Princess Way 5 NR35 . . . 123 F8
Prince St PE13 . . . . 152 D5
Princes Way PE30 . . . . . . 146 F5
Prince William Cl PE36 . . 132 C3
Pringle Way 5 PE38 . . . . . 97 B5
Prins Rd PE13 . . . . 152 D7
Prins Cts 3 PE13 . . . . 152 D7
Printing Mus ★ NR34 . . . 110 D1
Prior Bank Orch 3
 NR27 . . . . 139 C6
Prior Cl 5 NR15 . . . . 106 F6
Prior Rd NR7 . . . . 72 D5
Priors Dr NR6 . . . . 158 E6
Prior Stephen Way IP24 . 176 B3
Priorswood NR8 . . . . 155 E3
Priory Chase
 Downham Market PE38 . . 172 B5
 Wormegay PE33 . . . . 61 F8
Priory Cl
 Acle NR13 . . . . 166 C3
 Alpington NR14 . . . . 90 F5
 Caister-on-Sea NR30 . . . 168 D4
 2 Fritton & St Olaves
 NR31 . . . . 93 D2
 7 Hethersett NR9 . . . . . . 88 D7
 Palgrave IP22 . . . . 177 D1
 Sheringham NR26 . . . . . . 138 F5
Priory Cres NR21 . . . . 6 E2
Priory Dro IP25 . . . . 83 D4
Priory Gdns
 1 Fritton & St Olaves
 NR31 . . . . 93 D2
 12 Great Yarmouth NR30 . 169 C4
Priory La
 Ingworth NR11 . . . . 21 A1
 12 King's Lynn PE30 . . . 146 D6
 Shotesham NR15 . . . . 90 A2
Priory Maze & Gdns ★
 NR26 . . . . 138 F6
Priory Pk IP24 . . . . 176 C3
Priory Pl PE32 . . . . 65 D6
Priory Plain 13 NR30 . . . 169 C4
Priory Rd
 Bacton NR12 . . . . 23 E4
 Castle Acre PE32 . . . . 46 F1
 Downham Market PE38 . . 172 B5
 Fritton & St Olaves NR31 . 93 D2
 Great Cressingham IP25 . . 83 D5
 Hethersett NR9 . . . . 88 D7
 King's Lynn PE30 . . . . 148 C5
 Palgrave IP22 . . . . 177 C1
 Sheringham NR26 . . . . . . 138 E7
 Watton IP25 . . . . 84 E3
 Woodbastwick NR13 . . . . . 55 F1
Priory Row 11 NR30 . . . . 169 C4
Priory St NR31 . . . . 170 D6
Priory Terr PE38 . . . . 172 B5
Priscilla Cl NR5 . . . . 161 D5
Pristow Gn La NR16 . . . . . 120 E8
PRISTOW GREEN NR16 . . . 120 E8
Private Rd
 Earsham NR35 . . . . 123 D8
 Ormesby St Margaret
 NR29 . . . . 167 A3
Procession La PE32 . . . . . 153 F8
Proctor Ave NR14 . . . . 92 A2
Proctor Cl 4 NR14 . . . . 92 A2
Proctor Rd
 Chedgrave NR14 . . . . 91 F2
 5 Loddon NR14 . . . . 92 A2
 Norwich NR6 . . . . 158 F6
Proctors Cl PE30 . . . . 146 C2
Progress Way IP23 . . . . . . 130 B1
Promenade
 Overstrand NR27 . . . . 11 A4
 Sheringham NR26 . . . . . . 138 D7
Prophets Alley PE34 . . . . . 61 B6
Prospect Pl PE13 . . . . 152 C3
Proudfoot Way NR11 . . . . 150 B5
Provan Cres 6 NR5 . . . . . . 94 A5
Provence Pl 2 PE13 . . . . . 152 E3
Providence Pl
 Briston NR24 . . . . 142 E5
 Thorpe Hamlet NR1 . . . . 163 A6
Providence St 5 PE30 . . . 146 E4
Providence Terr PE13 . . . 153 A5
Provision Mkt NR3 . . . . . . 178 A3
Provost Rd PE30 . . . . 98 D1
Puddingmoor NR34 . . . . . 110 C1
PUDDING NORTON NR21 . 141 B1
Pudding Norton Medieval
 Village of ★ NR21 . . . . . . 31 E6
PUDDLEDOCK NR17 . . . . . 104 C3
Pug St IP21 . . . . 121 B2
Pulham CE Prim Sch
 IP21 . . . . 121 E5
PULHAM MARKET IP21 . . 121 E5
PULHAM ST MARY IP21 . . 121 F4
Pullover Rd PE34 . . . . 146 A1
Pump La NR30 . . . . 168 D3
Punsher Way PE34 . . . . 60 C8
Purbeck Cl PE14 . . . . 152 A4
Purdance Cl NR5 . . . . 160 D8
Purdy St NR25 . . . . 8 B6
Purdy Way NR11 . . . . 150 B6
Purfleet PE30 . . . . 146 D5
Purfleet St
 11 King's Lynn PE30 . . . 146 D5

Purfleet St continued
 8 King's Lynn PE30 . . . . 146 D5
Purland Rd NR7 . . . . 159 D2
Purley Ct NR31 . . . . 169 A1
Pursehouse Way IP22 . . . 177 E4
Purtingay Cl NR4 . . . . 162 A1
Putney Cl IP27 . . . . 175 A1
Pyebush La NR13 . . . . 166 B5
Pyecroft Rd PE14 . . . . 41 E3
Pyehurn La NR10 . . . . 53 A3
Pyehurn Mews NR8 . . . . . 155 E3
Pye La
 Cranworth IP25 . . . . 86 A6
 Deopham NR18 . . . . 86 E2
Pyes Cl 1 NR25 . . . . 7 C6
Pye's La
 Castle Acre PE32 . . . . 46 F2
 Swanton Morley NR20 . . . 50 C3
Pyes Mill Rd NR14 . . . . 92 A1
Pyes Yd NR3 . . . . 178 B4
Pyghtle The 4 NR16 . . . . 118 C5
Pyke Ct NR30 . . . . 168 D7
Pymar's La 6 NR15 . . . . . 107 C5
Pym Cl NR13 . . . . 72 E5
Pyrford Dr NR4 . . . . 161 F1

Q

Quaker La
 Fakenham NR21 . . . . 141 B4
 Norwich NR6 . . . . 53 E1
 8 Spixworth NR12 . . . . . 54 A1
 Tasburgh NR15 . . . . 106 E6
 Wisbech PE13 . . . . 152 E3
Quarry La NR9 . . . . 51 A5
Quay Angel NR31 . . . . 170 D1
Quay La NR25 . . . . 2 A7
Quay Mill Wlk 3 NR30 . . 169 C4
Quay Ostend NR31 . . . . . . 171 C8
Quay Rd NR31 . . . . 170 D4
Quay Side NR31 . . . . 178 B4
Quay The
 Blakeney NR25 . . . . 7 C6
 Wells-next-the-Sea NR23 . 136 C6
 Wiveton NR25 . . . . 7 E7
Quebec Cl 14 NR4 . . . . 89 B8
Quebec Rd
 Dereham NR19 . . . . 154 D7
 Norwich NR1 . . . . 163 A6
Quebec St NR19 . . . . 154 D5
Queen Anne's Rd NR31 . . 170 C8
Queen Elizabeth Ave
 PE30 . . . . 147 B7
Queen Elizabeth Cl NR3 . 178 C4
Queen Elizabeth Dr
 Dersingham PE31 . . . . . . 140 D3
 Wisbech PE13 . . . . 152 F8
Queen Elizabeth Hospl
 PE30 . . . . 147 A5
Queen Elizabeth Way
 Bawsey PE30 . . . . 147 F6
 Castle Rising PE30 . . . . . . 27 C1
Queen Mary Rd PE30 . . . 147 A5
Queens Ave PE30 . . . . 146 D2
Queens Cl
 6 Blakeney NR25 . . . . 7 C6
 Norwich NR4 . . . . 162 A3
Queen's Cl PE33 . . . . 80 E4
Queen's Cres
 Bircham PE31 . . . . 14 A3
 Great Yarmouth NR31 . . . 170 B3
Queens Ct 1 NR15 . . . . . . 106 E3
Queen's Ct NR17 . . . . 174 D6
Queens Dr PE36 . . . . 132 C6
Queen's Dr PE34 . . . . 77 A7
Queens Gdns PE36 . . . . . 132 C6
Queen's Hill Pr Sch NR8 156 A5
Queen's Pl 2 PE34 . . . . 43 B1
Queens Rd
 Attleborough NR17 . . . . . 174 C6
 Clenchwarton PE34 . . . . . 146 A5
 Fakenham NR21 . . . . 141 C4
 Great Yarmouth NR30 . . . 169 D2
 Hethersett NR9 . . . . 88 D8
 Holt NR25 . . . . 137 C5
Queens Sch The PE13 . . . 152 C5
Queen's Sq NR17 . . . . 174 D6
Queen St
 Great Yarmouth NR30 . . . 169 C3
 King's Lynn PE30 . . . . 146 D5
 New Buckenham NR16 . . 104 F1
 Norwich NR1 . . . . 178 B3
 Stradbroke IP21 . . . . 131 E1
 12 Sutton Bridge PE12 . . 41 B8
 Swaffham PE37 . . . . 153 B4
 Wisbech PE13 . . . . 152 C6
 Wymondham NR18 . . . . . 173 C3
Queensway
 Caister-on-Sea NR30 . . . 168 A4
 7 Earsham NR35 . . . . . . 123 F8
 King's Lynn PE30 . . . . 147 C6
 North Walsham NR28 . . . 151 A5
 Roydon IP22 . . . . 177 A5
 Thetford IP24 . . . . 176 C2
 Watton IP25 . . . . 84 D3
 Wymondham NR18 . . . . . 173 B5
Queensway Com Jun Sch
 IP24 . . . . 176 C2
Queensway Inf Sch IP24 176 C2

QUIDENHAM NR16 . . . . 118 F6
Quidenham Rd
  Harling NR16 . . . . 118 D5
  Kenninghall NR16 . . . . 119 A5
  Quidenham NR16 . . . . 118 F8

R

Rabbit La
  Downham Market PE38 . . . 172 D6
  Great Witchingham NR9 . . . 51 E6
Raby Ave PE30 . . . . 146 E6
Racecourse Rd NR7 . . . . . . 159 E1
Raceys Cl 4 PE14 . . . . 59 D2
Rachel Cl 7 NR5 . . . . 161 C5
Rackham Cl NR11 . . . . 171 C5
Rackham Rd NR3 . . . . 158 D2
RACKHEATH NR13 . . . . 72 E8
Rackheath La NR12 . . . . . . 54 B2
Rackheath Prim Sch
  NR13 . . . . 54 D1
Radcliffe Rd NR8 . . . . 155 E2
RAF Air Defence Radar
  Mus** NR12 . . . . 55 E5
Rafeman Cl 3 NR5 . . . . 160 E7
Raglan St 1 NR2 . . . . 162 C6
RAGMERE NR17 . . . . 104 D1
Ragmere Rd NR17 . . . . 104 D1
Railway App 2 NR26 . . . . . 138 D7
Railway Hill IP20 . . . . 122 C2
Railway La PE12 . . . . 41 B7
Railway Mus NR18 . . . . . . 173 D2
Railway Rd
  Downham Market PE38 . . . 172 A5
  King's Lynn PE30 . . . . 146 E5
  Wisbech PE13 . . . . 152 C3
Rainey Ct 17 IP20 . . . . 122 D2
Rainsborough Rise NR13 . 72 D5
Rainsthorpe PE30 . . . . 147 D8
Rainthorpe Hall NR15 . . . 106 F8
Raleigh Ave NR30 . . . . 169 D7
Raleigh Inf Sch IP24 . . . . 176 E6
Raleigh Rd PE30 . . . . 147 B4
Raleigh Way IP24 . . . . 176 E6
Ramblers The NR14 . . . . . . 90 B6
Rambouillet Cl NR31 . . . . 170 A4
Ram La NR15 . . . . 121 C4
Ramms Ct NR23 . . . . 136 D6
Ramm's La PE37 . . . . 66 A4
Ramnoth Cty Jun Sch
  PE13 . . . . 152 C4
Ramnoth Rd PE13 . . . . 152 D4
Rampant Horse St NR2 . . 178 A2
Rampart Rd NR30 . . . . 169 C5
Rampart Way IP24 . . . . . . 176 D3
Ramsay Cl PE36 . . . . 132 D3
Ramsey Cl
  Norwich NR4 . . . . 161 E3
  Thetford IP24 . . . . 176 E6
Randall Cl 1 NR11 . . . . . . 171 D5
Randell Cl NR28 . . . . 151 D4
Randle Gn NR5 . . . . 161 C8
Randolf Rd NR1 . . . . 162 E2
Rands Rd PE14 . . . . 60 C5
Rangoon Cl NR7 . . . . 159 C4
Ransome Ave IP21 . . . . . . 130 B5
Ransome's Cl PE14 . . . . . . 77 E5
Ranson Rd NR3 . . . . 163 B5
RANWORTH NR13 . . . . 55 F1
Ranworth 5 PE30 . . . . 147 D5
Ranworth Rd
  8 Belton NR31 . . . . 94 A6
  Swaffham PE37 . . . . 153 B1
Ranworth Dr NR29 . . . . . . 167 B2
Ranworth Fst Sch NR5 . . 161 E7
Ranworth Rd
  Blofield NR13 . . . . 165 F8
  Norwich NR5 . . . . 161 D7
  South Walsham NR13 . . . . . 74 A8
Rash's Cres IP22 . . . . 129 C6
Rash's Gn NR19 . . . . 154 F2
Ratcliffe Rd NR21 . . . . 141 C4
RATTEN ROW PE14 . . . . . . 59 F8
Rattle Row
  Mileham PE32 . . . . 48 C6
  Wymondham NR18 . . . . . . 173 B4
Rattlerow Hill IP21 . . . . . 131 F2
Rattler's Rd IP27 . . . . 175 C3
Raven Cl NR31 . . . . 170 A7
RAVENINGHAM NR14 . . . . 110 A7
Raveningham Gdns
  NR14 . . . . 110 A7
Raveningham Rd
  Gillingham NR34 . . . . 110 C4
  Stockton NR34 . . . . 110 A5
Raven's La PE31 . . . . 29 D5
Ravensway PE38 . . . . 172 C4
Ravine Rd NR31 . . . . 93 E1
Rawhall La NR20 . . . . 49 B5
Rawley Rd NR5 . . . . 161 B8
Rawlings Way 21 IP26 . . . 98 E1
Rawlinsons La NR15 . . . . 107 C7
Ray Bond Way NR11 . . . . 150 C4
Raymond Cl NR7 . . . . 157 F2
Raymond Rd NR6 . . . . 157 F7
Raymond St
  Thetford IP24 . . . . 176 D3
  15 Wisbech PE13 . . . . . . 152 C4
Rayner's Cl 6 NR20 . . . . . 68 E6
Rayner's La NR35 . . . . . . 109 D4
Rayner's Way NR20 . . . . . 68 E6
Raynham Cl NR30 . . . . 147 B4
Raynham Rd
  Dunton NR21 . . . . 31 C6

Raynham Rd continued
  Hempton NR21 . . . . 141 A2
  Whissonsett NR20 . . . . 31 C2
Raynham Ride NR19 . . . . 154 D7
Raynham St NR2 . . . . 162 B7
Rayns Cl NR6 . . . . 158 F5
READING GREEN IP21 . . . 131 C1
Read's Cross NR14 . . . . . 109 E8
Readscross La NR14 . . . . 109 E8
Recorder Rd NR1 . . . . 178 C3
Recreation Dr PE38 . . . . . 97 A5
Recreation Gd Rd NR7 . . 159 A4
Recreation Rd
  East Dereham NR19 . . . . . 154 C1
  Great Yarmouth NR31 . . . 170 C5
  Hethersett NR9 . . . . 88 C7
  North Walsham NR28 . . . . 151 B4
  Norwich NR2 . . . . 162 A5
  Stalham NR12 . . . . 39 A4
Rectory Cl
  Caister-on-Sea NR30 . . . . 168 E5
  Coltishall NR12 . . . . 54 D7
  21 Long Stratton NR15 . 106 E3
  2 Newton Flotman NR15 . 89 D1
  Rollesby NR29 . . . . 57 C2
  Roydon PE32 . . . . 27 F2
Rectory Ct NR3 . . . . 158 D2
Rectory Dr PE34 . . . . 145 E5
Rectory Gdns
  Hingham NR9 . . . . 86 B5
  Wisbech PE13 . . . . 152 E6
Rectory Hill IP22 . . . . 128 D2
Rectory La
  Bracon Ash NR14 . . . . 88 E3
  Bunwell NR16 . . . . 105 C4
  Great Ellingham NR17 . . . 103 E8
  Haddiscoe NR14 . . . . 110 F7
  Hedenham NR35 . . . . 108 D4
  Little Melton NR9 . . . . 160 A3
  Loddon NR14 . . . . 92 A2
  Mettingham NR35 . . . . 124 D8
  Mulbarton NR14 . . . . 89 B3
  North Runcton PE33 . . . . . 44 A3
  Poringland NR14 . . . . 90 D5
  Scole IP21 . . . . 121 C1
  Stuston IP21 . . . . 130 B4
  Watlington PE33 . . . . 61 D5
  Weeting IP27 . . . . 175 B7
  West Winch PE33 . . . . 43 F3
Rectory Mdw
  Diss IP22 . . . . 177 E4
  Litcham PE32 . . . . 48 A4
Rectory Rd
  Aldeby, Wheatacre, Burgh St
    Peter NR34 . . . . 111 B4
  Bacton NR28 . . . . 23 C3
  Brome & Oakley IP23 . . . . 130 B3
  Broome NR35 . . . . 109 B3
  Burston & Shimpling IP22 . 120 E2
  2 Coltishall NR12 . . . . . . 54 C6
  Dickleburgh IP21 . . . . 121 B1
  East Carleton NR14 . . . . . . 89 A4
  Edgefield NR26 . . . . 19 D5
  Elsing NR20 . . . . 50 F7
  Gillingham NR34 . . . . 110 B3
  Gissing IP22 . . . . 120 F4
  Haddiscoe NR14 . . . . 110 F7
  Hockering NR20 . . . . 69 B8
  Hoveton NR12 . . . . 55 A7
  Lyng NR9 . . . . 51 B4
  Northrepps NR27 . . . . 11 A1
  Outwell PE14 . . . . 77 F6
  Rocklands NR17 . . . . 103 B7
  Shelfanger IP22 . . . . 120 B2
  Sutton NR12 . . . . 39 C3
  Swanton Morley NR20 . . . 50 B4
  Tivetshall St Mary NR15 . 121 C4
  Topcroft NR35 . . . . 107 F4
  Weston Longville NR9 . . . . 51 D2
  Whissonsett NR20 . . . . 31 E2
  Wood Norton NR20 . . . . . . 33 A7
  Wortham IP22 . . . . 129 C8
Red Admiral Cl 1 NR18 . 173 E4
Red Barn La NR11 . . . . 9 D1
Redbrick Cotts IP27 . . . . 175 D5
Red Bridge La NR5 . . . . . 157 C2
Redcastle Furze Prim Sch
  IP24 . . . . 176 B3
Redcastle Rd IP24 . . . . . . 176 A4
Redcliffe Way NR18 . . . . 165 B4
Red Cottage Cl NR3 . . . . 158 A2
Redell Cl 3 NR13 . . . . 55 A1
Redenhall Rd IP20 . . . . . . 122 F3
Redenhall Rd IP20 . . . . . . 122 D2
Redfern Cl
  East Dereham NR19 . . . . . 154 B4
  King's Lynn PE30 . . . . 147 E8
Redfern Rd NR7 . . . . 159 D1
Redgate IP24 . . . . 176 E4
Redgate Hill PE36 . . . . . . 132 D2
Redgate Jun Sch PE36 . . 132 D2
Redgrave Rd IP22 . . . . 41 A4
REDGRAVE IP22 . . . . 128 E4
Redgrave & Lopham Fen
  National Nature Reserve *
  IP22 . . . . 128 A4
Redgrave Rd
  South Lopham IP22 . . . . . 128 E7
  Wortham IP22 . . . . 129 A5
Red Lion Cl
  Holme Hale IP25 . . . . 66 B2
  Hoxne IP21 . . . . 131 A3
Red Lion St
  3 Aylsham NR11 . . . . . . 150 C7
  Norwich NR1 . . . . 178 B2
Red Lion Yd NR23 . . . . . . 136 D6
Redman Rd NR28 . . . . 151 D3
Redmere Cl 4 NR12 . . . . . 54 A4

Redmere Dro CB7 . . . . . . 112 D5
RED PITS NR11 . . . . 34 D7
Red Robin Cl 9 NR15 . . . 106 D3
Redwell St NR2 . . . . 178 B3
Redwing Dr
  1 Great Yarmouth NR31 . 94 C7
  5 Hethersett NR9 . . . . . 152 D2
Redwing Gdns 7 NR10 . . 54 A1
Redways Horse Sanctuary
  (Caldecott) * NR31 . . . . . . 93 F4
Reeder Cl NR19 . . . . 154 D3
Reeder's La NR14 . . . . 90 E4
REEDHAM NR13 . . . . 92 E5
Reedham Prim Sch NR13 . 93 A4
Reedham Rd
  Acle NR13 . . . . 166 B1
  Beighton NR13 . . . . 74 E1
  Cantley NR13 . . . . 92 D6
Reedham Sta NR13 . . . . . . 92 F5
Reed La NR19 . . . . 48 F3
Reed Way 3 PE14 . . . . 77 A8
REEPHAM NR10 . . . . 149 B5
Reepham High Sch
  NR10 . . . . 149 B3
Reepham Prim Sch
  NR10 . . . . 149 B4
Reepham Rd
  Bawdeswell NR20 . . . . 50 F8
  Briston NR24 . . . . 142 E2
  Felthorpe NR10 . . . . 155 D5
  Foulsham NR20 . . . . 33 D3
  Guestwick NR20 . . . . 34 A5
  Horsford NR10 . . . . 157 D7
  Norwich NR6 . . . . 157 E2
  Swannington NR9 . . . . 52 B5
  Thurning NR20 . . . . 34 B8
  Wood Dalling NR11 . . . . . . 34 D5
Reeve Cl NR27 . . . . 130 D6
Reeve Pl NR27 . . . . 139 D4
Reeves Ave PE30 . . . . 147 B8
Reeves Ct NR28 . . . . 151 C5
Reeves La IP26 . . . . 114 A7
Reffley La PE30 . . . . 148 C5
Reffley Prim Sch PE30 . . 147 D8
Regal Ct 28 IP25 . . . . 84 D3
Regal Rd PE13 . . . . 152 B2
Regency Ave PE30 . . . . . . 147 C5
Regent Bvd 10 NR30 . . . . 169 D4
Regent Cl NR19 . . . . 154 D1
Regent Pl 1 PE30 . . . . . . 146 E4
Regent Rd
  Downham Market PE38 . . . 172 A4
  9 Great Yarmouth NR30 . 169 D4
Regents Cl NR25 . . . . 137 B5
Regents Ct NR28 . . . . 151 B5
Regents Pk PE30 . . . . 147 C5
Regent St
  Great Yarmouth NR30 . . . 169 C3
  Wickmere NR11 . . . . 20 E4
Regent Way 6 PE30 . . . . 146 E4
Reg Houchen Rd PE31 . . 140 C3
Regina Rd NR1 . . . . 178 A1
Regis Ave 8 NR27 . . . . 9 F5
Regis Pl NR26 . . . . 138 E7
Reid Way PE30 . . . . 147 A8
Renowood Cl PE32 . . . . . . 48 B8
Renson Cl NR3 . . . . 158 C4
Renwick Pk E NR27 . . . . . 10 A4
Renwick Pk W NR27 . . . . 10 A4
REPPS NR29 . . . . 56 F4
Repps Rd
  Ashby with Oby NR29 . . . . 57 B3
  1 Martham NR29 . . . . . . 57 D4
  Thurne NR29 . . . . 56 E3
Repton Ave NR6 . . . . 158 D7
Repton Cl NR11 . . . . 150 D5
Repton Rd NR28 . . . . 172 D6
Reve Cres 5 NR13 . . . . 73 C6
Revell Rd PE38 . . . . 172 B4
Reydon Cl 10 NR5 . . . . . . 161 A7
REYMERSTON NR9 . . . . 68 C1
Reymerston Rd NR9 . . . . . 68 B2
Reynolds Ave NR30 . . . . . 168 C8
Reynolds Gn NR5 . . . . 56 E7
Reynolds Way PE31 . . . . . 140 C3
Rhombus Bsns Pk NR6 . . 158 B5
Rhond The NR12 . . . . 164 C5
Rhone Pl 3 PE13 . . . . 152 E3
Rhoon Rd PE34 . . . . 144 E8
Rice Way NR7 . . . . 159 C2
Richard Easter Rd IP24 . 176 D6
Richard Haggard Cl 3
  IP25 . . . . 67 C2
Richard Hicks Dr 9
  NR19 . . . . 154 C4
Richardson Cres NR9 . . . . 88 C8
Richards Rd NR21 . . . . 15 D2
Richard Young Cl 2
  PE13 . . . . 152 C8
Richenda Cl 11 NR5 . . . . 161 C5
Riches Cl 2 NR15 . . . . 106 F6
Richmond Cl
  Honingham NR9 . . . . 69 E6
  Lyng NR9 . . . . 51 A5
Richmond Ct PE13 . . . . . . 152 A4
Richmond Pk NR17 . . . . . 174 F6
Richmond Pl NR1 . . . . 51 A4
Richmond Rd
  Brandon IP27 . . . . 175 A1
  Downham Market PE38 . . . 172 B4
  4 Long Stratton NR15 . 106 E3
  Norwich NR5 . . . . 156 E1
  Saham Toney IP25 . . . . 84 C4
Richmond Rise NR10 . . . 149 C5
RICKINGHALL IP22 . . . . . 128 E2
Rickinghall Rd IP22 . . . . . 128 C3
Riddlesworth Hall Sch
  IP22 . . . . 127 C8

Rider Haggard Rd NR7 . . 159 D1
Ridgeway
  Caister-on-Sea NR30 . . . . 168 D8
  Cromer NR27 . . . . 139 C4
Ridgeway The NR1 . . . . . 163 B8
Ridings The
  8 Cringleford NR4 . . . . . . 89 B8
  Fakenham NR21 . . . . 141 E4
Ridland's Rd NR24 . . . . . . 142 C1
RIDLINGTON NR28 . . . . . . 23 E1
RIDLINGTON STREET
  NR28 . . . . 23 E1
Rigby Cl 1 NR1 . . . . 90 D5
Rigbys Ct NR2 . . . . 178 A3
Rigg Cl 2 PE13 . . . . 152 B3
Rightup Dro IP27 . . . . 113 E5
Rightup La NR18 . . . . 173 D2
Riley Cl NR7 . . . . 159 D1
Rill Cl PE30 . . . . 148 B4
Rimer Cl NR5 . . . . 160 F6
Ringbank La NR11 . . . . 21 A6
Ringers Cl 3 NR18 . . . . . 173 D5
Ringers La NR9 . . . . 86 C5
RINGLAND NR8 . . . . 70 B8
Ringland La
  Costessey NR8 . . . . 156 B6
  Easton NR9 . . . . 70 B5
  Morton on the Hill NR9 . . . 52 A2
  Weston Longville NR9 . . . . 51 F3
Ringland Rd NR8 . . . . 155 A1
Ringmere Cl 2 NR25 . . . . 84 C3
Ringmere Rd 3 IP25 . . . . 84 C3
Ringmore Rd PE38 . . . . . . 97 B6
Ring Rd NR7 . . . . 163 F7
Ringsfield Rd NR34 . . . . . 124 F5
RINGSTEAD PE36 . . . . 2 A3
Ringstead Downs Nature
  Reserve * PE36 . . . . 1 F2
Ringstead Rd
  Burnham Market PE31 . . . 135 A2
  Docking PE31 . . . . 134 A6
  Heacham PE31 . . . . 133 E6
  Ringstead PE36 . . . . 2 A2
  Sedgeford PE36 . . . . 13 B8
  Thornham PE36 . . . . 2 D6
Ringwood Cl NR9 . . . . 160 B2
Ripley Cl NR2 . . . . 161 F5
Ripon Way NR7 . . . . 176 B5
Rippingall Cl 6 NR11 . . . 150 D6
Rippingall Rd NR11 . . . . . 150 D6
Rise The
  10 Loddon NR14 . . . . 92 A2
  Sheringham NR26 . . . . . . 138 E6
Riseway Cl NR1 . . . . 163 B8
Rising Way 83 NR9 . . . . . 57 C4
Risley Cl NR16 . . . . 117 E5
River Cl PE32 . . . . 63 E8
River Ct NR21 . . . . 141 A3
Riverdale Ct NR13 . . . . . . 165 D3
Riverdene Mews NR8 . . . 155 E3
River Dro NR13 . . . . 80 F2
Rivergreen Ct NR1 . . . . . 163 E6
River La
  Cranworth IP25 . . . . 85 F7
  King's Lynn PE30 . . . . 147 A6
Rivermead PE12 . . . . 39 B3
River Rd
  West Acre PE32 . . . . 46 B1
  West Walton PE14 . . . . 59 A8
Riverside
  Cockley Cley PE37 . . . . 82 D7
  Diss IP22 . . . . 177 B3
  King's Lynn PE30 . . . . 147 B7
  Norwich NR1 . . . . 178 C2
  Reedham NR13 . . . . 92 F4
  West Walton PE14 . . . . 59 A8
Riverside Cl NR1 . . . . 178 C1
Riverside Ctr NR6 . . . . . . 157 D2
Riverside Ctr NR12 . . . . . 164 C5
Riverside Est NR11 . . . . . 165 D1
Riverside Ind Ctr NR13 . 170 D5
Riverside Ind Est PE30 . 146 D2
Riverside Maltings IP22 . 177 F3
Riverside Rd
  Great Yarmouth NR31 . . . 170 D6
  Holt NR25 . . . . 8 A1
  King's Lynn PE30 . . . . 147 B7
  Wroxham/Hoveton NR12 . 164 C4
Riverside Swimming Ctr
  NR1 . . . . 178 C1
Riverside Way
  Brandon IP27 . . . . 175 C5
  1 Wisbech PE13 . . . . . . 152 B3
Riverside Wlk IP24 . . . . . 176 C4
Riversway PE30 . . . . 146 E7
River Terr PE13 . . . . 152 A8
River View
  Beccles NR34 . . . . 110 C2
  7 Beetley NR20 . . . . 49 D4
River View Cl NR21 . . . . . 141 E4
Riverview Dr NR13 . . . . . 166 B8
River Vw NR20 . . . . 49 D4
River Wlk
  Great Yarmouth NR30 . . . 169 D4
  King's Lynn PE30 . . . . 146 C6
RNLI Henry Blogg Mus *
  NR27 . . . . 139 B7
Roaches Ct NR3 . . . . 178 B3
ROAD GREEN NR15 . . . . . 107 E4
Robberds Way NR5 . . . . . 160 E8
Robert Andrew Cl NR18 . 87 B2
Robert Balding Rd PE31 . 140 C3
Robert Cl
  Trunch NR28 . . . . 22 E5
  5 Wymondham NR18 . . 173 C6
Robert Gybson Way NR2 178 A3
Robert Herb Way 5
  NR18 . . . . 173 E4

Robert Kett Jun Sch
  NR18 . . . . 173 C5
Robert Key Dr 2 NR20 . . . 68 E6
Robert Linge Cres IP27 . 175 D3
Roberts Cl 3 NR15 . . . . . 107 C5
Robertson Cl NR26 . . . . . 138 E6
Robert St 8 PE30 . . . . 146 E3
Robin Cl
  Great Yarmouth NR31 . . . 170 A3
  Mulbarton NR14 . . . . 89 A3
Robin Hill NR11 . . . . 133 D8
Robin Hood Rd NR4 . . . . . 162 C1
Robin Kerkham Way
  PE34 . . . . 61 B6
Robin La NR14 . . . . 152 C2
Robin Mews NR4 . . . . 161 F5
Robins La NR10 . . . . 149 B4
Robinson Rd IP21 . . . . . . 130 C5
Robin Wlk IP27 . . . . 175 F3
Robson Rd NR5 . . . . 161 B6
Robyns Rd
  3 Sheringham NR26 . . . . . 9 F5
  Sheringham NR26 . . . . . . 138 F5
Rocelin Cl NR3 . . . . 158 E3
Rochford Rd 4 NR29 . . . . 57 C4
Rochford Wlk 5 PE13 . . 152 E5
Rockall Way 4 NR30 . . . 168 C6
Rockingham Rd NR5 . . . . 161 B6
ROCKLAND ALL SAINTS
  NR17 . . . . 103 B7
Rockland Cl NR13 . . . . . . 153 B2
Rockland Dr NR7 . . . . 163 C6
Rockland La NR17 . . . . 85 F1
Rockland Rd NR14 . . . . . . 90 F7
ROCKLAND ST MARY
  NR14 . . . . 91 B7
Rockland St Mary Prim Sch
  NR14 . . . . 91 B6
ROCKLAND ST PETER
  NR17 . . . . 103 B8
Rocklands Prim Sch
  NR17 . . . . 103 B4
Rocklands Rd NR17 . . . . . 103 B4
Rode La NR16 . . . . 105 B3
Rodham Rd PE15 . . . . 77 A1
Rodinghead 1 PE30 . . . . 147 D5
Rodney Rd NR30 . . . . 169 D3
Rodwell Cnr NR10 . . . . 35 C1
Roedich Dr NR8 . . . . 155 C1
Roe Dr NR5 . . . . 161 E6
Roger Ride 3 NR19 . . . . . 154 D2
Rogers Cl 3 NR5 . . . . 161 B7
Roger's Cl NR31 . . . . 171 D5
Roger's La NR15 . . . . 89 F1
Roland Dr NR15 . . . . 107 D5
Rolfe Cres PE31 . . . . 133 E3
ROLLESBY NR29 . . . . 57 D2
Rollesby Ave NR31 . . . . . . 94 C5
Rollesby Fst Sch NR29 . . 57 D3
Rollesby Gdns NR29 . . . . 57 D2
Rollesby Pl NR10 . . . . 37 B2
Rollesby Rd
  Fleggburgh NR29 . . . . 57 C1
  King's Lynn PE30 . . . . 147 A3
  Martham NR29 . . . . 57 D3
  Swaffham PE37 . . . . 153 B2
Rolleston Cl NR5 . . . . 161 B7
Rollington La NR19 . . . . . 154 D4
Roman Cres PE37 . . . . . . 153 D2
Roman Dr NR13 . . . . 165 B3
Roman Pl 3 NR30 . . . . . . 169 D4
Roman Way
  Brancaster PE31 . . . . 3 B7
  Caister-on-Sea NR30 . . . . 168 D5
  Thetford IP24 . . . . 176 C7
Romany Cl 8 NR29 . . . . . 57 D2
Romany Rd NR3 . . . . 158 F1
Romany Wlk 6 NR14 . . . . 90 C5
Romer Dro NR25 . . . . 81 B3
Romney Mile NR19 . . . . . 154 D4
Romney Wlk NR19 . . . . . 154 D4
Rook Dr NR8 . . . . 155 E2
Rookery Cl PE14 . . . . 145 E5
Rookery Farm Rd NR28 . . 23 F2
Rookery Hill NR14 . . . . . . 91 B7
Rookery La NR35 . . . . 107 F3
Rookery Rd PE34 . . . . 145 E4
Rookery The IP27 . . . . . . 114 D5
Room La NR15 . . . . 122 D8
Ropemakers Row 5
  NR3 . . . . 158 C1
Ropes Hill NR13 . . . . 55 D4
Ropes Hill Dyke NR12 . . . 55 D4
Ropes Wlk NR13 . . . . 165 C6
Rope Wlk 5 IP24 . . . . 176 D4
Rosa Cl NR14 . . . . 54 B1
Rosalie Cl NR6 . . . . 158 B4
Rosary Cl 11 NR14 . . . . . 89 B3
Royal Rd NR1 . . . . 163 A6
Rosa Vella Dr 3 NR20 . . . 68 A8
Roseacre Cl NR12 . . . . . . 162 C2
Roseacre Est NR25 . . . . . . 9 A2
Rose Ave NR20 . . . . 129 D7
Rosebay 1 NR8 . . . . 148 C3
Rosebay St 4 NR6 . . . . . . 158 D5
Roseberry Rd PE14 . . . . . . 59 B1
Rosebery Ave
  King's Lynn PE30 . . . . 147 B6
  Poringland NR14 . . . . 90 D5
Rosebery Rd
  Cromer NR27 . . . . 139 D5
  Great & Little Plumstead
    NR13 . . . . 73 A4
  Norwich NR3 . . . . 158 D1
  3 Sheringham NR27 . . . 10 A5
Rose Cottage's NR19 . . . . 66 D8
Rosecroft 4 NR17 . . . . . . 174 C5
Rosecroft Rd NR14 . . . . . 176 F4
Rosedale Cres 5 NR1 . . . 163 A6
Rosedale Gdns NR31 . . . . 94 A5

Rose Dr NR20 . . . . 68 A8
Rosefields NR13 . . . . 165 E4
Rose La
  Botesdale IP22 . . . . 128 E3
  Diss IP22 . . . . 177 F3
  11 Elm PE14 . . . . 59 A1
  Norwich NR1 . . . . 178 C3
  Palgrave IP22 . . . . 177 D1
Rose La CI IP22 . . . . 177 D2
Rosemary La
  11 Gayton PE32 . . . . 45 C6
  2 New Buckenham NR16. 104 F1
  Norwich NR23 . . . . 178 A4
Rosemary Musker Cty High
  Sch IP20 . . . . 176 E7
Rosemary Rd
  Blofield NR13 . . . . 73 C6
  Norwich NR7 . . . . 159 A4
Rosemary Terr NR21 . . . . 141 B5
Rosemary Way PE38 . . . . 172 E6
Rosery The NR14 . . . . 89 C3
Rosery CI NR23 . . . . 136 D5
Rosetta Rd NR10 . . . . 54 A2
Rose Valley **4** NR2 . . . . . 162 B5
Roseville CI **2** NR1 . . . . 163 B5
Rose Wlk
  Brundall NR13 . . . . 165 C3
  Sculthorpe Airfield NR21. . 15 C2
  11 Wisbech PE13. . . . . . . 152 A6
Rosewood NR28 . . . . 151 E5
Rose Yd NR3 . . . . 178 A4
Roslyn Rd NR13 . . . . 170 C5
Rosslare NR4 . . . . 162 A1
Rossons Rd NR8 . . . . 155 C1
Rostwold Way NR13 . . . . 158 D2
Rosyth Rd **4** IP31 . . . . . . 126 E1
Rothbury CI NR18 . . . . 173 B4
Rothbury Rd NR18 . . . . . . 173 C4
Rotten Marsh NR13 . . . . . 166 C2
Rottenstone La NR29 . . . . 167 F3
Roudham Rd NR16 . . . . . . 117 F6
Rouen Rd NR1 . . . . 178 B3
ROUGHAM PE32 . . . . 47 B7
Rougham Cnr IP26. . . . . . . 99 F3
Rougham End PE32 . . . . . . 47 C8
Rougham Hall PE32 . . . . . . 47 A7
Rougham Rd PE32 . . . . 29 E1
Roughlands IP27 . . . . 113 E1
Rougholme CI
  6 Beetley NR19 . . . . 49 C3
  6 Gressenhall NR20 . . . . . 49 C3
Rought Ave IP27 . . . . 175 D2
ROUGHTON NR11 . . . . 21 E8
Roughton Rd
  Roughton NR27 . . . . 139 B2
  Thorpe Market NR11. . . . . 21 F7
Roughton Rd Sta NR27 . . 139 A4
Roundabout La NR14 . . . . 109 B8
Roundham Medieval Village
  of ★ NR16 . . . . 117 E6
Roundhead Ct **26** NR7. . . . 72 D4
Round House Way NR4 . . 161 B1
Roundtree CI NR7 . . . . . . 159 B2
Roundtree Way NR7 . . . . 159 B2
Roundway Down **17** NR7. . 72 D4
Round Well Rd NR5 . . . . . 156 D1
Rouse's La PE38 . . . . 172 D4
Rowan CI
  10 Great Yarmouth NR31 . 94 C7
  Thetford IP24 . . . . 176 B1
  7 Watlington PE33 . . . . . 61 D5
  Wisbech PE13 . . . . 152 F7
Rowan CI NR5 . . . . 156 F1
Rowan Dr
  Brandon IP27 . . . . 175 C3
  Gayton PE32 . . . . 45 C6
Rowan Rd
  King's Lynn PE34 . . . . 43 D4
  Marthan NR29 . . . . 57 D4
Rowan Way
  Fakenham NR21. . . . . 141 F4
  10 Great Yarmouth NR31 . 170 B6
  Holt NR25 . . . . 137 B2
Row Hill **6** PE33 . . . . 43 F2
Rowington Rd NR1 . . . . . 178 A1
Rowland Ct NR1 . . . . 178 B1
Rowley Cnr IP26 . . . . 83 A5
Row's Mdw **1** NR15. . . . . 107 C5
Row The
  Weeting IP27. . . . . 175 A7
  Wereham PE33 . . . . 80 D3
  West Dereham PE33 . . . . . 80 B4
Rowton Heath NR7. . . . . . 72 D4
Roxley CI NR7 . . . . 163 F5
Royal Albert CI **8** NR31 . 170 D4
Royal Arcade NR2 . . . . . . 178 B2
Royal Ave NR30 . . . . 169 D7
Royal CI **11** PE12 . . . . 41 B8
Royalist Dr **28** NR7 . . . . . . 72 D4
Royal Norfolk Regimental
  Mus ★ NR1 . . . . 178 B3
Royal PI **2** PE13 . . . . 152 C4
Royal Thames Rd NR30. . 168 D7
Royden Way **3** NR29. . . . . 57 C1
ROYDON
  Roydon IP22 . . . . 129 D7
  Roydon PE32 . . . . 28 A2
Roydon Comm National
  Nature Reserve ★ PE32 . 27 F1
Roydon Fen IP22 . . . . 177 A4
Roydon Gdns IP22 . . . . . 177 A4
Roydon Prim Sch IP22 . . 177 B5
Roydon Rd IP22 . . . . 177 C5
Royston Gn NR28 . . . . . . 151 D6
Rubens Way **6** PE38 . . . . 172 D6
Rudd's Drift PE32 . . . . 48 E5
Rudds La NR10. . . . . 149 B3

Rudham CE Prim Sch
  PE31 . . . . 30 A6
Rudham Rd
  Great Massingham PE32 . . 29 D2
  Syderstone PE31 . . . . 15 A3
Rudham Stile La NR21. . . 141 B6
Rudolf Steiner Sch NR12 164 B3
Rugge Dr NR4 . . . . 161 E2
Rugg's La NR29 . . . . 75 C8
Ruin Rd NR28 . . . . 38 A5
Rumburgh La NR35 . . . . . 124 D2
Rump CI **10** NR20 . . . . 50 B3
Runcton CI NR5 . . . . 161 B7
RUNCTON HOLME PE33 . . . 61 D3
Runcton Holme CE VA Prim
  Sch PE33 . . . . 61 E3
Runcton Rd PE33 . . . . 61 F2
RUNHALL 68 F2
Runhall Rd NR9 . . . . 69 A2
RUNHAM
  Great Yarmouth NR30 . . . 169 B5
  Mautby NR29 . . . . 75 E6
Runham Rd
  Great Yarmouth NR30 . . . 169 B5
  Stokesby NR29 . . . . 75 B5
Run La NR14. . . . . 91 B6
Runnel The NR5 . . . . 160 F6
Runton House CI NR27 . . . 10 A5
Runton Rd NR27 . . . . 139 A7
Rupert St NR2 . . . . 162 C4
RUSHALL IP21 . . . . 121 F1
Rushall Rd IP20 . . . . 122 B2
RUSHFORD IP24 . . . . 126 E8
Rushford Rd
  Coney Weston IP31 . . . . . 127 B5
  Euston IP24 . . . . 126 D7
RUSH GREEN NR9. . . . . 69 B1
Rushmead CI PE38 . . . . . 172 C2
Rushmeadow Rd NR10 . . 154 A5
Rushmer Way NR26 . . . . 138 C5
Rushmore Rd NR7 . . . . . . 159 A4
Ruskin Ave NR31. . . . . . . 170 B2
Ruskin CI **5** PE38 . . . . . . 172 D6
Ruskin PI **5** PE38 . . . . . . 172 D6
Ruskin Rd NR4 . . . . 161 E4
Russell Ave
  Caister-on-Sea NR30 . . . . 168 E5
  Great Yarmouth NR31 . . . 170 C3
  Norwich NR7 . . . . 159 B3
  9 Spixworth NR10 . . . . . . 54 A2
Russell CI NR23 . . . . 136 C5
Russell CI NR23 . . . . 136 D6
Russell Rd NR30 . . . . 169 D4
Russell Sq NR30 . . . . 169 D4
Russell St
  King's Lynn PE30 . . . . . . 146 F3
  Norwich NR2 . . . . 162 C7
  Wisbech PE13 . . . . 152 C6
Russell Terr
  Mundesley NR11 . . . . 143 C6
  Trowse Newton NR14 . . . 163 B2
Russell Way NR18 . . . . . . 173 C3
Russet CI NR17 . . . . 174 E4
Russet Gr NR4 . . . . 161 E5
Russet Rd IP22 . . . . 177 C5
Russets The PE14 . . . . 77 E6
Russett CI PE30 . . . . 147 C8
Russet Way NR19 . . . . . . 154 E3
Rustens Manor Rd **2**
  NR18 . . . . 173 C5
Rustons Rd PE14 . . . . 59 F3
Ruthen PI **11** NR19 . . . . . . 154 D5
Rutherford Way IP24. . . . 176 C6
Rutland St NR2 . . . . 162 C4
Ryalla Drift PE30. . . . . . . 148 B4
Ryburgh Dr NR20 . . . . 32 D5
Rydal CI NR5 . . . . 161 C6
Ryders Way IP22. . . . . . . 128 E2
Rye Ave NR3 . . . . 158 B3
Rye CI
  North Walsham NR28 . . . 151 E6
  Norwich NR3 . . . . 158 B2
Rye La NR17 . . . . 174 C4
Ryeland Rd IP24 . . . . 176 C5
Ryelands **5** NR29 . . . . . . 167 B7
Ryelands Rd PE30. . . . . . 148 D4
Rye's CI PE30 . . . . 147 D8
Rygil CI PE30 . . . . 147 E8
Ryrie CI NR4 . . . . 161 E2
Ryston CI PE38. . . . . 172 C4
Ryston End PE38 . . . . 172 C4
Ryston Pk PE38 . . . . 172 F1
Ryston Rd
  Denver PE38 . . . . 172 D2
  West Dereham PE33 . . . . . 80 B4

S

Sackville CI **4** NR30 . . . . . 169 C3
Sacred Heart Convent Sch
  PE37 . . . . 153 C5
Saddlebow Ind Est PE34. . 43 C4
Saddlebow Rd PE30 . . . . 146 D1
Sadler CI PE38 . . . . 146 F7
Sadler Rd NR6 . . . . 157 F7
Sadlers Ct **11** NR26 . . . . 138 D7
Sadlers Way NR28 . . . . . 151 E5
Saffron CI IP27 . . . . 175 B2
Saffron Sq NR6 . . . . 158 C3
Sage Rd PE38 . . . . 172 D7
SAHAM HILLS IP25. . . . . . . 84 C6
Saham Rd IP25 . . . . 84 C4
SAHAM TONEY IP25 . . . . . . 84 C4
Sainsbury Ctr for the Visual
  Arts ★ NR4 . . . . 161 C3
St Alban's Rd NR1 . . . . . 162 D3
St Albans Way IP24 . . . . . 176 B5

St Andrew CI **1** NR31. . . . 171 E5
St Andrews **5** NR7 . . . . . 72 D3
St Andrew's & Blackfriars
  Halls ★ NR1 . . . . 178 B3
St Andrews CE VA Prim Sch
  IP22 . . . . 119 A1
St Andrews CI
  Barningham IP31. . . . . . . 127 C3
  Buxton with Lammas NR10 . 36 E1
  Framingham Earl NR14 . . . 90 D5
  Great Yarmouth NR31 . . . 170 C5
  1 Hingham NR9 . . . . 86 C4
  Long Stratton NR15. . . . . 106 E4
  Poringland NR14. . . . . 90 D5
  West Dereham PE33 . . . . . 80 C4
  Worstead NR28 . . . . 38 A4
St Andrew's CI
  Blofield NR13 . . . . 165 E5
  Caister-on-Sea NR30 . . . . 168 D7
  Holme Hale IP25 . . . . 66 A2
  Hoit NR25 . . . . 137 C6
  Northwold IP26 . . . . 99 C8
  3 Old Buckenham NR17. . 104 D2
St Andrews Dr
  3 Norwich NR4 . . . . 89 C8
  Quidenham NR16. . . . . . 103 E1
St Andrews Drift **2** NR25. . 7 A4
St Andrews Hill NR2 . . . . 178 B3
St Andrew's La
  Necton PE37 . . . . 65 F5
  Roydon PE32 . . . . 28 A2
St Andrews Rd
  North Runcton PE30 . . . . 147 B3
  Norwich NR6 . . . . 157 D6
  Scole IP21 . . . . 130 D5
St Andrew's Rd
  Great Yarmouth NR31 . . . 170 C6
  Lingwood NR13 . . . . 73 F3
  Sheringham NR26 . . . . . . 138 D6
St Andrews Sch NR27 . . . . 10 B5
St Andrews St NR2 . . . . . 178 B3
St Andrews Way PE37 . . . . 65 F5
St Andrew's Way NR13 . . 165 E5
St Andrews Wlk PE33 . . . . 80 C5
St Anne's Cres
  Clenchwarton PE34 . . . . . 145 D6
  8 Great Yarmouth NR31 . 170 B4
St Annes Rd **4** NR14 . . . . . 90 D5
St Ann La NR1 . . . . 178 C2
St Anns Fort PE30. . . . . . 146 D6
St Ann's St PE30 . . . . 146 D5
St Anthony's Way IP27 . . 175 E4
St Antony's Ave NR31 . . . 170 B2
St Audreys IP24 . . . . 176 F3
St Augustines Gate **12**
  NR3 . . . . 162 D8
St Augustines RC Prim Sch
  NR8. . . . . 156 E1
St Augustines Rd PE13 . . 152 C5
St Augustine's St NR3 . . . 162 D8
St Augustines Way **3**
  PE30. . . . . 148 C4
St Austin's Gr NR26 . . . . 138 E7
St Barnabas CI **2** PE30 . . 148 D3
St Bartholomews CI **4**
  NR2 . . . . 162 B8
St Benedicts CI NR34. . . . 110 D5
St Benedicts Rd IP27 . . . 175 E4
St Benedicts St NR2 . . . . 178 A3
St Benet's Abbey ★ NR12 . . 56 C2
St Benets Ave NR26 . . . . 151 E4
St Benet's CI **9** NR12 . . . . 39 B4
St Benets Gr PE30 . . . . . 148 D3
St Benets Rd NR29 . . . . . . 56 C3
St Benet's Rd
  Great Yarmouth NR31 . . . 170 B3
  Stalham NR12 . . . . 39 B4
St Botolphs CE VC Prim Sch
  IP22 . . . . 128 F3
St Botolph's CI **3** PE30 . . 148 C3
St Catherine's Ave **5**
  NR29 . . . . 56 C8
St Catherines Rd NR7 . . . 163 F8
St Catherine's Way NR31 170 B4
St Christopher CI
  16 Belton NR31 . . . . 94 A6
  6 Caister-on-Sea NR30 . . 168 D7
St Christophers CI NR15 . 108 C7
St Christophers Sch NR6 158 E4
St Clare CI **5** NR31 . . . . . . 171 D5
St Clement CI **2** PE14 . . . . 77 F6
St Clement Mews **7**
  NR31 . . . . 171 D5
St Clements Dr **4** PE38 . 172 C6
St Clements High Sch
  PE34 . . . . 144 C6
St Clements Hill NR3 . . . 158 E2
St Clements Way NR13 . . 165 C4
St Crispins Rd NR3 . . . . . 178 A4
St Cross Rd IP20 . . . . 123 B4
ST CROSS SOUTH ELMHAM
  IP20 . . . . 123 D3
St Davids CI
  Brandon IP27 . . . . 175 D3
  Long Stratton NR15. . . . . 106 E4
St David's CI **17** NR31 . . . . 94 A6
St Davids Dr **8** NR31 . . . . 73 D6
St David's Rd NR9. . . . . . . 88 C7
St Dominic Sq **8** NR30 . . 146 D5
St Domonic's Dr IP27 . . . 175 E4
St Edmund CI
  Attleborough NR17 . . . . . 174 C5
  Great Yarmouth NR31 . . . 170 B3
  Poringland NR14 . . . . 90 B6
St Edmund Rd IP27 . . . . . 114 E8
St Edmunds NR17 . . . . . . 174 E5
St Edmund's Ave PE36 . . 132 D5

St Edmundsbury Rd
  PE30. . . . . 146 E7
St Edmunds CI
  Costessey NR8. . . . . 156 F5
  Norwich NR6 . . . . 157 E1
St Edmunds Com Sch
  PE30 . . . . 146 E8
St Edmunds Ct **1** IP24 . . 176 C1
St Edmunds Dr PE14 . . . . 59 D1
St Edmunds Gate
  Attleborough NR17 . . . . . 174 B4
  11 Honington IP31 . . . . . 126 B1
St Edmunds Prim Sch
  IP21 . . . . 131 A2
St Edmunds RC Prim Sch
  NR35. . . . . 124 B8
St Edmunds Rd NR13 . . . 166 B3
St Edmund's Rd
  Downham Market PE38. . . 172 D5
  Lingwood NR13 . . . . 73 F3
  Taverham NR8 . . . . 155 C1
St Edmund's Rise **2**
  NR8 . . . . 155 C1
St Edmunds Sq **18** IP31. . 126 B1
St Edmund's Terr
  Hunstanton PE36. . . . . . . 132 C4
  King's Lynn PE30 . . . . . . 146 C7
St Edmunds Wharf NR3 . . 178 B4
St Ethelberts CI PE31. . . . 135 C2
St Faith's Church ★ NR9 . . 51 F7
St Faith's Dr PE30 . . . . . . 147 A6
St Faiths La NR1 . . . . 178 C3
St Faith's Rd NR6 . . . . . . 158 D6
St Francis CI IP27 . . . . . . 175 E4
St Francis Way NR30 . . . 168 D7
St Furseys' Way **2** NR31 . 94 A6
St George's CI
  Saham Toney IP25 . . . . . . 84 B5
  Thurton NR14 . . . . 91 C4
St George's Dr
  Caister-on-Sea NR30 . . . . 168 D7
  East Dereham NR19 . . . . . 154 D1
St Georges Fst Sch **18**
  NR30. . . . . 169 D3
St Georges Mid Sch PE31 13 A1
St Georges Rd NR31 . . . . . 94 A6
St Georges Rd NR30 . . . . 169 D3
St George's Theatre **19**
  NR30. . . . . 169 D3
St Germans Prim Sch
  PE34 . . . . 43 B1
St Giles Gr PE14 . . . . 59 B1
St Giles' La IP24 . . . . 176 D4
St Giles Rd NR24 . . . . 18 B2
St Giles St NR2 . . . . 178 A3
St Giles Terr NR2 . . . . . . 178 A3
St Gregorys Alley NR2. . . 178 A3
St Guthlac CI PE37 . . . . . . 153 C6
St Helena Way NR10 . . . . . 53 A3
St Helens CI **11** PE24 . . . . 176 D6
St Helens Way IP24 . . . . . 176 C7
St Hilda CI NR19 . . . . 154 C6
St Hilda Rd
  Caister-on-Sea NR30 . . . . 168 D6
  East Dereham NR19 . . . . . 154 C6
St Hilda's Cres NR31 . . . . 94 A6
St Hugh's Gn NR31 . . . . . 170 B3
ST JAMES NR12 . . . . 54 E7
St James CI NR3 . . . . 178 C4
St James Cres **18** NR31 . . 94 A6
St James St NR3 . . . . 178 A4
St James Dr PE38 . . . . . . 172 B4
St James PI IP19 . . . . 124 A1
St James' Rd PE30 . . . . . 146 E4
St James Rd NR31 . . . . . . 170 B2
St James St PE30 . . . . . . 146 D4
St James Way NR15 . . . . 106 E4
St James Wlk **14** NR30 . . 169 D3
St John Maddermarket
  NR2 . . . . 178 A3
St John's Ave NR1 . . . . . 170 A4
St Johns CI
  3 Norwich NR1 . . . . 162 C2
  Swaffham PE37 . . . . 153 C4
St John's CI
  Coltishall NR12 . . . . 54 D7
  11 Hethersett NR9 . . . . . 88 D7
  Oxborough PE33 . . . . 81 E4
  St Johns CI PE13. . . . . . . 153 C4
ST JOHN'S FEN END PE14. . 60 B6
ST JOHN'S HIGHWAY
  . . . . 42 B1
St Johns La NR14 . . . . . . 109 A8
St Johns Prim Sch NR12 164 D5
St Johns RC Fst Sch
  NR2 . . . . 162 C6
St Johns Rd
  Belton NR31. . . . . 93 F6
  Stalham NR12 . . . . 39 B4
St John's Rd
  Bungay NR35. . . . . 124 A8
  Terrington St John PE34. . 60 C8
St John St NR1 . . . . 178 C2
St John's Terr
  8 Great Yarmouth
  NR30. . . . . 169 D3
  King's Lynn PE30 . . . . . . 146 E4
St Johns Way PE38. . . . . 172 A4
St John's Way PE38 . . . . 172 A4
St John the Baptist Cath ★
  NR2 . . . . 162 C5
St Joseph's Rd NR26 . . . 138 D6
St Julian Rd NR30 . . . . . 168 D6
St Julians Alley NR1. . . . 178 B2
St Laurence Ave NR13. . . 165 C4

St Lawrence Dr NR4. . . . 161 C1
St Lawrence La NR2. . . . . 178 A3
St Lawrence Prim Sch
  NR34. . . . . 124 F2
St Leger NR15 . . . . 106 E3
St Leonards CI
  Scole IP21 . . . . 130 D5
  Wymondham NR18 . . . . . 173 C6
St Leonards Rd NR1. . . . 163 A8
St Leonards St IP26 . . . . 100 B4
St Leonards Terr **6** NR1 . 163 A6
St Luke's Terr **1** NR1 . . . 169 B4
St Magdalen Way PE13 . . 153 E2
St Margarets Ave **8** PE33 63 B4
St Margarets CI NR10 . . . 155 F3
St Margaret's CI
  Upton with Fishley NR13 . . 166 B8
St Margaret's Cres IP24 . 176 C3
St Margarets Dr IP27 . . . 175 A2
St Margarets Gdns NR22 164 D6
St Margarets La NR7 . . . 159 B5
St Margaret's La
  2 Cromer NR27 . . . . 139 C6
  King's Lynn PE30 . . . . . . 146 D4
St Margarets Mdw PE34 . 145 E5
ST MARGARET SOUTH
  ELMHAM IP20 . . . . 123 E2
St Margarets PI NR12 . . . . 40 A5
St Margaret's Rd
  Bungay NR35. . . . . 124 A6
  Cromer NR27. . . . . 139 C6
St Margarets St NR2 . . . . 178 A3
St Margaret's Way
  1 Burgh St Margaret
  (Fleggburgh) NR29 . . . . . 57 C1
  2 Hopton on Sea NR31 . . 171 D5
St Marthas RC Prim Sch
  NR30. . . . . 147 C6
St Martin-at-Palace Plain
  NR3 . . . . 178 B4
St Martins CI NR3 . . . . . . 162 D8
St Martin's CI NR27 . . . . . 139 C5
St Martin's Gdns **1**
  NR16 . . . . 104 F1
St Martins La NR3. . . . . . 178 A4
St Martin's La IP24 . . . . . 125 E6
St Martin's Rd
  2 Norwich NR3 . . . . 162 D8
  Wisbech PE13 . . . . 152 E7
St Martin's Way IP24. . . . 176 B2
St Mary CI NR17 . . . . 174 C6
St Mary's **4** NR16. . . . . . . 104 F1
St Mary's CI
  Alpington NR14 . . . . 90 F5
  Flixton NR35 . . . . 123 E5
  Harleston IP20 . . . . 122 E2
  Heacham PE31. . . . . 133 E6
  Hemsby NR29 . . . . 167 A7
  Horsham St Faith & Newton St
  Faith NR10 . . . . 53 E2
  King's Lynn PE30 . . . . . . 148 C2
  Newton Flotman NR15. . . . 89 C1
  12 Snettisham PE31 . . . . 12 E4
  1 Watton IP25 . . . . 84 E3
  Wroxham/Hoveton NR12 . 164 B4
St Mary's Cres **5** IP24 . . 176 C3
St Mary's Ct **2** NR2 . . . . 176 C3
St Mary's Dr IP22 . . . . . . 177 E4
St Marys Endowed Prim Sch
  NR11. . . . . 21 E8
St Marys Gr NR7 . . . . 159 C5
St Marys La NR31. . . . . . 169 C3
St Marys La **1** NR31. . . . . 7 A4
St Marys Mid Sch NR15 . 106 E4
St Marys Plain NR3 . . . . 178 A4
St Marys Prim Sch NR30 . 93 C4
St Marys RC Prim Sch
  NR31. . . . . 170 C6
St Marys Rd
  Ashby St Mary NR14 . . . . 91 C4
  Hemsby NR29 . . . . 167 A6
  5 Norwich NR3 . . . . 162 D8
  22 Stalham NR12 . . . . . . 39 B4
St Mary's Rd
  Aldeby NR34 . . . . 111 A3
  Cromer NR27. . . . . 139 B6
  20 Long Stratton NR15 . . 106 E3
  Poringland NR14 . . . . 90 D5
  West Walton PE14 . . . . . . 59 B8
St Mary's Way **8** NR28 . . 151 C5
St Marys Wlk **3** NR15 . . . 89 C1
St Matthew's Dr PE12 . . . 41 B8
St Matthews Rd NR1 . . . . 178 C3
St Michael-at-Pleas
  NR3 . . . . 178 B3
St Michaels CI NR12 . . . . 39 C2
St Michaels CE Prim Sch
  Gillingham NR34 . . . . 110 B2
  King's Lynn PE30 . . . . . . 146 D1
St Michaels CI NR20 . . . . . 69 B7
St Michael's CI
  Aylsham NR11 . . . . 150 C7
  Thetford IP24 . . . . 176 C2
St Michael's Cres IP25. . . 83 D4
St Michaels Inf Sch
  NR11. . . . . 150 C7

St Michaels Mid Sch
NR5 . . . . 160 F8
ST MICHAEL SOUTH
ELMHAM NR35 . . . . 124 A2
St Michael's Rd PE30 . . 146 D1
St Michaels Way NR13 . . 165 F2
St Michels Rd NR15 . . . . 106 E4
St Mildreds Rd 3 NR5 . . 161 B7
St Nicholas Cl
Dersingham PE31 . . . . 140 E3
9 Gayton PE32 . . . . 45 C6
1 King's Lynn PE30 . . . . . 146 D5
St Nicholas Ct
1 Great Yarmouth NR31 . . 94 C6
6 North Walsham NR28 . 151 C5
St Nicholas Dr
Caister-on-Sea NR30 . . . . 168 D6
Feltwell IP26 . . . . 98 E2
St Nicholas Gdns 6 NR31 94 C6
St Nicholas House Sch
NR28 . . . . 151 D4
St Nicholas Pl 1 NR26 . . 138 D7
St Nicholas Priory Mid Sch
NR30 . . . . 169 D5
St Nicholas Rd
Great Yarmouth NR30 . . . . 169 D4
North Walsham NR28 . . . . 151 D5
St Nicholas Retail Park
PE30 . . . . 146 D6
St Nicholas's NR14 . . . . . . 88 F3
ST NICHOLAS SOUTH
ELMHAM IP20 . . . . 123 E2
St Nicholas St
Diss IP22 . . . . 177 D5
East Dereham NR19 . . . . . 154 D6
3 King's Lynn PE30 . . . . . 146 D5
Thetford IP24 . . . . 176 C4
St Nicholas Wlk IP27 . . . 175 E4
ST OLAVES NR31 . . . . 93 D2
St Olaves Rd
Herringfleet NR32 . . . . 111 D8
Norwich NR3 . . . . 162 E8
St Omer Cl NR14 . . . . 89 B4
St Pauls Cl NR6 . . . . 158 A5
St Paul's Cl
Brockdish IP21 . . . . 131 C6
4 Horsford NR10 . . . . 53 B3
6 Wisbech PE13 . . . . 152 E6
St Paul's Rd N PE14 . . . . . 59 D7
St Paul's Rd S PE14 . . . . . 59 E7
St Pauls Sq 1 NR3 . . . . . 178 B4
St Paul's Way NR30 . . . . . 169 C7
St Peter & St Paul Prim Sch
IP25 . . . . 85 A5
St Peter's App IP27 . . . . . 175 B3
St Peters Ave NR31 . . . . . 170 B2
St Peters CE Jun Sch
PE13 . . . . 152 E6
St Peters CE VC Prim Sch
NR9 . . . . 70 B5
St Peters Cl 3 NR4 . . . . . 89 B8
St Peter's Cl
Brockdish IP21 . . . . 131 C6
King's Lynn PE34 . . . . 146 B4
Swaffham NR13 . . . . 73 F2
Yaxham NR19 . . . . 68 A5
St Peters Dr NR9 . . . . 70 B5
St Peters Hill NR16 . . . . . . 87 A2
St Peter's La NR12 . . . . . 164 E8
ST PETER SOUTH ELMHAM
NR35 . . . . 124 A3
St Peter's Pl IP27 . . . . . . 175 B2
St Peters' Plain NR30 . . . 169 D3
St Peters Rd
Outwell PE14 . . . . 77 E5
Wattlington PE34 . . . . 61 C7
Wiggenhall St Germans
PE34 . . . . 61 B8
St Peter's Rd
Brooke NR15 . . . . 90 F2
Fakenham NR21 . . . . 141 B6
Great Yarmouth NR30 . . . . 169 D3
King's Lynn PE34 . . . . 146 C5
Lingwood NR13 . . . . 73 F3
5 Sheringham NR26 . . . . 138 D7
5 Wisbech PE13 . . . . 152 C4
St Peters St NR2 . . . . 178 A2
St Peters Terr PE34 . . . . . 146 C4
St Peter's Way 2 NR13 . . 165 F2
St Peter's Wlk IP26 . . . . . 113 F7
St Philips Rd NR2 . . . . . . 162 B6
St Roberts Way 12 NR31 . . 94 A6
St Saviors La NR3 . . . . . . 178 B4
St Stephen's Cres IP27 . . 175 E4
St Stephens Rd NR1 . . . . 178 A1
St Stephens Sq NR1 . . . . 178 A1
St Stephens St NR1 . . . . 178 A1
St Swithins Rd NR2 . . . . . 178 A3
St Thomas Cl IP27 . . . . . 175 E4
St Thomas Dr NR18 . . . . 173 C2
St Thomas' La NR18 . . . . . 88 C4
St Thomas More RC Mid Sch
NR2 . . . . 162 A5
St Thomas Rd NR2 . . . . . 162 A6
St Thomas's La
Ingoldisthorpe PE31 . . . . . 140 D8
Snettisham PE31 . . . . 12 F4
St Thomas's Rd NR29 . . . 167 C7
St Valery La PE30 . . . . . . 146 D2
St Vedast St NR1 . . . . 178 C3
St Vincent Wlk NR31 . . . . 171 E5
St Walstan's Cl
Norwich NR5 . . . . 156 D1
Taverham NR8 . . . . 156 D8
St Walstan's Rd NR8 . . . . 156 D8

St Williams Prim Sch
NR7 . . . . 163 D8
St Williams Way NR7 . . . 163 C7
St Winnold Cl PE38 . . . . . 172 B4
St Withburga La 8
NR19 . . . . 154 D5
Saker Cl 11 NR7 . . . . 72 D4
Salamanca Rd 7 NR15 . 106 D3
Salcott Dr PE13 . . . . 152 E5
Sale Ct 5 NR14 . . . . 92 A1
Sale Rd NR7 . . . . 159 D4
SALHOUSE NR13 . . . . 55 B1
Salhouse Dr PE37 . . . . . . 153 B2
Salhouse Prim Sch NR13 . 55 B1
Salhouse Rd
Great & Little Plumstead
NR13 . . . . 73 B6
New Rackheath NR13 . . . . . 72 E7
Norwich NR7 . . . . 159 C2
Sprowston NR13 . . . . 72 D6
Woodbastwick NR13 . . . . . 55 C1
Wroxham NR12 . . . . 164 B2
Salhouse Sta NR13 . . . . . 54 F1
Salisbury Rd
Cromer NR27 . . . . 139 D4
Great Yarmouth NR30 . . . . 169 D6
Norwich NR1 . . . . 163 A8
Sheringham NR26 . . . . 138 E7
Salisbury Way IP24 . . . . . 176 B4
SALLE NR10 . . . . 149 E8
Sallow La
Framingham Pigot NR14 . . . 90 E7
Snetterton NR16 . . . . 118 B8
Salmond Dr 1 IP24 . . . . . 125 F6
Salmond Rd 8 IP25 . . . . . 84 F3
Salmon Rd NR30 . . . . 170 D8
Salmon's Way NR21 . . . . 141 F5
Salter Ave NR4 . . . . 161 E5
Salter's La PE32 . . . . 48 E4
SALTERS LODE PE38 . . . . 79 A4
Salter's Rd PE30 . . . . 146 E7
Salters Way PE13 . . . . . . 152 A2
SALTHOUSE NR25 . . . . 8 B7
Salthouse Marshes Nature
Reserve ★ NR25 . . . . 8 B7
Saltings The PE34 . . . . . . 144 A5
Salts Rd PE14 . . . . 59 C8
Samphire 5 PE30 . . . . . . 147 B7
Sampson Rd NR28 . . . . . 151 C3
Samson Rd NR6 . . . . 157 F4
Samson's La IP22 . . . . . . 129 C7
Samuel Rd 1 NR1 . . . . . . 163 B7
Sancroft Way IP20 . . . . . 123 A3
Sandale Rd PE30 . . . . . . 147 C4
Sandall Rd PE13 . . . . 152 C3
Sandfield Rd 3 PE38 . . . 172 C6
Sandhole La NR13 . . . . . . 73 A7
Sandhole Rd NR14 . . . . . . 74 F1
Sandholme Cl NR1 . . . . . 163 B8
Sandover Cl 4 PE33 . . . . 43 F2
Sandown Rd
Great Yarmouth NR30 . . . . 169 D5
Wisbech PE13 . . . . 152 A2
Sandpiper Cl 1 NR31 . . . 170 A5
Sandpiper Ct 8 NR39 . . . 58 B6
Sandpit La
Gimingham NR11 . . . . 22 E8
Saxlingham Nethergate
NR15 . . . . 107 A8
Thorpe Market NR11 . . . . . 21 F7
SANDRINGHAM PE35 . . . . 27 F7
Sandringham Ave
Great Yarmouth NR30 . . . . 169 D7
12 Marham PE33 . . . . 63 B4
Wisbech PE13 . . . . 152 D6
Sandringham Cres PE30 148 D5
Sandringham Ct
Norwich NR22 . . . . 178 A1
6 Watton IP25 . . . . 84 D3
Sandringham Ctry Pk ★
PE35 . . . . 27 E7
Sandringham Dr
Downham Market PE38 . . . 172 E5
Fakenham PE31 . . . . 133 C4
Sandringham House Mus &
Gdns ★ PE35 . . . . 27 F7
Sandringham Private Hospl
PE30 . . . . 147 E6
Sandringham Rd
Dersingham PE31 . . . . 140 D4
Hunstanton PE36 . . . . 132 D4
King's Lynn PE30 . . . . 147 C7
Norwich NR2 . . . . 162 B6
Sandringham Way PE37 . 153 C2
Sandringham & W Newton
CE Prim Sch PE31 . . . . . . 27 F6
Sands Cl NR31 . . . . 171 E4
Sand Stone Way IP22 . . . 177 B4
Sandy Cl PE31 . . . . 140 C7
Sandy Cres PE31 . . . . . . 140 C7
Sandygate La PE34 . . . . . 144 F5
Sandy Hill La NR25 . . . . . . 8 F4
Sandy La
Aylsham NR11 . . . . 150 B6
Bacton NR12 . . . . 23 D3
Barningham IP31 . . . . 127 C4
Beighton NR13 . . . . 74 D2
Belton with Browston NR31 . 93 F5
Blackborough End PE32 . . . 44 C2
Bradwell NR31 . . . . 94 C8
Buxton with Lammas NR10 . 53 F8
Canadas NR11 . . . . 10 A3
Cantley NR13 . . . . 92 E6
Castle Acre PE32 . . . . 47 A2
Cromer NR27 . . . . 139 A6
Denver PE38 . . . . 172 C2
Dereham NR19 . . . . 154 C8
Diss IP22 . . . . 177 F4

Sandy La continued
Docking PE31 . . . . 134 D6
East Dereham NR19 . . . . . 154 C6
East Tuddenham NR20 . . . . 69 D8
Fakenham NR21 . . . . 141 A5
Fleggburgh NR29 . . . . 75 B8
Great Massingham PE32 . . 46 E8
Grimston PE32 . . . . 44 C8
Hardingham NR9 . . . . 86 D7
Hilgay PE38 . . . . 97 C8
Hoveton NR12 . . . . 55 C4
Ingoldisthorpe PE31 . . . . . 140 C7
King's Lynn PE30 . . . . 148 F1
Loddon NR14 . . . . 92 B1
Mundham NR14 . . . . 109 A7
Norwich NR4 . . . . 162 D1
Old Hunstanton PE36 . . . . 132 E8
Oulton NR11 . . . . 35 B7
Raveningham NR14 . . . . . 110 B8
Rocklands NR17 . . . . 103 A6
Runton NR27 . . . . 10 C4
Sheringham NR27 . . . . 10 A5
Somerton NR29 . . . . 57 E6
Southrepps NR11 . . . . 22 B7
South Wootton PE30 . . . . . 27 C1
St Mary, South Elmham
otherwise Homersfield
IP20 . . . . 123 B3
Taverham NR8 . . . . 156 C8
Thurning NR20 . . . . 34 C8
West Acre PE32 . . . . 46 B2
Weston Longville NR9 . . . . . 51 D4
Wisbech PE13 . . . . 152 F4
Sandy La E NR19 . . . . 154 C6
Sandyland PE13 . . . . 152 B5
Sandy Way PE31 . . . . 140 C7
Sankence La NR11 . . . . . . 35 E5
Santon Cl IP24 . . . . 176 A3
SANTON DOWNHAM
IP27 . . . . 115 C6
SAPISTON IP31 . . . . 126 D2
Sapiston Rd IP31 . . . . 126 D1
Sapwell Cl NR11 . . . . 150 A6
Sarahs Rd NR26 . . . . 157 F6
Sarahs Rd NR36 . . . . 132 C2
Sarah W Cl NR1 . . . . 162 C4
Sarah William Cl 2
NR4 . . . . 161 C5
Sardis Way NR19 . . . . . . 154 D4
Saturday Mkt Pl PE30 . . 146 D4
Saunders Ct 7 NR1 . . . . 163 A6
Savery Cl NR5 . . . . 161 B6
Savory Rd PE13 . . . . 152 B7
Sawmill Cl NR18 . . . . 173 B5
Saw Mill La
Brancaster PE31 . . . . 3 B6
7 Great Yarmouth NR31 . 169 B4
Sawston 1 PE30 . . . . 147 D6
Sawyers Cl NR5 . . . . 156 E1
Sawyer's La NR18 . . . . . . 87 D2
SAXLINGHAM NR15 . . . . . . 7 C2
SAXLINGHAM GREEN
NR15 . . . . 107 D7
Saxlingham La NR15 . . . 106 F7
SAXLINGHAM NETHERGATE
NR15 . . . . 107 C8
Saxlingham Prim Sch
NR15 . . . . 107 C8
Saxlingham Rd
Blakeney NR25 . . . . 7 C5
Saxlingham Nethergate
NR15 . . . . 107 C8
Shotesham NR15 . . . . 89 F1
SAXLINGHAM THORPE
NR15 . . . . 107 A8
Saxon Cres 9 IP31 . . . . . 126 B1
Saxon Ct PE37 . . . . 153 D2
Saxon Field PE31 . . . . 3 B6
Saxonfields NR14 . . . . . . 90 C4
Saxon Gdns NR30 . . . . . 168 D5
Saxon Pl
3 Thetford IP24 . . . . 176 C3
Weeting IP27 . . . . 175 A8
Saxon Rd NR30 . . . . 169 D4
Saxon Way
Dersingham PE31 . . . . 140 D4
Wormegay PE33 . . . . 62 C6
Saxon Wlk IP26 . . . . 100 A4
SAXTHORPE NR11 . . . . . . 19 F1
Sayer Ct NR25 . . . . 9 A2
Sayers St 9 NR2 . . . . . . 162 C7
Scama La IP22 . . . . 129 A2
Scania Way PE30 . . . . . . 147 A1
Scarborough Rd NR22 . . . 17 A8
Scarfield La PE14 . . . . . . 59 C2
Scarlet Rd NR4 . . . . 162 D1
Scarnell Rd NR5 . . . . 161 C6
SCARNING NR19 . . . . 67 B7
Scarning Fen NR19 . . . . . 154 C2
Scarning VC Prim Sch
NR19 . . . . 154 A4
Sceptre Cl NR6 . . . . 158 A3
Scholars Wlk IP22 . . . . . 177 C5
School Ave NR7 . . . . 163 F6
School Cl
Kenninghall NR16 . . . . 119 A4
Knapton NR28 . . . . 143 A1
3 Ludham NR29 . . . . 56 C5
Northrepps NR27 . . . . 11 A2
4 Rollesby NR29 . . . . 57 D2
School Comm Rd NR12 . . 24 C3
Schoolfield NR10 . . . . . . 155 C8
School Hill
Reedham NR13 . . . . 93 A4
Tasburgh NR15 . . . . 106 E6
Schoolhouse La 1 NR11 150 C7

School La
Brandon IP27 . . . . 175 C3
Cantley NR13 . . . . 92 B7
East Dereham NR19 . . . . . 154 E1
East Harling NR16 . . . . . . 118 C5
Gimingham NR11 . . . . 22 E8
Great Yarmouth NR31 . . . . 170 D6
17 Harleston IP20 . . . . . 122 D2
Heckingham NR14 . . . . . . 109 F8
Little Dunham PE32 . . . . . . 65 E7
Little Melton NR9 . . . . 160 C2
Neatishead NR12 . . . . 55 D7
North Runcton PE33 . . . . . 44 A2
Northwold IP26 . . . . 99 C7
Norwich NR7 . . . . 158 F3
Rockland St Mary NR14 . . . 91 B7
Runhall NR9 . . . . 68 F1
Skeyton NR10 . . . . 37 A5
Smallburgh NR12 . . . . 38 D3
Stoke Ferry PE33 . . . . 80 F2
Surlingham NR14 . . . . 73 B1
Thetford IP24 . . . . 176 D3
Walpole St Andrew PE14 . . 41 E3
Wereham PE33 . . . . 80 E4
1 Wisbech PE13 . . . . 152 C5
Wramplingham NR18 . . . . . 69 F1
Wymondham NR18 . . . . . . 105 A8
School Loke
Bodham NR25 . . . . 9 A2
Hemsby NR29 . . . . 167 A7
School Pastures PE31 . . . 3 E7
School Plain NR19 . . . . . 154 B5
School Rd
Alburgh IP20 . . . . 123 A5
Aldborough NR11 . . . . 21 A5
Ashmanhaugh PE12 . . . . . 55 B7
Bacton NR28 . . . . 23 B4
Barton Turf NR12 . . . . 38 E1
Bedingham NR35 . . . . 108 B3
Beetley NR20 . . . . 49 C5
Blofield NR13 . . . . 165 B8
Bracon Ash NR14 . . . . 89 A3
Bradenham IP25 . . . . 66 D3
Bressingham IP22 . . . . . . 129 B8
Brisley NR20 . . . . 49 A8
Catfield NR29 . . . . 56 C8
Colkirk NR21 . . . . 31 D5
Earsham NR35 . . . . 123 F8
East Ruston NR12 . . . . 38 E7
Erpingham NR11 . . . . 21 B2
Foulden IP26 . . . . 82 A1
Freethorpe NR13 . . . . 92 F7
Frettenham NR12 . . . . 54 A4
Great Massingham PE32 . . 29 D1
Great Yarmouth NR30 . . . . 169 B5
Haveringland NR10 . . . . . . 52 D7
Heacham PE31 . . . . 133 D5
Hindersclay IP22 . . . . 128 C3
Holme Hale IP25 . . . . 66 A2
Horning NR12 . . . . 55 F8
Kirby Cane NR35 . . . . 109 E4
Lessingham NR12 . . . . 24 D3
Lingwood NR13 . . . . 74 A3
Little Cressingham IP25 . . . 83 F2
Little Plumpstead NR13 . . . 73 B6
Ludham NR29 . . . . 56 B5
Marshland St James PE14 . 60 B4
Mautby NR29 . . . . 75 E5
Middleton PE32 . . . . 44 C2
Morning Thorpe NR15 . . . . 107 B3
Neatishead NR12 . . . . 55 E7
1 Necton PE37 . . . . 65 F4
Newton Flotman NR15 . . . . 89 D1
Outwell PE14 . . . . 77 D4
Potter Heigham NR29 . . . . 56 F6
Reepham NR10 . . . . 149 B4
Runcton Holme PE33 . . . . . 61 E3
Sculthorpe Airfield NR21 . . 15 C3
Seething NR15 . . . . 108 E8
10 Snettisham PE31 . . . . 12 E5
South Walsham NR13 . . . . 74 A8
St Andrew, Ilketshall
NR34 . . . . 124 E6
Strumpshaw NR13 . . . . 73 F1
Swanington NR9 . . . . 52 B5
Taverham NR8 . . . . 155 F1
Terrington St John PE14 . . 60 B7
Thompson IP24 . . . . 102 B7
Tilney All Saints PE34 . . . . 42 E4
Tilney St Lawrence PE34 . . 60 C7
Tivetshall St Mary NR15 . . 121 B5
Walpole Highway PE14 . . . 59 F8
Walton Highway PE14 . . . . 59 C8
Watlington PE33 . . . . 61 D6
Weasenham All Saints PE32 47 D8
Weasenham St Peter PE32 . 30 D1
West Rudham PE31 . . . . . . 29 F6
West Walton PE14 . . . . 59 B8
Whissonsett NR20 . . . . 31 C2
Wiggenhall St Germans
PE34 . . . . 61 B8
Worstead NR28 . . . . 38 A5
School Rd Back 4 NR30 . 169 C5
School Sq IP29 . . . . 102 E3
School Terr 3 NR14 . . . . 163 B2
School View NR34 . . . . . . 124 F1
SCOLE IP21 . . . . 130 D6
Scole Comm IP21 . . . . . . 130 C6
SCOLE COMMON IP21 . . . 130 C7
Scole Comm Rd IP21 . . . 130 D6
Scole Prim Sch IP21 . . . . 130 D6
Scole Rd IP21 . . . . 131 C6
Scolt Head Island National
Nature Reserve ★ PE31 . . . 3 E8
Sconch Beck Rd IP20 . . . 123 A2
SCO RUSTON NR12 . . . . . 54 E8
Scotch Hill Rd NR8 . . . . . 155 B1

Scotgate Cl IP24 . . . . 102 E3
Scott Cl IP24 . . . . 176 E6
Scotter Rise 7 NR26 . . . . 138 C5
SCOTTOW NR10 . . . . 37 D2
Scottow Rd NR10 . . . . 37 B2
Scott's Cl NR10 . . . . 163 B5
Scott's Cnr NR16 . . . . . . 105 B4
Scott's Hill NR14 . . . . 89 A4
Scott's La IP26 . . . . 99 A7
SCOULTON NR9 . . . . 85 E3
Scoulton Rd NR17 . . . . . . 85 F2
SCRATBY NR29 . . . . 167 E4
Scratby Cres NR29 . . . . . 167 E4
Scratby Rd NR29 . . . . . . 167 D3
Scrobie Sands Visitor Ctr ★
NR30 . . . . 169 E4
Scroby Ct NR29 . . . . 167 E3
Scrumpy Way NR16 . . . . 119 D7
SCULTHORPE NR21 . . . . . 16 B2
Sculthorpe Airfield NR21 . 15 E2
Sculthorpe Ave PE34 . . . 146 B5
Sculthorpe Bsd 7 NR21 . . 15 C2
Sculthorpe CE VA Prim Sch
NR21 . . . . 16 C2
Sculthorpe Eastgate
NR21 . . . . 141 A5
Sculthorpe Rd NR21 . . . . 141 A5
Seabank Rd
Heacham PE31 . . . . 133 B6
Wisbech PE13 . . . . 152 F6
Seabank Way PE30 . . . . . 146 E7
Seabird Cl 4 NR30 . . . . . 168 D7
Seabrook Ct 9 NR5 . . . . 161 A7
Sea Cl PE31 . . . . 133 B6
Seacliff NR26 . . . . 138 E7
Seafield Cl 20 NR30 . . . . 169 D2
Seafield Rd N NR30 . . . . 168 E6
Seafield Rd S NR30 . . . . 168 D6
Seafields Dr NR31 . . . . . 171 D4
Seaforth Dr NR8 . . . . 156 E8
Seagate PE36 . . . . 132 C3
Seagate Rd PE36 . . . . . . 132 B3
Seagull Rd NR29 . . . . . . 167 E5
Sea La PE36 . . . . 132 E7
Sea Palling Rd NR29 . . . . 86 D4
SEA PALLING NR12 . . . . . 40 A6
Sea Palling Rd NR12 . . . . 39 F3
Searle Cl NR21 . . . . 141 F5
Sears Cl NR21 . . . . 150 C6
Seaside La NR12 . . . . 24 E4
Seates The 6 NR8 . . . . . 155 D2
Seathwaite Rd PE30 . . . . 147 D8
Seaview Cres NR26 . . . . 138 D5
Sea View Rd
Hemsby NR29 . . . . 167 D7
Mundesley NR11 . . . . 143 B7
Sea View Rise NR31 . . . . 171 E4
Seawake Cl NR31 . . . . . . 170 A4
Seaward Cres NR11 . . . . 143 B6
Seaward Wlk NR30 . . . . . 168 E8
Seckar Dr NR19 . . . . 154 C4
Second Ave
Caister-on-Sea NR30 . . . . 168 D8
Wisbech PE13 . . . . 152 D4
Second Dro IP27 . . . . 113 C3
Second Marsh Rd PE14 . . 59 A7
Sedge Cl NR21 . . . . 141 E4
Sedge Ct NR21 . . . . 96 C7
Sedgefen Dro PE38 . . . . 112 E7
Sedgefen Rd IP27 . . . . . . 112 F3
Sedge Fen Rd PE38 . . . . 97 B3
SEDGEFORD PE36 . . . . . . 13 B7
Sedgeford Fst Sch PE36 . 13 B7
Sedgeford La 5 PE30 . . . 146 D4
Sedgeford Rd
Docking PE31 . . . . 134 D4
Snettisham PE31 . . . . 12 F5
Sedge Rd NR19 . . . . 154 B4
Seeche Abbey PE34 . . . . . 43 D1
SEETHING NR14 . . . . 108 F8
Seething & Mumdham Sch
NR15 . . . . 108 C8
Seething Old Hall Pk
NR15 . . . . 91 B1
Seething Rd NR35 . . . . . 108 D5
Seething St NR15 . . . . . . 108 E8
Seeview Cres NR12 . . . . . 24 A7
Sefton Ave PE13 . . . . . . 152 E6
Sefton La NR31 . . . . 169 C3
Sego Vale NR8 . . . . 156 E8
Segrave Rd 6 NR30 . . . . 147 A8
Selby Pl 19 NR30 . . . . . . 169 D2
Self's La IP22 . . . . 128 C7
Selwyn Dr NR31 . . . . 94 A5
Selwyn Gdns IP21 . . . . . 121 E5
Selwyn Rd NR31 . . . . . . 170 A5
Semere Gn La IP21 . . . . 121 D2
Semere La IP21 . . . . 121 D4
Sendall Rd NR28 . . . . . . 151 B3
Sennowe Rd NR20 . . . . . . 32 F4
Senter's Rd NR11 . . . . . . 140 D2
Seppings Rd NR21 . . . . . 141 A6
Seppings Way NR13 . . . . 72 E6
Serpentine La NR10 . . . . 53 C6
SETCHEY PE33 . . . . 61 E8
Setch Rd
Middleton PE33 . . . . 44 A1
West Winch PE33 . . . . 43 F1
Seton Rd NR8 . . . . 155 E1
Setons Halt Sta NR23 . . . . 5 C7
Seven Sisters Cl IP30 . . . 146 D4
Seventh Ave PE13 . . . . . 152 E4
Severalls Rd IP26 . . . . 98 D5
Sewell Rd
Lamas NR10 . . . . 36 F1
Norwich NR3 . . . . 158 E1
Sewells Cl 6 NR15 . . . . . . 89 C1
Sewell's La NR15 . . . . 90 D3

Sexton Rd NR35. . . . . 108 D2
Seymour Ave
  Brandon IP27 . . . . 114 D4
  Great Yarmouth NR30 . . . 169 D8
Shack La NR13 . . . . 165 C6
Shadingfield Cl 16 NR30 169 D2
SHADWELL IP24 . . . . 117 C2
Shadwell Cl IP27 . . . . 175 B7
Shakers' Rd
  Brandon IP27 . . . . 115 A1
  Wangford IP27 . . . . 114 F1
Shakespeare Rd NR30 . . . 169 E8
Shakespeare Way
  Taverham NR8 . . . . 156 E8
  Thetford IP24 . . . . 176 E6
Shannock Ct 14 NR26 . . . 138 C7
Shannon Dr 4 NR30 . . . . 168 C6
Shannons Cl NR17 . . . . . . 174 E4
Sharman Ave IP25 . . . . . . 84 D4
Sharmans Loke NR31 . . . . 93 F5
Sharon Cl
  2 East Dereham NR19 . . 154 D1
  Felmingham NR28 . . . . . . 37 A8
Sharper's Cnr IP27 . . . . . . 113 D2
Sharpe Way NR17 . . . . . . 167 B2
Sharp St NR29 . . . . 56 C7
SHARP STREET NR29 . . . . 56 C7
SHARRINGTON NR24 . . . . . 18 D7
Sharrington Rd NR24 . . . . 18 B5
Shavcross Rd NR27 . . . . . 10 A4
Shaw's Yd PE31 . . . . 30 B7
Shearwater Dr 2 NR31 . . 170 A7
Sheddick Ct NR19 . . . . . . 154 D6
Sheep Mdw Cl NR5 . . . . . 156 E1
Sheffield Rd NR18 . . . . . . 173 C5
Sheldonian Ct NR31 . . . . 170 A4
Sheldrake Cl NR21 . . . . . 141 F5
Sheldrick Pl NR10 . . . . . . 154 E2
Shelduck Dr 7 PE31 . . . . 12 E5
SHELFANGER IP22 . . . . . . 120 C2
Shelfanger Rd IP22 . . . . . 177 C7
Shelford Dr PE30 . . . . . . 147 B8
Shelley Cl NR30 . . . . 168 D6
Shelley Dr NR8 . . . . 156 D8
Shelley Way IP24 . . . . . . 176 E6
Shell Mus The* NR25 . . . . 7 E4
Shelly Cl 3 PE38 . . . . . . 172 D6
Shelterhouse Cnr IP24 . . 125 A4
SHELTON NR15 . . . . 107 B1
Shelton with Hardwick Sch
  NR15 . . . . 107 B1
Shepeard Cl 1 NR28 . . . . 151 C6
Shepeards Cl NR11 . . . . . 150 E8
Shepherd Cl
  Norwich NR6 . . . . 161 D5
  Sheringham NR26 . . . . . . 138 B6
Shepherds Cl
  Cromer NR27 . . . . 10 B5
  11 Horsford NR10 . . . . . . 53 A3
  Runton NR27 . . . . 10 A5
Shepherd's Fold PE37 . . . 153 D2
SHEPHERD'S GATE PE34 . . 42 D4
Shepherdsgate Rd PE34 . 144 C1
Shepherds La
  Burgate IP22 . . . . 129 B3
  Oulton NR11 . . . . 35 B6
Shepherd's La NR10 . . . . 36 A2
Shepherds Pightle PE36 . . 2 D6
SHEPHERD'S PORT PE31 . . 12 B4
Shepherd Way NR8 . . . . . 155 E2
Shepley Cres 2 NR30 . . . 147 D5
Sheppard Way NR17 . . . . 174 C5
Sherbourne Pl NR1 . . . . . 178 C1
SHEREFORD NR21 . . . . . . 31 A8
Shereford Rd
  Fakenham NR21 . . . . 141 A3
  Hempton NR21 . . . . 141 A3
Sheridan Cl NR8 . . . . 156 F8
Sheridan House Sch IP25 36 A7
SHERINGHAM NR26 . . . . . 138 C5
Sheringham Com Prim Sch
  NR26 . . . . 138 C5
Sheringham High Sch
  NR26 . . . . 138 D7
Sheringham Little Theatre
  NR26 . . . . 138 D7
Sheringham Mus* 138 D7
Sheringham Pk* NR26 . . . . 9 B6
Sheringham Pk Visitor Ctr*
  NR26 . . . . 9 B4
Sheringham Rd
  West Beckham NR25 . . . . . 9 B3
  Weybourne NR25 . . . . 8 F5
Sheringham Sta NR26 . . . 138 C7
Sheringham Woodfields
  Spec Sch NR26 . . . . 138 C5
SHERINGWOOD NR26 . . . . 138 C5
Sheringwood NR26 . . . . . 138 E4
SHERNBORNE NR31 . . . . . 13 B3
Shernborne Rd PE31 . . . . 140 E7
Sherwell Rd NR6 . . . . 157 E6
Sherwood Ave PE13 . . . . 152 D7
Sherwood Rd NR4 . . . . . . 162 C1
Sheval Cl NR31 . . . . 121 A8
Shickle Pl IP22 . . . . 127 F6
Shillgate Way NR8 . . . . . 155 B2
Shillito Rd NR13 . . . . 165 F6
SHIMPLING IP21 . . . . 121 A2
Shimpling Rd IP21 . . . . . 121 B1
SHINGHAM PE37 . . . . 82 A8
Shipden Ave NR27 . . . . . 139 A7
Shipden Ct NR27 . . . . . . 139 A7
SHIPDHAM IP25 . . . . 67 B2
Shipdham Airfield IP25 . . 67 E2
Shipdham Airfield Ind Est
  IP25 . . . . 67 F2

Shipdham Rd
  Carbrooke IP25 . . . . 85 A5
  East Dereham NR19 . . . . 154 D1
  Scarning NR19 . . . . 67 B6
  Shipdham NR19 . . . . 67 E5
Shipfield NR3 . . . . 158 F2
Shipgate Rd PE31 . . . . . . 29 B5
Ship La PE36 . . . . 2 C6
SHIPMEADOW NR34 . . . . 124 F8
Shippea Hill Sta CB7 . . . 112 C3
Shipstone Rd 11 NR3 . . . 162 D8
Shire Ave 5 NR31 . . . . . . 94 C8
Shiregreen NR30 . . . . 147 C4
Shires The NR8 . . . . 155 F2
Shirley Cl 3 NR12 . . . . . . 54 A4
Shoe Devil La NR35 . . . . 124 C4
Shoemakers La PE37 . . . . 64 E3
Shooters Cl NR8 . . . . 155 D1
Shop La
  Hethersett NR9 . . . . 88 E8
  Tunstead NR12 . . . . 38 A3
  Wells-next-the-Sea NR23 . 136 D6
Shop St NR19 . . . . 68 A3
Shorncliffe Ave NR3 . . . . 158 C1
Shorncliffe Cl 1 NR3 . . . 158 C1
Short Beck 18 PE36 . . . . . 98 E1
Short Cl NR8 . . . . 172 C6
Short Dro PE38 . . . . 172 C6
Short Gn IP22 . . . . 120 B5
SHORT GREEN IP22 . . . . . 120 A5
Short La
  Billingford NR20 . . . . 50 A8
  Feltwell IP26 . . . . 98 D1
  Happisburgh NR12 . . . . . 24 B3
  Harpley PE31 . . . . 29 D4
  Mautby NR29 . . . . 75 E6
  Swardeston NR14 . . . . . . 89 C5
Short Rd
  8 Attleborough NR17 . . . 174 C5
  Belton with Browston NR31 94 A4
Short St 8 NR15 . . . . 89 D1
Short-thorn Rd NR10 . . . . 52 F5
SHOTESHAM NR15 . . . . . . 90 A2
Shotesham La NR15 . . . . 107 C8
Shotesham Rd
  Howe NR15 . . . . 90 C2
  Poringland NR14 . . . . 90 B3
  Wootton NR35 . . . . 108 A6
Shotford Rd IP20 . . . . 122 D1
SHOULDHAM PE33 . . . . . . 62 D4
Shouldham Cl PE31 . . . . 140 C3
Shouldham La PE37 . . . . 153 A4
Shouldham Rd
  Marham PE33 . . . . 63 A3
  Shouldham Thorpe PE33 . 62 C2
SHOULDHAM THORPE
  PE33 . . . . 62 C3
Shreeves Rd IP22 . . . . . . 177 E4
SHROPHAM NR17 . . . . . . 103 B4
Shropham Rd IP24 . . . . . 102 E3
Shrub Cl NR17 . . . . 174 D5
Shrub Dro PE38 . . . . 112 E6
Shrub Hill PE38 . . . . 112 F7
Shrublands The
  Horsford NR10 . . . . 53 B4
  Norwich NR2 . . . . 162 B6
Shrublands Way NR31 . . 170 B5
Shuttleworth Cl NR31 . . 170 A8
Sidegate Rd
  Great Yarmouth NR30 . . . 169 C5
  Hopton on Sea NR31 . . . 171 B7
Sidell Cl 11 NR4 . . . . 89 B8
SIDESTRAND NR11 . . . . . 11 C2
Sidestrand Hall Specl Sch
  NR27 . . . . 11 B2
Siding Rd NR34 . . . . 111 C1
Sidings The IP24 . . . . 176 C5
Sidney Cl
  2 Great Yarmouth
    NR30 . . . . 169 D2
  8 Martham NR29 . . . . . . 57 C4
Sidney Rd
  Costessey NR8 . . . . 156 F4
  Ingham NR12 . . . . 39 D4
Sidney St PE30 . . . . 146 F3
Sienna Mews 3 NR1 . . . . 163 B7
Sigismund Rd NR1 . . . . . 162 D3
SILFIELD NR18 . . . . 88 A2
Silfield Ave NR18 . . . . . . 173 D1
Silfield Gdn PE36 . . . . . . 132 D4
Silfield Rd NR18 . . . . 173 C2
Silfield Sch NR18 . . . . . . 147 C6
Silfield St NR18 . . . . 88 A2
Silkmill Rd 2 NR30 . . . . . 169 D4
Silver St
  Nordelph PE38 . . . . 78 B2
  Runcton Holme PE33 . . . 61 C4
  Terrington St Clement PE34 25 F3
  Upwell PE14 . . . . 77 F1
Silver Cour NR27 . . . . 11 A2
Silver Dr PE31 . . . . 140 C4
Silver Drift PE37 . . . . 64 E5
Silver End NR10 . . . . 149 B6
Silver Gdns 5 NR1 . . . . . 94 A5
Silvergate La NR11 . . . . . 35 F6
SILVER GREEN NR15 . . . . 107 E3
Silver Hill PE30 . . . . 147 D6
Silver Rd NR3 . . . . 178 C4
Silver St
  Attleborough NR17 . . . . . 174 F6
  Besthorpe NR17 . . . . 104 D7
  Fleggburgh NR29 . . . . . . 75 C8
  Garvestone NR9 . . . . 86 C8
  Norwich NR3 . . . . 162 B8
  South Lopham IP22 . . . . 128 F7
  Wisbech PE13 . . . . 152 C6
Silvertree's Way PE33 . . . 43 E1

Simon Scotland Rd PE30 146 F2
Simpson Cl NR28 . . . . . . 151 B6
Sinclair Cl NR31 . . . . 170 A8
Sir Alfred Munnings Rd
  NR5 . . . . 156 A3
Sir Douglas Bader Espl
  PE36. . . . . 132 C4
Sir Edward Stracey Rd
  NR13 . . . . 72 D8
Sir Lewis St PE30 . . . . . . 146 E6
Sir Thomas Cl NR18 . . . . 173 C5
Sir William's Cl NR11 . . . 150 D6
Sir William's La NR11 . . . 150 D7
Siskin Cl NR31 . . . . 170 A6
SISLAND NR14 . . . . 91 E1
Sitka Cl PE31 . . . . 133 C6
Six Crossways NR14 . . . . 91 D3
Sixteen Foot Bank PE14 . 77 D1
Sixth Ave PE13 . . . . 152 E4
Skedge Way NR13 . . . . . . 73 C6
Skelton Cl 1 IP22 . . . . . . 177 E4
Skelton Rd
  Diss IP22 . . . . 177 E4
  Norwich NR7 . . . . 163 C8
Sketton View NR28 . . . . . 151 B3
SKEYTON NR10 . . . . 37 A4
Skeyton Cnr NR10 . . . . . . 37 B6
SKEYTON CORNER NR10 . . 37 B6
Skeyton New Rd NR28 . . 151 B5
Skeyton Rd
  Coltishall NR10 . . . . 37 B2
  North Walsham NR28 . . . 151 A4
Skinners La NR12 . . . . . . 164 B2
Skinner's La IP20 . . . . . . 122 B4
Skipping Block Row NR18 88 B6
Skippon Way NR13 . . . . . 72 D5
Skitfield Rd NR20 . . . . . . 33 E6
Skoner Rd NR5 . . . . 161 B8
Skoyles' La NR9 . . . . 88 A8
Skye Cl NR5 . . . . 161 A8
Slade La
  Framingham Pigot NR14 . 90 E6
  Old Buckenham NR17 . . . 104 B3
  Wortham IP22 . . . . 129 B6
  Yelverton NR14 . . . . 90 F6
Slade Rd NR21 . . . . 118 B7
Slad La NR20 . . . . 50 C6
Sleaford Gn NR3 . . . . 158 C2
Sleigh La IP25 . . . . 84 E2
Sleights Dr PE14 . . . . 59 C5
Slessor Cl 2 IP25 . . . . . . 84 F3
Slip Rd NR14 . . . . 93 A1
Slipshoe La NR15 . . . . . . 122 B7
Slip The PE36 . . . . 2 C3
Sloane Way IP24 . . . . 176 B2
Sloe La NR13 . . . . 72 D8
SLOLEY NR28 . . . . 37 F4
Sloley Rd NR28 . . . . 38 A3
Slopers Rd NR18 . . . . 87 F7
Slough La
  Attleborough NR17 . . . . . 174 E3
  North Tuddenham NR20 . . 68 E8
Slough Rd IP22 . . . . 129 A1
Slugs La NR31 . . . . 111 C8
Sluice Dro IP26 . . . . 113 E7
Sluice Rd
  Denver PE38 . . . . 172 B1
  Wiggenhall St Germans
    PE34 . . . . 61 A8
Slutshole La
  Besthorpe NR17 . . . . 104 D7
  Wymondham NR17 . . . . . 105 A7
SMALLBURGH NR12 . . . . . 38 D3
Smallburgh Rd
  Barton Turf NR12 . . . . 55 E8
  Smallburgh NR12 . . . . . . 38 D2
Smallholdings Rd PE34 . . 145 D4
Small Lode PE14 . . . . 77 F5
SMALLWORTH IP22 . . . . . 128 A7
Smallworth La IP22 . . . . 128 B7
Smea The NR12 . . . . 39 E1
Smeat St 2 NR5 . . . . 161 B7
Smee La NR13 . . . . 72 A4
Smee Rd NR13 . . . . 72 F4
Smeeth Rd
  Emneth PE14 . . . . 59 F2
  St John's Fen End PE14 . . 60 A5
Smith Ave NR30 . . . . 146 E6
Smithdale Rd NR5 . . . . . . 157 B1
Smithdon High Sch
  PE36 . . . . 132 D4
Smithfield Rd NR1 . . . . . 162 E3
Smiths Dr IP21 . . . . 121 B1
Smith's Dro PE38 . . . . . . 112 C8
Smith's Loke NR11 . . . . . 141 E5
Smith's Loke NR11 . . . . . 170 A6
Smithson Cl NR18 . . . . . 173 C4
Smithson Dr NR20 . . . . . 68 F5
Smithtyne Ave
  Dereham NR19 . . . . 68 A7
  3 East Dereham NR19 . . 154 F3
Smithy Cl PE31 . . . . 133 D5
Smithy Rd PE31 . . . . 140 D8
Smock Mill Loke NR18 . . 173 B5
Smugglers Cl PE36 . . . . . 132 F8
Smuggler's La NR10 . . . . 149 B4
Smugglers' Rd IP26 . . . . 100 F8
Snaefell Pk NR26 . . . . . . 138 D6
Snake's La
  Lound NR32 . . . . 94 C2
  Toproft NR35 . . . . 108 A4
Snape Hall Rd 11 NR35 . 106 E3
Snape Hill IP22 . . . . 128 C2
Snape La PE38 . . . . 172 B5
SNEATH COMMON NR15 . 121 A8
Sneath Rd NR15 . . . . 121 A8
SNETTERTON NR16 . . . . . 103 C2
Snetterton Circuit NR16 . 118 D8

SNETTISHAM PE31 . . . . . . 12 E5
Snettisham Beach PE31 . . 12 A3
Snettisham Nature Reserve*
  PE31. . . . . 12 A3
Snettisham Pk* PE31 . . . 12 E4
Snettisham Prim Sch
  PE31 . . . . 12 E5
Snoring Rd NR21 . . . . 17 C3
Snowberry Cl NR21 . . . . . 141 E5
Snowdrop Cl 20 NR31 . . . 94 C6
Snowdrop Dr NR17 . . . . . 174 B4
Snowhill Drift NR19 . . . . 154 D6
Snow's Hill 8 NR14 . . . . . 92 A2
Snow's La NR14 . . . . 92 A2
Snow St IP22 . . . . 177 A6
SNOW STREET IP22 . . . . . 129 D8
Soame Cl NR11 . . . . 150 D5
Soames Pl NR19 . . . . 67 B7
Soanes Cl NR9 . . . . 51 A5
Softley Dr NR4 . . . . 161 C2
Soken Dr
  8 Beetley NR19 . . . . 49 C3
  8 Gressenhall NR20 . . . . 49 C3
Solace Cl NR35 . . . . 124 C8
Sole Cl 6 NR10 . . . . 53 B3
Soleme Rd NR3 . . . . 158 B1
Solent Cl NR30 . . . . 168 C5
Somerleyton Gdns NR2 . . 162 C5
Somerleyton Hall & Gdns*
  NR32 . . . . 111 E8
Somerleyton Prim Sch
  NR32 . . . . 111 D8
Somerleyton Rd
  2 Norwich NR2 . . . . 162 C5
Somerleyton Sta NR32 . . 111 C7
Somersby 2 PE30 . . . . . . 147 A8
Somerset Pl 22 NR30 . . . 169 D4
Somerset Way NR8 . . . . . 155 A1
Somers Rd PE13 . . . . 152 B4
Somerton Rd
  Martham NR29 . . . . 57 D5
  Somerton NR29 . . . . 58 A6
Somerville Ave 170 B3
Somerville Rd 11 PE30 . . 146 E3
Sorrel Cl PE30 . . . . 147 C8
Sorrel Dr
  Attleborough NR17 . . . . . 174 B4
  8 Thetford IP24 . . . . 176 E4
Sorrel La NR20 . . . . 49 D5
Sorrel Rd 25 NR31 . . . . . 94 C6
Sorrel Way PE38 . . . . 172 C3
Sotherton Rd NR4 . . . . . . 161 F3
Soudan Cl 3 NR30 . . . . . 168 D7
SOUTH ACRE PE32 . . . . . . 46 F1
SOUTHBURGH NR9 . . . . . . 86 A4
Southacre Rd PE32 . . . . . 65 C7
South Acre Rd PE32 . . . . 46 F1
Southampton Pl 16
  NR30 . . . . 169 D4
South Ave
  Norwich NR7 . . . . 163 C5
  Swanton Morley Airfield
    NR20 . . . . 50 B5
South Beach Rd NR31 . . . 133 A3
South Beach Par NR30 . . 170 E6
South Beach Pl NR30 . . . 169 E2
South Beach Rd
  Heacham PE31. . . . . 133 A4
  Hunstanton PE36 . . . . . . 132 B3
South Brink PE13 . . . . . . 152 A3
South Burlingham Rd
  NR13 . . . . 74 B3
South Cl NR25 . . . . 7 A6
South Cnr PE31 . . . . 3 B7
SOUTH CREAKE NR21 . . . 15 D6
South Creake Maize Maze*
  NR21. . . . . 15 C5
South Croft NR9 . . . . 88 C7
SOUTH DENES NR30 . . . . 170 E5
South Denes Rd NR30 . . . 169 E1
SOUTH END NR16 . . . . . . 103 C1
Southend
  Bradenham IP25 . . . . 66 D3
  East Dereham NR19 . . . . 154 D4
Southend Rd PE36 . . . . . 132 C3
Southern La IP22 . . . . . . 128 D5
Southern Reach 7 NR14 . 89 B2
Southerwood 4 NR6. . . . 158 D5
SOUTHERY PE38 . . . . 97 F3
Southery Prim Sch PE38 . 97 A5
Southery Rd
  Feltwell IP26 . . . . 98 B2
  Methwold IP26 . . . . 97 F3
South Everard St PE30 . . 146 E3
Southfield PE32. . . . . 65 C5
Southfield Dr 8 PE33 . . . 43 F2
Southfield La NR13 . . . . . 55 C1
Southfields
  Downham Market PE38 . . 172 B4
  8 King's Lynn PE30 . . . . 147 B6
South Gage Cl NR7 . . . . . 159 C4
SOUTHGATE
  Cawston NR10 . . . . 35 B3
  South Creake NR21 . . . . 15 C5
Southgate 12 IP20 . . . . . 122 D1
Southgate Cl NR23 . . . . . 136 C5
Southgate La
  Norwich NR1 . . . . 178 C1
  Snettisham PE31 . . . . 12 E4
Southgates Dr NR31 . . . . 169 D2
Southgates Rd NR30 . . . . 169 D2
Southgate St PE30 . . . . . 146 F3
South Gdn NR31 . . . . 170 C1

South Gn 154 E3
  Terrington St Clement
    PE34 . . . . 144 B5
South Gn Gdns NR19 . . . 154 E3
SOUTH GREEN
  East Dereham NR19 . . . . 154 E3
  Hoxne IP23 . . . . 130 F1
  Mattishall NR20 . . . . 68 F5
  Pulham St Mary IP21 . . . 121 F2
  Terrington St Clement PE34 42 B6
South Harford Mid Sch
  NR4. . . . . 89 E8
South Hill Cl NR7 . . . . . . 163 F8
South Hill Rd NR7 . . . . . . 163 F8
South Icehouse Hill
  NR31. . . . . 170 D6
Southlands PE37 . . . . 153 B2
SOUTH LOPHAM IP22 . . . 128 C8
SOUTH LYNN PE30 . . . . . 146 E2
South Lynn Plain PE30 . . 146 E4
South Mkt Rd NR30 . . . . 169 D4
South Moor Dr PE31 . . . . 133 D4
SOUTH PICKENHAM PE37 . 83 D6
South Pk IP27 . . . . 175 B7
South Pk Ave 2 NR4 . . . . 162 A4
South Quay
  Great Yarmouth NR30 . . . 169 C3
  8 King's Lynn PE30 . . . . 146 D4
South Rd
  Great Yarmouth NR30 . . . 169 E8
  Hemsby NR29 . . . . 167 D7
  Watton IP25 . . . . 84 D3
SOUTHREPPS NR11 . . . . . 22 B7
Southrepps Rd
  Antingham NR28 . . . . 22 B4
  Gimingham NR11 . . . . . . 22 E6
South Rise NR28 . . . . 151 B3
SOUTH RUNCTON PE33 . . 61 F3
Southside PE34 . . . . 79 D8
South St
  Great Dunham PE32 . . . . 47 F1
  Hockwold cum Wilton PE33 113 F6
  2 King's Lynn PE30 . . . . 146 E4
  Sheringham NR26 . . . . . . 138 C7
SOUTHTOWN NR31 . . . . . 169 B1
Southtown Fst Sch NR31 169 B2
Southtown Rd NR31 . . . . 169 C2
SOUTH WALSHAM NR13 . . 74 A7
South Walsham Rd
  Acle NR13 . . . . 166 A5
  South Walsham NR13 . . . 74 B5
Southwell Rd
  8 Horsham St Faith & Newton
    St Faith NR10 . . . . 53 D2
  Norwich NR1 . . . . 178 A1
  Wisbech PE13 . . . . 152 C7
South Wlk NR13 . . . . 72 E5
SOUTHWOOD NR13 . . . . . 92 D8
South Wood Dr NR14. . . . 90 B6
Southwood Rd
  Beighton NR13 . . . . 74 C1
  Cantley NR13 . . . . 92 C8
SOUTH WOOTTON PE30 . . 148 C2
South Wootton Fst Sch
  PE30 . . . . 148 C2
South Wootton Jun Sch
  PE30 . . . . 148 B1
South Wootton La PE30 . 148 C1
Sovereign Cl 2 PE13. . . . 152 A6
Sovereign Way PE38 . . . . 172 A4
Sow's Loke 11 NR12 . . . . 55 E6
SPA COMMON NR28. . . . . 23 A1
Spa La
  Aylsham NR11 . . . . 150 B3
  Oulton NR11 . . . . 35 B8
Spalding's Chair Hill
  IP24. . . . . 126 E8
SPARHAM NR9 . . . . 51 B6
SPARHAMHILL NR9 . . . . . 51 C5
Sparhawk Ave NR7 . . . . . 159 C4
Sparhawk Cl NR7 . . . . . . 159 C4
Sparhawk Fst Sch NR7 . . 159 C4
Spar Rd NR6 . . . . 158 C5
Sparrow Cl 4 NR31 . . . . . 94 C7
Sparrowgate Rd PE14 . . . 59 C5
Speedwell Cl
  8 Attleborough NR17 . . . 174 B4
  2 Thetford IP24 . . . . 176 E4
Speedwell Rd NR18 . . . . 173 C4
Speedwell Way
  13 Redenhall with Harleston
    IP20 . . . . 122 D1
Speke St NR2 . . . . 162 A7
Spelman Rd NR2 . . . . 162 A4
Spencer Ave NR31 . . . . . 170 C6
Spencer Cl
  Great & Little Plumstead
    NR13. . . . . 73 B7
  11 Wymondham NR18 . . . 74 A3
  West Walton PE14 . . . . . . 59 B8
Spencer Ct 12 IP25 . . . . . 84 D3
Spencers Cl NR20 . . . . . . 49 E7
Spencers St NR3 . . . . 162 E8
Spens Ave NR31 . . . . 170 B3
Spenser Ave NR28 . . . . . 151 D4
Spenser Rd PE30 . . . . . . 148 B1
Spice Chase PE34 . . . . . . 60 C7
Spicer's La NR16 . . . . . . 106 B5
Spiers Way IP27 . . . . 177 B4
Spindle Cl NR18 . . . . 173 D4
Spindle Rd NR6 . . . . 158 D4

Spindrift Cl 1 NR29 .... 58 B6
Spinks La NR18 .... 88 B4
Spinks' La NR35 .... 108 C2
Spink's La NR18 .... 173 F6
Spinners Cl PE37 .... 153 B5
Spinners La PE37 .... 153 B5
Spinney Cl
  Beetley NR20 .... 49 D4
  Brandon IP27 .... 175 C2
  King's Lynn PE30 .... 148 B4
  9 Long Stratton NR15 .... 106 E3
  Norwich NR7 .... 163 F8
Spinney Rd NR7 .... 163 E8
Spinney The NR14 .... 110 B7
Spirkett's La IP20 .... 122 D1
Spitalfields NR1 .... 163 A7
Spitfire Rd NR6 .... 158 C6
SPIXWORTH NR10 .... 54 A2
Spixworth Fst Sch NR10 .. 54 A2
Spixworth Rd
  Hainford NR10 .... 53 F4
  Horsham St Faith & Newton St
    Faith NR10 .... 53 E2
  Norwich NR6 .... 158 E5
Splashes The PE37 .... 153 B7
Splash Leisure Complex
  NR26 .... 138 B7
Spong La
  Carleton St Peter NR14 ... 91 D5
  East Carleton NR14 .... 88 F4
  Shropham NR17 .... 103 C4
SPOONER ROW NR18 .. 105 A8
Spooner Row Prim Sch
  NR18 .... 105 A8
Spooner Row Sta NR18 .. 105 A8
SPORLE PE32 .... 65 C6
Sporle Fst Sch PE32 .... 65 D6
Sporle Rd
  Little Dunham PE32 .... 65 D7
  Swaffham PE37 .... 153 C5
Springbank NR1 .... 162 E2
Spring Cl PE30 .... 148 C1
Springdale Cres NR13 ... 165 B4
Springdale Rd NR13 .... 165 B4
Springfield NR13 .... 166 C3
Springfield Cl
  Crimplesham PE33 .... 80 B6
  Hemsby NR29 .... 58 A4
  4 Weybourne NR25 .... 8 F5
Springfield Rd NR29 .... 58 A4
Springfield Rd
  Great Yarmouth NR31 ... 170 D4
  Hemsby NR29 .... 58 A4
  Norwich NR7 .... 159 D2
  Taverham NR8 .... 155 C1
  Walpole St Andrew PE14 .. 41 D4
Springfields
  Attleborough NR17 .... 174 B5
  10 Poringland NR14 .... 90 C5
Springfield Way NR9 ... 86 B5
Springfield Wlk IP21 ... 121 E5
Spring Gr PE34 .... 144 B4
Spring La
  Forncett NR16 .... 106 B5
  Hempnall NR15 .... 107 E3
  King's Lynn PE30 .... 147 C2
  North Barsham NR22 ... 16 A7
  Shouldham PE33 .... 62 D4
  South Creake NR22 .... 16 A6
  Yaxham NR19 .... 68 A5
Springles The 6 NR27 .. 10 B5
Spring Rd IP31 .... 127 A1
Spring Sedge 4 NR30 .. 147 A8
Springvale 3 NR22 .... 45 C6
Spring View 6 PE21 ... 12 D4
Springwell La NR9 .... 51 F6
Springwell Rd NR20 ... 31 D2
Springwood
  Taverham NR8 .... 155 E1
  Woodton NR35 .... 108 A6
Springwood High Sch
  PE30 .... 147 C6
SPROWSTON NR7 .... 159 B3
Sprowston Fst & Mid Sch
  NR7 .... 159 A4
Sprowston High Sch
  NR7 .... 159 B3
Sprowston Rd NR3 .... 178 C2
Sprowston Ret Pk NR7 .. 159 C2
Spruce Ave 2 NR29 ... 167 A2
Spruce Cl PE31 .... 133 B6
Spruce Cres 4 NR14 ... 90 C5
Spruce Dr IP27 .... 175 D2
Spruce Rd PE38 .... 172 B6
Spurdens Cres NR28 ... 151 D3
Spurge Sq 3 NR18 .... 173 E4
Spur La NR14 .... 90 C6
Spur Rd NR9 .... 69 C2
Spynke Rd NR3 .... 158 B3
Squire's Dr PE14 .... 77 E3
Squire's Dro PE14 .... 78 A3
Squires Hill PE33 .... 63 B4
Squire's Rd NR13 .... 75 A2
Stablefields IP26 .... 99 C7
STACKSFORD NR17 .... 104 C1
Stacy Rd NR3 .... 162 E8
Staden Pk NR11 .... 11 D1
Stafford Ave NR5 .... 156 F1
Stafford Rd NR31 .... 169 B2
Stafford St NR2 .... 162 B6
Stag Pl PE30 .... 147 A7
Stainsby Cl PE31 .... 133 D4
Staithe Cl 3 NR12 .... 55 E4
Staithe La PE36 .... 2 C7

Staithe Rd
  Barton Turf NR12 .... 38 F1
  Burgh St Peter NR34 .... 111 C3
  Catfield NR29 .... 56 D8
  Halvergate NR13 .... 166 F1
  Heacham PE31 .... 133 C5
  Hickling NR12 .... 39 E1
  Langley with Hardley NR14 .. 91 F4
  Ludham NR29 .... 56 C5
  Marthan NR29 .... 57 D5
  Repps with Bastwick NR29 .. 56 F4
  Somerton NR29 .... 57 E6
  Stalham NR12 .... 39 E3
  Wisbech PE13 .... 152 E5
Staithe Stree NR23 .... 136 D6
Staithe The NR11 .... 150 D8
Staitheway Rd NR12 ... 164 C4
STALHAM NR12 .... 39 B4
Stalham Firehouse Mus*
  NR12 .... 39 B3
STALHAM GREEN NR12 .. 39 C3
Stalham High Sch NR12 .. 39 B4
Stalham Mid Sch NR12 .. 39 B3
Stalham Rd
  Ashmanhaugh NR12 .... 55 C8
  Hickling NR12 .... 39 E2
  Sea Palling NR12 .... 24 F1
  Wroxham/Hoveton NR12 .. 164 D6
STALLAND COMMON
  NR17 .... 86 C1
Stalland La NR18 .... 86 D2
Stalland The NR18 .... 86 D2
Stallett Way PE34 .... 60 C8
Standard Pl 10 NR30 .. 169 D3
Standard Rd
  Great Yarmouth NR30 .. 169 E3
  Wells-next-the-Sea NR23 .. 136 D6
Standley Cl NR18 .... 173 B4
STANFIELD NR20 .... 48 F7
Stanfield Rd
  Mileham PE32 .... 48 E6
  Tittleshall PE32 .... 48 C7
  Wymondham NR18 .... 173 F3
STANFORD IP24 .... 101 A5
Stanford Cres NR13 ... 73 B7
Stanford Tuck Rd NR28 .. 151 B7
STANHOE PE31 .... 14 E8
Stanhoe Rd PE31 .... 134 E4
Staniforth Rd IP24 ... 176 B2
Stanley Ave
  Great Yarmouth NR31 .. 170 C3
  Neatishead NR12 .... 55 E7
  Norwich NR7 .... 163 C5
Stanley Cl NR13 .... 92 B6
Stanley Dr PE12 .... 41 A8
Stanley Rd
  Diss IP22 .... 177 B4
  Great Yarmouth NR30 .. 169 C5
  North Walsham NR28 .. 151 D6
Stanleys La NR18 .... 173 C2
Stanley St 10 NR30 ... 146 E5
Stanley Terr NR30 .... 169 D4
Stanmore Rd NR7 .... 163 E6
Stannard Cl 4 IP22 ... 177 C4
Stannard Rd NR21 .... 161 F5
Stanninghall Rd NR12 .. 54 B4
Stan Petersen Cl NR1 .. 163 A6
STANTON CHARE IP31 .. 127 B1
Stanton Rd
  Barningham IP31 .... 127 C2
  Dersingham PE31 .... 140 C3
Star Farm Cl 1 NR31 ... 94 C6
Star Hill NR12
Stark Cl IP22 .... 177 C4
Star La
  Long Stratton NR15 .... 106 E3
  1 Thetford IP24 .... 176 C3
  Tivetshall St Margaret
    NR15 .... 121 C5
Starling Cl NR11 .... 150 C5
Starling Rd NR3 .... 162 D8
Starling Rise NR27 .... 11 B2
Star Mdw NR21 .... 141 B4
STARSTON IP20 .... 122 C3
Starston La IP20 .... 122 C1
Statham Cl NR4 .... 162 B2
Station App
  Norwich NR1 .... 178 C2
  12 Sheringham NR26 ... 138 D7
  Wymondham NR18 .... 173 C2
Station Cl
  East Dereham NR19 ... 154 D6
  4 Lingwood NR13 .... 74 A3
  6 Marthan NR29 .... 57 D4
  Sheringham NR27 .... 10 A5
  Swainsthorpe NR14 .... 89 D4
Station Dr
  Fransham NR19 .... 66 A8
  Reedham NR13 .... 92 F5
  Wisbech PE13 .... 152 C4
Station Gdns PE13 .... 153 B5
Station Halt NR11 .... 165 B3
Station Hill IP20 .... 122 D2
Station La
  Garvestone NR9 .... 68 D1
  Hethersett NR9 .... 88 E7
  Thetford IP24 .... 176 C5
  Thornham PE36 .... 2 C6
Station New Rd NR13 .. 165 D3
Station Rd
  Acle NR13 .... 166 B2
  Alburgh IP20 .... 123 A3
  Aldeby NR34 .... 110 F6
  Attleborough NR17 .... 174 E5
  Attlebridge NR9 .... 52 A4
  Aylsham NR11 .... 150 D6
  Barnham IP24 .... 125 E6
  Beccles NR34 .... 110 D1

Station Rd continued
  Brundall NR13 .... 165 D2
  Burnham Market PE31 ... 135 C3
  Burston & Shimpling IP21 .. 120 F2
  Cantley NR13 .... 92 C6
  Clenchwarton PE34 .... 145 B4
  Coltishall NR12 .... 54 C7
  Congham PE32 .... 27 F3
  Corpusty NR11 .... 19 F1
  Cromer NR27 .... 139 D5
  Dersingham PE31 .... 140 B4
  Diss IP22 .... 177 F3
  Ditchingham NR35 .... 160 F2
  Docking PE31 .... 134 D5
  Downham Market PE38 .. 172 A5
  2 Earsham NR35 .... 123 F8
  East Dereham NR19 ... 154 E4
  East Rudham PE31 .... 30 B5
  East Winch PE32 .... 44 F3
  Ellingham NR35 .... 109 D3
  Flordon NR15 .... 106 C4
  Forncett NR16 .... 106 C4
  Foulsham NR20 .... 33 C3
  Fransham NR19 .... 66 B7
  Fulmodeston NR21 .... 17 F4
  Geldeston NR34 .... 109 F2
  Great Moulton NR15 ... 121 A7
  Great Ryburgh NR21 ... 32 B6
  Great Yarmouth NR31 .. 169 B3
  Guestwick NR20 .... 33 F5
  Haddiscoe NR14 .... 93 D1
  Hardingham NR9 .... 86 E8
  Harleston IP20 .... 122 D2
  Heacham PE31 .... 133 D6
  Hilgay PE38 .... 96 C6
  Hindolveston NR20 .... 33 E8
  Holme Hale IP25 .... 65 F2
  Holt NR25 .... 137 C6
  Honing NR28 .... 38 C6
  Hopton on Sea NR31 ... 171 D4
  Kimberley NR18 .... 87 A6
  King's Lynn PE30 .... 148 B5
  Lakenheath IP27 .... 112 E3
  Lenwade NR9 .... 51 E5
  Lingwood & Burlingham
    NR13 .... 74 A3
  Middleton PE32 .... 44 C4
  Mundesley NR11 .... 143 B6
  North Elmham NR20 ... 49 F7
  North Walsham NR28 .. 151 B4
  Ormesby St Margaret with
    Scratby NR29 .... 167 B2
  5 Potter Heigham NR29 .. 56 F6
  Pulham Market NR15 ... 121 E4
  Quidenham NR16 .... 118 E8
  Rackheath/Salhouse NR13 .. 72 F8
  Reedham NR13 .... 92 F5
  Reepham NR10 .... 149 C5
  Roydon PE32 .... 28 A2
  6 Sheringham NR27 ... 10 A5
  Snettisham PE31 .... 12 D4
  Somerleyton, Ashby &
    Herringfleet NR32 ... 111 C7
  South Wootton PE31 ... 149 C5
  Stanhoe PE31 .... 14 E8
  Strumpshaw NR13 .... 91 F8
  Taverham NR8 .... 156 F8
  Terrington St Clement
    PE34 .... 144 C2
  Thetford IP24 .... 176 C5
  Thorpe Market NR11 ... 22 A6
  Tilney All Saints PE34 .. 144 F2
  Tivetshall St Margaret
    NR15 .... 121 B7
  Walsingham NR22 .... 16 F7
  Walsoken PE14 .... 59 E4
  Watlington PE33 .... 61 C6
  Wells-next-the-Sea NR23 .. 136 D5
  Wendling NR19 .... 66 F7
  West Dereham PE33 .... 80 B3
  Weybourne NR25 .... 8 F5
  Whinburgh & Westfield
    NR19 .... 68 A5
  Worstead NR28 .... 37 F3
  Wroxham/Hoveton NR12 .. 173 C3
  Wymondham NR18 .... 173 C3
Station Rd Ind Est NR17 .. 174 D4
Station Rd N
  Belton NR31 .... 93 F6
  Walpole Cross Keys PE14 .. 41 F5
Station Rd S
  Belton NR31 .... 93 F6
  Walpole Cross Keys PE14 .. 41 F5
Station St IP27 .... 153 B5
Station Terr IP27 .... 175 C5
Station Way IP27 .... 175 C5
Station Yd PE13 .... 153 B5
Steam Mill La NR31 .... 169 B4
Stearne Cl IP24 .... 176 B2
Stebbings Cl IP32 .... 28 A1
Steel's Dro PE38 .... 79 C1
Steepgreen Cl NR1 .... 163 C8
Steeple Chase NR8 .... 155 F2
Steeple La NR15 .... 106 A2
Steeple View PE13 .... 153 B4
Steeps The 6 NR30 ... 169 D1
Steer Rd PE31 .... 27 B8
Steggles Dr IP22 .... 177 C5
Stegg's La NR19 .... 124 F1
Stephen Beaumont Way
  NR19 .... 154 F2
Stephenson Cl
  3 Great Yarmouth
    NR30 .... 169 D5
  West Raynham Airfield
    PE31 .... 30 B3

Stephenson Way IP24 .. 176 A2
Stephenson Way Ind Est
  IP24 .... 176 A2
Steppings La NR15 .... 107 C3
Stepping Stone La NR12 .. 39 A4
Stepshort NR31 .... 94 A6
Stermyn St 2 PE13 ... 152 C5
Stevens Cl IP25 .... 84 D4
Steven's La
  Ashwellthorpe NR16 ... 106 B8
  Wreningham NR16 .... 88 E1
Stevenson Rd NR5 .... 161 B7
Steward Rd
  Cromer NR27 .... 139 C4
  2 Little Snoring NR21 .. 17 B3
Steward Cl 1 NR18 ... 173 D5
Stewards Cl NR10 .... 149 C4
Steward St 4 NR3 .... 162 E8
Steward Way NR14 .... 154 C5
Stewkis Hall Drift NR9 .. 51 B6
STIBBARD NR21 .... 32 C2
Stibbard Rd NR21 .... 17 F1
Stickfer La NR16 .... 106 A6
STIFFKEY NR23 .... 6 D5
Stiffkey Cl 8 PE33 .... 61 D6
Stiffkey Rd
  Warham NR23 .... 5 F5
  Wells-next-the-Sea NR23 .. 136 F5
Stigand's Gate NR19 ... 154 D7
Stile Cl NR20 .... 99 B3
Stile La NR18 .... 173 B5
Stileman Way 11 PE13 .. 12 E4
Stillington Cl NR7 .... 159 B3
Stilwell Dr NR19 .... 154 B6
Stirling Cl
  Downham Market PE38 .. 172 D6
  Taverham NR8 .... 155 F3
Stirling Rd
  Old Catton NR6 .... 158 C6
  Sculthorpe Airfield NR21 .. 15 C3
Stirrups La NR32 .... 171 E1
Stitch The PE14 .... 77 B8
Stockholm Way NR19 .. 154 C2
Stock Lea Rd 1 PE30 .. 148 C4
Stocks Hill NR9 .... 160 B8
Stocks La NR13 .... 165 E5
STOCKTON NR34 .... 109 F4
Stockton Rd NR34 .... 110 A3
STODY NR24 .... 18 F6
Stody Rd NR24 .... 18 D6
STOKE FERRY PE33 ... 80 F3
STOKE HOLY CROSS
  NR14 .... 89 F4
Stoke Holy Cross Prim Sch
  NR14 .... 89 F4
Stoke La NR14 .... 89 F5
Stoke Rd
  Barton Bendish PE33 .... 81 C5
  Bixley NR14 .... 162 F1
  Boughton PE33 .... 81 A4
  Caistor St Edmund NR14 ... 89 F7
  Methwold IP26 .... 99 A6
  Poringland NR14 .... 90 B5
  Wereham PE33 .... 80 E4
  Wormegay PE33 .... 62 A5
Stokes Ave IP25 .... 84 C3
Stokesby New Rd NR13 .. 166 F6
Stokesby Rd NR29 .... 75 D6
Stone Breck NR5 .... 156 E2
STONEBRIDGE IP24 ... 102 B1
Stonebridge Rd NR28 .. 23 D2
Stone Brigg NR18 .... 87 A7
Stone Cl 2 PE33 .... 61 D5
Stonecross Rd PE38 ... 172 D5
Stonecutters Way NR30 .. 169 C4
Stonefield Rd NR25 ... 20 A8
Stonegate
  Aylsham NR11 .... 150 A3
  Morley NR18 .... 87 A3
Stonegate St PE30 .... 146 D4
Stone Hill Rd NR30 ... 168 D6
Stonehill Way NR27 ... 10 C4
Stone House Cl NR6 ... 158 D2
Stonehouse Rd
  Norwich NR7 .... 159 B4
  Salhouse NR13 .... 54 F2
  Upwell PE14 .... 77 E5
Stone La
  Bintree NR20 .... 33 B3
  Bressingham IP22 .... 119 F2
  5 Hingham NR9 .... 86 C4
  Hoveton NR12 .... 164 D8
  Runhall NR9 .... 68 F3
Stonemasons Ct NR13 .. 166 C3
Stone Rd
  6 Beetley NR20 .... 49 D4
  6 Beetley NR20 .... 49 D4
  Briston NR24 .... 142 E2
  East Dereham NR19 ... 154 C2
  Great Yarmouth NR31 .. 169 B4
  Halvergate NR13 .... 75 A1
  Hockering NR20 .... 51 B1
  Mattishall NR20 .... 68 C6
  Norwich NR3 .... 158 C1
  Strumpshaw NR13 .... 73 F1
  Yaxham NR19 .... 68 B4
Stone St IP19 .... 124 F1
STONE STREET IP19 ... 124 F1
Stoney End 2 NR20 ... 68 F6
Stoney La
  Beetley NR20 .... 49 B6
  Reepham NR10 .... 149 B6
Stoney Rd PE32 .... 27 F2
Stony La
  Attleborough NR17 .... 174 B6

Stony La continued
  Pulham Market NR21 ... 121 E7
  Raveningham NR14 ... 110 B6
  Tivetshall St Margaret
    NR15 .... 121 B5
  Wortwell IP20 .... 122 F4
Storbeck Rd 2 PE13 .. 152 D7
Stores St IP27 .... 175 C3
Story's La NR15 .... 105 E5
STOW BARDOLPH PE34 .. 79 E8
Stow Barn Rd PE33 .... 80 A7
STOW BEDON NR17 .... 102 E4
Stow Bedon Rd IP24 .. 102 C2
Stowe Rd NR14 .... 61 B2
Stow Bridge Rd
  Stow Bardolph PE34 ... 61 D1
  Wimbotsham PE34 .... 79 E8
Stow Gdns PE13 .... 152 E4
Stow La PE13 .... 152 E4
Stowlay La NR17 .... 103 B6
Stow Rd
  Outwell PE14 .... 78 A7
  Runcton Holme PE33 ... 62 B3
  Wiggenhall St Mary Magdalen
    PE34 .... 61 B5
  Wisbech PE13 .... 152 F5
Stow Windmill* NR28 .. 143 D4
Stracey Rd
  Lamas NR10 .... 36 F1
  Norwich NR1 .... 163 A5
Strachan Cl PE31 .... 133 E5
STRADBROKE IP21 .... 131 E1
Stradbroke CE Prim Sch
  IP21 .... 131 E1
Stradbroke Prim Sch
  NR31 .... 170 D5
Stradbroke Rd NR31 ... 170 C5
STRADSETT PE33 .... 80 B8
Stradsett Cl 8 PE38 ... 172 D6
Straight La 10 IP20 ... 122 D2
Strangers Hall* NR2 ... 178 A3
Stranton Ave NR19 ... 68 A5
Strasbourg Way NR19 .. 154 B1
Stratford Cl
  Dersingham PE31 .... 140 E3
  Norwich NR1 .... 162 F2
Stratford Cres NR4 .... 161 C1
Stratford Dr NR1 .... 162 E3
Stratton Cl 6 PE37 ... 153 C3
Stratton Rd
  Hainford NR10 .... 53 E6
  Stratton Strawless NR10 ... 53 E8
  Wacton NR15 .... 106 D2
STRATTON ST MICHAEL
  NR15 .... 106 F4
STRATTON STRAWLESS
  NR10 .... 53 E6
Strawberry Cl 3 PE13 .. 152 A6
Strawberry Fields NR12 .. 39 B3
Straw Mus The* NR11 .. 21 D3
Strayground La NR18 .. 173 B2
Street Hill NR12 .... 55 E7
Street The
  Acle NR13 .... 166 C3
  Alburgh IP20 .... 122 F6
  Aldborough NR11 .... 20 F5
  Aldeby NR34 .... 110 F4
  Ashby St Mary NR14 ... 91 C5
  Ashwellthorpe NR16 ... 106 A8
  Aslacton NR15 .... 106 A1
  Aylmerton NR11 .... 10 A2
  Baconsthorpe NR25 ... 19 F8
  Bacton NR28 .... 23 B2
  Barnham IP24 .... 125 E6
  Barton Turf NR12 .... 55 E8
  Bawdeswell NR20 .... 50 E7
  Beachamwell PE37 .... 81 E8
  Beeston with Bittering PE32 .. 48 C2
  Belaugh NR12 .... 164 A6
  Bergh Apton NR15 ... 91 A3
  Billingford NR20 .... 50 B7
  Bintree NR20 .... 33 B2
  Blo' Norton IP22 .... 128 B5
  Booton NR10 .... 149 A4
  Botesdale IP22 .... 128 E2
  Bracon Ash NR14 .... 89 A3
  Bramerton NR14 .... 90 F7
  Brampton NR10 .... 36 E3
  Brandon IP27 .... 175 A3
  Bressingham IP22 .... 119 D2
  Bridgham NR16 .... 117 E4
  Brinton NR24 .... 18 D6
  Brockdish IP21 .... 131 D6
  Brome & Oakley IP23 ... 130 C3
  Brooke NR15 .... 90 E2
  Brundall NR13 .... 165 E5
  Burgh & Tuttington NR11 .. 36 E4
  Caston NR17 .... 102 E8
  Catfield NR29 .... 56 C8
  Claxton NR14 .... 91 D6
  Coltishall NR12 .... 54 E7
  Coney Weston IP31 ... 127 B4
  Corpusty NR11 .... 19 F1
  Costessey NR8 .... 156 E5
  Croxton IP24 .... 116 C6
  Dickleburgh IP21 .... 121 B1
  Dilham NR28 .... 38 D4
  Earsham NR35 .... 123 F8
  East Tuddenham NR20 .. 66 F6
  Erpingham NR11 .... 21 A2
  Felthorpe NR10 .... 155 C8
  Flixton NR35 .... 123 E6
  Flordon NR15 .... 106 D8
  Foxley NR20 .... 50 D8
  Framingham Pigot NR14 .. 90 D6
  Fulmodeston NR21 ... 17 F3
  Garvestone NR9 .... 68 B1
  Geldeston NR34 .... 109 F2

Street The *continued*
Gooderstone PE33. . . . . . 81 F5
Great Cressingham IP25. . 83 C4
Great Snoring NR21. . . . . 17 A5
Great Yarmouth NR30 . . . 76 F5
Halvergate NR13. . . . . . . 74 F1
Hempnall NR15. . . . . . . 107 C5
Hemsby NR29 . . . . 167 A7
Hevingham NR10. . . . . . . 53 C8
Heydon NR11. . . . . 34 F6
Hickling NR12 . . . . 39 F2
Hinderclay IP22. . . . . . . 128 C3
Hindolveston NR20 . . . . . 33 D8
Hindringham NR17 . . . . . 17 E7
Hockering NR20. . . . . . . 69 B6
Honingham NR9. . . . . . . 69 B6
Horsey NR29 . . . . 40 E1
Kelling NR25 . . . . 8 C5
Ketteringham NR18. . . . . 88 E6
Kettlestone NR21. . . . . . 17 C2
Knapton NR28. . . . . 143 B1
Lamas NR10. . . . . 37 A1
Lenwade NR9. . . . . 51 D5
Lessingham NR12 . . . . . . 24 D3
Little Barningham NR11. . 20 B4
Little Snoring NR21 . . . . 17 B3
Long Stratton NR15. . . . 106 E3
Lound NR32. . . . . 94 C2
Marham PE33 . . . . 63 B5
Market Weston IP22. . . . 127 E4
Marlingford NR9 . . . . . . 69 E4
Mautby NR29. . . . . 75 E5
Melton Constable NR24. . 142 A5
Mileham NR22 . . . . 48 D6
Morning Thorpe NR15 . . 107 C4
Morston NR25 . . . . 7 A6
Morton on the Hill NR9 . . 52 A3
North Lopham IP22 . . . . 119 C2
North Pickenham PE37 . . 65 E1
Norwich NR14 . . . . 163 B2
Ovington IP25 . . . . 84 E5
Poringland NR14 . . . . . . 90 C5
Pulham St Mary IP21. . . 122 A3
Redenhall with Harleston
  IP20. . . . . 122 F1
Redgrave IP22. . . . . 128 E6
Reepham NR10. . . . . . . 149 C3
Riddlesworth IP22. . . . . 127 D7
Ringland NR8. . . . . 70 B8
Rockland St Mary NR14. . 91 A7
Rocklands NR17. . . . . . . 103 C7
Rougham PE32. . . . . 47 B7
Ryburgh NR21 . . . . 32 C7
Salle NR10. . . . . 149 D8
Saxlingham Nethergate
  NR15. . . . . 107 B8
Scoulton NR9. . . . . 86 D3
Sculthorpe Airfield PE31. . 15 B3
Sculthorpe NR21 . . . . . . 16 B1
Sea Palling NR12 . . . . . . 40 A5
Shelton NR15. . . . . 122 B8
Shotesham NR15. . . . . . . 90 A2
Somerton Ashby &
  Herringfleet NR32 . . . 111 D8
Somerton NR29 . . . . 57 F6
South Lopham IP22 . . . . 128 D8
South Pickenham PE37. . . 83 D7
South Walsham NR13 . . . 74 A8
Sparham NR9. . . . . 51 B4
Sporle with Palgrave PE32 . 65 C7
Starston IP20 . . . . 122 C3
St Margaret, South Elmham
  IP20. . . . . 123 E2
St Michael South Elmham
  IP19 . . . . 124 A2
Surlingham NR14. . . . . . 165 B1
Sustead NR11 . . . . 20 E7
Swafield NR28. . . . . 151 D8
Swanton Abbott NR10 . . . 37 C4
Swanton Novers NR24. . . 18 C2
Taverham NR8 . . . . 156 B8
Tharston & Hapton NR15. 106 C2
Themelthorpe NR20. . . . . 33 F2
Thornage NR25 . . . . 18 E6
Thurlton NR14 . . . . 92 F1
Thurne NR29 . . . . 56 E2
Thurton NR14 . . . . 91 C3
Tibenham NR16 . . . . . . 120 E8
Tivetshall St Mary NR15 . 121 B5
Topcroft NR15 . . . . 107 F3
Warham NR23. . . . . 6 A4
Waterloo NR11. . . . . . . 130 C5
Wattisfield IP22. . . . . . . 128 A1
Wellingham PE32. . . . . . 47 F8
West Beckham NR25 . . . . 9 B2
Weybourne NR25. . . . . . . 8 E5
Winfarthing IP22. . . . . . 120 B4
Witton NR28 . . . . 23 E1
Wiveton NR25 . . . . 7 E6
Woodton NR35. . . . . . . 108 C5
Stretton Sch NR2. . . . . 162 C3
Strickland Ave 9 PE31. . 12 E4
Strickland Cl 8 PE31 . . 12 E4
Stringside Dro PE33. . . 81 B3
STRUMPSHAW NR13. . . . . 73 F2
Strumpshaw Rd NR13. . 165 E3
Strumpshaw Steam Mus★
  NR13. . . . . 73 E2
Stuart Cl
  Brandon IP27 . . . . . . 175 C3
  7 Great Yarmouth NR31 . 170 B4
  7 Hethersett NR9 . . . . 88 D8
Stuart Gdns NR1. . . . . 178 C3
Stuart Rd
  Aylsham NR11 . . . . . . 150 C7
  Norwich NR1 . . . . 178 C1
STUBB NR12 . . . . 39 F1

STUBBING'S GREEN
  IP22. . . . . 129 A1
Stubb Rd NR12 . . . . . . 39 F2
Stubbs Cl PE38 . . . . . . 172 E5
Stubbs Gn La NR14. . . 109 C8
STUBBS GREEN NR14. . 109 C8
Sturdee Ave NR30. . . . 169 D8
Sturdee Cl IP24. . . . . . 176 F6
Sturmy Cl 15 NR15. . . . 106 E3
STUSTON IP21 . . . . 130 B5
Stuston La IP21. . . . . . 130 B4
Stuston Rd IP21 . . . . . 130 B5
Style Loke NR9 . . . . . . 69 F2
Styles Cl NR14 . . . . . . 161 A7
Stylman Rd NR5. . . . . 161 A7
Suckling Ave NR3. . . . 158 B3
Suckling Dro PE14 . . . . 78 C5
Suckling La
  Framingham Pigot NR14 . . 90 D6
  Hickling NR12 . . . . 39 F3
Suckling Pl NR35 . . . . 108 C5
SUFFIELD NR11. . . . . . . 21 F3
Suffield Cl
  1 Cringleford NR4. . . . 89 B8
  3 Long Stratton NR15 . 106 D3
  North Walsham NR28 . . 151 A6
Suffield Ct NR28 . . . . . 151 D8
Suffield Rd NR31. . . . . 170 C4
Suffield Way PE30 . . . 147 B8
Suffling Rd NR30 . . . . 170 D8
Suffolk Ave IP31. . . . . 126 B1
Suffolk Cl NR31. . . . . . 170 C7
Suffolk Ct IP27 . . . . . . 175 C4
Suffolk Pl NR19. . . . . . 154 C1
Suffolk Rd
  Great Yarmouth NR31. . 170 C8
  King's Lynn PE30 . . . . 147 C6
  Norwich NR1 . . . . 161 C3
  Sheringham NR26 . . . . 138 D6
Suffolk Sq NR2 . . . . . . 162 C5
Suffolk Wlk NR1 . . . . . 161 D3
Sugar La PE31. . . . . . . 140 E4
Sukey Way NR5. . . . . . 160 F6
Summer Cl 4 PE14 . . . . 41 E4
Summer Dr NR12 . . . . 164 D6
SUMMERFIELD IP31. . . . . . 2 E1
Summerfield Cl PE13. . . 152 A6
Summerfield Rd NR29. . 58 A4
SUMMERHILL PE31. . . . . 133 C3
Summerhouse Ct NR27 . 139 A6
Summer La IP25 . . . . . . 85 A4
Sumpter Rd NR4 . . . . . 161 B3
Sunart Cl NR17 . . . . . . 174 E6
Sun Barn Rd NR10 . . . 149 B4
Sun Barn Wlk NR10 . . . 149 B4
Suncroft NR1. . . . . 162 F2
Sunderland Cl NR6. . . . 158 C6
Sundew Cl 6 IP24 . . . . 176 F4
Sunk Rd NR22 . . . . 16 F7
Sun La
  Great Yarmouth NR31 . . 94 C6
  Norwich NR3 . . . . 158 D1
Sunley Cl NR35 . . . . . . 109 C2
Sunningdale NR4 . . . . . 162 A2
Sunninghill Cl 14 NR8 . . 94 C8
Sunny Cl NR5. . . . . 157 B1
Sunny Cnr NR28 . . . . . 151 B4
Sunny Gr NR5. . . . . . . 161 B8
Sunny Hill NR1 . . . . . . 162 E2
Sunnyside
  Bedingham NR35. . . . . 108 C4
  Diss IP22. . . . . 177 D5
  Heacham PE31. . . . . . 133 C5
Sunnyside Ave 10 NR14 . 90 C5
Sunnyside Cl PE31 . . . 133 D5
Sunnyside Rd PE32. . . . 29 D2
Sun Rd NR35. . . . . 109 B2
Sunsalve Ride NR19 . . . 154 C1
Sunset Gdns PE13. . . . 152 E2
Sunset Wlk NR12 . . . . . 24 E4
Supple Cl NR1 . . . . 163 C7
SURLINGHAM NR14 . . . . 73 B1
Surlingham Dr PE37. . . 153 B1
Surlingham La
  Bramerton NR14 . . . . . 90 F8
  Rockland St Mary NR14. . 91 B8
Surlingham Prim Sch
  NR14. . . . . 73 B1
Surrey Cl NR7 . . . . 159 C5
Surrey Gr NR1 . . . . 178 B1
Surrey St
  Cromer NR27. . . . . . . 139 C7
  6 King's Lynn PE30 . . 146 D5
  Norwich NR1 . . . . 178 B2
  6 Wiggenhall St Germans
  PE34. . . . . 43 B1
Surrogate St NR17 . . . 174 D5
Sursham Ave NR6. . . . 158 F4
Sussex Rd NR3. . . . . . . 170 D5
Sussex St NR3 . . . . 178 A4
SUSTEAD NR11 . . . . 21 A7
Sustead La NR11. . . . . . 20 D8
Sustead Rd NR11 . . . . . . 9 F1
Suters Dr NR8. . . . . . . 155 E2
Sutherland Ave NR6. . . 158 A4
Sutherland Ct Gdns
  NR27. . . . . 139 C6
SUTON NR18 . . . . 87 D2
Suton La NR18. . . . . . . 173 A1
SUTTON NR12. . . . . 38 F2
SUTTON BRIDGE PE12 . . . 41 B7
Sutton Cres NR18 . . . . . 92 F8
Sutton Fst Sch NR12 . . . 39 C2
Sutton Lea PE31 . . . . . 135 C2
Sutton Mdws PE13 . . . 152 A8

Sutton Rd
  Catfield NR29. . . . . 39 C1
  Great Yarmouth NR30 . . 169 D1
  Hickling NR12 . . . . 39 D1
  Swaffham PE37 . . . . . 153 B1
  Terrington St Clement
  PE34. . . . . 144 A4
  Walpole Cross Keys PE34 . 42 A7
  Wisbech PE13 . . . . . . 152 A7
Suttons Cl 1 PE14. . . . . 77 F6
Sutton Windmill & Broads
  Mus★ NR12 . . . . 39 D2
SWAFFHAM PE37 . . . . . . 23 E3
Swaffham Com Hospl
  PE37. . . . . 153 C5
Swaffham Gap IP26. . . . 82 C1
Swaffham Greenhoe Mid Sch
  PE37. . . . . 153 B2
Swaffham Leisure Ctr
  PE37. . . . . 153 C4
Swaffham Mus★ PE37. . 153 B4
Swaffham Raceway PE37 . 64 C4
Swaffham Rd
  Ashill IP25. . . . . 84 A7
  Barton Bendish PE33. . . 63 C2
  Cockley Cley PE37. . . . . 82 D7
  East Dereham NR19 . . . 154 D6
  Mundford IP26 . . . . . . 100 B4
  Narborough PE32 . . . . . 63 F7
  Oxborough PE33 . . . . . 81 E4
  Raynham NR21 . . . . . . 30 F2
  Swaffham PE37 . . . . . . 64 A4
  Watton IP25 . . . . 84 C4
Swaffham VC Fst Sch
  PE37. . . . . 153 C4
SWAFIELD NR28. . . . . . . 22 E3
Swafield Rise NR28 . . . 151 D7
Swafield St NR5 . . . . . 160 F7
SWAINSTHORPE NR14 . . 89 D3
Swale The NR5 . . . . . . 160 F6
Swallow Cl 3 NR13. . . . 170 A7
Swallow Dr IP27 . . . . . 175 E3
Swallowfield Rd PE30 . 147 C4
Swallowtail Cl NR5. . . . 160 F5
Swamp La
  Great Ellingham NR17 . . 103 F7
  Roydon IP22 . . . . 177 A6
Swan Cl
  Aylsham NR11 . . . . . . 150 C6
  Swannington NR9 . . . . . 52 B5
Swan Cotts PE32. . . . . . 47 D5
Swan Dr NR20 . . . . 49 C3
Swan Entry 2 NR29 . . . 22 E7
Swangey La NR17 . . . . 103 D4
Swan La
  Coney Weston IP31. . . . 127 B4
  Fincham PE33 . . . . 62 E1
  King's Lynn PE30 . . . . 147 A6
  1 Norwich NR2 . . . . . 178 B3
  Redenhall with Harleston
  IP20. . . . . 122 D2
Swann's Rd NR30 . . . . 170 D8
Swan Terr 1 PE38. . . . . 172 A6
SWANTON ABBOTT NR10. . 37 A5
Swanton Abbott Com Sch
  NR10. . . . . 37 B5
Swanton Ave NR19 . . . 154 E7
Swanton Cl NR19 . . . . 154 E7
Swanton Dr NR20 . . . . 154 E6
Swanton Gr NR19 . . . . 154 E6
SWANTON HILL NR10. . . . 37 C5
SWANTON MORLEY NR20. . 50 B3
Swanton Morley Prim Sch
  NR20. . . . . 50 B4
Swanton Rd
  Hoe NR20. . . . . 50 A6
  North Elmham NR20 . . . 49 F6
  Swanton Morley NR20 . . 50 C3
Swanton St
  Dereham NR20. . . . . . . 50 A1
  East Dereham NR19 . . . 154 E6
  Gunthorpe NR24 . . . . . 18 B5
  Norwich NR3. . . . . . . 162 B8
SWARDESTON NR14. . . . 89 C5
Swardeston La NR14 . . . 89 B6
Swargate La NR15 . . . . 108 E8
Swash La NR13 . . . . 54 D2
Sweden Pl IP27 . . . . . . 175 B2
Sweetacres 1 NR29 . . . 167 B6
Sweetbriar Gdns NR20 . . 49 C4
Sweetbriar La
  Edgefield NR24. . . . . . . 19 D5
  Sheringham NR26 . . . . 138 C7
Sweet Briar Rd
  7 Long Stratton NR15 . . 106 E3
  Norwich NR6 . . . . 161 F8
Sweet Briar Rd Ind Est
  NR3. . . . . 157 F1
Sweyn Cl IP24. . . . . . . 176 B2
Swim Rd NR29 . . . . 75 F6
Swinbourne Cl NR6. . . . 158 F3
Swindells Cl NR5 . . . . . 157 A2
Swingy La NR18. . . . . . . 87 A3
Swirle's Pl 6 NR30 . . . 169 D4

Swiss Terr PE30 . . . . . 146 F5
Sybil Rd PE13 . . . . 152 C6
Sybil Wheeler Cl 5
  IP24. . . . . 176 D6
Sycamore Ave
  16 Great Yarmouth NR31 . 94 C7
  22 Marham NR29. . . . . . 57 D4
  Wymondham NR18 . . . . 173 E6
Sycamore Cl
  Attleborough NR17 . . . 174 C4
  King's Lynn PE30 . . . . 148 D2
  8 Loddon NR14 . . . . . . 91 F1
  North Walsham NR28 . . 151 C6
  Thompson IP24 . . . . . 102 A7
Sycamore Covert IP24. . 116 D2
Sycamore Cres NR21 . . 161 F7
Sycamore Gn 2 NR31 . . 170 B6
Sycamore Gr NR26 . . . 138 D5
Sycamores The NR19 . . 154 E3
Sycamore Way IP27. . . 177 F5
Sydenham Cl NR13. . . . 166 B4
SYDERSTONE PE31 . . . . . 15 B3
**Syderstone Comm Nature
  Reserve**★ PE31. . . . . . 15 A3
Syderstone Rd NR21 . . . 15 B3
Sydney Dye Ct PE32. . . 65 C5
Sydney Rd NR10. . . . . . 54 A2
Sydney Terr 2 PE30 . . . 146 D1
Syers La PE32. . . . . 48 D2
SYLEHAM IP21. . . . . . . 131 F5
Syleham Hall La IP21 . . 131 F5
Syleham Rd IP21 . . . . . 131 B4
Sylvan Cl NR6. . . . . . . 157 E6
Sylvan Way
  2 Blofield Heath NR13. . 73 C6
  Thetford NR8 . . . . 156 E8
Sylvden Dr PE13 . . . . . 152 F6
Symonds Ave NR29. . . 167 C2
Syon Cl PE38 . . . . 172 B4
Sywell Cl NR6. . . . . . . 158 F6
Sywell Gr 5 PE14. . . . . 59 A1

T

Tabernacle La NR16. . . 105 F4
TACOLNESTON NR16. . . . 105 F5
Tacolneston VC Prim Sch
  NR16. . . . . 105 F6
Tagg Way 3 NR13 . . . . . 72 E7
Talbot Cl NR18. . . . . . . 173 C5
Talbots Mdw IP21 . . . . 130 B5
Talbot Sq NR3 . . . . 178 A4
**Tales of the Old Gaol
  House**★ PE30. . . . . . . 146 D4
Taleworth Cl 11 NR5 . . 161 A7
Tallon St IP26 . . . . 82 A2
Tamarind Mews NR4 . . 161 E1
Tamarisk PE30. . . . . . . 148 B1
Tamworth La NR31. . . . 169 B2
Tanager Cl NR3 . . . . . . 158 D3
Tanaway Cl NR14 . . . . . 90 E6
Tanners Gn NR9 . . . . . . 68 C3
Tanner St 4 IP24. . . . . 176 C4
Tanning La 7 NR16 . . . 104 F1
Tanns La IP22 . . . . 119 A2
Tansy Cl NR6. . . . . 158 D4
Tantallon Dr NR17 . . . . 174 F6
Target Hill IP20. . . . . . 123 B2
Tarragon Cl 3 NR14 . . . 94 C6
Tarragon Rd PE38. . . . 172 D7
Tar Works Rd NR30. . . 169 C6
TASBURGH NR15 . . . . . . 106 F7
Tasburgh Rd NR15 . . . . 106 F8
Tasman Dr NR11. . . . . . 22 F8
Tas Valley Vineyard★
  NR16. . . . . 106 A3
TATTERFORD NR21. . . . . 30 E7
Tatterford Dr PE31. . . . 15 C1
TATTERSETT PE31 . . . . . 15 C2
Tattersett Pk Bsns Ctr
  NR21. . . . . 15 C1
Tattersett Rd PE31. . . . 15 B2
Tattle Hall IP21 . . . . . . 121 E5
TAVERHAM NR8 . . . . . . 155 C1
Taverham Chase NR8. . 156 D8
Taverham Hall Sch NR8 . 156 A8
Taverham High Sch NR8. 155 B2
Taverham Mid Sch NR8 . 156 C8
Taverham Rd
  Felthorpe NR10. . . . . . 155 C7
  Honingham NR9. . . . . . 69 F6
  Taverham NR8. . . . . . 156 D8
  Taverham NR10 . . . . . . 49 D4
Taverna La
  Diss IP22. . . . . 177 F3
  East Dereham NR19 . . . 154 E3
Tavistock Rd PE13 . . . . 152 D5
Tawny Sedge 3 PE30 . . 147 A8
Taylor Ave NR4 . . . . . . 89 B8
Taylor Rd
  Diss IP22. . . . . 177 B4
  Norwich NR5 . . . . 161 C6
Taylor's La
  Gressenhall NR20. . . . . 49 C3
  Norwich NR6. . . . . . . 158 D6
  Trimingham NR11. . . . . 11 E1
Taylors Loke
  5 Cley next the Sea NR25 . . 7 E6
  Hemsby NR29. . . . . . . 167 A8
Taymor Pl PE14. . . . . . . 95 D4
Teal Cl 3 PE31. . . . . . . 12 E5
Teal Wlk
  Brandon IP27 . . . . . . 175 D4
  16 Great Yarmouth NR31 . 94 C8
Teasel Cl NR20. . . . . . . 68 A8
Teasel Dr IP24. . . . . . . 176 E5

Teasel Rd NR17. . . . . . 174 B4
Teasel Rise 4 NR26. . . . 138 B6
Tebbutt Ave 6 NR19 . . . 154 C3
Tedder Cl
  5 Barnham IP24 . . . . . 125 F8
  13 Watton IP25. . . . . . 84 E3
Ted Ellis Nature Reserve★
  NR14. . . . . 91 D8
Tee Cl 1 NR14. . . . . 89 B2
Telegraph La E NR1. . . 163 B6
Telegraph La W 4 NR1 . 163 A6
Telford Cl
  King's Lynn PE30 . . . . 147 D4
  2 Norwich NR3 . . . . . 157 F1
Telford Way IP24 . . . . 176 B6
Temple Cl NR25. . . . . . . 8 F6
Temple Dr NR25. . . . . . . 8 F6
Templemere NR3 . . . . 159 A2
Temple Rd
  Great Yarmouth NR30 . . 169 D7
  King's Lynn PE30 . . . . 148 D1
  Norwich NR3 . . . . 158 D1
Templewood La PE31 . . 137 F8
Ten Bell La NR21. . . . . 178 A3
TEN MILE BANK PE38. . . 96 E7
Ten Mile Bank
  Hilgay PE38 . . . . 96 F6
  Littleport PE38. . . . . . 96 E1
Ten Mile Bank Prim Sch
  PE38. . . . . 96 F7
Tennyson Ave PE30 . . . 146 F4
Tennyson Rd
  3 Diss IP22 . . . . 177 E4
  3 Great Yarmouth NR30 . 169 D8
  King's Lynn PE30. . . . . 146 F4
Tennyson Way IP24 . . . 176 E6
Tensing St NR35 . . . . . 108 C5
Terence Airey Ct 28
  IP20. . . . . 122 D2
Terence Ave NR7 . . . . . 159 A4
Tern Cl 8 IP25 . . . . 84 C3
Tern Gdns NR31 . . . . . 170 A6
Tern Rd NR25 . . . . 167 E5
Terrace Wlk NR1. . . . . 178 B1
Terrington Cl 3 PE14. . . 59 D2
TERRINGTON ST CLEMENT
  PE34. . . . . 144 B4
Terrington St Clements Sch
  PE34. . . . . 144 C6
TERRINGTON ST JOHN
  PE34. . . . . 42 C2
Terrington St John Prim Sch
  PE14. . . . . 60 B8
Terr The 12 NR19 . . . . 154 C5
Testerton Cotts NR21 . . 32 A6
Texas Ave NR15 . . . . . . 15 C2
Texel Way NR11. . . . . . 143 A7
Thacker Way NR5. . . . . 160 F6
Thain's La NR27. . . . . . . 10 B5
Thamesfield Way NR31. . 169 B2
Thames Way 8 NR30 . . 168 C6
THARSTON NR15 . . . . . . 106 E5
Thatchwood Ave PE14. . 59 C2
THE ARMS IP25 . . . . 83 F1
Theatre Plain NR30 . . . 169 C4
Theatre Rd NR23. . . . . 136 C6
Theatre St
  East Dereham NR19 . . . 154 D6
  Norwich NR2 . . . . 178 A2
  Swaffham PE37 . . . . . 153 B4
THE BROOK IP22 . . . . . 129 C3
THE GRANGE NR10. . . . . 35 C1
THE GREEN NR18 . . . . . . 87 B4
THE HEATH
  Fakenham NR21. . . . . . 141 F4
  Hevingham NR10. . . . . 53 A8
  Stratton Strawless NR10. . 53 F8
THE LIMES IP25 . . . . . . 59 C5
THE LING NR15 . . . . . . 91 A1
THELNETHAM IP22 . . . . 128 B5
Thelnetham Rd
  Blo' Norton IP22 . . . . . 128 B6
  Hopton IP22 . . . . 127 F5
THELVETON IP21. . . . . . 130 D8
THE MARSH
  Thrandeston IP22 . . . . 129 F3
  Wortham IP22 . . . . . . 129 C4
THEMELTHORPE NR20. . . 33 F2
Themelthorpe Rd NR20. . 33 E1
Theobald Rd NR1 . . . . . 89 E8
THE SMEETH PE14 . . . . . 60 A5
THETFORD IP24 . . . . . . 176 B4
**Thetford Ancient House
  Mus**★ IP24 . . . . 176 C4
Thetford Cottage Hospl
  IP24. . . . . 176 C4
Thetford Gram Sch IP24 . 176 C4
Thetford L Ctr & Waterworld
  IP24. . . . . 176 D5
Thetford Priory★ IP24 . . 176 C4
Thetford Rd
  Brandon IP27 . . . . . . 175 E3
  Coney Weston IP31. . . . 127 B4
  Euston IP24 . . . . 126 B6
  Garboldisham IP22 . . . 127 F8
  Northwold IP26 . . . . . . 99 B8
  Santon Downham IP27 . 115 B5
  Watton IP25 . . . . 84 D3
  Wretham IP24 . . . . . . 117 A7
Thetford Sta IP24. . . . . 176 C5
Thetford Warren Lodge★
  IP24. . . . . 115 A3
Thetford Way PE30. . . . 148 C3
Thicket The 6 NR18 . . . 155 E2

Thiefgate La PE34 . . . . 43 D2
Thieves' Bridge Rd PE33 . 61 E5
Thieves La NR13 . . . . 55 A1
Thieves' La
  Attleborough NR17 . . . . 174 E5
  Burgh & Tuttington NR11 . . 36 E6
  Little Ellingham NR17 . . . 103 C8
Third Ave PE13 . . . . 172 E4
Third Marsh Rd PE14 . . . . 59 A7
Thirlby Rd NR28 . . . . 151 D3
Thirlmere 🔟 NR9 . . . . 88 D8
Thistle Cl
  Norwich NR5 . . . . 160 F5
  🔟 Thetford IP24 . . . . . 176 F5
Thistledown Rd NR10 . . . . 53 B2
Thomas Bole Cl IP22 . . . . 128 A8
Thomas Bullock Prim Sch
  IP25 . . . . 67 C2
Thomas Cl 🔟 PE31 . . . . . 61 D5
Thomas Dix Cl NR28 . . . . 151 D5
Thomas Drew Cl PE31 . . . 140 C3
Thomas Glover Ct NR6 . . . 158 C22
Thomas Manning Rd
  IP22 . . . . 177 E4
Thomas Paine Ave 🔟
  IP24 . . . . 176 C4
Thomas St PE30 . . . . 146 E3
Thomas Vere Rd NR7 . . . . 163 F7
Thomas Way NR30 . . . . . 168 C6
Thomas Wyatt Cl NR2 . . . 178 A1
THOMPSON IP24 . . . . 17 E4
Thompson Ave 🔟 NR25 . . 137 C5
Thompson Cl NR20 . . . . . . 50 B4
Thompson Prim Sch
  IP24 . . . . 102 B7
Thompson Rd
  Griston IP25 . . . . 85 A1
  Norwich NR7 . . . . 163 F8
Thompson's La PE33 . . . . . 81 A2
Thompsons Yd NR3 . . . . 178 B4
Thor Cl NR7 . . . . 163 E7
Thoresby Ave PE30 . . . . . 147 B4
Thoresby Coll PE30 . . . . . 146 D4
Thor Loke NR7 . . . . 163 E7
THORNAGE NR25 . . . . 18 F7
Thornage Rd NR25 . . . . . 137 A5
THORNHAM PE36 . . . . 2 D6
Thornham Cl NR7 . . . . . . 159 B2
Thornham Cnr PE36 . . . . . 2 E2
Thornham Rd
  Methwold IP26 . . . . 99 A6
  Norwich NR7 . . . . 159 B2
Thorn La NR1 . . . . 178 B2
Thorn Rd
  Catfield NR29 . . . . 56 C8
  Fakenham NR21 . . . . . . 141 D4
Thornton Cl NR24 . . . . . . 142 E4
Thornycroft Gdns 🔟
  NR33 . . . . 111 F1
Thoroughfare La NR29 . . . 167 B4
Thoroughfare The IP20 . . . 122 D2
Thorp Ct NR19 . . . . 154 D4
THORPE NR14 . . . . 93 B1
Thorpe Abbots Rd IP21 . . . 131 A8
THORPE ABBOTTS IP21 . . . 131 B6
Thorpe Ave NR7 . . . . 163 E8
Thorpe Cl NR7 . . . . 163 F7
Thorpe Dr NR17 . . . . 174 D4
THORPE END NR13 . . . . . . 72 D6
Thorpe Hall Cl NR7 . . . . . 163 F7
THORPE HAMLET NR1 . . . 163 B6
Thorpe Hamlet Fst Sch
  NR1 . . . . 163 B6
Thorpe Hamlet Mid Sch
  NR1 . . . . 163 B6
Thorpe House Sch NR7 . . . 163 C6
Thorpeland Cl 🔟 PE33 . . . 61 D3
Thorpeland La 🔟 PE33 . . . 61 D3
THORPE MARKET NR11 . . . 22 A6
THORPE MARRIOTT NR8 . . 155 F2
Thorpe Mews NR7 . . . . . 163 A4
Thorpe Mkt Rd NR11 . . . . 21 E7
Thorpe Rd
  Haddiscoe NR14 . . . . . 110 F8
  Norwich NR1 . . . . 178 C2
  Southrepps NR11 . . . . . 22 A7
THORPE ROW IP25 . . . . . . 67 C4
THORPE ST ANDREW
  NR7 . . . . 163 F8
Thorpe St Andrew Sch
  NR7 . . . . 72 D4
THORPLAND PE33 . . . . . . 61 D3
Thorpland Rd NR21 . . . . . 141 E6
Thor Rd NR7 . . . . 163 E7
THRANDESTON IP21 . . . . . 129 F3
Threadneedle St NR15 . . . . 91 A4
Three Acre Cl NR12 . . . . . 164 C6
Three Cnr Dr NR6 . . . . . . 158 F6
THREE COCKED HAT
  NR34 . . . . 110 D7
THREEHAMMER COMMON
  NR12 . . . . 55 E6
THREE HOLES PE14 . . . . . 77 E3
Three King La NR2 . . . . . 178 A3
Three Mile La NR5 . . . . . 156 F1
Three Oaks Rd 🔟 IP25 . . . 147 C5
Three Post Rd 🔟 IP25 . . . 84 C3
Three Score Rd
  Colney NR5 . . . . 161 A5
  Norwich NR5 . . . . 160 F5
Threxton Rd IP25 . . . . 84 C3
THRIGBY NR29 . . . . 75 D7
Thrigby Hall Wildlife Gdns★
  NR29 . . . . 75 E3
Thrigby Rd NR29 . . . . 75 E6

Throckmorton Yd 🔟
  NR3 . . . . 162 E8
Thrush Cl 🔟 NR14 . . . . . 89 B3
Thumb La NR20 . . . . 31 F2
Thunder La NR7 . . . . 163 E7
THURGARTON NR11 . . . . . 20 F5
Thurgarton Rd NR11 . . . . . 21 A5
Thurland's Dro PE14 . . . . . 77 D5
Thurlby Rd NR5 . . . . 160 E8
Thurling Loke NR7 . . . . . 159 E1
Thurling Plain NR7 . . . . . 159 E1
Thurlin Rd PE30 . . . . 147 B4
Thirlby Rd NR28 . . . . 151 C2
Thurlow Cl NR5 . . . . 160 E8
THURLTON NR14 . . . . 92 F1
Thurlton Prim Sch NR14 . . 92 F1
Thurlton Rd NR14 . . . . . . 110 B7
THURNE NR29 . . . . 56 E3
Thurne Rd NR29 . . . . 57 A2
Thurne Rise 🔟 NR29 . . . . 57 D5
Thurne Way NR29 . . . . . . 167 B3
THURNING NR11 . . . . 34 C7
Thurning Rd NR20 . . . . . . 33 E8
THURSFORD NR21 . . . . . . 17 E4
Thursford Collection★
  NR21 . . . . 17 D5
THURSFORD GREEN
  NR21 . . . . 17 D5
Thursford Rd
  Great Snoring NR21 . . . . 17 A5
  Hindringham NR21 . . . . 17 E6
  🔟 Little Snoring NR21 . . 17 B3
Thursford Wood Nature
  Reserve★ NR21 . . . . . . 17 D4
Thurston Cl 🔟 NR5 . . . . . 160 F8
Thurst Rd NR27 . . . . 11 A3
THURTON NR14 . . . . 91 D4
Thurton Prim Sch NR14 . . . 91 D4
THUXTON NR9 . . . . 68 D2
Thuxton Sta NR9 . . . . 68 C2
Thwaite Rd NR35 . . . . . . 109 A2
THWAITE ST MARY
  NR35 . . . . 109 A5
Thyme Cl
  Attleborough NR17 . . . . 174 B4
  🔟 Thetford IP24 . . . . . 176 F5
Thyne's La NR20 . . . . 68 E5
TIBENHAM NR16 . . . . 120 E8
Tibenham Rd NR15 . . . . . 121 A8
Tiercel Ave NR7 . . . . 159 C4
Tillett Cl NR29 . . . . 167 C2
Tillett Rd NR3 . . . . 158 E2
Tills Cl NR6 . . . . 158 F4
Tills Rd NR6 . . . . 159 A5
TILNEY ALL SAINTS
  PE34 . . . . 144 F1
Tilney All Saints Prim Sch
  PE34 . . . . 42 E4
TILNEY CUM ISLINGTON
  PE34 . . . . 60 F8
TILNEY FEN END PE34 . . . 60 C6
TILNEY HIGH END PE34 . . . 42 D4
Tilney Rd NR10 . . . . 69 C6
TILNEY ST LAWRENCE
  PE34 . . . . 60 D8
Tilney St Lawrence CP Sch
  PE34 . . . . 60 C8
Timberhill NR1 . . . . 178 B2
Timber Rd NR16 . . . . 118 C5
Time & Tide Mus of Great
  Yarmouth★ NR30 . . . . 169 D2
Timothy Cl NR1 . . . . 163 B8
Timperley La NR7 . . . . . . 31 D5
Tindall Cl PE13 . . . . 152 C8
Tinker's Dro PE13 . . . . . 152 D7
Tinkers' La
  Garvestone NR9 . . . . . . 68 C1
  Strumpshaw NR13 . . . . . 73 D1
Tinker's La NR15 . . . . . . 121 C4
Tintern Gr 🔟 PE30 . . . . . 148 C4
Tippett Cl NR5 . . . . 160 F6
TIPPS END PE14 . . . . 95 C6
Tipton Cl NR19 . . . . 154 D2
TITCHWELL PE31 . . . . 2 F7
Titchwell Marsh Nature
  Reserve★ NR31 . . . . . . 2 F7
Tithe Barn Cl IP26 . . . . . 100 C5
Tithebarn La
  Marham PE33 . . . . 63 D6
  🔟 Thurlton NR14 . . . . . 92 F1
Tithe Barn La NR24 . . . . . 142 F3
Tithing Cl 🔟 IP24 . . . . . 176 E5
Titlow Rd 🔟 IP20 . . . . . 122 D2
TITTLESHALL PE32 . . . . . 48 B8
Tittleshall Rd
  Litcham PE32 . . . . 48 A5
  Mileham NR20 . . . . 48 E8
  Stanfield NR20 . . . . 48 C6
Tivetshall Cty Prim Sch
  NR15 . . . . 121 B5
Tivetshall Rd IP21 . . . . . 121 D5
TIVETSHALL ST MARGARET
  NR15 . . . . 121 B5
TIVETSHALL ST MARY
  NR15 . . . . 121 B8
Toad Hole Cottage Mus★
  NR29 . . . . 56 A6
Toad La
  Ditchingham NR35 . . . . 108 F5
  Great & Little Plumstead
  NR13 . . . . 72 F5
  Thwaite NR35 . . . . 109 A5
Todhunter Ave NR34 . . . . 110 C2
Todkill's La PE12 . . . . 41 C8
Toftes Pl 🔟 NR5 . . . . . . 161 B8
TOFT MONKS NR34 . . . . . 110 D5
TOFTREES NR21 . . . . 31 B6
TOFTWOOD NR19 . . . . . . 154 E2

Toftwood Inf Sch NR19 . . 154 E1
Toftwood Jun Sch NR19 . . 154 E2
Tolhouse Mus★ NR30 . . . 169 C3
Tolhouse St NR30 . . . . . . 169 C3
Toll Bar NR21 . . . . 141 A6
Tollgate Rd NR14 . . . . . . 169 C1
Tollgate Way NR5 . . . . . . 161 A5
Tollhouse Rd NR5 . . . . . . 161 E7
Tolwin Wlk 🔟 NR6 . . . . . 158 F1
Tolye Rd NR5 . . . . 160 F7
Tombland NR1 . . . . 178 B3
Tooks Comm La NR34 . . . 124 F5
Topcliffe Ave 🔟 NR13 . . . 55 A1
TOPCROFT NR35 . . . . 107 F3
TOPCROFT STREET
  NR35 . . . . 107 F2
Top Driftway IP24 . . . . . . 117 C8
Top Rd
  Belaugh NR12 . . . . 164 A6
  St Andrew, Ilketshall
  NR34 . . . . 124 E5
  Wicklewood NR18 . . . . . 87 B4
  Wingfield IP21 . . . . 131 E3
TOPROW NR16 . . . . 88 E1
Topshill Rd NR11 . . . . 21 E6
Torrey Cl PE31 . . . . 133 E5
Tortoishell Way NR18 . . . 173 E4
Tottenham St 🔟 NR30 . . . 169 D5
TOTTENHILL PE33 . . . . . . 62 A5
TOTTENHILL ROW PE33 . . . 62 A5
Tottenhill Row PE33 . . . . . 61 F6
TOTTINGTON IP24 . . . . . 101 E6
Tottington Cl 🔟 NR5 . . . . 160 F8
Tottington La IP22 . . . . . 177 B4
Tottington Rd
  Little Cressingham IP25 . . 101 C8
  Thompson IP24 . . . . . . 102 A7
  Tottington IP24 . . . . . . 101 F7
Tower Cl
  Brandon IP27 . . . . 175 B3
  Costessey NR8 . . . . . . 156 C4
TOWER END PE32 . . . . . . 44 C4
Tower Hill
  Costessey NR8 . . . . . . 156 C4
  Norwich NR7 . . . . 163 D6
Tower Hill Pk NR8 . . . . . 156 C4
Tower La
  Middleton PE32 . . . . . . 44 D4
  Sidestrand NR27 . . . . . . 11 B3
Tower Mdws PE37 . . . . . 153 C5
Tower Mill Rd NR35 . . . . 124 A8
Tower Pl 🔟 PE30 . . . . . . 146 D4
Tower Rd
  Burgh St Margaret
  (Fleggburgh) NR29 . . . . 57 C1
  Burnham Overy PE31 . . . 135 E7
  Canadas NR11 . . . . 77 A4
  Elm PE14 . . . . 77 A7
  Hilgay PE38 . . . . 97 A8
  Repps with Bastwick NR29 . 57 A5
  Terrington St Clement
  PE34 . . . . 144 C7
Tower St PE30 . . . . 146 D4
Town Bridge 🔟 PE13 . . . 152 B5
Town Cl
  Corpusty NR11 . . . . 19 E1
  East Winch PE32 . . . . . 44 F3
  Holt NR25 . . . . 137 B6
Town Cl House Prep Sch
  NR2 . . . . 162 C3
Town Cl Rd NR2 . . . . . . 162 C3
Town Cnr NR10 . . . . 53 C8
Town End NR11 . . . . 143 C6
Town Est PE38 . . . . 172 B5
Town Gn NR18 . . . . 173 B4
Town Gn Rd IP25 . . . . 84 E3
TOWN GREEN
  Alby with Thwaite NR11 . . 21 C4
  South Walsham NR13 . . . 74 A7
Town House La IP22 . . . . 128 B2
Town House Mus★ NR30 . 146 D4
Town House Rd NR8 . . . . 156 F4
Town La
  Aylsham NR11 . . . . . . 150 C7
  Brancaster Staithe PE31 . . . 3 D7
  Castle Acre PE32 . . . . . . 46 F2
  Garvestone NR9 . . . . . . 68 C2
Townlands NR31 . . . . . . 170 B7
Town Lands Trading Est
  NR31 . . . . 170 B7
Townley Cl PE14 . . . . 77 E5
Townley Prim Sch PE14 . . . 95 A7
Town Rd
  Burgh St Margaret
  (Fleggburgh) NR29 . . . . 57 C1
  Ingham NR12 . . . . 39 C4
Townsend Gn N NR21 . . . 141 F5
Townsend Rd
  Norwich NR4 . . . . 162 C1
  Upwell PE14 . . . . 77 F6
Townshend Cl 🔟 NR30 . . 169 D3
Townshend Gn E NR21 . . . 141 F5
Townshend Gn W NR21 . . 141 F5
Townshend Pl 🔟 IP25 . . . . 6 F2
Townshend Rd
  Dereham NR19 . . . . . . 154 D7
  Wisbech PE13 . . . . 152 D6
Townshend Terr 🔟
  PE30 . . . . 146 E6
Town St
  Outwell PE14 . . . . 77 D5
  Swanton Morley PE20 . . . 50 B4
Town Wall Mews 🔟
  NR30 . . . . 169 C5
Town Wall Rd NR30 . . . . 169 C5
Town Yd 🔟 NR25 . . . . 7 E6
Tracey Rd NR7 . . . . 159 E1

Trafalgar Ct
  Cliftonville NR11 . . . . . 143 B7
  Great Yarmouth NR30 . . 169 E3
Trafalgar Ind Est PE38 . . 172 A4
Trafalgar Rd
  Downham Market PE38 . . 172 B4
  🔟 Great Yarmouth NR30 . 169 D3
Trafalgar Rd E NR31 . . . . 170 D6
Trafalgar Rd W NR31 . . . . 170 D6
Trafalgar Sq NR30 . . . . . 169 E3
Trafalgar St NR1 . . . . . . 178 B1
Trafford Est PE14 . . . . . . 59 C8
Trafford Pk 🔟 PE13 . . . . 152 E6
Trafford Rd
  Norwich NR1 . . . . 178 A1
  Wisbech PE13 . . . . 152 D5
Trafford Wlk NR12 . . . . . 164 B2
Traice Rd NR16 . . . . 105 D7
Transport La NR14 . . . . . 109 D7
Trap La NR21 . . . . 174 D3
Trelawny Rd 🔟 NR29 . . . 57 D4
Tremaine Cl NR6 . . . . . . 158 C7
Trenchard Cres 🔟 IP25 . . 84 F3
Trenchard Sq IP26 . . . . . . 98 D1
Trendall Rd NR7 . . . . . . 159 C4
Trenowaths Pl 🔟 PE30 . . 146 D5
Trent V C Cl IP26 . . . . 99 A5
Tretts Loke NR29 . . . . . . 57 C1
Trident Dr NR1 . . . . 163 A7
TRIMINGHAM NR11 . . . . 11 D2
Trimingham Rd
  Gimingham NR11 . . . . . 22 E8
  Trimingham NR11 . . . . . 11 E1
Trimming Wlk NR8 . . . . . 156 E8
Trinity Ave NR3 . . . . . . 170 B4
Trinity Cl NR19 . . . . 154 D6
Trinity Hospl (Bede House)★
  PE31 . . . . 27 C3
Trinity Pl 🔟 NR30 . . . . . 169 D2
Trinity Rd
  Walpole Highway PE14 . . 59 F8
  Wisbech PE13 . . . . 152 E6
Trinity Sq 🔟 NR30 . . . . . 169 D1
Trinity St NR2 . . . . 162 C5
Triple Plea La NR35 . . . . 108 A4
Triple Plea Rd NR35 . . . . 108 A4
Trix Rd NR2 . . . . 162 C5
Tropical Butterfly World★
  NR17 . . . . 103 F5
Trory St NR2 . . . . 162 C5
Troston Rd IP31 . . . . . . 126 C1
Troutbeck 🔟 NR9 . . . . . . 88 D8
TROWSE NEWTON NR14 . . 163 B3
True's Yd Fishing Heritage
  Mus★ PE30 . . . . 146 D6
Truman Cl
  🔟 Norwich NR4 . . . . . 161 C5
  Rackheath/Salhouse NR13 . 72 F8
Trumpery La NR14 . . . . . 90 C8
TRUNCH NR28 . . . . 22 E5
Trunch Hill IP20 . . . . . . 123 A7
Trunch Rd
  Denton IP20 . . . . 123 B6
  Mundesley NR11 . . . . . 143 B4
Tucker St NR27 . . . . 139 B7
Tucks Rd NR28 . . . . 38 A5
Tuckswood Ctr 🔟 NR4 . . 162 C1
Tuckswood Fst Sch NR4 . . 162 D1
Tuddenham Rd NR11 . . . . 150 B6
Tud La NR9 . . . . 69 E6
Tudor Cl NR29 . . . . 167 A4
Tudor Cl IP22 . . . . 177 A5
Tudor Cres PE36 . . . . . . 132 D2
Tudor Way
  Dersingham PE31 . . . . . 140 D4
  🔟 Mulbarton NR14 . . . . 89 B3
Tudor Wlk
  Great Yarmouth NR31 . . 170 C1
  🔟 Kenninghall IP31 . . . 126 B1
Tuesday Mkt Pl 🔟 PE30 . . 146 D5
Tuffen La IP22 . . . . 128 B4
Tulip Cl NR17 . . . . 174 C5
Tulip Tree Dr 🔟 NR14 . . . 90 C5
Tumbler Hill PE37 . . . . . 153 C6
Tumbleyhill Rd PE22 . . . . 46 C3
Tumbril La IP21 . . . . 131 D7
Tummel Way NR17 . . . . . 174 E6
Tunbeck Cl IP20 . . . . . . 123 A3
Tunbeck Rd IP20 . . . . . . 123 A4
TUNGATE NR28 . . . . 37 C8
Tungate Cres NR28 . . . . . 89 B8
Tungate Rd NR28 . . . . . . 151 A5
Tungate Way 🔟 NR12 . . . 57 D4
Tuneys La NR35 . . . . . . 109 B2
Tunn St 🔟 NR21 . . . . . . 141 B4
Tunns Yd NR23 . . . . 136 D6
Tuns Rd PE37 . . . . 65 F4
TUNSTALL NR13 . . . . 74 F3
Tunstall Cl 🔟 NR5 . . . . . 161 A7
Tunstall Rd NR13 . . . . . . 74 E2
TUNSTEAD NR12 . . . . 37 E1
Tunstead La NR12 . . . . . 164 D6
Tunstead Prim Sch NR12 . . 37 F1
Tunstead Rd
  Tunstead NR12 . . . . . . 37 E1
  🔟 Wroxham/Hoveton
  NR12 . . . . 164 C5
Turbine Way PE37 . . . . . 153 B6
Turbo Rd NR21 . . . . 15 D2
Turbus Rd PE30 . . . . . . 146 E7
Turf Fen La NR29 . . . . . . 56 B5
Turf Lot Dro PE14 . . . . . . 95 B5
Turin Way NR31 . . . . . . 171 E4
Turkey La NR24 . . . . 19 D6

Turner Cl
  Ditchingham NR35 . . . . 109 B2
  🔟 Great Yarmouth NR31 . 170 A7
  Wymondham NR18 . . . . 173 E5
Turner Rd NR2 . . . . 162 A7
Turner's Cl PE34 . . . . . . 79 E8
Turner Way PE38 . . . . . . 172 E5
Turnham Gn 🔟 NR7 . . . . 72 D4
Turning The NR26 . . . . . 138 C6
Turnpike Cl
  Foxley NR20 . . . . 50 D8
  🔟 Wisbech PE13 . . . . . 152 E6
Turnpike The
  Ashwellthorpe NR16 . . . 106 A7
  Carleton Rode NR16 . . . 105 D2
Turn The NR10 . . . . 53 A8
Tusser Rd NR8 . . . . 156 E8
Tusting Cl NR7 . . . . 158 F4
TUTTINGTON NR11 . . . . . 36 E6
Tuttington Rd NR11 . . . . 150 F8
Tuttles La E NR18 . . . . . 173 D6
Tuttles La W NR18 . . . . . 173 B6
Tuxhill Chase PE34 . . . . . 42 B2
Tuxhill Rd PE34 . . . . 42 B5
Twelveacre NR4 . . . . . . 161 F4
Twickenham Ave IP27 . . . 175 B1
Twickenham Rd NR6 . . . . 158 B5
Twiss Cl 🔟 IP22 . . . . . . 129 D7
Two Acres 🔟 PE32 . . . . . 44 B3
Two Fields Way 🔟 NR20 . . 50 F7
Two Furlong Hill NR23 . . 136 C5
Two Saints Cl NR12 . . . . 164 D7
Two Sisters Cl 🔟 PE12 . . 41 B8
Twrs The PE38 . . . . 172 C5
TWYFORD NR20 . . . . 33 B3
Twyford La NR20 . . . . . . 33 C3
Twyford Rd NR20 . . . . . . 33 A6
TYBY NR11 . . . . 34 B6
Tyndale PE30 . . . . 148 E5
Tyne Mews NR30 . . . . . . 168 C5
Tyrolean Sq NR31 . . . . . 169 A4
Tyrrell's Rd 🔟 NR31 . . . . 169 B4

U

UEA Sportspark NR4 . . . 161 D4
Ulfkell Rd IP24 . . . . 176 B2
Ullswater Ave
  Castle Rising PE30 . . . . . 27 C1
  King's Lynn PE30 . . . . . 148 F1
Ullswater Dr 🔟 NR9 . . . . 88 D8
Ulph Pl PE31 . . . . 135 D3
Uncle's La IP19 . . . . 124 E2
Unicorn Yd 🔟 NR11 . . . . 150 C6
Union Dr NR20 . . . . 68 A8
Union La
  🔟 King's Lynn PE30 . . . 146 D4
  Wortham IP22 . . . . . . 129 D5
Union Pl 🔟 PE13 . . . . . . 152 C5
Union Rd
  🔟 Great Yarmouth
  NR30 . . . . 169 D4
  Smallburgh NR12 . . . . . 38 C3
Union St
  Norwich NR2 . . . . 178 A2
  🔟 Wisbech PE13 . . . . . 152 C5
University Cres NR31 . . . 170 B4
University Dr NR4 . . . . . 161 C5
University of E Anglia
  Norwich NR4 . . . . 161 C3
  Norwich NR6 . . . . 157 D4
Unthank Rd NR4 . . . . . . 161 F2
UPGATE NR9 . . . . 52 C5
Upgate NR14 . . . . 90 D5
Upgate Rd NR15 . . . . . . 108 E7
Upgate St
  Carleton Rode NR16 . . . 105 A4
  Southery PE38 . . . . 97 B5
UPGATE STREET
  Bedingham NR15 . . . . . 108 B2
  Old Buckenham NR16 . . 105 A3
Uphalle NR8 . . . . 155 D1
Uplands Ave NR30 . . . . . 168 D5
Uplands Pk NR26 . . . . . . 138 C6
Uplands Way IP22 . . . . . 177 D5
UPPER BRANDON PARVA
  NR9 . . . . 68 E3
Upper Breckland Rd
  NR5 . . . . 156 F1
Upper Brook La IP20 . . . 131 E8
Upper Bunthouse La
  IP20 . . . . 131 E8
Upper Cliff Rd NR31 . . . . 170 D6
Upper Goat La NR2 . . . . 178 A3
Upper Grange Cres
  NR30 . . . . 168 D5
UPPER GUIST NR20 . . . . . 33 A5
Upper Hall La NR24 . . . . 18 D8
Upper Harmans La IP20 . . 122 B1
UPPER HELLESDON NR3 . . 158 C3
Upper Kiln La NR15 . . . . . 90 F4
Upper King St NR1 . . . . . 178 B3
Upper Mkt 🔟 NR21 . . . . 141 B4
Upper Oakley IP21 . . . . . 130 E4
Upper Olland St NR35 . . . 124 A8
Upper Rose La IP22 . . . . 177 E2
Upper St Giles St NR2 . . . 178 A3
UPPER SHERINGHAM
  NR26 . . . . 138 A5
Upper St
  Gissing IP22 . . . . 120 F4
  Salhouse NR13 . . . . . . 55 B2
Upper Stafford Ave NR5 . . 156 F1
Upper Staithe Rd 🔟 NR12 . 38 B4
UPPER STOKE NR14 . . . . 90 B5

UPPER STREET
Dickleburgh and Rushall
  IP21 . . . . 130 F6
Horning NR12 . . . . 55 F4
Hoveton NR12 . . . . 55 C5
Southrepps NR11 . . . . 22 B7
Tunstead NR12 . . . . 38 A3
Upper Tumbril La
Brockdish IP20 . . . . 131 D8
Needham IP20 . . . . 122 A1
Scole IP20 . . . . 130 E8
UPPER WEYBREAD IP21 . 131 E6
UPTON NR13 . . . . 166 A8
Upton Broad Nature
  Reserve★ NR13 . . . . 74 C8
Upton Cl NR4 . . . . 162 A3
Upton Dr PE37 . . . . 153 B2
UPTON GREEN NR13 . . . 166 B8
Upton Rd
Norwich NR4 . . . . 162 A3
South Walsham NR13 . . . . 74 B8
Uptons Way IP26 . . . . . . 82 A2
Upton Way NR12 . . . . . . 24 C5
UPWELL PE14 . . . . 77 F5
Upwell Prim Sch PE14 . . 77 D4
Upwell Rd PE14 . . . . 95 F7
Utopia Way NR12 . . . . . . 39 B3

V

Vale Cl 9 NR10 . . . . 53 B3
Vale Ct 5 IP27 . . . . 114 E1
Vale Gn NR6 . . . . 158 B1
Valentine Cl PE36 . . . . . 132 D5
Valentine Rd PE36 . . . . . 132 D4
Valentine St 3 NR2 . . . . 162 C6
Vale Rd
High Kelling NR25 . . . . 8 E2
Mundesley NR11 . . . . 143 A8
Thurton NR14 . . . . 91 C3
Valerian Rise IP24 . . . . 116 D2
Valinger's Pl 6 PE30 . . 146 E4
Valingers Rd PE30 . . . . 146 E3
Valley Dr The NR1 . . . . 163 B8
Valley Gdns 1 NR28 . . 151 E5
Valley La NR25 . . . . 137 B5
Valley Rd
Norwich NR5 . . . . 157 C1
  5 Sheringham NR26 . . . 105 F6
Valley Rise PE31 . . . . . 140 C4
Valleyside NR18 . . . . . . 173 C3
Valley Side Rd 3 NR1 . 163 C8
Valley View NR10 . . . . . 149 D6
Valley View Cres NR5 . 157 A1
Valpy Ave NR3 . . . . 158 A1
Vancouver Ave PE30 . . 146 E3
Vancouver Rd 4 NR7 . . 163 C8
Vane Cl NR7 . . . . 72 D4
Vanguard Cl
  2 Great Yarmouth NR31 . . 94 C8
Great Yarmouth NR31 . . . 170 A8
Varsity Rd IP25 . . . . 84 F3
Varvel Ave NR7 . . . . 159 C4
Vassar Ct 6 NR20 . . . . . 68 F6
Vaunces La IP21 . . . . . . 131 B8
Vaunce's La IP21 . . . . . 131 B8
Vauxhall St NR2 . . . . . . 162 C5
Vauxhall Terr NR30 . . . 169 C6
Vawdrey Rd NR8 . . . . . . 155 F1
Veltshaw Cl PE31 . . . . . 133 B4
Venables Cl NR1 . . . . . . 163 B7
Venta Icenorum (Roman
  Town)★ NR14 . . . . 89 E6
Ventura Cl IP26 . . . . 98 F5
Vera Cl 10 NR13 . . . . 72 E7
Vera Rd
New Rackheath NR13 . . . 72 F7
Norwich NR6 . . . . 158 B4
Verdon's La NR18 . . . . . 87 F2
Verdun Rd PE13 . . . . . . 152 D5
Veronica Gn 9 NR32 . . 170 B6
Vervain Cl 23 NR31 . . . . 94 C6
Vetch Cl NR18 . . . . 173 D4
Viburnum Way 6 NR31 . 170 B6

Vicarage Cl
Costessey NR8 . . . . 156 F5
Foulden IP26 . . . . 82 A1
  1 Potter Heigham NR29 . . 56 F6
Vicarage La
Bungay NR35 . . . . 124 C3
Hoveton NR12 . . . . 164 E5
Vicarage NR19 . . . . 154 C4
Vicarage Rd
Cromer NR27 . . . . 139 B6
Deopham NR18 . . . . 86 D3
East Ruston NR12 . . . . . . 24 A3
Foulden IP26 . . . . 82 A2
Hockham IP24 . . . . 102 D3
Norwich NR3 . . . . 158 C1
Paston NR28 . . . . 143 D2
Salhouse NR13 . . . . 55 A2
Sheringham NR26 . . . . . 138 C6
Thetford IP24 . . . . 176 D5
Wingfield IP21 . . . . 131 E3
Worstead NR28 . . . . 38 A5
Vicarage St NR28 . . . . . 151 C5
Vicarage Wlk 11 IP25 . . 84 E3
Vicar St NR18 . . . . 173 B4
Viceroy Cl PE31 . . . . . . 140 C4
Victor Charles Ct PE37 . 153 B7
Victoria Arc NR30 . . . . 169 C3
Victoria Ave
Brandon IP27 . . . . 175 C3
Hunstanton PE36 . . . . . . 132 D5
Victoria Cl
Diss IP22 . . . . 177 E3

Victoria Cl *continued*
Rushall IP21 . . . . 133 E6
Taverham NR8 . . . . 156 C8
Victoria Cotts PE31 . . . 133 D6
Victoria Ct
Sheringham NR26 . . . . . 138 E7
  22 Watton IP25 . . . . 84 D3
Victoria Gdns 7 NR30 . 169 D2
Victoria Hill IP23 . . . . 130 C1
Victoria La
Deopham NR18 . . . . 86 F3
Fakenham NR21 . . . . 141 E4
Victoria Pl 17 PE13 . . . 152 C4
Victoria Rd
Diss IP22 . . . . 177 D4
  5 Great Yarmouth NR30 . 169 D2
Great Yarmouth NR31 . . . 170 D3
Mundesley NR11 . . . . . . 143 C6
  1 Taverham NR8 . . . . . . 155 C1
Taverham NR8 . . . . 156 C8
Terrington St John PE34 . 42 C2
Wisbech PE13 . . . . 152 C4
Victoria St
Caister-on-Sea NR30 . . . 168 F4
  2 Downham Market PE38 172 A5
Great Yarmouth NR30 . . . 169 D6
Norwich NR1 . . . . 178 A1
Sheringham NR26 . . . . . 138 D7
Victoria Terr PE34 . . . . 146 C4
Victoria Way NR5 . . . . . 157 B2
Victory La PE34 . . . . 60 C8
Victory Rd
Downham Market PE38 . . 172 B4
Wisbech PE13 . . . . 152 B3
Vienna Wlk NR19 . . . . . 154 C1
Viking Cl
Great Yarmouth NR31 . . . 170 D2
Swaffham PE37 . . . . 153 D2
Viking Rd 1 NR31 . . . . . 94 C8
Village Cl 4 NR4 . . . . . 161 C5
Vilarome NR30 . . . . 168 C5
Villavon Way 4 NR13 . . 73 D6
Villebois Dr PE33 . . . . . 63 B4
Vimy Dr NR18 . . . . 173 D4
Vimy Ridge NR18 . . . . . 173 D4
Vincent Cl 6 IP26 . . . . . 98 E1
Vincent Pl 10 IP25 . . . . 84 D3
Vincent Rd
Norwich NR4 . . . . 163 A7
Sheringham NR26 . . . . . 138 E7
Vincents Rd NR9 . . . . . . 69 A4
Vince's Rd IP22 . . . . 177 F4
Vine Cl
Coney Weston IP31 . . . . 127 B5
Hemsby NR29 . . . . 167 B8
Vine Ct NR21 . . . . 141 B4
Vine Hill PE34 . . . . 61 C2
Vinery Cl 1 NR34 . . . . . 146 C5
Violet Cl
Attleborough NR17 . . . . 174 C5
  18 Great Yarmouth NR31 . 94 C6
Violet Dr NR26 . . . . 138 B6
Violet Elvin Ct NR5 . . . 161 F5
Violet Rd NR3 . . . . 158 F1
Violet Way NR19 . . . . . . 154 C4
Virginia Cl NR7 . . . . 159 C4
Vong La
Grimston PE32 . . . . 28 B1
Roydon PE32 . . . . 45 A8
Vulcan Rd N NR6 . . . . . 158 C5
Vulcan Rd S NR6 . . . . . 158 C4

W

WACTON NR15 . . . . 106 C2
Waddington Ct 6 NR2 . 162 B7
Waddington St NR2 . . . . 162 B7
Waddling La NR32 . . . . . 111 F7
Wade Cl NR11 . . . . 150 C5
Wadehall La NR34 . . . . . 111 B1
Wades Way NR28 . . . . . . 22 E5
Wadham Cl NR31 . . . . . 170 B3
Wadham Rd NR31 . . . . . 170 B3
Waggon & Horses La
NR3 . . . . 178 B3
Wagtail Cl 2 NR31 . . . . 170 A6
Wagtail Way IP24 . . . . . 176 D1
WAINFORD NR35 . . . . . . 109 B1
Wainford Mills Rd
Bungay NR35 . . . . 124 C8
Wainford NR35 . . . . 109 C1
Wainford Rd NR35 . . . . 124 C8
Wakefield Rd NR5 . . . . 161 C5
Wakehurst Cl 6 NR4 . . 161 F1
Wakes La NR19 . . . . 154 D5
Walcot Cl NR5 . . . . 161 A7
WALCOT GREEN IP22 . . 177 F6
Walcot Rd IP22 . . . . 177 F5
Walcot Rise IP22 . . . . . 177 F5
WALCOTT NR12 . . . . 24 A7
Walcott Road N12 . . . . . 23 E4
Walcup's La PE32 . . . . . . 29 D2
Waldeck Rd NR4 . . . . . . 162 A3
Waldegrave 3 NR5 . . . . 161 A8
Waldemar Ave NR8 . . . . 158 B5
Waldemar Pk NR8 . . . . . 158 B5
Wales Bank PE14 . . . . . . 59 A1
Wales Ct PE38 . . . . 172 C5
Walkers Cl PE31 . . . . . . 135 D2
Walker St 1 NR30 . . . . . 146 E6
Walks The NR34 . . . . . . 111 A4
Walk The
Great Yarmouth NR31 . . . 170 B6
Hicking NR12 . . . . 39 F3
Oulton NR11 . . . . 35 A8
Walkway The NR12 . . . . 24 A7

Wallace Cl
Dereham NR19 . . . . 154 B6
King's Lynn PE30 . . . . . . 147 D4
Wallace Twite Way PE31 140 C3
Waller Cl NR13 . . . . 72 C5
Wallers La NR20 . . . . 33 C3
Wallgate La NR21 . . . . . . 17 D5
Wall La PE31 . . . . 29 C4
Wall Rd
Erpingham NR11 . . . . 20 F3
Norwich NR3 . . . . 158 E2
Wall's La NR25 . . . . 7 F3
Walnut Ave 3 PE33 . . . . 43 E2
Walnut Ave N 2 PE33 . . 43 E2
Walnut Cl
Brandon IP27 . . . . 175 E2
Foulden IP26 . . . . 82 A2
Hopton IP22 . . . . 127 F5
Taverham NR8 . . . . 155 D2
Walnut Gr
  1 Fakenham NR21 . . . . 141 E4
Watton IP25 . . . . 84 D4
Walnut Hill NR14 . . . . . . 73 A1
Walnut Rd PE33 . . . . 82 A5
Walnut Rd PE14 . . . . 41 E3
Walnuts The
Grimston PE32 . . . . 28 B1
Norwich NR4 . . . . 162 A2
Walnut Tree Ave 24 NR29 57 D4
Walnut Wlk PE33 . . . . . . 63 B4
Walpole Bank PE14 . . . . 41 E4
WALPOLE CROSS KEYS
PE34 . . . . 41 F7
Walpole Cross Keys Prim Sch
PE34 . . . . 42 A6
WALPOLE HIGHWAY PE14 . 59 F8
Walpole Highway Prim Sch
PE14 . . . . 59 F8
Walpole La PE14 . . . . . . 41 C4
WALPOLE MARSH PE14 . 41 C4
Walpole Rd
Great Yarmouth NR30 . . . 169 D7
King's Lynn PE30 . . . . . . 146 E3
WALPOLE ST ANDREW
PE14 . . . . 41 D4
WALPOLE ST PETER PE14 . 41 E3
Walpole St NR2 . . . . . . 178 A2
Walpole Wlk PE33 . . . . . 43 E2
Walpole Wr Gdns★ PE14 41 E3
Walsham 2 PE30 . . . . . 147 D5
Walsingham Abbey Grounds
& Shirehall Mus★ NR22 . 16 F7
Walsingham Cl 2 PE13 . 152 A7
Walsingham Dr NR8 . . . 155 E3
Walsingham Prim Sch
NR22 . . . . 16 F8
Walsingham Rd
Binham NR21 . . . . 6 C1
Burnham Thorpe PE31 . . 135 F3
Grear Balsingham NR22 . . 17 B8
WALSOKEN PE13 . . . . . 152 F6
Walsoken Rd PE14 . . . . . 59 D3
Walter Howes Cres PE32 . 44 C3
Walters Cl NR31 . . . . . . 171 D5
Walters Rd NR8 . . . . . . 156 C8
Walton Cl PE30 . . . . 148 C4
WALTON HIGHWAY PE14 . 59 D8
Walton Rd
Norwich NR1 . . . . 163 A8
St John's Fen End PE14 . . 60 A3
West Walton PE14 . . . . . . 59 F5
Wisbech PE13 . . . . 152 F6
Waltons Way IP27 . . . . . 175 D2
WALTON WARREN PE32 . 45 E2
WANGFORD IP27 . . . . . . 114 C2
Wangford Rd IP27 . . . . . 113 F3
Wansbrough Rd 10 NR15 106 F3
Wanton La PE34 . . . . . . 144 A5
Waples Way NR19 . . . . . 154 D3
Wapping NR29 . . . . 167 A2
Warbler Cl 13 NR31 . . . . 94 C7
Wardley Hill Rd NR35 . . 109 D3
Ward Rd NR13 . . . . 55 B1
Ward's Chase PE34 . . . . 79 B8
WARHAM NR23 . . . . 6 A4
Warham Rd
Binham NR21 . . . . 6 E2
Wells-next-the-Sea NR23 . 136 E4
Warham St Mary's Halt Sta
NR23 . . . . 5 F4
Waring Rd NR5 . . . . 161 B6
Warner Ave NR19 . . . . . 154 E7
Warnes Cl 4 NR27 . . . . 139 C6
Warnett Rd NR7 . . . . . . 159 D1
Warren Ave
Fakenham NR21 . . . . 141 F4
Norwich NR6 . . . . 158 A5
Warren Cl
Brandon IP27 . . . . 175 D3
High Kelling NR25 . . . . . . 8 E3
  15 Horsford NR10 . . . . . 53 A3
Thetford IP24 . . . . 176 A3
Watlington PE33 . . . . 61 D5
Warren Dr NR11 . . . . . . 143 B5
Warren Gn NR13 . . . . . . 72 F8
Warren Loke NR31 . . . . . 93 E3
Warren Pl 4 NR19 . . . . 154 D1
Warren Rd
Great Yarmouth NR31 . . . 171 D8
High Kelling NR25 . . . . . . 8 E3
Hopton on Sea NR31 . . . 171 D5
Shouldham PE33 . . . . 62 D4
Southrepps NR11 . . . . . . 22 C6
Warren's La NR17 . . . . . 174 A6
Warren's Rd NR15 . . . . . 106 C4
Warren's Way 5 NR16 . . 105 F5

Warrens Yd NR23 . . . . . 136 C6
Warren The
Cromer NR27 . . . . 139 C6
Horsham St Faith & Newton St
  Faith NR10 . . . . 53 D2
Little Snoring NR21 . . . . . 17 C3
Norwich NR6 . . . . 158 A5
Warren View NR14 . . . . 109 D8
Warstade Way NR37 . . . 153 B4
Warwick Dr NR18 . . . . . 173 C5
Warwick St 4 NR2 . . . . 162 B5
Washbridge 10 NR19 . . 154 D5
Wash La
Alburgh IP20 . . . . 122 E2
Aslacton NR15 . . . . 106 A1
Banham NR16 . . . . 119 D6
Burgh St Peter NR34 . . . 111 C4
Clenchwarton PE34 . . . . 145 E6
Gissing IP22 . . . . 120 E5
Hales NR14 . . . . 109 E6
Hinderclay IP22 . . . . 128 C4
Howe NR15 . . . . 90 C2
Redgrave IP22 . . . . 129 A5
Saxlingham Nethergate
  NR15 . . . . 107 D8
Shelfanger IP22 . . . . 120 B2
Shotesham NR15 . . . . 89 F1
St Peter, South Elmham
  NR35 . . . . 123 F3
Topcroft NR35 . . . . 108 A4
Wacton NR15 . . . . 106 B2
Whissonsett NR20 . . . . . . 31 E2
Wash National Nature
  Reserve The★ PE30 . . 26 B5
Washpit Dro
South Acre PE32 . . . . 64 D8
Swaffham PE37 . . . . 153 C8
West Acre PE32 . . . . 64 D8
West Rudham PE31 . . . . . 29 F6
Wash Rd PE14 . . . . 155 D8
Watch House Hill NR35 . 124 C8
Watch House La NR12 . . 23 E4
Waterbank Rd 10 PE34 . 138 D7
Watercress La NR20 . . . . 68 E6
Waterden Cl 5 NR28 . . . 147 A8
Water End La PE32 . . . . . 48 D2
Waterfield Ave NR21 . . 141 D5
Waterfield Cl 2 NR21 . . 141 C5
Waterfield Mdws NR28 . 151 E5
Water Gdns The PE13 . . 152 A5
WATERHEATH NR34 . . . 110 E5
Waterheath Rd NR34 . . 110 E5
Watering La PE33 . . . . . . 43 E2
Watering Piece La NR29 . 56 C7
Wateringpit La NR12 . . . 55 A8
Watering Rd IP21 . . . . . 131 B1
Watering The 3 NR3 . . 162 D8
Water La
Barnham IP24 . . . . 125 E6
Barsham NR21 . . . . 16 F4
Botesdale IP22 . . . . 128 D1
Cringleford NR4 . . . . 161 D1
Garboldisham IP22 . . . . 128 A8
Great & Little Plumstead
  NR13 . . . . 73 A5
Ingham NR12 . . . . 24 D2
  4 King's Lynn PE30 . . . 146 D5
Letheringsett with Glandford
  NR25 . . . . 8 A2
Middleton PE32 . . . . 44 C1
Mundesley NR11 . . . . . . 143 C4
Neatishead NR12 . . . . . . 55 E7
Runton NR27 . . . . 10 A5
Theinetham IP22 . . . . . . 128 B5
Thetford IP24 . . . . 176 C4
Waterland Dr NR30 . . . . 168 C7
Waterlees Rd
Walsoken PE13 . . . . 59 A6
  2 Wisbech PE13 . . . . . 152 E7
WATERLOO
Alderby NR34 . . . . 110 C4
Dickleburgh and Rushall
  IP21 . . . . 130 C6
Hainford NR10 . . . . 53 E6
Waterloo Ave 4 IP22 . . 129 D7
Waterloo Cl 3 NR10 . . . 53 D2
Waterloo Pk Ave NR3 . . 158 C1
Waterloo Pk Cl 6 NR3 . 158 C1
Waterloo Rd
Great Yarmouth NR30 . . . 169 E2
Hainford NR10 . . . . 53 D6
Horsham St Faith NR10 . . 53 E2
Norwich NR3 . . . . 162 D8
Waterloo St 13 PE30 . . 146 E5
Waterlow Rd PE34 . . . . . 42 C4
Waterman Rd NR2 . . . . 162 C5
Waterman's La PE38 . . . 79 D1
Waterman's Way PE38 . 79 A4
Water Mdw NR20 . . . . . 167 A3
Water Mdw Way 2
PE38 . . . . 172 A6
Watermeadow Cl 3 NR14 91 F1
Watermill Cl NR11 . . . . . 9 F1
Watermill Gn IP27 . . . . 176 C3
Watermill La IP27 . . . . . 82 A6
Water Mill La IP21 . . . . 131 A4
Water Moor La NR21 . . 141 C6
Watersfield Way NR19 . 154 D2
Waterside PE30 . . . . 146 F7
Waterside The NR6 . . . 157 D3
Waters La NR29 . . . . 167 A7
Water Sports Ctr PE34 . 43 C3
Water Twr Rd NR14 . . . . 88 E4
Waterworks Rd
Norwich NR2 . . . . 162 A7
Old Hunstanton PE36 . . 132 F7
Watery La
Beeston with Bittering
  PE32 . . . . 48 B3

Watery La *continued*
Grimston PE32 . . . . 45 B8
Guist NR20 . . . . 33 A4
Mattask NR11 . . . . 20 D5
Necton PE37 . . . . 66 B4
Scarning NR19 . . . . 154 A1
Shipdham IP25 . . . . 67 C2
Wathen Way NR10 . . . . 150 C1
Watkin Rd NR4 . . . . 89 E8
Watling Cl NR30 . . . . . . 168 C6
Watling Rd
Attleborough NR17 . . . . 174 F6
Norwich NR7 . . . . 159 D1
Watlings Ct 8 NR2 . . . . 162 C6
Watlings The NR19 . . . . 67 B6
WATLINGTON PE33 . . . . 61 E5
Watlington Prim Sch
PE33 . . . . 61 D5
Watlington Rd PE33 . . . . 61 F6
Watlington Sta PE33 . . . 61 D5
Watson Gr 8 NR2 . . . . . 162 B8
Watsons Cl NR31 . . . . . 171 E4
Watson-Watt Gdns
NR11 . . . . 143 A7
WATTISFIELD IP22 . . . . 128 B1
WATTLEFIELD NR18 . . . 105 C7
Wattlefield Rd
Tacolneston NR16 . . . . . 105 C6
Wymondham NR18 . . . . . 88 A1
WATTON IP25 . . . . 84 E3
WATTON GREEN IP25 . . 84 E4
Watton Jun Sch IP25 . . 84 D3
Watton Rd
Ashill IP25 . . . . 84 A6
Barford NR9 . . . . 69 E2
Colney NR4 . . . . 160 F4
Great Cressingham IP25 . 83 D4
Great Ellingham NR17 . . 103 D8
Great Melton NR9 . . . . . . 70 B2
Griston IP25 . . . . 85 A2
Hingham NR9 . . . . 86 B5
Hockham NR16 . . . . 102 E4
Larling NR16 . . . . 118 A8
Little Cressingham IP25 . 83 F2
Little Melton NR9 . . . . . 160 B4
North Pickenham PE37 . . 83 C8
Shipdham IP25 . . . . 67 B1
Shropham NR17 . . . . 103 A4
Stow Bedon NR17 . . . . . 102 D7
Swaffham PE37 . . . . 153 D2
Thompson IP25 . . . . 102 A8
Waunci Cres NR31 . . . . 170 D2
Wavell Rd NR19 . . . . . . 154 C7
Waveney Cl
Hoveton NR12 . . . . 164 E6
Hunstanton PE36 . . . . . . 132 D3
Wells-next-the-Sea NR23 . 136 D4
Waveney Dr
  10 Belton NR31 . . . . 94 A6
Wroxham/Hoveton NR12 164 D5
Waveney Fst Sch NR31 . 94 A5
Waveney Hill NR32 . . . . 111 F3
Waveney Hts IP21 . . . . . 131 C6
Waveney Rd
Bungay NR35 . . . . 124 B8
Diss IP22 . . . . 177 B3
Ditchingham NR35 . . . . 109 B2
Great Yarmouth NR31 . . . 169 C1
Hunstanton PE36 . . . . . . 132 C3
King's Lynn PE30 . . . . . . 147 D5
Waveney Valley Swimming
  Pool NR35 . . . . 124 B7
Waverley Rd NR4 . . . . . 162 A2
WAXHAM NR12 . . . . 40 C5
Waxham Ct NR12 . . . . . . 40 A5
Waxham Rd NR12 . . . . . . 40 B5
Waxworks 22 NR30 . . . 169 D4
Wayford Rd NR12 . . . . . . 38 F4
Wayland Ave 4 IP25 . . . 84 C3
Wayland Cl NR17 . . . . . 174 D5
Wayland Com High Sch
IP25 . . . . 84 D3
Wayland Ct NR17 . . . . . 174 C5
Wayland Hospl NR17 . . 174 A7
Wayland Rd NR17 . . . . . 103 C8
Wayland Way NR16 . . . 119 D7
Wayland Wlk PE38 . . . . 172 B7
WEASENHAM ALL SAINTS
PE32 . . . . 47 C8
Weasenham La 1 PE13 . 152 D2
Weasenham Prim Sch
PE32 . . . . 47 D8
Weasenham Rd
Great Massingham PE32 . 29 E1
Litcham PE32 . . . . 47 E7
WEASENHAM ST PETER
PE32 . . . . 30 D1
Weatherby Rd NR5 . . . . 160 D8
Weavers Cl 4 NR10 . . . . 53 D2
Weavers Croft 8 IP20 . 122 D2
Weavers Ct IP22 . . . . . . 177 D5
Weavers View NR12 . . . . 37 F1
Webb Dr 4 NR13 . . . . . . 72 E7
Webbs Ct 2 NR28 . . . . . 151 E5
Webdell Ct 3 NR1 . . . . 162 E1
Webster Cl
  5 Norwich NR5 . . . . . . 161 B8
  8 Stoke Holy Cross NR14 . 89 F4
Webster Way NR30 . . . . 168 D6
Wedgewood Ct NR31 . . 170 C3
Wedgwood Dr PE13 . . . 152 D5
Weedon Way PE30 . . . . 147 D4
WEETING IP27 . . . . 175 B8
Weeting Castle★ IP27 . 114 E8

Weeting Heath National
  Nature Reserve★ IP27 . .114 C7
Weeting VC Prim Sch
  IP27 . . . . .175 B8
Welbeck Ave ⓑ NR29 . . . . .57 D4
Welbeck Rd PE13 . . . . .152 E4
WELBORNE NR20 . . . . .69 A4
Welborne Rd NR20 . . . . . . .68 F5
WELBOURNE COMMON
  NR20 . . . . .68 F4
Welden Rd NR19 . . . . .154 B4
Welgate Cl ⓑ NR20 . . . . . .68 E6
Welgate Rd NR20 . . . . .68 E5
Welholme's Cl ⓑ NR15. .106 E13
Wellbeck NR15 . . . . .90 F2
Wellbeck Rd NR15 . . . . . . .91 A2
Well Cl NR9 . . . . .51 A6
Well Creek Rd PE14 . . . . . . .77 F6
Well End PE14 . . . . .77 A7
Wellesley Ave NR1 . . . . . .163 B7
Wellesley Ave N ④ NR1 . .163 B7
Wellesley Ave S NR1 . . . .163 B6
Wellesley Fst Sch ★ NR1 . .163 B7
Wellesley Rd
  Great Yarmouth NR30 . . .169 D5
  ⑧ Long Stratton NR15 . .106 D3
Wellesley St ⑪ NR30 . . . .146 E5
Well Hall La PE32 . . . . .45 A6
Well Hill NR19 . . . . .68 C5
WELLINGHAM PE32 . . . . . . .30 F1
Wellingham Rd
  Litcham PE32 . . . . .47 F6
  Tittleshall PE32 . . . . .48 A8
Wellington Cl
  Brandon IP27 . . . . .175 D3
  Gimingham NR11 . . . . . . .22 F8
Wellington Cres NR21 . . . .15 C3
Wellington Gn ⑦ NR2 . . .162 C6
Wellington La NR2 . . . . . . .162 C6
Wellington Pl ⑲ NR30 . .169 D4
Wellington Rd
  Briston NR24 . . . . .142 B4
  East Dereham NR19 . . . . .154 D5
  ⑧ Feltwell IP26 . . . . .98 E1
  Great Yarmouth NR30 . . .169 E2
  ⑧ Long Stratton NR15 . .106 D3
  Norwich NR2 . . . . .162 B6
Wellington Terr ❶ PE13 . .152 C4
Well La NR9 . . . . .51 A6
Well Loke NR3 . . . . .158 B3
Well Medieval Village of★
  PE32 . . . . .45 B7
Well Opening ㉔ NR30. . .169 D2
Well Rd
  Cantley NR13 . . . . .92 D6
  Great Yarmouth NR30 . . .169 D2
Wells Ave NR28 . . . . .151 A3
Wells Cl ② NR10 . . . . .53 E5
Wells' La IP20 . . . . .122 C1
Wells Maritime Mus★
  NR23 . . . . .136 B6
WELLS-NEXT-THE-SEA
  NR23 . . . . .136 E5
Wells next the Sea Prim Sch
  NR23 . . . . .136 E5
Wells next the Sea Sta
  NR23 . . . . .136 F4
Wellspring Rd NR11. . . . . .22 C8
Wells Rd
  Burnham Overy Staithe
    PE31 . . . . .135 E7
  Fakenham NR21. . . . . . . .141 B4
  Hindringham NR21 . . . . . .17 D6
  Needham IP20 . . . . .122 C1
  North Creake NR21 . . . . . .4 D1
  Stiffkey NR23. . . . . .6 C6
  Walsingham NR22 . . . . . . .16 F8
  Wighton NR23 . . . . .5 F3
Well St
  Docking PE31 . . . . .134 C5
  Great Yarmouth NR30 . . .169 D4
  Thetford IP24 . . . . .176 D3
  Witton NR28 . . . . .23 D3
WELNEY PE14 . . . . .95 D4
Welney Wildfowl Refuge★
  PE14 . . . . .95 F6
Welsford Rd
  ⑤ Norwich NR4 . . . . .89 D8
  Norwich NR4 . . . . .162 B1
Weltons Loke NR9 . . . . . . .52 A6
Wendene NR5 . . . . .160 F7
WENDLING NR19 . . . . .66 F8
Wendling Rd NR19 . . . . . . .48 F2
Wendover Rd NR13 . . . . . . .72 D8
Wenman Cl ⑤ NR5 . . . . .160 F8
Wensom Cl ⑤ PE33 . . . . . .61 D6
Wensum Cres NR6 . . . . . .157 D3
Wensum Ct NR21 . . . . .32 C6
Wensum Dr NR20 . . . . .49 F7
Wensum Gdns ❶ NR20. . .50 B3
Wensum Mdws Mental
  Health Hospl NR6. . . . . .157 D4
Wensum Mid Sch NR2. . . .162 A7
Wensum Rd NR9 . . . . .51 A4
Wensum St NR3 . . . . .178 B3
Wensum Valley Cl NR6 . .157 D4
Wensum Way
  ⑪ Fakenham NR21 . . . . . .94 A6
  ⑧ Fakenham NR21. . . . . .141 E4
Wensum Wlk NR8 . . . . . . .155 F3
Wentworth Cl ⑥ IP27 . . .114 E1
Wentworth Gn NR14 . . . . .161 F2
WEREHAM PE33 . . . . .80 E4
Wereham Row PE33 . . . . . .80 D3
Wesley Ave PE34 . . . . .144 B5

Wesley Cl
  Downham Market PE38 . .172 B5
  ④ Mattishall NR20 . . . . . .68 E6
  Mundesley NR11 . . . . . . .143 D5
  Terrington St Clement
    PE34 . . . . .144 B5
Wesley Rd
  King's Lynn PE30 . . . . . . .148 C5
  Terrington St Clement
    PE34 . . . . .144 B5
Wessex St NR2. . . . . .178 A1
WEST ACRE PE32 . . . . .46 B2
Westacre Dr NR1. . . . . . . .158 E7
West Acre Gdns★ PE32. . .46 D4
West Ave
  Great Yarmouth NR31 . . .170 C3
  Ormesby St Margaret
    NR29. . . . . .167 A3
WEST BARSHAM NR21. . . .16 C4
WEST BECKHAM NR25. . . . . .9 C2
WEST BILNEY PE32 . . . . . . .45 B2
Westbourne Rd NR12 . . . . .54 D7
Westbriggs Dro PE33. . . . . .62 B5
Westbrook Ave ⑧ NR13. .170 B6
WESTBROOK GREEN
  PE22 . . . . .177 C7
WEST CAISTER NR30 . . . .168 C4
WEST CARR Rd NR17. . . . .174 A4
West Church St NR16 . . . .119 A5
West Cl NR5 . . . . .157 A2
West Cliff
  Cromer NR27. . . . . .139 B7
  Sheringham NR26 . . . . . .138 D7
Westcliff Ave NR27. . . . . .139 A7
West Cres NR20. . . . . .50 A5
West Croft NR9 . . . . .88 C7
WEST DEREHAM PE33. . . . .80 B3
West Dereham Rd PE33 . . .80 D3
West Dr
  Brandon IP27 . . . . .175 A2
  ❶ Friday Bridge PE14 . . . .77 A8
West Dro N PE14. . . . . .59 D8
West Dro S PE14. . . . . .59 E8
West Earlham Fst Sch
  NR5. . . . . .161 D6
West Earlham Mid Sch
  NR5. . . . . .161 D6
WEST END
  Necton IP25. . . . . .66 C4
  West Caister NR30 . . . . . .76 B6
West End
  Briston NR24 . . . . .142 F5
  Costessey NR8. . . . . .156 C4
  Hilgay PE38 . . . . .79 D1
  Northwold IP26. . . . . .99 B8
West End Ave
  Brundall NR13 . . . . .165 A4
  Costessey NR8. . . . . .156 C5
West End Ct ⑥ IP25 . . . . .84 C3
West End St NR2. . . . . . . .162 B7
Westerley Cl NR30 . . . . . .168 D4
Westerley Way NR30 . . . .168 D4
Western Ave NR7 . . . . . . .163 E6
Western Bypass NR11 . . .150 B5
Western Cl ⑧ IP26. . . . . . .98 D1
Western Rd NR31 . . . . . . .170 C4
WESTFIELD NR19 . . . . .67 F4
Westfield Ave NR23 . . . . .136 C6
Westfield Cl ② NR29 . . . . .57 C1
Westfield Inf Sch IP25 . . .84 D3
Westfield La NR19 . . . . . . .154 F1
Westfield Rd
  Brundall NR13 . . . . .165 A4
  East Dereham NR19 . . . . .154 E2
  Swaffham PE37 . . . . .153 B4
  Wisbech PE13 . . . . .152 E7
Westfields
  Attleborough NR17 . . . . .174 B4
  King's Lynn PE30 . . . . . . .147 C4
  Narborough PE32 . . . . . . .63 E7
Westfields Cl
  Terrington St John PE14 . .60 C8
  Tilney St Lawrence PE34. . .42 C1
West Flegg Mid Sch
  NR29. . . . . .57 D5
WESTGATE
  Binham NR21. . . . . .6 D3
  Burnham NR21. . . . . .135 B3
Westgate
  Hevingham NR10. . . . . . . .53 B8
  Hunstanton PE36. . . . . . .132 C4
  Norwich NR8 . . . . .157 F5
  Shropham NR17 . . . . . . .103 B4
  Walsingham NR22 . . . . . . .16 F8
West Gate NR18 . . . . .173 B4
Westgate Cl NR2 . . . . .162 A4
Westgate Gn NR10 . . . . . . .53 B8
Westgate Rd PE36 . . . . .1 F6
Westgate St
  Hevingham NR10. . . . . . . .52 B8
  Hilborough IP26 . . . . .83 A3
  Holme next the Sea PE36 . .2 A6
  Shouldham PE33 . . . . .62 D4
  Southery PE38. . . . . .97 A5
WESTGATE STREET NR10 . .53 B8
Westhall Rd
  Dersingham PE31 . . . . . .140 D3
  Mundford IP26 . . . . .100 B4
WEST HARLING NR16. . . . .118 A3
West Harling Rd NR16. . .118 B4
WEST HEAD PE34 . . . . .78 F8
West Head Rd PE34 . . . . . .78 F8
West Herne La IP22 . . . . .128 D5
Westhorpe Cl ⑧ PE30. . . .147 A8
West La NR10. . . . . .53 D1

Westland Chase PE33 . . . . .43 F1
Westlegate NR1 . . . . .178 B2
WEST LEXHAM PE32 . . . . . .47 C4
West Lexham Hall PE32. . .47 C4
WEST LYNN PE34. . . . . . . .146 C5
West Lynn Cty Prim Sch
  PE34. . . . . .146 C5
Westmark PE30 . . . . .147 C4
Westmead Ave PE13 . . . . .152 E2
Westmead Rd NR21 . . . . . .141 C4
WEST NEWTON PE31. . . . . .27 F6
Weston Cl ❶ NR29. . . . . . .73 C6
Weston Ct NR6 . . . . .158 F6
WESTON GREEN NR9. . . . . .51 E1
WESTON LONGVILLE NR9. . .51 E3
Weston Miller Dr PE13 . .152 C7
Weston Rd
  Easton NR9 . . . . .70 A7
  Norwich NR3 . . . . .158 C3
  ⑰ Norwich NR3 . . . . . . .152 C4
Weston Rise NR30 . . . . . .168 D5
Weston Sq ❸ NR25 . . . . .137 B6
Weston Terr NR26 . . . . . . .138 C7
Weston Wood Cl NR7 . . .163 E7
Weston Wood Rd NR7. . .163 D7
West Parade
  Norwich NR2 . . . . .162 B6
  Wisbech PE13 . . . . .152 B7
WEST PORINGLAND NR14. .90 B4
West Pottergate NR2. . . .162 B6
WEST RAYNHAM NR21 . . . .30 E4
West Raynham Prim Sch
  NR21. . . . . .30 F4
West Raynham Rd NR21. . .30 F4
West Rd
  Caister-on-Sea NR30. . . .168 D4
  Dersingham PE31 . . . . . .140 D3
  Great Yarmouth NR30 . . .168 F1
  Norwich NR5 . . . . .157 A2
  Ormesby St Margaret
    NR29. . . . . .167 A2
  Shouldham Thorpe PE33 . .62 C2
  Tacolneston NR16 . . . . . .105 F8
  Watton IP25 . . . . .84 D3
  West Caister NR30 . . . . .168 B4
WEST RUDHAM PE31 . . . . .29 F7
WEST RUNTON NR27 . . . . .10 A5
West Runton Sta NR27 . . .10 A5
Westry Cl PE13 . . . . .55 C5
WEST SOMERTON NR29. . .57 E6
West St
  North Creake NR21 . . . . . .4 D1
  Wisbech PE13 . . . . .152 C5
West Stree ⑱ NR30. . . . .169 D2
WEST TOFTS IP26 . . . . . . .100 F4
West Tofts Rd IP26 . . . . .100 D3
West View
  Dereham NR19 . . . . .154 E1
  South Pickenham PE37 . . .83 D7
West View Dr NR13 . . . . . .74 A2
West View Rd NR13 . . . . .165 E6
WEST WALTON PE14 . . . . . .59 B8
West Way
  Downham Market PE38 . .172 B4
  Stow Bardolph PE34 . . . . .61 D1
  Tacolneston NR16 . . . . . .105 E5
  Wimbotsham PE34. . . . . . .79 D8
WESTWICK NR10 . . . . .37 D6
Westwick Dr NR28 . . . . . .151 A4
Westwick Rd NR2 . . . . . . .178 A3
Westwick St NR2 . . . . . . .178 A3
WEST WINCH PE33. . . . . . . .43 E2
West Winch Rd PE33. . . . . .43 F4
West Wood Cotts NR21. . .32 B5
Westwood Dr NR6 . . . . . .157 D6
Westwood Gdns NR18. . .173 A6
Westwood La NR21 . . . . . .32 B5
WEYBOURNE NR25. . . . . . . .8 F5
Weybourne St ❶ NR25. . . .8 F5
Weybourne Sta NR25. . . . . .8 F5
Weynor Gdns NR25 . . . . . . .8 E5
Wharf St PE12 . . . . .41 B8
Wharton Dr NR28 . . . . . . .151 E7
Whartons La ❶ NR18 . . .173 B3
WHEATACRE NR34 . . . . . . .111 B5
Wheatacre Cl ❸ NR10. . . .53 A3
Wheatacres PE13 . . . . .24 A4
Wheatcroft Way NR20. . . .68 A8
Wheatfields
  Hillington PE31 . . . . .28 B4
  Rickinghall Superior IP22. .128 E2
Wheat Fields NR8 . . . . . . .155 F2
Wheatfield Way NR15 . . .106 F4
Wheatley Bank PE14 . . . . .59 C5
Wheatley Dr PE30. . . . . . .148 B4
Wheatley Rd NR21 . . . . . .141 F7
Wheelbarrow La IP20 . . .123 F1
Wheeler Rd NR3 . . . . .158 A1
Wheelers La NR15 . . . . . . .108 E8
Wheel Rd NR14 . . . . .90 E4
Wheelwright Rd PE30 . . .147 C5
Wheelwrights Cl NR13 . . .92 E8
Wherry Cl NR28. . . . . .151 E7
Wherry Rd
  Bungay NR35. . . . . .124 C8
  Norwich NR1 . . . . .178 C1
Wherry Reach ❷ NR13 . .166 D4
Wherry Way NR30 . . . . . .169 C7
Whimbrel Dr
  ⑧ Great Yarmouth NR31. . .94 C8
  ❶ Great Yarmouth NR31. .170 A7
WHIMPWELL GREEN
  NR12 . . . . .24 C4

Whimpwell St NR12. . . . . .24 C4
WHINBURGH NR19 . . . . . . .68 A3
Whinburgh Rd NR19 . . . . .67 F3
Whinchat Way ❸ NR31. . .94 C7
Whin Comm Rd
  Denver PE38 . . . . .172 D1
  Tottenhill PE33 . . . . .61 F6
Whinmere Rd NR12 . . . . . .39 E3
Whipp's La NR16. . . . . . . .105 F7
Whisson Cl ❶ PE30 . . . . .147 A8
WHISSONSETT NR20 . . . . . .31 D2
Whissonsett Rd NR20 . . . .48 E8
Whistle Dro IP28 . . . . .112 D1
Whitby St ❸ PE13. . . . . . .152 C5
White City Rd PE14. . . . . . .78 D6
White Clover Rd ㉘ NR31. .94 C6
White Cross
  Burgh & Tuttington NR11. . .36 E4
  Hardingham NR9. . . . . . . .86 E8
Whitecross La PE34 . . . . .144 E4
White Cross Rd PE37 . . . .153 C4
Whitedike Dro IP26 . . . . .113 B8
White Farm La NR7 . . . . .163 C6
White Hart Cl NR7 . . . . . .178 B4
Whitefriars CE Prim Sch
  PE30 . . . . .146 D3
Whitefriars Rd PE30. . . . .146 D3
Whitefriars Terr NR1 . . . .146 D3
White Gate La NR11 . . . . . .11 D2
White Gates NR5 . . . . .156 E1
Whitegates Cl ⑥ NR9. . . .88 D7
Whitegates Rd NR11 . . . . .22 B7
White Hall PE34 . . . . .78 C4
Whitehall Rd NR2 . . . . . . .162 B5
Whitehall Yd ⑧ NR26. . .138 D7
Whitehart La IP27 . . . . . . .175 C4
Whitehart St ⑥ IP24. . . .176 C4
White Horse La
  Bixley NR14 . . . . .89 F8
  Trowse with Newton NR14 .163 A1
  Worstead NR28 . . . . .38 B6
Whitehorse Plain ⑦
  NR3 . . . . .169 C5
Whitehorse St
  ❶ Fakenham NR21. . . . . .141 C3
  Wymondham NR18 . . . . .173 B3
White Horse St IP27 . . . . .175 A2
White House Ct NR3 . . . .158 B3
White House Dr ㉓ NR6. .158 E6
White House Rd NR27. . . .139 D4
White House Farm La
  IP21. . . . . .122 B2
White House Gdns ⑫
  NR14 . . . . .90 D5
Whitehouse La
  Earsham NR35. . . . . .108 C1
  Wicklewood NR18 . . . . . . .87 C4
White House La NR17 . . .174 F5
White House Rd CB7 . . . .112 A7
White La PE33 . . . . .63 A3
Whitelands NR21 . . . . . . .141 D5
White Lion Rd
  Coltishall NR12 . . . . .54 D6
  Wheatacre NR34 . . . . . . .111 B4
White Lion St
  Holt NR25 . . . . .137 B6
  Norwich NR2 . . . . .178 A2
White Lodge Bsns Est
  NR4. . . . . .89 E8
White Oaks PE37 . . . . .65 E2
Whiteplot Rd IP26 . . . . . . .98 D5
White Post Rd NR11. . . . . .21 D5
White Rd
  Barton Bendish PE33. . . . .63 D1
  Methwold IP26 . . . . .99 A5
White Rose Cl NR5. . . . . .161 D8
White Sedge PE30 . . . . . .147 A8
White St NR29 . . . . .57 D5
Whitethorn Cl ⑥ NR6. . .158 D5
Whiteway Rd PE31 . . . . . .135 B3
White Woman La NR6 . . .159 A6
White Woman La Mid Sch
  NR6. . . . . .158 F6
Whiting Rd NR4 . . . . .162 D1
Whiting's La NR17 . . . . . .103 A6
Whitley Cl NR6 . . . . .158 C6
Whitlingham Ctry Pk★
  NR7. . . . . .163 E4
Whitlingham La NR14 . . .163 C4
Whitsands Rd PE37 . . . . .153 A5
WHITTINGTON PE33. . . . . . .81 B2
Whittington Hill PE33 . . . .81 B2
Whittome Mill PE38. . . . . .79 D1
Whitwell Rd
  Norwich NR1 . . . . .163 A7
  Reepham NR10 . . . . .149 A2
  Sparham NR9 . . . . .51 B6
  Swanton Morley NR20 . . .149 C3
WHITWELL STREET
  NR10 . . . . .149 C3
Whitworth Ave ❶ NR17. .174 C5
Whytehead Gdns IP22. . .177 D4
WICKEN GREEN VILLAGE
  NR21 . . . . .15 D2
Wick Farm Cl ❸ IP25. . . .84 D3
WICKHAMPTON NR13 . . . . .93 A8
Wickhampton Rd NR13 . . .93 A8
Wick La NR9 . . . . .57 D2
WICKLEWOOD NR18 . . . . . .87 B5
Wicklewood Prim Sch
  NR18. . . . . .87 B5

Wicklewood Rd NR18 . . . .87 B6
WICKMERE NR11 . . . . .20 F4
Wickmere Rd NR11 . . . . . .20 C5
Wiclewood Way PE31 . . .140 C3
Widgeon Cl NR31 . . . . . . .170 A6
Wier Ave NR20. . . . . .68 F6
Wiggenhall Rd PE34 . . . . .42 E3
WIGGENHALL ST GERMANS
  PE34. . . . . .43 C1
WIGGENHALL ST MARY
  MAGDALEN PE34 . . . . . .61 B6
Wiggenhall St Mary
  Magdalen Prim Sch
  PE34. . . . . .61 B5
WIGGENHALL ST MARY THE
  VIRGIN PE34 . . . . .61 A8
WIGGENHALL ST PETER
  PE34. . . . . .61 C8
Wiggets La NR11. . . . . .34 D7
Wigg Rd NR21 . . . . .141 B6
Wiggs Rd NR14 . . . . .110 F7
Wight Dr NR30. . . . . .168 C6
Wightmans La NR11 . . . . .170 D5
WIGHTON NR23 . . . . .6 A2
Wighton Halt Sta NR23. . . .5 F3
Wigwam Hill IP22 . . . . . . .129 C5
Wilberforce Rd
  Norwich NR5 . . . . .161 B6
  Wisbech PE13 . . . . .152 D5
WILBY NR16. . . . . .119 A8
Wilby Rd
  Norwich NR1 . . . . .162 E1
  Quidenham NR16 . . . . . .118 F8
Wildbriar Cl PE33 . . . . .43 E1
Wilde Rd ❶ NR13 . . . . . . .72 E7
Wilderness Cl ❸ IP20. . .122 D1
Wilderness La IP20 . . . . . .122 D2
Wildfields Cl PE34 . . . . . .145 D5
Wildfields Rd PE34 . . . . . .145 C6
Wild Flower Cir★ NR25. . . .7 F2
Wildflower Way NR35 . . .109 A2
Wild Radish Cl ⑱ NR14. . .89 B3
Wild Rd NR3 . . . . .158 D1
Wilkins Ct NR5. . . . . .161 C7
Wilkinson Rd NR13. . . . . . .72 E7
Wilkinson Way NR28 . . . .151 D4
Wilkins Rd PE14 . . . . .59 D3
Wilks Farm Dr NR7. . . . . .159 A5
Willbye Ave IP22 . . . . .177 E5
William Booth Rd PE30. .147 D5
William Booth St NR2 . . .178 A2
William Brown Way ❶
  IP22. . . . . .177 A5
William Bush Cl NR10 . . . .35 B2
William Childerhouse Way ❶
  NR5 . . . . .160 E7
William Cl
  ⑤ Watton IP25. . . . . .84 D3
  ⑥ Wymondham NR18. . .173 C6
William Cowper Cl NR19 .154 E1
William Kett Cl NR1. . . . .163 A6
William Marriot Mus★
  NR25. . . . . .137 E8
William Marshall CE Prim
  Sch PE14 . . . . .95 D4
William Mear Gdns NR1 .163 B6
William O'Callaghan Pl ❶
  NR19 . . . . .154 D5
William Paston Rd NR28 .151 D6
William Peck Rd ❼ NR10. .54 A2
William Rd
  Fakenham NR21. . . . . . . .141 F5
  Wisbech PE13 . . . . .152 C5
Williams Loke NR7. . . . . .163 D8
Williamson Cl
  Diss IP22. . . . . .177 D6
  Norwich NR7 . . . . .159 C2
Williamson Cres ❹ IP24 .176 C2
William St ❸ PE30 . . . . . .146 E3
Williams Way
  ❸ Holt NR25. . . . . .137 C5
  North Walsham NR28 . . .151 C6
William Way NR19 . . . . . .154 C1
Williman Cl PE31 . . . . . . .133 D6
Willis St NR3 . . . . .178 B4
Willoughby Way ❺ NR13. .72 E7
Willow Ave NR31. . . . . .94 C7
Willowbrook Cl ❹ NR33. .111 F1
Willow Cl
  Brandon IP27 . . . . .175 D2
  Lingwood NR13. . . . . .74 A2
  Long Stratton NR15. . . . .106 E2
  ⑩ Mattishall NR20 . . . . . .68 E6
  Middleton PE32 . . . . .44 B4
  North Walsham NR28 . . .151 D7
  Wortwell IP20. . . . . .123 A4
  Wymondham NR18 . . . . .173 D5
Willow Cres ❸ PE13. . . . . .152 A5
Willow Ct
  ❸ Attleborough NR17. . .174 B5
  Beetley NR20 . . . . .49 D4
Willow Dr
  Clenchwarton PE34 . . . .145 E5
  Dersingham PE31 . . . . . .140 D3
  King's Lynn PE33 . . . . . . .43 F4
  Tilney All Saints PE34 . . . .42 E4
  West Winch PE33 . . . . . . .43 F1
Willow Gr
  East Dereham NR19 . . . . .154 D2
  Sheringham NR26 . . . . . .138 E5
Willow Heath Rd PE33. . . .80 B7
Willow Herb Wlk ❹
  NR8 . . . . .173 E4
Willow La
  Bedingham NR35. . . . . . .108 B3
  Broome NR35 . . . . .109 C3
  Carbrooke IP25 . . . . .85 B5

Willow La continued
Norwich NR2 . . . . 178 A3
Willow Pk PE30 . . . . 147 C8
Willow Pl PE33 . . . . 62 A5
Willow Rd
Downham Market PE38. . 172 B6
East Dereham NR19 . . . . 154 B4
Hunstanton PE36. . . . . . . 132 C3
King's Lynn PE30 . . . . . . 148 D2
Willows Ct 18 NR29 . . . . 57 D4
Willow Way
2 Ludham NR29 . . . . 56 C5
18 Marthan NR29 . . . . 57 D4
Wisbech PE13 . . . . 152 D3
WILNEY GREEN IP22 . . . 129 A8
Wilshere Ct 11 NR30 . . . 169 D3
Wilson Dr PE32 . . . . 44 F3
Wilson Rd 5 NR1. . . . . . 163 B5
Wilson's Dro PE32 . . . . . . 45 E3
Wilson's Way NR25 . . . . . . 7 D6
Wilton Cres 2 NR20 . . . 148 C5
Wilton Rd
Feltwell IP26 . . . . 98 E1
Heacham PE31. . . . . 133 C6
Wilton View NR28 . . . . . 151 D5
Wimbledon Ave IP27 . . . 175 A1
Wimbledon Way PE38 172 E7
WIMBOTSHAM PE34. . . . . 79 D8
Wimbotsham Rd PE38 . 172 C6
Wimpole Cl PE30 . . . . . . 148 E1
Wimpole Cl 15 NR7 . . . . 72 D4
Winchcomb Rd NR2 . . . . 161 F7
Winchester Twr NR2 . . . 162 C5
Winchester Way IP24 . . 176 B5
Winch Rd PE32 . . . . 45 C5
Windermere Cl NR15 . . . . 90 E2
Windermere Rd PE30 . . 148 F2
Windle The NR13 . . . . 74 C5
Windmill Ave NR20 . . . . . 68 A8
Windmill Cl
Poringland NR14 . . . . 90 C4
Thetford IP24 . . . . 176 D5
Windmill Ct 7 PE30 . . . . 147 C5
Windmill Hill PE31 . . . . . 14 E3
Windmill La
Costessey NR8 . . . . 157 A4
Syleham IP21 . . . . 131 D4
Thetford IP24 . . . . 102 B1
Windmill Rd
Gimingham NR11 . . . . 22 F8
1 Marham PE33. . . . . . . 63 B4
Norwich NR3 . . . . 158 F2
Worstead NR28 . . . . 38 A6
Wortwell IP20 . . . . 123 A3
Windsor Cl NR4 . . . . 169 D7
Windsor Chase NR8 . . . 155 D1
Windsor Cl IP24 . . . . 125 F6
Windsor Cres PE31 . . . . 133 C5
Windsor Ct 4 IP25 . . . . . 84 D3
Windsor Dr
Dersingham PE31 . . . . . . 140 D3
Wisbech PE13 . . . . 152 D8
Windsor Pk
East Dereham NR19 . . . . 154 D8
2 King's Lynn PE30 . . . . 146 E3
Windsor Pk Gdns NR6 . . 159 A6
Windsor Rd
Caister-on-Sea NR30 . . . 168 E6
Cantley NR13 . . . . 92 C6
King's Lynn PE30 . . . . . . 146 E3
Norwich NR6 . . . . 158 A5
Windsor Rise PE36 . . . . 132 C2
Windsor St 1 PE38 . . . . 172 A5
Windsor Terr PE30 . . . . 146 E3
Windsor Way NR31 . . . . 170 B4
Windy Cres PE33. . . . . . . 63 B3
Windy La NR15. . . . . 107 B8
Windy Ridge PE33 . . . . . 63 B3
WINFARTHING IP22 . . . . 120 B4
Winfarthing Ave PE30 . 146 D4
Winfarthing Rd
Banham NR16 . . . . 119 D6
Shelfanger IP22. . . . . . . 120 B2
Wingate Way NR2. . . . . 162 C7
WINGFIELD IP21 . . . . 131 E4
Wingfield PE30 . . . . 147 D5
WINGFIELD GREEN IP21 . 131 D4
Wingfield Rd
Lakenheath IP27 . . . . . . 113 E2
Norwich NR3 . . . . 158 D1
Syleham IP21 . . . . 131 D5
Weybread IP21 . . . . 131 F6
Wing's La NR20 . . . . 33 B7
Wings Rd IP27 . . . . 113 D4
Winifred Ct NR26 . . . . . . 138 E7
Winifred Rd NR13 . . . . . 169 B3
Winifred Way NR30 . . . . 168 D8
Winmer Ave 6 NR29 . . . 58 B6
Winners Wlk NR8 . . . . . . 155 E3
Winn's Ct NR25 . . . . 137 A7
Winsford Way NR5. . . . . 157 C1
Winstanley Rd 21 NR7. . . 72 D4
Winston Churchill Dr
PE30. . . . . 147 C4
Winston Dr NR12 . . . . 15 E6
Winter Gdns NR30. . . . . 169 E2
Winter Rd NR2. . . . . 162 A6
Winterton Dunes National
Nature Reserve NR29. . 58 B7
Winterton Fst Sch NR29. . 58 B6
WINTERTON-ON-SEA
NR29 . . . . 58 C6
Winterton Rd
Hemsby NR29 . . . . 167 B8
Somerton NR29 . . . . 57 F6
WISBECH PE13 . . . . 152 A6
Wisbech Castle PE13 . 152 C4

Wisbech & Fenland Mus
PE13. . . . . 152 C4
Wisbech Gram Sch PE13 152 B5
Wisbech Rd
King's Lynn PE30 . . . . . . 146 D2
Manea PE15. . . . . 95 A2
Nordelph PE38. . . . . 78 D4
Outwell PE14 . . . . 77 F7
Walpole PE14 . . . . 41 D4
Walsoken PE13 . . . . 152 E8
Welney PE14 . . . . 95 D5
Wissey View IP26. . . . . . 100 B4
Wistaria Rd PE13 . . . . . 152 F7
Wisteria Cl NR20. . . . . . 154 C4
Witard Cl NR7 . . . . 159 D1
Witard Rd NR7. . . . . 163 D8
WITHERGATE NR28 . . . . . 38 A6
Withersdale Rd IP20 . . . 123 A1
Withington St 1 PE12. . . 41 B8
Withy Way NR8 . . . . 155 E1
WITTON NR13 . . . . 165 A6
WITTON BRIDGE NR28 . . 23 E2
Witton Cl
Heacham PE31. . . . . 133 C5
Reedham NR13 . . . . 92 F5
Witton Gn NR13. . . . . 92 F5
Witton La NR13 . . . . 165 A8
Wittons La IP21. . . . . . . 131 A3
WIVETON NR25 . . . . 7 E6
Wiveton Rd NR25 . . . . 7 D6
Woburn St NR22 . . . . . . 162 C5
Wodehouse Cl 1 NR12. . 39 B4
Wodehouse Ct 11 IP25. . 84 D3
Wodehouse Rd
Bacton NR12 . . . . 23 D4
Old Hunstanton PE36. . . 132 E7
Wodehouse St NR3 . . . . 162 E8
Wolfe Rd NR1. . . . . 162 E3
WOLFERD GREEN NR15. . 90 B2
WOLFERTON PE31. . . . . . . 27 B7
Wolferton Dr PE37. . . . . 153 B2
Wollaston Ave NR19. . . 154 D7
Wolseley Rd NR31 . . . . . 169 B2
Wolterton La NR25 . . . . . 20 E2
Wolterton Rd 6 NR11 . . . 20 E2
Wolterton Rd
Wickmere NR11 . . . . 20 C2
WOODBASTWICK NR13 . . 55 D2
Woodbastwick Rd
Blofield Heath NR13 . . . . 73 C6
Blofield NR13. . . . . 165 E7
Woodbastwick NR13 . . . . 55 E1
Woodbine Cl
North Walsham NR28 . . . 151 F5
Potter Heigham NR29 . . . 56 F6
Woodbridge Way PE30 . 147 D4
Wood Cl
Brandon IP27 . . . . 175 D2
Kenninghall NR16 . . . . . 119 A4
Woodcock La PE34. . . . . . 41 B6
Woodcock Mews 4
NR31 . . . . 170 A6
Woodcock Rd NR3 . . . . . 158 D3
Woodcock Rise IP27. . . 175 F4
Woodcock's La NR9. . . . . 88 A8
Woodcote Pk PE13. . . . . 152 A4
Woodcroft NR7. . . . . 159 E2
WOOD DALLING NR11. . . . 34 D6
Wood Dalling Rd
Guestwick NR20 . . . . 34 A6
Reepham NR10 . . . . 149 C6
Wood Dene Sch NR11. . . . 9 F3
Wood Dr
11 Beetley NR20 . . . . 49 D4
1 Beetley NR20 . . . . 49 D4
Woodend Rd NR31 . . . . 133 E5
Woodfarm La NR31 . . . . 170 A2
Woodfield
Briston NR24 . . . . 142 E4
1 East Dereham NR19. . 154 D1
Woodfield Rd NR21 . . . . 137 C2
Woodforde Rd NR7 . . . . 159 D2
Woodfordes Brewery &
Visitors Ctr NR13. . . . . 55 C2
WOODGATE NR27 . . . . 10 A4
Woodgate 12 NR4. . . . . . . 89 B8
Woodgate La NR20. . . . . . 50 B3
Woodgate Rd NR20 . . . . . 50 B3
Woodgate Way PE31 . . . 134 F4
Wood Gn NR13. . . . . 72 F8
Woodhall Rd DF29 . . . . . . 97 B8
Woodham Leas NR6. . . . 158 E6
Wood Hill NR8 . . . . 156 D8
Woodhill Rise NR5. . . . . 161 C8
Woodhouse Cl 1 NR26. . 138 B6
Wood La
Aldeby NR34 . . . . 110 E5
Bedingham NR35 . . . . . 108 C2
Bradenham IP25 . . . . 66 A2
Bressingham IP22 . . . . . 119 E2
Bunwell NR16 . . . . 105 D3
Burgh & Tuttington NR11. . 36 D5
Dickleburgh & Rushall
IP21 . . . . 130 F4
Great Ellingham NR17 . . 103 D8
Hepworth IP22 . . . . 127 E2
Holme Hale IP25 . . . . 66 B1
Honingham NR9. . . . . 69 E8
Kelling NR25 . . . . 8 C5
Little Ellingham NR17 . . . 86 B1
Long Stratton NR15. . . . 107 A2
Morley NR18 . . . . 87 A1
Pulham Market IP21 . . . 121 E8
Scole IP21 . . . . 130 F3

Wood La continued
Starston IP20 . . . . 122 C5
Strumpshaw NR13. . . . . . 73 F2
Swardeston NR14 . . . . . . 89 C5
Thelnetham IP22 . . . . . . 128 A2
Wicklewood IP25 . . . . 87 B4
Wicklewood NR18. . . . . . . 87 B4
Woodland Dr
Bungay NR35 . . . . 124 A7
Ellingham NR35 . . . . . . 109 E3
Norwich NR6 . . . . 158 E6
Thorpe End NR13. . . . . . . 72 D5
Woodland Farm Ind Units
NR10. . . . . 53 A6
Woodland Gdns PE30 . . 148 D5
Woodland La NR14 . . . . 142 F2
Woodland Rd NR6 . . . . . 157 E6
Woodland Rise
Sheringham NR26 . . . . . 138 E5
12 Tasburgh NR15. . . . . 106 F6
Woodland Rise W NR26. 138 D4
Woodlands
35 Harleston NR20 . . . . 122 D2
2 Thorpe Marriott NR8 . 155 B2
Woodlands Cl
Holt NR25 . . . . 137 D7
4 Thetford IP24 . . . . . 176 E6
Woodlands Cres 1 NR7 . . 72 D5
Woodlands Ct PE13 . . . 152 F7
Woodlands Dr IP24 . . . . 176 D6
Woodlands Mid Sch NR31 94 C6
Woodlands Rd NR5 . . . . 157 A2
Woodlands Rise IP27 . . 175 A2
Woodlands The IP25. . . . 84 A7
Woodlands Way Rd NR12. 55 D4
Woodland View Mid Sch
NR10. . . . . 54 A2
Woodland View Mobile
Home Pk NR10. . . . . . . 53 D6
Woodlark Cl 2 IP24 . . . 176 D2
WOOD NORTON NR20 . . . 33 A7
Wood Norton Rd
Foulsham NR20 . . . . 33 C5
Stibbard NR21 . . . . 32 E3
Woodpecker Dr 8 IP25. . 84 C7
Woodpecker Mews 5
NR31 . . . . 170 A6
WOODRISING NR9 . . . . . . 85 E6
Woodrising Rd NR9 . . . . . 85 D4
Wood Rising Rd NR9 . . . . 86 A5
Woodrow Ave NR25 . . . 137 B5
Woodrow La NR15 . . . . . 121 A8
Woodrow Pl NR1. . . . . . . 163 B6
Woodruff Cl 3 NR6. . . . . 158 D5
Wood St Rd NR29 . . . . . . 56 B8
Woods Cl 3 NR29 . . . . 88 C7
Woods End NR11 . . . . . . 174 C4
Woodside
Burnham Market PE31. . . 135 A2
5 King's Lynn PE30 . . . 147 C4
North Walsham NR28 . . . 151 E4
Woodside Ave
Dersingham PE31 . . . . . . 140 C5
Heacham PE31. . . . . 133 D4
Woodside Cl
Attleborough NR17 . . . . 174 C3
Dersingham PE31 . . . . . . 140 C5
1 Taverham NR8 . . . . . 155 C1
Woodside Ct NR7 . . . . . . 159 E1
NR7. . . . . 159 E1
Woodside Fst Sch NR8 . . 88 D7
Woodside Pk NR17 . . . . 174 C3
Woodside Rd NR7 . . . . . 159 E1
Wood's La NR20 . . . . 49 B8
Wood St
Norwich NR1 . . . . 178 A1
Wisbech PE13 . . . . 152 B6
Woodstock La NR15 . . . 120 F8
Woodton Rd NR35 . . . . . 108 A2
Woodton Prim Sch
NR35 . . . . 108 C5
Woodview NR28 . . . . 38 A4
Wood View NR28 . . . . . . 151 A4
Woodview Ct IP25 . . . . . . 84 C4
Wood View Ct NR5. . . . . 157 A2
Woodview Rd NR5 . . . . . . 70 B5
Wood View Rd NR6 . . . . 157 E5
Woodward Cl PE33. . . . . . 62 D4
Woodward Rd NR31. . . . 169 C3
Woodwark Ave 3 PE30 . 146 E6
Woodyard Cl 9 NR14 . . . 89 B3
Woodyard Sq The NR35 . 108 C5
Wooll Dr NR28. . . . . 151 A6
Woolner's La NR14 . . . . . 90 E7
Woolstencroft Ave NR6 . 146 F7
Wootton Rd PE30 . . . . . . 147 B7
Worcester Cl 3 NR29 . . 167 A2
Worcester Rd PE13 . . . . 152 C7
Worcester Way
Attleborough NR17 . . . . 174 E4
Great Yarmouth NR31 . . 170 B4
Wordsworth Cl PE38 . . . 172 D5
Wordsworth Gn IP24. . . 176 E7
Wordsworth Rd
2 Diss IP22 . . . . 177 E4
Norwich NR5 . . . . 161 C6
Workhouse La
Foulsham NR20 . . . . 33 D4
Tilney St Lawrence PE34. 42 C1
Upwell PE14 . . . . 77 E4
Workhouse Rd NR12 . . . . 38 C3
Worlds End NR13 . . . . . . 74 C1
WORMEGAY PE33. . . . . . . 62 C7
Wormegay Prim Sch
PE33 . . . . 62 A6

Wormegay Rd
Blackborough End PE32. . 44 C1
Wormegay PE32 . . . . 62 D8
WORSTEAD PE28 . . . . 38 A5
Worstead Prim Sch NR28. 38 A5
Worstead Rd NR28 . . . . . 38 B4
Worstead Sta NR28 . . . . . 37 F4
WORTHAM IP22 . . . . 129 B4
Wortham Cl 3 NR5 . . . . 161 A8
Wortham Prim Sch IP22 129 C4
WORTHING NR20 . . . . 49 F6
Worthing Rd
North Elmham NR20 . . . . 49 F7
Swanton Morley NR20. . . 50 B6
Wortley Rd IP22. . . . . . . 128 D4
WRAMPLINGHAM NR8 . . . 69 E1
Wramplingham Rd NR18 173 D8
Wrench Cl 4 NR11. . . . . 150 D6
Wrench Rd NR5. . . . . . . 161 D6
Wren Cl
Brandon IP27 . . . . 175 E3
Necton PE37 . . . . 66 A3
Norwich NR4 . . . . 161 E2
Wren Dr
2 Great Yarmouth NR31 . 94 C7
Great Yarmouth NR31. . . 170 A6
WRENINGHAM NR16 . . . . . 88 D1
Wreningham Prim Sch
NR16. . . . . 88 D1
Wrens The 11 IP24. . . . . 176 D2
WRETTON PE33 . . . . 80 E3
Wretton Fen Dro PE33 . . 80 D1
Wretton Rd PE33. . . . . . . 80 F2
Wretton Row PE33 . . . . . 80 E3
Wright Ave NR19. . . . . . 154 D1
Wright Cl NR30 . . . . 168 E7
Wright Dr NR19. . . . . . . 154 C4
Wrights Cl NR11 . . . . . . 150 C7
Wright's Cl
Holt NR25 . . . . 137 C7
North Walsham NR28 . . . 151 B4
Wright's La PE12. . . . . . . 41 B8
Wright's Loke NR28 . . . . 22 E5
Wright's Wlk 12 NR19 . . 154 D5
Wroe The PE14 . . . . 59 C1
Wroo Rd NR17 . . . . 103 F5
Wroughton Infant Sch
NR31. . . . . 170 B6
Wroughton Jun Sch
NR31. . . . . 170 B7
WROXHAM NR12. . . . . . . 164 D3
Wroxham Ave PE37 . . . . 153 C2
Wroxham Rd
Coltishall NR12 . . . . 54 E8
Rackheath NR13 . . . . 72 D8
Salhouse NR13 . . . . 54 E2
Sprowston NR7 . . . . 159 C5
Wroxham Sta NR12 . . . . 164 C6
Wyatt St NR30 . . . . 146 E5
Wyatt Way IP24 . . . . . . 176 B7
Wycliffe Rd NR4 . . . . . . 161 D3
Wylde Croft NR8 . . . . . . 155 D2
Wymans Way NR21. . . . 141 E5
Wymer Dr NR11 . . . . . . 150 C4
Wymers La NR13 . . . . 74 B8
Wymer St NR2. . . . . 162 B6
WYMONDHAM NR18 . . . . 173 E5
Wymondham Abbey (rems)*
NR18. . . . . 173 B3
Wymondham Abbey Sta
NR18. . . . . 173 A3
Wymondham Coll NR18 . 87 B1
Wymondham Heritage Mus
NR18. . . . . 173 C3
Wymondham High Sch
NR18. . . . . 173 C5
Wymondham Hist Rly Sta
NR18. . . . . 173 D3
Wymondham Leisure Ctr
NR18. . . . . 173 C4
Wymondham Rd
Bracon Ash NR14. . . . . . . 88 E2
Bunwell NR16 . . . . 105 B5
East Carleton NR14. . . . . 88 F4
Flordon NR15. . . . . 106 C8
Kimberley NR18 . . . . 87 B6
Morley NR18 . . . . 87 A3
Wreningham NR16 . . . . . . 88 B2
Wymondham NR18 . . . . 105 A8
Wymondham Sta NR18 . 173 C2
Wyndfields 10 PE37 . . . . 65 F4
Wyndham Pk NR27 . . . . . 10 C5
Wyndham St NR26 . . . . 138 D7
Wyngates NR13 . . . . 165 F6
Wynne's La PE34. . . . . . 145 C4

Yarmouth Rd continued
Kirby Cane NR35 . . . . . . 109 E3
Lound NR32. . . . . 94 B3
Ludham NR29 . . . . 56 C5
North Walsham NR28 . . . 151 C4
Norwich NR7 . . . . 163 E5
Ormesby St Margaret
NR29. . . . . 167 C1
Postwick with Witton
NR13. . . . . 165 A5
Raveningham NR14 . . . . 110 B8
Stalham NR12 . . . . 39 B3
Thurlton NR14 . . . . 93 A1
Toft Monks NR34. . . . . . 110 C5
Worstead NR28 . . . . 38 A6
Yarmouth Stadium NR30 168 E2
Yarmouth Way NR30 . . . 169 C3
Yarn Mews 2 NR3 . . . . . 178 B4
Yarrington Way NR5 . . . 160 E8
Yarrow Cl IP24 . . . . 176 F5
Yarrow Rd
Bintree NR20 . . . . 33 B2
2 Dereham NR20. . . . . . 68 A8
YAXHAM NR19 . . . . 68 A5
Yaxham CE Prim Sch
NR19. . . . . 68 C6
Yaxham Rd
East Dereham NR19 . . . . 154 E4
Mattishall NR20. . . . . 68 C6
Yaxham Sta NR19 . . . . . . 68 A4
YAXLEY IP23 . . . . 130 A1
Yaxley's La NR11. . . . . . 150 C5
Yaxley's Rd NR30 . . . . . 169 B6
Yaxley Way NR5 . . . . . . 161 A8
Yeats Way NR19 . . . . . . 154 D4
YELVERTON NR14 . . . . . . 90 E5
Yelverton Cl NR6. . . . . . 157 D5
Yelverton Rd NR14 . . . . . 90 E5
Yesmere 16 NR14 . . . . . . 89 B3
Yesterday's World *
NR30. . . . . 169 E3
Yew Cl NR7 . . . . 159 D4
Yew Tree Cl 24 NR13 . . . 94 C7
Yew Tree Ct NR20. . . . . . . 69 C3
Yew Tree Rd NR17 . . . . . 174 C5
York Ave PE36 . . . . 132 D5
York Gdns PE13 . . . . . . 152 D6
York La 15 NR12 . . . . 39 B4
York Rd
4 Cromer NR27 . . . . . . 139 D5
Great Yarmouth NR30 . . 169 D3
King's Lynn PE30 . . . . . . 146 E3
Wisbech PE13 . . . . 152 C6
York Row PE13 . . . . 152 C5
York St NR2 . . . . 162 B4
York Terr
Cromer NR27 . . . . 139 D5
Wisbech PE13 . . . . 152 C6
York Villa Cl NR29 . . . . . 75 B8
York Way IP24 . . . . 176 B5
Youell Ave NR31 . . . . . . 170 D1
Youngmans Cl NR28 . . . 151 D3
Youngmans La NR12 . . . . 38 E6
Youngman's La NR10. . . . 37 C5
Youngmans Rd NR13 . . 173 C8
Young's Cres NR13 . . . . . 92 E7
Young's Row PE12 . . . . . 41 A8

Z

Zara Way NR19 . . . . 154 C5
Zephyr Cl NR30 . . . . 168 D7
Zig-Zag La NR15 . . . . . . 108 C8
Zobel Cl NR3 . . . . 157 F2
Zurich Cl NR31. . . . . 171 E4

Y

Yallop Ave NR31 . . . . . . 171 D8
Yare Cl
Caister-on-Sea NR30. . . 168 D6
Great Yarmouth NR30 . . 169 C6
Yare Rd NR31. . . . . 94 A6
Yare Valley Dr NR4. . . . 161 C2
Yare Valley Rise NR13. . 165 C3
Yare View Cl NR13 . . . . . 92 F4
Yarmouth Bsns Pk NR31. 169 B2
Yarmouth Rd
Blofield NR13. . . . . 165 F6
Broome NR35 . . . . 109 C3
Brundall NR13 . . . . 165 C5
Caister-on-Sea NR30. . . 168 E2
Corton NR32 . . . . 171 D1
Dilham NR28 . . . . 38 D1
Geldeston NR34. . . . . . . 110 A3
Hales NR14 . . . . 109 F8
Hemsby NR29 . . . . 167 A6

PHILIP'S MAPS

the Gold Standard for drivers

◆ **Philip's street atlases cover all of England, Wales, Northern Ireland and much of Scotland**

◆ Every named street is shown, including alleys, lanes and walkways

◆ Thousands of additional features marked: stations, public buildings, car parks, places of interest

◆ Route-planning maps to get you close to your destination

◆ Postcodes on the maps and in the index

◆ Widely used by the emergency services, transport companies and local authorities

BEST BUY • BEST BUY
Auto EXPRESS
BEST BUY • BEST BUY

For national mapping, choose
Philip's Navigator Britain
the most detailed road atlas available of England, Wales and Scotland. Hailed by Auto Express as 'the ultimate road atlas', Navigator shows every road and lane in Britain.

● Britain's best-selling UK road atlas

Street atlases currently available

England

Bedfordshire and Luton	Surrey
Berkshire	East Sussex
Birmingham and West Midlands	West Sussex
Bristol and Bath	Tyne and Wear
Buckinghamshire and Milton Keynes	Warwickshire and Coventry
Cambridgeshire and Peterborough	Wiltshire and Swindon
Cheshire	Worcestershire
Cornwall	East Yorkshire Northern Lincolnshire
Cumbria	North Yorkshire
Derbyshire	South Yorkshire
Devon	West Yorkshire
Dorset	
County Durham and Teesside	**Wales**
Essex	Anglesey, Conwy and Gwynedd
North Essex	Cardiff, Swansea and The Valleys
South Essex	Carmarthenshire, Pembrokeshire and Swansea
Gloucestershire and Bristol	Ceredigion and South Gwynedd
Hampshire	
North Hampshire	Denbighshire, Flintshire, Wrexham
South Hampshire	Herefordshire Monmouthshire
Herefordshire Monmouthshire	Powys
Hertfordshire	
Isle of Wight	**Scotland**
Kent	Aberdeenshire
East Kent	Ayrshire
West Kent	Dumfries and Galloway
Lancashire	Edinburgh and East Central Scotland
Leicestershire and Rutland	Fife and Tayside
Lincolnshire	Glasgow and West Central Scotland
Liverpool and Merseyside	
London	Inverness and Moray
Greater Manchester	Lanarkshire
Norfolk	Scottish Borders
Northamptonshire	
Northumberland	**Northern Ireland**
Nottinghamshire	County Antrim and County Londonderry
Oxfordshire	County Armagh and County Down
Shropshire	
Somerset	Belfast
Staffordshire	County Tyrone and County Fermanagh
Suffolk	

Philip's maps and atlases are available from bookshops, motorway services and petrol stations.

For further details visit
www.philips-maps.co.uk